ENCYCLOPEDIA OF
AMERICAN
IMMIGRATION

Volume 3

James Ciment

Editor

SHARPE REFERENCE

An imprint of M.E. Sharpe, INC.

SHARPE REFERENCE

Sharpe Reference is an imprint of *M.E. Sharpe,* INC.

M.E. Sharpe, INC.
80 Business Park Drive
Armonk, NY 10504

© 2001 by *M.E. Sharpe,* INC.

All rights reserved.

Library of Congress Cataloging-in-Publication Data

Encyclopedia of American Immigration / James Ciment, editor
p. cm.
Includes bibliographical references and index.
ISBN 0-7656-8028-9 (set; alk. paper)
1. United States—Emigration and immigration—Encyclopedias. 2. Immigrants—United States—Encyclopedias. I. Ciment, James.

JV6465.E53 2000
304.8′73′03—dc21

00-026560

Printed and bound in the United States of America

The paper used in this publication meets the minimum requirements of American National Standard for Information Sciences—Permanence of Paper for Printed Library Materials,
ANSI Z 39.48-1984.

BM (c)   10   9   8   7   6   5   4   3   2   1

CONTENTS

FILM, RADIO, AND TELEVISION

For over a century, the images, words, and sounds presented by film, radio, and television have been an integral part of the acculturation and assimilation process for new immigrants in the United States. Social scientists and cultural historians have shown that, along with interpersonal communication, mass media consumption is central to immigrants' cultural learning process and the establishment of intercultural and ethnic identity. In other words, film, radio, and television teach newcomers how to be "American." At the same time, the portrayal of immigrants in the mass media reveals much about American society's attitudes toward different social groups at a given historical juncture. To adequately address this complex relationship between the mass media and American immigration, it is essential to examine three subjects (a) the role of immigrants within each medium's industrial history; (b) the representation of immigrant groups in each mainstream medium; and (c) the consumption of mainstream and alternative media by immigrant audiences.

FILM

EARLY CINEMA AND THE NICKELODEON ERA

When commercial cinema debuted in New York in 1896, it was only one of several acts on a vaudeville theater bill. Less than ten years later, films would become the star attraction in storefront five-cent movie theaters (called nickelodeons) in cities across the United States. The year 1896 was also the first year that more immigrants came to the United States from southern and eastern Europe than from northern and western Europe, and the future entrepreneurs of the Hollywood film industry were among this new immigrant population. The multiplicity of working-class immigrants in major urban areas that patronized early film—e.g., eastern European Jews, Italians, and the Irish—presented film producers and exhibitors with myriad, and often conflicting, sets of desires, beliefs, and sensibilities to which to appeal. The nickelodeon provided a space in which illiterate or foreign-speaking workers and immigrants could be entertained by silent movies which overcame language barriers through their focus on visual images. Yet these films also assimilated recent immigrants to the culture of American urban life, including—albeit in a limited way—teaching newcomers the English language through the use of intertitles (printed words indicating dialogue) and exhibitors' lectures.

Economics, affordability, geography, accessibility, age, sex, ethnicity, race, and religion all affected whether or not one might see a film. When motion pictures were still a novelty in the 1890s, they often attracted elite audiences. According to Charles Musser, however, "With the advent of the nickelodeons [after 1900], moving pictures became a democratic art, at least by the standards of the day. Inside the new movie houses, particularly in the downtown areas, an Italian carpenter in need of a bath might sit in an orchestra seat next to a native-born white-collar salesman or a Jewish immigrant housewife." Unlike vaudeville and melodrama theaters, which segregated seating by social class through ticket pricing, the single admission price of nickelodeons collapsed class and gender boundaries among its audience. This economic egalitarianism was reflected in early advertisements for the movies, which often featured their low admission prices and encouraged women to attend the movies, which they did in large numbers. Film historians have disagreed about the function and influence of early movies on American immigrants. Some scholarship stresses the common cultural experience among ethnic groups, presenting film as a guide or instructor for new arrivals. Counter to this assimilationist thesis, others have argued that the early filmgoing experience constituted an alternative public sphere or oppositional social space in which immigrant identities could survive and thrive, allowing newcomers to resist the assimilationist impulse of the content of early film.

Several early American films had immigrant characters and presented anti-immigrant themes through negative stereotypes despite the fact that many European immigrants worked for the early film production companies and were a large segment of the film audience. In the early film *Skyscrapers* (1906), for instance, the Italian immigrant "Dago Pete" steals from his boss and blames a native-born co-worker for the crime. One would expect that immigrants would have an ambivalent relationship at best to mass-mediated images of their respective ethnic groups, rejecting the negative portrayals while also internalizing a wide range of representations, from demeaning images of working-class immigrants to positive portrayals of middle-class Anglo-Americans. There were also early documentary films (or "actualities"), such as *Emigrants Landing at Ellis Island* (1903) and *Arrival of Emigrants, Ellis Island* (1906), which show immigrants arriving from Europe at Ellis Island, and *Move On* (1903) and *New York City "Ghetto" Fish Market* (1903), which show street scenes of turn-of-the-century immigrant life in New York's Lower East Side.

By 1907, nickelodeons were predominantly frequented by the working class (of which immigrants made up a large portion), especially in larger cities, although films continued to be exhibited to the upper classes and other culturally elite groups in alternative venues such as museums, lecture halls, universities, and churches. The earliest films normally lasted between fifteen and ninety seconds, and were comprised of scenes of everyday life, exotic locales, famous people and political figures, important current events, as well as staged fictional films. Filmmakers soon began to edit several scenes together in order to tell longer and longer stories, leading to the development of the narrative feature film, and eventually to the Hollywood studio system of film production. By 1915, most film programs consisted of a single feature film supplemented by one or two shorter films, and most of the leading film companies had relocated to Hollywood for better weather and real estate values. That the established film companies in the east had a virtual monopoly on early film production and distribution also prompted film entrepreneurs to move west.

EUROPEANS

Several important figures involved with the early film industry were immigrants, such as Stuart Blackton, a British-born director who founded the Vitagraph film company and was a pioneer of film animation, and Sigmund Lubin, a German-Jewish immigrant who produced and distributed films under his own name. Lubin's films appealed to immigrant and working-class audiences due in part to their sensationalism, but also because they were inexpensively produced and exhibited in venues with low admission fees. Most of the major moguls during the later Hollywood studio era also were Jewish immigrants. Louis B. Mayer (MGM) emigrated from Russia, Samuel Goldwyn (MGM) and Harry and Jack Warner (Warner Bros.) from Poland, William Fox (20th Century Fox) and Adolph Zukor (Paramount) from Hungary, and Carl Laemmle (Universal Studios), the only non-eastern European, was a German Jew. In the face of anti-Semitism and anti-immigrant sentiment from within established industries, the movies' status as both a new and culturally illegitimate business provided Jewish immigrants with the opportunity to become entrepreneurs in this risky and unpredictable field.

Several of the Hollywood film moguls (like many actors and directors) adopted Americanized versions of their names and attempted to recruit a more respectable middle-class audience by replacing nickelodeons with spectacular movie palaces that would provide a high-class cultural experience in comparison to the lowly nickelodeon storefronts. Feature films were more palatable to the middle class because they adopted the narrative form of legitimate theater and adapted their stories from middle-class novels and plays. By 1916, movie palaces had replaced nickelodeons as the dominant venue for film exhibition, and the Hollywood studios would supply those theaters with their product through the 1950s.

As part of the attempt to reach a more affluent "legitimate" audience (and to legitimize themselves and the film business), the Hollywood studios and their immigrant owners made films that mythologized assimilation and the concomitant social values of the WASP middle and upper classes. And although American-born directors such as Thomas Ince and D. W. Griffith were leading figures in the 1910s and 1920s, Hollywood enlisted many immigrant directors, some of whom were already influential in their native countries during the silent period and escaped from repressive conditions, including Erich von Stroheim, Josef von Sternberg, Mauritz Stiller, Ernst Lubitsch, Victor Sjöström, Fritz Lang, F. W. Murnau, E. A. Dupont, Frank Capra, William Wyler, and Maurice Tourneur. In addition, several foreign-born stars, such as Greta Garbo, Pola Negri, Marlene Dietrich, Carmen Miranda, Rudolph Valentino, Ramon Navarro, and Rod La Rocque, became part of the Hollywood studio's star system of film production in the late 1920s, the 1930s, and the 1940s.

Nickelodeon filmgoing did continue alongside movie palace exhibition through the 1910s and 1920s. For instance, unlike D. W. Griffith's 1915 blockbuster *The Birth of a Nation*, which targeted the middle and upper classes (including President Woodrow Wilson who watched a private screening of the film in the White House), Charlie Chaplin's short comedy *The Immigrant* (1917) was still aimed at the working-class audience that frequented nickelodeons. In the film's account of emigrating to the United States, Chaplin's "Little Tramp" travels in steerage, falls in love, and faces many obstacles as a new immigrant in America. While *The Immigrant* is perhaps the best-known film about the immigrant experience during the silent era, immigrants would commonly appear in films for the simple reason that immigrants were part of the fabric of American life, especially in urban areas, and films reflected and responded to aspects of that social and historical reality.

In *The Italian,* produced by Thomas H. Ince in 1915, immigrant Beppo Donnetti (George Beban) leaves his sweetheart in Italy to find a better life in the ghettos of New York. Although the lovers are reunited and marry in the United States, like Chaplin's *The Immigrant*, their new life in America is filled with hardship. *Hungry Hearts* (1922) tells the story of an immigrant Russian Jewish mother in the slums of New York who tries, at tremendous costs, to make a better life for her family. Warner Bros. early partial sound film *The Jazz Singer* (1927) is also set within the context of Jewish immigrant life in the Lower East Side of New York. Jakie Rabinowitz (Al Jolson) is torn between his love for performing jazz music in blackface, and the pressure from his father to continue a family tradition by becoming a cantor (presented in the film as an "ancient tradition of his [Jewish] race"). The "Cohen" vaudeville routines that inspired Jewish caricatures in early films like *Cohen's Advertising Scheme* (1904) and *Cohen's Fire Sale* (1907) were revived to exploit the coming of sound in *Cohen on the Telephone* (1929), in which a Jewish immigrant has trouble using the phone and communicating with his landlord. Charles Musser has also pointed out that the popular Marx Brothers films, such as *Animal Crackers* (1930) and *The Cocoanuts* (1929), are "directly connected to the immigrant experience" through their indebtedness to the cultural relations between Jewish and Italian immigrants on New York's Lower East Side.

The 1931 film *Delicious* (1931) centers on a group of Russian, Scottish, and Scandinavian immigrants headed for America aboard the S. S. *Mauronia* and the difficulties one of the characters faces at Ellis Island.

In *Paddy O'Day* (1935), an immigrant learns on arrival in America that her mother is dead, but friends facilitate a career for her as an entertainer with the hope of convincing immigration officials to let her remain in the United States. Similarly, in *Romance in Manhattan* (1935), co-starring Ginger Rogers, a Czechoslovakian immigrant almost does not achieve his dream of coming to America when he learns at Ellis Island that he cannot afford the entrance fee. He jumps ship on his way back, and eventually finds work as a cab driver. Worried about his status as an illegal immigrant, however, he consults a corrupt lawyer who promptly hands him over to immigration authorities. In *Gateway* (1938), a female Irish immigrant (Arleen Whelan) meets a returning war correspondent (played by Don Ameche) on the journey who rescues her when she is unjustly detained at Ellis Island. Taken together, although these films can be viewed as melodramatic exploitations of the immigrant experience, one could also argue that in order to resonate with the historical sensibilities of filmgoers, the films were careful not to romanticize or uncritically celebrate the realities of American immigrant life.

LATINOS

Hollywood films have been consistent with U.S. anti-immigration policies and sentiments, often criminalizing immigrants without addressing the material reasons and economic causes behind immigration, such as the cheap manual labor Mexican immigrants provide in the United States. The majority of Hollywood films depicting Mexican immigrants (and potential immigrants) are usually in the action genre, featuring a strong native-born American male protecting the U.S. southern border from the "invasion of immigrants." Other films about Mexican immigrants reflect the historical anxieties and ambivalences within mainstream American culture toward immgration. *Bordertown* (1935), for instance, stars Paul Muni as Johnny Ramirez, a hard-working student who graduates at the top of his class and becomes a lawyer, only to lose his temper in court and attack another attorney. As a result of this stereotypical behavior of the hot-tempered Latin, he is disbarred and resorts to a life of gambling and connections with crime. *Forbidden Passage* (1941), part of MGM's "Crime Doesn't Pay" series, tells the story of the Department of Immigration's attempts to stop the smuggling of illegal aliens into the country. Nominated for an academy award in the best short category, the film warns that desperate immigrants tired of waiting for legal entry often risk their lives and pay exorbitant fees to enter the United States illegally. MGM's *Border Incident* (1949) dramatized the Mexican and American governments' efforts to stop the smuggling of Mexican migrant workers across the border. Earlier films cast Latinos as the violent "greaser" or "bandito," which became a stock villain character among early Mexican stereotypes (e.g., D. W. Griffith's *The Greaser's Gauntlet* [1908] [which also has an early example of Griffith cutting into a scene], *Tony, the Greaser* [1914], *The Greaser's Revenge* [1914], and *Broncho Billy and the Greaser* [1914]).

Between 1934 and 1968 the Production Code Administration (PCA), or Hays Office, regulated the production and censored the content of Hollywood films. By monitoring the moral and political messages of films, the PCA could withhold its seal of approval, thereby severely hampering a film's exhibition. In conjunction with the House Un-American Activities Committee (HUAC) in the 1950s, the PCA prevented the mass distribution of two important independently produced films about Mexican-American immigrants: *Salt of the Earth* (1954), based on an actual miners' strike in New Mexico, and *The Lawless* (1950), about a xenophobic small town whose residents falsely accuse a Mexican-American youth of attempted rape and murder.

Although the violent "bandito" reappeared in films such as *The Magnificent Seven* (1960), *Bring Me the Head of Alfredo Garcia* (1974), and the "spaghetti westerns" (e.g., *The Good, the Bad, and the Ugly* [1967] and *Duck, You Sucker* or *A Fistful of Dynamite* [1971]), in the 1980s more nuanced representations of Latinos began to appear. *Zoot Suit*, directed by Latino Luis Valdez, was based on the 1940s Los Angeles "Sleepy Lagoon" murder trial of Mexican-American gang members who are convicted for a crime they may not have committed. The academy award nominee *El Norte* (1983) follows Mayan Indian peasants who flee Guatemala with the help of other immigrants who have already traveled successfully through Mexico. The peasants make their way to Los Angeles where they start to build a new life as illegal immigrants. In *Born in East L.A.* (1987), a native-born Mexican American (Cheech Marin) is accidentally caught up in an immigration raid on a factory. After he is mistakenly deported to Mexico as an undocumented immigrant, he is forced to smuggle his way back into the United States.

According to the public interest group Fairness & Accuracy In Reporting (FAIR), the news coverage in 1993 of the controversy surrounding attorney general nominees Zoe Baird and Kimba Wood's hiring of undocumented immigrant childcare workers excluded the viewpoint of immigrant Latina, Caribbean, and Asian women. In addition, since the early 1990s, the major networks have used military metaphors in reports about illegal immigration from Mexico such as "army of invaders" and "border battleground." Media critics have argued that the overall effect of many of these reports is to implicitly condone vigilante violence against immigrants in the "war on illegal immigration." The HBO Pictures political satire *The Second Civil War* (1997) addresses the issue of anti-immigrant sentiment by having the governor of Idaho (Beau Bridges) refuse to accept orphan immigrants from Pakistan and India. He eventually closes his state's borders, and as xenophobia leads to ethnic factionalization among the native-born population, the president (Phil Hartman) is forced to intervene. While *The Second Civil War* critiques anti-immigration sentiment by moving the debate to Idaho, in a very different way, the blockbuster *Independence Day* (1996) presented a world threatened by alien outsiders, while the government agents in *Men in Black* (1997) controlled and subverted dangerous extraterrestrial immigrants invading the planet.

In the late 1980s and early 1990s, the box office hit *La Bamba* (1987) and low-budget sleeper *El Mariachi* (1992) also demonstrated the crossover potential of Latin-themed films. In 1995, *My Family/Mi Familia* (1995) countered Hollywood stereotypes by telling the epic story of a Mexican immigrant family over three generations, beginning with the parents' emigrating to Los Angeles in the 1930s, where they immediately faced possible deportation. Latino Hollywood stars such as Andy Garcia, Antonio Banderas, Salma Hayek, Jennifer Lopez, Jimmy Smits, Edward James Olmos, Cheech Marin, and Esai Morales, continue to exert greater influence in Hollywood at the turn of the century, playing a wider range of characters with proven crossover potential.

ASIANS

Just as Jews found themselves economically coerced through social discrimination into the entertainment industry, Chinese immigrants' occupational options in the nineteenth century were often limited to laundry, restaurant, manual labor, and household services. Arriving as laborers in large numbers in the late nineteenth and early twentieth centuries, Asian immigrant characters appeared in film from the medium's inception, usually as the stereotypical "coolie." Coolies were usually presented as exotic characters with queues or braids, caps, slippers, and buttoned jackets. As early as 1894, a Chinese immigrant character appeared in *Chinese Laundry Scene*, one of the earliest film comedies, providing comic gags by eluding an Irish policeman. Dressed in a "coolie" laborer costume and wearing a wig with queues, a white actor from the Robetta and Doretto vaudeville team plays the part of the Chinese immigrant. According to the coolie stereotype, Chinese men are economically and sexually inferior, speak with a heavy accent, and are submissive, yet sneaky and untrustworthy. Images of Chinese immigrants in San Francisco appear in the early nonfiction films or "actualities" of life and events in San Francisco, such as *Arrest in Chinatown, San Francisco, Cal.* (1897), *Parade of Chinese* (1898), *Scene in Chinatown* (1900), and *San Francisco Chinese Funeral* (1903). Hollywood studios later cast Asians to play a variety of Asian roles, making no distinction between Japanese, Korean, Chinese, or Vietnamese. Asian women have consistently been exoticized in American film and portrayed as being silently submissive to men. In addition, Korean and Chinese women were consistently referred to as mama-san in American films during the post–World War II period, despite the specifically Japanese origin and meaning of the term.

This disregard for ethnic and national differences among Asians is also evidenced by the fact that whites and Latinos also played Asians in leading roles with the use of exaggerated features through makeup and costuming. For instance, Ricardo Montalban was the Japanese lead in *Sayonara* (1957), and the Swedish actor Warner Oland played the Charlie Chan character in several popular films. And although the Charlie Chan character may have been an immigrant, he is still described as a "Chinese detective" in the films, even though he lives in Hawaii with his Americanized children. (Chinese-American immigrant Wayne Wang's *Chan Is Missing*, a 1982 low-budget film set in San Francisco's Chinatown, can be viewed as a critical response to these earlier stereotypes.)

While Charlie Chan is the archetypal fictional representation of the clever, benign, and lawful Asian hero, Chan has his counterpart in the archetypal Fu Manchu character (also played by Warner Oland in *The Mysterious Dr. Fu Manchu* [1929] and *The Return of Dr. Fu Manchu* [1930]), which represents the threatening and evil foreigner. As Gina Marchetti has also demonstrated in *Romance and the "Yellow Peril,"* since the turn of the century, Asians have been cast in the cultural role of the "yellow peril" and social "other," intent on undermining Western religion and values. The mysterious and exotic East was often presented as a sexual (as well as cultural) threat that needed to be contained in order to preserve the established social order. Films such as Cecil B. DeMille's *The Cheat* (1915), D. W. Griffith's *Broken Blossoms* (1919), and Frank Capra's *The Bitter Tea of General Yen* (1933) (with another Swedish actor, Nils Asther, in the male lead)

either warned against the dangers of miscegenation (i.e., interracial sexual relations or marriage) or punished those involved with interracial romance (often with death). This category of representation depicts Asians as sexually compulsive and morally inferior. While many of these films may not be directly about Asian-American immigrants, because American film rarely distinguishes between Asians and Asian Americans, the larger repertoire of representations is especially relevant.

Of course, representations of all ethnic immigrant groups in the mass media reflect the cultural, political, and historical contexts in which they are produced, and as immigration patterns have shifted historically (due in large part to changes in immigration law, political policy, and social anxieties) media portrayals have also resonated with those changes. According to Ana López, for instance, after decades of the occasional inclusion of Latin American stereotypes such as the lazy peasant, greaser, and wily señorita, in response to President Franklin D. Roosevelt's revival of the Good Neighbor Policy and the disappearance of European film markets during World War II, Hollywood made over 100 films with Latin American stars and themes between 1939 and 1947. According to López, "A special kind of . . . [Latin American] was needed to reinforce the national self, one that—unlike the German or Japanese other—was nonthreatening, potentially but not practically assimilable (that is, nonpolluting to the purity of the race), friendly, fun-loving, and not deemed insulting to Latin American eyes and ears." The Brazilian singer and actress Carmen Miranda exemplified this Latin American image, earning her more money than any other woman in the United States in 1945.

Although films from the 1980s and 1990s presented the Japanese as a business threat to Americans, as in *Gung Ho* (1986) (in which the Japanese invade a working-class auto town) and *Rising Sun* (1993) (in which we learn from a Japanese businessman that "business is war"), during World War II, Hollywood films reflected the demonization of the Japanese enemy in newsreels, cartoons, and other forms of government propaganda. Films such as the critically acclaimed *Wake Island* (1942) and *Objective, Burma!* (1945) portrayed the Japanese as the vicious Fu Manchu archetype, while the Chinese began to be differentiated from the Japanese through heroic and sympathetic portrayals. In *Dragon Seed* (1944), for instance, Katharine Hepburn plays a Chinese woman who confronts the barbaric Japanese who invade her village. After the Korean War and during the Cold War, however, Chinese Communists were portrayed in *The Manchurian Candidate* (Frankenheimer, 1962) as Chinese agents (with assistance from the Russians) who brainwash Americans into committing ruthless political assassinations, and the James Bond film *Dr. No* (1962) features an evil and unscrupulous Chinese scientist in the title role.

Although images of Japanese-American immigrants emphasized the patriotism of those who enlisted in the U.S. armed forces, many Japanese immigrants and native-born Japanese Americans were evacuated from their homes and relocated to internment camps during World War II. This historical reality has a fictional counterpart in *The Siege* (1998), in which the American military confines Arab immigrants and Arab Americans in detention centers because the entire ethnic group is seen as potential terrorists. The film is at once complicit with and critical of the Hollywood stereotypes, which have long presented Arabs as greedy, lustful, and exotic villains. More specifically, the Arab stereotype in fictional films and on the television news has been of the evil international terrorist at war with Judaism, Christianity, and the Western world in the name of Islamic fundamentalism (e.g., *True Lies* [1994]). After the 1993 Oklahoma City terrorist bombing, the media scapegoated immigrants by running stories about people seeking asylum from the Middle East and Pakistan, and the 1990–91 Persian Gulf War, which received 24-hour news coverage on CNN, was facilitated by years of dehumanizing stereotypes and the overall marginalization of Arab history and Islamic culture.

America's military involvement in Southeast Asia in the 1960s and 1970s was also reflected in the mass media. In addition to the spate of Vietnam War films in the 1970s and early 1980s, Disney's made-for-television docudrama *The Girl Who Spelled Freedom* (1985) told the story of a young refugee from Cambodia who emigrates to Tennessee with her family in 1979 and eventually wins a national spelling bee. In Louis Malle's *Alamo Bay* (1985), a despondent Vietnam veteran in danger of losing his livelihood is pushed to the edge when he sees Vietnamese immigrants moving into the fishing industry in a Texas bay town. Television news journalism in the 1970s and 1980s complemented these fictional portrayals through exaggerated coverage of the presence of gang activities among young immigrants from Southeast Asia. Other popular representations of Asian Americans and immigrants that could be viewed as more positive representations include *The Karate Kid* films (1984–89) and *The Joy Luck Club* (1993), which tells the story of four Chinese mothers who emigrate to the United States after World War II and struggle with their relationship to a younger generation of assimilated Chinese-American women.

The term Asian, like Hispanic, is problematic because it encompasses a wide range of ethnicities and nationalities, including East Indian. As has been the case historically for other ethnic groups (such as Arab immigrants), Indian immigrants are for the most part absent from or peripheral to mainstream American film. One important exception to this rule is *Mississippi Masala* (1991), which tells the story of an Indian family forced from Uganda by Idi Amin's regime in the 1970s. They emigrate to Mississippi and twenty years later their Indian-American daughter falls in love with an African-American man (Denzel Washington), forcing the family to face their prejudices. East Indian characters are even more invisible on American television, although the animated situation comedy *The Simpsons* (Fox, 1989–) includes a character named Apu Nahasapeemapetilon who is an illegal immigrant from India with an exaggerated accent and a stereotypical job as the manager of the local convenience store.

THE AMERICAN IMMIGRANT DREAM

Whatever the historical shifts in the relationship between the mass media, American society, and immigrant groups, the traditional nineteenth-century narrative of American immigration has continued to be told and mythologized on film and television. In Paul Mazursky's *Moscow on the Hudson* (1984), for instance, a Russian saxophone player working in a circus defects in the middle of Bloomingdales during a tour in the United States. He is befriended by the African-American security guard (Cleavant Derricks), falls in love with the Italian immigrant from behind the perfume counter (Maria Conchita Alonso), and is aided by an immigration attorney (and onetime Cuban immigrant) played by Alejandro Rey. He ultimately succeeds, getting the girl, a job, and achieves his American immigrant dream. Like the radio and television series *Life with Luigi* in the late 1940s and early 1950s, the ethnically diverse situation comedy *What a Country!* (Syndicated, 1986–87) was set in a citizenship class for immigrants in Los Angeles. The program starred Yakov Smirnoff as a Russian immigrant (which he was in real life), and a cast of immigrant characters from Pakistan, Hungary, Latin America, Korea, and Africa. Another version of the traditional immigrant story formed the basis for the sitcom *Perfect Strangers* (ABC, 1986–93) as sheepherder Balki Bartokomous (Bronson Pinchot) emigrates to the United States from the fictional European island nation of Mypos to live the American Dream with his cousin in Chicago.

Avalon (1990) told the story of a Jewish family

coming to America at the beginning of the twentieth century to make a better life for themselves in the promised land, while American independent filmmaker Jim Jarmusch has told the immigrant story in more subtle, less celebratory ways. His 1984 *Stranger than Paradise* has an Eastern European immigrant woman make her way from New York to the Midwest, and his 1991 *Night on Earth*, follows an endearing East German immigrant cab driver around New York where he is educated by African American and Latino New Yorkers. Although less conventional and obvious than *Moscow on the Hudson*, Jarmusch also valorizes the mythology of the American melting pot in these films. The saga of the Corleone Mafia crime family continued with *The Godfather, Part III* (1990), completing a trilogy that began with a young Don Vito Corleone emigrating from Sicily to New York in the early 1900s. In 1992, *Far and Away*, directed by Ron Howard and starring Tom Cruise and Nicole Kidman, offered an historical epic romance that told the story of late-nineteenth-century Irish immigrants struggling to overcome class differences during the Oklahoma Land Rush. Taken together, all of these films point to the continued centrality of the immigrant experience in the American popular imagination.

RADIO AND TELEVISION

DAVID SARNOFF

Radio broadcasting developed very rapidly during the first decades of the twentieth century. In the early period, the airwaves were dominated by amateurs (or "hams") who built their own receivers. The range of amateur broadcasts was only a few miles, and the receivers were mostly made by other experimenters, who, like the broadcasters, pursued radio as a hobby. Soon the demand for music and words over the air led to the development of a radio receiver for the general public. The increase in the number of listeners in turn justified the establishment of stations, especially for the purpose of broadcasting entertainment and information programs. Two years after the first commercial (i.e., advertising-driven) radio station went on the air in 1920 (KDKA in Pittsburgh), over 550 broadcasting stations had been licensed.

In *The Box: An Oral History of Television, 1920–1961*, author Jeff Kisseloff rightly points out that David Sarnoff "is easily the most important figure in the history of telecommunications." Like the moguls of Hollywood, this broadcasting pioneer was a Jewish immigrant who helped build the broadcasting industry not as an inventor or artist, but as a skilled businessman and manager with the ability to promote and market the new technologies of radio and television to the American public. Born in Russia, Sarnoff came to Albany, New York, in 1900, and later moved to New York City, where he found work as a paper boy and then as a radio operator for the Marconi Wireless Telegraph Company (Sarnoff's claim to having been the first Marconi operator to receive distress signals from the *Titanic* have been discredited by media historians). As early as 1916, Sarnoff had come up with the idea of mass-marketing a wireless "radio music box" for the home, but the idea was not implemented until 1921, the year Sarnoff was named general manager of the newly formed Radio Corporation of America (RCA). By the time Sarnoff formed the National Broadcasting Company (NBC) in 1926, over $100,000,000 worth of radio receivers had been sold in the United States. The growth of radio broadcasting in the United States led to unregulated business arrangements between manufacturers of radio equipment and broadcasters. To protect against monopolies, Congress took antitrust measures by passing the Radio Act of 1927, which also created the Federal Communications Commission (FCC) to assign broadcast wavelengths and licenses. The government's antitrust actions eventually resulted in four radio networks—the National Broadcasting Company (NBC), Columbia Broadcasting System (CBS), Mutual Broadcasting System, and American Broadcasting Company (ABC).

The history of television is closely tied to radio because the companies, networks, and businessmen from the radio industry were also central to establishing television as the dominant mass medium of the twentieth century. After World War II, several radio programs were adapted for the new medium of television in an attempt to retain their large audiences and because the advertising-driven model had proved to be cost-effective and profitable. The most influential figure responsible for orchestrating this transition was also broadcasting pioneer David Sarnoff (or "The General" as he preferred to be addressed after being awarded the honorary rank of Brigadier General in 1944). Even before Sarnoff had formed NBC in 1926, he had already committed to developing television (or "radio with pictures"), and he launched an experimental NBC television station in 1928, before introducing the new medium to the American public in 1939 through a widely publicized demonstration at the New York World's Fair. Shortly after World War II (which halted commercial television development in favor of military research), CBS and ABC also launched their own television networks, and the competition among the "big three" for the television viewing public had begun. (Dumont, a small network founded by Allen B. Dumont in 1946, was never profitable or competitive and went out of business in 1955.)

RADIO AND TELEVISION PROGRAMMING DURING THE "GOLDEN AGE"

There were several programs during radio's "golden age" that reflected the immigrant experience. *Americans All, Immigrants All* was a dramatic documentary series that ran for twenty-six episodes during the 1938–39 radio season, highlighting the historical contributions of immigrant groups to building America. Produced by the Department of the Interior and the Works Projects Administration, the thirty-minute episodes were devoted to topics such as *Our Hispanic Heritage, The Negro, The Germans, The Irish*, and *The Jews*. Largely intended to unite the country in preparation for war, NBC found the topic too politically controversial, so CBS ended up broadcasting the series on Sundays at 2 P.M.

One of the most popular programs in radio history was the serialized comedy-drama *The Goldbergs* (or *The Rise of the Goldbergs*), which was broadcast in various forms on NBC and CBS from 1929 through 1950. Created by Gertrude Berg, the program centered on the daily life of a Jewish immigrant family in a New York City ghetto. *Abie's Irish Rose* was an NBC situation comedy in the early 1940s that was first produced as a hit Broadway play and a 1929 film directed by Victor Fleming. The radio sitcom revolved around the interethnic marriage between Abie Levy (Sydney Smith) and Rosemary Murphy (Betty Winkler). The cultural clash between the respective Jewish and Irish Catholic immigrant families, especially the fathers, provided the theme or situation for many of the episodes. From 1948 to 1953 on CBS, the popular situation comedy *Life with Luigi* (titled *The Little Immigrant* until shortly before its premiere) also entertained audiences with the "clash of cultures" theme. In the sitcom, Luigi Basco emigrated to Chicago from Rome to open an antique shop with the hope of becoming an American citizen. Other immigrant characters in the program included Pasquale, the owner of Pasquale's Spaghetti Palace in Chicago's Little Italy, and Schultz, Horowitz, and Olsen, who attended night school with Luigi to study American citizenship, government, and history. Each episode was framed by Luigi writing a letter that began "Dear-a Mamma-mia" (accompanied by the accordion and the song "Oh Marie" playing in the background) and ended with the signature line, "Luigi Basco, the li'l immigrant."

In the late 1940s and 1950s (television's "golden age") there were several popular television programs that represented the American immigrant experience. *Mama* was an extremely popular sitcom that ran on CBS from 1949 to 1957. It depicted the experiences of the Hansens, a Norwegian immigrant family living on Steiner Street in San Francisco at the turn of the twentieth century. *Mama* was based on the book *Mama's Bank Account* by Kathryn Forbes, which was adapted into a play in 1945 and a movie in 1948, both titled *I Remember Mama*. Each episode began with the daughter Katrin (Rosemary Rice) leafing through the pages from the family photo album and reminiscing, "I remember . . . my little sister Dagmar, and my big brother Nels, and Papa. But most of all, I remember mama." Peggy Wood played the loving mama and Judson Laire played papa, a carpenter who made just enough money to support his family. Each week's episode would focus on a small family event, usually relating to one of the children. The program reflected a strict Victorian sensibility, while also offering a warm-hearted, reassuring portrait of Scandinavian Americans. *Life with Luigi* also made the transition from radio to television for one full season in 1952 before being dropped midseason by CBS in 1953. The main character was originally played by J. Carrol Naish (who also did the radio role). The popular *I Love Lucy* (CBS, 1951–57) centered around the marriage between Lucille Ball and the Cuban-American immigrant Desi Arnaz. Although Arnaz's accent was at times used for comic relief, the interracial marriage between Lucy and Ricky Ricardo remains a rare exception to televison's prohibition against miscegenation.

When *The Goldbergs* (CBS/NBC/Dumont, 1949–55) moved from radio to network television in 1949, Molly, her husband Jake, Uncle Dave, and children Sammy and Rosalie still lived in a crowded Bronx apartment on Tremont Avenue with other working-class Jews, many of them immigrants like Molly and Jake. In 1954, the series changed its name from *The Goldbergs* to the more ethnically neutral *Molly*, and like many Americans, the Goldbergs bought a house in the fictional suburb of Haverville. The trajectory of *The Goldbergs* series from radio to television and the city to the suburbs reflects the history of broadcasting and historical migration of many actual immigrants out of urban areas after the war. In later episodes, Molly and Jake's Depression-era immigrant sensibilities of thrift and frugality were transformed into the 1950s consumerism embodied in their native-born children, who often educated their parents (and the viewing audience) on topics essential to the new consumer economy, such as the advantages of buying on credit. In 1956, CBS premiered *Hey, Jeannie!*, a sitcom about an immigrant woman from Scotland (Jeannie Carson) who finds work in a New York donut shop, only to see it canceled in 1957. By 1958, then, *The Goldbergs, Mama, Life with Luigi, I Love Lucy*, and *Hey, Jeannie!*, as well as the working-class sitcoms *The Honeymooners* and *The Life of Riley*, were canceled and replaced by middle-class WASP family situation comedies such as *Ozzie and Harriet* (The Nelsons [ABC, 1952–66]), *Leave it to Beaver* (The Cleavers [CBS/ABC, 1957–63]), *The Donna Reed Show* (The Stones [ABC, 1958–66]), and *Father Knows Best* (The Andersons [CBS/NBC, 1954–62]).

TELEVISION PROGRAMMING SINCE 1960

Although American television networks had abandoned immigrant sitcoms by the end of the 1950s, immigrant characters have, of course, continued to appear on television in news broadcasts and as characters in fictional television genres. The 1974 series *The New Land* (ABC) was based on the Swedish epic films *The Emigrants [Utvandrarna]* (Troell, 1971) and *The New Land [Nybyggarna]* (Troell, 1972). The television show starred Max von Sydow and Liv Ullmann as an immigrant Swedish couple who immigrates to the American Midwest in the 1850s. This one-hour historical drama could not survive opposite the new political sitcom *All in the Family* (CBS, 1971–79) and was canceled mid-season.

The long-running *Bonanza* (NBC, 1959–73) inherited the Asian immigrant domestic coolie character in Hop Sing (Victor Sen Yung) who frenetically runs around his employer's home completing all the domestic tasks and providing comic relief. While Hop Sing's character speaks with a Chinese accent, the more Americanized Chinese immigrants on *Bonanza* also work in service positions. (This coolie character has its Japanese counterpart in the manservant "Charlie" stereotype present in many Hollywood films.) For the most part, however, regular Asian-American immigrant characters have been absent from mainstream television, or relegated to supporting or guest parts (see Darrell Y. Hamamoto's book *Monitored Peril*). In 1994, stand-up comic Margaret Cho starred in the ABC sitcom *All-American Girl*, which was premised on the differences between an Americanized daughter of Korean immigrant parents, but which was canceled after only one season. Asian-American women such as Connie Chung (*CBS Evening News*, 1993–95 and ABC's *20/20*, 1999–), have been assigned positions as anchors (especially in local news) but largely, according to Darrell Y. Hamamoto, to exploit their "exotic looks." One of the few popular Asian stars on mainstream television in the late 1990s was Sammo Hung Kam-Bo, the Hong Kong native and star of the martial arts action program *Martial Law* (CBS, 1998–), which, like the earlier *Kung Fu* (ABC, 1972–75) capitalizes on the association of Asians with the mysterious and supernatural powers of martial arts and the karate/kung fu subgenre popularized by Bruce Lee (e.g., *Enter the Dragon* [1973] and *Game of Death* [1978]) and more recently by Jackie Chan (*Rush Hour* [1998] and *Shanghai Noon* [2000]).

Chico and the Man (NBC, 1974–78) starred Freddie Prinze (who was of Puerto Rican and Hungarian descent) as a Mexican-American mechanic in the barrio of East Los Angeles. In response to Chicano organizations' protests over the lack of Chicanos in the cast (and the television industry in general), as well as the use of the derogatory nickname "Chico," several Mexican Americans were added to the cast. The show was canceled shortly after Prinze committed suicide in 1976, and remains a rare example, however brief, of a Chicano or Latino character in a leading television role. In 1984, producer Norman Lear attempted to launch his own sitcom entitled *a.k.a. Pablo* about a Mexican-American comic named Paul (Pablo) Rivera (played by Paul Rodriguez) and his family, but it was canceled after a few episodes. Although no racial groups besides black and white appeared on daytime television before 1980 (the year that Latinos became the fastest growing immigrant group in the United States), in the 1980s, Latinos began to get guest or temporary roles on soap operas. During the 1990s Latinos were given regular parts, such as the Santos family on *All My Children* (NBC, 1970–) and the maid Carlotta Vega (Patricia Mauceri) and her son Cristian (Yorlin Madera) on *One Life to Live* (ABC, 1968–). During the 1990s, in prime-time programming, Latino actor Hector Elizondo played a non-Latino role on *Chicago Hope* (CBS, 1994–2000), while Jimmy Smits played a Latino role as a detective on *NYPD Blue* (ABC, 1993–) from 1994 to 1998. The Associated Press reported in June 2000 that the coverage of the Elian Gonzales controversy had received an inordinate amount of news coverage, surpassing even the O. J. Simpson murder trial. A major aspect of the news stories was immigrant rights in relation to issues of family and international politics. Elian was a big star during the 1999–2000 television season largely due to his good looks and pleasant smile, but also because the Elian Gonzales story provided a convenient synergy across genres and formats with the larger increased presence and marketing of Latinos in American media culture.

THE MEDIA INDUSTRY AND IMMIGRATION IN THE TWENTY-FIRST CENTURY

NARROWCASTING

The presence of topical sitcoms like *All in the Family* and other Norman Lear programs in the early 1970s was due in part to the restructuring of the television industry after cigarette advertising (a major source ot television revenue) was banned from television in 1970. The rise in spot and niche advertising, and the increased concern for demographics and audience market research was another result of this change in the financial stability and structure of the television industry. In the 1960s, the radio and television industries had already begun "narrowcasting" by directing information, programming, and advertising to specific, or narrow, segments of the audience or consumer market, as opposed to broadcasting, which tried to capture the entire viewing public as a homogeneous mass market. Of course, narrowcasting can still be considered a form of mass communication because it reaches large numbers of people from a demographic group, yet the movement toward targeting specific demographics has important consequences for a consideration of immigration and the mass media.

Throughout the 1940s, 1950s, and 1960s, the television industry was dominated by the "big three" networks (ABC, NBC, and CBS). Increased deregulation and the growth of cable channels facilitated by satellite distribution in the 1970s and 1980s (e.g., HBO, ESPN, C-SPAN, CNN, MTV, Nickelodeon, the Playboy Channel, the Disney Channel, QVC, and Lifetime) challenged the dominance of the broadcast television networks. The multiplicity of channels and rise of narrowcasting by advertisers and programmers have been viewed by some as the media equivalent to societal segregation as each cultural group is supposed to watch a separate channel intended for its specific ethnicity. The development in the 1990s of Black Entertainment Television (BET) and Spanish language networks such as Univision and Telemundo, continue this trend of targeting groups, in these cases by categories of race, ethnicity, and/or language. Rather than integrating within programs (i.e., having a multiethnic cast), or into the established prime-time schedules, critics argue that cable has "ghettoized" minority groups into channels with lower advertising revenue and smaller programming budgets. Others, however, have celebrated the increased competition as inaugurating a more democratic media culture that gives viewers more consumer choices and a wider range of cultural representation than any other point in media history (i.e., "there is something for everyone").

Although it is often assumed that programs "hit" their desired demographic "targets," media content may also communicate cross-culturally in ways other than producers intended. The crossover potential of music media has long been recognized by the recording and radio industries, as most recently evidenced by the increased presence of "Latin pop" and by the popularity of rap music and hip-hop culture (once predominantly consumed by African Americans but now popular among white youth markets). Television network executives seem to assume that because television is a primarily visual medium, that it is more difficult to cross over to other demographic groups that are not explicitly represented in the program. Yet the popularity in the 1980s of *The Cosby Show* (NBC, 1984–92) suggests that images of the American Dream and middle-class values can transcend putative barriers of racial identification. Network executives and programmers also seem unable to account for the inconsistent inclusion of minority ethnic groups within their programs and in production and personnel positions when compared to the presence of those groups in the actual U.S. population. For instance, in the 1990s, African Americans have been represented in greater numbers on television than in the U.S. population, while Latinos, which have made up over 10 percent of the U.S. population through the 1990s, have comprised between 1 and 4 percent of the roles in film and television. Asian Americans have been similarly underrepresented. Having said that, it is important to consider when one quantifies images of ethnic groups in the media, that an increase in representation does not address the quality of those roles and images which through negative stereotyping can have regressive rather than progressive effects.

The term "ethnic" (e.g., "ethnic media") is currently used in popular discourse and professional trade publications to refer to minority cultures in the United States, which suggests that those in the cultural majority (i.e., whites) are not ethnic. Nevertheless, as articles in the advertising and media industries have begun point out, the ethnic population of the United States will change dramatically over the next twenty to fifty years according to projected immigration patterns and immigrant family growth. The targeting of new immigrant groups by mainstream media and advertisers, however, already lags behind the demographic realities. Beginning in 1997, the Latino, or Hispanic, population—which comprises the fastest-growing segment of the U.S. population—has been included (along with African Americans) as a distinct market demographic by Nielsen Media Research's television ratings. Although this recognition of the Latino market was reflected in 1999–2000 by the increased popularity of Latino music (for example, performers Ricky Martin, Carlos Santana, Jennifer Lopez, Marc Anthony, and Christina Aguilera), Hispanic organizations were critical of the television industry for the lack of Latino actors and characters during the 1999–2000 programming season. One of the most salient representations of Latino ethnicity on television during 1999–2000 was not even human, but a dog named Dinky, the Chihuahua with the Spanish accent from the popular Taco Bell commercials. Dinky revived the dehumanizing and degrading stereotypes from the "Frito Bandito" advertisements of the late 1960s that warned, "Caution: He loves 'cronchy' Frito corn chips so much he'll stop at nothin to get yours. What's more, he's cunning, clever—and sneaky!"

MEDIA OWNERSHIP AND GLOBALISM

Just as the visual language of silent film during the nickelodeon period lent itself to the multiethnic makeup of early film audiences, so, too, does the popularity of low dialogue, high special effects and action-oriented blockbusters (including martial arts films) appeal to a multilinguistic global marketplace, especially as American films consistently make more money from international sales than domestic box office. In addition to the influence of a global international audience, because the film industry receives more revenue in domestic sales and rentals from nontheatrical distribution of films through video (VHS and DVD format), this format facilitates for niche marketing (the film industry's equivalent of narrowcasting) to ethnic and immigrant audiences. At the same time, video also allows recent immigrants to retain a sense of participation their native culture through low cost distribution of popular films from their home countries.

The coming of sound films of high technical quality in the late 1920s and early 1930s precipitated several important mergers within the film industry. By acquiring first-run theater chains, eight major studios owned by five companies became vertically integrated companies that controlled the 95 percent of all feature film production, distribution, and exhibition in the United States. In 1948, the Supreme Court's Paramount Consent Decrees forced the studios to divorce their exhibition holdings from production and distribution. It would take until 1985, however, before independent film producers would release more films than the major studios (largely as a result of the burgeoning cable and video industries). During the 1980s,

cable networks, satellites, and videocassettes provided new methods of film distribution, while advances in computer technology allowed for lower-cost filmmaking. By the late 1980s, Universal and Columbia were primarily producing films for the television networks, and all of the major studios began negotiating cable and video deals for their theatrical features.

Since the 1960s, the history of film, television, and radio has been one of mergers, conglomeration, and convergence across different media industries. As early as 1955, RKO had been sold to the General Tire and Rubber Corporation. Seven years later, MCA (the Music Corporation of America) acquired Universal. In 1966, Gulf and Western Industries, Inc., bought Paramount; in 1967, Transamerica Corporation bought United Artists; in 1969, Kinney National Services Inc., bought Warner Bros. (renamed Warner Communications); and in 1970, Las Vegas investor Kirk Kerkorian bought MGM. In 1981, Colorado oil magnate Marvin Davis acquired 20th Century Fox (the ownership of which he later shared with publisher Rupert Murdoch's News Corporation), and in 1982, the Coca-Cola Company purchased Columbia. United Artists merged with MGM in 1981 to form MGM/UA, which was later acquired by Turner Broadcasting in 1986.

Also in 1986, Capital Cities Communications purchased ABC, creating Capital Cities/ABC, and General Electric bought RCA, the parent company of NBC (in what was at the time the largest non-oil acquisition in U.S. history). In 1989, Sony bought Columbia Pictures Entertainment from Coca-Cola, and in 1990, Warner Communications and Time Inc. completed a $14.1 billion merger, creating what was then the world's largest media conglomerate. In 1991, Matsushita Electric of Japan acquired MCA, and in 1994 Viacom bought Paramount and the Blockbuster video chain. In 1995, the liquor company Seagram purchased MCA from Matsushita and renamed it Universal Studios, while later that year Westinghouse Electric Corporation bought CBS. In 1996, Disney bought Capital Cities/ABC; Time Warner and Turner Broadcasting System merged; and Westinghouse's CBS unit bought rival radio network Infinity Broadcasting Company. In 1997, Westinghouse changed its name to CBS Inc. after selling its traditional electrical businesses, and in 1998, Seagram bought PolyGram, a leading music company. In 1999, CBS purchased King World Productions, the leading syndicator of television programs, and Viacom bought CBS for $34.5 billion in the biggest media merger in history. In January 2000, however, Internet service provider America Online announced plans to acquire Time Warner forming the media conglomerate AOL-Time-

Warner, which would be worth approximately $350 billion. (The Federal Trade Commission approved this arrangement in December 2000.) In response to this, Seagram announced plans to merge with the European telecommunications company Vivendi to give them Internet and cable delivery systems for their film, television, and music products.

The major film production companies have thus become one of many corporations owned by transnational conglomerates for which films and television programs are secondary to other products and services. For instance, General Electric (GE) makes billions of dollars more annually from military weapons contracts than it does from its television network NBC. Consequently, when the United States takes part in a military conflict, such as the 1990–91 Persian Gulf War, GE has more invested (literally) in promoting the performance of those weapons through its NBC news division than it does in educating viewers and offering balanced journalism. Media conglomerates often own several different media outlets and are thus able to promote a film, television program, radio personality, book, magazine, or theme park across media formats and genres. This is the method of the New Hollywood studio system, which may hire independent companies to produce films, but monopolizes the distribution and promotion of content through different media. Disney, the only studio-era company to remain controlled by industry veterans, now owns the television network ABC and has launched the Go.com Internet portal (formerly Infoseek.com), giving it ownership of two important media outlets (television and the Internet) for distributing and promoting products and theme parks in American homes.

The current unprecedented level of media concentration is significant for any consideration of American immigration because it means that fewer and fewer voices are being represented through the mainstream media, making it extremely difficult for newcomers to have access to the media to express their views. The media performs a crucial role in the check and balance system of democracy by serving as a watchdog for unethical government and businesses practices and by providing the public with the necessary information it needs to make informed decisions. The undemocratic structure of the media industry lends itself to propagating the stereotypes and portrayals of minority immigrant groups in ways that best serve the interests of the elite group who control the media. This affects not only when, where and if immigrant-related issues are deemed newsworthy by the media, but also how those issues are presented and framed. To have the major media and entertainment industries in the control of a small handful of corporations gives those interests an inordinate amount of influence and constitutes a dangerous crisis in American democracy. Recent antitrust rulings against the Microsoft Corporation may signal a trend toward antitrust regulation that could possibly affect the structure of the media industry. Although the Microsoft case has received media coverage, it is not in the media's interest to report on its own monopolistic structures or to criticize the structure of its parent companies. Because we live in an increasingly mass-mediated world in which media becomes more and more responsible for constructing our understanding of reality—including how people view immigrant groups and immigration issues—some observers and critics deem it essential to democratize the media and its representations so that alternative voices can be heard.

ALTERNATIVE MEDIA AND DEMOCRATIC MEDIA CULTURE

While the mainstream mass media's portrayal of the immigrant experience has changed in degree and kind throughout the twentieth century, there is also a rich tradition of alternative media that has provided important avenues of ethnic expression and cultural exchange in the United States. For instance, Yiddish film production and exhibition flourished in the United States between the two world wars, until its decline after the Holocaust, Stalinism, and assimilation in America by new immigrants. Jonas Mekas's experimental film diaries, entitled *Lost, Lost, Lost* (1976), between 1949 and 1963, tell the story of Mekas's emigration from Lithuania and the Lithuanian immigrant community's painful attempts to adapt to life in the United States while also fighting for the independence of their homeland. Pioneer avant-garde filmmaker Maya Deren (*Meshes of the Afternoon* [1943]) emigrated to America in 1922 from Kiev with her parents (as Eleanora Derenkowsky) to escape pogroms against Russian Jews. More recently, there is also a strong tradition of Latino and Chicano media art being exhibited at film and video festivals, museums, and galleries, rather than at mainstream theaters, and distributed through alternative media.

Many of the ethnic radio stations formed in the 1920s and 1930s to appeal to new immigrants have been forced to changed their programming from Yiddish, Polish, Czech, Greek, German, and Swedish to Spanish as immigration from European regions has slowed and Latin American immigration has increased since the mid-1960s. Foreign-language stations have also been increasing in the 1990s because the time-brokered or rental approach (buying programming time on a station) has become very popular in the age of duopolies and deregulation. Because the cost of buying a station is prohibitive as well as illegal if you are not an American citizen, many foreign-language broadcasters enter into local agreements with established businesses and markets.

Always in search of untapped consumer markets, several firms have begun to use data from the Immigration and Naturalization Service to help market, promote, and distribute media content to specialized immigrant populations in the United States. All mainstream media content is driven by advertising revenue, which, in turn, is premised on delivering an audience of consumers to businesses. Although the mass media are profit-driven, some segments of the audience (or markets) matter to advertisers more than do others. If a television or radio program is not reaching a very large audience, but is being viewed by a desired (i.e., affluent or ethnic) demographic segment of the population, the program is likely to stay on the air. Media executives' and advertising agencies' perceptions of, and attitudes toward, immigrant or "minority" ethnic groups have at times caused advertisers and businesses to overlook immigrant audiences and "ethnic media" outlets, in addition to either under-representing members of immigrant groups in their programming and production staffs, or portraying stereotypes.

The 1990s, however, witnessed the growth of Latino and Chicano media from a newly recognized niche to a dominant consumer market in cities with a large Latino/Chicano population. By 1995, Spanish-language stations KLVE in Los Angeles, WSKQ in New York, and WRMA in Miami had all reached number one in the Arbitron radio audience ratings. This success has led to the acquisition of some of these stations by larger media companies, such as Paxson Communications Corporation, which owns six stations in the Miami market. In 1995, Sony bought the Spanish-language television network Telemundo in an attempt to challenge Univision for a share of the Latino market. In Los Angeles, there are at least thirteen ethnic radio stations, including KBLA (Korean), KKHJ (Spanish/News Radio), KORG (Talk/Various foreign languages), KRRA (Spanish/Mexican), KTNQ (Spanish/Talk), KWKW (Spanish), KWRM (Spanish), KALI (Asian), KBUE (Spanish/Mexican), KLAX (all Spanish), KLVE (Spanish), KSCA (Spanish/Mexican), and KSSE (Spanish/Mexican). This points to the growing commercial viability of niche ethnic radio in smaller U.S. markets. For instance, the Portuguese-language station WJDF in New Bedford, Massachusetts, has no competition, so its 150,000 listeners each week are enough to keep the station profitable. Many

other ethnic stations, such as the Asian-language stations KVTO in San Francisco and KALI in Orange County, California, are returning to the multiformat (talk, news, and music) model of radio from the 1930s through the 1950s.

Similarly, Los Angeles's station KSCI-TV Channel 18 is an independent station that provides twenty-four-hour programming in at least sixteen languages (Arabic, Armenian, Cambodian, Mandarin, French, Tagalog, German, Hungarian, Persian, Italian, Japanese, Hebrew, Korean, Russian, Vietnamese, and English). Most of its programming is produced in the United States by and for immigrant and ethnic groups. The cable networks Univision and Telemundo provide Latino immigrants with twenty-four-hour Spanish-language television programming in several genres, from telenovelas from Mexico and South America to variety, talk, and news magazine programs. The Ethnic-American Broadcasting Company (EABC) provides foreign-language and ethnic programming across North America through satellite distribution. According to its promotional material, EABC provides "a service which meets the specific needs of today's growing immigrant population." EABC imports programming over satellite, while also producing its own foreign-language shows. Its flagship channel is the Russian-language WMNB with over 60,000 subscribers, making EABC the "largest non-Hispanic, ethnic pay-TV network in North America." EABC has more than twenty channels of ethnic-specific foreign-language programming, including Russian, Arabic, Ukrainian, Greek, Italian, East Indian, Filipino, Chinese, Japanese, Korean, German, Polish, French, Persian, Turkish, and Serbian.

In addition to satellite technology, cable programs, and niche radio, all of which allow immigrants to participate in their native cultures, the Internet also provides low-cost global access to radio and television through digital streaming technology. Similarly, the Internet provides access to news and entertainment Web sites and to personal home pages, and allows e-mail communication between people from one's home country to nations around the world. Although the proposed merger between America Online and Time Warner may signal a movement toward the kind of corporate ownership and control of the Internet that currently exists with television and film in the beginning of the twenty-first century, the Internet and World Wide Web are still promising and exciting media with democratic cultural potential for American immigration.

James Castonguay

See also: Public Opinion and Immigration (Part II, Sec. 6); Arts I: Literature, Arts II: Performing Arts, Language, Media Portrayal of Immigrants, Press, Sports (Part II, Sec. 10).

BIBLIOGRAPHY

Barnouw, Erik. *A History of Broadcasting in the United States.* 3 vols. New York: Oxford University Press, 1966–70.

———. *Tube of Plenty: The Evolution of American Television.* Rev. ed. New York: Oxford University Press, 1990.

Cook, David A. *A History of Narrative Film.* 3rd ed. New York: W. W. Norton, 1996.

Dunning, John. *On the Air: The Encyclopedia of Old-Time Radio.* New York: Oxford University Press, 1998.

Friedman, Lester D., ed. *Unspeakable Images: Ethnicity and the American Cinema.* Chicago: University of Illinois Press, 1991.

Genco, Louis V., ed. "The Original Old Time Radio (OTR) WWW Pages." http://www.old-time.com/.

Hamamoto, Darrell Y. *Monitored Peril: Asian Americans and the Politics of TV Representation.* Minneapolis, MN: University of Minnesota Press, 1994.

Jones, Dorothy P. *The Portrayal of China and India on the American Screen, 1896–1955: The Evolution of Chinese and Indian Themes, Locales, and Characters as Portrayed on the American Screen.* Cambridge, MA: Center for International Studies, MIT, 1955.

Kim, Young Yun. "Communication Patterns of Foreign Immigrants in the Process of Acculturation." *Human Communication Research* 4:1 (Fall 1997): 66–77.

Kisseloff, Jeff. *The Box: An Oral History of Television, 1920–1961.* New York: Penguin, 1995.

Lester, Paul M., ed. *Images That Injure: Pictorial Stereotypes in the Media.* Westport, CT: Praeger, 1996.

López, Ana M. "Are All Latins from Manhattan?: Hollywood, Ethnography, and Cultural Colonialism." In *Unspeakable Images: Ethnicity and the American Cinema,* ed. Lester D. Friedman, pp. 404–24. Chicago: University of Illinois Press, 1991.

Maciel, David R., and María Herrera-Sobek, eds. *Culture Across Borders: Mexican Immigration and Popular Culture.* Tucson: University of Arizona Press, 1998.

Marchetti, Gina. *Romance and the "Yellow Peril": Race, Sex and Discursive Strategies in Hollywood Fiction.* Berkeley, CA: University of California Press, 1993.

Musser, Charles. *The Emergence of Cinema: The American Screen to 1907.* New York: Charles Scribner's Sons, 1990.

———. "Ethnicity, Role-Playing, and American Film Comedy: From *Chinese Laundry Scene* to *Whoopee* (1894–1930)." In *Unspeakable Images: Ethnicity and the American Cinema,* ed. Lester D. Friedman, pp. 39–81. Chicago: University of Illinois Press, 1991.

Naficy, Hamid. "Narrowcasting in Diaspora: Middle Eastern Television in Los Angeles." In *Living Color: Race and Television in the United States,* ed. Sasha Torres, pp. 82–96. Durham, NC: Duke University Press, 1998.

Rogin, Michael. *Blackface, White Noise: Jewish Immigrants in the Hollywood Melting Pot.* Berkeley, CA: University of California Press, 1996.

Taylor, Ella. *Prime-Time Families.* Berkeley, CA: University of California Press, 1989.

$\mathscr{F}$OREIGN AND IMMIGRANT INFLUENCE ON AMERICAN POPULAR CULTURE

$\mathscr{A}$fter World War II, immigrant groups actively participated in American popular culture as both cultural consumers and cultural contributors. While the period immediately following the war was a time when Allied victory came to represent an affirmation of American values, and cold war tensions reinforced the need for a strong national identity, the second half of the twentieth century is most important because it saw, for the first time, the major integration of foreign cultural elements into America's popular culture not only as curiosities, but as viable alternatives to the mainstream. Beginning with the so-called Beat movement of the 1950s and continuing through the counterculture moment in the 1960s, the deterioration of popular confidence in the American way (accelerated particularly during the Vietnam War) coupled with increasing popular exposure to foreign countries through the expansion of television and air travel resulted in a fetishism for the exotic and the new. As confidence in American core values decreased over a half century and the producers and products of mainstream American culture (represented in the popular imagination by such products and producers as Hollywood studios, Coca-Cola, and Nike) came to be viewed by many as monolithic and bland, immigrant and foreign influence on popular culture grew stronger.

The impact of immigration and immigrants on American popular culture in the post–World War II era has been, of course, contingent on the ebb and flow of immigration. With restrictive immigration laws in place through the Immigration and Nationality Act of 1965, few immigrants were able to make their way to the United States for almost two decades. Thus, the influence of newly arrived immigrants on American society was relatively slight, even as Americans became increasingly receptive to foreign cultural influences primarily through the counterculture of the 1960s and 1970s. Moreover, the impact of the 1965 lib-eralization of immigrant law, the Immigration and Nationality Act, took some time to play itself out in terms of cultural impact. That is to say, until the upturn in immigration produced by the law had created a critical mass of the foreign-born, the cultural influence of immigrants on American society remained relatively slight. Because the increase in immigration gradually gained momentum, it is difficult to say when that critical mass was achieved, although many students of modern American immigration would place it sometime in the late 1970s or early 1980s.

1940s AND 1950s

The impact of immigrants on American popular culture during the latter half of the twentieth century can be linked to the level of popular confidence in the economy and social stability at a particular time. Despite the civil unrest and turmoil over civil rights throughout the South after World War II, for most of the country this period was marked by prosperity and a high level of national confidence. Immigrant impact on popular culture was therefore limited to the cultural fringes—the Beat fetishism for Eastern religions, for example—or mainstream representations that held to traditional and often stereotypical models, such as in the popular Charlie Chan films of the 1940s. During the 1940s and 1950s, immigrant and foreign cultural elements did not so much become part of the American mainstream as foreign cultures continued to be mastered by an American popular culture that demonstrated a remarkable power to disempower and devalue foreign cultures by rendering them quaint. Nonetheless, during this period many immigrants were able to take advantage of a booming economy and increased public mobility to lay the economic foundations—in the form of small businesses such as

A sign of immigrant influence on American customs is the fact that salsa now outpaces ketchup as the number one condiment on the nation's dinner tables. *(AP/Wide World Photos)*

restaurants, grocery stores, car dealerships, and motels—that later enabled them to institutionalize elements of their cultures in the American mainstream. After World War II, businesses such as Chinese, Indian, and Mexican restaurants first became firmly integrated parts of American popular culture rather than foreign cultural curiosities.

The 1940s and 1950s were a time of popular confidence in America balanced by rapid social, demographic, and economic change. In 1943, Congress repealed legislation dating to 1882 that had barred Chinese immigration. At the time, the repeal (which still established small quotas of 105 immigrants per year) was largely a statement of sympathy for China, an ally in the war against Japan. Nonetheless, it was the first in a series of steps that would reinvigorate the flow of immigrants to America, culminating in the

Immigration and Nationality Act of 1952, which repealed laws excluding Asians from settling in the United States and eliminated race as a barrier to nationalization, making it possible for Asian immigrants to become American citizens. Moreover, provisions within the act that permitted family reunification allowed 45,000 Japanese and 32,000 Chinese to emigrate during the 1950s. An estimated 450,000 Mexicans emigrated to the Southwest and California during the 1950s as well.

The practical effect of these new laws and reinvigoration of immigration on American popular culture, though, was not immediately very great. However, the 1950s saw an expansion of popular consumer culture unprecedented in the United States. The baby boom—the huge number of children born between 1947 and 1961—saw the juvenile-products market bring in $33 billion in one year. Diapers alone were a $50 million industry in 1957. Between 1948 and 1955 the number of televisions in America increased from 172,000 to 32 million, and over the same period the number of television stations grew from thirty-two into the hundreds.

While much of the music, film, and television produced during this period now occupies the place of kitsch in the eyes of many Americans (witness the popularity of 1950s fashions during the 1980s or of swing music in the late 1990s), this period nonetheless saw the emergence of an uncondescending attention to minority groups in popular media that was later to serve a vital function in helping to integrate immigrant elements into American popular culture. Films such as *Imitation of Life, Gentleman's Agreement*, and *Touch of Evil* told the stories of African Americans, Jews, and Mexican Americans and presented members of these groups not as obviously foreign curiosities living in the United States but as active members of the American postwar consumer culture. Different from the popular works of social crusaders of the nineteenth century, such as Jacob Riis's *How the Other Half Lives*, new books and films often approached minority groups as integrated parts of a larger American culture, whose lives and problems could be presented through mainstream media. In doing this, American popular culture became prepared for the explosion of immigrant influence that was to occur during the 1960s.

Ultimately, though, the widespread popular confidence and economic prosperity during this period made the expanding American popular culture largely monolithic. While parents expressed anxiety about the dangers of the teenage-oriented consumer culture that developed around rock-and-roll music, immigrant groups contributed little to this. By the end of the 1950s, millions of Americans were enjoying an affluence the likes of which they could not have imagined just twenty years earlier. In the process, however, popular expectations were growing, and older cultural norms were beginning to be gradually and subtly undermined. As the value of the American way came into question, people began to look for alternatives in other cultures, both those represented by immigrants living within the borders of the United States and those thousands of miles away. Popular norms, however, did not truly face a strong challenge until the 1960s, when social unrest and popular dissatisfaction reached a scale not seen since the time of the Civil War.

1960s AND 1970s

If one can say that the 1950s were a time when hidden tensions were applying pressure to long-standing cultural norms, one can also say that it was during the 1960s that this pressure finally exploded and these tensions manifested themselves in the counterculture movement. While preexisting tensions concerning the nuclear arms race, U.S. foreign policy, and civil rights broke forth most noticeably in the decade of the 1960s, immigrant and foreign influences similarly began to penetrate American popular culture, due largely to the economic base that many immigrants had been able to establish in the growing economy of the 1950s. At the same time, the widespread unrest centered around the civil and women's rights movements and, most important, the war in Vietnam produced for many dissatisfaction with the government and mainstream American society. The explosion of popular consumer culture in the 1950s had created fear among parents, as for the first time the culture of teenagers and adults began to take paths with no recognizable similarities. Yet by the 1960s and 1970s, this consumer culture had become institutionalized, and young people, to whom popular culture producers most vigorously cater, began to seek modes of expression in dress, music, and political and sexual orientation and behavior unlike those that had been radically new just a decade earlier. In such an environment, products and practices not traditionally associated with the United States took on a strong appeal for many Americans. Not only were they new and exotic, but, because they were associated with foreign cultures, they did not carry the negative connotations that being American began to represent to many people.

It has been said that the 1960s can best be understood by the fact that the Beatles began the decade dressed like accountants and ended it dressed like hobos. Indeed, popular culture during this decade was characterized by a general loosening of attitudes and a breaking down of taboos. One of the most important of these concerned the visibility of minority figures. In the 1950s, rock-and-roll producer Sam Phillips had needed a white singer (Elvis Presley) to sing songs by African Americans in order to make them publicly acceptable. By the mid-1960s, though, music in particular had become tolerant of publicly visible minority figures, and in that environment immigrant performers such as Ravi Shankar of India and later in the 1970s the Jamaican Bob Marley were able to integrate not only their music but themselves into the canon of popular culture. At the same time, many observers of the music industry, witnessing the bubblegum music fad of the early 1960s, wondered aloud if rock and roll had not exhausted its possibilities. In response, by the late 1960s, mainstream popular artists such as the Beatles, the Who, and the Doors had begun to turn to foreign influences, unfamiliar to American audiences, in order to make their music sound new and different.

Still, the strongest possible appeal of foreign cultural elements to the consumers of popular culture in the 1960s was the implicit rejection of the American mainstream that the adoption of foreign modes carried, even as these elements gradually became part of the mainstream themselves. Opposition to the Vietnam War and American foreign policy, along with growing awareness of the nation's long history of racism and discrimination, led many college students into racial politics and Marxism. Foreigners such as the Argentinean Che Guevara became not only ideological heroes of the left, but figures of popular culture who appeared on posters and t-shirts. So-called hippies acted on the perception that the United States had become so obsessed with money and power and so driven by technology that it had lost its spiritual element (many residents of communes simply referred to the outside world as "Babylon"). Included in this perception of the soullessness of modern life was organized religion, which many felt served only to reinforce outdated cultural norms. In response, these people turned to Eastern faiths such as Buddhism and Hinduism, which seemed far beyond the American mainstream. Indeed, hippies expressed a particular interest in the culture of India and Tibet, adopting colorful Indian fashions and practices such as burning incense. Affiliating themselves with a foreign culture, rather than a reactionary ideology, was a powerful statement of rejection of the mainstream, because it was actually a rejection in favor of a clearcut cultural alternative and not for an ideological system such as Marxism that could be dismissed as idealistic.

One peculiar side effect of the counterculture movement, though, was that the more mainstream gains of immigrant groups largely fell by the wayside. By the beginning of the 1980s, immigrant groups had become an established part of American popular culture, particularly as small-business owners, and as part of the mainstream, they were rejected by the counterculture. In a sense, from the end of the World War II to 1980, cultural elements such as Chinese food underwent a remarkable progression, one where they first entered popular culture as exotic novelties, inseparable from their foreign identities, and gradually became part of the American mainstream, largely inseparable from the mainstream identity. During the last two decades of the twentieth century, though, such institutions were to have their foreign identities reestablished from without, in the form of stereotypes.

1980s AND 1990s

As the 1950s had been, the 1980s and 1990s were decades of great economic expansion in America. There were crucial differences between these two boom periods, though, which produced widely different environments for immigrants in the arena of popular culture. The boom of the 1950s had affected Americans with recent memories of the crippling poverty and material deprivation of the Great Depression. Buoyed by an era of good feelings in the wake of the Allied victory, the explosion of consumer culture in the 1950s created a high level of popular confidence among many Americans. By the 1980s, though, Americans, on average, had much greater expectations, particularly economically, than those who had lived through the Depression and World War II. Consequently, the boom of the 1980s did not produce a similar era of good feelings among many Americans but instead led to increasing frustration as the gap between rich and poor widened.

In the field of popular culture, this frustration fused with several other factors to reintroduce into popular culture stereotypes of immigrants that had faded somewhat during the 1960s and 1970s. The fact that, since 1945, certain immigrant groups (Chinese, Koreans, Japanese, Mexicans, and Indians, for example) were able to achieve economic footholds and that these footholds (primarily in the form of small businesses such as Chinese restaurants and Korean grocery stores) became institutionalized in the popular imagination made them open to criticism along with the rest of mainstream culture. Especially in the late 1980s and throughout the 1990s, a widespread push for multiculturalism emerged that celebrated the contributions of many different groups to American society. At the same time, many Americans reacted to what they considered the fragmentation of a unified national identity. New stereotypes emerged in popular culture. Television shows such as *The Simpsons* and *Saturday Night Live* gained widespread popularity by appealing to these stereotypes, with characters such as Apu, the Indian convenience-store owner, in the former and a pidgin-English-speaking Korean grocer in the latter. The Arab terrorist proved to be one of the firmest stereotypes of this new era, and countless films stocked their productions with these characters, who by the end of the 1980s had come to replace the Soviets as Hollywood's most reliable villains.

At the same time that stereotypes returned strongly during this period, though, immigrant and foreign influence on American popular culture remained persistent. While stereotypes were one reaction to multiculturalism and an expression of frustration, many other Americans absorbed the increasing foreign presence in the popular culture canon with great enthusiasm. The most powerful force by far in popular culture is the new and exotic. During the 1960s, foreign modes of cultural expression had appealed to many in the counterculture not only because they presented alternatives to the American mainstream (in which many had lost confidence), but because they were ways of asserting personal separation from the mainstream and, in that way, allowed the individual a certain claim to superiority over others who lacked this separation. Ever-expanding media and possibilities for world travel in the 1980s and 1990s allowed the producers of popular culture to flood the market with items such as Indonesian cigarettes, Jamaican clothing, and Japanese cartoons, whose primary appeal to the consumer seeking to assert his or her individuality through conspicuous consumption was their newness and relative obscurity.

Yet the economic prosperity of this period, coupled with relatively little popular unrest, meant that, unlike during the 1960s, the consumption of foreign elements for the popular culture consumers of the 1990s no longer contained an implicit rejection of the American way. In this sense, even as many in America reacted to immigrant economic footholds with a reinvigorated stereotyping, immigrant impact on American popular culture continued to gain strength because it presented a seemingly endless supply of new and different possibilities for individual differentiation from the mainstream.

By the year 2000, it has become clear that the new post-1965 immigration has had a broad, profound, and lasting impact on American culture. First, daily life has been profoundly changed, most notably in American dietary habits. Ethnic restaurants have sprouted across the American landscape, with Ethiopian, Indian, Japanese, and Thai establishments, among others, joining those eateries (such as Chinese and Italian) opened by earlier waves of immigrants. At the same time, Mexican cuisine has spread across America from its previous bastions in California, Texas, and the Southwest. Indeed, this growth in Mexican restaurants follows the spread of Mexican immigrants to much of the rest of the country in the 1980s and 1990s. Nor is the impact of immigrant cultures on U.S. eating habits solely restricted to restaurants. Today, salsa—rather than ketchup—is the number one condiment on American tables.

American music, as well, has been heavily influenced by the new immigration. While Americans, as noted earlier, have been increasingly listening to foreign popular music since the 1960s and 1970s, the explosion in the popularity of "world music" in the 1980s and 1990s could, at least in part, be directly related to the influx of peoples from diverse cultures. Immigration from the far corners of the globe has also fundamentally affected the way American children learn about their own country and the world around them. Beginning at the primary level—but particularly in college—educational institutions have incorporated world history into their curricula, often at the expense of courses in Western civilization. This educational emphasis on world history and culture impacts popular culture as students take their newfound awareness of international cultures out into the world, influencing the popular culture that they so effectively maintain through their enthusiasm and their pocketbooks.

But education also underscores the unevenness of the impact of immigration on American popular culture. Always linguistically challenged, America's educational establishment has done little to promote bilingualism. Indeed, many Americans have come to see bilingualism as a threat to national unity and social cohesiveness, while voters in several immigrant-heavy states—such as California and Arizona—have gone so far as to pass referenda severely limiting bilingual education. While much of this linguistic backlash is aimed at immigrants themselves, it has had the side effect of de-emphasizing bilingual studies for native-born, English-speaking students.

Another sign of the unevenness of immigration's impact on American popular culture has been in the mass media, most notably television. While recent decades have seen a proliferation of Spanish-language programing and radio franchises in many American cities, Hispanics, Asians, and other immigrant groups have barely been able to penetrate prime-time television on major English-language networks and cable stations, as recent protests by Hispanic and Asian advocacy groups have made clear.

As the twenty-first century dawns, however, there are increasing signs that this resistance is beginning to break down. As with the growing immigrant popular culture impact of the 1980s and 1990s, this phenomenon is driven by numbers. By 2000, California—home state of so much of American media and the source of innumerable cultural fads—had become a minority-majority state. That is to say, no single race or ethnic group claimed more than 50 percent of the population. Within the next 50 or so years, this development is expected to spread from state to state until, perhaps by mid-century, it is expected that non-whites will become a majority of the population of the country as a whole. Some early evidence of the influence this demographic tide is having came in the ballyhoo over the rise of Hispanic pop stars at the start of the twenty-first century. As Asians and other non-European immigrant groups begin to make their numerical presence felt, their cultural impact will also undoubtedly increase.

Michael Lloyd Gruver

See also: Arts I: Literature, Arts II: Performing Arts, Arts III: Visual and Religious Arts, Film, Radio, and Television, Language, Media Portrayal of Immigrants, Sports (Part II, Sec. 10).

BIBLIOGRAPHY

Bigsby, C. W. E., ed. *Approaches to Popular Culture*. London: Edward Arnold, 1976.

Hawkins, Harriet. *Classics and Trash*. New York: Harvester Wheatsheaf, 1990.

Patterson, James T. *Grand Expectations: The United States, 1945–1974*. New York: Oxford University Press, 1996.

Tyson, Lois. *Psychological Politics of the American Dream*. Columbus: Ohio State University Press, 1994.

GENEALOGY: SEARCHING FOR ROOTS

" "To begin my life with the beginning of my life, I record that I was born (as I have been informed and believe). . . ." These words, the opening lines of Charles Dickens's *David Copperfield,* express the motives of genealogists. In the twenty-first century, the study of family history has become one of the greatest hobbies of Americans. Recent issues of popular magazines such as *Time* and *U.S. News and World Report* have devoted several pages to articles on the search for family history. Genealogy received a boost in the 1970s with the publication of Alex Haley's *Roots* and the resulting 1977 television miniseries. No longer was genealogy only a pastime for the wealthy to enable them to validate their lineage. Haley made it apparent that the average person could trace his or her ancestry as he had traced his African-American ancestry from his slave origins in the United States to the original roots in Africa. With the increasing interest in the Internet and Web site searches in the latter part of the twentieth and the beginning of the twenty-first centuries, genealogy has gained credibility as more people begin the quest to determine where they came from. The editor of the magazine *The Computer Genealogist* has commented, "The Internet has helped democratize genealogy."

In her article, "For Every Soul There is a Trace," genealogist Michelle Adam observed, "If learning about those who came before us is the key to understanding who we are in the present, there is perhaps no more fulfilling project than putting together a family tree." Genealogy crosses all ethnic boundaries. For example, in 1999, a quarter of the 300,000 amateur genealogists who visited the Denver Public Library were Hispanic, while in San Francisco educator Albert Cheng leads groups of Chinese-American youths on tours each summer to their ancestral villages in China. Furthermore, the oldest genealogical library in the United States, the New England Historic Genealogical Society, operates with a staff of seventy, and contains over 1 million items, in addition to publishing four genealogical journals through its two publishing houses.

GENEALOGICAL RESEARCH

Genealogical research requires the researcher to be part historian and part detective. The modern outlook on genealogy is quite different from that of earlier centuries. For example, in Ireland during the fifth through seventh centuries, genealogists played an important role in assuring the accession to power. However, written records from this time period are scarce, and records from more recent centuries are often just as impossible to retrieve. In Ireland, for example, the defeat of the Gaelic order resulted in a change in land ownership, and consequently, many records were destroyed. Due to the distrust of Roman Catholicism, early records are often difficult to follow and records were often misplaced. Census records documenting the increase in the Irish population from 5 million in the early nineteenth century to 8.5 million by the Great Famine in 1846 were destroyed during the Irish Civil War in 1922. Therefore, modern researchers attempting to find ancestors from much of the nineteenth century often have difficulty tracing Roman Catholic tenant farmers and landowners to an era before 1800.

Researchers in the United States often begin their research at the National Archives and its thirteen regional branches, and modern researchers are also able to do preliminary research on-line as well. The National Archives houses the United States census returns, which have been made every ten years beginning with the 1790 census. However, it was not until the 1860 U.S. census that details such as the names of all the household occupants and their country or state of origin were listed. Unfortunately, just thirty years later, almost all of the 1890 census returns were de-

This flag sculpture in the Ellis Island, New York, immigrant museum celebrates the diverse genealogy of America. *(Richard Renaldi/ Impact Visuals)*

stroyed by fire, so genealogical researchers have gaps in their search from 1880 to 1900. The U.S. census, however, is only made public after seventy-two years have elapsed from the year in which it was taken. This is a provision meant to protect the privacy of the individuals covered in the census. Therefore, the next census to be made available, the 1930 census, will be released in 2002.

The thirteen regional archives offices, including New York, Boston/Pittsfield, Massachusetts, Philadelphia, Atlanta, Chicago, Kansas City, Missouri, Fort Worth, Denver, Seattle, Anchorage, Los Angeles, and San Bruno, California, contain immigrant passenger records from 1800 to the 1950s. This information is also cited on the National Archives Web site, but the records prior to 1860 contain name and country, or port of origin, while those after the Civil War contain additional information, including the passenger's occupation and exact address. The regional offices also maintain naturalization petitions, port arrivals, a federal census for every state, and information on

whether or not a relative was naturalized in a federal court. As Michelle Adam points out, the earliest naturalization records are from the late eighteenth century and provide dates of citizenship, country, and in some cases, the locality of origin. Naturalization files also provide more detailed information, such as the occupation, address, and name of a witness, as well as the original names (if known) of those who changed their names after immigrating to the United States.

For those immigrants who arrived before 1893, information is scant. Prior to 1893, passenger lists included only name, age, gender, occupation, and nationality. Between 1893 and 1907, changes were made to the process for recording facts about passengers, and by 1907, the information on passenger lists included name, specific age (in both years and months), gender, occupation, literacy level, nationality, race, last place of residence, name and address of nearest relative, final destination, who paid for the passage to America, how much money the person had with him or her, physical characteristics, and whether or not the person had ever been to the United States. The year 1907 is crucial, since it was the peak year for immigration to the United States; over 1.3 million immigrants entered the United States, mostly through the port at Ellis Island. Immigration remained high until World War I began in 1914, and dropped off considerably after passage of anti-immigration laws in the 1920s.

State and town registries also provide significant information, specifically birth, marriage, and death certificates. These documents may list parents' names and often, in New England repositories, will contain information dating back to the early eighteenth century. Information on property ownership can often be found in the county clerk's offices, which maintain records of mortgages, deeds, federal liens, or court cases. Further research in federal records may provide information on military records. The National Archives catalogues military records prior to 1912, while the National Personnel Records Center in St. Louis archives all military records after 1912. Prison logs can also be helpful in determining the negative elements of family history.

CHURCH RECORDS

Church records, including information on local baptism, marriage, and death records, can offer additional assistance in uncovering genealogical data prior to the civil registration periods. Church records can augment gaps if civil files are missing, since these records predate civil records. These records may also contain minutes of meetings, annual reports, correspondence, publications, genealogical charts, and event programs. Occasionally, information regarding missionary and women's societies is also included. For the researcher seeking information on ancestors prior to the American Revolution, details can be uncovered in the church records of the locality in which the original colonist settled. In these situations, often entire ethnic groups settled in an area together. For example, the Congregationalists, or the Puritans of the Massachusetts Bay Colony and the Separatists of Plymouth Colony, as well as the Anglicans in Virginia, comprised almost 85 percent of the European-born population in the American colonies in 1660. In New York and New Jersey, members of the Reformed Dutch Church predominated, and until about 1800, the Dutch employed strict nomenclature procedures that help genealogists determine parentage. Baptismal and marriage records for members of the Dutch Reformed congregations often provide the wife's maiden name, and this is unique to their records.

By the middle of the eighteenth century, members of the Presbyterian denomination, representing colonists from Scotland and Northern Ireland, had spread throughout the thirteen colonies and claimed nearly as many members as the combination of Anglicans and Congregationalists. The Methodists doubled their numbers from 1775 to 1781, increasing from fewer than seven thousand in 1775 to approximately fourteen thousand in 1781. The knowledge of such statistics can help genealogical researchers determine the accuracy of their information and lead them to the discovery of church membership lists, which may include both new and departing members, as well as those who had been excommunicated or censured.

The repositories of the Church of Jesus Christ of Latter-Day Saints (LDS), or Mormons, provide more than merely the local baptism, marriage, or death records found in most church records. The LDS Family History Library in Salt Lake City, Utah, established in 1894, has 3,200 Family History Centers in sixty-four countries worldwide, each of which is overseen by a local Mormon church. Through the LDS Web sites, www.lds.org, or www.familysearch.org, research can also be conducted via the Internet. The LDS church also created the International Genealogical Index (IGI) so that researchers can track religious ordinances on behalf of deceased family members. Originally created only for LDS members, it has since blossomed to include over 100 million names, including either birth or marriage dates, as well as the names of either parents or spouses. In addition, the LDS library also contains extensive parish records of many religious denominations, as well as county courthouse records, and land, tax, birth, marriage, and death records.

OBSTACLES TO RESEARCH

Although the number of on-line and print resources can be overwhelming, genealogical researchers are often faced with their share of obstacles. Information is often omitted due to wars and natural disasters, as in the case of the fire that destroyed most of the 1890 United States census. During the Civil War, the Union army burned Southern courthouses. During the Cultural Revolution in China, ancestral records were declared "feudal garbage," and the records of entire villages were destroyed. For researchers looking for clues to their Indian heritage, most vital statistics were (and are still) left unrecorded, with the exception of Hindu holy spots in which priests recorded births, deaths, and marriages. In the case of interpreting nomenclature, adoptions, divorces, and illegitimacy cloud records. Census takers often recorded inaccurate names or may have had indecipherable penmanship. Immigrants disembarking at Ellis Island often changed their names to conform to the Anglo spelling. For African Americans, the problem is often worse; slaves did not always carry the last name of their last master. They often changed masters several times during a lifetime, and they rarely changed their surname, making their origins difficult to trace. In the case of biracial children, records often do not make clear if the father was the master, overseer, or another white male who took liberties with the female slave.

While genealogical research can be frustrating, the lack of knowledge of family history can be just as frustrating. As one scholar noted while "genealogy is an entertaining hobby, it can also be a matter of life and death." A knowledge of family history can help a person determine the most beneficial health behaviors. For example, certain diseases can be found only in specific ethnic groups. Cystic fibrosis can occur in descendants of immigrants from northern Europe, while Tay-Sachs disease can occur in descendants of Eastern and Central European Jews, as well as French Canadians. Sickle-cell anemia is typically associated with black Africans and African Americans. Medical researchers have discovered that it is quite likely that there is a strong hereditary influence over disease.

"Genealogy" has become the buzzword of the twenty-first century, and it is no longer only for the white Anglo-Saxon Protestant individual wanting to confirm blue-blood status in society. Genealogy is fueled by a sense of nostalgia, a search for lost roots, and this has resulted in an impetus to make a connection with the past in an attempt to leave a legacy of identity for future generations.

Jennifer Harrison

See also: Elderly, Family (Part II, Sec. 4); Foreign and Immigrant Influence on American Popular Culture (Part II, Sec. 10).

BIBLIOGRAPHY

Adam, Michelle. "For Every Soul There is a Trace." *World of Hibernia* 5:1 (Summer 1999): 1–11.

Haley, Alex. *Roots*. New York: Doubleday, 1976.

Hornblower, Margot et al. "Roots Mania." *Time* 153 (1999): 54–66.

Kemp, Thomas J. "The Roots of Genealogy Collections." *Library Journal* 124: 6 (1999): 57–61.

McClure, Rhonda. *The Complete Idiot's Guide to Online Genealogy*. New York: Macmillan USA, 2000. 230–57.

"Prepare for the Future: Know Your Ancestors." *Consumer Reports on Health* (September 1999): 1–6.

Vanderpool-Gormley, Myra. "Exploring Church Records of Colonial America." *Colonial Homes* 25 (July 1999): 20–22.

LANGUAGE

Although the United States has been a land of immigrants—and immigrant languages—since colonial times, its immigrant multilingualism has been transitional. Over the last two centuries, the United States has incorporated huge numbers of bilinguals—perhaps more than any other country—but in no major country has bilingualism so quickly turned to monolingualism. With the exception of a few, small groups, immigrants have lost the languages of their countries of origin by the third generation and, sometimes, even the second, making America a graveyard for immigrant languages. At the same time that immigrant languages have been replaced by English, however, these languages have contributed to American English, and many U.S. ethnic/racial identities have been maintained in part through the resulting, distinctive varieties of English.

The most compelling explanation for the rapid language shift is the tangible, socioeconomic rewards that the United States has extended to those who engage in English-speaking life. Participation in the educational, political, and economic mainstream in the United States, which has long required English, has made possible upward social and economic mobility for countless immigrants. Groups that have maintained languages other than English for longer periods have typically been outside of this reward system, for example, Native Americans on reservations and isolated Spanish Americans on formerly Spanish lands in the Southwest. Other small groups that have maintained immigrant languages, such as Old Order Amish and some Hasidim, have created and maintained social worlds that require immigrant languages for full participation. In these latter two cases, language is linked to religious practices and identities, which are particularly resistant to the secular socioeconomic rewards available in the wider society.

There are many stories of American immigration, and the role of language in these stories has varied with the specifics of different immigrant groups and different historical time periods. Popular and social scientific understandings of language and immigration have long been dominated by patterns of immigration and acculturation documented among early-twentieth-century immigrants and their descendants. These European immigrants, many from southern and eastern Europe, entered a country socially and politically dominated by northwestern European immigrants and their descendants. The co-occurrence of language shift, cultural change, and socioeconomic mobility among 1880–1920 immigrants and their descendants led to a theory of *assimilation*. Assimilation is the idea that linguistically and culturally distinct immigrants lose their distinctiveness over several generations, gain a degree of economic mobility, and become "American." In this model of assimilation, immigrant languages are a symbol of difference, and the language shift to English across generations both symbolizes assimilation to American identities and enables upward economic mobility.

For most immigrants, the move to the United States involves wrenching change. Migration involves not only change in geographic location but movement into a new and different social world. These differences in social worlds are confronted and negotiated by migrants in their everyday lives after immigration. Language is deeply intertwined, at several levels, with these negotiations of cultural and historical differences.

Language is both a *reflection* of particular understandings of the world and a medium through which to *constitute* particular social worlds. Because of these dual functions—both reflector and constitutor of sociocultural worlds—language is a quintessential symbol of identity for both group members and outsiders. While many practices or artifacts can serve as symbols of identity—for example, clothing, food, music, or patterns of worship—language is distinctive because its use is part and parcel of other sociocultural activities and institutions that maintain and reproduce

New York City is home to a veritable Tower of Babel of languages, as this no smoking sign makes clear. *(Anne Burns)*

identities. Use of a particular language can call into being a distinct social world associated with that language. Even the most mundane utterances in an immigrant language can imply particular social relationships, expectations, and values associated with immigrant identities and experiences. The language shift experienced by immigrants across generations is both reflective of and instrumental to other shifts in sociocultural realities.

LANGUAGE SHIFT ACROSS IMMIGRANT GENERATIONS

The historical pattern of language shift in the United States—from immigrant languages to English—occurs by generation. In the conventional pattern, first-generation adult immigrants learn only as much En-

glish as they need to function, and they maintain the immigrant language as the home language. Members of the second generation are monolingual in the home language during their first years of life but then rapidly become fluent in English as they attend school. Among children who have older, native-born siblings or other playmates raised in the United States, this acquisition of English can occur earlier and faster. By their teenage years, members of the second generation prefer English to their parents' language, their skills in English are stronger than those in the home language, and they can function across a wider range of contexts in English. When members of this English-dominant second generation establish their own households, the home language is overwhelmingly English, and third-generation children achieve little to no bilingualism. The shift is thus complete within three generations.

The speed and generational organization of this

language shift is partly a function of biological, developmental aspects of language acquisition. Children who are exposed to American English during childhood are much more likely to speak it without apparent effects from other languages (e.g., "accent"). Second-generation children who spend their childhood in the United States are not only socialized in an environment different from that of their parents but are also able to acquire varieties of English and fluency that are beyond their parents, who were not exposed to American English until later in life. Intensive exposure to two languages through childhood thus leads to the bilingualism that is typical of the second generation but not the first or third. It is this developmental character of language learning that makes language shift more closely linked to generation than any other aspect of immigrant acculturation. Language shift is a phenomenon that occurs at the intersection of historical time—for example, the forces leading to immigration and the contexts of reception—and individuals' developmental time.

Even relatively newly arrived immigrants—if they arrive during childhood—can be fluent English speakers. In the 1990 census, 43 percent of the five- to seventeen-year-olds in non-English-speaking households that had arrived over the previous ten years reported speaking English "very well."

SECOND-GENERATION BILINGUALISM

Language shift between first and second generations results in bi- or multilingual language use within the home. The language used for any individual utterance, or portion of an utterance, depends on a number of situational factors including the topic, the particular metaphorical associations of the languages, and who is speaking to whom. First-generation parents commonly address each other in their native language. Second-generation children typically speak to each other increasingly in English by the time that they attend school. Talk between children and parents can be in English, a second language, or some combination of the two. It is not uncommon for increasingly English-dominant children to address their parents in English even as their parents address them in their immigrant language. In three-generation households, interactions with grandparents commonly occur in the grandparent's native language, as older immigrants are even less likely than their adult children to achieve fluency in English.

Language use is compartmentalized by social domains and activities in many immigrant community contexts. For the second generation, the immigrant language is the language of home, older generations, tradition, church, and family, including both relatives who are newly arriving and those whom one occasionally visits abroad. In larger, more vibrant ethnolinguistic enclaves, the immigrant language can also be the language of certain local businesses and language-based media such as newspapers, radio, and television stations.

English, in contrast, is the language of public school education and the larger society, and it has great pull for children growing up in the United States. It is the language of Hollywood, Madison Avenue advertising, and the wealth of the wider society. It is the language through which children and youth are most targeted by marketers with cartoons, movies, toys, and other products. For many second-generation youth, English is associated with economic opportunity, glamorous popular culture, and modernity. It is associated with the seductive, individualistic freedoms made available to many American teenagers—for example, dating without chaperons, choosing one's friends, and developing personal interests and activities.

The parental language is often associated with a contrasting sociocultural and immigrant framework for seeing the world. This parental framework commonly includes relative strictness and parental control in childrearing, obligations to both nuclear and extended family, and delay of gratification through hard work in education or employment to achieve socioeconomic security, a primary motive for immigrating. For the second generation, few functions can be filled only by the parental language, while many can be filled by either language or only by English. With English-language schooling, literacy skills and academic discourse are much more developed in English, although this varies somewhat with the level of education of first-generation parents.

The bilingualism of the second generation reflects their bridging of social worlds. Their lives straddle national, linguistic, and ethnic boundaries in ways that the lives of the first and third generations do not. Their access to both sending and host society languages and sociocultural roles can result in distinctive forms of bilingual language use. Among coethnic peers, for example, members of the second generation will often code switch—that is, alternate between languages in the same conversation—in ways that are distinct from the ways that they code switch in intergenerational contexts.

Code switching between immigrant generations is often done to accommodate or exclude speakers with varying degrees of fluency in one language or the other, or to claim metaphorically particular sociocultural frameworks through their talk. In intragroup second-generation interaction, by contrast, codes are not always so compartmentalized from each other, and speakers see both languages as their own. Code switching can be frequent and within sentences in such peer interactions, serving local conversational functions such as emphasis or contrast, rather than broader social or metaphorical meanings.

First-generation parents usually express the desire that their children maintain the parental language, but research shows that their practices are not always consonant with this desire. Investment in second-generation language maintenance is often seen as at odds with a goal of greater urgency: that the painful, disruptive act of immigration yield a better life for one's children. The desire that children maintain their parents' language in the second generation is thus tempered by the desire that their children enjoy all the educational and socioeconomic opportunities available to fluent English speakers in the United States.

Because the second generation become English-dominant, the language of homes established by second-generation adults is English, and the third generation grow up speaking English. When the home language has shifted to English, there is little chance of gaining active use of the immigrant language. Although such third-generation individuals may be exposed to first-generation coethnics, the home is the last redoubt of the immigrant language in a society dominated numerically, socially, and economically by English monolinguals.

While the shift to English with time and generations is virtually categorical, generations and home language shift are not always as discrete as in this idealized characterization. Many immigrants, for example, arrive at ages intermediate between adulthood and early childhood and are not as clearly dominant in one language or the other as adult arrivals or those born in the United States. Coethnic spouses may represent different immigrant generations, so the home language may remain the immigrant language despite one second-generation parent. Many immigrant households include monolingual grandparents who care for younger children, so such third-generation children may gain some fluency in childhood. Finally, return and circular migration are not uncommon among many immigrant groups, so the second and third generations may receive varying periods of intensive language acquisition and socialization in the source countries of migration.

HISTORICAL BACKGROUND TO ENGLISH DOMINANCE IN THE UNITED STATES

The United States has never had an official language, and there have always been multilingual and non-English-speaking peoples in the geographic area that the country now occupies. From its first European settlements, however, English speakers numerically and politically dominated its colonization. Even though immigration has become increasingly non-British across the centuries, the early dominance of English in what is now the United States became self-perpetuating.

In colonial times, the sheer numerical superiority of English-speaking residents and immigrants—and their power over indigenous and African groups—made English the de facto language of the colonies. As early as 1660, the population of the North American English-speaking colonies was 70,000 as opposed to 5,000 Dutch speakers in New Netherlands, 3,000 French, and an even smaller number of Spanish. By 1700, the English-speaking population had grown to 250,000, while French and Spanish speakers totaled only 7,500.

The predominance of British-born immigrants continued to the mid-nineteenth century. As late as 1860, 53 percent of the foreign-born population in the United States were from the British Isles. English was thus firmly established as the language of social and economic mobility, higher education, and political power by the time that English-speaking immigrants became a minority of immigrants.

During the 1880–1920 period of increased migration, the foreign-born percentage of the population counted in the census peaked at 14.7 percent in 1910. Despite the high rate of immigration during this period, the foreign-born never accounted for even 1 in 6 Americans. The relatively low number of foreign-born residents and the language shift to English among the United States–born generation—speeded by compulsory school attendance that was instituted in the 1870s—precluded any threat to the dominance of English.

IMMIGRANTS AND AMERICAN ENGLISH

While America English has, with few exceptions, replaced immigrant languages within two to three generations, American English itself has been shaped, at various levels, by immigrant languages. Unlike countries such as France and Spain that have official academies to codify and promote specific varieties of language and grammar, the United States has not had a central language governing body. Standards of American English have thus evolved, in part, following the usage of immigrants and those in contact with immigrant communities. Some of these immigrant language contributions to English are most prominent in certain geographic areas or among certain ethnic/racial groups, while others have achieved widespread adoption. Effects of these immigrant languages on varieties of American English range from discrete words and expressions to more subtle variations in pronunciation or communicative style.

From the Dutch, whose New Netherlands colony (1621–64) included what is now New York City, we have such terms as "poppycock," "waffle," "cookie," "sleigh," "Santa Claus," "dumb" (as in "stupid"), and "pit" (as in "stone of a fruit"), and the expression "How come?" (as in "Why?"). Some terms of Dutch origin remain more strongly represented in the geographic areas where the Dutch were once dominant: the word "stoop," for example, is used in the urban Northeast to refer to a staircase and entry platform in front of a house.

From the German immigrants of the eighteenth and nineteenth centuries, American English has the terms "check" (as in "bill in a restaurant"), "fresh" (as in "impertinent"), "hoodlum," "hex," and "kindergarten." Various German expressions also became American English expressions through direct translation of the German: "And how!" and "No way."

Although Irish immigrants to America were English speakers, their forms of English had been influenced by the indigenous Gaelic in Ireland, resulting in distinctive forms. To American English, Irish immigrants contributed explanatory expressions based on "must not" (e.g., "He *must not* have seen me, or he would have waved") and the second-person plural pronoun "youse," heard in some dialects of northeastern United States cities.

Italians contributed many words closely associated with the food dishes that they introduced or popularized in the United States, such as "pasta," "lasagna," and "spaghetti," including some that are no longer specifically associated with Italian cooking, as with "broccoli" and "zucchini."

Yiddish speakers and their descendants have contributed many terms with ethnic associations such as "schmaltz," "kosher," and "schlock." From Yiddish speakers comes the pattern of dismissive rhyme in which "schm-" is made a word's initial sound, as in "Rockefeller, Schmockefeller." Other expressions derived from Yiddish that have been integrated into many varieties of English include "Get lost," "Enjoy," and "If you'll excuse the expression."

Many Spanish terms entered English not through immigration, per se, but through U.S. incorporation of formerly Spanish peoples and lands in the Southwest during the mid-nineteenth century. Many of these words refer to distinctive topographic features of the Southwest ("canyon," "arroyo," and "chaparral"), or to animal husbandry practices in that region, ("ranch," "rodeo," "bronco," "stampede," "lariat," and "lasso"). French terms specific to topography, such as "levee" and "bayou," similarly entered English through incorporation of French speakers in the 1803 Louisiana Purchase.

Enslaved Africans brought with them to the United States words including "tote," "goober," "jazz," "banjo," "yam," "gumbo," and "okra." Africans brought to the United States may also have contributed the positive expression of affirmation/consent "uh-huh" and the negative response of denial/refusal "uh-uh." These expressions occur in Africa and countries of the New World that had African-descent slavery. Some scholars have also traced the American expression "okay" to African roots, although others have attributed it to other sources.

While contributing relatively few words to American English, Africans affected language practices deeply, particularly in the South and among the descendants of African slaves. Sociolinguists and creolists have traced distinctive grammatical features of African-American English to Africa and subsequent creolization processes among Africans in the Americas. Such forms as the "habitual be" of African-American English, as in "He be late" (that is, "He is recurringly or habitually late"), have no corresponding tense/aspect form in varieties of non-African English. Grammatical structures and words of African origin are most frequent in Gullah, the variety of English spoken by the descendants of African slaves on the relatively isolated Sea Islands of the South Carolina coast.

African languages were quickly lost through the deliberate dispersion of coethnic slaves, but various pan-ethnic West African communication patterns have been retained in the language of many African Americans and have affected many varieties of American English. Certain forms of storytelling, mimicry, speech making, and ritual teasing have all survived in American English. These patterns are variously evident in the sermons of African-American preachers and politicians, such as Martin Luther King Jr.; in the rhyming boasts of heavyweight boxing champion

Muhammed Ali; and in the rhythmic rapping of hip-hop music artists.

LANGUAGE RIGHTS FOR LANGUAGE MINORITIES

Beginning in the 1960s, both courts and federal legislators began to recognize the educational, political, and civil rights of minority language speakers. Civil rights legislation of the 1960s was originally aimed at low-income Americans and African Americans but was extended to cover the rights of U.S. speakers of languages other than English. These extensions to minority language speakers officially countenanced the difficulties faced by members of such groups in taking full advantage of the political and educational opportunities available to Americans.

The 1968 Bilingual Education Act (Title 7 of the Elementary and Secondary Education Act) provided funds for the planning and implementation of special programs for minority language speakers. These programs were "designed to meet the special educational needs of children of limited English-speaking ability in schools having a high concentration of such children" from families under particular income thresholds. This act was an amendment to 1965 legislation that had provided federal funds for local school districts for the education of low-income students. While schools had used languages other than English to instruct immigrants and their children—for example, German was used in schools in Cincinnati, St. Louis, and Milwaukee in the mid-1800s—such programs had always been initiated and funded at the local level, rather than federally.

Bilingual education (as well as specialized English as a Second Language programs) in the United States received further support from the 1974 *Lau v. Nichols* Supreme Court decision. In this class-action suit brought by Chinese language–speaking students in San Francisco, the Court ruled that school districts must take affirmative steps to ensure that non–English speakers are not excluded from the effective participation in the educational programs offered by the district. This decision did not set a precedent as such but was rather an affirmation of the 1964 Civil Rights Act (Title 6, section 601).

Like the Bilingual Education Act, the *Lau v. Nichols* decision did not specify what affirmative steps school districts were required to take for language minority speakers or how they were to be carried out. The very vagueness of the Bilingual Education Act and the *Lau*

v. Nichols decision allowed for competing and conflicting visions of bilingual education. Some proponents of bilingual education have seen it as a brief program to *transition* students into English-speaking classrooms. Other advocates have framed it as a language and culture *maintenance* program that serves simultaneously to raise the esteem, ethnic consciousness, and achievement of participants. These competing visions of bilingual education have regularly erupted in conflict, visibly and notably in a 1998 California referendum (Proposition 227) that outlawed bilingual education in that state.

Language rights legislation was extended to domains outside of schools in 1975 amendments to the 1965 Voting Rights Act. While the 1965 act had been aimed at enfranchising black Americans in the South, the 1975 amendments were triggered by disenfranchisement of Mexican Americans in southwest Texas. The amendments extended protections, such as bilingual ballots, to members of four groups in voting districts matching a set of criteria for constituent literacy, voting rates, and percentage of linguistic minorities. The four groups officially recognized by the amendments as linguistic minorities included both indigenous and immigrant groups: Alaskan natives, American Indians, Asian Americans, and those "of Spanish heritage."

A third sphere in which the rights of non–English speakers have been recognized is in criminal court proceedings. The Second Circuit Court of Appeals found in the 1970 *U.S. ex rel. Negron v. New York* case that there is a constitutional basis for criminal defendants to have interpreters. The 1978 Court Interpreters Act, passed by Congress, extends the right to courtroom interpreters to certain civil trials, those initiated by the United States in a U.S. District Court. Courts have repeatedly found, in contrast, that there is no right to interpreters in civil or administrative proceedings more generally, although some states have provided for such interpretation through state-specific statutes.

HISTORY OF LINGUISTIC NATIVISM

Nativism is the ideology and policy of favoring the interests of residents of a polity over the interests of immigrants. In the United States, nativism has historically arisen during periods of increased migration or when spatial concentration of immigrants makes their ethnolinguistic communities more salient. Nativism in the last decades of the twentieth century manifested itself largely in various "English Only" and "Official

English" movements that attempted to restrict the use of languages other than English in government and public life.

Language is closely associated with ethnic, racial, and national identity, and it is easily activated as a symbol of difference. There is a Western tradition of equating race, language, and nation that has its roots in eighteenth-century Romantic philosophy, notably that of Johann von Herder, and subsequent European nation building. The unity of language, nation, and identity proclaimed by Herder is at odds with the multilingual reality of most nation-states—for each nation-state in the world there are over thirty languages—but dominant national languages still function as symbols of unity. Because of the salience of language as an emblem of identity, it is a readily available target for discrimination that may have economic, racial, or other political origins.

Linguistic nativism waxes and wanes with the political moment. In the decades before the Revolutionary War, for example, German immigrants and their descendants made up as much as one-third of the population of Pennsylvania. There were German-language churches, press, and even publicly funded schools. Although the numerically dominant English speakers always controlled the Pennsylvania Assembly, the size and vibrancy of the German-speaking community led Benjamin Franklin to nativist editorializing in 1751: "Why should *Pennsylvania*, founded by the *English*, become a Colony of *Aliens*, who will shortly be so numerous as to Germanize us instead of our Anglifying them, and will never adopt our Language or Customs, anymore than they can acquire our complexion?"

These nativist sentiments from Franklin abated when English- and German-speaking colonists found themselves allied in both the French and Indian War and the Revolutionary War. English-speaking leaders were then very ready to make accommodations to language-minority German speakers to encourage political support. Extracts of Votes and Proceedings of the Congress (1774), the Declaration of Articles Setting Forth Causes of Taking up Arms (1775), and Resolves of Congress (1776), among other government documents, were officially published in German as well as in English.

During the large-scale European migration at the turn of the twentieth century, nativist attacks on immigrants sometimes took the form of discriminatory legislation based on language. In 1897, Pennsylvania enacted an English proficiency requirement for miners, seeking to bar Italians and Slavs from the coalfields. In 1921, New York Republicans passed an English literacy test for voting, hoping to disenfranchise

the 1 million Yiddish speakers who voted heavily Democratic.

CONTEMPORARY LINGUISTIC NATIVISM AND SPANISH-SPEAKING IMMIGRATION

In the 1980s, nativist language organizations such as Official English and English Only began to lobby for legislation that would restrict the use of languages other than English in government and public life. This rise of linguistic nativism can be explained largely by the spatial concentration of Spanish-speaking immigrants. Despite assertions that the United States was being overrun by immigrants, the rate of immigration (relative to the existing U.S. population) in the last decades of the twentieth century was not as high as early in the century. During the 1900–30 period, for example, the per capita rate was more than 1.5 times as high as during the 1970–90 period.

Post-1965 immigration has been linguistically and geographically more concentrated, however. While the largest linguistic group between 1900 and 1930 consisted of Italian speakers, they represented only 19 percent of the total flow of immigrants during that time. In the first two decades of the post-1970 influx, Spanish speakers—from a variety of countries—accounted for over 38 percent of the total flow of immigrants.

Relative to the turn-of-the-century migration, the new migration has also been more concentrated spatially. Whereas the five states receiving the most immigrants in 1910 accounted for 54 percent of the total flow, five states in 1990 (California, New York, Texas, Illinois, and Florida) accounted for 78 percent of the flow. Immigrants in 1990 were further concentrated in only a handful of metropolitan areas: nearly half of all new immigrants clustered in New York, Chicago, Houston, and the greater Los Angeles area.

This spatial concentration of Spanish speakers in vibrant ethnolinguistic communities is both reflected and reproduced by their growing commercial and political power. Univision, the Spanish-language television network, more than doubled its affiliated stations and cable providers in the 1980s, and then doubled again in the 1990s to over 900, reaching over 90 percent of Spanish-speaking households in the United States. Mainstream companies now advertise their products in Spanish to tap into the large market, and politicians, both locally and nationally, have begun to use the Spanish that they have learned to address

Spanish-speaking audiences. Spanish speakers in the United States represent the northernmost tip of a community of over 250 million Latin American Spanish speakers. Mexico, with a population of over 80 million, is by far the largest single source country for immigration to the United States, representing 21.6 percent of the foreign-born persons counted in the 1990 census.

Despite this vitality of Spanish in the United States, only one in four foreign-born individuals counted in the 1990 census reported speaking English "not well or not at all." The number of people reporting little English would be even smaller if not for the many new arrivals counted in the 1990 census: the 1980s had the greatest number of immigrants since the 1901–10 period, and nearly as many arrived in the 1980s period as during the entire twenty-year period preceding 1980. Recent arrivals who are isolated from mainstream English-speaking institutions—the elderly, the undocumented, and the least educated—account disproportionately for these foreign-born persons reporting that they speak little English.

Although Spanish-speaking immigrants are spatially concentrated and Spanish-language institutions and media have gained unprecedented significance, the cross-generational shift from Spanish to English has not stopped or slowed significantly. The salience and strength of Spanish in the United States is not from the second and third generations but from the ongoing immigration of Spanish speakers. Spanish-speaking communities in the United States do not have a distinctive form of linguistic self-perpetuation separate from ongoing and circular migration.

If immigration were suddenly cut off, Spanish would quickly become an active language only for grandparents, and only vestiges of its use would remain in the second and third generations. Even in dense enclaves of Spanish-speaking immigrants such as Miami and Los Angeles, second-generation individuals not only speak English but also prefer it to Spanish. Despite nativist fears, there is little sign that current Spanish-speaking immigrants will differ significantly from earlier waves of immigrants in this century, who quickly shifted languages across generations.

ISSUES OF LANGUAGE AND IDENTITY RAISED BY THE NEW IMMIGRATION

Although immigrants shift to English across generations, this does not mean that language ceases to func-

tion as a marker of immigrant or ethnic/racial identity. Particular communicative styles or linguistic features associated with immigrant groups, for example, can persist in English for generations, even after immigrant languages themselves are lost. These intra-English differences are particularly salient where socioeconomic or political marginalization has prevented group members from fully participating in the wider society.

The ways in which the descendants of immigrants use varieties of American English have much to do with the historically specific ways in which they have been incorporated into the United States. The differing contexts faced by European and non-European groups in the United States, for example, have shaped the varieties of English adopted and maintained by such groups. While 88 percent of immigrants arriving to the United States before 1960 counted as white by current standards, only 38 percent of the immigrants arriving in the 1980s counted as such. The cultural and linguistic emblems of difference that disappear across generations are very different from the phenotypic differences that do not disappear with acculturation across generations.

Differences in historical patterns of linguistic acculturation between European immigrants and non-European American groups can suggest the issues raised by contemporary migration. Among the many European groups who have had the opportunity to engage fully in the political and economic systems of the country, there has been relatively little incentive for maintaining, re-creating, or emphasizing linguistic or cultural distinctiveness. Assimilation to unmarked white identities with attendant privileges has been an available and attractive pathway, and language shift to dominant standard varieties of American English has been a symbol of this assimilation. For many third- and fourth-generation descendants of European immigrants, ethnic or linguistic distinctiveness is something that is only occasionally, and voluntarily, invoked.

Groups such as African Americans, Native Americans, and some Chicanos, in contrast, have been in the United States for centuries but have retained distinctive social identities and associated linguistic practices. Exclusion from participation in the traditional power structures has both allowed—through social isolation—and encouraged—through activation of identity politics—such groups to maintain distinct languages or distinctive varieties of English much longer than among voluntary European immigrants.

Such groups have not had the option of assimilating to unmarked, white identities, and language has served many members of these groups as an emblem of difference rather than assimilation. For many African Americans, for example, being authentically African American includes being able to use distinctive linguistic forms and practices associated with African-American communities. Situational use of African-American English as an identity marker is thus a political statement of identity in a broader context that disparages such forms. Particular sociopolitical conditions such as discrimination can thus have more effect on linguistic assimilation—or linguistic divergence—than the passage of time and generations since arrival in the United States.

The language choices facing the children of contemporary immigrants are thus intimately intertwined with the trajectories of acculturation/assimilation available in the United States. Several characteristics of the post-1965 immigration have led to predictions of *segmented assimilation*—that is, the acculturation of contemporary immigrants and their children will vary and fall into distinct types. The basic question is to *which* American groups new immigrants acculturate. Immigrants and their children with higher levels of education and economic means will be likely to use education as a means to social and economic mobility, approximating the traditional notion of assimilation and socioeconomic mobility over time. The English language of second- and third-generation members of this group will thus acculturate to dominant middle-class and educated standards.

Many new immigrants without such resources, however, will face specific obstacles to the socioeconomic mobility and trajectories of assimilation that the 1880–1920 immigrants and their descendants have achieved. Changes in the economy after the first half of the century resulted in the loss of the low-skilled industrial jobs that provided earlier immigrants with secure employment and a basis for incremental upward mobility across generations. The combination of discrimination faced by nonwhites—the majority of contemporary immigrants—and the lack of apparent pathways to upward mobility may encourage the second generation to identify with the practices and values of marginalized and impoverished ethnic/racial minority groups already in the United States. There is already widespread evidence of this type of acculturation. Second-generation teenagers in groups ranging from Puerto Ricans to Cambodian refugees, for example, who see their opportunities for educational success and socioeconomic mobility blocked, have adopted features of African-American English as a language of resistance to dominant United States ideologies.

A third potential trajectory of acculturation for members of the second and third generations is toward immigrant/ethnic identities rooted in dense immigrant social networks. The barriers to economic and social mobility encountered by nonwhite immigrants with less formal education could encourage the second and third generations to identify with coethnic immigrants. When such communities are large and vibrant enough, they can provide economic resources in terms of ethnic enclave jobs, psychological support for immigrant identities, and an immigrant language milieu. The second and third generations following these trajectories can become English dominant but identify strongly with the immigrant language, even as active fluency is lost across generations.

The size of the Spanish-speaking immigrant community and the salience of language as an identity marker has already led to the constitution of the widely and officially recognized ethnolinguistic category "Hispanic." Individuals from Latin America who can be differentiated by national boundaries, phenotype, culture, and socioeconomic class find themselves united, at least from official perspectives, under such rubrics as Hispanic, Latino, or Spanish. For many Spanish-speaking immigrants and their children, the label "Spanish" has come to stand for ethnic/cultural identity and is used by many as a term for ethnic and racial self-identification.

CHANGING RELATIONS AMONG LANGUAGE, ASSIMILATION, AND ECONOMIC MOBILITY IN CONTEMPORARY IMMIGRATION

Assumptions about relationships between language shift, assimilation, and economic mobility that were based on the early-twentieth-century immigration are being undermined by both the English proficiency of many contemporary immigrants and the overall socioeconomic diversity of the immigration stream. While language shift to English is central to the classic story of American immigration, large numbers of contemporary immigrants *already* speak English upon arrival in the United States. Following centuries of British imperialism and a briefer period of American hegemony, English is an official language in many countries and a well-known second language for many immigrants. English-speaking immigrants to the United States come not only from the British Isles but also from former British colonies, for example, Jamaica, India, Hong Kong, and Canada. Other English speakers arrive from countries such as the Philippines, where the educated classes have high levels of proficiency in English because of long-standing political and economic ties to the United States. Of foreign-born persons, that is, the *first* generation, counted in the 1990 census, 21 percent described themselves as speaking *only* English.

In addition to arriving as fluent English speakers, many immigrants also arrive as highly educated professionals. Between the late 1960s and the early 1990s, over one in four immigrant heads of household was a high-status professional, executive, or manager in his or her country of origin. The education and resources of these immigrants may enable them to help their children become more fully bilingual, acquiring literacy and academic skills in two languages. Acquisition of English in U.S. immigrant contexts has historically been approached as a zero-sum process, in which fluency English is seen as precluding fluency in an immigrant language. However, as is evident from countries with sustained bilingualism, various bilingual outcomes are possible in such contexts, given the proper support and community contexts. Given the resources spent in the United States on second-language training in secondary schools and universities, support for such bilingualism may develop more broadly.

The role of language in the lives of immigrants is intimately intertwined with other aspects of their social lives and the conditions under which they arrive in the United States. Although many immigrants in the second half of the twentieth century came from educated elites, many others arrived with low levels of education and resources. Among United States ethnic/racial groups in the 1990s, both native and foreign-born, immigrant groups accounted variously for both the *highest* and the *lowest* rates of education, homeownership, poverty, and welfare dependency. While language shift and loss have been a common experience of virtually all non-Anglophone immigrants to the United States, the vast differences in education, financial resources, and prior knowledge of English among contemporary immigrants make for multiple and distinct stories of language shift and acculturation.

Benjamin Bailey

See also: Arts I: Literature, English as a Second Language, Foreign and Immigrant Influence on American Popular Culture, Press (Part II, Sec. 10); *Lau v. Nichols*, 1974, California Proposition 227, 1998 (Part IV, Sec. 1).

BIBLIOGRAPHY

Conklin, Nancy Faires, and Margaret Lourie. *A Host of Tongues: Language Communities in the United States*. New York: Free Press, 1983.

Dillard, J. L. *American Talk*. New York: Random House, 1976.

———. *Toward a Social History of American English*. New York: Mouton, 1985.

Fishman, Joshua. *Language and Ethnicity in Minority Sociolinguistic Perspective*. Philadelphia: Multilingual Matters, 1989.

Fishman, Joshua, R. L. Cooper, and R. Ma. *Bilingualism in the Barrio*. Bloomington: Indiana University Press, 1971.

Franklin, Benjamin. *The Papers of Benjamin Franklin*, ed. Leonard W. Labarre. New Haven: Yale University Press, 1959.

Glenn, Charles Leslie, Ester J. De Jong, and Edward R. Beauchamp. *Educating Immigrant Children: Schools and Language Minorities in Twelve Nations*. New York: Garland Publishing, 1996.

Gordon, Milton. *Assimilation in American Life: The Role of Race, Religion, and National Origins*. New York: Oxford University Press, 1964.

Lieberson, Stanley, G. Dalto, and M. E. Johnston. "The Course of Mother Tongue Diversity in Nations." *American Journal of Sociology* 81 (July 1975): 34–61.

Massey, Douglas. 1995. "The New Immigration and Ethnicity in the United States." *Population Development Review* 21:3 (1995): 631–52.

McCrum, Robert, William Cran, and Robert MacNeil. *The Story of English*. New York: Viking/Elisabeth Sifton Books, 1986.

Mufwene, Salikoko, John Rickford, Guy Bailey, and John Baugh. *African-American English: Structure, History, and Use*. New York: Routledge, 1998.

Piatt, Bill. *Only English: Law and Language Policy in the United States*. Albuquerque: University of New Mexico Press, 1990.

Portes, Alejandro. "Children of Immigrants: Segmented Assimilation and Its Determinants." In *The Economic Sociology of Immigration: Essays on Networks, Ethnicity, and Entrepreneurship*, ed. Alejandro Portes, 248–79. New York: Russell Sage, 1995.

Portes, Alejandro, and Richard Schauffler. "Language and the Second Generation: Bilingualism Yesterday and Today." In *The New Second Generation*, ed. Alejandro Portes, 8–29. New York: Russell Sage Foundation, 1996.

Portes, Alejandro, and Rubén Rumbaut. *Immigrant America: A Portrait*. 2d ed. Berkeley: University of California Press, 1996.

Rumbaut, Rubén. "Paradoxes (and Orthodoxies) of Assimilation." *Sociological Perspectives* 40:3 (1997): 483–511.

Zentella, Ana Celia. *Growing Up Bilingual: Puerto Rican Children in New York*. Malden, MA: Blackwell Publishers, 1997.

MEDIA PORTRAYAL OF IMMIGRANTS

Media portrayal of immigrants has to a large extent been a portrayal of ethnic stereotypes. And for many, images gathered throughout the years from many sources of popular culture—stage, print, film, and television—are their only exposure to immigrants and immigrant life.

Both positive and negative images of immigrants have occurred throughout the years. Reflecting both the anti-immigrant sentiment that has occurred at various times and the social conscience of a nation viewing prejudice and discrimination against immigrants as inherently evil, images of immigrants have had a prominent place in media forms of all kinds.

Portrayals of immigrants in the media have waxed and waned with the waves of immigration. Immigrants have been a favorite topic of the media during peak immigration periods—the "old" immigration of the mid–nineteenth century, the "new" immigration period from about 1880 to 1924, and the "modern" immigration period that has occurred since immigration restrictions were eased in the mid-1960s. But although found less often outside of peak migration periods, immigrants have still played a prominent role as the subject matter in the media of all kinds.

One of the unique features of the portrayal of immigrants in the media is the shifting attitude of the descendants of those who were immigrants. When the great influx of immigrants from southern and eastern Europe began in the 1880s, much of the opposition that occurred in the media was initiated or supported by the children and grandchildren of those who had emigrated from northern and western Europe a generation before. There has been general opposition in public opinion to the arrival of immigrants from Asia and Latin America that began when immigration restrictions were eased in the 1960s, though much less has occurred in the media. This opposition reflected in popular opinion has often come from the second- and third-generation descendants of those who arrived from southern and eastern Europe. And although stereotyping of immigrants continues and immigrant themes still abound in the popular media, the strong anti-immigrant sentiment and rhetoric has largely disappeared.

IMMIGRANT PORTRAYALS ON THE STAGE

Prior to the advent of movies, radio, and television, the stage play was one of the primary forms of popular culture and entertainment media. From traveling troupes and medicine shows to vaudeville and elaborate Broadway productions, immigrants have always been a favorite subject of the theater. Often, although not always, cultural images have reflected the anti-immigrant sentiments of the late nineteenth and early twentieth centuries, but several themes recur in theatrical productions about immigrants. Among the themes commonly seen are the reasons for migration; the immigrants' reactions and dealings with American life; the prejudices expressed by Americans toward -the immigrants; and the immigrants' way of life, including religion, marriage practices, food and cultural customs, ethnic character and values, and assimilation.

Perhaps one of the earliest and best-known stage portrayals has been that of Shakespeare's character Shylock from *The Merchant of Venice*. Listed in the Dramatis Personae only as "a Jew," the portrayal of Shylock as the scheming and conniving persona of evil became a standard for showing Jewish characters that has lasted into the twentieth century. Synonymous with one who is sly, cheating, and scheming, the term "shylock" has eventually become a derogatory epithet for Jewish people.

Besides Jewish immigrants, the Irish and later the Italians also became favorite topics of stage productions, again with prevailing stereotypical images emerging. The Irish man was usually portrayed as tough, crude, loud-talking, brash, and often fighting, brawling, and drinking; he invariably worked as a policeman, politician, or priest. The Irish woman was usually seen as the strong yet self-effacing force behind the family who held it together at all costs. The Italian immigrant was typically shown in two ways: either as the sinister and evil criminal element or the lazy but happy-go-lucky peasant, always eating, singing, and drinking wine.

Although the stereotyping of immigrants continued into the twentieth century, not all stereotypes were negative. The idea of a "melting pot," first popularized by French immigrant J. Hector St. John de Crèvecoeur in 1782, was again brought to the forefront in playwright Israel Zangwill's play of the same name in 1908. In his play, Zangwill envisioned "the American" as a product of "God's crucible . . . a fusion of all races." By the time anti-immigrant sentiment reached its peak and the quota laws of the 1920s effectively shut off immigration for the next forty years, the passing of the "threat" of immigration allowed playwrights to examine other aspects of immigration as well. While stock and less important immigrant characters were most often stereotyped in more shallow roles, deeper themes and the immigrant experience itself increasingly became the subject of many stage productions as the country moved deeper into the twentieth century. Even the comedic aspects of immigration themes emerged; audiences could now laugh with the immigrant characters instead of just laughing at them.

Some of these plays became so popular that they persisted and have been resurrected in remakes or in different form for years. *The Jazz Singer*, for example, premiered on Broadway in 1925 and explored the agony and the conflict of the immigrant Jewish cantor Rabinowitz and his son, who was torn between following his father into the synagogue as a cantor or following the lure of stardom as a popular singer. Besides being made into what is commonly billed as the first "talking" movie in 1927, *The Jazz Singer* was remade into popular and successful movie versions in 1952 and 1980. Likewise, *Abie's Irish Rose*, which premiered on Broadway in 1922 and ran for well over 2,500 performances, took a comedic look at the pairing of children of two immigrants, the Jewish boy Abie Levy and the Irish girl Rose Mary Murphy. *Abie's Irish Rose* was so successful that it later ran as a popular radio series of the 1930s, was made into movie versions in both 1929 and 1946, and was the basis for the television series of the early 1970s *Bridget Loves Bernie*.

IMMIGRANT PORTRAYALS IN PRINT

Beginning in the nineteenth century, most portrayals of immigrants in popular print reflected either the anti-immigrant sentiment of the period or took the form of debate: Should large-scale immigration continue, and what would happen if it did?

As large-scale immigration of northern and western Europeans, particularly the Irish, to America began in the mid–nineteenth century, print media started to overflow with anti-immigrant sentiment. Mostly poor, unskilled, and lower-class, immigrants appeared in print articles that highlighted these immigrants and the problems of overcrowded and squalid conditions in the cities in which they lived, either condemning them for "despoiling" the American landscape or speculating as to just what long-term effects immigration would have. Famed cartoonist Thomas Nast often portrayed the Irish—the largest immigrant group of the mid–nineteenth century—as stupid, simian, and vicious.

At about the same time, large numbers of Chinese immigrants began arriving in the West, coming to work in the mining camps and on the building of the railroads. Because they fulfilled a pressing need for labor, some welcomed the Chinese at first, but anti-Chinese sentiment grew and soon began appearing in the popular press. Chinese were depicted as devious, untrustworthy "heathens," and Americans began to fear them as a peculiar, dangerous, and "mysterious" people. The print media played an important role in expressing and perpetuating the anti-Chinese feelings that led to the passage of the Chinese Exclusion Act in 1882.

Anti-immigrant sentiment escalated again in the popular press with the coming of the "new" European immigration of the 1880s. Mostly from southern and eastern Europe, these immigrants were non-English-speaking and often physically differentiated more easily from other Americans or their earlier immigrant counterparts from northern and western Europe. Most of the same fears and objections appeared in the popular press that had been raised earlier to the northern and western European immigrants and to the Chinese. Concern about the loss of jobs, the harmful effect on the American economy, and the "purity" of the American race were the major themes raised by the press.

With the rise in popularity of social Darwinism, immigrants of the nineteenth and early twentieth centuries were often depicted in print as subhuman and lesser-evolved species than the "superior" white race and "as lacking the purity" of the white, Anglo-Saxon

Protestant (WASP). Editorial cartoons, especially, were able to promote this idea, often depicting immigrants as animals in human clothing, usually "infringing" or "taking" from the "good and decent" Americans. One popular cartoon of the 1890s, for example, shows an ape in a cage and an ape-like Irishman dressed in a suit staring at each other with a caption that reads "Mutual: Both are glad there are bars between 'em!"

The idea of these immigrants as "lesser-evolved" or more "animal-like" was also prominent in academic circles and the legitimate press. The rise in urban crime and among immigrant populations was one of the major issues raised against immigrants and was fueled by the publication of such works as *The Criminal Man* (1887) by the Italian physician and criminologist Cesare Lombroso. Lombroso offered "scientific proof" of the "born criminal," saying that they were "throwbacks" to earlier human forms. The popularity of *The Criminal Man* spread throughout Europe and then the United States, and although its thesis soon fell out of favor in Europe, its popularity in the United States continued for years. Popular magazines such as the *North American Review* and the *Saturday Evening Post*, for example, continued anti-immigrant articles, once publishing data from army intelligence tests calling the minds of immigrants "scarcely superior to [those of] an ox."

The attitude of the popular press toward immigrants has, to a large extent, reflected the political leanings of the publication in general or the attitudes of the editorial boards at any given time. Some, such as the *Saturday Evening Post* and *Atlantic Monthly*, consistently carried negative views of immigrants and immigration for several years. Others, such as *Harper's* and *The Nation*, were consistently positive and some, such as *Commentary, Reader's Digest, Time, Newsweek, Life*, and *U.S. News and World Report*, varied in their coverage.

Since the 1960s, most (though not all) of the coverage of immigration issues in the popular press has been positive. Some publications, such as the *Saturday Evening Post*, have significantly changed their views on immigration issues. After publishing anti-immigrant articles throughout most of its history, the *Post* did an abrupt about-face in the 1960s and began publishing editorials and articles condemning the discriminatory practices of quota laws and biases against immigrants. Some magazines continue to carry mixed messages, even in the generally immigration-favorable period since the 1960s. *Reader's Digest*, for example, has carried articles in recent years that reflect both a favorable and unfavorable view of immigration, featuring items that both promote the contributions of recent immigrants and yet decry the drain that some claim immigrants place on the American economy. And although mostly favorable, many periodicals seem to vary their stance depending on the immigrant group: Mexican immigration has generally been seen in a more negative light, whereas Asian immigration has been seen more positively.

IMMIGRANT PORTRAYALS IN THE MOVIES

Immigrant characters and immigration issues have abounded in cinema houses throughout the country. The *Internet Movie Database* alone lists over 150 movie titles under the keyword "immigrant" or "immigration"; 49 biographies of those with immigrant origins; and 108 characters playing immigration officials. And this list is far from complete.

Movie plots and subjects about immigrants were an early staple with the rise of movie houses in the first decades of the twentieth century. Newsreels showed the influx of immigrants through Ellis Island and the crowded conditions of large cities to audiences across the country. Immigrants and immigration supplied plots and movie story lines as well. The 1915 silent film *The Italian*, for example, portrayed the difficulty of an immigrant and the young woman he loves, as he comes to America amid trials, tribulations, and separation before they are eventually reunited and able to marry. In what some have called the best short feature of his career, Charlie Chaplin used his already established character of the Little Tramp in a mix of comedy and pathos in his 1917 film *The Immigrant*. Chaplin portrays the hardships and comedic adventures of the tramp character and his love interest, Edna, in their steerage-class voyage across the sea as well as upon arrival in America. Ironically for Chaplin, an Englishman, incidents portrayed in *The Immigrant* were later cited as evidence of anti-Americanism in his political troubles and eventual deportation after World War II.

Immigrant movies remained popular in the 1920s, with films such as *Mother Machree* (1928) and *The Younger Generation* (1929), among others. Movies such as these explored the difficulties of acculturation, assimilation, and struggles between the older immigrant generation and the younger American-born generation. But as with stage productions, immigrant themes in movies began to wane after quota laws took effect and immigration issues and problems diminished as national concerns. To be sure, these themes remained popular, as evidenced in *Huddle* (1932), *Paddy O'Day*

(1935), and *I Remember Mama* (1948), but more pressing national issues such as the Great Depression and World War II overwhelmed immigrant issues. With the exception of the popularity of ethnic gangster movies, most of them about Italians, it was not until the civil rights movement in the 1950s and 1960s that immigrant themes again reemerged. After the easing of immigration quotas in the mid-1960s and the modern influx of immigrants, this time more from Asia and Latin America and political refugees from third-world countries, immigration themes regained prominence in the cinema and its new cousin, television.

Movie audiences began to see bigotry and bias emerge as a leading cinematic theme. Shakespeare's *Romeo and Juliet* took on a new form as *West Side Story*, first as a successful Broadway production and then in a movie version. The story examined the lives of a white boy and a Puerto Rican girl who fall in love and the competition between rival gangs in New York City. Partly a reflection of the civil rights movement, interracial relationships were also seen in such films as *Sayonara* (1957), in which an American serviceman and a Japanese woman encounter difficulties owing to the opposition to their romance and her subsequent immigration to America.

The political nature of immigration, postwar refugees, and the Cold War also became movie themes during this time. Among films that explore these issues are *Gambling House* (1951), which depicts struggles of European refugees; *Popi* (1969), a story about a Puerto Rican father who hatches a plot to pass his sons off as Cuban refugees in order to obtain special treatment for them; and propaganda films such as *The Million Dollar Nickel* (1952), in which foreign-born American film stars attempt to defeat Soviet anti-American propaganda.

With the 1970s came a new ethnic consciousness, and millions of Americans began "rediscovering" their ethnicity. Motion pictures with immigrant and ethnic themes began to appear, and the genre grew and continues to be a popular theme today. The list of movies dealing with immigrant characters and themes produced since the 1970s through the present day is extensive. Several themes repeat themselves and recur throughout. Many of these films took a historic and sometimes nostalgic look backward at immigration issues of the past, often exploring issues once considered too daring and taboo for the large screen. *Free Country*, for example, looks at an immigrant Lithuanian family that settles in New York in 1909. The movie *'68* (1988) tells the story of a year in the life of a Hungarian family and their adjustments to a new life in San Francisco. *My Family* (1995) tells the story of generations of a Latino family that settle

in Los Angeles, while *Out of Ireland* (1994) looks at Irish immigration through the stories of several Irish immigrant families. *The Long Way Home* (1997) deals with the issue of refugees and displaced persons with the story of the hardships faced by World War II Holocaust survivors and their eventual immigration to Israel and the United States.

Contemporary immigration issues recur throughout these modern productions as well. *Alamo Bay* (1985) concerns a disturbed Vietnam veteran and the difficulties he experiences with the postwar influx of Vietnamese immigrants. *Moscow on the Hudson* (1984) tells the story of the defection of a Soviet clown from a Russian circus visiting New York, while *Midnight Mambo* (1998) combines both comedy and serious issues as it details the problems of Latin American immigrants in the story of a hardworking Guatemalan immigrant.

Romance and romantic comedy themes, long a staple of immigrant-centered movies, abound during more recent years as well, often with a story line revolving around attempts to keep from being deported through marriage. *Sophie's Choice* (1982) and *Come See the Paradise* (1990), for example, take a serious look, whereas *Born in East L.A.* (1987) and *A Million to Juan* (1994), among others, take a more lighthearted view.

Crime and immigrants is another theme that has constantly been repeated. Although Italian-American groups have long decried the association of Italian immigrants and gangsters, the popularity of such movies has remained constant. *The Godfather: Part II* (1974), the immensely popular sequel to *The Godfather* (1972), presents the story of Vito Corleone as a child in Sicily, his coming to America to escape death at the hands of the Sicilian Mafia, and his eventual rise to crime boss in New York. A host of Italian-American gangster films have followed in the ensuing years, some of which have achieved great popularity. *The Untouchables* (1987), for example, is a remake of the 1950s television series about Al Capone and the Italian gangsters of Chicago in the 1920s. Italians are not the only immigrant group linked with crime, however. Movies such as *Boulevard Nights* (1979), *Colors* (1988), *Gong pu II* (1995), *China Girl* (1987), *Hollow Point* (1995), and *Once Upon a Time in America* (1984), are just a sampling of films dealing with Asian, Latino, Jewish, and Russian crime themes. Even the science fiction genre has used immigration as a plot in movies. *Alien Nation* (1989), for example, is a futuristic story that concerns Los Angeles's newest immigrant group—extraterrestrials.

IMMIGRANT PORTRAYALS ON TELEVISION

Television programming, meanwhile, was slower to catch up with the burgeoning social consciousness reflected in the movie theaters. Most of the on-air immigrant characters in the early decades of television continued to depict the immigrant stereotype. Although some were benign, all-in-fun characters, some were offensive to the immigrant groups they portrayed. In its infancy, television had little or no heritage to draw on and, as such, drew from the other media and entertainment forms that preceded it. As a consequence, many of the stereotypical immigrant images in the early days of television were carry-overs from stage, screen, and vaudeville.

Television series such as *The Goldbergs*, starring Gertrude Berg; *Life with Luigi*, starring J. Carroll Naish; and *Mama*, based on the movie *I Remember Mama*, along with such characters as Ricky Ricardo of *I Love Lucy* and Jose Jimenez of *The Bill Dana Show*, were typical of the immigrant portrayals in television sitcoms. Interestingly, the Ricky Ricardo character, portrayed by Desi Arnaz, was felt to be offensive when the pilot was pitched to the networks, not because of the ethnic stereotype but because the network was hesitant to present a Cuban character married to an American woman, despite the fact that Lucille Ball and Desi Arnaz were real-life husband and wife. The American public, however, not only tolerated but also embraced the ethnically mixed couple, and *I Love Lucy* became one of the most successful TV sitcoms ever. And despite his portrayal of the hotheaded, temperamental Cuban bandleader who always cautioned his wife that she had "some 'splainin" to do, Arnaz was in fact an astute businessman who, with his wife, built their Desilu Studios into one of the largest and most successful television production companies of all time.

Immigrant characters were usually not the stars of the show, however, but often secondary or stock characters. As was also the case with many African-American characters, immigrant characters showed up in a variety of roles, often as servants, hired help, comic relief, or as foil to the main characters. These characters were portrayed as they had been for years, in stereotypes as the Asian house servant, Mexican migrant laborer, Jewish mother, Irish brawler, and Italian street vendor. Yet despite these stereotypes, some of these characters were welcome and even beloved parts of the show, as was the Lebanese Uncle Tonoose on *Make Room for Daddy*, starring Danny Thomas.

The Italian mobster reached television through both the periodic appearances of the stereotypical gangster character and with the debut of the television drama *The Untouchables*. Throughout its 1959–63 run, the show about the 1920s federal law enforcement unit dedicated to bringing down a variety of bootleggers and organized crime racketeers, mostly with Italian surnames, continued to receive a barrage of criticism from Italian-American groups nationwide.

Besides sitcoms, immigrant characters often appeared in the myriad of comedic sketches on the many variety programs that were immensely popular, many of which had their origins in vaudeville. Stand-up comedy, another staple of the variety show, also often featured ethnic and immigrant humor. With New York as the center of American television broadcasting, many of these stand-up comics had acts that had played to ethnic and immigrant audiences in nightclubs and resort circuits in the Northeast for years.

A variety of new ethnic characters appeared in the 1970s. Although not always immigrants, these characters showed a different type of ethnic hero at a time when viewers had become much more aware of the offensiveness of earlier stereotypes. Most prominent in TV dramas about detectives, high-powered lawyers, and private investigators, such ethnic characters as Kojak, Baretta, and Petrocelli filled the small screen. Yet as that ethnic consciousness waned, an overabundance of ethnic and immigrant stereotypes again filled television programming in the 1980s and 1990s.

Although some of the demeaning characters and the ridicule of immigrants was gone, many TV roles still featured the classic lovable-but-buffoonish immigrant characters of old. Perhaps a combination of the insensitivity of the past and the backlash against the political correctness of the 1990s, the stereotypical roles of these characters are often buffered by their well-meaning nature and the everything-works-out-well-in-the-end plots in which they were featured. It was difficult, for example, for audiences to dislike Andy Kaufman's character of Latka Gravas on *Taxi*. Yakoff Smirnoff's *What a Country* featured a variety of these characters as well. Set in a night school that was supposed to help immigrants pass their citizenship exams, the program featured individuals from Russia, Pakistan, Africa, Hungary, and elsewhere. *Perfect Strangers* was another 1980s/1990s sitcom, with Bronson Pinchot in the starring role as Balki, the lovable immigrant character who comes to live with his American cousin.

Much of the television programming dealing with immigrants and immigration issues has been in the form of made-for-television movies and miniseries, however, not a part of the regular programming schedule. Like their large-screen counterparts, a number of themes repeat themselves in this type of program—the nostalgic or historical view, the ethnic crime drama, the bigotry and prejudice encountered in the new country, and the romance or romantic comedy. Television movies and miniseries continue to the present day to be a lucrative vehicle for immigrants and immigrant issues.

Stereotyping in television drama has remained the most common criticism of immigrant characters throughout the 1990s and into the twenty-first century as well. For some, current issues and events dictate that Latinos be portrayed as gang members, Arabs and other Middle Easterners as terrorists, Cubans as political refugees, and Russians as international smugglers. Although commonly protested by immigrant groups, these stereotypes persist and show no signs of abating.

And just as television commercials have been a part of the industry since its inception, so too have immigrant characters been part of commercials from the beginning. Although some of these advertisements have become memorable "classics," they have often been protested and decried by immigrant groups as prejudicial and offensive. Jolly German characters hawk beer, the efficient Japanese sell cars, the British remain aloof as they sell mustard, while Italians usually specialize in two things: any type of food and anything that can be sold by a gangster character. From yesterday's Gertrude Berg, who once used her "Jewish Mother" character to sell soap pads ("with soap it's loaded," she once declared), to today's chameleon-like little girl, who enters an Italian restaurant and in her best gangsterlike voice expresses her discontent over the lack of respect shown by being served the wrong soft drink, immigrant characters remain prominent in television advertising today. In between, American consumers have been sold corn chips by the Frito Bandito, water conditioners by the owner of a Chinese laundry ("Ancient Chinese secret, eh?"), antacids by Italian actors ("Mama mia, atsa spicy meat ball-a"), wine by a little Swiss fellow ("That little old winemaker, me"), and tacos by a Mexican-accented Chihuahua.

Paul Magro

See also: Film, Radio, and Television, Press (Part II, Sec. 10); New York State Report on Multicultural Textbooks, 1991 (Part IV, Sec. 2).

BIBLIOGRAPHY

Allen, James Paul, and Eugene Turner. *We the People: An Atlas of America's Ethnic Diversity.* New York: Macmillan, 1988.

Beirne, Piers, and James Messerschmidt. *Criminology.* Boulder, CO: Westview Press, 2000.

Leon F. Bouvier, ed. *U.S. Immigration in the 1980s: Reappraisal and Reform.* Boulder, CO: Westview Press, 1988.

Barolini, Helen, ed. *Images: A Pictorial History of Italian Americans.* New York: Center for Migration Studies of New York, 1981.

Erdman, Harley. *Staging the Jew: The Performance of American Ethnicity.* New Brunswick, NJ: Rutgers University Press, 1962.

"Folklore, Culture, and the Immigrant Mind." In *American Immigration and Ethnicity.* Vol. 18, ed. George E. Pozzetta. New York: Garland Publishing, 1991.

"Images of Mexico in the United States." In *Dimensions of United States–Mexican Relations,* ed. John H. Coatsworth and Carlos Rico. San Diego: Center for U.S.-Mexican Studies, 1989.

The Internet Movie Database. 2000. http://us.imdb.com

Marcuson, Lewis R. *The Stage Immigrant: The Irish, Italians, and Jews in American Drama, 1920–1960.* New York: Garland Publishing, 1990.

Martin, Philip, and Elizabeth Midgley. "Immigration to the United States: Journey to an Uncertain Destination." In *Population Bulletin,* ed. Mary Mederios Kent, Washington, DC: Population Reference Bureau, 1994.

McClellan, Robert. *The Heathen Chinee: A Study of American Attitudes toward China.* Columbus: Ohio State University Press, 1971.

Parenti, Michael. *Make-Believe Media: The Politics of Entertainment.* New York: St. Martin's Press, 1992.

———. "The Media Are the Mafia: Italian-American Images and the Ethnic Struggle." *National Review* 30, no. 10 (1979): 20–27.

Parillo, Vincent N. *Strangers to These Shores: Race and Ethnic Relations in the United States.* New York: Macmillan, 1994.

Shakespeare, William. *The Complete Works of William Shakespeare.* New York: Avenel Books, 1975.

Simon, Rita J., and Susan H. Alexander. *The Ambivalent Welcome: Print Media, Public Opinion, and Immigration.* Westport, CT: Praeger, 1993.

Thernstrom, Stephen, ed. *Harvard Encyclopedia of American Ethnic Groups.* Cambridge: Harvard University Press, Belknap Press, 1980.

Ungar, Sanford J. "Coping with Diversity: The Magnitude and the Impact of Immigration since World War II." In *The New American Immigrants,* ed. Sanford J. Ungar, pp. 91–114. New York: Simon and Schuster, 1995.

PRESS

It is generally assumed that the history of the American ethnic press began as early as 1732 with the publication, in Pennsylvania, of the first German-language newspaper: *Philadelphische Zeitung*, edited by Benjamin Franklin. However, even though foreign-language periodicals have been published in the United States for over two centuries, historians have shown little interest in the study of what was deemed for a long time a minor research field.

As part of a project conducted by the Chicago School of Sociology aiming at evaluating the immigrants' contribution to American society, Robert Park was, in the 1920s, the first scholar to dedicate an in-depth comparative study to the immigrant press in the now classic book *The Immigrant Press and its Control*. After World War II, when "loyalty" became one of America's priorities and McCarthyism created a general climate of suspicion in the country, the foreign-language press was more than ever subjected to close scrutiny. Edward Hunter's poorly documented volume *In Many Voices: Our Fabulous Foreign-Language Press* was quite emblematic of postwar xenophobic preoccupations and proposed a political analysis of ethnic periodicals the purpose of which was to check their orthodoxy. In the 1960s, as ethnic studies developed, the importance of minority groups' print culture was reassessed, and many research centers began collecting foreign-language newspapers, while several books focusing on the experience of specific nationalities were published. In 1971, the creation by Lubomyr R. Wynar of the Center for the Study of Ethnic Publications at Kent State University, Ohio, marked the beginnings of a more systematic examination of diverse cultural productions and led to the publication of an essential research tool: the *Encyclopedic Directory of Ethnic Newspapers and Periodicals in the United States* (1972).

It was not until the 1980s, however, that studies on ethnic journalism started coming into their own, as periodicals were studied not solely for their doc-umentary value as sources of information on the immigrant experience but also for the active part they played as institutions in the development of ethnic communities. *The Ethnic Press in the United States* and *The Immigrant Labor Press in North America, 1840s–1970s*, edited respectively by Sally Miller and Dirk Hoerder in 1987, are good examples of this new approach and paved the way for more recent surveys such as those compiled by James Danky and Wayne Wiegand in *Print Culture in a Diverse America* (1998) and Frankie Hutton and Barbara Strauss Reed in *Outsiders in Nineteenth-Century Press History: Multicultural Perspectives* (1995). In fact, the relative economic strength shown by ethnic media at a time when the mainstream American press is facing increasing survival problems justifies the growing attention now paid to this traditionally neglected domain and allows the work of ethnic editors to be finally recognized as an integral part of American journalism.

PROBLEMS OF DEFINITION

Wynar and Miller have both raised the important question of terminology when defining the ethnic press. Many terms serve as substitutes for the words "ethnic press," but each unfolds a distinct sociological—and sometimes political—approach to the phenomenon. Park, like many other sociologists after him, referred to the "immigrant press." Nevertheless, this concept was inappropriate even in the 1920s, for it could not apply to the papers published by the second and third generations of immigrants. The second most commonly selected term is "foreign-language press," which covers only ethnic publications issued in their "native" tongues, thus failing to characterize numerous bilingual and English-language periodicals. The labels "foreign," "alien," or "non-English" have

The diversity of the nation's immigrant press is captured in this New York City newsstand. *(Anne Burns)*

also been extensively used, particularly by observers who either meant to depict the ethnic press as unfriendly, unreliable, and possibly disloyal (in wartime, for example) or saw it as an entity that was completely separate from standard American journalism. The choice of words is therefore all the more significant as it can lead to misrepresentations of the press and its position vis-à-vis American society. Unlike the above terminology—including "immigrant" and "foreign-language"—the term "ethnic press," which is most frequently used now, offers a wider perspective because it clearly encompasses black and native journalism. Some scholars presently associate the ethnic press with "radical," "specialized," or "women's" publications, and define it as a part of "alternative," "dissident," "diverse," or "other" journalistic productions (see bibliography). This trend of thought is quite

revealing of the complex position of a press belonging of right to American journalism yet still remaining at its margin.

FUNCTIONS OF THE ETHNIC PRESS

In 1835, Alexis de Tocqueville described as a typically American compulsion the fact that every village in the United States, however small and remote, had to publish a newspaper of some kind. Similar views were expressed by Park, who claimed that in New York City there was "no language group so insignificant that it does not maintain a printing press and publish some sort of periodical." It is undeniable that the United States is probably the country with the greatest number of ethnic publications. Those periodicals were born in a national tradition of news printing but perform specific functions differing from mainstream journalism. In fact, they serve the needs of their communities at four different levels.

First, their role consists in preserving the cultural heritages of ethnic groups. When published in a foreign language, they aim at reaching both an audience whose proficiency in English is not sufficient to access American news media and bilingual individuals who want to maintain a linguistic link with the land of their ancestors. The immigrant press is also an essential provider of information on the country from which the community originally came and which American standard media often overlook in their reports. This function of cultural preservation and language maintenance has been, in times of crisis, at the center of scorching debates over the dangers of keeping alive a press that, by fostering the distinctiveness of ethnic groups, might also be deemed responsible for retarding the assimilation process.

Second, ethnic publications are instrumental in shaping the community into a cohesive group. By definition, they remain close to their readers' daily preoccupations and supply information related to the life of local cultural, political, and religious associations and mutual aid societies. They deal with the specific problems that confront their audience, stimulate contacts with people of a similar background, and thus contribute to the elaboration of a sense of ethnic belonging, serving, says Wynar, as a "cementing element within the community."

Third, the ethnic press plays an influential part in helping the new immigrant adjust to American society by publishing news about the government, customs, laws, and language of the United States. Its educational value has been emphasized by most scholars, as well as its function of interface between minorities and the dominant group. Park argued that the press prepared readers for citizenship and credited it for being an "agent of assimilation." Years later, Yaroslav Chyz, manager of the Foreign Language Press Division of the Common Council for American Unity, still maintained that ethnic journalism acts as "an interpreter of American institutions and ideals, a guide to the American scene and way of life." Ethnic editors today still insist on this aspect of their work, explaining, as does Albor Ruiz—first Latino member of the *New York Daily News's* editorial board—that they teach their readers "how to navigate the system," bringing "diverse communities closer to the mainstream" in the process.

Finally, the ethnic press serves as a mirror of minorities by exposing their viewpoints on American events and offering a new perspective on stories published in mainstream newspapers. It can then be used as a channel voicing ethnic groups' claims and aspirations, since it is directed not only at diverse communities—as is generally assumed—but also at a larger American audience. In that regard, it also constitutes, as Miller notes, "the best primary source for an understanding of the world of non-English-speaking groups in the United States, their expectations and concerns, their background and evolution as individual communities."

TYPES OF PUBLICATIONS

Because the ethnic press is, in itself, regarded as a specific category of American journalism, the incredible diversity of its content is often overlooked. Nonetheless, the rich variety existing in that field has been emphasized by scholars ever since the 1920s, when Park proposed to divide the press into three main, yet somewhat limited, categories: commercial papers, organs of institutions or societies, and propagandist papers. In the 1970s, Wynar established a more comprehensive classification which is still valid today and which distinguishes among the following twelve categories of ethnic periodicals: political and ideological, fraternal, religious, scholarly and academic, educational, professional and trade, cultural, youth-oriented, women-oriented, sports and recreational, veteran's, and bibliographic publications. Papers can be dailies, weeklies, monthlies, or be published irregularly, according to the needs of their audiences and

the financial possibilities of their managers. They are owned by an ever greater variety of business professionals, political leaders, religious congregations, benevolent societies, regional leisure clubs, or even single individuals.

NUMBER OF PERIODICALS

There are no reliable statistics on the number and circulation of ethnic periodicals published in the United States. Figures vary greatly from one source to another, and available estimations must therefore be considered with caution. The most dependable sources are the Foreign Language Information Service (FLIS) (which in 1939 became the Common Council for American Unity [CCAU], an institution that itself evolved into the American Council for Nationalities Service [ACNS] in 1959) and the *Ayer Directory of Newspapers and Periodicals*, which was succeeded by the *Gale Directory of Publications and Broadcast Media*. The regular surveys of foreign-language periodicals published by the FLIS, CCAU, and ACNS are relevant indicators as to the general development of the ethnic press but do not provide definite comprehensive data. The Ayer directory dedicates specific chapters to the "foreign language" and "Negro" publications, while its successor also includes, along with the "foreign language" and "Black" sections, listings of the "Jewish" and "Hispanic" publications. Because both directories are meant to inform possible American advertisers, they cannot be relied on for registering all of the existing publications but certainly account for the major trends in the numerical evolution of the ethnic press (see Tables 1 and 2).

Table 1 Number of Ethnic Publications in the United States, 1999				
	Foreign-language	Hispanic	Black	Jewish
Newspapers	149	90	183	60
Magazines	165	67	58	46
Total	314	157	241	106

Source: Gale Directory of Publications and Broadcast Media, 133d ed. Farmington Hills, MI: Gale Research, 1999.
Note: Most of the "Hispanic publications" are included in the foreign-language section under the label "Spanish."

Table 2
Number of Foreign-Language Publications, 1890–1990

Year	Number of publications	Source
1890	1,028	Park
1910	1,198	Park
1930	1,052	Fishman
1950	739	Ayer
1970	903	Wynar
1990	572	Gale

Note: Includes Hispanic and Yiddish publications.
Source: Park, Robert. *Immigrant Press and Its Control.* New York: Greenwood Press, 1970; Fishman, Joshua. *Language Loyalties in the United States.* London: Moulton & Company, 1966; Percy, J., and M. Johnson. *Directory of Newspapers and Periodicals, 1950.* Philadelphia: N.W. Ayer and Sons, 1950; Wynar, Lubomyr, and Anne Wyner. *Encyclopedic Directory of Ethnic Newspapers and Periodicals in the United States.* Littleton, CO: Libraries Unlimited, 1976; Boyden, Donald P., and John Krol, eds. *Gale Directory of Publications and Broadcast Media.* Detroit: Gale Research, 1990.

BRIEF HISTORY OF THE IMMIGRANT/ETHNIC PRESS

It would be impossible to cover thoroughly the history of all the thousands of ethnic newspapers published in the United States over nearly three centuries in no fewer than forty different languages. Because the emphasis is on immigration, the black and native presses will not be examined, and many groups must be omitted, due to obvious space constraints. Nonetheless, the following table, though not comprehensive, provides a more pluralistic idea of the immense variety of groups and languages that constitute the American ethnic press.

PIONEER JOURNALISM: 1730s–1820s

The history of the ethnic press is closely connected to the development of American immigration, each new wave of immigrants bringing along a potential readership for enterprising professional or scratch publishers. It began in the eighteenth century with Benjamin Franklin's attempt to launch a German-language newspaper that failed to survive after only two issues. At that early stage, ethnic journalism was extremely fragile, for it was frequently the result of single individuals' efforts. Owning an immigrant paper required multiple skills and a strong deter-

mination because it meant collecting the news, writing opinion pieces, editing the articles, printing the paper, and even selling it. The first groups to get involved in this highly risky venture were those which were large enough to rely on at least a small readership. Among the pioneers were the Germans, French, and Irish, who all started newspapers before the 1820s.

The Germans' endeavors in the publishing business proved remarkably successful over the years, as estimations credit that community for having established up to 5,000 publications since the 1730s. Yet in 1739, when Christophe Sauer started a monthly in Germantown entitled *Der Hoch-Deutsch Pennsylvanische Geschichts-Schreiber* (High German Pennsylvania Annalist), no one could have predicted his paper would outlive him and be taken over by his son Christophe Sauer II, finally to become the influential loyalist *Germantauner Zeitung* (Germantown Times, 1758). As James M. Berquist shows in his essay "The German-American Press" (in Miller), those publications did not only reflect the specific concerns of the German communities but were also dealing with American colonial debates, discussing issues such as the Stamp Act and British oppression. They were journals of opinion, offering opposing viewpoints that were very similar in substance to those developed by the English colonial press. Some, like Sauer's paper, would defend peace, while others, such as John Heinrich Miller's *Wochentliche Philadelphische Staatsbote* (Weekly Philadelphia Public Messenger, 1762), supported the Revolution. In fact, it seems that the fate of the German press of the time was intrinsically linked to that of American journalism in general. Between the end of the Revolution and 1800, the number of German newspapers increased by thirty-eight, and these publications continued to thrive as more Germans came to Pennsylvania, Maryland, Virginia, and even Ohio.

According to the 1790 census, the French accounted for only 1.7 percent of the American white population, while the Germans represented 8.7 percent. Therefore, the Franco-American press could not benefit, especially in the beginning, from as large an audience as that of the German-language newspapers. Robert B. Perreault, author of several monographs on the French press, listed only ten newspapers appearing before 1800, in Boston, Philadelphia, New York, and New Orleans. Among them were the *Courrier de Boston* (Boston Courier, 1789), and *Le Moniteur de la Louisiane* (The Louisiana Monitor, 1794), both of which were deeply committed politically. The latter lasted for twenty years in New Orleans (then Spanish Louisiana) and was owned by Louis Duclot, a printer

Table 3
First Newspapers Published by Major Ethnic Groups, 1732–1905

Year	Title	Translation	Ethnic group	Place of publication
1732	*Philadelphische Zeitung*	Philadelphia News	German	Philadelphia, PA
1776	*The New York Packet and American Advertizer*		Irish	New York City (NYC)
1780	*La Gazette Française*	The French Gazette	French	Newport, RI
1823	*The Jew*		Jewish	NYC
1827	*Freedom's Journal*		Afro-American	NYC
1828	*The Cherokee Phoenix*		Native American	New Echota, GA
1834	*El Crepúsculo de la Libertad*	The Dusk of Freedom	Mexican	Taos, NM
1847	*Nordlyset*	The Northern Light	Norwegian	Norway, WI
1847	*Skandinavia*	Scandinavia	Scandinavian	NYC
1849	*De Sheboygan Nieusbode*	The Sheboygan News Messenger	Dutch	Sheboygan, WI
1849	*L'Europeo Americano*	The European American	Italian	NYC
1854	*The Golden Hills' News*		Chinese	San Francisco
1855	*Hemlandet, det Gamla Och det Nya*	The Homeland, Old and New	Swedish	Galesburg, IL
1857	*Scottish American Journal*		Scottish	NYC
1863	*Echo z Polski*	Echo of Poland	Polish	NYC
1865	*La Voz de America*	The Voice of America	Puerto Rican	NYC
1868	*Svoboda—The Alaska Herald*		Russian	San Francisco
1869	*Slavenska itaonica*	Slavic Reading Room	Serbian-Montenegrin	San Francisco
1870	*Yiddishe Tseitung*	The Jewish Journal	Jewish (in Yiddish)	NYC
1876	*Amerikan Suomalainen Lehti*	The American Finnish Journal	Finnish	Hancock, MI
1877	*Journal de Notícias*	News Journal	Portuguese	Erie, PA
1879	*Lietuwiszka Gazieta*	Lithuanian Gazette	Lithuanian	NYC
1886	*Ameryka*	America	Ukrainian	Shenandoah, PA
1886	*Amerikanszko-Szlovenszke Noviny*	American-Slovak News	Slovak	Pittsburgh, PA
1886	*Shinonome*	Dawn	Japanese	San Francisco
1888	*Arekag*	The Sun	Armenian	Jersey City, NJ
1891	*Amerikanski Slovenec*	The American Slovene	Slovene	Chicago
1892	*Kawkab Amrika*	Star of America	Arabic (Syrian)	Boston
1892	*Slavenska Sloga*	Slavic Unity	Croatian	San Francisco
1892	*Neos Kosmos*	New World	Greek	NYC
1896	*Amerikas Vëstenis*	American Herald	Latvian	Unknown
1900	*Curierul Româno-American*	The Romanian-American Courier	Romanian	NYC
1905	*Filipino Students' Magazine*		Filipino	Berkeley, CA
1905	*Konglip Sinbo*	Public News or United Korean	Korean	San Francisco

Source: Park, Robert. *Immigrant Press and Its Control.* New York: Greenwood Press, 1970; Fishman, Joshua. *Language Loyalties in the United States.* London: Moulton & Company, 1966; Percy, J., and M. Johnson. *Directory of Newspapers and Periodicals, 1950.* Philadelphia: N.W. Ayer and Sons, 1950; Wynar, Lubomyr, and Anne Wyner. *Encyclopedic Directory of Ethnic Newspapers and Periodicals in the United States.* Littleton, CO: Libraries Unlimited, 1976; Boyden, Donald P., and John Krol, eds. *Gale Directory of Publications and Broadcast Media.* Detroit: Gale Research, 1990.

originally from Santo Domingo. Its motto, "Bombalio, Clangor, Stridor, Tarantantara, Murmur," was quite representative of the tone adopted by a certain fringe of strongly opinioned ethnic newspapers. Yet, as specialist Edward Larocque Tinker noted, not all the French papers proved that successful, most of them springing up "like mushrooms" and dying "like flies."

EXPANSION OF THE PRESS: 1820s–1880s

Between the 1820s and the 1860s, new ethnic groups came to the United States, while others became more visible. As German publications expanded thanks to the arrival of the forty-eighters, the Scandinavian, Dutch, Scottish, Mexican, Jewish, Italian, and Chinese communities—along with natives and black Americans—began to contribute to the ethnic press. The papers that were born in that period represented various ideological and religious trends, often echoing the political struggles that were sweeping the immigrants' motherlands. Most of them were confronted with great financial difficulties and proved ephemeral for lack of sufficient audience. In the 1840s, for example, neither the Swedes nor the Danes could find within their own ranks enough readers to sustain a paper. Nonetheless, to circumvent this problem, they joined their efforts and issued a periodical written in both Swedish and Danish: *Skandinavia*. Such bilingual or trilingual publications were not uncommon in the ethnic press. In fact, *Skandinavia* was following in the footsteps of *El Correo Atlantico* (The Atlantic Courier), which had been founded by an Italian exile in Mexico in 1835, had moved to New York City a year later, and had been featuring at the same time French, Spanish, and Italian articles.

When the all-Danish newspaper *Emigranten* (The Immigrant) was finally launched in 1852, it aimed at offering religious support and guidance to the immigrants. The same ambition also characterized the early Jewish, Swedish, and Chinese journalistic enterprises as is shown by the birth of such periodicals as *The Occident and American Jewish Advocate* in 1843, *Hemlandet* (The Homeland) in 1855, and the *Chinese Daily News* in 1858.

Before the 1860s, the Mexican and Italian journalists were essentially concerned with the political changes affecting their motherlands. In his essay "Mexican American Press" (in Miller), Carlos E. Cortès mentions the existence of over 130 papers established by Mexicans in the Southwest (Arizona, California, Colorado, New Mexico, and Texas) during the nineteenth century. All of them were said to hold "strong editorial positions" with respect to the status of Mexico and that of the newly annexed Chicano population. The Italian press, though quite scarce in the 1840s, also assumed a political role and spoke for the Italian Mazzinian exiles in America. The first yet short-lived Italian periodical, *L'Europeo Americano*, as well as the more successful *L'Eco d'Italia* (Echo of Italy), were both started in 1849 by Giovanni Francesco Secchi de Casali and epitomized the needs of a small community of political refugees for the freedom of expression provided by the American Constitution. In the United States, they could expose the very opinions that had caused their exile. Their papers were then sent back to the motherland, where they served as underground subversive organs used by those who championed the cause of the Italian Republic. Very similar concerns led Puerto Ricans in 1865 to establish *La Voz de America* (The Voice of America), which supported the struggle for independence of Puerto Rico and the Caribbean nations from Spain. The paper was not addressed only to the Puerto Ricans of New York City but also to those who had remained on the island, and it was meant to influence local politics. In like manner, *Echo z Polski* (Echo of Poland), founded by Romuald Jaworowski in 1863, advocated insurrection in Poland against the Russian overlords, thus being emblematic of all the ethnic papers that used their freedom to give voice to oppressed or dissident factions in their homelands.

The arrival of Slovaks, Russians, and Ukrainians in the late 1860s, as well as the settling of the Finns in the Midwest a decade later, enriched ethnic journalism with such new publications as *Svoboda* (freedom)—*The Alaska Herald*, created in 1868 by Aga Pius Honcharenko for the Russians who had migrated to Alaska, and *Amerikan Suomalainen Lehti* (The American Finnish Journal) established by the Finnish Lutheran community in 1876. The 1870s were also marked by the emergence of the immigrant radical press. As an increasing number of foreign workers participated in the expansion of American industry, immigrants began to organize and to edit papers that dealt with the difficulties of their working experience. Although the first German-language labor paper, *Beobachter am Ohio* (Observer on the Ohio), dates back to 1844, the most successful ones, such as *Der Vorbote* (The Harbinger, 1874–1924) or *Chicagoer Arbeiter-Zeitung* (Chicago Labor News, 1876), appeared later, to blossom fully in the early 1900s. The Czechs, the Danes, and the French-speaking communities were also active in unions and gave birth to several publications, including the long-lasting *New Yorské Listy* (New York Papers, 1874); *Den Nye Tid* (The New

Time, 1877), edited by the Danish socialist Louis Pio; and *La Commune* (The Commune), set up in New Orleans in 1871.

THE GOLDEN AGE: 1880s–1930s

In the last two decades of the nineteenth century, massive immigration from eastern and southern European countries fostered the expansion of the ethnic press. In the 1890s, thanks to the modernization of printing equipment and the development of advertising, the Germans were still leading the way with 800 publications, whose circulation could reach peaks after fifty years of existence, as was the case for the New York daily *Staats-Zeitung* (Public News), which claimed a readership of over 70,000 in the 1890s. No other group even came close to that score, but Park's figures show that the communities that were already rather well established in the United States saw their presses develop steadily. Between 1884 and 1895, the number of publications issued by Scandinavians, French/French Canadians, and Hispanics rose from 53 to 135, 46 to 49, and 35 to 60, respectively. As to the new waves of immigrants, they increased the diversity of languages printed in the United States, with the foundation, among others, of the Lithuanian *Wienibe Lietuwnink* (Unity of Lithuanians, 1886), Ukrainian *Svoboda* (Liberty, 1893), Croatian *Slavenska Sloga* (Slavic Unity, 1892), Greek *Neo Kosmos,* (New World, 1892), Armenian *Arekag* (The Sun, 1888), and even the Japanese *Shinonome* (Dawn, 1886) and Syrian *Kawkab Amrika* (Star of America, 1892). The Chinese, whose immigration had been restricted by the Chinese Exclusion Act of 1882, also contributed to the expansion of foreign-language newspapers by giving birth to three major and long-lived dailies in that period: *Sai Gai Yat Po* (The Chinese World, 1892–1969), organ of the Reform Party; *Young China* (1910 to present) established on behalf of the Chinese Revolutionary Party; and *Mun Hey Daily* (Chinese Nationalist, 1915–58), set up by the Kuomintang in New York City.

In the first decade of the twentieth century, the configuration of the ethnic press began to change significantly. While the German and Scandinavian publications started declining slowly, the Bohemian, Russian, Ukrainian, Jewish, Mexican, Polish, and Italian presses dramatically increased. Most of the newly born papers shared common characteristics with the publications established by other ethnic groups before them. They still suffered from a high mortality rate, they often depended on a single person's endeavors, and they were published, as Father Moise Balea, editor of the Romanian newspaper *Amerika,*

put it, "when I have time, money, and disposition" (in Miller). In spite of their difficulties, they played an important role in their communities, not only by providing news about the Old Country but also by participating in the building of the cultural identity of their respective groups.

Community activism was particularly the case for Jewish and Italian papers. When the first Jewish periodicals appeared, they were published essentially in English, and it was only in the 1880s, with the arrival of the eastern European Jews who had fled the Russian pogroms, that the Hebrew and Yiddish papers began to flourish, a variety of dailies and weeklies among which were: *Yiddishes Tageblatt* (Jewish Daily News, 1885); *Der Teglicher Herold* (The Daily Herald, 1890); and *Die Yiddishe Aben Post* (Yiddish Evening Post, 1889). In 1916, the Yiddish press could thus boast eleven dailies with a total peak circulation of 650,000. Yiddish journalism had by then become an essential educational tool and proved instrumental in uniting the very diverse New York Jewish communities. Moreover, as Mordecai Soltes emphasizes in his book *The Yiddish Press* (1925), it played an active part in the Americanization process.

In the 1880s, when Carlo Barsotti founded the most famous Italian-American newspaper, *Il Progresso Italo-Americano* (The Italian-American Progress, 1880–1988), the Ayer directory listed fewer than ten Italian periodicals. By 1918, after 3 million immigrants from the peninsula had passed through the gates of Ellis Island, the number of Italian papers had risen to 110, including such different journalistic productions as *La Gazzetta del Massachusetts* (1903) in Boston; *L'Italia* (1886) in San Francisco; *La Follia di New York* (New York Follies, 1893) in New York City; *L'Opinione* (1906) in Philadelphia; and *Il Corriere dell'Italia* (The Italian Courier, 1886) in Chicago.

During the same period, the immigrant radical press extended the range of its anarchist, anarcho-syndicalist, socialist, communist, and revolutionary publications, welcoming within its ranks *Vorwaerts* (Jewish Daily Forward, 1897), edited by the socialist Abraham Cahan; *Il Martello* (The Hammer, 1916), led by Italian anarchist Carlo Tresca; *Il Proletario* (The Proletarian, 1896), founded by the Italian socialist Paolo Mazzoli; *California Arbeiter-Zeitung* (California Labor News, 1887), representing the official organ of the German Unions and Workers Associations; *Raivaaja* (The Pioneer, 1905), created by the Finnish socialist Taavi Tainio; and *Novii Mir* (New World, 1911), supported by the Russian Mensheviks. In fact, as the labor movement was growing, the Industrial Workers of the World (IWW), the Amalgamated Clothing Workers' Union (ACWU), the International Ladies' Garment Workers' Union (ILGWU), and other unions created foreign sections that also published several non-English periodicals, adding to the already industrious but often short-lived radical press.

The First World War marked a turning point in the relationship between the ethnic press and American authorities. The tense context of preparedness and rising xenophobia led more and more Americans to question the existence of "alien" papers. The nativists accused ethnic publications of thwarting the Americanization process and supporting foreign nations' interests. When the United States entered the conflict, the loyalty issue became more acute, as it was feared that ethnic journalists would foster enemy propaganda. The German publications were all the more vilified because they were produced by so-called old immigrants, who were expected to have abandoned their native tongue and to have been completely assimilated. To the "one hundred percent" Americans, the fact that Germans took pride in their cultural heritage was but another proof of their disloyalty. Therefore, they recommended the suppression of the "alien" press, which they felt was both useless and dangerous. The alternative to suppression was offered by the Committee on Public Information (CPI). Created in 1918 by the American government to organize war propaganda, the CPI set up its Foreign Language Division, which aimed at controlling "alien" media and ensuring their loyalty. Foreign-language papers were for the first time acknowledged by American authorities as partners in their dealings with diverse communities, at the same time as they were regarded with caution and mistrust as possible promoters of adverse ideology.

The Trading with the Enemy Act of 1917 took its toll on foreign-language newspapers because it required that a translation of all articles related to political issues be submitted to government censors for approval before publication. Not all the editors could afford this additional burden, and some papers died in the process. The position of immigrant and ethnic editorialists was very uncomfortable because they had to support the war effort with even more eagerness than did the all-American press. In that context, the pacifist periodicals that refused to advertise for war bonds, along with the papers that defended the German viewpoint, all had to conform or cease publication.

In 1920, the four most active groups in the publishing business were the Germans, the Scandinavians, the Hispanics, and the Italians with 276, 111, 100, and 98 publications, respectively. Strongly affected by the war, the German-American press continued to decline in the early twenties because it could not renew its readership. Italian newspapers kept on thriving until the late 1930s and saw the rise of new titles that mirrored the political changes affecting Italy. Agostino de Biasi, owner of the nationalistic review *Il Carroccio* (The Battle Wagon, 1915), and Domenico Trombetta, founder of the fascist *Il Grido della Stirpe* (The Cry of Race, 1923), supported the new Italian government, while Italian-American antifascist groups tried to counter Mussolinian propaganda in *Il Nuovo Mondo* (New World, 1925), created by trade unionist Vincenzo Vacirca, as well as in other labor newspapers.

In the same decade, the Americanization movements intensified their relationship with the ethnic press, using the latter as a vehicle for spreading American values. Keeping a benevolent yet prudent eye on the "non-English" papers was notably the task that the Foreign Language Information Service (FLIS) assigned itself after the war. The FLIS, which was founded by former members of the CPI, was not directly connected to the American government. But it provided the main ethnic editors with official government information to be used by immigrants and supplied American authorities with all relevant data concerning the numerical and political evolution of the foreign-language press.

DECLINE AND REVIVAL: 1930s–1990s

In the 1930s, the ethnic press was severely hit by both the Great Depression and the consequences of the 1920s immigration quota laws. The Polish and Italian publishers, who could equally rely on over 120 periodicals in 1930, were unable to produce more than 80 publications by 1940. Ethnic papers suffered from the loss of a large portion of their advertisers. The new restrictive immigration policy of the United States also caused them to be deprived of new potential readers. As to the second and third generations of immigrants, they were losing interest in what they considered to be the press of their parents and thus tended to turn to the mainstream American papers. This evolution of the concerns of the readership of the ethnic press led publishers to launch bilingual editions of their publications. Danish, Chinese, Italian, Polish, Ukrainian, and Lithuanian papers introduced English sections that were meant to attract a younger and more Americanized audience. When the Ukrainian *Rising Star* in Detroit or *The Chinese Digest* in San Francisco appeared in the thirties, they were emblematic of a new generation of ethnic periodicals written completely in English and dealing essentially with the American experience of their readers and the daily life of their communities in the United States rather than with the past heritage of their ancestors. Moreover, being exposed to a general decrease of circulation, many ethnic periodicals chose to merge in order to strengthen their position on the market, while numerous small publications could not survive.

After Pearl Harbor, the foreign-language press was once more asked to prove its loyalty to the United States by actively supporting war propaganda in its editorials. At the end of the conflict, the ethnic papers' endeavors in this matter won the recognition of American military authorities who praised the part played by the foreign-language press in selling war bonds and spreading official American news. The historian Arthur Goren explains how the Jewish press underwent major changes during that period with the creation of literary publications that responded to the new generation's needs and benefited from the arrival of such intellectuals as the future Nobel laureate Isaac Singer (in Miller). Acclaimed for its quality, *Commentary*, founded in 1945, is representative of those Jewish literary journals born as World War II drew to a close.

In the postwar era, the Scandinavian, German, and Italian presses continued to dwindle. However, the passage of the Displaced Persons Act of 1948, by allowing eastern European political émigrés to find refuge in America, led to a revitalization of the declining Russian and Ukrainian papers. While the Mexican press had been struck by the Great Depression and the repatriation program, it expanded in the aftermath of the war because of the large-scale immigration of Mexican workers that took place in the two decades following the enforcement of the Bracero Program (1951). Puerto Rican journalists also enjoyed a larger audience, as more immigrants from the island came to New York City, and the reporters found new organs of expression when *El Diario de Nueva York* was established in 1948 and *La Prensa* (The Press, 1913) was given a Puerto Rican editor in 1960. The Chinese papers similarly increased their readership when a wealthier Chinese-American middle class began to emerge in the 1950s.

In 1960, the ACNS listed 789 ethnic papers, including 134 publications issued in English by 27 different nationality groups. In spite of the decline of its press, the German-American community still produced then the largest number of ethnic periodicals (85) and was closely followed in numbers by the Italians (57), Hispanics (54), Poles (53), Ukrainians (45), Russians (42), and Chinese (17). In his analysis of the new trends characterizing the foreign-language press of the 1960s, Joshua Fishman noted a decrease of non-English dailies and an increase of monthly publications that were chosen by editors as a successful

alternative. The revival of the ethnic press in the sixties and seventies observed by Wynar and Miller was due to a combination of social, political, and demographic factors. The arrival of new waves of immigrants such as the Cubans in 1965, for example, contributed to the strengthening of Hispanic papers. In the mid-1970s, the admission of South Asian refugees into the United States permitted the birth of *Nguoi Việt* (1978), a daily that still represents the dynamism of Vietnamese journalism in California. The influence of the Civil Rights movement also proved essential in the development of ethnic media. In fact, it was responsible for the creation of many publications discussing the concept of ethnicity, thus sharpening among their readers "the sense of group cohesion, shared identity and pride." The Mexican press grew with the Chicano movement and mirrored the political aspirations of a community whose self-awareness was building up. *La Raza* (1967–75) and *La Luz* (1971–81) were born in that context, along with the scholarly publication *Aztlan; International Journal of Chicano Studies Research*, published by the University of California, Los Angeles, which attempted in its first issue to answer such difficult questions as, "To what extent do Mexican Americans constitute a separate racial entity?"

In the 1980s, a new exodus from the Soviet Union provided Russian and Ukrainian papers with a fresh readership and led to the establishment of new titles, among which were *Novii Amerikanets* (New American, 1980) and *Strelets* (Sagittarius, 1984). The development of Chinese communities in California, as well as the expansion of Taiwanese immigration in New York, drove publishers to launch new Chinese-American papers (*Taiwan Tribune*, 1981), while investors from China supported the creation of U.S. editions of Taipei's dailies (*World Journal*, in San Francisco and New York). In 1988, Sally Miller described the immigrant press as "an enduring phenomenon."

In fact, despite most predictions, ethnic papers have not passed away and even feature publications by older groups, as is shown by the subsistence in the new millennium of the *Danish Pioneer* (1872) or the *California Staats-Zeitung* (California State News). In 1990, the *Gale Directory of Publications and Broadcast Media* still mentioned the existence of over 570 ethnic periodicals (not including 249 black publications), and six years later the *New York Times* admitted that "as mainstream papers cut back, the ethnic press expands." With the growth of Hispanic communities, the number of papers issued in Spanish or published by Spanish-speaking investors has risen considerably in the last decade of the twentieth century. American advertising agencies trust ethnic newspapers to sell their telephone cards and other targeted products because they know they are dealing with a well-defined market. The ethnic media now represent a strong and active component of American journalism, whose power cannot be overlooked. Established in 1982 "to promote Hispanic media, provide incentives and opportunities for Hispanics to enter the media, encourage advertisers to place advertisements in Hispanic publications, and conduct research on the role and development of Hispanic media in the United States," the National Association of Hispanic Publications claims its staff comes from no less than "400 Hispanic newspapers, magazines and newsletters published in the United States." This spectacular boom of the Hispanic press could not be ignored by mainstream publishers who thus started collaborating with the major Spanish-language papers. The *New York Times*, for example, has been promoting a joint subscription with the daily *El Diario* to sell the two papers together. Moreover, "ethnic" journalists are invited to contribute their share to standard American periodicals, in an effort on behalf of the mainstream editors to capture a larger and more diverse readership.

The expansion of the ethnic press on the Internet certainly constitutes the most striking development of the last decade. The Web offers an amazingly rich panel of newspapers serving the various American ethnic communities. Old publications such as the *Danish Pioneer* or the Dutch-American *Windmill Herald* (1954) are as well represented as such recent productions as the Russian-American *Kontakt* (1994), the Lebanese-American *Beirut Times* (1984), or the Arab-American *Al Watan* (1991). The Internet also reveals the dynamism of the Asian-American press, providing access to the Vietnamese *Nguo Viêt Daily News* and featuring over thirteen Chinese-American papers, among which are *The China Press, Sing Tao Daily, World Journal*, and *China News Digest*. The Hispanic press is obviously very active in this field too, with numerous online papers including *El Nuevo Herald, La Raza, Diario las Americas, Dos Mundos-Two Worlds, El Sol de San Diego*, and *La Oferta Review*. Many of those publications are bilingual, and they all deal with the particular experience of the communities they serve in the United States, while offering an alternative understanding of American and foreign news. Interestingly enough, although the major foreign papers all have a Web site of their own and can therefore furnish the latest news on their countries in their respective tongues, it does not seem to affect the success of the American ethnic press, which fulfills a specific mission that neither the foreign nor the mainstream papers can. In her book on the Latino press, América

Rodriguez explains: "Latino-oriented journalism will exist as long as Latinos are outside the center of the U.S. society." She adds: "The central challenge of Latino media is . . . to preserve a Latino ethnoracial identity and worldview, while at the same time embracing the defining values of the majority society and its media markets." One can assume that all ethnic papers will be confronted with a similar challenge in the new millennium.

Bénédicte Deschamps

See also: Public Opinion and Immigration (Part II, Sec. 6); Arts I: Literature, Film, Radio, and Television, Language (Part II, Sec. 10).

BIBLIOGRAPHY

Chyz, Yaroslav. *225 Years of the U.S. Foreign-Language Press in the United States.* New York: American Council for Nationalities Service, 1959.

Danky, James, and Wayne Wiegand, eds. *Print Culture in a Diverse America.* Urbana: University of Illinois Press, 1998.

Fishman, Joshua. *Language Loyalties in the United States.* London: Moulton and Co., 1966.

Hardt, Hanno. "The Foreign-Language Press in American Press History." *Journal of Communication* 39:2 (Spring 1989): 114–31.

Harzig, Christine, and Dirk Hoerder, eds. *The Press of Labor Migrants in Europe and North America, 1880s–1980.* Lexington: Lexington Books, 1985.

Hoerder, Dirk, ed. *The Immigrant Labor Press in North America, 1840s–1970s.* New York: Greenwood Press, 1987.

Hunter, Edward. *In Many Voices: Our Fabulous Foreign-Language Press.* Norman Park: Norman College, 1960.

Hutton, Frank and Barbara Strauss Reed, eds. *Outsiders in Nineteenth-Century Press History: Multicultural Perspectives.* Bowling Green: Bowling Green State University Popular Press, 1995.

Ireland, Sandra L. Jones. *Ethnic Periodicals in Contemporary America: An Annotated Guide.* New York: Greenwood Press, 1990.

Kessler, Lauren. *The Dissident Press:, Alternative Journalism in American History.* Newbury Park, CA: Sage, 1990.

———, ed. *The Ethnic Press in the United States: A Historical Analysis and Handbook.* New York: Greenwood Press, 1987.

Miller, Sally. "Immigrant and Ethnic Newspapers: An Enduring Phenomenon." *Serials Librarian* 14:1–2 (1988): 135–43.

O'Brien Ruth. "Ethnic Media Help New Immigrants Adjust to U.S." *Professional Journalism* (www.freedomforum.org), November 19, 1998.

Park, Robert. *The Immigrant Press and Its Control.* Reprint, New York: Greenwood Press, 1970.

Rodriguez, América. *Making Latino News: Race, Language, Class.* Thousand Oaks, CA: Sage Publications, 1999.

Soltes, Mordecai. *The Yiddish Press: An Americanizing Agency*. 1925. Reprint, New York: Arno Press and the New York Times, 1969.

Sreenivasan, Sreenath. "As Mainstream Papers Cut Back, the Ethnic Press Expands." *New York Times*, July 22, 1996, D7.

Tinker, Edward Larocque. *French Newspapers and Periodicals of Louisiana*. Worcester, MA: American Antiquarian Society, 1933.

Wynar, Lubomyr. "The Study of the Ethnic Press." *Unesco Journal of Information Science* 1:1 (January–March 1979).

Wynar, Lubornyr, and Anna Wynar. *Encyclopedic Directory of Ethnic Newspapers and Periodicals in the United States*. Littleton, CO: Libraries Unlimited, 1976.

Zubrzycki, Jerzy. "The Role of the Foreign-Language Press in Migrant Integration." *Population Studies* 22 (1958): 73–82.

SCIENCE

Rational immigration policies have resulted in large numbers of scientists immigrating to the United States and contributing significantly to the advancement of science. American immigrant scientists have revolutionized all the sciences, including physics, chemistry, and biology, but may have deprived their home country of its most valuable human resources.

THE LAW

This section outlines the requirements for immigration based on a profession in science. Many immigrant scientists originally arrived in the United States as nonimmigrant F-category students or H1B-category professional temporary employees and subsequently adjusted their status to lawful permanent resident by applying to the Immigration and Naturalization Service in the United States; other scientists have applied for and received immigrant visas at United States embassies abroad before immigrating. Below is a brief outline of the law as it applies to a scientist seeking to immigrate to the United States or to adjust status to that of permanent resident based on profession. The immigration laws change so frequently that the description that follows must be read more as a guide to the overall philosophy of the immigration laws as they pertain to scientists than as a practical how-to guide or legal advice.

FIRST PREFERENCE SCIENTIST

Section 203 of the Immigration and Nationality Act (8 U.S.C. 1153) established in 1965 an almost "too logical to be an immigration law" hierarchy based on the documented ability of prospective immigrants, with those at the extreme right end of the bell-shaped curve of renown—that is, those of the most coveted skills—receiving the most favored treatment.

Section 203(b)(1) of the act, defines "Employment Based First Preference" to include three categories of "priority workers" and allocates the first 28.6 percent of available employment-based visas to this group. The first two of the three categories ("Aliens of Extraordinary Ability" and "Outstanding Professors and Researchers") clearly have application to immigrant scientists; the third category ("Multinational Managers and Executives") could apply to a scientist acting in an executive or managerial position.

First Preference Category One: Extraordinary Ability

Aliens of "Extraordinary Ability" in the sciences, as well as arts, education, athletics, or business, are the "small percentage to have risen to the very top of the field of endeavor" and who can demonstrate with extensive documentation that they have sustained national or international acclaim in the "field of endeavor." In a highly specialized world, it becomes apparent that how one defines "the field of endeavor" will often be decisive in determining whether an alien is "at the very top." Consider a biologist and a physicist. For the biologist, is the "field of endeavor" defined as "science," "biology or chemistry," "genetics," "Polymerase Chain Reaction (PCR) genotyping," or use of a particular procedure to identify DNA? For the physicist, is the field "science," "astronomy and physics," "astrophysics," "big bang theory," measurement of background radiation, or use of a particular instrument to measure radiation? In each example, the first two categories are too broad and thus exclude too many scientists, and the final category is too narrowly drawn and thus includes too high a percentage of scientists working in that field. Consider the irony that however one defines the field of endeavor, the more highly populated fields, which presumably are more well staffed in terms of both quantity and quality of researcher, may have roughly the same number

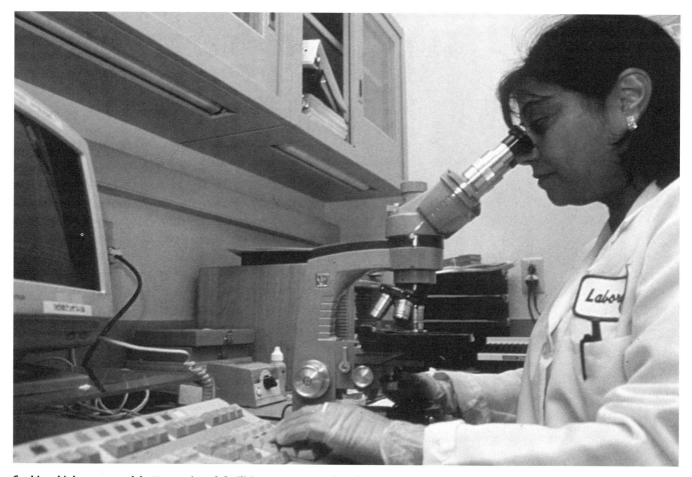

Seeking higher pay and better-equipped facilities, many scientists from the developing world—like this Arab-American biologist— come to the United States, thus creating a phenomenon known as the "brain drain." *(David Bacon/Impact Visuals)*

"at the top" as less populated and likely less critical fields. Also note the requirement of "sustained" acclaim, so that presumably a single well-publicized episode (cold fusion, perhaps) is likely insufficient to meet the requirement.

Extraordinary ability requires either a major, internationally recognized award (the Nobel Prize) or the fulfilling of at least three of the following ten criteria, most of which apply to scientists:

1. Receipt of lesser national or international awards

2. Membership in associations requiring outstanding achievement in the field

3. Published material about the alien

4. Evidence that the alien is a judge of the work of others (as, for example, a referee in a peer-reviewed journal)

5. Evidence of original contribution of major significance to the field (more than the standard Ph.D. thesis)

6. Authorship of scholarly articles (for example, publication in a peer-reviewed journal)

7. Evidence the alien has performed in a leading or critical role for organizations with a distinguished reputation

8. Evidence the alien is paid more than others in the field

9. Other evidence, if the enumerated standards do not apply

10. Display at artistic exhibitions

11. Evidence of commercial success in the performing arts

All but the last two criteria apply to scientists. Considering that many scientists, especially in academia, publish (6) and review (4) articles, this type of immigration is within the realm of possibility for many experienced scientists. Kary Mullis, 1993 Nobel laureate in Chemistry, has said the Nobel Prize will open any door, at least once. While this manner of immigrating is for the rarefied few Nobel Prize winners, it can also be used by other very highly qualified scientists not in the Nobel category because of the three-out-of-eleven-criteria rule.

First Preference Category Two: Outstanding Professor or Researcher

The second type of priority workers in the Employment Based First Preference category are "Outstanding Professors or Researchers." This requires that the scientist be "internationally recognized as outstanding" in a specific area in which the scientist has at least three years of experience and that the scientist be immigrating to a tenured or tenure-track or comparable teaching or research position at an institution of higher education or an "accomplished" private company with at least three full-time research employees. To be "recognized internationally as outstanding," at least two of the following six criteria must be met:

1. Receipt of major prizes or awards

2. Membership in associations requiring outstanding achievements

3. Material published in professional journals about the alien's work

4. Evidence that the alien judges the work of others

5. Original scientific or scholarly research

6. Authorship of scholarly books or articles in internationally circulated journals

These criteria place immigration within the reach of an experienced, competent, successful science professor who has published original research.

The immigration laws have a history of being supportive of college and university instructors. For example, concerning labor certifications, which under prior law almost all employment-based immigrants required, the prospective employer had to establish, to the Department of Labor's satisfaction, minimum requirements for the position before advertising it. If any available United States worker met the minimum requirements, the certification would be denied, notwithstanding the fact that the alien was more qualified. This strict rule was inapplicable to college and university instructors; committees of the college or university were able to select the most qualified individuals, and the government did not review the committee's decision.

First Preference Category Three: Multinational Manager and Executive

The third type of priority workers in Employment Based First Preference, "Multinational Managers and Executives," could apply to a manager or executive who for at least the immediately preceding three years has directed a scientific or technical area (for example, research and development or computer information management) of a corporation. This category is not geared primarily toward scientist immigration. However, as science has progressed from individual efforts to large teams with specialized subsections requiring significant management intervention and as research has progressed from primarily academic to the private sector, the role of the scientist-manager is apt to grow.

Most aliens seeking employment-based immigration require a specific job offer and certification from the Department of Labor that their immigration will not adversely affect conditions for United States workers. One benefit of first-preference immigration is that neither a job offer nor labor certification is required. However, the alien must intend to continue work in the field, and the alien's immigration must "substantially benefit" the United States.

SECOND PREFERENCE SCIENTIST

Section 203(b)(2) of the Immigration and Nationality Act allocates 28.6 percent of employment-based visas to two categories of second-preference immigrants: aliens of exceptional ability in the sciences, arts, or business who will substantially benefit the economy or cultural or educational interests, and aliens who are members of the professions holding advanced degrees.

Second Preference Category One: Exceptional Ability

In the legislative scheme, second-preference "exceptional" is less demanding than "extraordinary" as used in first preference. To qualify as an immigrant of "exceptional ability" in the sciences, arts, or business, an alien must meet at least three of the following seven criteria, all of which have applicability to scientists:

1. An academic record showing virtually any degree, diploma, or certificate in the field

2. A license to practice in the field

3. Ten or more years' documented experience

4. High salary

5. Professional association membership

6. Recognition for achievement by organizations, peers, or government

7. Any other evidence

These requirements are not onerous for a competent scientist who has a master's degree (1), professional association membership (5), and one other criterion. Professional association membership is easy to meet; unlike for first preference, which requires membership in a selective organization, any professional organization membership suffices.

Except in the unusual event that the "national interest" is affected, a second-preference "exceptional ability" alien also requires either a labor certification or a specific exemption. The Department of Labor maintains a schedule of aliens exempted from the individual certification process based on either a known insufficient supply of the type of employee needed or on the alien's exceptional ability. However, Labor's definition of "exceptional" is more stringent than that in the Immigration and Nationality Act.

To qualify as an employment-based, second-preference member of the professions holding advanced degrees, a scientist requires any degree beyond the baccalaureate (or a baccalaureate plus five years' experience) in an occupation where entry requires at least a baccalaureate. A master's degree clearly qualifies, as do some foreign higher-education degrees that are evaluated as less than a master's but beyond the baccalaureate.

THIRD PREFERENCE SCIENTIST

Section 203(b)(3) of the Immigration and Nationality Act allocates 28.6 percent of employment-based visas to other workers, which include "professionals" who have and whose job offer requires at least a baccalaureate degree and who have a labor certification (or a scheduled exemption). Compared with first and second preference, it is much easier for a scientist to meet the requirements for third-preference immigration, but there is often a prohibitively long wait to immigrate in this category.

THE STATISTICS

The National Science Foundation (NSF), Division of Science Resources Studies, Human Resources Statis-

tics Program maintains a comprehensive system of information about the demographic characteristics of scientists and engineers in the United States, including citizenship and birthplace. The database is called SESTAT (Scientists and Engineers Statistical Data System) and can be accessed at http://www.sestat.nsf.gov. However, the NSF data collection procedures focus on United States–trained scientists, thus excluding foreign-trained immigrants. Only data based on the census, conducted once a decade, provide the NSF with information on immigrant scientists trained in other countries. Therefore, the NSF has "an undercount in (the) database of people who were trained abroad and entered the U.S. after 1990."

Despite the undercount of immigrant scientists, immigrants are significantly overrepresented in the population of U.S. scientists. According to the National Science Foundation, while only 10 percent of employed persons in the United States are foreign-born, 17 percent of scientists and 17 percent of engineers in the United States are foreign-born. Non-native-born engineers have attained higher levels of education than native-born engineers: 12 percent of the former versus 4 percent of the latter have a doctorate. Reflecting these higher levels of academic credentials, non-native-born engineers comprise about one-third of the engineers working in the academic sector, which is twice the level of their representation overall. Further reflecting this trend, immigrants make up 23 percent of residents with doctorate degrees in science and engineering. As about two-thirds of scientists educated in the United States are here only temporarily as nonimmigrants—for example, F-category students—the percentage of foreign-born who receive doctorate degrees from U.S. institutions is even higher. Fully 40 percent of science and engineering doctorates awarded by U.S. institutions are awarded to foreign-born. Considering only the natural sciences, more than half (51 percent) of doctorates are awarded to foreign-born. Asians received over 70 percent of these doctorates, and, in order of frequency, the countries most represented are the People's Republic of China (PRC), Taiwan, India, and Korea. In 1995, of the 26,515 science and engineering doctorates awarded in the United States, 10,493 were awarded to noncitizens, of whom 7,660 were from Asia and 1,253 from Europe. Of the Asians, 2,751 were from the PRC; 1,239 from Taiwan; 1,204 from India; and 1,004 from Korea. A significant proportion of nonimmigrant scientists educated in the United States do in fact stay in the United States. An Oak Ridge study concluded that 42 percent of scientists who received degrees as nonimmigrants were working in the United States eight years after graduation.

The alien overrepresentation in academia and at the doctorate degree level can be explained as a natural consequence of the immigration laws. Once in the United States as a nonimmigrant F student, the safest way to assure continued legal status is to continue as a student. Further, under the immigration laws, universities were given discretion to select the best candidate for a faculty position, as opposed to other employers who could sponsor an alien applicant only if no citizen who meets the minimum requirements is available.

As for aliens who obtained permanent residence based on employment, during the 1980s, the immigration of scientists and engineers was relatively stable, about twelve thousand annually. However, the Immigration Act of 1990 increased the available number of visas, so that in the early 1990s scientist immigration rose markedly, almost doubling to 23,534 in 1993. Immigration patterns have changed over time. Most recently, the majority of scientists immigrating to the United States came from the Far East, followed by Eastern and Western Europe. The region contributing the fewest was Africa. While certainly there have been some U.S. scientists who emigrated, there has been a net gain for the United States and a "brain drain" in other countries.

IMPACT ON HOME COUNTRY— THE BRAIN DRAIN

The term "brain drain" refers to the movement of persons with scientific or technological knowledge, skills, or experience from one country to another. The United States has experienced a net gain of scientists for many reasons. More economic and scientific opportunity exists in the United States; taxes are sometimes lower; younger people are given more responsibility; and scientists in the Third World often feel professionally isolated.

The Russian press reported in June 1996 that following the collapse of the Soviet Union, Russia had lost 75 percent of its mathematicians and 40 percent of its scientists and researchers. Russia's technology minister stated in January 1998 the country's elite universities, such as Moscow State University, have lost 20 percent of the scientific staff to emigration. The United States gained 22 percent of these scientists, the remainder dispersed to Europe 26 percent; Canada and Australia, 9 percent; South Africa, 5 percent; Israel, 2 percent; and 27 percent from the rest of the world. Very low wages, lack of research funds, and lack of control over the content of research motivate Russian scientists to emigrate. In 1993, only 61 of over 3,550 Russian academic and research institutions were assured of government funding. This massive migration from a nuclear power causes concern about weapons proliferation. To stem the flow, in 1992 the United States, the European Union, and Japan set up the International Scientific Research Center in Moscow to give Russian scientists and researchers the chance to continue to work at home. By some estimates, the research at the center is being performed for 1 percent of what the same research would cost in the United States, Europe, or Japan.

Canadian scientists, especially in the lucrative information technology field, often immigrate south for higher pay and lower taxes. In the mid-1990s, about 15 percent of Canadian scientists and physicians immigrated to the United States, including such irreplaceable talent as Canada's only pediatric liver transplant specialist. At McGill University's electrical engineering department, 25 percent of faculty immigrated to the United States. Estimates are that half the graduates in highly specialized technical fields migrate, usually to the United States, for their first jobs. According to a Canadian official, "Talent is mobile . . . and it will go where the market is."

In addition to low pay and insufficient research support, scientists from Third-World countries often face professional isolation. When Abdus Salam, a physics Nobel laureate, returned to his native Pakistan, he found it difficult to stay because of a lack of professional peers. China loses one-third of its scarce physics graduates to emigration. Thailand and other countries have established organizations attempting to decrease the brain drain flow.

While the United States benefits from the brain drain, other countries suffer and call the effect "brain theft." Critics, according to journalist Andrew Purvis, hypothesize that there are three reasons for the United States's "inability to supply its own brains": a poor elementary and secondary school education system that "compares unfavorably even to many underdeveloped countries"; the "corrupting" effect of U.S. society in which children are "inculcated in passivity," watching excessive television and "adults are encouraged to squander their time in material acquisition and self-indulgence"; and the "dysgenic effect of professional families having few children." These critics conclude that the United States fails to produce the skilled workers needed for the next generation and "steals brains." While there may be an element of truth to this analysis, it is certainly incomplete, because it fails to address the blatant lack of opportunity elsewhere and ignores the rapid technological and economic progress of the United States, which can be measured in weeks or months, not "generations."

The National Science Foundation uses the term "brain circulation" in an attempt to ameliorate the consequences of the "brain drain." For scientists, a cycle of study and work abroad may be followed by a return to the home country to take advantage of high-level opportunities there. Statistics show the "brain circulation" pattern to be more likely for some countries (Taiwan and South Korea) and the "brain drain" more likely for others (China and India). In total, roughly half of all foreign science and engineering doctoral recipients leave the United States immediately after completing their graduate education, and others leave after some years of teaching or industrial experience in the United States. Many of those who remain in the United States network productively with scientists in their home country and, like other immigrant workers, help support their extended family abroad.

THE PEOPLE

AMERICAN IMMIGRANT NOBEL PRIZE LAUREATES

It would be very difficult to overestimate the contributions that immigrants to the United States have made to science. The universally recognized preeminent award in science is the Nobel Prize. In 1999, immigrants to the United States received prizes in each science for which a Nobel Prize is awarded: physics, chemistry, and physiology and medicine. Since the inception of the Nobel Prize, Americans, including immigrants, have been awarded more Nobel Prizes than those from any other country. Considering all Nobel Prizes awarded to Americans (the three science awards and literature, economics, and peace), approximately a third were awarded to American immigrants. Remarkably, only two countries, England and Germany, received more Nobel awards than American immigrants alone. Since 1975, roughly 40 percent of the science awards have been to U.S. immigrants.

Presented in this entry is a partial summary of the Nobel Prizes awarded in the sciences to immigrants. Listed are the year of the award; the recipient's name; the recipient's year and place of birth; the American or international institution with which the recipient was or is affiliated; and a brief synopsis of the nature of the award-winning work. The given country of birth is based on sovereignty at the time of the scientist's birth, notwithstanding subsequent geopolitical changes. Many Nobel laureates are associated with

multiple institutions, but just one domestic institution is presented for each scientist. The names on the list represent an overwhelming contribution to science and humanity.

These Nobel laureates include a diversity of immigration, career, and life patterns. Some, including Polycarp Kusch, Sidney Altman, Charles Pederson, William Shockley, Arno Penzias, Roald Hoffmann, and Isidor Rabi, immigrated early in life and were raised and educated in the United States. Some, including Tsung-dao Lee, Chen Ning Yang, Yuan T. Lee, Ivar Giaever, Susumu Tonegawa, Nicolaas Bloembergen, and Ahmed Zeweil, began their higher education abroad and migrated to the United States to complete their education, usually obtaining a doctorate from a U.S. institution. Many, including Henry Taube, George Palade, David Hubel, Torsten Wiesel, Alan Cormack, Renato Debecco, Roger Guillemin, and Maria Goeppert-Mayer, completed their education abroad and did most or all their work in the United States. Some, including Rudolf Mossbauer, Wolfgang Pauli, Paul Dirac, and, possibly, even Albert Einstein, did most of their work before immigrating, and others, including Enrico Fermi, Albert Szent Gyorgyi, Karl Landsteiner, Martinus Veltman, Peter Doherty, Carl Cori, and Rolf Zinkernagel, worked in both the Europe and America. The majority, including Walter Kohn, Andrew Schally, and Subramanyan Chandrasekhar, did their most notable work in the United States.

Motivating factors for immigration differed markedly. Some came as children with their parents, for example, Isidor Rabi, whose parents migrated for economic opportunity and opened a small grocery after working in a garment factory in New York City. Many fled anti-Semitism in Europe in general and from Nazi Germany in particular (Konrad Bloch, Jack Steinberger, Arno Penzias, Albert Szent-Györgyi). Adolf Butenandt was forced by the Nazi government to decline the 1939 Chemistry Prize and received it only after the war. Similarly, some fled from fascist Italy (Enrico Fermi, Salvador Luria), and some sought to avoid the upheaval in Europe caused by war (Nicolaas Bloembergen). Penzias and Steinberger came to the United States quite poor. Maria Goeppert-Mayer, the first female American physics laureate, immigrated in 1930 because of her marriage to a United States citizen. Hans Dehmelt's first interaction with America was as a member of the German army during World War II and later as a prisoner of war in an American camp in France. Charles Pederson fit perfectly into America's polyglot society in that he was born in Korea to an ethnic Japanese mother and Norwegian father, who was employed by a U.S. company. The majority immigrated because of the sterling reputation of

Table 1
American Immigrant Nobel Laureates

Year	Nobel Laureate	Birth Year/Country	Affiliation	Awarded for:
Physics				
1999	Martinus J. G. Veltman	1931/Netherlands	University of Michigan	gauge theory creating more precise calculations for predicting and confirming the existence and behavior of subatomic particles and elucidating the quantum structure of the electroweak interaction
1990	Richard E. Taylor	1929/Canada	Stanford University	inelastic scattering of electrons on protons and bound neutrons leading to the quark model
1989	Hans G. Dehmelt	1922/Germany	University of Washington, Seattle	development of the ion trap technique
1988	Jack Steinberger	1921/Germany	CERN (international organization)	neutrino beam method and demonstration of the doublet structure of the leptons through the discovery of muon neutrino
1984	Carlo Rubbia	1934/Italy	CERN, Harvard University	discovery of W and Z particles
1983	Subramanyan Chandrasekhar	1910/India	University of Chicago	studies of the structure and evolution of stars
1981	Nicolaas Bloembergen	1920/Netherlands	Harvard University	development of laser spectroscopy
1978	Arno A. Penzias	1933/Germany	Bell Laboratories, NJ	discovery of cosmic microwave background radiation
1973	Leo Esaki	1925/Japan	IBM Watson Research Center, NY	discoveries regarding tunneling phenomena
1973	Ivar Giaever	1929/Norway	General Electric Co., NY	discoveries regarding tunneling phenomena
1967	Hans A. Bethe	1906/Germany	Cornell University	contributions to the theory of nuclear reactions and energy production in stars
1963	Eugene P. Wigner	1902/Hungary	Princeton University	contributions to the theory of atomic nucleus and elementary particles, particularly through the discovery and application of fundamental symmetry principles
1963	Maria Goeppert-Mayer	1906/Germany	University of California, San Diego	discoveries concerning nuclear shell structure
1961	Rudolf L. Mössbauer	1929/Germany	California Institute of Technology	research concerning the resonance absorption of gamma radiation (Mössbauer Effect)
1959	Emilio Gino Segre	1905/Italy	University of California, Berkeley	discovery of the antiproton
1957	Chen Ning Yang	1922/China	Institute for Advanced Study, Princeton, NJ	investigation of parity laws regarding elementary particles
1957	Tsung-Dao Lee	1926/China	Columbia University, NY	investigation of parity laws regarding elementary particles

(continued)

Table 1
American Immigrant Nobel Laureates (continued)

Year	Nobel Laureate	Birth Year/Country	Affiliation	Awarded for:
1956	William Shockley	1910/Great Britain	Beckman Instruments, Inc., Mountain View, CA	research on semiconductors and discovery of the transistor effect
1955	Polykarp Kusch	1911/Germany	Columbia University	precision determination of the magnetic moment of the electron
1952	Felix Bloch	1905/Switzerland	Stanford University	development of new methods for nuclear magnetic precision measurements
1949	Hideki Yukawa	1907/Japan	Columbia University	prediction of the existence of mesons on the basis of nuclear force theory
1945	Wolfgang Pauli	1900/Austria	Princeton University	discovery of the Exclusion Principle, also called the Pauli Principle
1944	Isidor Isaac Rabi	1898/Austria-Hungary	Columbia University	resonance method for recording the magnetic properties of atomic nuclei
1943	Otto Stern	1888/Germany	Carnegie Institute of Technology	contributions to the development of the molecular ray method and discovery of the magnetic moment of the proton
1938	Enrico Fermi	1901/Italy	University of Chicago	demonstrating the existence of new radioactive elements produced by neutron irradiation and discovering nuclear reactions caused by slow neutrons
1933	Paul Dirac	1902/Great Britain	Florida State University	discovery of new productive forms of atomic theory
1921	Albert Einstein	1879/Germany	Institute for Advanced Study, Princeton, NJ	theoretical physics and especially for the discovery of the law of the photoelectric effect

Chemistry

Year	Nobel Laureate	Birth Year/Country	Affiliation	Awarded for:
1999	Ahmed H. Zewail	1946/Egypt	California Institute of Technology	pioneering studies of the transition states of chemical reactions using femtosecond spectroscopy
1998	Walter Kohn	1923/Austria	University of California, Santa Barbara	development of the density-functional theory
1998	John A. Pople	1925/United Kingdom	Northwestern University	development of computational methods in quantum chemistry
1994	George A. Olah	1927/Hungary	University of Southern California	contributions to carbocation chemistry
1992	Rudolph A. Marcus	1923/Canada	California Institute of Technology	contributions to the theory of electron transfer reactions in chemical systems
1989	Sidney Altman	1939/Canada	Yale University	discovery of the catalytic properties of ribonucleic acid (RNA)

Year	Nobel Laureate	Birth Year/Country	Affiliation	Awarded for:
1988	Johann Deisenhofer	1943/Germany	University of Texas	determination of the three-dimensional structure of a photosynthetic reaction center
1987	Charles J. Pedersen	1904/Korea	Du Pont Co., Wilmington, DE	development and use of molecules with structure-specific interactions of high selectivity
1986	Yuan T. Lee	1936/Taiwan	University of California, Berkeley	contributions concerning the dynamics of chemical reactions
1983	Henry Taube	1915/Canada	Stanford University	work on the mechanisms of electron transfer reactions, especially in metal complexes
1981	Roald Hoffmann	1937/Poland	Cornell University	theories concerning the course of chemical reactions
1979	Herbert C. Brown	1912/Great Britain	Purdue University	developing catalysts for difficult chemical reactions
1977	Ilya Prigogine	1917/Russia	University of Texas	contributions to nonequilibrium thermodynamics
1968	Lars Onsager	1903/Norway	Yale University	discovery of reciprocal relations, fundamental for the thermodynamics of irreversible processes

Physiology and Medicine

Year	Nobel Laureate	Birth Year/Country	Affiliation	Awarded for:
1999	Günter Blobel	1936/Germany	Rockefeller University	studies of how proteins find their places in cells
1996	Peter C. Doherty	1940/Australia	St. Jude Children's Research Hospital, Memphis, TN	discoveries concerning the specificity of the cell-mediated immune defense
1996	Rolf M. Zinkernagel	1944/Switzerland	Scripps Institute, La Jolla, CA	discoveries concerning the specificity of the cell-mediated immune defense
1993	Richard J. Roberts	1943/England	New England Biolabs, Beverly, MA	discovery of split genes
1992	Edmond H. Fischer	1920/China	University of Washington	discoveries concerning reversible protein phosphorylation as a biological regulatory mechanism
1987	Susumu Tonegawa	1939/Japan	Massachusetts Institute of Technology	discovery of the genetic principle for generation of antibody diversity
1986	Rita Levi-Montalcini	1909/Italy	Institute of Cell Biology, Rome, Italy	discovery of growth factors
1981	David H. Hubel	1926/Canada	Harvard Medical School	discoveries concerning information processing in the visual system
1981	Torsten N. Wiesel	1924/Sweden	Harvard Medical School	discoveries concerning information processing in the visual system

(continued)

Table 1
American Immigrant Nobel Laureates (continued)

Year	Nobel Laureate	Birth Year/Country	Affiliation	Awarded for:
1980	Baruj Benacerraf	1920/Venezuela	Harvard Medical School	discoveries concerning genetically determined structures on the cell surfaces that regulate immunological reactions
1979	Allan M. Cormack	1924/South Africa	Tufts University, Medford, MA	the development of computer-assisted tomography (CAT)
1977	Roger Guillemin	1924/France	The Salk Institute, San Diego, CA	discoveries concerning the peptide hormone production of the brain
1977	Andrew V. Schally	1926/Poland	Veterans Administration Hospital, New Orleans	discoveries concerning the peptide hormone production of the brain
1975	Renato Dulbecco	1914/Italy	residence USA	discoveries concerning the interaction between tumor viruses and the genetic material of the cell
1974	Christian de Duve	1917/Belgium	Rockefeller Institute, NY	discoveries concerning the structural and functional organization of the cell
1974	George E. Palade	1912/Romania	Yale University School of Medicine, CT	discoveries concerning the structural and functional organization of the cell
1969	Max Delbrück	1906/Germany	California Institute of Technology	discoveries concerning the replication mechanism and the genetic structure of viruses
1969	Salvador E. Luria	1912/Italy	Massachusetts Institute of Technology	discoveries concerning the replication mechanism and the genetic structure of viruses
1968	Har Gobind Khorana	1922/India	University of Wisconsin	interpretation of the genetic code and its function in protein synthesis
1964	Konrad Bloch	1912/Germany	Harvard University	discoveries concerning the mechanism and regulation of the cholesterol and fatty acid metabolism
1961	Georg von Békésy	1899/Hungary	Harvard University	discoveries of the physical mechanism of stimulation within the cochlea
1959	Severo Ochoa	1905/Spain	New York University College of Medicine	discovery of the mechanisms in the biological synthesis of ribonucleic acid (RNA)
1956	André F. Cournand	1895/France	Columbia University	discoveries concerning heart catherization and pathological changes in the circulatory system
1953	Fritz A. Lipmann	1899/Germany	Harvard Medical School	the discovery of co-enzyme A and its importance for intermediary metabolism
1952	Selman A. Waksman	1888/Russia	Rutgers University, NJ	discovery of streptomycin, the first antibiotic effective against tuberculosis

Year	Nobel Laureate	Birth Year/Country	Affiliation	Awarded for:
1951	Max Theiler	1899/South Africa	Rockefeller Foundation, NY	discoveries concerning yellow fever and how to combat it
1947	Carl F. Cori	1896/Czech Republic	Washington University, St Louis, MO	discovery of the course of the catalytic conversion of glycogen
1947	Gerty T. Cori	1896/Czech Republic	Washington University, St. Louis, MO	discovery of the course of the catalytic conversion of glycogen
1937	Albert Szent-Györgyi von Nagyrapolt	1893/Hungary	Institute of Muscle Research, Woods Hole, MA	discoveries in connection with the biologic combustion processes
1930	Karl Landsteiner	1868/Austria	Rockefeller Institute, NY	discovery of human blood groups

Source: www.nobelprizes.com

American institutions, as well as the availability of resources and opportunity.

These immigrant laureates occasionally became active, famous or infamous, in areas far afield from their expertise. William Shockley upset many by espousing views of differential intelligence, which many perceive as racist. Salvador Luria and Albert Szent-Györgyi became active antiwar protestors during the Vietnam era. Sidney Altman became dean at Yale College.

Albert Einstein

Albert Einstein exerted influence far beyond his incredible accomplishments in theoretical physics and even today is quoted or misquoted on a variety of issues including pacifism, theology, philosophy, and politics. One instance of his influence commenced during the early days of World War II. Albert Einstein was on vacation sailing a small boat in Long Island Sound, when two acquaintances, the physicists Szilard and Wigner, tracked him down and asked him to write a letter to Belgium's queen mother warning her not to let Germany ship uranium ore from the Belgian Congo. The economist Alexander Sachs learned of this letter and imposed on Einstein to write to President Roosevelt and indicate the potential military application of uranium ore. The upshot of this letter was the $2 billion Manhattan Project, which succeeded in making the atomic fission bomb, radically changing the world. Einstein was the most influential scientist of his time and has contributed the most to our understanding of the world since Sir Isaac Newton. The majority of his work, done part-time while a patent clerk in Bern, Switzerland, revolutionized science and humankind's understanding of the world. In later years, Einstein could live virtually anywhere he pleased and was offered the presidency of Israel. Instead, he chose to remain in Princeton, New Jersey, from 1933 until his death in 1955.

OTHER EXTRAORDINARY AMERICAN IMMIGRANT SCIENTISTS

In addition to distinguishing themselves as Nobel laureates, many other immigrant scientists, engineers, inventors, and mathematicians have had undeniably productive careers in the United States. It would be impossible to credit every scientist, but I will some of the more prominent whose work has affected everyone.

Alexander Graham Bell was born in 1847 in Scotland to a family known as leading authorities in elocution and speech. He was educated in England and in 1871 immigrated to the United States, where he taught speech at Boston University, specializing in teaching the deaf. He married one of his former students, whose father was the founder of the National Geographic Society. It was Bell who suggested that geography could be taught best using pictures. In 1875, the first telephone transmitted sound, and the following year, voices. The British scientist Lord William Kelvin called Bell's telephone "the most wonderful thing in America." Bell was naturalized in 1882.

Nikola Tesla was born in 1856 in Croatia to Serbian parents and immigrated to the United States in 1884. The next year, Westinghouse Electric Company bought the patent rights to Tesla's dynamos, transformers, and motors and used Tesla's current system to illuminate the 1893 World's Exposition in Chicago. In 1891, he invented the Tesla coil, used in electronic equipment including radio and television.

Edward Teller was born in 1908 in Budapest, Hungary. Teller immigrated in 1935 and naturalized in 1941. During World War II, he participated in the

Manhattan Project and during the Cold War led the U.S. efforts to make the nuclear fusion bomb, thus earning the title "father of the hydrogen bomb."

Wernher von Braun, born in 1912, was a German rocket pioneer during World War II. He was jailed briefly for initially refusing to help the war effort but later designed the V2 rocket, which gave rise to Mort Sahl's quip, "We aim for the stars, but sometimes we hit London." After the war, von Braun was brought to the United States along with 112 of his coworkers by Operation Paperclip, a scheme to keep top German minds out of Russian hands. Von Braun developed ballistic missiles and the Redstone and Saturn rockets used in early space exploration. He was naturalized in 1955, served as a National Aeronautics and Space Administration (NASA) official, and was awarded the National Medal of Science by President Gerald Ford in 1977.

Andrew Grove was born 1936 in Budapest, Hungary. He immigrated to the United States and graduated from City College of New York in 1960 with a bachelor's degree in chemical engineering and received his Ph.D. from the University of California, Berkeley, in 1963. As much a businessman as a scientist, in 1968 he participated in the founding of Intel Corporation and later became its chief executive officer. He has many patents on semiconductor technology, has authored technical and business books, and was named *Time* magazine's 1997 "Man of the Year."

Immigrants have made incalculable contributions to all fields of science and have affected our everyday lives. Telephone (Bell), radio and television (Tesla), transistors, electronics, computers (Shockley, Andrew Grove), rockets, space exploration (von Braun), nuclear power (Fermi), CAT scans (Alan Cormack), antibiotics (Selman Waksman), cell biology (Christian De Duve, George Palade), heart catheterization (André Cournand), and human blood groupings (Karl Landsteiner) are but a few of the things we take for granted today that came through the efforts of immigrant scientists.

In addition to practical, tangible contributions, immigrant scientists have been instrumental in determining the way modern humans perceives the world. Consider the two main theories of modern physics. Einstein monopolized relativity theory, and Wolfgang Pauli, Paul Dirac, and other immigrant scientists made important contributions to the development of quantum mechanics. The big bang theory was reinforced by Arno Penzias's discovery of universal background radiation. The transition of stars to black hole, brown dwarf, nova, or other state was explained by Subramanyan Chandrasekhar. The quark theory of hadron matter, or matter like protons and neutrons

(but not electrons), developed after scattering experiments led by Richard Taylor. Consider the major tenants of biology: the organization of the cell was elucidated by De Duve and Palade; the replication of viruses by Max Delbruck; and immune reactions by Baruj Benacerraf, Torsten Wiesel, David Hubel, and Peter Doherty. As for chemistry, contributions to femtochemistry or high-speed chemistry were made by Ahmed Zewail; quantum chemistry, by John A. Polpe; and electron transfer, by Henry Taube and Rudolf Marcus. Einstein said, "Only a life lived for others is a life worthwhile." Many immigrant scientists have had worthwhile and influential lives.

The immigration laws follow a logical sequence in facilitating the immigration of scientists to the extent that the scientist can demonstrate qualifications in her or his field. The proverbial door is wide open for scientists at the top of their field and open a crack for neophytes whose skills are in demand.

The technology and theories of our twenty-first-century world have been shaped by scientists who have immigrated to the United States. Statistically, immigrant scientists are overrepresented in academia and at the doctorate level and play a key role in maintaining America's technological society. Yet America's gain of the most qualified scientists in the world may adversely affect the countries losing human resources.

I. Steven Krup, J.D.

See also: Professionals and the Brain Drain (Part II, Sec. 8); Higher Education (Part II, Sec. 9); Report on the Shortage of Technology Workers, 1997 (Part IV, Sec. 2).

BIBLIOGRAPHY

The Plundering of Ukraine (A Preliminary Overview), *InfoUkes Posting*, October 17, 1997, http://www.ukar.org/97100351.shtml.

Purvis, Andrew. "Brain Drain from Canada to the U.S." *Time* (Canadian Edition), May 11, 1998, http://www.ukar.org/purvis01.shtml.

Title 8, *U.S. Code*.

Title 8, *Code of Federal Regulations*.

WEB SITES

Canadian Medical Association	www.mcma.ca
Encyclopaedia Britannica	www.Britannica.com
National Science and Technology Development Agency, Thailand	www.rbd.nstda.org.th
National Science Foundation	www.nsf.gov
Nobel Prize Internet Archive	www.nobelprizes.com

SPORTS

The rise of popular, organized sports in the United States began in the middle of the nineteenth century. It coincided with the rise of industrialization, urbanization, and immigration, when many Americans left the farm for the city and desperate Europeans sailed into America's seaports in search of new opportunities. In their new, crowded, concrete environments, these urban dwellers began playing sports in an attempt to reclaim a part of their rustic pasts. Immigrants especially looked for a respite from their low-wage, unskilled jobs. Historians link the rise of sports to the rise of cities, but Americans didn't play sports just in the cities. In small towns and frontier areas, people found that organized sports provided a sense of community and security in a world that was rapidly changing.

BASEBALL

By the middle of the nineteenth century, native-born Americans as well as immigrants were increasingly playing sports, especially baseball. Legend has it that the first game took place in Cooperstown, New York, in 1839, though this is disputed by some historians of the game. Nonetheless, within a few years the best players were being paid to play in professional leagues. The game was played nearly everywhere by almost everyone. From New York City to Chicago and all the way to California, by the time of the Civil War it was clear to many that baseball was evolving into America's pastime. The first professional ballplayers were working-class Anglo-Americans, but by the end of the century, the number of foreign, especially Irish and German, players increased; it was a sign of things to come.

Baseball is a cultural institution that stands as a symbol of American diversity. Consequently, it is in baseball that immigrants have had the greatest impact on American sports. At the beginning of the twentieth century, the success of ethnic stars coincided with coverage of the games in the popular press. Game reports traveled along telegraph wires while players and fans rode the railroads to get to the games. The game served as a metaphor for the nation's emerging modernization. When immigrants came to America, they followed the success of fellow landsmen in either American papers or papers printed in their native languages. Irish, Germans, Italians, and other immigrants were conspicuous in the early baseball crowds, where they felt welcome. For many, the game provided the first positive cultural experience in America. Baseball was an American game, played by myriad groups of people. For immigrants, the game symbolized the potential for them to fit, or even melt, into society. The decision to follow American baseball was for many a first step toward assimilation.

For the immigrant athlete, baseball not only provided a vehicle toward assimilation it also became a means of achieving economic success. Yet these men struggled with their identities and at times found it difficult to appease all of their fans. While most fans took great pride in the accomplishments of ballplayers of similar nationality and faith, a minority of fans castigated these athletes for sacrificing their ethnicity in an effort to achieve success. The careers of Joe DiMaggio and Hank Greenberg provide examples. Born in 1914 to Italian immigrants, DiMaggio became one of the greatest baseball players of all time as well as a cultural icon. Known as the Yankee Clipper, he played in ten World Series and won the American League Most Valuable Player award in 1939, 1941, and 1947. His most impressive accomplishment, however, was hitting safely in fifty-six consecutive games in 1941, a record that still stands today. Greenberg was born on New York's Lower East Side in 1911 to Romanian-Jewish immigrants. He quickly took to baseball and signed a professional contract with the Detroit Tigers when he was nineteen years old.

Greenberg led the Tigers to the pennant in 1934 and four years later, fell short of breaking Babe Ruth's sixty home-run record by two. His refusal to play ball on a religious holiday, Yom Kippur, made him an even greater star among his Jewish fans. While the media and fans stressed DiMaggio's nationality and Greenberg's religion, the athletes themselves downplayed them. When they put their baseball careers on hold to serve in the United States Army during World War II, they further emphasized their implicit desire to be seen as Americans rather than something else. When they returned to the major leagues following military service, sports reporters placed noticeably less emphasis on their backgrounds. The war changed many people's minds about race and ethnicity. DiMaggio and Greenberg started their careers as a great Italian and a great Jewish player respectively, but they retired as two of the greatest American players of all time.

After Jackie Robinson broke professional baseball's color line in 1947, African-American athletes began filtering into the major leagues. Light-skinned Hispanics had played professionally in America before, but now dark-skinned Hispanics started to join the ranks of the major leagues. Some immigrated to the United States hoping to secure a professional contract; others were recruited. Arguably the greatest such athlete in American sports history was Roberto Clemente, who was born near San Juan, Puerto Rico, in 1934. This precocious athlete grew up surrounded by poverty, and he never forgot it. Playing with the Pittsburgh Pirates from 1955 to 1972, Clemente led the team to two world championships, while winning four National League batting titles. Nonetheless, his greatest contributions may have come off the field, where he spent his time helping others. In 1972, when he was traveling to assist Nicaraguan earthquake victims, Clemente's small plane crashed, killing the baseball star. The following year, he became the first Hispanic athlete inducted into Major League Baseball's Hall of Fame. Today, an award in his name is presented annually to the player that best displays the human compassion and charity that this immigrant athlete demonstrated throughout his life.

Immigrant athletes continue to play a large role in professional baseball. In 1990, for example, 13 percent of Major League players were Hispanic, and by 1997, the number had risen to 24 percent. No team symbolizes professional baseball's diversity more than the New York Yankees. Playing in the city where so many immigrants arrived after the long journey to America, the Yankees have been one of professional sports' greatest franchises, and they owe much of their success to immigrant ballplayers. Since the first World

Series took place in 1903, the team has won twenty-four. In 1998 and 1999, the Yankees again won the World Series, led by a number of immigrants from around the world, including Orlando Hernandez from Cuba, Hidecki Irabu from Japan, Mariano Rivera from Panama, and Bernie Williams from Puerto Rico.

BOXING

Baseball was America's first great spectator sport, but by the end of the nineteenth century, tens of thousands of Americans also watched boxing matches. To working-class white men and immigrants in the nation's urban areas, this violent, bloody, and, at times illegal sport had a lot more to offer than did baseball's orderliness. A cult of masculinity attracted these men, who rejected the effete Victorian values of the era in favor of those put forward in this manly art. Part of the reason for boxing's early popularity among immigrant groups, especially Irish Americans, was the phenomenal success of immigrant athletes, men like Yankee Sullivan and John Morrissey.

Sullivan, the Irish immigrant with the American nickname, is recognized as America's first boxing champion. He gained notoriety not only for the strength and endurance that he displayed in the ring but also for his illicit activities outside it. Morrissey's reputation was likewise unfavorable. He came to America from Ireland at an early age and immediately began working countless dead-end jobs. Along the way he developed an intense passion to succeed as well as a name for himself as a ruffian. Eventually, he turned to bare-knuckle boxing for income. After gaining fame and only a modest fortune during his short-lived professional career, Morrissey entered politics. Capitalizing on his popularity among New York's substantial Irish population, he served two terms in the New York State senate and two in the U.S. House of Representatives. Morrissey's rise from Tipperary, Ireland, to Troy, New York, and on to Washington, D.C., made him an Irish-American legend. An American sport had served as a vehicle toward his economic and professional success. For immigrants especially, the example was not lost.

In spite of the success of these fighters, the most popular nineteenth-century American athlete was unquestionably John L. Sullivan, the son of Irish immigrants, who on February 2, 1882, beat Paddy Ryan, another Irish American, becoming the first official American world champion. His fans knew him affectionately as John L., and Americans from all walks of life followed his exploits, anointing him America's first cultural hero. But in northern cities, Irish Americans were routinely discriminated against. They were offered the worst jobs at the lowest pay and were in many respects a despised race. They looked to John L. for proof that they could succeed in a foreign land, and he did not disappoint them. He was living proof that, if given the opportunity, Irish Americans would make it in America.

When Sullivan fought, boxing was open to Native Americans, English, Germans, Irish, and Italians. The sport appealed to first- and second-generation Americans because ethnicity was of little importance to succeed in it. Fighters' ethnicity, religion, and nationality were routinely remarked upon, but they were not obstacles to participation. Most boxers, however, regardless of their background, refused to fight African Americans. Sullivan, for example, claimed to take on all comers, yet he refused to fight Peter Jackson, a black heavyweight champion. Ironically, like Sullivan's parents, Jackson's were also immigrants. The refusal of immigrants' sons to fight African Americans demonstrated the rapidity with which immigrant athletes could be assimilated into American culture and adopt contemporary racist practices.

Boxing remains an outlet for youths trapped in the midst of the harsh realities of urban life. Today, the ranks of amateur and professional boxing are filled with African Americans from poor urban areas and Hispanic athletes from the American Southwest as well as Mexico, Latin and Central America, and the Caribbean. Immigrant fighters continue to display intense national pride, just as have others before them. During the first decades of the twentieth century, boxing was largely an ethnic sport dominated by Irish and Jewish athletes from American cities. Many were second- and third-generation Americans who learned to use their fists defending their names and nationalities on America's streets. Between 1900 and 1910, eight of the twenty-six world champions were Irish. In the next three decades, Jewish boxers won twenty-six world titles. The most well-known Jewish boxers were Benjamin Leiner and Barney Ross. The son of orthodox, immigrant Jewish parents, Leiner changed his name to Benny Leonard to keep his career hidden from them. Known as the Ghetto Wizard, Leonard was the world lightweight champion from 1917 to 1923 and finished his career with a record of eighty-five wins, five losses, and one draw. Barnet David Rasofsky was also the son of orthodox Jewish immigrants. His family moved from New York to Chicago when he was two years old, and when he was fourteen, he came home from school one day to see his father dead, the victim of a robbery. The death hit the son hard, and he vented his anger by participating in the amateur sport of boxing. Assuming the name Barney Ross to hide his identity from his mother, who detested sports, Ross won amateur boxing's highest prize, the Golden Gloves championship, in 1929. Later that year, he began fighting professionally and won his first title in 1933. He eventually held the lightweight, junior welterweight, and welterweight titles. Ross finished his career with seventy-four wins, four losses, three draws, and one no-decision.

Proud of their heritage, Leonard, Ross, and other prominent Jewish boxers of their time wore the six-pointed Star of David on their shorts and robes. The careers of both of these fighters illustrate the precarious position that sports held among immigrants. Europeans emigrated to the United States to better provide for their families through hard work and determination, and they expected nothing less from their children. Many of their children, however, became enthralled with popular American culture. They attended public schools and played sports with diverse groups of children. They at times shunned the church and the synagogue for the ball field. Their parents struggled for control. Sports became a symbol of the industrialization, urbanization, and massive demographic changes that threatened immigrants' families and communities. They were an American invention, and immigrants did not readily accept their children's infatuation with them.

As Jewish Americans began moving out of urban areas, the Irish- and Italian-American presence in boxing became more pronounced. Fighting three decades after the great John L., Jack Dempsey became Irish Americans' next athletic superstar. The descendant of Irish immigrants, Dempsey, whose real name was William Henry, left home at sixteen and began fighting at mining camps and in saloons in the American West, winning the heavyweight title in 1919. Irish Americans weren't his only fans, however. Like that of other exceptional athletes, Dempsey's popularity overcame ethnic boundaries. In 1921, a crowd of 80,000 paid nearly $2 million to see him fight in Jersey City. Six years later, 104,000 fans watched him at Soldier Field in Chicago. Many experts consider Rocco Francis Marchegiano, better known as Rocky Marciano, the greatest American boxer of all time. His father emigrated from Italy to America during World War I, and at a young age Marciano displayed athletic promise. He won the heavyweight championship in 1952 and held the title until his retirement four years later. To this day, he remains the only undefeated heavyweight champion in the sport's history.

BASKETBALL

Because many immigrants worked long hours outside of the home, social reformers organized clubs like the Young Men's Christian Association (YMCA) to provide safe havens for the immigrants' unsupervised children. The groups used organized sports as an enticement. One YMCA instructor, a Canadian immigrant named James Naismith, invented the game of basketball in 1891. It was a sport ideally suited for America's cities, since all that was needed to play was a hard-surface court, a ball, and a basket. Spacious outdoor fields were unnecessary. Not surprisingly, then, urban athletes—Jews, Irish, and Italians—became the first great basketball players. During the 1920s and 1930s, amateur basketball games between ethnic groups attracted large crowds. In some cities, crowds of more than ten thousand attended these in-

In the 1990s Nigerian immigrant Hakeem Olajuwon led the Houston Rockets to two National Basketball Association championships. *(NBA Photos)*

terethnic contests. Soon professional contests became just as popular. By 1920, the Celtics, a team of Irish and Jewish players from Manhattan, became the most successful professional team. Other teams were similarly organized along ethnic or racial lines—including the South Philadelphia Hebrew All-Stars, the Irish Brooklyn Visitations, the Polish Detroit Pulaskis, and the all-black Harlem Renaissance Five. It is estimated that prior to 1940, 75 percent of the most prominent professional basketball players were German, Irish, or Jewish, many of whom were second- or third-generation Americans.

The best basketball players have typically come from the ethnic and racial groups that have held the lowest position in the urban, economic, and social hierarchy. Thus, when Jewish, Irish, Italian, and other European ethnic groups moved out of the cities in the latter half of the twentieth century, African Americans began to dominate the sport. Today, approximately 80 percent of the National Basketball Association's (NBA) players are African-American. Nevertheless, some of the league's most talented players remain immigrants. Hakeem Olajuwon, who was born in Lagos, Nigeria, in 1963, led the Houston Rockets to the NBA title in 1994 and 1995. Patrick Ewing was born in Jamaica and emigrated to the United States with his family when he was thirteen years old. In 1984, he led the Georgetown Hoyas to the NCAA championship and has since twice led the New York Knicks to the NBA finals. Tony Kukoc, a native of Split, Croatia, and three-time European Player of the Year, came to the United States in 1993 and helped the Chicago Bulls win the NBA championship in 1996, 1997, and 1998.

FOOTBALL

Originally, football was a sport reserved for Anglo-Saxon athletes at prestigious colleges such as Harvard and Princeton. But in the twentieth century, immigrants increasingly made their way onto collegiate and, eventually, professional rosters and overall had a profound impact on the game. Born in Norway in 1888, Knute Rockne came with his family to the United States in 1893. Although a Protestant, he attended the Catholic university of Notre Dame, where he excelled as a football player. In 1918, he accepted the position of head football coach and athletic director at the school. During his tenure, his teams won 105 games, lost 12, and had 5 ties. They went undefeated in five seasons. Known as the Fighting Irish, his teams attracted a national following. To Irish and Catholic Americans everywhere, Rockne's Fighting

Irish were sacrosanct. In 1940, Hollywood immortalized the coach in a film entitled, *Knute Rockne—All American*. Vince Lombardi, born to Italian immigrants, did for professional football what Rockne did for the collegiate game. In 1959, Lombardi accepted the head coaching position for professional football's unsuccessful Green Bay Packers and immediately reversed the team's fortunes. He led the Packers to 105 wins, against only 35 losses and 6 ties. The team won nine of ten playoff games and five National Football League championships, including the first two Super Bowls. Rockne and Lombardi were passionate, hard working, driven men who demonstrated that through athletics, the American dream could become a reality. To immigrants everywhere they were an inspiration.

Heading into the twenty-first century, the proliferation of immigrants in American sports continues, and not only do immigrant athletes participate—they excel. In basketball, Tim Duncan, a native of St. Croix, won the NBA's Rookie of the Year award in 1998 and a year later led the San Antonio Spurs to their first world championship. That same year major league baseball's National and American Leagues' Most Valuable Player awards were both awarded to immigrants—Sammy Sosa and Juan Gonzales, respectively. In 1999, Chicago Cubs slugger Sosa, a native of the Dominican Republic, became the first player in league history to hit more than sixty home runs in a season more than once. Ironically, he wears number 21 on his jersey in memory of his childhood idol, Roberto Clemente.

The success of immigrants in American sports is not limited to the few mass-media sports mentioned above or just to men, which is not surprising because athletics were the entree to America for many immigrants. America professes to welcome the tired, poor, and the huddled masses. It claims to be a place where dreams can come true. A look at American sports indicates that the nation is still, in many respects, living up to these ideals.

Matt Clavin

See also: Film, Radio, and Television, Foreign and Immigrant Influence on American Popular Culture (Part II, Sec. 10).

BIBLIOGRAPHY

Bodner, Allen. *When Boxing Was a Jewish Sport*. Westport, CT: Praeger, 1997.

Dulles, Foster Rhea. *A History of Recreation: America Learns to Play*. New York: Meredith Publishing Company, 1965.

Gorn, Elliot J. *The Manly Art: Bare-Knuckle Prize Fighting in America*. Ithaca, NY: Cornell University Press, 1986.

Hickok, Ralph. *A Who's Who of Sports Champions: Their Stories & Records*. New York: Houghton Mifflin Company, 1995.

Isenberg, Michael T. *John L. Sullivan and His America*. Urbana and Chicago: University of Illinois Press, 1988.

Levine, Peter. *Ellis Island to Ebbets Field*. New York: Oxford University Press, 1992.

Michener, James A. *Sports in America*. New York: Random House, 1976.

Mrozek, Donald J. *Sport and American Mentality*. Knoxville: The University of Tennessee Press, 1983.

Riess, Steven A. *The American Sporting Experience: A Historical Anthology of Sport in America*. West Point, NY: Leisure Press, 1984.

———. *City Games: The Evolution of American Urban Society and the Rise of Sports*. Chicago: University of Illinois Press, 1989.

Roberts, James B., and Alexander G. Skutt. *The Boxing Register: International Boxing Hall of Fame Official Record Book*. Ithaca, NY: McBooks Press, 1997.

White, G. Edward. *Creating the National Pastime, Baseball Transforms Itself, 1903–1953*. Princeton, NJ: Princeton University Press, 1996.

RELIGION

INTRODUCTION

In Part II, Section 11 of the *Encyclopedia of American Immigration,* the entries cover the topic of religion. The section is divided into seven entries, corresponding with major faiths. The topics covered include Buddhism, Catholicism, Evangelical Christianity, Hinduism and Sikhism, Islam, and Judaism, as well as alternative faiths.

In her entry on alternative faiths, Cecelia M. Espenoza examines the various nontraditional religions that have been brought to these shores and practiced here by various immigrant groups or, in one case, are practiced by the native peoples of America. Offered in alphabetical order, these include the Amish, the Bahai, Confucianism, indigenous faiths, Jainism, Rastafarianism, Santeria, Taoism, Wicca, Zen Buddhism, and Zoroastrianism.

The entry on Buddhism by Paul David Numrich begins with a discussion of the first Buddhists who came to this country, the Chinese in the midnineteenth century, before continuing the history through the 1920s. The author next goes on to explore the various trends in immigrant Buddhism through the 1960s and then brings the discussion up to the present.

In his entry on Catholicism and immigration, Ted G. Jelen first considers the waves of Catholic immigrants who came to this country from the midnineteenth to the early twentieth centuries, before discussing the communal basis of Catholic ethnicity.

Turning to the political, Jelen examines how Catholicism and anti-Catholicism have affected American elections over the years.

Arlene M. Sánchez-Walsh starts her entry on evangelical Christianity by examining its history in America and American immigration. She then goes on to look at evangelism among contemporary immigrant groups, including the Koreans, Chinese, Filipinos, and various Latino groups. In the essay on Hinduism and Sikhism, Prema Ann Kurien opens with a discussion of Hindu organizations in America and then goes on to consider American Hindu practices and interpretations.

In his entry on Islam, Daniel James examines the basic precepts of the religion and its expansion throughout much of the Eastern Hemisphere in the medieval age, before turning to an overview of the history of Islamic immigration to the United States. The article concludes with a brief description of four major Islamic immigrant groups in the United States: Bangladeshis, Egyptians, Iranians, and Pakistanis.

In her entry on Judaism, Susanna Smulowitz first discusses early Jewish immigration to the United States and then considers the huge waves of Jewish immigration at the turn of the twentieth century. Finally, the author examines the recent history of Jewish immigration, including those who have come from the former Soviet Union.

ALTERNATIVE FAITHS

Religious diversity in the United States has been profoundly affected by immigration. Early U.S. immigrants were mainly Christians who practiced such faiths as Roman Catholicism or Protestantism, and who were seeking religious freedom. In time, believers in Judaism, Buddhism, Islam, and Hinduism also traveled to the United States. However traditional, the United States's religious fabric has never been monolithic, and new immigrant groups have brought a variety of religious practices with them.

Much of the research regarding religious traditions of immigrants is spurred by the interests of scholars in assessing the role that assimilation, acculturation, or continuation of tradition plays in the life of an immigrant. Many religious traditions of immigrants remain small and obscured from mainstream life, but some religious expressions have found the American society fertile ground for growth and expansion. Religion provides many with a strong framework for maintaining self-identification in the United States, and today there are thousands of immigrant religious institutions.

Mayan Indians from Guatemala congregate in places such as Los Angeles, and Rastafarians congregate in Queens, New York. Jains and Sikhs are coming together in the suburbs of Boston. The Baha'is are holding conferences in Chicago, and Zoroastrians are also forming enclaves in the United States. There are even Santeria practitioners honoring the Orishas in South Carolina. Immigrants all over the country are eating, drinking, singing, and reciting prayer in their native languages in their homes, at festivals, and in neighborhood centers. Immigrants in the United States are no longer wed to structures; they do not embrace the notion that religious practice can only be found in temples, mosques, or churches.

Religious and sociological experts believe that immigrants have come to the United States with the intent of building institutions to perpetuate their respective faiths and traditions. Of the numerous faiths that immigrants embrace in the United States, even those that have been long existent were rarely documented. This was either due to their small presence, lack of knowledge about the particular faith, or the absence of any feasible way of conducting research. As the number of new religions has grown, research about them and how immigrants have relied on their faiths for spiritual and social needs to adapt to life in this country has also developed. This research has been difficult because many of the practices involve private rituals that were not meant to be shared. New investigations involve how these faiths and religions have served as avenues to pass on traditional customs and beliefs to new generations. This, in turn, has demonstrated that religion serves as a method of affirmation and survival for immigrants who are displaced from their native countries.

THE AMISH

The first documented Amish colonists, who fled Germany seeking religious freedom, came to America on a ship called the *Adventurer*, which arrived in Philadelphia in 1727. The Amish faith traces its roots to the time of the Reformation and the Anabaptist movement, whose followers were persecuted by Catholics and Protestants. In 1536, a Catholic priest from Holland named Menno Simons joined the Anabaptist movement, and under his leadership the Mennonites split from the Anabaptists. Approximately 150 years later, Jacob Amman led a new denomination, which came to be known as the Amish.

In the United States, the Amish retain elements of their immigrant heritage in that most are trilingual. They speak High German, English, and Pennsylvania Dutch, which is similar to *Plattdeutsch*, a dialect

Alternative faiths, like Haitian voodoo, that combine Christianity with various African and Native American religions flourish in many Latin American and Caribbean immigrant neighborhoods, like this one in New Orleans. *(David Rae Morris/Impact Visuals)*

spoken in parts of northern Germany. There are no Amish in Europe today, as they were all absorbed into other sects. It is estimated that about sixty thousand to ninety thousand members can be found in the United States, most living in Pennsylvania. (These figures do not include Mennonites, who practice a related faith.)

THE BAHA'I FAITH

With its origins in present-day Iran, the Baha'i faith was founded by Mirza Hussein Ali, known by his followers as Bahaullah, in 1863. The immigrant Ibrahim George Kheiralla established the Baha'i faith in the United States in 1894. Initially, he spread his faith through the healing practice he established to earn in-

come. The founders of the Baha'i community in the United States called themselves the First Assembly of Baha'ists in America.

The sacred text written by Bahaullah is known as Kitab-i-Aqbas. The Baha'i faith believes there is only one God, who is unknowable and who is revealed throughout history by a number of divine messengers that include Zoroaster, Moses, Buddha, Jesus, Krishna, and Muhammad. According to the faith, Bahaullah is the latest messenger of the word of God. The role of the messenger is to educate humanity. Some basic Baha'i principles include (a) independent search of truth; (b) oneness of the human race; (c) unity of religion; (d) equality of the sexes; and (e) elimination of prejudice.

Recent statistics show that there are more than one hundred and thirty-three thousand Baha'is living in the United States. In January 2000, the Baha'i official Web page claimed that it is the second most widespread independent religion. Although relatively new to the United States, the Baha'i are established in 235 countries and territories throughout the world and come from over twenty-one hundred ethnic, racial, and tribal groups numbering 5 million followers.

CONFUCIANISM

The Chinese community is one of the largest immigrant communities in the United States, and the primary religion of this immigrant population is found in the teachings of Confucius, or K'ung Chiu (551 B.C.–479 B.C.). His teachings have strongly influenced Chinese culture and are in evidence in many U.S. Chinese communities. According to tradition, Confucius was born in Lu, China, in 551 B.C. He promoted peace and social harmony, and is said to have collected, edited, and written five canonical works, including the *I Ching*. Besides these five canonical works, there are four classical works of dogma. Their doctrines promote righteousness, ancestor worship, devotion to family elders, benevolence toward others, order in the state, and conduct based on the inherent goodness of man.

INDIGENOUS FAITHS

Central and South American immigrants have brought indigenous religious practices to the United States. Although the majority of immigrants who come from these countries are also practicing Christians, many of these groups supplement the traditional Christian faith with religious practices found in the Mayan culture, which comes from the regions of Mesoamerica and such places as Guatemala and Honduras. Mayan religious practice grew primarily out of milpas agriculture, which required accurate predictions of time and accommodation to the cycles of life in the rainforest. At its essence, the religion is based on accommodating humanity to the cycles of the universe. The calendar system has served as the primary source for Mayan cyclical predictions. The Mayans believe that the world has been created five times and destroyed four times. Religious ceremonies involve dancing, competitions, dramatic performances, and prayer.

JAINISM

Due to the increasing number of East Indians immigrating to the United States, Jainism has grown in America in the last twenty-five years. A world religion that began as a reform movement of Hinduism, Jainism has been around since 500 B.C. It was also known as Shraman Dharma or Nirgranth Dharma. It was established by the Tirthankaras (prophets), who were also called Jina. A Tirthankara is one who revitalizes the Jain order. Jainism was reestablished by Lord Mahāvira, who was the twenty-fourth and last Tirthankar. Jains believe that the universe is eternal and imperishable, and the universe was not created or sustained by a supernatural being. They believe that the world operates in accordance with natural law. They promote nonkilling, nonviolence, and noninjury. The law of karma, in the sense of cause and effect, is also an integral part of this faith. Jains reject attachments to material objects, and their goal in life is to attain *kevala* (liberation). There are many Jain centers in the United States.

SANTERIA

Santeria is a religious practice that mixes non-Christian religious traditions with those of Christianity. It is found in places such as Florida, New York, and South Carolina, as a result of immigration from Caribbean countries. It is estimated that the number of practitioners of Santeria in the United States surpasses 5 million. Santeria, also known as La Regla Lucumi and the Rule of Orisha, has roots in West Africa, the transatlantic slave trade, and the Caribbean. Religious historians attribute its creation in the 1700s as a combination of West African Yoruba religion and Iberian Catholicism, developed by African slaves in order to continue their native practice of worship. Slaves in Cuba created this religion to maintain a faith system in the face of official Catholicism. Santeria uses Catholic saints and personages as equivalents for their own god and Orishas (spiritual envoys). For some time the religion was practiced in secret, because the slave masters outlawed the traditions of the African slaves.

SIKHISM

In 1995, there were 139 ashrams, or teaching centers, in the United States, professing Sikhism to more than two hundred and seventy-five thousand Sikhs. Sikhism, a religion based mostly in the Punjab province of India, attempts to unite Hinduism and Islam on the basis of monotheism, and without images of any deities. It is based on the teachings of the founder, Nanak, who lived from 1469 to 1538. Orthodox and unorthodox sects of Sikhs differ slightly in the extent to which each follows beliefs and practices, but both groups believe in one supreme God, which cannot take human form. Their goal of human life is to break the cycle of births and deaths and merge with God. There is great emphasis placed on daily devotion to the remembrance of God. The Sikh holy book is the *Aji Granth*. Community service is an integral part of these groups. The free community kitchen, or *langar*, found at every *gurdwara*, or temple, is open to people of all religions.

TAOISM

Taoism, also known as Daoism, has survived for centuries in Chinese communities. It is recognized as the most mystical belief of the Chinese philosophic school of thought. Tao is believed to be the natural flow of the cosmos; nature follows the Tao. The goal of the Taoist is to harmonize with the Tao and thereby become one with the cosmos and with nature. The Tao is composed of conflicting opposites (Yin and Yang), which should be balanced or harmonized through yoga, or meditation, to promote spiritual wholeness. According to legend, Taoism founder Lao-tse wrote *Tao Te Ching* (*Classic of the Way of Power*) about 550 B.C. His teaching was developed and spread in the third century B.C. by Chuang-tzu, whose writings inspired the *Tao Tsang,* or twelve hundred volumes of Taoist scripture. While both are of Chinese origin, Taoism and Confucianism differ in important ways. Confucianism thought is geared to the state and community, and it attempts to reestablish the pre-550 B.C. civilization and heritage of the Chinese. Taoism, on the other hand, espouses "quietistic individualism" and asceticism, and urges the believer toward meditation, simplicity, and freedom from desire.

WICCA

Wicca is the name of a contemporary neopagan religion, largely promulgated and popularized by the works of such early-twentieth-century writers as Margaret Murray and Gerald B. Gardner. In 1962, two of Gardner's students, Raymond and Rosemary Buckland (religious names: Robat and Lady Rowen), emigrated from England to the United States, where they began teaching Gardnerian witchcraft. At the same time, other groups of people became interested through reading books by Gardner and others. Many covens were spontaneously formed, using rituals created from a combination of research and individual inspiration. These self-created covens are today regarded as just as valid as those that can trace a lineage of teaching back to England.

In 1975, a very diverse group of covens that wanted to secure the legal protections and benefits of church status formed the Covenant of the Goddess (CoG), which is incorporated in California and recognized by the Internal Revenue Service. CoG does not represent all or even a majority of Wiccans. A coven or an individual need not be affiliated with CoG in order to validly practice the religion. But CoG is the largest single public Wiccan organization, and it is cross-traditional (i.e., nondenominational).

In the last few decades, Wicca has spread, in part due to its popularity among feminists and others seeking a more woman-positive, earth-based religion. Like most neopagan spiritualities, Wicca worships the sacred that is immanent in nature, drawing much of its inspiration from the non-Christian and pre-Christian religions of Europe. Neopagan means "new pagan" and is derived from the Latin *paganus,* or country-dweller. Neopaganism hearkens back to times before the spread of today's major monotheistic religions. Many claim that Wicca is the fastest-growing religion in the Western Hemisphere with an estimated fifty thousand Wiccans in the United States.

ZEN BUDDHISM

Buddhism originated in India around 500 B.C. It is founded on the teachings of a prince known alternately as Buddha, Siddhartha, and Bodhisattva. About a thousand years later, in 526 A.D., an Indian Buddhist named Bodhidharma landed in China and established a Chinese school of Buddhism: Chan Buddhism. Chan Buddhism was carried to Japan around 1200 A.D., where it was known as Zen Buddhism.

Zen Buddhists seek *satori* (sudden illumination enabling bliss and harmony), which cannot be explained but only experienced. In general, Zen is different from other beliefs; it is not a religion in the sense in which religion is generally understood. Zen has no god to worship, no ceremonial rites to observe, and no future abode to which the dead are destined. Zen is free of all dogmatic principles; a Zen Buddhist seeks to attain nirvana, or salvation, through correct conduct, breaking away from selfish craving, and meditation.

ZOROASTRIANISM

There are two hundred thousand Zoroastrians worldwide, and temples practicing this faith have sprouted in the United States in the past several years. Zoroastrianism is a religion thought to be founded about 600 B.C. in Persia, present-day Iran. The founder, Zoroaster, sought to reform the polytheistic religion of Persia into monotheism. According to legend, Zoroaster received enlightenment by the Daitya River when, at age thirty, he received a vision of Vohu Manah, or Good Thought, who took him into the presence of Lord Ahura-Mazda. The main belief is in a single God named Ahura Mazda, or Ohrmazd. Ahura Mazda is good, holy, supreme, and the creator of all things. But Zoroastrianism also identifies an active force of evil—a powerful spirit by the name of Angra Mainyu, or Ahriman. Within this system of opposing good and evil forces, humans must choose one side or the other. However, in the end, Ahura Mazda will triumph over evil. Zoroastrianism calls for its followers to incorporate good thoughts, good words, and good deeds. Examples include promoting justice, self-reliance, charity, and civic service.

Cecelia M. Espenoza

See also: Settlement Patterns (Part II, Sec. 3); Agriculture (Part II, Sec. 8); Central America, Mexico

(Part III, Sec. 2); Philippines, Southeast Asia (Part III, Sec. 3); California's Farm Labor Law, 1975 (Part IV, Sec. 1).

BIBLIOGRAPHY

Civilizations in America, www.wsu.edu:8000:8000/~dee/CIVAMRCA/MAYAS.HTM.

Classic Chinese Philosophy, www.geocities.com/Tokyo/Springs/6339/philosophy.html.

Crim, Keith. *The Perennial Dictionary of World Religions.* San Francisco: Harper and Row, 1989.

Ebaugh, Helen Rose, and Janet Saltzman Chafetz. *Religion and the New Immigrants: Continuities and Adaptations in Immigrant Congregations.* Walnut Creek, CA: AltaMira Press, 2000.

Warner, R. Stephen. "Approaching Religious Diversity: Barriers, Byways, and Beginnings." *Sociology of Religion* 59 (September 22, 1998).

BUDDHISM

Buddhism began in India around 500 B.C. as a movement of followers of Siddhartha Gautama, a noble of the Shakya people who claimed to have discovered a transcendent consciousness called Nirvana, or enlightenment, and who thereafter became known by honorific titles such as Shakyamuni (Sage of the Shakyas) and Buddha (Enlightened One). From its Indian homeland, Buddhism spread throughout Asia, eventually dividing into three major branches, each with distinctive practices, beliefs, and cultural expressions: the Theravada Buddhism of south and southeast Asia (the modern countries of Sri Lanka, Myanmar, Thailand, Laos, and Cambodia), the Mahayana Buddhism of east Asia (China, Korea, Japan, Tibet, Nepal, Mongolia, Taiwan, and Vietnam), and the Vajrayana Buddhism of central Asia (mainly Tibet). In the last two centuries, Buddhism has established a presence outside of Asia through population migration and conversions. Today, more than 300 million people practice Buddhism worldwide, perhaps as many as 3 million in the United States (the majority ethnic Asians).

The history of Buddhist immigration to the United States is part of the larger history of Asian immigration. Buddhist immigrants are a double minority in America, differing both racially and religiously from the majority population of the nation. Reception has been a mixture of hostility and fascination, the former riding the ebb and flow of nativism and anti-Asian bias, the latter evident in Buddhism's attractiveness to certain segments of the non-Asian population and its periodic emergence in pop culture. American Buddhist immigration history falls into three periods: (1) early immigration, late 1840s to 1920s; (2) pre– and post–World War II trends, 1930s to early 1960s; and (3) immigration reform, 1965 to the present.

EARLY IMMIGRATION, LATE 1840s TO 1920s

Tens of thousands of Chinese immigrants arrived in Hawaii and California beginning in the late 1840s, "pushed" out of China during the decline of the Manchu Dynasty (1644–1911) and "pulled" by economic opportunities in the United States. The lure of California's gold rush in 1849 was especially powerful initially—the Chinese dubbed California Gam Saan, or Gold Mountain—but soon other occupations opened up, most notably in construction of the transcontinental railway in the 1860s. Chinese immigrants had spread throughout the western states and territories by the 1880s, the peak decade for the Chinese population in this early period (about 100,000). During that decade, however, several anti-Chinese riots erupted, forcing many Chinese to retreat into the Chinatowns of the major cities. In 1882, Congress passed the Chinese Exclusion Act, the first law restricting immigration based on race or nationality passed by the United States. This pattern of hostility and exclusion extended to other Asian groups in subsequent years, culminating in the 1924 Oriental Exclusion Act, which cut off virtually all Asian immigration.

Chinese immigrants brought a type of folk religion that mixed Mahayana Buddhist practices with native Chinese traditions. Their temples featured statues of the Buddha as well as Chinese deities, and many rituals centered around the honoring of deceased ancestors. The first Chinese temple in America was established in San Francisco's Chinatown in 1853; by 1892, as many as fifteen Chinese temples could be found there, and by 1900, hundreds of temples and small shrine facilities had been established in the western states.

Japanese immigration to the United States began

Buddhism is the common faith of many Chinese immigrants, as this temple in New York's Chinatown shows. *(Clark Jones/Impact Visuals)*

during the Meiji modernization period (1868–1912). The primary "pull" came from agricultural opportunities in Hawaii and California, most of the immigrants having been farmers in Japan. By 1920, the Japanese population on the mainland exceeded 100,000. But anti-Japanese bias mirrored anti-Chinese bias, and discriminatory legal actions were taken in the years leading up to passage of the Oriental Exclusion Act, including the 1907–8 Gentlemen's Agreement that restricted the flow of Japanese labor to the United States, the alien land laws in several western states beginning in 1913 that targeted Japanese farmers, and the 1922 Supreme Court decision *Ozawa v. United States*, which denied Japanese immigrants naturalized citizenship rights.

The first Japanese Buddhist organization on the U.S. mainland was called the Young Men's Buddhist Association (YMBA), established in San Francisco in 1899 by two Buddhist priests sent from Japan and leaders within the local immigrant community. In 1914, the YMBA changed its name to the Buddhist Mission of North America (BMNA), a reflection of its institutional connection to the home temple in Kyoto,

which represented one sect within Jodo Shinshu, itself one tradition within the larger Mahayana Buddhism of Japan. By the end of the 1920s, more than thirty temples belonged to the BMNA, most of them located in California. The first temple in San Francisco served as national headquarters; its sacred status was greatly enhanced with the enshrinement of relics from the historical Buddha, a gift from the king of Siam (modern Thailand). The BMNA temples typically featured an altar with a statue of Amida Buddha, a spiritual being (not to be confused with the historical Buddha) who offers aid in reaching a place of bliss called the Pure Land.

Anti-Japanese bias seems to have led the early BMNA director Reverend Koya Uchida, who headed the organization from 1905 to 1923, to encourage temples to adopt the name "church" in the hope that American Christians would be more sympathetic to their situation (the original temple, for instance, was called the Buddhist Church of San Francisco). Many BMNA temples refurbished former Christian churches, and most sought not to stand out from their surroundings at least in part because of potential hostility from neighbors. Even so, Buddhist missionary success among Japanese immigrants seemed fueled by anti-Japanese incidents, especially after the Oriental Exclusion Act.

Whereas the early Chinese immigrants were mostly males, the early Japanese immigrant community included many married couples. Thus by around 1920, BMNA temples faced the special needs of their second (nisei) generation. The first (issei) generation of immigrants instituted programming with the dual purpose of preserving ethnic heritage and facilitating the Americanization process, for instance through local youth groups called the Young Men's and Young Women's Buddhist Associations (YMBA and YWBA).

PRE- AND POST–WORLD WAR II TRENDS, 1930s TO EARLY 1960s

Previous exclusionary legislation brought Asian immigration to a near standstill in the 1930s and early 1940s. During these years, Chinese and Japanese Buddhists continued to adapt their religion to its new American homeland. Especially in the Japanese case, the second generation, American citizens by birth, began to take leadership within the community and in the BMNA temples. Jodo Shinshu practices and terminology underwent a process called "Protestantization," in certain ways becoming more like the dominant religion of the society. Some traditional Japanese cultural festivals came to be overshadowed by American holidays such as the Fourth of July, Thanksgiving, and even Christmas.

The internment of Japanese Americans during World War II under Executive Order 9066 had a profound effect on Japanese-American Buddhists in the United States. More than 55 percent of the internees were Buddhists from a variety of traditions, the largest number from the BMNA, which moved its headquarters from San Francisco to the Topaz Relocation Center in Utah during this period. In 1944, the BMNA changed its name to the Buddhist Churches of America (BCA). The BCA's nisei leadership would accelerate the Americanization process, distancing the BCA from the home temple in Japan and increasing English language usage in temple activities.

As the Japanese-American historian Ronald Takaki points out, World War II marked a watershed in Asian-American history. Anti-Asian bias at home proved increasingly untenable in the light of foreign wars against racial-supremacist regimes in Europe and Asia. Release from the internment camps began

as early as 1943, the same year in which Congress repealed the Chinese Exclusion Act and granted Chinese immigrants naturalized citizenship rights. These rights were extended to Japanese immigrants under the McCarran-Walter Act of 1952, and more than 45,000 issei had taken the citizenship oath by 1965. Asian immigration began a slow rise between World War II and the early 1960s; Buddhist immigrants came from China, Japan, and Korea, many as so-called war brides under the provisions of the 1945 War Brides Act.

IMMIGRATION REFORM, 1965 TO THE PRESENT

Passage of the Hart-Celler Reform Act in 1965 created a powerful "pull" factor for immigrants from traditionally Buddhist countries in Asia. Implemented in 1968, the act reversed previous exclusionary trends—Asians would constitute more than one-third of all legal immigrants in the decades following the 1960s—and gave preference to skilled and educated people. Eight of the top ten Asian groups in the 1990 census came from home countries in which Buddhism is practiced by a majority of the population: Chinese, Japanese, Koreans, Vietnamese, Laotians, Cambodians, Thais, and Hmong (from Southeast Asia). (It should be noted that post-1965 selection trends for some of these groups favored non-Buddhist immigrants, e.g., Christians from Korea.) The large showing of groups from Southeast Asia in this list points to the major "push" factor for the new Buddhist presence in the United States, namely, the social upheaval following the end of the Vietnam War, which brought a wave of refugees in the late 1970s and 1980s.

The post-1965 immigrant/refugee influx tipped the foreign-born percentage of the Asian-American population back to earlier levels (nearly two-thirds according to the 1990 census). The Asian-American Buddhist community today has a varied configuration, comprising fourth- and fifth-generation descendants of Chinese- and Japanese-American pioneers as well as first- and second-generation newcomers. This dichotomy of established descendants versus relative newcomers can be seen even among Chinese Americans, who themselves distinguish between the pre-1965 Lo Wa Kiu (old overseas Chinese) and the post-1965 *San Yi Man* (new immigrants). A socioeconomic dichotomy has also emerged as a result of post-1965 trends, both within groups (e.g., so-called Uptown Chinese professionals versus Downtown Chinese workers) and between groups (relatively successful East Asian immigrants versus less successful Southeast Asian refugees).

Hundreds of immigrant and refugee Buddhist temples now dot the cultural landscape of America, and Buddhist shrines adorn the homes and businesses of uncounted numbers of Asian Americans. Extrapolating from 1990 census data, we can assume that most Asian-American Buddhists live in six states (California, New York, Hawaii, Texas, Illinois, and New Jersey, in that order of numbers), mostly in large metropolitan areas. Their temples range from the magnificent Hsi Lai Temple in suburban Los Angeles, a vast complex built in traditional Chinese architectural style at a cost of more than $30 million, to the more typical remodeled facility, often a former residence, church, or public building, which may exhibit little external evidence of its present temple function. Nationwide, Mahayana organizations may outnumber Theravada by as much as two to one, while few ethnic Vajrayana organizations have been established to date. In the Chicago metropolitan area, for instance, thirty-three ethnic Buddhist organizations existed in 1999, twenty-three of them Mahayana, ten Theravada, and none Vajrayana.

In most cases, such temples serve as centers of a larger ethnic culture beyond the expression of specifically Buddhist practices and beliefs. Like all immigrant religions, immigrant Buddhism continues to face a process of cultural negotiation as Asian traditions undergo transformation in the American context and as "Asians" become "hyphenated" Asian Americans. Ethnic-Asian Buddhist temples provide a crucial venue for this negotiation process through religious and other cultural activities, as well as social services to their ethnic constituencies and educational programming for American-born generations. Post-1965 immigrant Buddhists have begun a process familiar to their pre-1965 predecessors. To date, the vast majority of Buddhist clergy (monks, nuns, priests, and trained religious teachers) staffing the most recent temples are themselves immigrants or hold visa status. It remains to be seen whether second- and later-generation clergy will emerge from within these immigrant communities, as occurred within the Japanese Buddhist community.

Three aspects of the Buddhist immigrant experience in the United States stand out. The first has to do with minority identity. As a "visible" or racial minority in American society, Asian-American Buddhists have suffered prejudice and discrimination for most of their history. Although progress has been made in recent decades, it remains to be seen whether Asians, both immigrants and descendants of immi-

grants, will find full acceptance in a more pluralistically configured America. Religiously, as well, many Asian Americans hold minority status as Buddhists in predominantly Christian America, and any perceptual shift by the majority society again remains an open question. Many Americans perceive Buddhism as a strange, even threatening religion. One telephone poll in the mid-1990s found that a third of its respondents considered Buddhism one of the most negative influences on American society (only atheists and Scientologists had a more negative rating).

A second important aspect of the Buddhist immigrant experience in the United States may hold the key to the eventuation of the first. Upon arrival, Asian Buddhist immigrants have always encountered a significant number of non-Asian Americans who find Buddhism attractive. In all periods of Buddhist immigration to this country, a "convert" form of Buddhism has run parallel to the "culture" Buddhism practiced by ethnic-Asian Americans, and in some periods, Buddhism has attained a trendy status in American pop culture (most notably in the late 1800s, the 1950s and 1960s, and the 1990s). Such sympathetic perspectives may ease the lot of Buddhist immigrants.

A final point concerns the evolution of Buddhism as a world religion as it migrates out of its Asian homeland in the modern period. The intersection of various forms of ethnic/immigrant and convert Buddhism in Western contexts such as the United States has created an unprecedented awareness of Buddhism's multiplicity of expressions. Although it is too early to predict whether a fusion of the various historical expressions will create a single, new branch of Buddhism called "American" (or "Western") Buddhism, it is already clear that interaction among Buddhists in America (and the West) has resulted in significant dialogue about commonalities underlying historic divisions of practices, beliefs, and cultural expressions.

Paul David Numrich

See also: Chinese and Chinese Exclusion Act (Part I, Sec. 2); Japanese Internment (Part I, Sec. 4); Arts III: Visual and Religious Arts (Part II, Sec. 10); China, Japan, Korea, South Asia, Southeast Asia, Taiwan and Hong Kong (Part III, Sec. 3).

BIBLIOGRAPHY

Fawcett, James T., and Benjamin V. Carino, eds. *Pacific Bridges: The New Immigration from Asia and the Pacific Islands.* New York: Center for Migration Studies, 1987.

Fong, Timothy P. *The Contemporary Asian American Experience: Beyond the Model Minority*. Upper Saddle River, NJ: Prentice Hall, 1998.

Kashima, Tetsuden. *Buddhism in America: The Social Organization of an Ethnic Religious Institution*. Westport, CT: Greenwood Press, 1977.

Numrich, Paul David. "Buddhists." In *Buddhists, Hindus, and Sikhs in America*, ed. Jane Podell. Religion in American Life Series. New York: Oxford University Press, forthcoming.

———. "Buddhists." In *Encyclopedia of Chicago History*, ed. James Grossman. Chicago: University of Chicago Press, forthcoming.

———. *Old Wisdom in the New World: Americanization in Two Immigrant Theravada Buddhist Temples*. Knoxville: University of Tennessee Press, 1996.

Prebish, Charles S. *Luminous Passage: The Practice and Study of Buddhism in America*. Berkeley: University of California Press, 1999.

Prebish, Charles S., and Kenneth K. Tanaka, eds. *The Faces of Buddhism in America*. Berkeley: University of California Press, 1998.

Seager, Richard Hughes. *Buddhism in America*. New York: Columbia University Press, 1999.

Takaki, Ronald. *Strangers from a Different Shore: A History of Asian Americans*. Updated and rev. ed. Boston: Little, Brown, 1998.

Tweed, Thomas A. "Buddhists." In *American Immigrant Cultures*, ed. David Levinson and Melvin Ember, pp. 104–12. New York: Macmillan, 1997.

Williams, Duncan Ryuken, and Christopher S. Queen, eds. *American Buddhism: Methods and Findings in Recent Scholarship*. London: Curzon Press, 1999.

CATHOLICISM

For much of the political history of the United States, questions involving immigration and the status of Roman Catholics have been intimately related. Successive waves of Catholic immigrants have provided potential voters for several major shifts in American electoral politics, and the recurring presence of large numbers of Catholic immigrants has periodically occasioned the rise of important political issues in the United States. More specifically, anti-Catholicism has often provided a religious and intellectual scaffolding for certain occurrences of nativist sentiment in the nineteenth and twentieth centuries. More recently, the children and grandchildren of previous generations of Catholic immigrants have demonstrated remarkable stability in their political attitudes and loyalties, even though the circumstances of these second-, third-, and fourth-generation Catholics are substantially different from those of their ancestors.

WAVES OF CATHOLIC IMMIGRANTS

In general, there have been three major waves of Catholic immigration in American history. Although Catholics were among the earliest Europeans to settle in North America, the first numerically important wave of Catholic immigration arrived in the United States in the 1840s and 1850s. These immigrants were primarily Irish and German, with the Irish wave responding to a general famine in Ireland during the 1840s. The second wave began arriving around the turn of the twentieth century and consisted primarily of Catholics from the nations of southern and eastern Europe. The years surrounding the First World War brought to the United States large numbers of Slavs, Italians, Croats, Ukrainians, Poles, Hungarians, and Lithuanians. A third wave, arriving during the final third of the twentieth century, consisted mostly of immigrants from Mexico, Central and South America,

and Cuba. Included in this third wave of Catholic immigrants are substantial numbers of Asians from nations in which there is a strong Catholic presence, such as South Korea, Vietnam, and (especially) the Philippines.

To some extent, subsequent generations of American immigrant Catholics have assimilated into the dominant culture and no longer bear the distinctive cultural stamp of the nations from which their ancestors emigrated. To a remarkable degree, however, the American church carries the stamp of its European origins. Many American Catholics maintain ties to "the Old Country," and subsequent generations of immigrants have followed their families to America. For example, even though the Irish and Germans comprised the earliest wave of Catholic immigration, as recently as 1964, approximately a third of American Catholics of Irish or German descent were of the first or second generation. While geographic mobility and intermarriage outside the ethnic group (or Catholicism itself) have become increasingly common, many American Catholics appear to be quite conscious of their immigrant roots.

It is perhaps a matter of some importance that the first wave of Catholic immigration included substantial numbers of immigrants from Ireland. The Irish church is often considered a "sectlike" religious denomination, which, due in large part to the long-standing issue of English colonialism, stands in opposition to the dominant culture. That is, Irish Catholicism has traditionally provided alternatives to existing secular authority, rather than supporting and reinforcing the power of government. In the nineteenth and early twentieth centuries, Irish Catholics dominated the American church at the level of the diocese, and for much of American history, American Catholic bishops have been largely of Irish descent. The importance of this pattern may lie in the fact that the American church has generally sought religious and organizational autonomy and has not

A Creole-language mass offering a prayer for peace in their native land brings immigrants to the Haitian Catholic church of Notre Dame d'Haiti in the Little Haiti district of Miami. *(Jack Kurtz/Impact Visuals)*

necessarily been eager to accelerate the process of assimilation.

THE COMMUNAL BASIS OF CATHOLIC ETHNICITY

Catholic immigrants to the United States often experienced a church much different from the one they had left behind. Typically, the church in the Old Country enjoyed a near monopoly status among the laity, lacking serious competition from other religious bodies. These religious semimonopolies often held the status of a quasi-established church, in which governments provided local parishes with a variety of supports and services. In such a situation, some analysts have suggested that the Catholic Church assumed the position of a "lazy monopoly," in which it did not need to compete with other religious bodies for members. As a consequence, Catholic clergy may not have

been particularly responsive to the needs and desires of the laity, which in turn appears to have occasioned a decline in active religious participation. Church attendance, participation in the sacraments, and membership in Catholic social organizations appears to have been relatively low in heavily Catholic nations of Europe.

The situation encountered by Catholic immigrants to the United States could not have been more different. Here, not only was Catholicism typically a minority faith, but it was often a despised minority church as well. The combination of religious and ethnic prejudice, along with an easily asserted nativism among American Protestants, created a good deal of stress for newly arrived Roman Catholics. Thus, from the "demand side" (to use an economic metaphor), there was a strong need among Catholic immigrants for structures of social support, in which their faith, language, and customs were not automatic disadvantages.

Further, when viewed from the "supply side," parish priests and diocesan bishops could not count on automatic government or public support for Catholic organizations. Thus, Catholic clergy in the United States were forced to recruit potential members quite actively and to accommodate their religious pronouncements and services provided to the needs and desires of their potential lay members. There is some evidence of relatively high levels of lay participation in the governance of such parishes, which perhaps provided lay immigrants with political skills that could be transferred to the secular areas of business and politics.

Thus, in many urban areas, the early twentieth century witnessed the formation of numerous ethnically homogeneous parishes, in which recent immigrants could find religious consolation, social (and occasionally economic) support, and means of access to the broader American culture. Among the most important of these structures was an extensive network of Catholic elementary and secondary schools and an increasingly broad network of Catholic colleges and universities.

Thus, the combination of an immigrant population with extensive and diverse needs and an entrepreneurial clergy brought about the existence of a large, relatively devout, and increasingly skilled Catholic population of immigrants and their descendants. The American ethnic parish produced a relatively comprehensive set of social and economic structures virtually unprecedented in nations with large Catholic majorities. Such institutions appear to have empowered Catholic immigrants individually (by providing skills necessary to succeed outside the religious/ethnic enclave) and collectively (by creating large blocs of potentially mobilizable voters). The social, educational, political, and economic services provided by Catholic parishes enabled individual Catholics to adapt to the majority Protestant culture and to force that culture to adapt to the needs of Catholic immigrants as well.

CATHOLICISM AND ANTI-CATHOLICISM IN AMERICAN ELECTIONS

Although few Catholic immigrants would have ties or affiliations with American political parties, such nonnative Catholics provided both voters and controversies for several American elections. The presence of large numbers of Catholic immigrants in the mid-nineteenth century occasioned a great deal of nativist, anti-immigrant, and anti-Catholic sentiment, and reactions to Catholicism provided a backdrop for most presidential elections held during the final two-thirds of the nineteenth century.

Aside from (perhaps inevitable) prejudice against large numbers of economically disadvantaged foreigners, there were two major political issues associated with Catholicism during the 1840s and 1850s. One of these was public education: Catholics tended to resist the trend toward free, compulsory public education which began in the Northeast during this period, on the grounds that such public schools would likely teach Protestant versions of religion and morality and thus undermine the religious training of Catholic children. A second divisive issue was that of temperance. Throughout much of the nineteenth century, various movements sought to limit or prohibit the sale and consumption of alcoholic beverages. Such movements were not popular among immigrants of Irish or German descent. In addition to the social and recreational use of alcohol, some Catholic leaders feared that temperance, if enacted, would restrict the use of wine during the Sacrament of Communion.

Prior to the twentieth century, anti-Catholic votes were likely more politically consequential than those actually cast by Catholic immigrants. Not only were such immigrants numerically rather weak, they were, for the most part, poorly integrated into participation in American politics. Nevertheless, nativist movements of one sort or another were quite common during the mid-nineteenth century. Still, some Catholic

votes mattered, as in the two pivotal elections of 1844 and 1852. In both cases, Catholic votes were widely believed to have caused the defeat of Whig candidates Henry Clay and Winfield Scott. In the election of 1844, Catholic votes cast for a pro-Irish, third-party candidate (James G. Birney of the Liberty Party) were thought to have cost Clay New York State's electoral vote, and with it, the presidency. In 1852, the election of Democrat Franklin Pierce was widely attributed to the "foreign, Catholic" vote.

Throughout this period, the American Party (more commonly known as the Know-Nothing Party) made impressive gains in the Northeast with an explicitly anti-Catholic, anti-immigrant appeal. In the 1850s, the Know-Nothings were absorbed into the new Republican Party and appear to have been the source of rumors that Democratic candidate Stephen Douglas of Illinois was a "secret Catholic."

During the period following the Civil War, anti-Catholicism was a major component of the appeal of the Republican Party. Charging that the Democrats were the party of "Rum, Romanism, and Rebellion," the Republicans sought to use nativism as a source of popular appeal. For example, in 1875, President Grant introduced a measure, later dubbed the Blaine Amendment, that would have provided for the taxation of church property and eliminated much public support for sectarian institutions. The period between the Civil War and World War I saw a Democratic Party largely divided between its southern wing, which was hostile to civil rights and explicitly supportive of the Ku Klux Klan, and its northern, Catholic wing, which was generally unsuccessful in influencing the party's presidential nominating process.

The loyalty of the Catholic wing of the Democratic Party was weakened somewhat by the presidential campaigns of William Jennings Bryan in 1896, 1900, and 1908. To a large extent, Bryan's appeal was one of agrarian populism, temperance, and Protestant fundamentalism. These themes had little appeal for a largely Catholic, urban, working-class immigrant population. While most Catholics who were active in the electorate remained loyal to the Democratic Party in the early twentieth century, the Republicans made substantial inroads as the result of the Democrats' repeated nominations of Bryan. Moreover, analysis of the returns of the elections in which Bryan was a candidate suggests that his candidacy depressed the voting turnout of first- and second-generation Catholic immigrants. The southern wing of the Democratic Party was able to dominate the party's presidential nominating process until the pivotal election of 1928.

AL SMITH, THE NEW DEAL, AND THE ELECTION OF JOHN F. KENNEDY

Although most American Catholics who were politically active identified with the Democratic Party, ethnic Catholic communities often contained large numbers of new Americans who were not affiliated with either party. And, as noted above, The Democratic Party's repeated flirtations with "Bryanism" also caused a consequential minority of urban Catholic immigrants to identify with the Republican Party. Thus, it seems likely that the net contribution of Catholic immigrants to election outcomes in the United States was fairly minimal during the last quarter of the nineteenth century or the first quarter of the twentieth.

This situation appears to have changed drastically during the presidential elections of 1928, 1932, and 1936. In 1928, after multiple convention ballots, the Democrats nominated Governor Al Smith of New York for president. Despite his apparently English surname, Smith was (incorrectly) widely regarded as the son of Irish immigrants and spoke in a distinctive ethnic accent. Smith was a Catholic (indeed, the first Roman Catholic to be nominated for the presidency) and was a prominent and highly visible "wet" (opponent of Prohibition). Some Republican spokespersons raised the issue of Smith's loyalty to the United States, arguing that, as a Roman Catholic, his ultimate allegiance was to the pope (the head of a foreign state). In an electorate dominated by Republican identifiers, these characteristics proved to be insurmountable political barriers, and Smith went down to a decisive defeat at the hands of the Republican secretary of commerce Herbert Hoover. Indeed, Protestant reaction to Smith's candidacy was uniformly negative and undoubtedly contributed to Republican gains across the nation, and particularly in the South. Hoover was the first Republican presidential candidate after Reconstruction to win electoral votes in the South, carrying the former Confederate states of Florida, North Carolina, Tennessee, Texas, and Virginia, as well as the border states of Kentucky, Maryland, Missouri, and Oklahoma.

However, Smith's defeat may have laid the groundwork for an important component of the New Deal Democratic coalition that dominated American electoral politics from the 1930s through the 1960s. A large number of first-time voters entered the electorate in 1928, and most evidence suggests that many of these were first- or second-generation urban, Catholic immigrants. While analysis of the 1930 midterm elec-

tions suggests that these new voters were not immediate converts to the Democratic Party, the election of 1928 provided an opportunity and an incentive for these voters to involve themselves in the American political process.

Thus, the importance of the presidential election of 1928 is that it put into place an important component of Franklin Roosevelt's "New Deal" coalition. Catholic voters proved to be a reliable bloc of support for Democratic candidates at all levels of government. Moreover, Catholic immigrants and their descendants were especially important at the level of presidential elections. Because presidents are not elected by direct popular vote but by the electoral college, campaigns for the presidency are often focused on large, populous states rich in electoral votes. Because Catholics tended to be concentrated geographically in large cities, the Catholic vote became strategically, as well as numerically, important in presidential elections.

The mobilization of first- and second-generation Catholics from nonvoters to voters in the Smith-Roosevelt era occasioned the recruitment of Catholics to government posts at a variety of levels. Catholic candidates for state and local offices and for Congress were more viable due to the influx of Catholic voters. Given the ethnic homogeneity of many urban parishes, big-city political organizations (sometimes pejoratively termed "machines") provided ethnically balanced tickets, which accelerated the assimilation of recent immigrants into the electoral process. Moreover, presidents and governors, mindful of the importance of the Catholic vote, were increasingly likely to appoint Roman Catholics (often with ethnically identifiable surnames) to visible appointive offices.

Many analysts regard the election of 1960 as the occasion of full Catholic participation in American politics. The narrow election of John F. Kennedy over Vice-President Richard M. Nixon brought to the White House America's first Catholic president. Undoubtedly, the appearance of a young, handsome, wealthy, Harvard-educated Catholic did a great deal to minimize the connection between Catholics and immigrants in the minds of many voters, and many journalists and pundits declared the 1960 result to be the end of religious prejudice in the United States. However, analyses of public opinion data suggest that religion was a very strong predictor of voter choice in 1960 and that, on balance, Kennedy's religion slightly reduced his share of the popular vote. Thus, while Kennedy managed to eke out a very narrow victory in 1960 and thus accomplished what Al Smith was unable to do, the result of the 1960 election can be regarded as a testament to the persistence of the importance of religious identity in American politics.

THE POLITICAL INERTIA OF AMERICAN CATHOLICS

Since the election of 1960, Catholics have generally responded to the same sorts of political forces that have caused changes in other segments of the American electorate. Nevertheless, even though the Democratic share of the Catholic vote has waxed and waned according to the short-term forces unique to each election and the Democrats have experienced some defections to the Republican Party, Catholics have remained more Democratic in their vote choices and partisan loyalties than any other group of white Christians.

Most accounts of the political behavior of American Catholics have emphasized the socioeconomic nature of the connection between Catholics and the Democratic Party. Many analysts have suggested that Catholic identification with the Democratic Party has been the result of the historical maginalization of Catholic immigrants. That is, Catholic immigrants and their descendants have traditionally been poorly educated, working class, and inhabitants of large northern cities. In the years following the large waves of European Catholic immigrants in the early twentieth century, however, most of these demographic distinctions between Catholics and others have been reduced or eliminated. Contemporary American Catholics have become as affluent and well educated as Protestants and are as likely to live in suburban or rural areas. As such, the affinity between Catholics and the Democrats would seem to have outlived its usefulness, and a Catholic shift to the Republican Party has seemed long overdue.

Thus, the continuing loyalty of American Catholics to the Democratic Party remains something of an enigma. The solution to the puzzle of Catholic political inertia may have its roots in the content of Catholic theology and in the immigrant roots of the American Catholic Church.

Some analysts have suggested that there exists a discernible "Catholic ethic," which, unlike Max Weber's more famous account of the "Protestant ethic," is rather communal and egalitarian. In part because of the sacramental nature of their religion, Catholics encounter God's sanctifying grace in concert with others, rather than in isolation. The sacraments are *collective* interactions with the sacred and suggest that God relates to communities as opposed to particular individuals. Owing to the social availability of the sacraments, God is not regarded as separated from a sinful humanity but as omnipresent. Thus (in very brief

summary), Catholicism provides a counterweight to the pervasive individualism of the American culture.

Catholic socialization, in turn, may have been quite effective, and the effectiveness with which the Catholic clergy have transmitted Catholic doctrine to the laity may again be attributable to the immigrant roots of the American church. As noted earlier, Catholic parishes in the United States found themselves without the traditional means of support that characterized their European counterparts and were thus forced to recruit members actively. This suggests that Catholic church attendance may have been unusually strong, which provided clergy with many opportunities to instruct the laity in the particulars of the faith. Similarly, the extensive network of Catholic schools certainly contributed to the socialization of young Catholics. Moreover, the ethnic homogeneity of many urban parishes provided frequent opportunities for social interaction with the clergy and with one's coreligionists. The social, apparently secular aspects of urban Catholic parishes may have served to reinforce the message of the priests and the nuns.

A good deal of evidence suggests that Catholics retain distinctive political and economic attitudes, despite the increasingly remote immigrant roots of contemporary American Catholics. Even when their economic and educational characteristics are taken into account, Catholics tend to be more liberal on social welfare issues and, under many circumstances, more skeptical about the use of military force. American Catholics tend to be more sympathetic to demands of more recent ethnic immigrants (and of African Americans) for autonomy and diversity. These attitudes provide a basis for continued affinity between Catholics and the Democratic Party.

Conversely, the conservatism of some Catholics on issues such as abortion has not occasioned any sustained movement toward the Republican Party. Although Catholics are not nearly the Democratic monolith of the Roosevelt era, a solid plurality retains its identification with the Democratic Party. Further, the basis of new Catholic recruits to the Republicans is much different from that observed for Protestants. During the 1980s and 1990s, there has been a steady drift of white Protestants (especially in the South) toward the Republican Party. This shift toward the Grand Old Party (GOP) has, in large part, been occasioned by attitudes on social issues such as abortion, gay rights, and feminism and is most pronounced among Protestants who attend church frequently. Conversely, contemporary Catholic Republicans are slightly *less* religious than their Democratic counterparts and seem motivated by issues involving economic policy or race relations.

The American Catholic Church is no longer a church of immigrants. Nevertheless, the experience of immigration and (partial) assimilation has left deep roots in the social and political life of the United States. While not "liberal" in either the classical or contemporary senses, American Catholicism is a continuing source of communal attitudes and of support for public assistance for those who are disadvantaged.

Ted G. Jelen

See also: The Great Irish Immigration (Part I, Sec. 2); Culture and Assimilation (Part I, Sec. 3); Nativist Reaction (Part I, Sec. 4); Andean Countries, Brazil and the Southern Cone, Central America, Cuba, Dominican Republic, Haiti and French-Speaking Caribbean, Mexico, Puerto Rico (Part III, Sec. 2); Philippines (Part III, Sec. 3); Ireland, Western and Southern Europe (Part III, Sec. 4); Emigration, Emigrants, and Know-Nothings, 1854, Irish Response to Nativism, 1854 (Part IV, Sec. 3).

BIBLIOGRAPHY

Abramson, Harold J. *Ethnic Diversity in Catholic America*. New York: Wiley, 1973.

Andersen, Kristi. *The Creation of a Democratic Majority, 1928–1936*. Chicago: University of Chicago Press, 1979.

Clubb, Jerome M., and Howard W. Allen. "The Cities and the Election of 1928: Partisan Realignment?" In *Electoral Change and Stability in American Political History*, ed. Jerome M. Clubb and Howard W. Allen, pp. 236–54. New York: Free Press, 1971.

Converse, Phillip E. "Religion and Politics: The 1960 Election." In *Elections and the Political Order*, ed. Angus Campbell, Phillip E. Converse, Warren E. Miller, and Donald Stokes, pp. 96–124. New York: Wiley, 1966.

Finke, Roger, and Rodney Stark. *The Churching of America, 1776–1990*. New Brunswick, NJ: Rutgers University Press, 1992.

Jelen, Ted G. "Culture Wars and the Party System: Religion and Realignment, 1972–1992." In *Culture Wars in American Politics: Critical Reviews of a Popular Thesis*, ed. Rhys H. Williams, pp. 145–58. New York: Aldine de Gruyter, 1997.

O'Connor, Len. *Clout: Mayor Daley and His City*. Chicago: Henry Regnery Company, 1975.

Prendergast, William B. *The Catholic Voter in American Politics: The Passing of the Democratic Monolith*. Washington, DC: Georgetown University Press, 1999.

Royko, Mike. *Boss: Richard J. Daley of Chicago*. New York: Signet, 1971.

Sundquist, James L. *Dynamics of the Party System*. Washington, DC: Brookings Institution, 1973.

Tropman, John E. *The Catholic Ethic in American Society: An Exploration of Values*. San Francisco: Jossey-Bass, 1995.

Verba, Sidney, Kay Lehman Scholzman, and Henry E. Brady. *Voice and Equality: Civic Voluntarism in American Politics*. Cambridge: Harvard University Press, 1995.

EVANGELICAL CHRISTIANITY

Almost every aspect of American evangelicalism has been affected by the successive waves of immigration that have reshaped the contours of what historian Randall Balmer calls "America's folk religion." Beginning with the first immigrant wave during the colonial era that brought varieties of evangelicals to North America—English Puritans, Baptists, Scots-Irish Presbyterians, German Lutherans, and various Anabaptist groups—today's latest wave of immigrants, chiefly Latinos and Asians, are also contributing to evangelicalism's historical traditions. But they are also bringing imported traditions that are largely nondenominational, ethnic, and growing—often faster than the Euro-American churches. Ethnic Chinese and Korean churches and Latino churches have revitalized several evangelical denominations. They have kept the evangelical presence in America's cities, decades after the Euro-American flight to the suburbs. Moreover, the new immigrant evangelicals may be a part of a larger global decentralization of evangelicalism from northern and western Europe to the developing world.

In keeping with the spirit of the Reformation, immigrants have taken the initiative to reshape their traditions and import new varieties to America. The Christian Reformed Church was brought over by Dutch immigrants, and Scandinavians imported the Evangelical Covenant and Evangelical Free Churches. The immigration wave beginning after the 1965 Immigration Act has radically altered the evangelical landscape, once the bastion of white northern Europeans. It is now common to see Christian Reformed, Evangelical Covenant, Brethren, and other denominations growing because Asian and Latino immigrants have filled some of their near-empty pews. Latinos and Asians are changing the nature of evangelical America in how it looks and worships. In the 1990s, the growth of two of the largest evangelical denominations in the country, the Southern Baptists and the Assemblies of God, is due primarily to an increase in Asian and Latino churches. Evangelicalism in the United States has been infused with the cultural and linguistic diversity of the new immigration. This has helped to recast the idea that to be part of one of the largest, most influential movements in American society one need be of European stock. Such new dynamics require stepping back to examine how this trend developed by considering the histories of both evangelicals and immigrants during the points at which they have intersected throughout U.S. history.

HISTORY

The United States was the first Western society founded by evangelical Protestants. From colonial times until the middle part of the twentieth century, evangelicals in general were northern and western European immigrants from Reformed, Anabaptist, and Wesleyan traditions. Beginning in 1965, when immigration laws were reformed to emphasize family reunification instead of quotas, a substantial number of the new immigrants—Asians and, to a lesser degree, Latinos—have arrived in the United States as evangelicals, or have become evangelicals. They have planted churches, begun new ones, and imported their own evangelical traditions. It is probably one of the more ironic trends in American history that one pillar of society that has traditionally defined virtue, civility, and providence—the Protestant faith—should be, if population trends hold, home to more Asians and Latinos than Euro-Americans during the next century. Immigrant evangelicals from the developing countries of the world, once viewed as a dark, uncivilized wilderness, will be at least partially responsible for maintaining an evangelical presence in the Western world.

The obstacles these new immigrants have had to face go back to the founding of the nation when citizenship was restricted in the 1790 Naturalization Act to white people with some means, usually property. The fact that they would be Protestant was taken to be a given. From the beginning, being a part of this citizen class acted as a barrier against other groups that comprised colonial America. Citizens presumably represented civilization, virtue, and Christianity. Conversely, noncitizens (blacks, Native Americans, and, later, Asians) often represented the opposite of those valued traits: barbarity, immorality, and heathenism. What formed evangelical Protestantism in America was a blending of English Puritanism and several strains of European Pietism. What formed the basis for citizenship was ethnicity. American immigration was equated with Anglo conformity, and native-born Anglos insisted on the rapid assimilation of the immigrant into the prevalent American culture that was English. Groups that did not assimilate and refused to acquiesce to the dominant society's demands were set off from the larger society. Catholics congregated in the cities, formed alternative schooling systems, and built up their own institutions to insulate them from the dominant English culture. Groups of Pietists also refused to abandon their use of a German-based language known as Pennsylvania Dutch or their religious traditions that often called on them to be pacifist and sectarian.

Ethnic differences between colonial evangelicals did not seem to hinder their preaching alongside one another. Anglican preacher George Whitfield was especially effective in reaching Dutch immigrants. Puritan Jonathan Edwards worked among the Scots-Irish. Throughout the eighteenth and nineteenth centuries, evangelical immigrants, perhaps because of their common European Protestant heritage, began to submerge whatever distinct ethnic differences remained under a rubric called Anglo-America. The Dutch, Germans, Scots-Irish, and English forged religious and racial bonds to form the largest body of evangelical Protestants in the world. By the middle of the nineteenth century, however, after the Civil War, a rapid succession of events began to collapse the once unified force of the Euro-American evangelical establishment.

The next significant wave of immigrants arrived from 1880 to 1924, when 26 million newcomers came to the United States. Before this era, evangelicals controlled all major denominations, seminaries, divinity schools, mission boards, and other agencies. A series of events and trends caused this once solid evangelical empire to fracture and lose much of its dominance. Urbanization, industrialization, and immigration all forced evangelicals to deal with pressures they had not foreseen: city living and the allure of worldly ac-

coutrements, industrialization and its revolution in how people worked, and immigration of Catholics, Jews, and an array of non-Western faiths. When it came to responding to these challenges, particularly immigrants, many evangelicals (as some do today) viewed immigrants as an extension of missions work, a home mission field. Ethnic Catholics were targeted for a variety of reasons: Their alleged allegiance to the pope made them disloyal. Their faith rituals cast a suspicious eye on them as idolaters, and their often squalid living conditions in the cities of the Northeast displayed a lack of moral fortitude and intemperance. Asians were targeted because they came from "heathen" countries, were morally suspect, and generally were inassimilable. Evangelicals began homes for Chinese prostitutes and for immigrant women and their children, because it was thought that a woman could civilize and domesticate her husband—in effect be the vessel for the message of evangelical virtue. Toward the end of the nineteenth century, evangelicals turned their home missions work toward the southwest United States. Latinos, like other ethnic Catholics, were viewed in the same unflattering ways as other Catholic immigrants and Asians. Latinos were living in the "darkness" of Catholicism and idolatry and, because of their indigenous lineage, had a propensity for violence. Presbyterian, Methodist, Baptist, and later Assemblies of God missionaries spread out throughout the borderlands to civilize and to evangelize.

Along with these bewildering changes, evangelicals found themselves battered by liberals for failing to appreciate scientific inquiry, biblical criticism, and the Social Gospel, which preached social reform and justice as the goal of the church over evangelicalism. The Holiness evangelicals especially found themselves surprised by a series of revivals that purported to be a continuance of the biblical Pentecost. Beginning in Texas, then Kansas, and finally Los Angeles, this revival culminated at the Azusa Street Mission in Los Angeles in 1906. The significance of this event is twofold: First, it displayed a multiethnic church where Asians, Latinos, eastern Europeans, African Americans, and Euro-Americans worshiped together. Such a display was probably the reason why the revival was over by 1909. Second, it introduced on a major scale to American soil the Pentecostal movement that in a few decades has become the fastest growing segment of Christianity worldwide, largely in the developing world, homeland to many of today's immigrants.

By the end of the nineteenth century and well into the twentieth, calls for restrictions on immigration succeeded with a series of national and state prohi-

Many Central American immigrants, like these Salvadoran women, have converted from the region's traditional Catholicism to one of the evangelical Protestant sects. *(Donna DeCesare/Impact Visuals)*

bitions: the 1882 Chinese Exclusion Act, 1906 California Alien Land Law, and the 1924 Quota Act, which cumulatively effectively ended Asian and restricted eastern European immigration. It would not be until the 1965 Immigration Act that a significant number of Asians would be allowed to emigrate. As for Latinos, primarily Mexicans, who make up 65 percent of the Latino population in the United States, immigration, legal or otherwise, has continued unabated since the Mexican Revolution era from 1910 to 1920, with spurts of great activity in the last several decades owing primarily to Mexico's economic downturns. Other significant waves of Latino immigration occurred with Cubans leaving largely for political reasons from the 1960s to the 1980s; Puerto Ricans (who hold the distinction of being American citizens), in the 1950s–1970s; and Central Americans, who arrived during the time of war and political strife in their countries, from the late 1970s to the 1980s. If population projections

hold, Latinos will be the largest ethnic/racial group in America next to Euro-Americans by 2025. And if current trends hold with regard to the 10 percent loss the Catholic Church has experienced every year in its once staunchly loyal Latino population, Latinos could play a major part in recasting the image of evangelical America.

The character of American immigration underwent a significant transformation with the passage of the Immigration Act of 1965. The legislation abolished the discriminatory quotas based on national origins that had favored northwestern Europeans and substituted a system based on family reunification. Once immigrants became citizens, they could bring over family members. Congress anticipated that most immigrants would continue to be Europeans. Newcomers from Asia and Latin America quickly began to outnumber Europeans with 3–4 million immigrants arriving from these areas in the 1970s. Between 1951 and 1965, 53 percent of all immigrants came from Europe and only 6 percent from Asia. In the twelve-year period after 1966, Europeans represented only 24 percent of the total, and Asians, 28 percent. The recasting of American evangelicalism occurred over the last thirty-five years. As recently as 1960, evangelicalism was largely a movement concentrated in Western Europe and North America. Of the one-half billion evangelicals in the world, 70 percent are non-Western, living in Africa, Asia, Oceania, and Latin America. By 1990, only 37 percent of all evangelicals lived in Western nations.

CONTEMPORARY SCENE

Evangelicals in America are sprawling and loosely organized, encompassing varied traditions. They are now part of the Protestant establishment, the single largest religious faction in the country. They are religious innovators in radio, television, religious movies, advertising, publishing, Christian pop and rock music, foreign missions, seminary education, and cyberspace. So what part, if any, do the new evangelical immigrants play in this movement? The array of immigrant evangelicals is incredible: Asians of dozens of different ethnic and linguistic groups, Latinos from a dozen or so different countries, small groups of African and Oceanian immigrants. These groups have added not only numbers to evangelical denominations but also linguistic and cultural differences, theological distinctness, and, in general, vigor to the evangelical establishment's churches, seminaries, and foreign missions.

Of particular interest are Koreans, Chinese, Southeast Asians, and Filipinos, who have made significant contributions in terms of churches and membership, to such established evangelical denominations as the Presbyterians, Christian Missionary Alliance, Methodists, Baptists, Assemblies of God, Seventh-Day Adventists, Church of the Nazarene, and a host of nondenominational evangelical churches. Among all these Asian groups, the most stunning growth has come from Koreans.

KOREANS

American missionaries introduced Koreans to evangelical Christianity in the late nineteenth and early twentieth centuries. The same missionaries encouraged Koreans to emigrate. Koreans arrived first in Hawaii and worked as plantation workers; 40 percent of all Korean immigrants were evangelicals. While working in the plantations, they built churches and restricted gambling and drinking in the migrant camps. Throughout the first part of the twentieth century, Korean immigration was small, numbering between 5,000 and 7,000. After the immigration reforms of 1965, Koreans began arriving in steady streams. Today, there are close to 1 million Koreans in Los Angeles alone. Their presence in evangelical America has been startling. Koreans have over 2,000 churches of varying evangelical persuasions in the United States. There are over 1 million in attendance at those churches, with over 70 percent of the first-generation immigrants affiliated with a Korean church in the United States. The denominational affiliations are overwhelmingly evangelical: Presbyterian and Methodist comprise over 50 percent of the churches; 27 percent are either nondenominational or spread across varied denominations. Korean seminary students form one of the largest ethnic blocks in such divinity schools as the School of Theology in Claremont, California, a United Methodist school, and Fuller Theological Seminary, the largest evangelical seminary on the West Coast. Many seminaries have instituted Korean ministerial programs to account for the rise in student population. That nearly all this growth has occurred within the last thirty-five years makes it all the more remarkable. Korean immigrants have been hugely successful not only at building churches but also at revitalizing established churches whose diminishing attendance was stemmed by immigrant evangelicals. Another area of growth has been missions. Many, if not all, of these Korean churches have active mission programs: to urban centers in the United States and to the republics of the former Soviet Union, Asia, and Europe.

CHINESE

Once one of the most despised of immigrant groups, Chinese, like Koreans, began as migrant workers in Hawaii. American missionaries introduced them to evangelical Christianity. The Chinese were once viewed as so incompatible with the assimilationist goals of many American politicians that they were effectively excluded from the country for nearly forty years. That this group, once portrayed in the most unflattering light as "heathens," would be one of the largest, proportionate to the population, of evangelical Americans is quite amazing considering the rather shameful treatment of past generations of Chinese immigrants. Chinese evangelicals, unlike Koreans, tend to belong to nondenominational churches, many of which are transnational imports from the mainland, Hong Kong, or Taiwan. At least 40 percent of Chinese churches are nondenominational. Chinese, like their evangelical immigrant brethren before them, have founded their own branches of existing denominations: the Chinese Evangelical Free Church and the Evangelical Formosan Church. Between 1968 and 1990, there has been a 500 percent increase in the number of Chinese churches in the United States. Of the 644 churches, most, if not all, are evangelical. The churches are split with 50 percent affiliating with such denominations as Baptist and 40 percent affiliated with nondenominational churches. Many of these nondenominational churches resemble Reformed and Baptist churches in theology and polity. Many Chinese evangelicals are adult converts from non-Christian families, which means that growth is coming from conversion and generational sources. The growth of evangelical Christianity in the Chinese community is phenomenal considering that in the 1950s there were about fifty Chinese churches in the United States. Today, Chinese evangelicals form a significant block of new churches in the Southern Baptist denomination. Thirty-two percent of the Chinese community identifies itself as Christian, the highest rate in Chinese-American history. Like Koreans, Chinese make up a significant ethnic block in many evangelical seminaries in the United States. Regarding foreign missions, Chinese evangelicals are heavily involved in planting churches in the United States and throughout Asia.

SOUTHEAST ASIANS

Southeast Asians, chiefly Vietnamese, Cambodians, Hmong, and, to a smaller extent, Laotians, have begun to make inroads into evangelical America. Usually their allegiance to a denomination has been based on whether that group helped them emigrate as refugees or if that denomination had mission work in their country. The growth of the Christian Missionary Alliance, a Holiness Wesleyan group that began in the late nineteenth century, has been particularly impacted by the involvement of Vietnamese and Cambodian evangelicals. Of the denomination's 2,000 churches, fully 25 percent are ethnic churche, all of them either Asian or Latino. The American Baptist Church is another denomination that has benefited from church-sponsored refugee programs of the 1970s. Today, Southeast Asian immigrant evangelicals are a presence in Baptist, Methodist, and many non-denominational churches. Southeast Asians have lagged behind the Koreans and Chinese in terms of economic success, therefore their ability to attend seminaries and do large-scale foreign missions work has not grown as it has with Koreans or Chinese.

FILIPINOS

And in another striking example of the dramatic demographic shift that has occurred and will continue to occur, fully 90 percent of new growth in the Seventh-Day Adventist Church of New York has come about by infusion of immigrants: Asian, Latino, and African. Filipino immigrants planted many of those churches. In Los Angeles, some of the Seventh-Day Adventist's largest churches are Filipino. Filipinos have also contributed to the ever changing evangelical landscape by importing a Filipino evangelical church, the Iglesia Ni Cristo, a fundamentalist church whose members believe that it is the only church that one need to be baptized into for purposes of salvation. Mission work by this and other Filipino churches has seen many churches planted not only in the Philippines but also around the world where Filipinos comprise much of the manual labor force: Indonesia, Saudi Arabia, and India.

LATINOS

Commonalities between Asian and Latino immigrants exist in that they have traditionally been unwanted, viewed as economic burdens, incapable of assimilation, and objects of missions. In the mid to late nineteenth century, Latinos became the object of conversion by an array of American evangelicals such as the Presbyterians and the Methodists, later joined by Assemblies of God in the early twentieth century. Assembly of God missionaries worked along the borderlands and made successful inroads, building bible institutes in the 1920s to be used as launching pads for further ministry to Latinos. Today, Latinos and Asians represent one of the fastest growing segments of evangelical Christianity around the world, including in the United States. With Asians, the trend seems to be toward Reformed and Baptist evangelical persuasions; with Latinos, the evangelicalism has taken on the added dimension of a large Pentecostal presence. Latinos comprise at least 15 percent of the Assemblies of God, and there are an estimated 1,500 Spanish-speaking Assemblies of God churches in the United States.

In Mexico, from where most Latino immigrants arrive, the growth of evangelicalism has been startling. In 1970, non-Catholics represented less than 1 million people. By 1980, there were 2 million, and in 1990, 7 million. Of the 6,000 religious associations in the country, 75 percent are evangelical, and of those, 60 percent are Pentecostal. There can be little doubt that as Mexican immigrants continue to arrive in the United States, many more of them will be evangelical;

if not, they will have been exposed to the faith back home. Many Latino Pentecostals have not chosen or did not have the means to go to seminary, but they do populate Bible institutes of many evangelical and Pentecostal denominations. Mexican evangelicals have largely been responsible for the growth of Spanish-speaking churches in the Assemblies and other denominations. They also are training to go back to Latin America and become missionaries there and in other parts of the Spanish-speaking world, such as the Caribbean and Spain.

In other Latin American countries, the growth of Pentecostalism has been even more exponential than in Mexico and has directly affected the growth of evangelical immigrants in the United States. In Guatemala, a shift from Catholicism to evangelical Protestantism will soon find evangelicals being the largest religious group in the country. Independent Guatemalan Pentecostal churches have taken to viewing the United States as a mission field and have begun planting churches here. Guatemalans and other Central Americans are forming significant portions of the growth not only among Pentecostal denominations such as the Church of God, but also within the American Baptists and other noncharismatic denominations. Again, like Mexicans, Central Americans have either by choice or circumstance gone to Bible institutes to train for church ministry or missions.

On a smaller scale are the arrivals of imported churches in Latino communities, usually Pentecostal in theology and practice. One such church, the Igreja Universal, a Brazilian import, has begun planting churches in major U.S. cities, chiefly within immigrant Latino neighborhoods. Being a Latin American import, this church has brought with it some theological and practical distinctiveness. Heavily influenced by the cultural ethos of spiritual warfare (exorcism of spirits), Brazilian Pentecostalism has transmitted that emphasis on exorcism to its U.S. churches along with Pentecostal practices of divine healing and speaking in tongues. Additionally, because Pentecostalism in the developing world first began in the poorest areas, offering refuge and help for social ills, a unique prosperity gospel that equates personal salvation with wealth is also a part of how immigrant evangelicals have reshaped the religious landscape of the United States.

AFRICA

A young Ugandan missionary will serve as a final example of how evangelical immigrants have begun and will continue to change what was, until the 1960s, a largely Euro-American religious movement. The Ugandan has been sent to the United States as a missionary to Episcopalians; he was chosen because the Anglican Church in Uganda has grown to over 21,000 churches in the country, whereas its American counterpart, the Episcopal Church, has declined steadily for decades.

A stark reversal of historic mission roles is in the works. In decades past, Euro-American missionaries viewed the developing countries of Latin America, Asia, and Africa as the most benighted areas of the world, bound by superstition and backwardness and in desperate need of a dose of Christianity in the guise of civilization. Today, it is becoming more common for missionaries from these areas to see the United States as a mission field. A once great, shining city on a hill lost in secularism, violence, and consumerism in need of a dose of imported evangelical Christianity—or so the idea goes.

Watching all these trends with anticipation and more than a little trepidation are scores of evangelical denominations, many of which have already initiated plans to reach the growing communities of immigrants. National and regional strategies to reach immigrant groups have been initiated by denominations as varied as the Lutherans (both the Evangelical Lutheran and Missouri synod varieties), Baptists (Southern and American), Wesleyan Holiness (Christian Missionary Alliance and Salvation Army), Pentecostal (Assemblies of God and Church of God) and a host of nondenominational churches, many of which began in the home countries of the immigrants. What this signals for the future of American evangelicalism is that it will grow to look more like a global religious movement. With this new infusion of immigrant evangelicals, as with the waves past, innovations in practice and theology will also recast what so far has been a stable mix of Western European Reformed and Baptist theology. If the center of evangelical Christianity will move to the developing world, will it follow that the theological trends will also move to the developing world to address issues as varied as how to deal with indigenous faiths, internal ethnic tensions, social justice issues revolving around poverty, and immigrant's rights? In effect, will the new wave of immigrant evangelicals seek to retain more of their ethnic identity than the immigrants of the past? After all, it was relatively easy for the amalgamation of German, Dutch, Scots-Irish, and eventually Irish to become anglicized. The 1965 generation of immigrants will have a whole host of different problems fitting in because they cannot readily blend in with the anglicized majority. Will the added specter of a larger number of immigrants arriving in the United States as evangelicals add to their assimilation into the larger Euro-American society? Judging from the persistence of ethnic churches—separated from the larger religious bodies based on language and culture—such assimilation figures are not to be the case for the 1965 generation. What appears to be happening is that immigrant evangelicals are carving out their own religious and cultural space where they can be evangelical without losing their ethnic identity. Similarly to the ethnic revitalization of the past, where Germans in particular insisted on having at least some church services held in the mother tongue, Asian and Latino immigrants tend to congregate in churches that speak their language, and they work very hard at trying to inculcate that loyalty in their children. Watching how the larger Euro-American evangelical world responds to this radical demographic shift will say much about how talk about diversity has been internalized by the movement and whether this acceptance of diversity has taken root.

Arlene M. Sánchez-Walsh

See also: Puritans and Other Religious Dissenters (Part I, Sec. 1); Segmented Assimilation (Part II, Sec. 4); Southern Africa, West Africa (Part III, Sec. 1); Andean Countries, Central America, English-Speaking Caribbean (Part III, Sec. 2); Korea, Oceania, Taiwan and Hong Kong (Part III, Sec. 3).

BIBLIOGRAPHY

Balmer, Randall. *Blessed Assurance: A History of American Evangelicalism.* Boston: Beacon Press, 1999.

Bodner, John. *The Transplanted: A History of Urban Immigrants.* Bloomington: Indiana University Press, 1985.

Warner, Stephen R., and Judith G. Wittner, eds. *Gatherings in Diaspora: Religious Communities and the New Immigration.* Philadelphia: Temple University Press, 1998.

HINDUISM AND SIKHISM

Hinduism, a religion that originated in India, is different from other major world religions in many ways. It does not have a founder, a single text or deity, or even a central belief system. Although the religion is ancient and has its roots in the beliefs, practices, and texts of the Vedic period (1500–1000 B.C.), the term "Hinduism" was introduced only in the early 1800s. The British colonialists who coined the term used it to refer to the culture and practices of the non-Islamic people of the Indian subcontinent. In that sense, Hinduism referred both to the Indian civilization and to a group of related religions that were indigenous to India. Currently, however, the term is used more specifically to refer to a religion under whose umbrella falls a vast diversity of practices, deities, and schools of thought. Because of this diversity, the nature and character of Hinduism have varied greatly by region, caste, and historical period, and Hinduism in diaspora manifests certain distinctive features.

One of the earliest groups of Indian immigrants (mostly from Punjab province) to the United States arrived in California between 1899 and 1914. Numbering around 6,800, most were Sikh (85 percent) and another 10–12 percent were Muslim. Despite the fact that people from Hindu backgrounds constituted less than 5 percent of this group, all of them were classified as "Hindu" in the United States (at the time the term applied to anyone from the Indian subcontinent). These immigrants were mostly male, and because of laws restricting Asian immigration and marriage across "racial" lines, most of them married Mexican women. Since the mothers oversaw domestic life, the culture, religion, and practices of the mothers predominated in the home. However, most of the Punjabi–Mexican children identified themselves as "Hindu" as a means to distinguish themselves from the poorer Mexican-American population around them.

Based on a theory first formulated by European scholars during the British colonization of India, upper-caste Hindus were believed to be descendants of a branch of the Aryan race. Thus the early immigrant "Hindus" were classified as "Caucasians." Court decisions in 1910 and 1913 held that Indians were therefore to be considered "white persons" and eligible for citizenship. In 1923, however, the Supreme Court ruled that Indians were Caucasians but not "white" and were thus ineligible for naturalized citizenship. The classification of Indian Americans as "Caucasian" continued until the 1980 census when, under pressure from Indian-American leaders, they were reclassified as "Asian Indians" and therefore as a "minority group" eligible for affirmative action.

As a consequence of the exclusion acts that prevented further immigration of Indians (and other Asians), the Indian population fell sharply. According to the 1940 census, there were only 2,405 Indians in the United States, most of them living in California. Thus, most people of Indian origin in the United States today are immigrants who arrived during the second phase of immigration, after the passage of the 1965 Immigration and Naturalization Act. Currently, there are probably more than 1.3 million people of Indian origin in the United States. There are no figures on the proportions of Indians in the United States belonging to various religions. In India, Hindus constitute more than 80 percent of the population, but indirect evidence indicates that the proportion of Indian immigrants in the United States who are Hindu is smaller because religious minorities are overrepresented. However, Indian Hindus are still the majority religious group among Indian immigrants.

Scholars have argued that religion often becomes more important to immigrants, for a variety of reasons. First, sociologist Stephen Warner and other commentators indicate that the disruptions and questions raised by migration and resettlement in a new environment have a "theologizing" effect. More important, religion becomes more salient because religious

Indian immigrants offer sacrifices at a Hindu shrine in Queens, New York. *(Clark Jones/Impact Visuals)*

institutions become the means to construct ethnic communities and identities in the immigrant context. Both religion scholar Raymond Williams and Warner argue that this is particularly the case in the United States because Americans view religion as the most acceptable and nonthreatening basis for community formation and ethnic expression. Immigrant parents also view religion as the best way to transmit their culture and values to their children. For all these reasons, religious organizations become multifunctional institutions in the immigrant context.

AMERICAN HINDU ORGANIZATIONS

Two types of organizations have proliferated among the immigrant Hindu Indian community in the United States, *satsangs* (religious congregations) and *bala-vihars* (child-development organizations). Both satsangs and bala-vihars consist of a group of Hindu families who typically meet once a month. Satsang

groups conduct a *pooja* (worship), generally led by lay leaders and consisting of prayers, chants, the singing of *bhajans* (devotional songs), and frequently also a discussion of Hindu texts. Bala-vihar groups conduct religious education classes for children. Both of these types of organizations are generally based on linguistic background and region of origin in India. Although these two types of organization have become typical in the Hindu Indian community in the United States (and in other overseas communities around the world), both are organizations that do not generally exist in India. Group religious activity is not typical in traditional Hinduism except during temple and village festivals. In India, Hindus worship largely as families or as individuals, in their homes or a temple. However, in the diaspora, there is a tendency for Hindus to adopt "congregational" forms of worship and learning.

The primary reason for Hindu Indian immigrants to adopt congregationalism is the need for community. Immigration generally results in the isolation of the family from relatives and friends. For Indians—

who are the most dispersed ethnic group in the United States—the only way they can meet other Indians on any regular basis is through attending the meetings and functions of religious organizations. One consequence of immigration is that Hindu Indians who were part of the majority group in India are transformed into a minority group in the United States. As nonwhite immigrants and practitioners of a religion and culture that is generally misunderstood and negatively stereotyped in the United States, many Hindu Indians soon feel the need for a support group, both for themselves and for their children.

Two other types of Hindu institutions that are widespread in the United States are temples and pan-Hindu federations or umbrella groups. Although these institutions are prevalent in India, both manifest certain unique features in the United States. Hindu temples have now mushroomed all over this country. One distinctive feature of American Hindu temples is that they tend to be more "ecumenical" than temples in India. In India, many temples are devoted to a single regional deity and the local language is used for rituals and worship. In the United States, however, Hindu temples mostly house only the major Indian deities but also enshrine deities from several, sometimes opposing, traditions. Rituals and worship are generally conducted in Sanskrit and are frequently explained in Hindi or English for the benefit of the eclectic audience. American Hindu temples also perform a range of cultural services that are not performed by temples in India. In the United States, temples become cultural and social centers for Hindu Americans. Satsang and bala-vihar groups frequently meet at the temple. Temples also offer Indian language, music, and dance classes and have a central hall where dance, drama, and music recitals are performed.

Several Hindu umbrella organizations have sprung up in the United States with the goal of uniting, educating, and mobilizing Hindu Indian Americans of different backgrounds in support of Hindu interests. In India, there are two major Hindu umbrella groups—the Vishwa Hindu Parishad (VHP) and the Rashtriya Swayamsevak Sangh (RSS)—and one political party, the Bharatiya Janata Party (BJP), with branches all over the country. In the United States there is a greater number and variety of such groups. In addition to branches of the VHP, a parallel organization to the RSS called the Hindu Swayamsevak Sangh (HSS), and the BJP, there are several regional Hindu groups. In general, such organizations are strong supporters of *Hindutva* (Hinduness), the Hindu nationalist movement that is currently the leading political force in India. Typically, they consist of a small core of dedicated, largely male activists, who try to

disseminate their message through speeches and writings and by organizing meetings, youth programs, and celebrations of Hindu festivals. They also sponsor the visits of Hindutva leaders from India, meet with American public officials to discuss concerns of Indian Americans, and frequently raise money to support causes in India.

In August 1999, under the sponsorship of the VHP of America and several Hindu umbrella organizations, a group of eminent Hindu spiritual leaders from India undertook a nine-day, coast-to-coast pilgrimage across the United States, passing through and holding programs in ten major cities. By all accounts the programs drew thousands in each city and were highly successful in energizing Hindus around the country. Following this pilgrimage, a summit meeting of Hindu spiritual and political leaders was held in Austin, Texas.

Another type of Hindu umbrella organization that has recently developed in the United States is not found in India and is a distinctly diasporic phenomenon. This type of organization has as its goal the defense of Hinduism against defamation, commercialization, and misuse. Hindu deities, icons, and music are not infrequently used in the advertising and entertainment industries in the United States. In the past few years, Hindu watchdog organizations have launched protest campaigns against the Om perfume sold by The Gap stores, a Sony music CD that featured a distorted image of a Hindu deity on its cover, an episode of the Fox television program *The Simpsons* that caricatured the Hindu god Ganesh, an episode of *Xena Warrior Princess* in which Hindu gods were characters, and the use of a verse of the *Bhagavad Gita* (an important Hindu text) as background music during an orgy scene in the film *Eyes Wide Shut*. In all of these instances the groups have been successful in getting the company concerned to issue an apology and in most cases to withdraw or modify the offending product or show.

AMERICAN HINDU PRACTICES AND INTERPRETATIONS

American Hindu practices and interpretations reflect both the adaptations to being immigrants in a non–Hindu country and the attempts to make Hinduism more compatible with American culture and society. As mentioned, Hinduism in India consists of an extraordinary array of diverse interpretations and practices. However, Hindu Indian Americans have taken upon themselves the task of simplifying, standardizing, and codifying the religion to make it easier for their Americanized children to understand. The publications and activities of an umbrella group, the Federation of Hindu Associations (FHA), based in Southern California, provide good examples. The FHA circulates a publication entitled *Hinduism Simplified*. One of the first few pages lists what they claim are the twelve central beliefs of Hindus. The publication also asserts that "the one Hindu holy book containing the essence of Hinduism is the Bhagavad Gita." The caste system, *Hinduism Simplified* states, was never religiously sanctioned by Hinduism and is not central to Hindu practice. Each of these assertions can be challenged by providing examples of Hindu groups whose ideas and practices differ from these interpretations. Over the past few years the organization has been collecting funds to build what they term will be an "Ideal Hindu temple," which will be nonsectarian and in which all the major Hindu deities will be given equal status. This again is an innovation born of the American context. Another good example of the way Hinduism is being formalized in the United States is the *Encyclopedia of Hinduism*, to comprise eighteen volumes, being prepared at the University of South Carolina and sponsored by the India Heritage Research Foundation (based in Pittsburgh). This is the first such encyclopedia, and once completed it is likely to be considered the authoritative word on Hinduism.

Although temples in the United States try to adhere to orthodox practices as far as possible, many modifications have to be made to accommodate to the American context. Thus temples in the United States celebrate new festivals such as graduation day, fathers' day and mothers' day. Religion scholar Vasuda Narayan provides several other examples. She discusses the way that temples adapt the Hindu ritual calendar so that major rituals and festivals are celebrated over the weekend or on other American holidays. Traditional Sanskrit chants are modified and new ones composed that make America sacred as a holy land for Hindus. Narayan also uses examples from a temple on the East Coast to make the point that Hinduism has been used to cater to American popular psychology. Thus this temple sponsored workshops and lectures that used Indian scriptures to examine topics such as "Living in Freedom," "Stress Management," and "Positive Thinking and Living." Again, she says that the temple publications have offered many interpretations of practices and scriptures that fit in with American culture but are not seen in temples in India, such as the tendency to provide symbolic interpretations for Hindu traditions.

There have been some changes in gender practice and the interpretation of traditional Hindu gender images in the American context. In this country, Hindu Indian women's socialization function and their role as "cultural custodians" has greatly increased. Children in India breathe in the values of Hindu life, but in the immigrant situation, the meaning and content of religion and culture have to be explicitly articulated and explained. Much of this task is performed by women at home and at bala vihar classes. Women also play active roles in many satsangs and temples. When women are the primary transmitters of religious and cultural traditions, they are also able to reinterpret the patriarchal images more in their favor. This, together with the fact that such interpretations are made in an American context, has had the result that Hindu norms regarding gender roles and relations are generally accorded more egalitarian interpretations.

As in the case of other immigrant religions, Hinduism in the United States becomes the axis around which Hindu Indian Americans construct community and ethnic identity. The content and meaning of this ethnic identity are explicitly articulated by the Hindu umbrella organizations. They describe Hindu Indian Americans as being the proud descendants of the world's oldest living civilization and religion and counter the negative American image of Hinduism as primitive and bizarre by arguing that, contrary to American stereotypes, Hinduism is very sophisticated and scientific. The "model minority" label is used explicitly by American Hindu leaders, who attribute the success of Indians in the United States to their Hindu religious and cultural heritage which, according to them, makes them adaptable, hard working, and family oriented.

One consequence of Hinduism and Hindu organizations becoming more important in the immigrant context is that many immigrants become susceptible to the appeal of Hindu nationalist leaders, who use the message of Hindu unity and pride to recruit members. That there is a close relationship between the Hindu renaissance that is currently taking place in India and the development of an American Hinduism has frequently been pointed out. Investigations in India and the United States have established that much of the financial resources and support for the Hindutva movement in India comes from Indian Americans.

Many Hindu Indians in America who participate in the activities of Hindu organizations in this country claim that they are "better Hindus here" and "more Indian" than many Indians in India, who they feel, are abandoning their cultural traditions and becoming more "Westernized." American Hindutva organizations similarly see themselves as the torchbearers and guardians of Hindu Indian tradition and values. The FHA position on this is fairly typical. FHA leaders claim that this is because Indians living outside India are able to understand India and India's problems more clearly. They also point out that Indians in the United States have greater resources (including access to modern communications) and power than Indians in any other part of the world and thus have the responsibility to use them to further the cause of Hinduism. They claim that they want to develop a model for Hindu pride, unity, and activism through their organization and then export the model back to India. In their speeches and advertisements, the FHA stresses the need for American Hindus to be more aggressive about defending and disseminating Hinduism.

Thus, in a variety of ways, Hindu Indian Americans are reinterpreting and restructuring Hindu theology and practice. Because this group wields considerable influence among the leadership and masses in India and within the global Hindu community, these interpretations and practices are being transmitted to India and around the world through the mass media and the Internet. Undoubtedly, then, American Hindus will shape the face of global Hinduism in the next century.

Prema Ann Kurien

See also: Arts III: Visual and Religious Arts (Part II, Sec. 10); English-Speaking Caribbean (Part III, Sec. 2); South Asia (Part III, Sec. 3).

BIBLIOGRAPHY

Anderson, Benedict. "Long Distance Nationalism." In *The Spectre of Comparisons: Nationalism, Southeast Asia and the World*, ed. Benedict Anderson. London: Verso, 1998.

Benei, Veronique. "Hinduism Today: Inventing a Universal Religion?" *South Asia Research* 18:2 (1998): 117–24.

Federation of Hindu Associations. *Hinduism Simplified*. Diamond Bar, CA: FHA, n.d.

———. *Directory of Temples and Associations of Southern California and Everything You Wanted to Know about Hinduism*. Artesia, CA: FHA, 1995.

———. "How to Be a Good Hindu" full-page advertisement. *India Post*, July 25, 1997, A15.

———. "A Call for Dharma Raksha" full-page advertisement. *India Post*, August 8, 1997, A15.

———. "To Our Hindu Youth" full-page advertisement. *India Post*, August 15, 1997, A 51.

Ghosh, Ajay. 1999. "Dharma Prasar Yatra Ends in Whippany, NJ." *India Post*, August 27, 1999, 26.

"Hindu Philosophy Has No Place for Caste System Says FHA." *India Post*, March 17, 1995, A6.

Kurien, Prema Ann. "Becoming American by Becoming Hindu: Indian Americans Take Their Place at the Multi-cultural Table." In *Gatherings in Diaspora: Religious Communities and the New Immigration*, ed. R. Stephen Warner and Judith G. Wittner, 37–70. Philadelphia, PA: Temple University Press, 1998.

———. "Gendered Ethnicity: Creating a Hindu Indian Identity in the U.S." *American Behavioral Scientist* 42:4 (1999): 648–70.

———. "Constructing 'Indianness' in the United States and India: The Role of Hindu and Muslim Indian Immigrants in Southern California." In *Asian and Latino Immigrants in a Restructuring Economy: The Metamorphosis of Los Angeles*, ed. Marta Lopez-Garza and David R. Diaz. Palo Alto, CA: Stanford University Press, 2001.

———. "We Are Better Hindus Here—Religion and Ethnicity among Indian Americans." In *Building Faith Communities: Asian Immigrants and Religions*, ed. Jung Ha Kim and Pyong Gap Min. Walnut Creek, CA: Altamira Press, in press.

Leonard, Karen Isaksen. *Making Ethnic Choices: California's Punjabi Mexican Americans*. Philadelphia: Temple University Press, 1992.

McKean, Lise. *Divine Enterprise: Gurus and the Hindu Nationalist Movement*. Chicago: University of Chicago Press, 1996.

Narayan, Vasuda. "Creating the South Indian 'Hindu' Experience in the United States." In *A Sacred Thread: Modern Transmission of Hindu Traditions in India and Abroad*, ed. Raymond Williams, 147–76. Chambersburg, PA: Anima Press, 1992.

Prashad, Vijay, "Culture Vultures." *Communalism Combat*, February 1997.

Portes, Alejandro, and Ruben Rumbaut. *Immigrant America: A Portrait*. Berkeley: University of California Press, 1990.

Rajagopal, Arvind. "Better Hindu Than Black? Narratives of Asian Indian Identity." Presented at the annual meetings of the Society for the Scientific Study of Religion and the Religious Research Association, St. Louis, MO, 1995.

Seshagiri Rao, K. L. "Encyclopedia of Hinduism: Questions and Answers." *India Post*, August 27, 1999, p. 38.

Smith, Timothy. "Religion and Ethnicity in America." *American Historical Review* 83 (December 1 (1978), pp.1155–85.

Warner, Stephen. "Work in Progress toward a New Paradigm for the Sociological Study of Religion in the United States." *American Journal of Sociology* 98 (March 1993). pp. 1047–1193.

Williams, Raymond. *Religions of Immigrants from India and Pakistan: New Threads in the American Tapestry*. Cambridge, UK: Cambridge University Press, 1988.

———. "Sacred Threads of Several Textures." In *A Sacred Thread: Modern Transmission of Hindu Traditions in India and Abroad*, ed. Raymond Williams, 228–57. Chambersburg, PA: Anima Press.

$\mathcal{I}$SLAM

Islam is one of the three major Western religions, along with Judaism and Christianity. And like Judaism and Christianity, Islam is a monotheistic faith. The word "Islam" in Arabic means "submission," as in submission or surrender to the will of an all-powerful God, known as Allah. Muslims, as practitioners of the faith are known, accept the Old and New Testaments as holy scripture (although they believe that Christ is a prophet, not the son of God) but believe that God's latest word was revealed to Muhammad in the seventh century C.E. (common era, also known in the West as A.D.) and was written down in the holy book of the Koran. Thus, as the latest revelation, the Koran is the final and definitive word of God.

PILLARS OF ISLAM

Islam is based on five "pillars" or precepts: *shahadah* (witness); *salat* (prayer); *zakat* (alms for the less privileged); *sawm* (fasting); and *hajj* (pilgrimage). First and foremost is witness, the acceptance of Allah as the one, true God and Muhammad as His prophet (a discussion of Muhammad and his revelations follows below). Every Muslim opens his or her prayers with the words, "There is only one God, Allah, and Muhammad is His prophet."

Muslims are required to stop all their activities five times per day, prostrate themselves on the ground, facing Mecca (a city on the Arabian Peninsula, now Saudi Arabia, where the word of Allah was revealed to Muhammad), and pray to Allah. The third precept, alms, requires Muslims to help the poor and the less fortunate at every opportunity. Specifically, it requires practitioners of the faith to give 2.5 percent of their wealth to charity every year.

Fasting represents the fourth precept and is practiced during the holy month of Ramadan, the ninth month of the Islamic calendar, when Allah revealed His word to Muhammad. (As the Islamic calendar is a lunar one, Ramadan shifts across the Western calendar, which is based on a solar year.) During Ramadan, Muslims do not eat from sunrise to sunset, although exemptions are made for those who are sick, the elderly, and those who are traveling (though the latter must make up the days later).

Finally, there is the precept of the pilgrimage. At least once in the course of their life, all Muslims are expected to make a pilgrimage to Mecca, providing they have the financial means to do so. Once a difficult and even dangerous journey, the rigors of the hajj have been eased significantly in recent decades by the development of jet travel; today, several million Muslims travel to Mecca each year. There, they engage in a series of rituals over the course of five days that reaffirm their faith and connect them to the larger *umma*, or Islamic community.

ISLAMIC THOUGHT AND PRACTICE

Like Judaism and Christianity, Islam is based on the revealed word of God. But it differs significantly especially from Christianity, in the emphasis it places on different parts of that message. While Christianity places a greater emphasis on achieving grace—that is, a way into heaven—Islam, like Judaism, emphasizes right and moral living in this world. (Naturally, this dichotomy oversimplifies things; Islam speaks of heaven and ways to get there, just as Christianity offers moral precepts. The point here is tendencies, not absolutes.)

Indeed, Islam possesses an elaborate body of law and political theory largely absent from Christian thought. Some of this law is laid out in the Koran, but most of it derives from the *sharia*, a body of thought

At the start of the holy season of Ramadan, Middle Eastern immigrant girls learn their Islamic prayers from a teacher in Kansas City, Missouri. *(Jeffry D. Scott/Impact Visuals)*

that comes in part from the Koran but also from the sayings of Muhammad and the early interpretations of sayings and actions of the Prophet made by Islamic scholars. The sayings and actions of the Prophet are known as the Sunna, and they are recorded in the Books of the Hadith. These provide a guide to right living for all Muslims, but they are not the word of God, which is confined to the Koran alone. The Koran, itself, is divided into verses, or *suras*.

Other important Muslim concepts include community, equality, justice, and toleration. The umma, as noted above, refers to the Islamic community. More than anything else, Islam emphasizes the equality of believers, all equally in Islam, or submission, to Allah. In fact, Islam divides the world into two parts, or "houses"—the "house of peace," where Islam predominates, and the "house of war," where it does not. Because Islam places such an emphasis on law and political theory, it also concerns itself deeply with questions of justice. Originating in the tribal milieu of medieval Arabia—where blood feuds predominated—

Islam emphasized justice over vengeance. Muslims also believe that Islam is an inherently tolerant faith and the historical record bears this out to a degree. While European Christians of the Middle Ages persecuted Muslims and Jews mercilessly, Islam offered them a protected, if secondary, status within society. Known as *dhimmi*, or fellow people of the "book" (that is, also believing in the revealed word of God), Christians and Jews could go about their business, so long as they did not proselytize and did not object to a special tax.

Finally, a word should be said about one of the most controversial—as least to non-Muslims—aspects of Islam: *jihad*, which in Arabic means "struggle." As in English, that word has a variety of meanings. On the grandest scale, *jihad* refers to the struggle between the Islamic and non-Islamic worlds. And all Muslims—like Christians—are reminded that their duty to God includes spreading the faith. But *jihad* can also be interpreted in personal terms, as the struggle each believer undergoes within his or her own soul to live by the word of God and the teachings of the Prophet.

HISTORY OF ISLAM

As noted above, Islam was born in Mecca, a trading city on the Arabian Peninsula, in the seventh century C.E. There, a wealthy merchant named Muhammad—a deeply spiritual man by all accounts—used to go off to meditate in nearby caves. In 610 C.E., Allah—always referred to as "the Compassionate and the Merciful"—revealed His word to Muhammad through the Angel Gabriel. Muhammad returned to Mecca and converted a few followers, including his wife. As the community of believers grew, it attracted the hostile opposition of the established pagan priests of the city. In 621, Muhammad fled to Jerusalem and there, where the current Dome of the Rock mosque now stands, ascended to heaven and received a vision from the prophets of the Old and New Testaments.

Muhammad then returned to Mecca, but the persecution of the Muslims continued. In 622, they fled to the nearby city of Medina, now the second holiest city of Islam. The Muslim calendar dates from this exodus, or *hejira*. Thus, the year 2000 C.E. is 1379 in the Islamic calendar. In Medina, the Islamic umma continued to grow and expand, so that by the end of the Prophet's life in 632, most of the Arab tribes of the peninsula had been converted. Within the next 100 years, the religion spread westward—both by conquest and proselytizing—across the Middle East and North Africa and into the Iberian Peninsula. Eastward it encompassed Persia and northern India. Over the coming centuries, it would continue to grow—largely through trading networks—to Southeast Asia and West and East Africa. The Turks, themselves converts to Islam, would bring it to southeastern Europe.

Efforts to halt the spread of Islam were largely futile. The Christian Crusades of the early part of the last millennium to reconquer the Holy Land, for example, did not last. Only in western Europe was Islam stopped at Poitiers (France) in 732 and then rolled back from the Iberian Peninsula between the eighth and fifteenth centuries. Then, after 1500, the tide turned against Islam. Between the 1400s and the early part of the twentieth century, Europeans would conquer most of the Islamic world. But while the rise of European imperialism after 1500 would see much of the Islamic world subjugated, the Europeans, through the construction of modern transportation, would also help in the expansion of Islam into remoter areas of

Table 1	
Islamic Nations	
Predominantly Islamic nations	Large Islamic minority
Afghanistan*	Armenia*
Albania*	Benin
Algeria	Bulgaria
Azerbaijan	Canada
Bahrain	Central African Republic
Bangladesh*	China
Bosnia-Herzegovina*	Côte d'Ivoire
Brunei	Cyprus
Burkina Faso	Eritrea
Chad	Ethiopia
Comoros	Fiji
Djibouti	France
Egypt*	Gambia
Indonesia	Georgia
Iran*	Germany
Iraq*	Ghana
Jordan*	Guinea
Kazakhstan	Guinea-Bissau
Kuwait	Holland
Kyrgizstan	India*
Lebanon*	Kenya
Libya	Liberia*
Malaysia	Mozambique
Mali	Nigeria*
Mauritania	Philippines
Morocco	Russia*
Niger	Senegal*
Oman	Serbia*
Pakistan*	Sierra Leone
Palestine*	Sweden
Qatar	Tanzania
Saudi Arabia	Togo
Somalia	Trinidad*
Sudan	Uganda
Syria*	United Kingdom
Tadjikhistan	United States
Tunisia	
Turkey*	
United Arab Emirates	
Uzbekistan	
Western Sahara	
Yemen*	

*Significant immigration to United States.
Source: Central Intelligence Agency. *The World Factbook, 1999–2000.* Washington, DC: Brassey's, 1999.

Africa and, through the use of Muslim indentured servants, to the Caribbean (Trinidad) and the South Pacific (Fiji). Eventually, like most of the non-European areas of the globe, the Islamic world would throw off the rule of the imperialists in the twentieth century. Today, there remains a strong mistrust among Muslims for the West, caused partly by the Crusades, partly by imperialism, and partly by Western support for the creation of Israel.

Currently, there are roughly 1 billion practitioners of various forms of Islam. The largest predominantly Islamic country in the world is Indonesia with about 180 million people, followed by Pakistan with about 135 million people and Bangladesh with around 125 million. But the heart of the Islamic world is the Middle East, the region in which Islam was born. Other areas of the world in which Islam predominates are North Africa and Central Asia. Significant Muslim minorities also exist in Southeast Asia, West and East Africa, and the Balkans region of southeastern Europe. These are all traditional areas of Muslim dominance or presence, dating back at least 500 years. In addition, postcolonial-era immigration patterns over the past forty or so years have brought millions of Muslims to Western Europe and North America.

MUSLIM IMMIGRATION TO AMERICA

For most of U.S. history before the post-1965 immigration reform era, Muslims were rare among immigrants. There were several reasons for this. First, America was a largely Christian country that neither welcomed Muslims nor seemed particularly welcoming to Muslims. Indeed, the one Muslim area of the world that sent large numbers of immigrants to the United States in the late nineteenth and early twentieth centuries—the Levant, or eastern Mediterranean region that is now Syria and Lebanon—did not send Muslims. That is to say, the vast majority of immigrants from this region were part of the Christian minority. With the passage of U.S. immigration quota laws in 1921 and 1924, few openings were set aside for people from Islamic regions of the world.

A second reason for the lack of Muslim immigrants to America was that most of them in the nineteenth century and early twentieth centuries lived within the spheres of European empires. Those few who decided—or were permitted by their colonizer—to emigrate to Christian countries were likely to make their way to the country that had colonized them, as was the case with Algerians to France, for example.

Finally, there were economic factors. Economic change rather than poverty has always been the main economic cause of immigration. Much of the Islamic world was economically stagnant and backward in the nineteenth and early twentieth centuries, with few of the modernizing disruptions that sent, for example, large numbers of southern and eastern Europeans to North America. And those parts that were modernizing were doing so under the control of European imperialists, who preferred to keep the population available to work on European-controlled plantations.

But the post–World War II era witnessed three significant developments that would spur Muslim immigration to the United States. First, there was the end of European political domination. With the ebbing of imperialism, Islamic countries came under the rule of indigenous governments that could make policy based on the needs of those countries rather than the needs of the colonizers. Second, the postwar era saw the spread of economic modernization, in the form of capitalist development in some countries and as part of socialistic planning in others. In either case, modernization disrupted traditional economies, particularly in rural areas, sending millions of peasants to local urban areas and then abroad. Most immigrants from a Muslim country first went to the European country that had colonized them—Pakistanis to the United Kingdom, North Africans to France, Indonesians to Holland.

Then came the U.S. Immigration and Nationality Act of 1965. The law contained two key provisions—one with an immediate effect and the other with a delayed but cumulative effect—that helped open the gates to immigrants from Islamic countries. The provision with the immediate effect was the end to national quotas. Under the 1924 quota law, the United States allowed in emigrants from a given country at the following annual rate: 2 percent of the number from that country already living in the United States in 1880. Since almost no persons from Islamic states lived in the United States before 1880, this rule effectively barred all immigration from those countries. The second and more delayed effect was the provision within the 1965 law that emphasized family unification. As more immigrants came in from Islamic countries, more family members back home became eligible for immigration. And because many Islamic societies—like almost all rural and economically underdeveloped societies—consist of large families, this had the effect of accelerating rates of immigration from Islamic countries over the past several decades. Today, it is estimated that between 6 and 8 million Muslims live in the United States, making them the

Table 2
Immigration to the United States from Predominantly Islamic Nations

Nation	1981–1990	1991–1996
Afghanistan	26,600	12,600
Azerbaijan	NA	3,900*
Bangladesh	15,200	35,400
Egypt	31,400	27,900
Iran	154,800	79,400
Iraq	19,600	26,800
Jordan	32,600	25,000
Lebanon	41,600	29,900
Pakistan	61,300	70,500
Syria	20,600	16,600
Turkey	20,900	15,700
Uzbekistan	NA	8,300*

*1995–96
Source: Census Bureau. *Statistical Abstract of the United States, 1998*. Washington, DC: Census Bureau, 1999.

largest non-Christian group in the country, slightly more numerous than Jews.

KEY ISLAMIC IMMIGRANT GROUPS IN THE UNITED STATES BY NATION

BANGLADESH

One of the most crowded (2,300 persons per square mile) and impoverished ($1,130 per capita income in 2000) countries in the world, Bangladesh is situated in the northeastern corner of the Indian subcontinent. The nation was founded in 1971, when East Pakistan broke away from the rest of the country amid a bloody civil war. (Bangladesh represents the Muslim half of the Bengali-speaking community of the subcontinent. Hindu Bengalis largely live in the Indian state of West Bengal.) Most Bengalis—both from Bangladesh and from West Bengal—tend to immigrate to the United Kingdom, which ruled over them from the 1700s through 1947. Bengal was one of the first areas colonized by the British in the subcontinent of India. Many Muslim Bengalis also immigrate to the oil-rich countries of the Middle East, where they work largely as construction workers and domestic servants.

According to the Census Bureau, approximately fifty thousand Bangladeshis immigrated to the United States between 1980 and 1996. Unofficial estimates put the total Bangladeshi population within the United States at between 100,000 and 150,000, with as many as half of them living in the New York City metropolitan area. Most legal Bangladeshi immigrants are well educated, particularly the men, who have an average fourteen years of schooling. Many of them, however, are forced to take jobs below their skill levels, with taxi driving a common occupation for New York Bangladeshis.

EGYPT

The most populous nation in the Arabic world (65 million), Egypt is also one of the most impoverished ($2,760 per capita income) and, despite its vast area (387,000 square miles), crowded—the vast majority of its people live in the narrow fertile belt of the Nile valley. Most Egyptians are Islamic (about 95 percent), with the remaining 5 percent largely consisting of Christian Copts, who make up a far bigger proportion of the Egyptian immigrant population in the United States. Egyptian immigration to the United States before 1965 was dominated by Copts. Since 1965, the Muslim contingent has predominated.

According to the U.S. census, approximately 78,000 people living in the United States in 1990 said that they were of Egyptian ancestry. Between 1989 and 1996, roughly 59,000 Egyptians entered the United States legally, with the rate increasing over the years. While an average of about 3,000 Egyptians entered the United States legally during each year of the 1980s, that figure climbed to about 4,000 annually between 1990 and 1994. Over 5,000 and over 6,000 came to the United States in 1995 and 1996, respectively. Most Egyptians have settled in major metropolitan areas, with the largest populations in Chicago, Los Angeles, New York City, and Washington, D.C.

IRAN

Iran is a vast country in Central Asia, situated just to the east of the Arab Middle East. It has a population of just under 70 million and ranks in the middle tier of nations economically with a per capita income of $4,700 annually. While the country is predominantly Islamic (with a tiny minority of Baha'is and Jews), it is ethnically quite mixed, with the dominant Persian ethnic and linguistic group accounting for barely over 50 percent of the population. Other significant minorities include Azeris and Kurds. The vast majority of Iranians follow Shiite Islam, which broke off from the dominant Sunni branch of the religion over 1,000 years ago. Many Shiites see themselves as looked down upon by Sunnis as deviationists and even heretics.

Until 1979, Iran was ruled by the Shah, who emphasized secularism and economic modernization. But the Shah's rule was also marked by gross human rights violations and great inequalities in wealth. During the 1970s, unrest in the country grew, with millions rallying around the Shiite leader the Ayatollah Khomeini. In 1979, the Shah was overthrown and Khomeini came to power. At that point, tens of thousands of Iranians who were associated with the Shah's government or who simply did not want to live in an Islamic state fled the country. Many came to the United States, which had been the main foreign backer of the Shah's government. Thus, most Iranians in the United States are not particularly scrupulous in their practice of Islam.

According to the Census Bureau, roughly 235,000 persons in the United States in 1990 said that they had Iranian ancestry. Between 1981 and 1990, just over 150,000 Iranians immigrated to the United States legally. These have been augmented by another 80,000 between 1990 and 1996. The vast majority of Iranians in the United States live in California, mostly in the Los Angeles metropolitan area, though significant Iranian communities exist in Texas and New York.

PAKISTAN

Among the most populous (135 million) and impoverished nations in the world ($2,100 in per capita income), Pakistan is located in the northwestern part of the Indian subcontinent. The country was established in 1947, when independence came to all British India. Originally, the entire subcontinent was supposed to be united in a single country. But the region's Muslims—fearful of being subjugated by the Hindu majority—insisted on a nation of their own. The result was Pakistan, divided into a western and an eastern half. In 1971, East Pakistan broke away violently to form the independent nation of Bangladesh. While Pakistan is a predominantly Muslim nation, like India it consists of numerous ethnic and linguistic groups, although Urdu-speaking people predominate.

Like their former compatriots from Bangladesh, most Pakistanis tend to immigrate to the United Kingdom, the former colonial ruler of the country. Still, increasing numbers are making their way to the United States, many of them highly educated. During the 1980s, roughly 61,000 Pakistanis legally entered

the United States, and the pace has picked up in the 1990s, with more than 70,000 coming between 1990 and 1996 alone. Most Pakistanis have settled in such major metropolitan areas as Chicago, Los Angeles, New York, and San Francisco. Three states—New York (with 19.2 percent of all Pakistanis in the United States), California (17.7 percent), and Illinois (11.2 percent)—contain nearly half the total Pakistani population in the United States.

Islamic immigration is a relatively recent phenomenon in the United States. But it is a growing one, as the numbers for just these few countries indicate. Indeed, Islam is the fastest growing religion in the United States, as the numerous mosques being erected in cities around the country attest. Already, this growing Islamic population is having an effect on the nation's culture and society. Imams, or Islamic religious figures, are becoming increasingly important spokespersons in communities large and small. The political impact of the rapidly expanding Islamic population has yet to be felt, but it certainly will be in coming years. Still, how it will affect United States policy—particularly toward the Middle East and the Israeli-Palestinian question—remains uncertain.

Daniel James

See also: Immigration to Western Europe (Part II, Sec. 13); East Africa, North Africa (Part III, Sec. 1); Iran, Middle East, South Asia (Part III, Sec. 3).

BIBLIOGRAPHY

Barakat, Halim. *The Arab World: Society, Culture, and State.* Berkeley, CA: University of California Press, 1993.

Bozorgmehr, Mehdi, and George Sabagh. "High Status Immigrants: A Statistical Profile of Iranians in the United States." *Iranian Studies* 21:3–4 (1988): 4–34.

Bureau of the Census. *Statistical Abstract of the United States, 1998.* Washington, DC: Bureau of the Census, 1999.

Haddad, Yvonne Yazbeck. *The Muslims of America.* New York: Oxford University Press, 1991.

Novak, J. J. *Bangladesh: Reflections on the Water.* Bloomington: Indiana University Press, 1993.

Sayyid-Marsot, A. L. *A Short History of Modern Egypt.* New York: Cambridge University Press, 1985.

Williams, R. B. *Religions of Immigrants from India and Pakistan: New Threads in the American Tapestry.* New York: Cambridge University Press, 1988.

*J*UDAISM

*T*raditional Judaism is founded on belief that the laws of the Torah, given by God to Moses as 2 million Jews watched at Mount Sinai, are forever binding. From the year 2448, when the Torah was given, or 1213 B.C.E., the terms of what its laws are, who has the authority to establish in what way they be kept, and what it means to be a "believing Jew" have been under debate. Migrating from Israel to what is now Italy, Iran, Iraq, North Africa, and later to western Europe in the centuries starting before the common era, Jews became not only a religious group but also an ethnic and national "other" inhabiting dozens of countries. In the different regions in which Jews lived, practice of the same laws acquired different aspects; Jewish religious observance was flavored by the general culture in each place. Nevertheless, the body of laws remained largely the same.

At the same time as the Americas were becoming the focus of mercantile and colonization interests, profound changes were occurring within the Jewish world. The medieval European Jew, whose horizons extended little beyond the Jewish quarter of his or her city, and whose learning was restricted to Jewish subjects, Torah and Talmud, whose economic interests were confined to trade or mercantile pursuits, was seeing new possibilities open before him. In small numbers, Jews were being admitted to universities. As America began its nationhood, modernity was sweeping through Jewish communities of western Europe. Especially in Germany, Jews would begin to learn secular subjects, become fluent in the language of their birthplace, and become part of its general culture, encouraging secular governments to accord Jews the rights of citizenship.

EARLY JEWISH IMMIGRATION

When the first colonists in New England, members of radical Protestant sects, arrived on American shores, they were eager to meet Native Americans. They believed them to be of the "ten lost tribes," the tribes who lived in the northern provinces of ancient Israel and were "lost" after the destruction of the first temple, when they went into exile and were not heard of by the rest of the world. Some Puritan clergymen approached the natives speaking Hebrew, expecting it to be their tongue. They looked forward to consulting them on original meanings of biblical texts.

In reality, the first Jews in America landed in New Amsterdam in 1654. They were a group of twenty-three, originally from Holland, who had made their home in Recife, Brazil, while that province was owned by the Dutch. These Dutch Jews' parents had, in turn, come from Portugal and before that perhaps from Spain, where Jews had lived since the fourth century. Thus, they were called Sephardic Jews, Jews from the Iberian Peninsula, North Africa, Iran, and Iraq (from the Hebrew word for Spain, *Sefarad*). Many of their prayers and customs differ from those of Ashkenazim, Jews hailing from Germany and eastern Europe. When the Jews were forcibly converted to Christianity in Portugal in 1497, the ancestors of the first twenty-three Jews became *conversos*, those who converted outwardly while retaining a loyalty to Judaism in their hearts, disparagingly called *marranos* (swine) by the Spanish and Portuguese. Thus, the original twenty-three were Jews who had maintained their observance of the commandments and their identity as Jews in the face of adversity, loss of finances, and loss of homeland. They established Congregation Sheirith Israel in New York in the Sephardic rite.

The first five synagogues established in America were in Newport, Rhode Island; New York, New York; Charleston, South Carolina; Savannah, Georgia; and Philadelphia, Pennsylvania. They all followed the Sephardic rite, even though from the

Rabbi Shimon Hecht, a descendant of Jewish immigrants, celebrates the opening of a new synagogue in the Park Slope section of Brooklyn. *(Rommel Pecson/Impact Visuals)*

earliest times, Ashkenazim outnumbered Sephardim in America. The first Ashkenazic synagogue would not be established until 1825 in New York. There was a sense that the Sephardic rite must be the "American rite."

It was difficult for the fledgling Jewish communities across America to sustain themselves religiously. Jewish practice was a challenge: rabbis had to be imported, as did *shochtim*, ritual slaughterers to provide kosher meat and religious articles required for observance. In the early days of America, the small Jewish communities faced the challenge that later waves of immigrants would face as well: the attractive pull of American culture. Greater tolerance in America than Jews experienced in most of Europe allowed them to become part of the general culture and life. The earliest Jewish settlers intermarried, were educated in American schools, and came to think of themselves as Americans. The smallness of their communities made integration desirable to them.

NINETEENTH-CENTURY JEWISH IMMIGRATION

As America became a nation, Jews desirous of equality under the law and economic opportunity trickled to the shores of America. In the mid-nineteenth century they founded mostly Reform congregations. Reform Judaism began in the second decade of the nineteenth century in Germany with a group of men who wished to make what they viewed as certain improvements in the Jewish community. They wanted to improve the image of the Jew in the eyes of non-Jews. They valued secular learning. Instead of being cloistered in small, insular communities, they wished to be part of the common culture—to attend university, to engage in academic and professional pursuits. As a means to this end, they sought to reform the Jewish community: to make synagogue services more dignified with organ music and many prayers in the vernacular. Orthodox prayer services, with worshipers calling out responses to the cantor and proceeding each at his own pace rather than in unison, were, to their mind, "unruly and caused them to be despised by their German neighbors, who loved order and decorum." They largely omitted reference to return to the Jewish homeland and the coming of the Messiah, central to traditional prayers, in order not to be accused of dual loyalty. They aimed to be considered Germans of the most loyal ilk, though of the Mosaic tradition. They rejected many of the observances that made Jews seem different from their non-Jewish neighbors: the requirement to eat only kosher food, the traditional Jewish garb and head covering, and the prayer services held completely in Hebrew, a language many of them understood imperfectly. All this would facilitate acceptance into German society.

America was not a country to which the more traditional minded came. The immigrants were able to rise socially, blending well into the American milieu; they sought to appear not as "foreigners," as Jews had always been classed in Europe, but to blend in indistinguishably as Americans. Trends at work in Europe helped shape America. Jewish immigration from Germany increased in the 1830s and 1840s. Other German Jews had supported the liberal, unsuccessful German revolution in 1848 and had to leave after it failed. They were successful in business in America, rising socially and financially. They went west. By the mid-nineteenth century, there were several Jewish communities in California. Between 1850 and 1860, the Jewish population in America rose from 50,000 to 150,000.

Political conditions worsened for the Jews in eastern Europe toward the end of the century. This would prepare the ground for the "great waves" of Jewish immigration. The first such wave of Jewish immigration began in the 1880s. It would steadily increase, with the peak year being 1888 and then 1914, due to World War I. The Jews who came from eastern Europe, mostly Russia and Poland, as well as Lithuania and the Baltic states, not only prayed differently from their Reform and now American brethren but also looked different. The overwhelming majority were devout in religious practice and were dressed in eastern European Jewish garb: long coats, earlocks, hats; the women wore wigs, as married Jewish women are commanded to cover their heads. They were from rural villages or from the Jewish quarters of cities where they had led lives in which they intermingled only minimally with non-Jews. They had a Jewish education and perhaps a rudimentary secular education in Polish or Russian, but nothing beyond that. They believed in the coming of the Messiah. They believed that Jewish observances were binding whether in Eu-

rope or America. Disembarking in such American cities as Boston, Chicago, and, overwhelmingly, New York, some were sick from the months-long ocean voyage. Families were poor and came with many children. They did not speak English. Their mannerisms were not the polite western European ones that appealed to Americans, nor were they accepted with open arms by their Americanized Jewish brethren, who thought they presented a negative image of Jews to America.

With the great waves of immigration, Orthodox Judaism became ensconced in America. Dozens of Orthodox Ashkenazic and Hasidic rite synagogues joined the few already in existence. The Orthodox houses of worship sprang up in the areas of cities with dense immigrant populations. These *shteiblach* functioned like the traditional eastern European model and like that model it also served as a *beit midrash*: a place for men to learn Jewish texts. But in America, it remained open late so that Jewish workers, after a long day of work in the textile mills or the garment factories, could study. It was open from very early in the morning, for those who wanted to begin morning prayers before sunrise, until late, for those who wanted to pray into the night. The beit midrash was a place of congregation: the poor could come to collect funds; communal announcements were made.

Despite the devout observance of the majority of eastern European immigrants, their children assimilated quickly. At the turn of the century, becoming American meant becoming less Jewish. Synagogues drew immigrants who earned better salaries and could build grand buildings and support their houses of prayer. Yet at the same time the religious observance of their children decreased. Public schools and universities showed them that they could excel in the secular and professional world. They could attend college in the United States and be accepted (some anti-Semitism notwithstanding) in the American world. This was an attractive prospect.

Hebrew Union College, the Reform rabbinical seminary, was founded in Cincinnati in 1875. The Jewish Theological Seminary was founded in 1886 in New York to train rabbis of all denominations but quickly became associated with the Conservative movement. Its president, Solomon Schechter, would be credited with forming the character of this movement in America. Conservative Judaism would, by the mid-twentieth century, become the branch of Judaism with the most adherents. It was a comfortable synthesis of Americanism and Jewish tradition.

Several movements, led by Orthodox elements concerned with the loss of Jewish practice among the young, sprang up to address the challenge present for youth who wanted to take part in American life while finding meaning in their religion. The Young Israel movement began in the 1920s with one Orthodox synagogue on Manhattan's Lower East Side. There, young people were involved in leading the prayer service. The cultural divide had grown too great between them and the older men who led services in most synagogues for them to feel that the same tradition could hold meaning for both. With their synagogue under their own leadership, American Jewish young men could give old traditions meaning in their new American lives. This notion formed the backbone of what became known as "modern Orthodoxy," which incorporates modern ideas, thought, and education into an observant and active Jewish life.

Conservative Judaism became "American Judaism," as the majority of congregations adopted this form. Jewish Community Centers and Hebrew schools formed for Americans a Judaism by which they could live. Conservative Judaism was the ideological child of positive-historical Judaism, an idea put forth by Zacharias Frankel in nineteenth-century Germany. Frankel called for retaining the traditions that the Jewish masses had always held dear—holidays, time-honored prayers, use of Hebrew in prayers, the Sabbath—while adapting dogma and theology to the modern world. American lifestyle lent itself to this type of Judaism: Jews lived in suburbs rather than in thickly Jewish neighborhoods congregated around a synagogue. They could not observe the prohibition to refrain from driving on Saturday. Attending a Conservative synagogue, they were permitted to drive there. They socialized with non-Jewish friends and coworkers and were permitted to eat nonkosher food with them and enjoy wine together, prohibited by traditional Judaism. At the same time, they held dear many traditions and believed it important to marry within the Jewish fold.

Orthodox Judaism was embodied in America in a scattering of synagogues, mostly in large cities. Yeshiva Rabbi Isaac Elchonon in New York City became the premier seminary for Orthodox rabbis. It later became a university, Yeshiva University, based on the motto "Torah U'Mada," that the learning of Jewish subjects should be combined with worldly knowledge of sciences, liberal arts, and the professions but still regarded as most important. Other yeshivas that did not believe university education to be important but favored full-time immersion in the Torah and Talmud imitated Isaac Elchonon, creating a base of intensive Jewish scholarship in America.

Orthodox Judaism's ranks would swell as refugees from the Second World War made their homes on American soil. Settling in New York and other large cities, they changed the face of American Judaism in these locales. Within two decades, they built hundreds of yeshivas that tried to retain the character and mission of European yeshivas. In the past half a century, these yeshivas offered from high school to postgraduate programs to tens of thousands of students. After the Second World War, the first large numbers of Hassidim came to America. Hasidim, the followers of a movement begun in eighteenth-century Russia and Poland, believe in the study of Cabala, stressing the worship of God out of love and joy, dancing, and singing. They venerate the person of the rebbe as a conduit to God. Through studying his teachings and spending time in his holy presence, Hasidim believe, they become better Jews, which is their chief goal. The Hasidic leader, in turn, cares for his flock's temporal and spiritual needs, giving advice on business and childrearing as well as on devotions. In America, Hasidim were the most staunch in insulating themselves from American culture, which they feel would dilute their Jewish ideology and values. Dressing in European garb, much of it dating from the eighteenth century, and discouraging higher secular education and social interaction with non-Jews, they congregated in insulated neighborhoods that would help them preserve, as much as possible, the lifestyle they considered closest to what God intended.

RECENT JEWISH IMMIGRATION

The most recent wave of Jewish immigration has come full circle since the turn of the century. Since immigration started from the Soviet Union in the 1970s, eighty-two years since the peak year of immigration from Russia to this country, it has grown enormously. It climaxed in the early 1990s, when permission to leave the former Soviet Union became easier to attain. This group of Jews came to America with a unique Jewish experience, the absence of tradition. The Soviet education system and the culture had tried to ensure that Jews would not learn about their religion or traditions. The immigrants came to America without knowledge of their heritage but with a strong Jewish identity.

The American Jewish community responded to the Russian immigration in ways that are both similar and dissimilar to the response from earlier in the century. Myriad educational apparatuses sprang up in the major areas of settlement. Funded by Jewish organizations, classes taught the Russian émigrés about their religion while teaching them the English language and helping them find jobs in America. Prayer groups led in Russian, elementary classes in Hebrew language for Russian speakers, communal Passover seders and other holiday events, and even yeshivas geared toward admitting Russian Jewish children became numerous.

The intensity of the Orthodox feeling of responsibility for Russian Jews' spirituality was part of a larger movement in American Jewish life—the Return movement. From the 1960s on, the trend toward assimilation seemed, for small numbers, to turn in the opposite direction. People whose parents or grandparents had rejected Jewish observance were seeking to know more about their heritage and, some, to become Orthodox Jews. Jewish organizations and individuals responded, setting about establishing "outreach" classes, seminars, and schools. Chabad Lubavitch, a group of Hasidim based in Crown Heights, Brooklyn, had been undertaking to involve their estranged coreligionists in *mitzvoth* since the 1950s, but the movement took on larger proportions as it became the sole focus of dozens of organizations. The real numbers of assimilated Jews who became observant is hard to estimate, but the spirit of thousands of returnees seeking Judaism for its spiritual fulfillment fed feelings of ascendancy within the Orthodox ranks. Not only was it possible to wear one's *yarmulke* in a top law firm and not only were thousands of brands of food kosher by the end of the century, but Orthodoxy's ranks were also swelling. Within Orthodoxy itself there was a renewed appreciation for prewar Jewish Europe and all that the shtetl, or small Jewish town, had held dear. Yet the trend of movement to the right is best symbolized by Reform Judaism: In 1999, Reform Judaism in America decided at a Reform Judaism-wide conference to encourage tradition and ritual as part of Reform Jewish practice.

Susanna Smulowitz

See also: Culture and Assimilation (Part I, Sec. 3); Collapse of Communism (Part I, Sec. 5); Immigration to Israel (Part II, Sec. 13); Middle East (Part III, Sec. 3); Former Soviet Union (Part III, Sec. 4).

BIBLIOGRAPHY

Eisen, Arnold M. *The Chosen People in America: A Study of Jewish Religious Ideology.* Bloomington: Indiana University Press, 1983.

Feingold, Henry L. *Zion in America: The Jewish Experience from Colonial Times to the Present.* New York: Hippocrene, 1981.

———, ed. *The Jewish People in America.* Baltimore: Johns Hopkins University Press, 1986.

Hertzberg, Arthur. *The Jews in America: Four Centuries of Uneasy Encounter, a History.* New York: Simon and Schuster, 1989.

Karp, Abraham J. *A History of Jews in America.* Northvale, NJ: J. Aronson Publishing, 1997.

Rischin, Moses. *The Promised City: New York's Jews, 1870–1914.* Cambridge, MA: Harvard University Press, 1962.

DESTINATIONS

INTRODUCTION

The entries in Section 12 of Part II of the *Encyclopedia of American Immigration* focus on the subject of immigrant destinations, that is, those places in the United States where immigrants have settled in large numbers. Most of the entries in this section are devoted to cities and include pieces on Houston, Los Angeles, Miami, New York City, San Francisco, and Washington, D.C. In addition, there are entries on Mex-America, or the border region; New Jersey and suburban America; and rural America.

In her entry on Houston as an immigrant destination, Cecelia M. Espenoza begins by discussing the various immigrants who helped found and build Houston in the nineteenth century before going into the subject of modern immigration to the Texas city. In the discussion of recent immigration, Espenoza looks at people from Mexico and Latin America, as well as Asian immigrants.

The entry on Los Angeles by Kevin Keogan opens with immigrants' role in the historical development of the city and then goes on to explore the immigrants in the contemporary period. Keogan examines the various immigrant groups, including Latinos and Asians. Next, the author looks at the reaction of native-born Angelenos to the tide of immigrants coming to their city, then goes into a comparison of Los Angeles with other immigrant cities. Finally, he discusses the future prospects of immigrants in the southern California metropolis.

With the entry "Mex-America," Ronald L. Mize examines the region of the United States that borders on Mexico and includes parts of four states: Texas, New Mexico, Arizona, and California. He begins with a discussion of the historical origins of the border region before discussing its demographics. An examination of the economic restructuring of Mex-America follows, as well as a discussion of the physical and social construction of the border itself and what it means to the inhabitants of the region. Finally, the au-

thor takes a look at immigrant identities and social inequalities in Mex-America.

In her entry on Miami, Sandra Dalis Alvarez opens with an exploration of the demographic changes immigration has brought to this southern Florida city. In addition, the author goes into the historical aspects of immigration to Miami, including a discussion of the Cuban exodus that followed the Castro revolution of the 1950s and 1960s and the Mariel Boat Lift of the 1980s. Next, she goes into the subject of Haitian refugees before discussing the implications of immigration policy for the city. Two final subsections deal with the contemporary and future situations of immigrants in Miami.

The phenomenon of immigration settlement in American suburbs is the subject of Vincent Parillo's entry, with a close look at New Jersey as an example. The entry begins with a discussion of historical trends in immigration to the Garden State through the seventeenth, eighteenth, nineteenth, and early twentieth centuries. Next, Parillo examines contemporary immigration to New Jersey before going on to discuss the question of suburban ethnicity in general.

America's largest city and number one immigration destination is the focus of Kevin Keogan's entry on New York City. The author begins with a discussion of the immigration to New York in its historical context before looking at the city's major immigrant groups of the past and present. Finally, Keogan examines how various immigrant groups have adapted themselves to living in New York.

In her entry on rural America, Gretchen S. Carnes opens by exploring the historical immigration patterns of Europeans to the American countryside. Next, the author looks at the historical patterns of Asian and Hispanic groups before discussing how U.S. immigration policy affects immigration to rural America.

Horacio N. Roque Ramírez's entry on San Francisco as an immigrant destination opens with a history of the city going back to the pre-Spanish era and continues through the present day. Finally, the author looks at how immigration has changed the face of to-day's San Francisco.

In their entry on Washington, D.C., Audrey Singer and Amelia Brown begin with a discussion of the city's growth and change due to immigration in the nineteenth and twentieth centuries. Next, the authors go into the historical sources of immigration to the nation's capital, beginning with the earliest immigrant groups and continuing through contemporary ones.

HOUSTON

When Alvar Nuñez Cabeza de Vaca ascended the San Jacinto River in 1529 to trade with the woodland Indians, he was one of the first Europeans to explore the area that comprises present-day Houston. From all accounts and data, his visit did not inspire additional settlements at that time.

American settlement began some three hundred years later when land speculators Augustus C. and John K. Allen from upstate New York purchased the eventual site of Houston for $5,000 on August 26, 1836. The Allens mapped out a town and offered plots for sale. Located near what was to become a significant port, the city became a point of commerce in 1911 when voters approved the Harris County Ship Channel Navigation District. In 1914, the United States Army Corps of Engineers finished deepening the channel to twenty-five feet, from the Gulf of Mexico to Galveston Bay. From those modest beginnings, the port continued to expand, and by the 1980s it was the second-largest port in the nation.

As a port city, Houston views itself as valuing cultural and ethnic diversity. In fact, ordinary people have come to view diversity not as a problem, but as a source of great strength for the city. This cooperative attitude fosters a welcoming attitude in which civic leaders, intent on minimizing racial and ethnic intolerance, work to solve problems. The new immigrants are encouraged to share in the American Dream, and as a result they find that by contributing hard work and optimism, those dreams can become a reality. The 1990 census identified eighty-five foreign-born groups located in Houston. The four largest immigrant groups are from Mexico, Central America, China, and Vietnam.

MODERN IMMIGRATION

Greater Houston area is the fourth-largest city in the country, and it enjoys a great economic viability. Despite its close proximity to Mexico and Central and South America, the existence of a substantial immigrant population is a relatively new phenomenon in the Houston area. The city of Houston has a population of over 1.6 million. Until the late 1900s, immigrant growth was less than that of northern and eastern cities. In fact, by 1960, only 3 percent of the city's population was foreign-born. In contrast, at the same time, cities of comparable size and populations, such as Milwaukee, Minneapolis, Buffalo, and Pittsburgh, had up to four times the proportion of foreign-born residents. By 1997, the foreign-born population in Houston had risen to 23 percent.

Houston remained relatively free from recession during the 1970s. In fact, huge economic expansion during the 1970s and early 1980s caused employment to grow an astonishing 145 percent. Houston's business community has a free-enterprise attitude that sees value in diversity; as a result, efforts to restrict immigration have not flourished there.

After a hundred years of sustained growth, Houston's oil-based economy came to a screeching halt in 1982. Suddenly the young Anglo professionals who had been pouring into the city throughout the 1970s stopped coming; many of those who were already in Houston moved out, and a ghost town of empty high-rise apartment buildings remained. The economic recession, which lasted from 1982 to 1987, forced Houston to rely less on its petrochemical industries and more on a diversified industrial base. One source of new business came into existence because the city became a major transportation hub for Hispanic immigrants. Local van and bus companies initiated routes between cities as far north as New York and as far south as San Luis Potosí and Veracruz, Mexico.

During the same time period, an estimated one hundred thousand Anglos left Houston for work in other parts of the country, while thousands of new immigrants arrived from Asia and Latin America. These new immigrants from China, Vietnam, Mexico,

Houston, a traditional destination for many Latino immigrants, has become home also for many newcomers from Asia, including this Southeast Asian woman now living in the Allen Parkway Village housing project. *(Sharon Stewart/Impact Visuals)*

and other countries gave rise to new communities within the city.

Over the next five years, one out of seven jobs disappeared. The ensuing recovery resulted in a radically different kind of economy for Houston. After the recession, growth of knowledge and expertise in the oil and gas industry emerged to form a solid base for Houston's economy. In addition, the convention and tourism industry, NASA, the Port of Houston, and applied technologies, especially biotechnologies, were incorporated into the fabric of Houston's economy and growth.

Houston embraced a cosmopolitan character that is dependent upon international trade, particularly

with Mexico and Latin America. An estimated one-third of all jobs in Houston are now related to such trade. The Port of Houston handles more cargo bound for Mexico than does any other American port. According to a recent *Wall Street Journal* article, Houston's current "economic boom is so powerful that some companies see hiring problems ahead" due to an anticipated worker shortage. In addition, although Houston had 1.6 million inhabitants in 1990, it was the least densely populated major city in America, with 25 percent of the land still available for development.

In 1995, the largest immigrant groups came to Houston from Mexico (3,362), Vietnam (1,836), El Sal-

The largest city in Texas, Houston has been a draw for Mexican immigrants since the early part of the twentieth century. In recent years, the population of Houston has also been augmented by large-scale immigration from Southeast Asia and a smaller influx from Africa. *(CARTO-GRAPHICS)*

vador (1,055), India (984), the Philippines (693), mainland China (468), Nigeria (469), and Pakistan (359). According to recent figures, Houston's racial and ethnic breakdown shows Anglos at 41 percent; African Americans at 28 percent; Hispanics at 28 percent; and Asians at 4 percent of the city's total population. The comparable 1980 figures were Anglos, 52.3 percent; African Americans, 27.1 percent; Hispanics, 17.6 percent; and Asians, 2.1 percent. The Houston-Harris County metropolitan area now contains one of the densest immigrant concentrations in the United

States. (As percentages are rounded off, they do not always add up to 100.)

IMMIGRANTS FROM MEXICO AND LATIN AMERICA

The 1850 census counted six Mexican-born persons in Houston, while the 1880 census counted less than ten.

It is estimated that by 1900, there were one thousand people of Mexican origin that called Houston home, and by the 1910 census approximately two thousand Mexicans were counted as residents. The Mexican Revolution of 1910 created the first major wave of immigration into the city. Mexicans, unlike other immigrants, formed *barrios* (communities) where family and friends established their homes and businesses in close proximity to one another. El Crisol, which is now known as Denver Harbor, was located next to the Southern Pacific Railroad lines. It derived its name from the pungent smell of the creosote ("crisol" in Spanish) used for the preservation of railroad ties. Another Mexican barrio was the *segundo barrio* (Second Ward) which extended from the center of Houston into Buffalo Bayou. Southeast from there, Magnolia became a Mexican barrio by 1915, as its location next to the shipyards provided many Mexican workers easy access to their jobs on the channel.

The Mexican Revolution pushed many Mexicans out of Mexico, while the favorable economic factors pulled them to the Houston area, which was a labor magnet. Railroad construction, the construction and development of Houston's port and shipping industry, agricultural work, and new manufacturing industries made the city attractive to immigrant workers.

The Catholic Church also helped the Mexican community establish itself in Houston. As early as 1911, the Oblate Fathers arrived in Houston in order to provide their religious services to the Mexican barrios. By 1912, they had built the original parish of Our Lady of Guadalupe. By 1923, catechetical centers had been built throughout Houston, teaching around one thousand children of Mexican descent. At about the same time, the Sisters of Divine Providence built Our Lady of Guadalupe Parochial School, which educated thousands of Mexican and Mexican-American children.

As more and more Mexicans were attracted to Houston for work, businesses catering to Mexican clientele emerged. By 1929, Mexican and Mexican-American merchants opened restaurants, theaters, furniture stores, dance halls, parlors, and bookstores, all catering to the rapidly growing Mexican population. A growing Mexican immigrant population meant greater business opportunities, which made Houston a more livable city for future Mexicans.

The introduction and proliferation of ethnic festivities also helped the Mexican immigrant population establish roots in the Houston area. In 1917, the first Fiestas Patrias, celebrating Mexican Independence Day, was celebrated by the Mexican community of Houston. By 1925, this yearly celebration included a parade through downtown, baseball games, beauty contests, dances, and patriotic speeches about Mexican history. The Sociedad de Benito Juarez helped organize the first Cinco de Mayo celebrations in Houston. This mutual aid society also sponsored musical, social, and other patriotic activities that were favored by workers.

The Mexican community in Houston began to organize politically during the Great Depression. A number of businessmen came together in order to form the Latin American Club (LAC). In 1938, LAC became the No. 60 Council for the League of United Latin American Citizens (LULAC). By the 1940s and 1950s, LULAC had become a contributing element in the protection of Mexicans' and Mexican Americans' rights—especially against police brutality—in recruitment of the Mexican into the political process, and in education and the betterment of the Mexican community. By the early 1980s, there were seventeen LULAC councils in Houston. Today, the Latino community is much more diverse, but it still manages to work in a cooperative fashion.

POST-1965 MEXICAN IMMIGRATION

The economic downturn that accompanied the Great Depression created a fear that immigrants would turn to public assistance. Mexicans were encouraged to repatriate in the 1930s to alleviate the potential economic drain. Records indicate that 2,000 left Houston for Mexico, but it is uncertain how many of these people were forced to leave. Immigration from Mexico did not increase until after 1965.

The increase in oil prices caused by OPEC policies in the mid-1970s and the passage of the Immigration and Nationality Act of 1965 created heightened opportunity for a new wave of Mexican immigrants, who came by the tens of thousands. The construction industry preferred cheap Mexican labor, usually undocumented workers who seemed amenable to working for less money and interested in leaving for Mexico when work slowed down in the winter. There was no law against employment of undocumented workers, and therefore those who reached Houston could count on finding work the next day, often earning twice as much as they could in Mexico.

In 1970, census figures indicated that the Latino population in metropolitan Houston was 212,444; by 1980, that population was at 424,903; in 1990, it had reached 707,536, outpacing the total population growth. Houston's economic boom helped support an increasing number of arrivals, who found work not only in industrial plants but in construction and service industries as well. As the city's economy grew, so did the need for new homes, office buildings, shopping centers, and apartment projects.

During the growth of the 1970s, the Latino immigrant prospered from the development of new manufacturing plants that sprouted along east-side, Mexican neighborhoods. Well-paid positions attracted Latino commuters from all over Houston. What did not change was the limited upward mobility many Latinos continued to face and their prospect of being employed in low-skilled manual labor jobs and clerical positions.

Mexican women also came to Houston in record numbers during the 1970s. They found jobs in the service industries and were usually employed as waitresses, chambermaids, and in-home maids in the city's middle- and upper-class homes. Office-cleaning companies, some national and international in scope, sought Mexican women immigrants for their crews as vigorously as the construction industry sought men.

The growing Latino population moved into neighborhoods not traditionally known as barrios. An example of one such transitional zone is the Heights neighborhood, located in Houston's northwest inner city, where Mexican Americans and Latino immigrants helped introduce their language and customs to the predominantly white, middle-class residents. By the 1980s, the transition had led to the opening of a number of small businesses catering to Mexican-American and other Latino immigrants. Many white-owned businesses catered to the Latino community by placing ethnic decorations and flags in their stores and shops.

The total increase in Mexican immigration in the 1970s is reflected by the 1980 census. Of the 93,718 foreign-born Mexicans counted, 68 percent had immigrated since 1970. As the economic boom was ending, the 1986 Immigrant Reform and Control Act (IRCA) offered amnesty for those who had entered the United States by 1982 and remained. Over ninety thousand Mexican immigrants from the Houston area sought relief through the implementation of IRCA. Under provisions of the new act, sanctions were imposed on those who hired undocumented workers, which meant that IRCA spelled out a new, tougher barrier for immigrants. The act put those immigrants at the mercy of employers, making them more susceptible to coercion and salary abuse. By the 1990 census, Mexican immigrants accounted for 69 percent of the 192,220 foreign-born Hispanic residents in the city of Houston. The Mexican-origin population age twenty-five and older suffered from a major educational disadvantage: Only 6 percent had a bachelor's degree or higher. As a result, the median household income for Mexican-origin residents was only $22,447. During the 1990s, Mexican immigration increased as a result of the growing regional economy, family reunification petitions filed by thousands of newly legalized immigrants, and a dramatic economic downturn in Mexico.

CENTRAL AMERICAN IMMIGRANTS

Up until the 1980s, Hispanic immigration to the city of Houston was primarily Mexican. However, during the 1980s, social and political turmoil in several Central American countries displaced thousands, ultimately changing the pattern of immigrantion to Houston. The new wave of immigrants came from Guatemala, Honduras, Nicaragua, and El Salvador and helped diversify Houston's Hispanic population.

In the 1980 census, 5,400 Central American immigrants were counted. By 1990 that number was 47,244. Salvadorans dominated the Central American influx. Most immigrants arrived after 1982, and thus they were not eligible for legalization under IRCA. Only about 25,000 Central American immigrants in the Houston area applied for relief under IRCA.

Because their displacement was prompted by war, political violence, and political instability instead of flight from economic hardships, their presence stimulated domestic activism, which was not present among Mexican immigrants. Protests about the military intervention in their native countries led to a religious sanctuary movement. The refugees depended on this private assistance because, unlike Cuban and Indochinese refugees, they were ineligible for federal assistance. Casa Juan Diego was founded in Houston to assist Central American refugees, and it remains as a shelter today.

Central Americans arrived during the economic slump of the 1980s, and they settled in the city's west side, away from the predominantly Mexican barrios located on the east side. The attraction to the west side of Houston was due in part to the bold marketing tools utilized by apartment-project owners. The real estate market dropped in the early to mid-1980s, leaving many desperate owners in search of new tenants. Faced with the huge exodus of Anglos, property owners focused their sights on the only large homogeneous group to be constantly arriving—the Central Americans. Apartment owners slashed their rent, sometimes by as much as 50 percent, in an effort to attract the financially strapped refugees. New bilingual staff helped bring in potential tenants. Some complexes offered English classes, had nightclubs on the premises, and changed the apartment names to attract Spanish-speaking tenants. These initiatives transformed many west-side neighborhoods from white, middle-income apartment areas to communities of ethnic diversity. Nevertheless, the national and ethnic separation of Central American immigrants remained intact in a complex social structure. National identities were often the basis of residential, workplace, and recreational groupings in Houston. By 1990, many Central Americans approached the economic mobility levels of Mexican immigrants. Despite these gains, however, only 6 percent of the Central Americans age twenty-five or older had a bachelor's degree, and their median income was only $17,429.

IMMIGRANTS FROM ASIA

Current immigration to Houston includes a large Asian population that emerged after the adoption of the 1965 Immigration and Nationality Act, which eliminated quotas on Asian immigration. The current Asian population began to emerge in the 1970s and has steadily continued to rise. A 1997 census report placed Asian immigration in Harris County at 202,685. The sending countries are diverse—as demonstrated by the fact that the 1990 census lists twenty-four different Asian nationalities in Houston.

THE INDOCHINESE

Since 1975, more than 1 million Indochinese have sought refuge in various parts of the world. Houston has not escaped the settlement and, in fact, because of several factors has become the second most popular destination for immigrants from Indochina. First, Houston was the nearest large metropolitan area for many of the initial immigrants, who accompanied military spouses stationed at Fort Chaffee in Arkansas. Second, Houston's semitropical climate and proximity to the Gulf attracted many Indochinese arrivals because of the similarities to the country they had left. Finally, many of the immigrants arriving after 1975 came to join family members already living in Houston.

Immigration of the Indochinese was not without problems. One faced by many is that of housing. Because many of the Indochinese immigrants came to the United States as entire families and prior to the early 1980s, Houston was ill-prepared to meet the surge in demand for housing. Even when the new

Indochinese immigrants were able to secure housing, it was usually subsidized and government-based, and they confronted many language obstacles. Many of these problems are solved by community organizations that have developed to assist Indochinese immigrants assimilate into the United States. The three main sending countries for Indochinese immigrants are Vietnam, Laos, and Cambodia.

Vietnamese Immigrants

Prior to 1975, the first wave of immigrants from Vietnam who arrived in Houston were accompanying U.S. servicemen husbands or seeking job opportunities. After 1975, the second wave were refugees from homelands severely affected by war and political turmoil. These Vietnamese newcomers were resettled by the federal refugee resettlement program, which was developed through the Indochinese Assistance Act of 1975. Between 1975 and 1988, the program resettled 1.2 million refugees in the country, and Texas, especially Houston, was one of the major resettlement sites for Vietnamese and other Indochinese.

The total U.S.– and foreign-born Vietnamese population in the Houston greater metropolitan area reached 33,000 in 1990. Notably, of the total 18,453 Vietnamese counted in the city of Houston in 1990, 84 percent were foreign-born. This was an increase from the 1980 census, which had already demonstrated the impact of immigration for the growth of the Vietnamese population in the Houston metropolitan area: 83 percent of the total 14,000 Vietnamese residents concentrated in the metropolitan area in 1980 were foreign-born. The overall impact can be illustrated by the fact that 95 percent of the foreign-born Vietnamese counted in the metropolitan area in 1980 had entered the United States only since 1975, with only eleven persons entering before 1950.

Laotian and Cambodian Immigrants

Immigrants from Laos typify those who have come to the United States in order to escape poverty and political instability. Laos is mostly agricultural—85 percent of its population makes a living through farming. The advent of communism did not establish a highly educated population, and civil strife continues to divide the country—but in the aftermath of the conflict in Vietnam, many thousands of refugees were resettled to the United States. The temperate climate and availability of farmland made Houston attractive to these immigrants.

Cambodian refugees escaped a public atrocity: With the 1975 fall of the capital of Phnom Penh to the

Communists came the murderous reign of Pol Pot and the now infamous "Killing Fields" of Cambodia's countryside. The solution for many was to flee their country, and, through international relief efforts, many relocated to the United States.

Two recurring problems faced by many of the new immigrants from Indochina have been language and education. Those coming from Laos and Cambodia have had great difficulty learning English. The Vietnamese that came prior to 1975, for example, had been in European-style schools and had been exposed to thousands of American GIs, while citizens of Laos and Cambodia had led a much more isolated existence. Later, Communist-based educational systems had an impact on students who immigrated and then attempted to make full assimilation into American schools.

For adults, English classes are available through the city's school system. Several support groups and volunteer agencies also assist adults in learning English. Vocational training is also readily available at Houston Community College, giving adults an opportunity to receive some specialized training and easing the job search.

JAPANESE IMMIGRANTS

Today, the Japanese in Houston can be categorized into three different groups—the largest of which is made up primarily of temporary immigrants, who arrive in the Houston area for various reasons but do not extend their visit for more than a few years before returning to Japan. This category includes businessmen, doctors, government officials, and students. Many of these men and women bring their families with them while they conduct activities ranging from improving international relations to completing medical training or simply opening and operating a new corporate office.

The strong ties between Houston and Japan really began with the opening of the Port of Houston. Consulates in Chicago and New Orleans had been interested in the development of the region for some time, and by the time the port opened, it was quickly inundated with commerce headed to and from Japan. The start of World War II interrupted this commerce, and it would take some time before prewar levels of trade would resume. From 1960 to 1980, exports to Japan out of the Port of Houston increased more than six times, while imports grew from less than $25 million to more than $1.6 billion.

A development that has shadowed this increase in trade was the growth of Japanese firms operating out of Houston that handle a myriad of different prod-

ucts. Because of this rich trade, from oil-field machinery to ceramic tiles, Houston is home to such companies as Sony and Mitsubishi, and the need for business travel and temporary visas has grown dramatically.

One of the results of this temporary visitor status, however, is that many of the businessmen and their accompanying families have little opportunity to integrate with the local population. Several factors give rise to this pattern, the temporary nature of their status being among the strongest reasons. Although the local consulate has made attempts to create a greater awareness in Houston of Japanese culture, the language barrier tends to isolate these temporary visitors.

The second largest group of Japanese in Houston are the Japanese Americans whose relatives immigrated to the United States half a century or more ago. Japanese Americans categorize themselves according to which generation of descent they represent. For example, first-generation immigrants are called *issei,* second-generation are referred to as *nisei,* and the third and fourth generations are called *sansei* and *yonsei,* respectively. Although their numbers remain relatively small, they are an excellent example of the speed and success some immigrants have had at assimilating to life in Houston.

Led and promulgated by the younger generations, many third- and fourth-generation Japanese share relatively little with their first-generation immigrant grandparents. The relatively small permanent Japanese population has interacted more with the local population, with acculturation spurred primarily by the potential risk of isolation. Japanese in Houston, therefore, were perhaps less likely to create congregated communities like those found on the West Coast.

The newer immigrants comprise the third group of Japanese in Houston. Many are Japanese Americans who, for various reasons, move to Houston from other parts of the United States. The group is relatively small, estimated to be at around one thousand.

One of the few things that all three groups share is their middle- and upper-middle-class backgrounds. Japanese in Houston, regardless of their level of acculturation or the expected length of their stay, have a generally high level of education, and hold technical and professional jobs. Many have tended to settle in west Houston and the surrounding suburbs to the north. The groups' small sizes, however, have tended to lead to a fragmented community with relatively little cultural similarities. Temporary immigrants from Japan remain quite isolated—their post in America is seen as a brief sojourn and the expectation is that they will retain their language and customs. For second- and third-generation Japanese, however, nothing could be further from the truth. While many continue to socialize within their own cultural group, the manner and style of their activities are more American than Japanese. Many have tended to break normal associations with Japanese-dominant social groups, as evidenced by more interracial marriages and membership in American organizations.

INDIAN IMMIGRANTS

In the late 1970s, Houston experienced the rapid growth of Indian immigrants in all professions. Gradually, the need to meet with their fellow countrymen and -women and celebrate religious festivals became very evident. Gujaratis, the largest group of Indian immigrants in Houston, became the leading community to start meeting informally to celebrate Diwali and Navratri. In 1978, with very few members, Gujarati Samaj took formal birth in Houston. Later, in 1980, it was incorporated in the state of Texas as Gujarati Samaj of Houston, Inc. (GSH). On the principle of a broader basis of Hindu religion coupled with educational and cultural activities to promote Indian heritage, nonprofit status under 501 (C)(3) was granted by the U.S. Internal Revenue Service. Today, with a membership of 1,500, GSH is the largest Indian organization in Houston.

Cecelia M. Espenoza

See also: East Africa, West Africa (Part III, Sec. 1); Central America, Mexico (Part III, Sec. 2); Middle East, Southeast Asia (Part III, Sec. 3); *LULAC et al. v. Wilson et al.,* 1995 (Part IV, Sec. 2).

BIBLIOGRAPHY

Bureau of the Census. *1980 Census of Population and Housing Characteristics for Census Tracts and Block Numbering Areas, Houston-Galveston-Brazoria, TX CMSA (Part), Houston, TX PMSA. CPH-3–176C.* Washington, DC: Government Printing Office, 1993.

———. *1980 Census of Population and Housing, Houston, Tex., Standard Metropolitan Statistical Area, Census Tract. PHC80–20184.* Washington, DC: Government Printing Office, 1983.

———. *1980 Census of Population, Detailed Population Characteristics, Texas. PC80–1-D45.* Washington, DC: Government Printing Office, 1983.

———. *1980 Census of Population: Social and Economic Characteristics, Texas.* Washington, DC: Government Printing Office, 1993.

———. *Statistical Abstract of the United States: 1997.* Washington, DC: Government Printing Office, 1997.

De Leon, Arnoldo. *Ethnicity in the Sunbelt: A History of Mexican Americans in Houston.* Houston: Mexican American Studies, University of Houston, 1989.

Ebaugh, Helen Rose. Center for Immigration Research, Religion, Ethnicity and New Immigrants Research Project I & II, (RENIR) I and RENIR II, 1999.

Feagin, Joe R. *Free Enterprise City: Houston in a Political and Economic Perspective.* New Brunswick, NJ: Rutgers University Press, 1988.

Hagan, Jacqueline Maria. *Deciding to Be Legal: A Maya Community in Houston.* Philadelphia: Temple University Press, 1994.

Henson, Margaret Scott. "Harris County" in *The Handbook of Texas Online.* www.tsha.utexas.edu/handbook/online/articles/view/HH/hch7.html

Rosales, Arturo F. "Mexicans to Houston: The Struggle to Survive." *Houston Review* 3 (1981): 249–52.

$\mathcal{L}$OS ANGELES

$\mathcal{L}$os Angeles is currently grappling with its prominent new role as a primary destination for immigrants. Although there have always been immigrants in the area, it is only during the past few decades that Los Angeles has emerged as a powerful immigrant magnet. Thus, unlike many other large urban areas such as New York, Chicago, or even San Francisco, Los Angeles has neither an established tradition nor extensive experience in dealing with a large foreign-born population. Moreover, long-present immigrant-ethnic groups such as the Mexicans—by far the largest group in the area—have not been effectively incorporated into the mainstream. The relative lack of a European immigrant tradition, combined with the post-1965 dominance of Latin American and Asian immigrants, has made Los Angeles the unofficial capital for "third world" immigration to the United States.

These rapid and unprecedented changes have rekindled nativism throughout the United States, and Southern California has been exceptional in this regard. Perhaps the most obvious example of this was the passing of Proposition 187 during statewide elections in 1994. This legislation called for the exclusion of undocumented immigrants, including children, from welfare, public education, and all but emergency health care. The vehemence of the anti-immigrant backlash was certainly fueled by the recent and large influx of immigrants, both legal and illegal. Although Proposition 187 was directed specifically at undocumented or "illegal" immigrants, some in the area, especially Mexican Americans, understood this measure as just another in a long history of discriminatory tactics aimed at the nonwhite population. To better understand these recent events, we must first get a sense of Los Angeles's general historical development and, more specifically, past immigrant-ethnic relations in the City of Angels.

THE HISTORICAL DEVELOPMENT OF LOS ANGELES

While cities on the East Coast and in the Midwest were attempting to deal with the first large wave of European immigrants from places such as Germany and Ireland in the mid-1800s, California was just being incorporated into U.S. territory. As a result of the Mexican-American War (1846–48) and the Treaty of Guadalupe Hidalgo in 1848, the United States annexed from Mexico the bulk of the present-day Southwest. The Southwest traces its origins to the indigenous population and to later incursions on the part of Catholic missionaries and Spain's military, both looking to further their sphere of influence. For about three decades between Mexican independence from Spain and the Mexican-American War, Los Angeles—or Nuestra Senora la Reina de Los Angeles de Porciuncula, as it was formerly and formally known—was officially a Mexican city. Many of the Mexican nationals within "old" Los Angeles stayed on after its official conversion to an American town in 1848.

Historically, Los Angeles never had a very large proportion of foreign-born residents. Rather, it was internal migration from other areas of the country, especially the Midwest, that provided most of Los Angeles's huge population growth over the last 100 years. During the city's "century of growth," this small town rose from geographic obscurity to join New York and Chicago as one of the nation's largest cities by the 1970s. This demographic ascendancy is truly remarkable: Los Angeles did not even make the ranks of the fifty largest U.S. cities in 1890 and appeared thirty-sixth in 1890 with a population of about one hundred thousand—under 20 percent of which was then foreign-born. By 1920, Los Angeles had risen to become the tenth largest urban area in the United States, with a population of 576,673, but

America's second-largest city, Los Angeles, is also the country's second-largest magnet—after New York—for immigrants from around the world. *(CARTO-GRAPHICS)*

the foreign-born component of the population stayed relatively steady at 21 percent. Los Angeles rose to fifth place in 1930 with about 1.2 million people, while the foreign-born population continued at 20 percent. In 1970, as large-scale immigration to the region was about to begin, Los Angeles was the third largest city in the United States with 2.8 million peo-

ple. The foreign-born population would rise dramatically after 1970, when it was at a relatively low 15 percent of the total population. Thus, despite one hundred years of rapid growth, during most of the twentieth century the foreign-born population of Los Angeles was never much more than 20 percent. This is in sharp contrast to most other large cities in the

The car culture of Los Angeles infects immigrants as much as native-born Americans. This vintage Volkswagen Beetle advertises La Curaçao, a store geared to immigrant shoppers. The sign reads: "A little bit of your country." *(Donna DeCesare/Impact Visuals)*

United States. Much of the urban population growth in the United States has traditionally been the result of increases in immigration.

This huge growth was encouraged by an orchestrated marketing of Southern California to residents and commercial enterprises based in other areas of the country. Projecting an image of itself as a sort of Eden, the geographic setting for the American dream, Los Angeles has provided a strong attraction for the tired and restless within the nation. When there was a complementary relationship between population growth and urban economic expansion, Los Angeles evidenced its familiar "boom" character of suburban growth. But the area's prolonged expansion has also been characterized by a series of "busts" ushered in by some combination of either too many people or too little material resources (e.g., water, employment). Of course, it is likely that many of the more affluent have realized the image of Los Angeles as a coastal paradise, replete with a warm climate, pristine beaches, and economic opportunity. As with all urban development, however, some had to do the dirty work necessary to transform the barren landscape from utopian image into an urban reality. But reality has not always coincided with the image and this discrep-

ancy has been felt most strongly by the immigrant population of Southern California. As economic crises periodically arose, paradise seemed increasingly crowded and unstable, prompting many residents to pose the question: Eden for whom?

Although the "white" or "Anglo" inhabitants of Southern California have European origins, they are not likely to identify as immigrants, at least when compared with people in cities such as New York. Because most came after extended residence elsewhere in the United States, they had a decidedly "American" character upon arrival. Migrants to Southern California tended to identify along state lines (e.g., as fellow Iowans), rather than as immigrant-ethnics. In fact, many "state societies" were formed, acting in a similar manner as immigrant aid societies in eastern cities, helping newcomers get in touch with "others of their kind." Writing over fifty years ago, Carey McWilliams claimed that "there is no more significant Southern California institution than the state society." In general, the journey to the West Coast has further removed European-origin individuals from the coethnic networks and tight-knit communities characteristic of the East Coast and the Midwest. Although many ties were likely transplanted to the new region, the ethnic flavor of residential patterns was less robust. Perhaps the state societies were an effort to recapture some of that which was lost due to the moving experience. Nevertheless, over time, the immigrant-ethnic component of Southern California's white population seems to have "melted under the California sun."

The sociologists Allen Scott and Edward Soja have described the 1920–70 population shift toward Southern California as the largest internal migration in American history. The initial phase of this mass movement of people was dominated by midwestern Protestant whites who quickly gained control of Los Angeles political and economic institutions. The 1930s witnessed another surge in white migrants, but this time they were typically poorer and not very well received by more established residents. Many of the depression era migrants came from the dust bowl region and were often derogatorily referred to as Okies or Arkies. These newcomers left their previous home owing to drastic conditions and were desperate for employment upon arrival in California. Therefore, they were willing to take the sort of jobs that most whites in the area would not consider. However, the depression era saw little economic expansion, so these newcomers had to compete for the least desirable jobs present in the local economy.

As global events escalated the U.S. role in World War II, Los Angeles's manufacturing sector grew rapidly. This industrial expansion coincided with a sharp increase in the number of blacks migrating into the region. Although whites were most likely to gain the good jobs that were generated during this boom period, blacks were also able to make some gains, especially in areas such as shipbuilding. As is generally the case during large-scale urban expansion, the production of Los Angeles's landscape required an influx of laborers from outside the area. While these labor market needs have been met by both migrants and immigrants, the labor market has become increasingly dependent on foreign labor during the twentieth century. For instance, Southwest farmers repeatedly lobbied to obtain increases in Mexican immigration to fill domestic labor shortages. As agricultural work diminished in importance and the manufacturing and service sectors expanded, new jobs were created. Again, newcomers would pour into the area and fill the many jobs being created, further expanding the local commercial market. But the contemporary newcomers to the Los Angeles region have been predominantly international, rather than domestic, migrants.

THE CONTEMPORARY PERIOD

Like the nation as a whole, the contemporary period in Los Angeles has been marked by a general trend toward immigration from Latin America and Asia. But the most salient feature of the recent immigrant flows has been the predominance of Mexican nationals. As the recent arrivals have swollen the ranks of the Mexican-origin population already present, they have become, by far, the most numerous immigrant-ethnic group in the region. As Table 1 shows, Mexicans in Los Angeles are more than three times the size of the next largest immigrant-ethnic group. In fact, Mexicans alone (34.2 percent) account for more of the total for the top ten immigrant-ethnics in Los Angeles than all the major European-origin ethnics combined (29 percent). Moreover, Mexicans are more than ten times the size of the next highest non-European immigrant-ethnic group, the Salvadorans at just 3.4 percent.

As Table 2 shows, the total immigrant-ethnic population for Mexicans in 1970 consisted of 830,000 Mexican Americans (i.e., native-born) and an additional 283,900 Mexican immigrants, putting the entire Mexican-origin population at over 1.1 million. The rapid growth of Mexican ethnics over the next two decades was due to both natural increase, a product

Table 1 The Top Ten Ethnic Groups in the Los Angeles Area, 1990		
Ethnic Group	Number (000s)	Percentage
Total specified nationalities	7,374	100.0
Mexican	2,520	34.2
German	692	9.4
English	465	6.3
Irish	370	5.0
Salvadoran	253	3.4
Chinese	248	3.4
Italian	236	3.2
Filipino	223	3.0
U.S./American	168	2.3
Russian	151	2.0
Totals for top ten	5,326	72.2

Source: Bureau of the Census. 1990 CensusCD, version 1.1. Washington, DC: Bureau of the Census, 1991.
Notes: The "Los Angeles Area" refers to the Los Angeles Primary Metropolitan Statistical Area (PMSA), as defined by the Bureau of the Census. Ethnic groups are ranked according to specified nationalities.

Table 2
Population of Specific Ethnic Groups by Nativity, Los Angeles Region, 1970–1990

	1970	1980	1990
Latinos			
Mexican NB[a]	830,000	1,380,200	2,000,472
Mexican FB[b]	283,900	928,660	1,717,911
Salvadoran NB	—	7,560	60,058
Salvadoran FB	4,800	54,060	241,509
Guatemalan NB	—	6,040	32,431
Guatemalan FB	3,500	32,780	126,837
All Latinos	1,399,600	2,862,120	4,697,509
Native-born	1,001,400	1,665,980	2,338,369
Foreign-born	398,200	1,196,140	2,359,140
Asians			
Chinese NB	26,800	36,160	75,649
Chinese FB	29,000	80,420	231,361
Filipino NB	19,300	32,200	81,080
Filipino FB	24,700	80,100	203,138
Korean NB	4,200	11,960	36,322
Korean FB	9,200	64,740	155,568
Japanese NB	88,600	108,300	123,345
Japanese FB	32,200	45,240	57,094
Vietnamese NB	—	4,200	26,597
Vietnamese FB	—	44,120	116,293
All Asians	256,200	596,080	1,326,559
Native-born	147,600	222,640	414,427
Foreign-born	108,600	373,440	912,132
Middle Easterners			
Native-born	25,100	51,300	90,622
Foreign-born	27,300	92,800	209,924
Non-Hispanic whites			
Native-born	6,577,500	6,425,560	6,494,372
Foreign-born	506,000	450,980	398,884
Total Population			
Native-born	8,868,600	9,485,340	10,576,033
Foreign-born	1,090,300	2,136,840	3,919,394

Source: Sabagh, Georges, and Mehdi Bozorgmehr. "Population Change: Immigration and Ethnic Transformation." In *Ethnic Los Angeles*, ed. Waldinger and Borzorgmehr (1996:95–96), Table 3.2.
Notes: "Los Angeles Region" refers here to the very broad, five-county area of Los Angeles, Orange, San Bernardino, Riverside, and Ventura counties. Therefore, the numbers here are not commensurate with those in Table 1.
[a] NB = Native-born.
[b] FB = Foreign-born.

of the relatively high fertility rates for Mexican Americans, and a sharp increase in the number of immigrants. The 1990 census recorded over 3.7 million Mexican ethnics in the greater Los Angeles area—roughly 25 percent of the total population. Since Mexican Americans have not been effectively incorporated into the mainstream, even many among the older generations still exhibit a rather strong identification with their Mexican roots. These factors have combined to account for the *numerical* dominance of this ethnic group. Their large numbers, however, have not translated into political power, at least not yet.

Further bolstering the ranks of the Latino population in Los Angeles are recent arrivals from Central America, in particular those from El Salvador and Guatemala. Although there were few immigrants from Central America before 1970, many have since arrived as a result of both economic and political turbulence in that region. By 1990, there were roughly 450,000 immigrants and another 120,000 native-born, mostly second-generation Central Americans in the Los Angeles region. Central Americans have helped to make the Spanish-speaking component of Los Angeles's immigrant population the clear majority. Not factoring in other Latin American immigrants, Mexicans and Central Americans accounted for over half of the Los Angeles region's immigrants in 1990. Mexicans alone accounted for over 40 percent of the entire foreign-born population in 1990, and they were nearly three-quarters of all Latino immigrants. All together, Latinos accounted for 2.4 million, or about 60 percent, of all immigrants.

As with the rest of the nation, Asians are the next most numerous pan-national immigrant category. The total for Asian/Pacific Island immigrants was about 900,000 in 1990. This accounted for another 23 percent of the total and makes Latinos and Asians well over four-fifths of Los Angeles's total immigrant population. The top four Asian countries of origin since 1970, in descending order, are China, the Philippines, Korea, and Vietnam. The top two Asian immigrant groups also have a longer presence in the area, which combines to make them significantly larger than all other Asian groups. However, Koreans have been very prominent as small business owners in the region, and the Vietnamese were the most prominent refugee group in Los Angeles as of 1990. The Japanese, a once prominent component of Los Angeles's Asian population, have seen their relative weight decline as a result of post-1965 Asian immigration. The combined Chinese native-born and foreign-born population in the Los Angeles region is over 300,000 strong, followed by Filipinos with about 284,000. Because there were only 36,000 native-born Koreans in 1990, the total for this immigrant-ethnic group was only about 192,000, despite a strong immigrant flow since the 1970s. Although there are relatively few first-generation Japanese immigrants in the area, their large native-born population enabled them to outnumber the ethnic Vietnamese in 1990 (180,000 and 143,000, respectively).

Aside from the bulk of the immigrant population accounted for by Latinos and Asians, the next largest region of origin is Europe. European and Canadian immigrants, along with immigrants and refugees from the former Soviet Union, accounted for the vast majority of the non-Hispanic white foreign-born in Los Angeles as of 1990. Middle Easterners accounted for about 5 percent of the Los Angeles region's foreign-born individuals, with Armenia and Iran being the largest source countries for that category. All told, there were almost 4 million foreign-born persons in the Los Angeles region in 1990, accounting for 27 percent of the entire population. We now turn to a more detailed look at the some of the largest immigrant-ethnic groups among the many Latinos and Asians in the Los Angeles area.

MAJOR IMMIGRANT GROUPS

LATINO IMMIGRANTS

As noted above, Mexicans are by far the largest immigrant-ethnic group in the Los Angeles area, and they have not been effectively incorporated into the city's mainstream economic and political institutions. As the scholar Peter Skerry has argued, Mexican Americans are an ambivalent minority. On the one hand, most wish to enter the American mainstream. On the other hand, an established political tactic for Mexicans has been to stress their "minority" status, highlighting similarities between their own historical experience in the United States and that of marginalized groups such as Native Americans and African Americans. A strong case can, and has, been made for granting minority status to Mexican Americans. Their low socioeconomic position is due, in large part, to past prejudice and discrimination. Although there are multiple and complex reasons for Mexican Americans' lack of mobility, their history of exclusion is a particularly familiar and salient theme for members of this ethnic group. To complicate the situation even further, the past few decades have seen a surge in the number of Latin American immigrants in the Los Angeles area, which has brought about a decline in the educational levels and wages for the Mexican immigrant-ethnic population.

Los Angeles was one of the last major urban areas to undergo development within the southwestern United States and therefore did not attract a large number of Mexican immigrants until well into the twentieth century. The sociologist Ricardo Romo reports that in 1900, 69 percent of the Mexican-origin population was concentrated in Texas, while only 2 percent resided in California. Although the vast majority of Los Angeles's inhabitants were of Mexican descent in 1850, by 1920 they were less than 20 percent of the population. While the Mexican population of Los Angeles remained stagnant, new arrivals from other areas of the country actively attempted to exclude Mexicans from the city's economic, political, and cultural institutions. This destroyed the preexistent basis for a long-established Mexican elite and thwarted the assimilation of the wider Mexican population into the American mainstream.

White Protestants from the Midwest became the dominant group, as Mexicans became the largest immigrant group in the area. Mexican workers were the backbone of the area's agricultural workforce, and southwestern farmers lobbied Congress to exclude Mexico from the national-origin quotas that were established by the 1924 Quota Act. Less than a decade later, the Mexican-origin population was subjected to mass deportations that resulted in many civil rights abuses and the loss of personal assets. This was one of the earliest and clearest examples of the cyclical relationship between U.S. commercial interests and Mexico: When there is a shortage of workers to fill the least desirable jobs in the labor market, Mexican laborers are welcomed; when there is a downturn in the economy, Mexicans are seen as an illegitimate burden.

In the 1940s, as the U.S. role in World War II escalated, Mexico was again viewed as an attractive source for much-needed labor. The Bracero Program made American dependency on Mexican labor explicit when the government contracted directly with Mexico for the provision of agricultural laborers. Bracero labor was used for over two decades until the program was officially ended in 1964; however, U.S. linkages to Mexican labor were well developed during this period. California prospered in the postwar period, which brought renewed prosperity to most of Los Angeles's inhabitants. The Civil Rights era also brought increased struggles for desegregation and full participation in the area's social institutions. This period was one of relative economic stability for Mexican Americans, and they did manage to make some significant strides in terms of political representation. But it was also during the postwar period that Southern California became more segregated, as the more affluent started the process of mass suburbanization and "white flight" from downtown, leading to Los Angeles's characteristic urban sprawl. As the historic heart of Los Angeles was abandoned for newly incorporated areas, Mexicans and other minorities were left behind.

Central Americans are the second largest of the Latino immigrant groups. Although small in number by comparison with the Mexicans, immigrants from El Salvador and Guatemala have experienced rapid growth since they first arrived in Los Angeles in substantial numbers during the 1970s. Ironically, many of the Central Americans who emigrated due to the effects of civil war and political repression in their native land have been labeled as illegal immigrants rather than refugees upon arrival in the United States.

Aside from sharing a common language, immigrants from El Salvador and Guatemala are similar to Mexicans in other respects. Salvadorans and Guatemalans are concentrated in relatively low-wage and semiskilled occupations and have relatively low educational levels. Thus, although they have a distinct history and cultural background, Central Americans find themselves with a similar socioeconomic situation as that of recent immigrants from Mexico. While their paths are likely to diverge somewhat in the future (perhaps more so with the second generation), Central Americans' economic and political adaptation is likely to mirror that of Latinos in general and Mexican immigrant-ethnics in particular.

ASIAN IMMIGRANTS

Asians have always been present in Los Angeles, and they have often been the targets of mob violence. Over 100 years after the Chinese Massacre of 1871 focused national and international attention on Los Angeles, where some twenty Chinese were murdered by an angry mob of Anglo vigilantes, the Koreans of Los Angeles became a prime scapegoat during the 1992 Los Angeles riot. However, Asians have made impressive strides despite prejudice and discrimination. For instance, the once highly isolated Chinese community is now considered by many to be one of Los Angeles's main success stories, helping to forge an image of Asians as a "model minority." Since the enactment of the 1965 legislation facilitating the entry of Asian immigrants, this group has become the fastest growing segment of the American population.

Prior to the "new" immigration, there was always a single national-origin group that accounted for the vast majority of the Los Angeles Asian population. As noted above, the Chinese were the first predominant Asian group in Los Angeles. Although there were well over 4,000 Chinese in Los Angeles in 1890, it was largely a bachelor society, and it therefore declined steadily after the Chinese Exclusion Act of 1882. The Japanese were a majority of the region's Asian population as late as 1970, but since they were not a major immigrant group during the contemporary period, other Asian groups have surpassed them in numbers.

In general, Asians have done very well as compared with other nonwhite ethnic groups. More specifically, Asian immigrants have excelled in comparison with Latinos, the other large pan-national category of immigrants in the region. But broad pan-national categories mask crucial differences and diversity within such groupings, as the Asian case clearly demonstrates. The Asian population of Los Angeles is heterogeneous on many variables, including national origin, time of arrival, immigration status, and mode of economic incorporation, to name a few. Because the term "Asian" includes so many distinct ethnicities, I will focus on the four largest immigrant groups since 1970: the Chinese, Filipinos, Koreans, and Vietnamese. These groups were doing relatively well as of 1990, although some fared better than others. In particular, the Vietnamese lagged behind the other main Asian groups in terms of educational achievement and occupational attainment.

Every immigrant group arrives from a national context that is distinct in terms of its collective history, culture, and economic system, which influences who emigrates, when and why they leave, and how they adapt to American society. For example, natives of the Philippines were not subject to exclusions on Asian immigration owing to the country's status as a U.S. territory between 1898 and 1935. This made them a source of agricultural labor in California during the early twentieth century. Even after independence, the United States continued to have a strong influence on the Philippines as a result of strong cultural, economic, and (perhaps most important) military connections. For instance, English is still a principal language spoken in the Philippines, and it is a medium for instruction in the educational system there. The American influence on the development of the Philippines's economic institutions has also facilitated linkages for immigration. Moreover, the large American military presence in the Philippines enabled many American servicemen to marry and return to the United States with Filipina brides. In San Diego, Southern California's other immigrant mecca, more than half of all Filipinos there are employed by the U.S. Navy. Vietnamese refugees (and to a lesser degree Koreans) are another example of how the leading role of the United States in international political, economic, and military affairs can provide important linkages for chain immigration.

Regardless of the forces that brought immigrants to the United States, their time of arrival can influence their process of adaptation. Immigrants need time to adjust to a new society, especially those who arrive unable to speak English well or lack work skills. In general, contemporary Asian immigrants have improved their economic lot over time, and native-born Asians do better than their foreign-born coethnics. This is one possible explanation for why the more recent Vietnamese immigrants are not as successful as "older" immigrant-ethnics such as the Chinese and Japanese. But perhaps the biggest difference between the Vietnamese and other Asians is their status as a refugee group. Due to rather generous government programs, refugee status enables the Vietnamese to survive economically despite war scars, relatively low levels of education, and few marketable skills. In stark contrast to undocumented immigrants, refugees and their families are given direct government assistance to facilitate their adaptation to American society.

Finally, Asian immigrants differ in terms of their employment patterns. For example, some groups—most notably the Koreans—tend toward self-employment, starting small businesses that often rely on family members as employees. A fairly large number of Asian professionals live in the Los Angeles area. Filipinos and the Chinese have a particularly strong presence in professional and other high-skill occupations. The Vietnamese were the Asian group most likely to land a job in low-skill occupations, although in general, Asian women provide much of the cheap labor necessary to keep Los Angeles's many sweatshops in business.

CONTEMPORARY REACTIONS TO IMMIGRANTS IN LOS ANGELES

As previously mentioned, the influx of immigrants into the Los Angeles area over the past few decades was unprecedented, providing a huge increase in the nonwhite population of the area. In general, Los Angeles has a long history of exclusionary tactics toward its nonwhite residents, and nativism has periodically arisen. The anti-immigrant propensity has been compounded by the fact that the vast majority of new immigrants are Latinos and Asians, two racialized groups that have long been the targets for collective frustration and insecurity.

Anti-immigrant sentiments generally increase during economic downturns, and Southern California was in a deep economic recession during the early 1990s. Major restructuring was under way as a result of Cold War downsizing, and there was a lack of decent jobs for the burgeoning population. Although many of the new immigrants were able to find work in the growing manufacturing and service sectors, these jobs were mostly nonunion and paid low wages, making them an undesirable option for American citizens. Whites and nonwhites alike were thrust into an increasingly precarious situation. Thus, Los Angeles was again experiencing one of its periodic "busts" characterized by a sharp increase in the population and an unstable economy.

In addition to economic disruptions in the early

1990s, the area also faced a plethora of natural disasters as well as one major social explosion—the Los Angeles riot of 1992. In the midst of the apparent chaos, many residents felt as if Los Angeles were under siege: Eden seemed to be rapidly disintegrating into an urban nightmare. Almost on cue, the "native" population of Los Angeles pointed a collective finger at immigrants, seeing them as an illegitimate burden on the area's scarce resources. The logic seemed to be that if enough of these "undesirables" were sacrificed, material relations would improve and help restore some of the luster to the city's tarnished image. Rather than the various efforts to foster solidarity and promote urban renewal, it has been reactionary, interethnic conflict that has garnered the most popular attention in Los Angeles.

Contrary to popular media images, the Los Angeles riots were not simply a black/white conflict. Although the Rodney King beating and the subsequent acquittal of the white police officers provided the spark for this collective behavior, much of the physical aggression and destruction was directed at Latino and Asian immigrants. Furthermore, the particularly hard-hit Korean enclave was targeted not only by African Americans but also by Latinos who felt they were not dealt with fairly as customers and employees of Korean-owned small businesses. While the riot directed physical aggression toward Los Angeles's various immigrant-ethnic groups, white Angelenos would vent their frustrations toward immigrants in a much more "civilized" manner, using the legal and political system.

Immigration was a central issue in California politics during the early 1990s, peaking with the passage of Proposition 187 in November 1994. Many politicians used the measure as an easy way to gain support for their campaigns during statewide elections. Although whites in Los Angeles are no longer the numerical majority, they still account for a majority of the voting population there. Despite a strong campaign against the measure from organizations such as the teachers' union, health professionals, the Catholic Church, and various pro-immigrant groups (especially those with a Mexican-American base), the measure passed by a significant margin. While this was a statewide measure, some of the strongest support was in Southern California. For instance, a *Los Angeles Times* article from just before the 1994 election indicated that voters in the San Francisco Bay Area were *against* the measure by almost 60 percent (despite a large immigrant population there). Voters in Los Angeles County *approved* the measure by over 56 percent; in the counties south of Los Angeles closer to the U.S.-Mexico border, it was approved by 67 percent of voters. The biggest ethnic difference in statewide voting patterns was between whites and Latinos: 67 percent of whites voted for Proposition 187, whereas only 23 percent of Latinos did so. Asians and African Americans were both evenly split in their voting on the measure.

Although illegal immigrants were the overt target for the most draconian of the recent immigration legislation, legal immigrants have also been excluded from various public benefits. Historically, during periods of increased nativism, there was little distinction made between native-born and foreign-born Mexicans. Therefore, it is not surprising that many among the Mexican-origin population have seen Proposition 187 and subsequent anti-immigrant policies as simply the most recent evidence of prejudice and discrimination toward their immigrant-ethnic group. Voting patterns and political demonstrations clearly showed the vast differences in Mexican and Anglo definitions of the situation.

Although some news reports challenged the stereotypical conception of Latinos as a monolithic and cohesive ethnic group, the measure seemed to reassert a common bond among many of the area's Mexican ethnics. The ethnic solidarity theme was displayed most vividly in the coverage of "the largest demonstration in recent Los Angeles history" in which "enthusiastic organizers and participants . . . expressed hope about a new political activism among Latinos." Other news stories also noted the effect that Proposition 187 had in terms of creating political activism. Ironically, others observed that the large political demonstration *against* Proposition 187 bolstered support *for* the measure. Protestors were seen by many as subversive in their support of illegal immigrants. For instance, one article in the *Los Angeles Times* from October 1994 reported that "several Latino activists privately expressed fears that a sea of brown faces marching through Downtown Los Angeles would only antagonize many voters." Other news reports claimed that the carrying of Mexican flags (usually without an American counterpart) by protesters helped to clarify the need for passage of Proposition 187 on the part of undecided voters: "The flags were intended as a show of pride [but] among non-Latino voters they were widely interpreted as a symbol of anti-American defiance, of suspicious allegiance to a foreign land—a lightning rod that dramatically increased emotional support for the measure." Paradoxically, it was the measure itself that brought about the surge in Latino activism and protest.

COMPARING LOS ANGELES TO OTHER IMMIGRANT CITIES

Based on the discussion so far, it might be tempting to conclude that the contemporary situation in Los Angeles is extraordinary, if not unprecedented. However, there are other examples, both historical and contemporary, that help put Los Angeles's current situation into perspective. The most important characteristics of the city's contemporary foreign-born population are the total number and large proportion of the population accounted for by the foreign-born; the predominance of one national-origin group as compared with all other immigrant-ethnic groups; and the relatively large number of undocumented immigrants within the geographic area.

First, Los Angeles is not the city with the highest percentage of foreign-born residents. Using Census Bureau data from the 1997 *Current Population Survey*, the sociologist Ruben Rumbaut estimates the foreign-born population of Miami at approximately 49 percent of the total population there; Los Angeles is second with about 37 percent of its population being foreign-born. Although Los Angeles has the highest number of immigrants with about 3.5 million in 1997, New York City is not far behind with almost 3 million, or approximately 33 percent of its population. However, New York City differs from both Los Angeles and Miami because of its long history of immigration and its past experience in adapting to a large foreign-born population.

Miami is similar to Los Angeles in that immigration contributed little to the city's growth prior to the 1960s, and Miami also has a dominant immigrant-ethnic group: the Cubans. The Cuban population of the United States is highly concentrated in southern Florida. Miami was almost 50 percent Hispanic in 1990, and Cubans constituted almost 60 percent of this pan-ethnic grouping. But important differences exist between Miami and Los Angeles. Unlike the Mexicans in Los Angeles, Cubans have become not only the largest immigrant-ethnic group but also the dominant group within the city's economic, political, and cultural institutions. A variety of reasons have been put forth to explain the Cubans' unprecedented ascendancy to economic and political power: the middle-class origins and entrepreneurial skills of the Cubans, especially the first wave of refugees; the role of the U.S. government programs that provided direct aid, as well as professional and vocational retraining programs, to Cuban exiles; and the creation of a strong collective identity that has facilitated economic and political community.

Rather than a large foreign-born population of political refugees, the Los Angeles area is home to mostly economic immigrants. Although the Vietnamese and various other refugee groups are a significant part of Los Angeles's foreign-born population, it is undocumented immigrants who have received a disproportional amount of popular attention. This is an important point because those who believe most immigrants are in the country illegally tend to have more negative views of immigrants in general. While estimates do point to a disproportional number of undocumented immigrants in California, most immigrants, including Mexicans, are legal residents. This is an especially critical point since the 1986 Immigration Reform and Control Act (IRCA) legalized the status for millions of previously undocumented immigrants; the single largest group filing applications for amnesty were Mexicans, with a demographic preponderance in the Los Angeles area. Although the IRCA amnesty gave a dramatic boost to the number of legal immigrants from places such as Mexico and Central America, there are still many undocumented immigrants in the Los Angeles region. Other provisions of IRCA were meant to discourage the flow of illegal immigrants and make it more difficult for them to find work if they do enter the United States.

While recent federal legislation has restricted eligibility for social services for all Americans, immigrants have been an especially easy target for such budget cuts. More important, there is a new status hierarchy among the American population seeking public assistance: American citizens (both native-born and naturalized) are the least restricted from government assistance, while the foreign-born are increasingly excluded from benefits, at least until they achieve citizenship. Illegal immigrants are at the bottom of the ladder and are "almost entirely ineligible for federal benefits." These recent changes in the distribution of public benefits based on immigration status have led to a huge increase in the number of legal permanent residents applying for citizenship, which could have a considerable impact on urban politics, as the number of immigrants eligible to vote in future elections increases.

Although recent legislation increases the potential to exclude immigrants (especially the undocumented) from various social services, much depends on the initiative of leaders and political organizations at the state and local levels. New York provides a stark contrast to Los Angeles in this regard. Despite its large proportion of foreign-born residents (both legal and illegal), New York City has demonstrated a much more welcoming posture toward immigrants than has Los Angeles. The economic and political structures of

New York seem to be rather favorable to immigrant adaptation. Comparing the economic and political adaptation of immigrants in Los Angeles and New York, the sociologist Roger Waldinger observes that "immigrant New Yorkers have an earnings advantage in six of the seven industries that rank as the top immigrant employers in both towns." This is largely due to the more unionized workforce in the New York City area and its positive effect on real wages. The scholars Charles Hirschman, Philip Kasinitz, and Josh DeWind argue that New York has developed a "dense network" of institutions such as labor unions, public education, charitable organizations, and so on that are relatively inclusive of immigrants, and they contend that this is partly the result of earlier immigrant struggles over access and fair representation within such institutions.

Finally, New York City's political culture and political structures are much more favorable to immigrants than those in Los Angeles. New York's political culture encourages a positive identification with immigrants owing to its central place in the production and re-production of the "nation of immigrants" mythology. Popular symbols such as the Statue of Liberty and Ellis Island create a cultural landscape highly conducive to pro-immigrant politics and identity formation. Furthermore, the demographic and political structure of New York City facilitates the effective incorporation of immigrant groups by creating the conditions conducive to interethnic coalition formation and grassroots political participation.

FUTURE PROSPECTS

Undoubtedly, the future of Los Angeles will be profoundly influenced by the short- and long-term adaptations made by the many and diverse immigrants living in the metropolitan area. Although any grand predictions are far from certain, the foreign-born population of Los Angeles presents a mix of both good and bad prospects. The two largest groupings that make up the vast majority of the area's immigrants, Latinos and Asians, have divergent experiences within the Southern California labor market. Although there is considerable diversity within these pan-ethnic categories (especially among the Asian immigrants), some general trends are notable.

All of the area's large Asian immigrant-ethnic groups, with the possible exception of the Vietnamese, seem to be poised at the threshold of the middle class. At the very least, we can say that Asians are doing much better than Latinos. In terms of occupational ad-

vancement, educational attainment, and median household wages, Asians are doing far better than Mexicans, both native-born and foreign-born. Moreover, most of the large Asian immigrant groups in the Los Angeles area (again, with the exception of the Vietnamese) outperform native-born whites in their completion of college degrees, a main determinant of future occupational advancement. Remarkably, they seem to have made these economic advancements without any major political representation, although a more active political role may be needed to maintain their position and avoid future discrimination and prejudice.

Mexicans are the single largest immigrant-ethnic group in Southern California, and this makes their role in the region's social institutions crucial. But the present economic situation and future prospects for Latinos in the Los Angeles area are far from optimistic, and this makes their ethnic political incorporation all the more important. The future political adaptations for Latinos in the Los Angeles area present both problems and possibilities. Stressing the primacy of politics, scholar Peter Skerry asks: "Will Mexican Americans see themselves as individual citizens or as members of an oppressed racial group? The critical question is therefore not *whether* Mexicans will become Americans, but *how*—on what terms?" Although reality is always more complex than such extreme contrasts suggest, many Asians in Los Angeles do seem to approximate the "model minority" stereotype, while many Mexicans and Central-American immigrants seem to be on a course for the permanent underclass. This is especially the case for undocumented immigrants, who have been left without a safety net and are most likely to be excluded from full participation in other crucial social institutions. At the same time, due to IRCA legalizations and a huge surge in applications for citizenship, Latinos and other immigrants may be an increasingly attractive bloc of voters to be courted by the political status quo in Los Angeles.

However, the real litmus test for immigrant-ethnic group adaptation over time will be the second generation and beyond. Much recent scholarship on immigrant adaptations has stressed the importance of immigrant children and the children of immigrants. Although the immigrant proportion of the entire Los Angeles population in 1997 was about 37 percent, the second generation (i.e., children with at least one foreign-born parent) accounted for another 25 percent. Thus, the first and second generations combine for about 62 percent of the entire Los Angeles population. Moreover, due to the recent arrival and high fertility rates of many immigrant groups, the second generation is likely to see further growth well into the future. Like all children, the children of immigrants will spend much of their formative years in school. Because the U.S. educational system is the main mechanism for intergenerational economic mobility, studies have focused on this social institution in particular.

As the sociologists Robert Dentler and Anne Hafner have argued, major improvements in education and other social services for students "hinge mainly upon local community politics, political culture and school organization." Although California has not been very receptive toward the children of immigrants (especially undocumented immigrants), many have done quite well through the educational system. Again, we see divergence in the performance among various immigrant groups, especially between Asians and Latinos. For example, one study of the children of immigrants in San Diego found that all Asian immigrant groups (including Chinese, Koreans, Filipinos, and Vietnamese) had higher grade point averages (GPAs) than those of Latino (mostly Mexican) students. Moreover, once they gained English proficiency, all of the main Asian immigrant groups were outperforming native white students in terms of their collective GPAs. Whether or not immigrant students see school as an avenue for socioeconomic advancement depends on many factors, but one important variable found through case studies is coethnic peers' definition of the situation. Again, this may put Mexican students at a disadvantage. Because there is a prevalent "oppositional identity" among Mexican-origin youth, Rumbaut says, a rejection of schoolwork and other conformist behavior is common.

In summary, the future prospects seem brightest for the Asian immigrant-ethnic groups and dimmest for Latino groups such as Mexicans and Central Americans. The adaptive process for the first and second generations will be influenced by both their coethnic communities as well as their interactions with other immigrant and native groups. The current anti-immigrant posture on the part of many area natives may discourage successful adaptation within the area's major social institutions, at least in the short run. However, the sheer number of first- and second-generation immigrant-ethnics in Los Angeles will make their future political potential formidable. The question that remains is whether or not (or perhaps *how*) the various immigrant-ethnic groups will translate their demographic might into economic and political gains.

Kevin Keogan

See also: Central America, Mexico (Part III, Sec. 2); China, Iran, Japan, Korea, Middle East, Oceania, Philippines, Southeast Asia, Taiwan and Hong Kong (Part III; Sec. 3); Great Britain (Part III, Sec. 4); California Proposition 187, 1994, California Proposition 227, 1998 (Part IV, Sec. 1).

BIBLIOGRAPHY

Bergesen, Albert, and Max Herman. "Immigration, Race, and Riot: The 1992 Los Angeles Uprising." *American Sociological Review* 63 (1998): 39–54.

Bozorgmehr, Mehdi, Georges Sabagh, and Ivan Light. "Los Angeles: Explosive Diversity." In *Origins and Destinies*, ed. Pedraza and Rumbaut.

Bureau of the Census. *Nativity of the Population for the 50 Largest Urban Places: 1870–1990*. Table 19.www.census.gov/population/www/documentation/twps0029/tab19.html (3/9/99 release date).

Bureau of the Census. *Statistical Abstract of the United States: 1997*. Washington, DC: U.S. Bureau of the Census, 1997.

Bureau of the Census. 1990. CensusCD version 1.1. "Area Snapshots" for selected Primary Metropolitan Statistical Areas (PMSAs). Washington, DC: Bureau of the Census, 1990.

Carino, Benjamin. "Filipino Americans: Many and Varied." In *Origins and Destinies*, ed. Pedraza and Rumbaut.

Chavez, Leo. "Borders and Bridges: Undocumented Immigrants from Mexico and Central America." In *Origins and Destinies*, ed. Pedraza and Rumbaut.

Cheng, Lucie, and Philip Yang. "Asians: The 'Model Minority' Deconstructed." In *Ethnic Los Angeles*, ed. Waldinger and Bozorgmehr.

Davis, Mike. *Ecology of Fear: Los Angeles and the Imagination of Disaster*. New York: Metropolitan Books, 1998.

———. *City of Quartz: Excavating the Future in Los Angeles*. New York: Vintage Books, 1990.

Dear, Michael. "In the City, Time Becomes Visible: Intentionality and Urbanism in Los Angeles, 1781–1991." In *The City*, ed. Scott and Soja.

Dentler, Robert, and Anne Hafner. *Hosting Newcomers: Structuring Educational Opportunities for Immigrant Children*. New York: Teachers College Press, 1997.

Espenshade, Thomas. "Unauthorized Immigration to the United States." *Annual Review of Sociology* 21 (1995): 195–216.

Espenshade, Thomas, and Gregory Huber. "Fiscal Impacts of Immigrants and the Shrinking Welfare State." In *Handbook of International Migration*, ed. Kasinitz and DeWind.

Fogelson, Robert. *The Fragmented Metropolis: Los Angeles, 1850–1930*. Cambridge: Harvard University Press, 1967.

Garcia, Maria Christina. *Havana USA: Cuban Exiles and Cuban Americans in South Florida*. Los Angeles: University of California Press, 1996.

Gonzalez-Baker, Susan. "The 'Amnesty' Aftermath: Current Policy Issues Stemming from the Legalization Programs of the 1986 Immigration Reform and Control Act." *International Migration Review* 31 (1997): 5–27.

Grenier, Guillermo, and Lisandro Perez. "Miami Spice: The Ethnic Cauldron Simmers." In *Origins and Destinies*, ed. Pedraza and Rumbaut.

Griswold del Castillo, Richard. *La Familia: Chicano Families in the Urban Southwest, 1848 to the Present*. Notre Dame: University of Notre Dame Press, 1984.

Johnson, James, Walter Farrell, and Chandra Guinn. "Immigration Reform and the Browning of America: Tensions, Conflict, and Community Instability in Metropolitan Los Angeles." *International Migration Review* 31 (1997): 1055–95.

Kasinitz, Philip, and Josh DeWind, eds. *The Handbook of International Migration: The American Experience*. New York: Russell Sage Foundation, 1999.

Laslett, John. "Historical Perspectives: Immigration and the Rise of a Distinctive Urban Region, 1900–1970." In *Ethnic Los Angeles*, ed. Waldinger and Bozorgmehr.

Lopez, David, Eric Popkin, and Edward Telles. "Central Americans: At the Bottom, Struggling to Get Ahead." In *Ethnic Los Angeles*, ed. Waldinger and Bozorgmehr.

Massey, Douglas, and Kristin Espinosa. "What's Driving Mexico-US Migration? A Theoretical, Empirical, and Policy Analysis." *American Journal of Sociology* 102 (1997): 939–99.

McWilliams, Carey. *Southern California Country: An Island on the Land*. New York: American Book—Stratford Press, 1946.

Mollenkopf, John. "Urban Political Conflicts and Alliances: New York and Los Angeles Compared." In *Handbook of International Migration*, ed. Kasinitz and DeWind.

Ong, Paul, and Tania Azores. "Asian Immigrants in Los Angeles: Diversity and Divisions." In *The New Asian Immigration in Los Angeles and Global Restructuring*, ed. Paul Ong, Edna Bonacich, and Lucie Cheng. Philadelphia: Temple University Press, 1994.

Ortiz, Vilma. "The Mexican-Origin Population: Permanent Working Class or Emerging Middle Class?" In *Ethnic Los Angeles*, ed. Waldinger and Bozorgmehr.

Pedraza, Silvia, and Ruben Rumbaut, eds. *Origins and Destinies: Immigration, Race, and Ethnicity in America*. New York: Wadsworth Publishing, 1996.

Portes, Alejandro, and Ruben Rumbaut. *Immigrant America: A Portrait*. Expanded 2d ed. Los Angeles: University of California Press, 1996.

Romo, Ricardo. "Mexican Americans: Their Civic and Political Incorporation." In *Origins and Destinies*, ed. Pedraza and Rumbaut.

Rumbaut, Ruben. "The New Californians: Comparative Research Findings on the Educational Progress of Immigrant Children." In *California's Immigrant Children*, ed. Rumbaut and Cornelius.

Rumbaut, Ruben. "Origins and Destinies: Immigration to the United States Since World War II." *Sociological Forum* 9 (1994): 583–621.

Rumbaut, Ruben. "Transformations: The Post-Immigrant Generation in an Age of Diversity." Paper presented at the annual meeting of the Eastern Sociological Society, Philadelphia, March 1998.

Rumbaut, Ruben, and Wayne Cornelius, eds. *California's Immigrant Children*. San Diego: Center for US-Mexican Studies, 1995.

Sabagh, Georges, and Mehdi Bozorgmehr. "Population Change: Immigration and Ethnic Transformation." In *Ethnic Los Angeles*, ed. Waldinger and Bozorgmehr.

Sanchez, George. "Face the Nation: Race, Immigration, and the Rise of Nativism in Late-Twentieth-Century America." *International Migration Review* 31 (1997): 1009–31.

Scott, Allen, and Edward Soja, eds. *The City: Los Angeles and Urban Theory at the End of the Twentieth Century*. Los Angeles: University of California Press, 1996.

Skerry, Peter. *Mexican Americans: The Ambivalent Minority*. Cambridge: Harvard University Press, 1993.

Swartz, Mimi. "Letter from Miami: The Herald's Cuban Revolution." *New Yorker*, June 6, 1999, pp. 36–63.

Waldinger, Roger. 1996. "From Ellis Island to LAX: Immigrant Prospects in the American City." *International Migration Review* 30 (1996): 1078–86.

Waldinger, Roger, and Mehdi Bozorgmehr, eds. *Ethnic Los Angeles*. New York: Russell Sage Foundation, 1996.

Waldinger, Roger, and Michael Lichter. "Anglos: Beyond Ethnicity?" In *Ethnic Los Angeles*, ed. Waldinger and Bozorgmehr.

Zhou, Min. "Growing Up American: The Challenge Confronting Immigrant Children and Children of Immigrants." *Annual Review of Sociology* 23 (1997): 63–95.

MEX-AMERICA

The term *Mex-America* was coined by commentator Joel Garreau in *The Nine Nations of North America*. Mex-America is characterized by the predominant Mexican-American influence in the states of California, Texas, Arizona, New Mexico, and portions of Colorado, Wyoming, Nevada, and Utah. Mex-America is

> a place . . . that appears on no map. It's where the gumbo of Dixie gives way to the refried beans of Mexico. The land looks like Northern Mexico. And the sounds of Spanish in the supermarkets and on the airwaves are impossible to ignore. The news stories it produces point up the trouble Anglo institutions have in dealing with enormous cultural strain. It's a place where cops sometimes shoot third-generation Americans of Mexican descent for very controversial reasons, a region faced with the question of whether the American Dream applies to innocent kids born of people who have crossed the border illegally. It's hot and dry. It has more big dreams per capita than any other place you'll ever know. Its capital is Los Angeles, but it stretches all the way to Houston. The politicians have difficulties comprehending it, because it ignores political boundaries. But it's there, it's there.

Mex-America is definable less by its geographical borders than by the similarities in living conditions and the Mexican cultural influence in the southwestern United States. But for the purposes of understanding the region and its relationship to migration, it is equally important to view the border states of northern Mexico (Baja California, Sonora, Chihuahua, Coahila, Nuevo Leon, and Tamaulipas) as part of Mex-America as well. The last thirty-five years have witnessed major changes along the U.S.-Mexico border. Demographic shifts, economic restructuring, the physical and social construction of the border, and growing inequalities constitute these important changes. But to understand the contemporary realities of Mex-America, a look at the historical formation of the area is also equally essential.

HISTORICAL ORIGINS OF MEX-AMERICA

The defining historical moment in the construction of Mex-America, the border region, was the U.S.-Mexico War of 1846–48 and its resultant Treaty of Guadalupe Hidalgo. In the treaty, Mexico ceded nearly 50 percent of its northern territories to the United States for a sum of $15 million. Literally overnight, the estimated one hundred thousand Mexican citizens who resided in the ceded territory were no longer living on Mexican soil. The newly designated inhabitants of the United States had three choices: move themselves south of the newly designated border to rejoin Mexico, publicly declare their Mexican citizenship in the now foreign land, or do nothing and become designated as U.S. citizens. A few opted for one of the first two options, but most become de facto citizens of the United States. Article Nine of the treaty was aimed specifically at the rights of the Mexican-origin population. Those who chose to remain in the United States were accorded "the enjoyment of all the rights of citizens of the United States, according to the principles of the Constitution; and in the meantime, shall be maintained and protected in the free enjoyment of their liberty and property, and secured in the free exercise of their religion without restriction." Article Ten, which specifically secured land rights by recognizing prior Spanish and Mexican land grants, was struck from the treaty by the U.S. Senate.

The Gadsen Treaty was engineered in 1853 and resulted in Mexico ceding an additional portion of its northern frontier. With the purchase of the land that now is the southern portion of Arizona and New Mexico, the border that divides the United States and

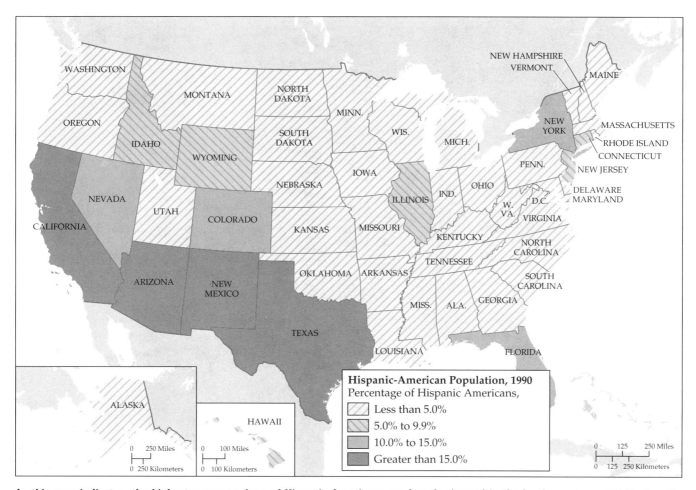

Hispanic-American Population, 1990
Percentage of Hispanic Americans,

	Less than 5.0%
	5.0% to 9.9%
	10.0% to 15.0%
	Greater than 15.0%

As this map indicates, the highest concentrations of Hispanic Americans are largely situated in the border regions with Mexico, the Pacific Coast, the southern mountain states, and South Florida. *(CARTO-GRAPHICS)*

Mexico was defined, and the same boundary has been maintained to the present day.

The U.S. border region was defined by the institutionalization of three major economic sectors: agriculture, mining, and rail transportation. Agricultural production provided the backbone of economic development and thus, provided the majority of positions available for Mexican migrants. By 1929, California had become the largest producer of fruits and vegetables in the Southwest. The state accounted for 40 percent of the total output of agricultural goods in the United States. For the Mexican-origin population, the employment options in mining were limited to the most dangerous, dirty, and difficult tasks. Restrictions, such as the 1849 California Foreign Miners Tax, were put in place to deny job advancement and ensure the marginal status of Mexican miners. Employment in rail transportation was directly linked to the infrastructure developments in Mexico. The majority of migrants who entered the United States originated from Mexico's cities and small towns *(pueblos)* that

were located within a day's walk of the burgeoning railway system. This railway system was financed by many of the U.S. capitalists who also funded the U.S. rail transportation network. As a result, the Mexican economy was dependent on U.S. markets for the commodities they produced.

In Mexico, the Porfiriato, or reign of Mexican President Porfirio Diaz (1876–1911), resulted in the entire *ejido* system of communal landholdings crumbling in the wake of export-based capitalist agriculture. This led to a push of landless peasants *(campesinos)* into the urban centers of Mexico's central plateau and northern border states. The Porfiriato also served as an important catalyst for the subsequent mass migrations to the United States. The creation of a landless peasantry in Mexico (it is estimated that 5 million *campesinos* were displaced by the Porfiriato) went hand in hand with attempts to implement capitalist development and modernization.

The Porfiriato utilized four means to destroy the *ejido* system. First, the 1883 Law of Vacant Lands was

Despite increasing security, people on both sides of the Mexican-American border cross frequently for daily errands, jobs, and—as with these Mexican children from Las Palomas—school. *(Jack Kurtz/Impact Visuals)*

established providing that any private colonizing company (an organization set up with the stated purpose of encouraging European immigration to the area in order to foster economic development) would receive up to one-third of the land it surveyed and subdivided. The second measure was an enforcement of Mexico's constitution of 1857 that forbid civil corporations (i.e., *ejidos*) from owning any land at all. This began to be enforced by the Porfiriato dictatorship in 1889 and 1890. Third, the Porfiriato was characterized by a rise in the number of hacienda land encroachments. With the spread of railways in Mexico, *hacendados* (owners of the large ranches) seized the majority of productive agricultural land from communal landholders for the express purpose of producing export-based commodities to be traded on the newly connected markets. The final means of expropriating land from peasants was the legal process of the denunciation of title, which allowed individuals to "lay claim to occupied lands that did not have a registered title simply by going to the local authorities and 'denouncing' the pretended title to the land in his

name." Coupled with the push factors associated with the Mexican Revolution, the Porfiriato led to a huge displacement of rural Mexican citizens.

As a result, labor became a very important export for Mexico. U.S. capitalists in the railroad, agricultural, and mining industries sent recruiters *(enganchadores)* to the populous central plateau of Mexico for cheap, desperate labor. El Paso, Texas, became the central way station for labor recruitment and distribution to not only the southwestern United States but also industrial centers such as Kansas City, Chicago, and Detroit. Historian George J. Sanchez estimates that three-fourths of all Mexican immigrants who settled in Los Angeles during the 1930s entered the United States through El Paso. The termination point of the Mexican Central Railroad, which originated in central Mexico, was El Paso. Most U.S. lines that headed westward, such as the Southern Pacific Railroad, went through El Paso. During that time, a number of labor contractors began business operations in El Paso to take advantage of the northward migration and link Mexican citizens with U.S. employers, pre-

Mexicans living in the Mexican border town of Anapra protest the erection of a border fence separating them from Sunland Park, New Mexico. The large sign reads: "No walls that separate." *(Jack Kurtz/Impact Visuals)*

dominantly in agriculture, mining, and railroads but also in meatpacking, cannery, and automobile factory work. Individual contractors, El Paso–owned employment agencies, representatives of southwestern and national corporations, and government-operated employment offices all established labor recruitment operations in El Paso.

One of the most important components of this recruitment strategy can be seen in the labor recruitment practices of the Great Western Sugar Company. Headquartered in northern Colorado, Great Western controlled sugar beet fields and processing plants on the plains of Colorado, Wyoming, Nebraska, and Kansas. In 1920, they established a labor recruitment office in El Paso and additionally began door-to-door canvassing campaigns, held public meetings, ran newspaper ads, and offered free transportation to the residents in the Mexican communities of New Mexico, Colorado, Texas, Kansas, Missouri, and Nebraska. Their labor recruitment strategies of targeting impoverished Mexicans and the reliance on *enganchadores* set the stage for later migration patterns.

These recruitment strategies were officially codi-

fied by the United States with the institution of the Bracero Program, 1942–64. A series of accords between the federal governments of Mexico and the United States brought Mexican laborers into agriculture and, for a time, the railroad industry. Initially intended to serve as a wartime relief measure, the temporary-worker arrangements were allowed to continue until 1964. The vast majority of workers were sent to three states (California, Arizona, and Texas), but a total of thirty states participated in the program. It is estimated that more than 4.5 million contracts were signed during the program's twenty-two-year duration. The federal governments of Mexico and the United States served as the recruitment agents of contract laborers. The Mexican government established recruitment centers in the northern border states of Mexico, and the U.S. government constructed processing centers in U.S. border towns.

From the history of U.S.-Mexico relations in the borderlands, where the two countries meet, it is much easier to comprehend how contemporary patterns were shaped by these historical forces. The demographics, economics, politics, culture, and identities in Mex-America today have many of their roots in the past.

DEMOGRAPHICS OF MEX-AMERICA

In 1990, an estimated nine million people resided in the U.S.-Mexico border region. The population was concentrated in two sets of sister cities: San Diego, California/Tijuana, Baja California, and El Paso, Texas/Ciudad Juarez, Chihuahua. In those four cities, an estimated 3,153,830 people reside within the city limits (35 percent of the total border population). According to sociologists Roberto Ham-Chande and John Weeks, the San Diego metropolitan area encompasses nearly one-half of the total U.S. border population.

But the large populations along the border were not always present. For instance, in 1900 Tijuana had a population of 242 people, and San Diego's population numbered nearly 18,000. As historian Oscar J. Martínez notes, the regional economies and populations of the border towns have historically tended to follow boom-and-bust cycles. Due to the fact that Mex-America was heavily dependent on extractive industries, the regional economies fluctuated with mineral prices, trade relations between Mexico and the United States, the market value of agricultural commodities, and the relative global supply of raw materials. U.S. Prohibition also provided a stimulus for demographic growth in Mexico's border towns. The Mexican border towns capitalized on the lack of sanctions on serving alcohol, and a number of nightclubs, bars, resorts, racetracks, and gambling halls arose in Tijuana and Ciudad Juarez. For example, Agua Caliente in Tijuana entertained patrons with cockfighting, horse racing, dog racing, gambling, theatrical performances, nightclubs, and golf. Hollywood entertainers made their way to Agua Caliente, a hot spot during the days of Prohibition.

One of the unique phenomena that define the U.S.-Mexico border region is the rise of sister cities on both sides of the border. Where California meets Baja California, the sister cities of San Diego–Tijuana and Calexico-Mexicali come together. On the border of Arizona and Sonora, one finds the sister cities of Nogales-Nogales, Yuma–San Luis Colorado, and Douglas–Agua Prieta. And along the Texas-Mexico border, a number of sister cities have developed: El Paso–Ciudad Juarez, Del Rio–Ciudad Acuña, Eagle Pass–Piedras Negras, Laredo–Nuevo Laredo, McAllen-Reynosa, and Brownsville-Matamoros.

THE ECONOMIC RESTRUCTURING OF MEX-AMERICA

Concomitant with the rise of sister cities along the border, there also developed a number of twin or sister *maquiladoras, or maquilas*. The *maquilas* (factories built in the border regions of Mexico) are part of a much larger global economic trend as the cheap labor of underdeveloped nations is utilized to assemble (and sometimes produce) goods at a very low cost of production. In the United States, sister plants were built to facilitate the shipping and distribution of goods produced and assembled in Mexico's *maquilas*. In Mexico, a number of foreign-owned assembly plants located operations along the border after the Mexican government initiated the Border Industrialization Program of 1965. In many ways, the Border Industrialization Program was developed to fill the void left by the termination of the Bracero Program. As stated in the *Mexican Newsletter:* "The advantages of setting up assembly plants became evident when the agreement governing the entry of seasonal workers into the United States ceased to function. They were particularly interesting as new sources of employment in an area beset by unemployment and underemployment."

The border region of northern Mexico has a long history of economic dependence on the markets of the United States. This is due to the Mexican federal government's special concessions to Mexican companies that wanted to do business with the United States. A *zona libre,* or free-trade zone, was established in the immediate border region of Tamaulipas and Chihuahua in 1858. Looking northward to U.S. markets, firms produced goods for export. The ascension of dictator Porfirio Diaz saw an expansion of the *zona libre* to the entire U.S.-Mexico border in 1885. The zone was challenged by U.S. merchants and their government representatives and also within Mexico. In 1891, a new clause was introduced that "stipulated that any goods manufactured in the Zona, whether composed of foreign or domestic raw materials, were subject to 90 percent of regular duties if shipped into the [Mexican] interior." The *zona libre* was eventually struck down in 1905, and it was not until the early 1930s that free-trade border zones were again officially designated by the Mexican government. Under the aegis of promoting migration to the northern border states, the free-trade zones were implemented to boost the Mexican border economies, which were ravaged by the Depression and end of Prohibition. The prior, exclusive dependence of regional Mexican economies on U.S. tourism and alcohol production was expanded with the redefining of free-trade border zones. Manufacturing, mineral extraction, textiles, and smelting plants were all developed with the aid of the Mexican government's policy shift in favor of northern Mexico's "special status" as a U.S. trading partner.

The Border Industrialization Program of 1965 can be seen as an extension of the notion of viewing the northern border region as a free-trade zone. The program was designed to encourage U.S. companies to send raw materials and components to the Mexican *maquilas* for assembly. Finished goods would then be returned to the United States and sold through U.S. distribution channels. In 1998, the number of *maquiladoras* was almost three thousand and the number of employees exceeded 1 million. The establishment of assembly plants in Mexico by U.S. and other transnational corporations relates to the global economic shifts in labor and capital. The increasing global division of labor and accompanying strategies of capital flight to low-wage nations by multinational corporations are demonstrated quite clearly along the U.S.-Mexico border.

The ratification of the North American Free Trade Agreement (NAFTA) in 1993 by the nations of Mexico, Canada, and the United States attempted to develop a tariff-free trade bloc. Using the *maquiladoras* as the main source of cheap labor, assembly plants were established in Mexico and expanded to capitalize on the labor of predominately Mexican women. In 1975, nearly 80 percent of all *maquila* operators were female. In 1985, 69 percent of the operators were women, and in 1990, an estimated 62 percent were women. But the *maquila* industry is still segregated by gender, and depending on the job task and industrial section, Mexican women are found in the lowest-paid and most hazardous job positions. Women occupy at least three-quarters of the positions in the service sector, food processing, and assembly line work.

THE PHYSICAL AND SOCIAL CONSTRUCTION OF THE BORDER

One of the other defining characteristics of contemporary Mex-America is the increasing militarization of the border. Sociologist Timothy Dunn has quite successfully argued that the military doctrine of low-intensity conflict (LIC) has been applied by the U.S. Immigration and Naturalization Service (INS) to "defend" the southern border of the United States. The equipment used to patrol the border (helicopters, night-vision equipment, electronic intrusion-detection ground sensors), operational tactics and strategies of border enforcement (combining police, military, and paramilitary forces), and overall aim of social control of a targeted civilian population all embody the LIC doctrine that has been put into action by the U.S. military in Vietnam, Somalia, Libya, Kuwait, Panama, and Grenada.

What has become the most visible physical manifestation of this militarization of the border region has been the construction of walls and fences to separate the urban sister cities. A series of INS campaigns from 1993 to the present (such as Operation Blockade and Operation Hold-the-Line in El Paso, Operation Gatekeeper in San Diego, and Operation Guardian—the "Light up the Border" campaign—in Douglas and Nogales, Arizona) have all had the result of physically defining the line in the sand or rivers that have symbolically marked the divisions between Mexico and the United States. As sociologist Néstor Rodríguez notes, "Nation-state boundaries are social constructions. They do not exist independent of our volition. . . . Nation-state borders exist primarily because state governments agree, voluntarily or through coercion, that they delimit political divisions. Solemn treaties formalize international boundaries, but it is the daily reproduction of ideas and myths that socially construct borders."

INEQUALITIES AND IDENTITIES IN THE BORDERLANDS

The lived realities of the citizens of Mexico in comparison to the lives of U.S. citizens point to the very real differences between the two nations. The intense level of inequality is demonstrated by a few recent statistics published by the San Diego Association of Governments (SANDAG). When data are collected by U.S. agencies on the labor force, the assumption is that wage labor does not begin until eighteen years of age, or after the completion of high school. When the Mexican government collects statistics on labor force participation, they include numbers that begin with those age twelve. The differential between the federally mandated minimum wages in the United States and Mexico is representative of the inequalities between the two nations. In the United States, the federal minimum wage is currently $5.15 per *hour*. In Mexico, the conversion of pesos into U.S. dollars puts the comparative wage from Mexico at $5 per *day*. In Table 1, the numbers demonstrate both the inflationary ten-

Table 1
Mexican Minimum Wage (per day)

Year	Mexican Pesos	U.S. Dollars
1985	1,250	3.42
1986	2,480	3.14
1987	6,469	2.93
1988	8,000	3.62
1989	9,160	3.72
1990	11,990	4.41
1991	13,330	4.30

Source: SANDAG. "Baja California Demographic Profile." *INFO Update Newsletter* May-June 1992.

dencies of the peso and the exchange value in U.S. dollars as indicative of the differential in wages (through 1991).

In terms of education, the relatively high dropout rate of students living in U.S. border towns cannot compare to the barriers facing the population in Mexico. For example, of the Mexican citizens age fifteen or older living in Baja California, 44.9 percent have no education beyond grade school. Out of these vast inequalities have emerged both a redefinition of identities and border cultures as well as new migration patterns.

Mexican Americans living in Mex-America have drawn upon the cultures of Mexico and been influenced by U.S. popular culture, as well as invented new modes of self-expression. The Chicano movement of the 1970s was as much about exerting political rights as it was a time of artistic and cultural redefinition. For instance, San Diego's Chicano Park has drawn inspiration from the Mexican revolutionary muralist art movement to take control of *la tierra mia* ("my land") and adorned the Coronado Bridge columns with images of Emiliano Zapata, Our Lady of Guadalupe, Aztec warriors and goddesses, and depictions of current Chicano struggles over the environment, labor, and land. Coming out of the Chicano movement, Gloria Anzaldúa writes in her highly acclaimed *Borderlands/La Frontera:*

> The actual physical borderland that I'm dealing with in this book is the Texas-U.S. Southwest/Mexican border. . . . I am a border woman. I grew up between two cultures, the Mexican (with a heavy Indian influence) and the Anglo (as a member of a colonized people in our own territory). I have been straddling that *tejas*-Mexican border, all my life.

Writing from the standpoint of an immigrant from Mexico, performance artist Guillermo Gómez-Peña similarly states that border cultures are hybrids. Writing from his experience, he states:

> From 1978 to 1991, I lived and worked in and among the cities of Tijuana, San Diego, and Los Angeles. Like hundreds of thousands of Mexicans living at the border, I was a binational commuter. . . . My art, my dreams, my family and friends, and my psyche were literally and conceptually divided by the border. . . . No matter where I was, I was always on "the other side," feeling ruptured and incomplete, ever longing for my other selves, my other home and tribe.

The prevalence of "commuter" migrants who live in either Mexico or the United States and work and shop *en el otro lado* (on the other side) has not been fully examined by researchers. The most recent estimates cited by geographer Lawrence Herzog are that nearly 160,000 Mexican workers commute to jobs in the United States each day. A Target department store in Chula Vista, California (south San Diego), estimates that 80 percent of its customers live in Mexico. Studies still need to be conducted on U.S. citizens who work in Mexico or shop in the pharmacies and other local businesses that offer items that cannot be readily found in the United States. From the history of U.S.-Mexico relations, the contemporary contours of Mex-America, the border region, can be more fully elucidated.

Ronald L. Mize

See also: Central America, Mexico (Part III, Sec. 2).

BIBLIOGRAPHY

Anzaldúa, Gloria. *Borderlands/La Frontera: The New Mestiza.* San Francisco: Aunt Lute Books, 1999.

Calavita, Kitty. *Inside the State: The Bracero Program, Immigration, and the I.N.S.* New York: Routledge, 1992.

Cardoso, Lawrence. *Mexican Emigration to the United States.* Tucson: University of Arizona Press, 1980.

Dunn, Timothy. *The Militarization of the U.S.-Mexico Border.* Austin: University of Texas Press, 1996.

García, Mario T. *Desert Immigrants.* New Haven: Yale University Press, 1981.

García y Griego, Manuel. "U.S. Importation of Mexican Contract Laborers." *The Border That Joins: Mexican Migrants and U.S. Responsibility,* ed. Peter G. Brown and Henry Shue, pp. 49–98. Totowa, NJ: Rowman and Littlefield, 1983.

Garreau, Joel. *The Nine Nations of North America*. Boston: Houghton Mifflin Company, 1981.

Gómez-Peña, Guillermo. *The New World Border*. San Francisco: City Lights Books, 1996.

Ham-Chande, Roberto, and John R. Weeks. *Demographic Dynamics of the U.S.-Mexico Border*. El Paso: Texas Western Press, 1992.

Herzog, Lawrence. "Border Commuter Workers and Transfrontier Metropolitan Structure Along the U.S.-Mexico Border." In *U.S.-Mexico Borderlands: Historical and Contemporary Perspectives*, ed. O. Martínez, pp. 176–89. Wilmington, DE: Scholarly Resources, Inc., 1996.

Kiser, George C., and Martha W. Kiser. *Mexican Workers in the United States*. Albuquerque: University of New Mexico Press, 1979.

Martínez, Oscar J. *Border Boom Town: Ciudad Juarez Since 1848*. Austin: University of Texas Press, 1975.

———. *Border People: Life and Society in the U.S.-Mexico Borderlands*. Tucson: University of Arizona Press, 1994.

Peña, Devon. *The Terror of the Machine*. Austin: University of Texas Press, 1999.

Rodríguez, Néstor. "The Social Construction of the U.S.-Mexico Border." In *Immigrants Out! The New Nativism and the Anti-Immigrant Impulse in the United States*, ed. J. Perea, pp. 223–43. New York: New York University Press, 1997.

Sanchez, George J. *Becoming Mexican American*. New York: Oxford University Press, 1993.

SANDAG (San Diego Association of Governments). "Baja California Demographic Profile." *INFO Update Newsletter* (May–June 1992).

Sklair, Leslie. *Assembling for Development: The Maquila Industry in Mexico and the United States*. Boston: Unwin Hyman, 1989.

MIAMI

Immigration has effectively changed the American urban landscape. There is no better example of this transformation than the case of Miami, the second largest city in Florida and the county seat of Miami-Dade County. Incorporated in 1896, after millionaire Henry Flagler extended the railroad from northern Florida, Miami was envisioned as a tropical paradise. The Florida East Coast Railroad would connect Miami to the East Coast, fulfilling Flagler's dream of making the area an enticement to the wealthy of the Northeast. Consequently, in the early 1920s through the 1950s, what began as a resort for the affluent members of American society, with its tropical breezes on beachfront properties, nightclubs, and hotels, would become a refuge for immigrants fleeing political persecution and economic despair.

Its proximity to the Caribbean has been beneficial in providing opportunity to those seeking the safety of democracy and the economic freedom that capitalism has to offer. Miami came to represent independence and the pursuit of the American Dream. It was as true for these new immigrants as it was for their early European predecessors. As a newly emerging city, Miami was readily looking for growth, and the immigrants would come to provide the human capital and the resources needed to make it happen.

In preparation for the continuing immigration from the Caribbean basin, Miami was adapting to the change. For example, in 1963, Miami-Dade County was the location for the first bilingual education program in public schools. Responding to the demographic changes within the county, the Board of Commissioners declared Miami-Dade County to be officially bilingual and bicultural in 1973. Moreover, in 1976, the most widely circulated newspaper serving the greater Miami area created a supplement titled *El Herald* to serve the growing population of Hispanic residents. These changes were instrumental in demonstrating the effects the new immigrants were having within Miami.

However, some changes would be short lived. As the immigrant population grew, a backlash soon followed. What has continued to make Miami unique was that it has one of the largest proportions of foreign-born people of any major metropolitan area in the United States, with approximately 35 percent. Yet Miami was also the birthplace of the antibilingual referendum, also known as the "English-only" ordinances. Shortly after the Mariel boat lift in 1980, the Board of County Commissioners passed a measure prohibiting the use of county funds for publications in any other language than English. With a population of over 2 million, Miami-Dade County, Florida, is home to residents speaking over 120 languages.

Although the majority of Miami-Dade residents in the year 2000 are Hispanic, it is very much a heterogeneous group made up predominantly of Cubans who emigrated following the collapse of the Batista regime in 1959, Nicaraguans escaping civil war in the 1980s, Mexicans who migrated for winter crops, and others from locations in Central and South America who have been coming for several decades. With over 77,000 migrating from 1977 to 1982, Haitian immigrants also represent a large component of recent newcomers affecting how Miami views itself. Although the educated class of Haitian society speaks French, the more common language spoken remains Creole. All have come together to create a vital cosmopolitan city tied to the global economy. This change is quite dramatic considering the number of immigrants was extremely low before 1950 when compared to the post–1960 era.

DEMOGRAPHIC CHANGES

The population of Miami-Dade County is predominantly Latino. With a demographic composition of 49.2 percent Latino, 20.8 percent black, 22 percent

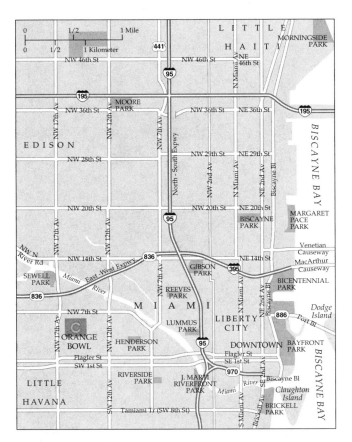

A key destination for Cubans since the late 1950s, in recent decades Miami has also become a magnet for immigrants from South and Central America and the Caribbean, earning the city the unofficial title, "Capital of Latin America." *(CARTO-GRAPHICS)*

white, and 8 percent other, Miami reflects the diversity of the Caribbean and Latin America with an Anglo presence primarily of European descent. A shift in the population occurred primarily due to migration from the Caribbean basin and the subsequent out-migration by Anglos, a phenomenon known as "white flight." Many Anglos, uncomfortable with the rapid changes occurring within Miami, moved to northern counties in Florida such as Broward and Palm Beach. The evacuation of Anglos from Miami-Dade County made available additional housing and employment opportunities for the new arrivals.

The growth and subsequent prosperity experienced in Miami is often attributed to the strong immigrant presence. Immigrants with the language ability and business acumen facilitated a relationship with Latin America that has led the city to replace New Orleans as the principal trade center between Latin America and the United States. The black presence in Miami also became strong, as southern blacks from Georgia and northern Florida and immigrants

from the Bahamas and Jamaica provided a pool of unskilled, low-wage labor. This small population of African Americans experienced a tide of booms and busts. It was during a period of economic bust that Miami experienced its most dramatic change.

THE CUBAN EXODUS

The first and largest wave of immigration occurred from 1958 to 1962. This migration stream that began as flight from the incoming Communist regime, which nationalized industry and seized private property, would continue until the political standoff of the Cuban Missile Crisis. The crisis would provide the political incentive needed to allocate funds to the new refugees, while validating their beliefs in the danger of communism to the United States citizenry.

Cubans escaping the collapse of the Batista regime and the political persecution associated with the incoming Castro regime caught some of the last flights to leave Havana or chartered boats to Miami. They strongly believed they could find a temporary refuge until they could one day return to Cuba. Florida, after all, had been well known to the elites of Cuban society. It was a popular location for both family vacations and financial dealings. Seeking self-exile in Miami was a natural course for those intent on waiting for the collapse of the Cuban revolution, so as to return to the life they had left behind on the island. By 1961, the U.S. government had established the Cuban Refugee Program, which gave special refugee status to Cubans and provided them economic assistance for resettlement.

Following the fall of the Batista regime and the failure of the Bay of Pigs invasion in 1961, thousands of Cuba's wealthiest and most elite members fled to Miami. Castro had touted his intent to nationalize businesses, and those who were his greatest foes were fleeing for their lives. By 1965, nearly 570,000 had relocated to Miami. Cubans were part of a large immigration stream creating an exile community in Miami. The self-designation of "exile" gave the immigrants cohesiveness in the belief that they were experiencing a temporary situation. They hoped and expected that when Castro was deposed from power they would be able to return to the life they had once led. The belief was pervasive that his coming to power was merely a temporary setback.

The first wave of immigrants from Cuba facilitated the transformation to an enclave by opening enterprises that would offer culturally defined goods and services. These enterprises gave newly arrived Cu-

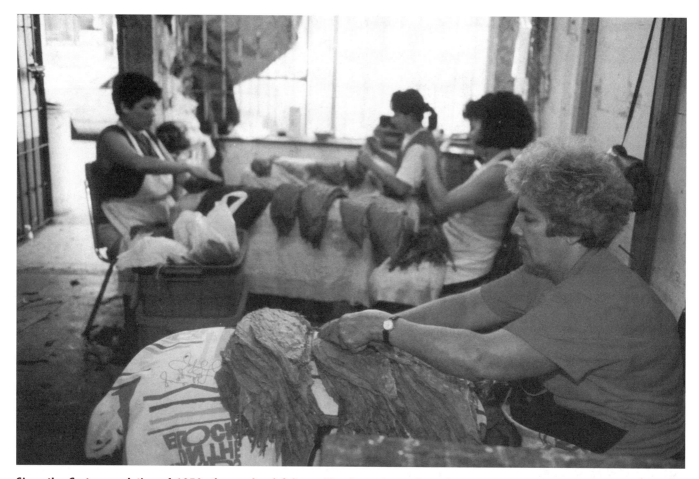

Since the Castro revolution of 1959, thousands of Cubans, like these cigarmakers, have made their homes in the "Little Havana" section of Miami. *(Jack Kurtz/Impact Visuals)*

bans a taste and feel of Havana; in turn, they were likely to frequent the new enterprises and assist in their success. These enterprises were also a source of employment, therefore facilitating the absorption of Cuban immigrants into the community. There was a shift in the demographics of subsequent waves of immigrants from Cuba.

The second wave of immigration from Cuba, 1963–65, brought a more representative sample of the island's population. This wave, although predominantly middle class, also included some working-class individuals. These people would provide the needed low-wage labor to work in the newly emerging small businesses opening throughout the area that would be known as Little Havana. Within this transitional neighborhood, Cuban immigrants were able to find employment and housing. This became an integral means for the absorption of the Cuban immigrants who continued to arrive.

The Cuban government, looking for a means to relieve mounting pressure on the island from those

eager to emigrate, allowed the use of the port of Camarioca for relatives from Miami to pick up family members. Approximately five thousand Cubans took advantage of the relaxation of policy. This ended when the United States and Cuba set forth a plan to resume daily flights from Cuba to Miami.

In December 1965, the airlift known as "freedom flights" was initiated to assist Cubans wishing to emigrate from Cuba. Daily flights to the United States brought more than 260,000 persons until their end in 1973. Those wanting to emigrate from Cuba after that time would need to find other means to leave the island.

The U.S. government in cooperation with American religious communities, initiated a program to allow for the emigration of children from Cuba. The Catholic diocese, Protestant denominations, and the Jewish community participated in locating placement for the incoming children. Designated Operation Pedro Pan (or Peter Pan), this program devised a strategy to provide visas to the youth from middle- and upper-middle-class families in Cuba, bring them to the United States, and place them in temporary foster care programs until the parents could arrive in the United States and reunite the family. Approximately fourteen thousand children were placed in foster care between 1960 and 1962.

Additional social programs were funded to assist in the assimilation of the immigrants into the population. With the greatest proportion of Cubans wishing to stay in Miami-Dade County, a relocation assistance program was needed to facilitate the resettlement of parties willing to move to other regions of the country. Resettlement programs in New York, New Jersey, Los Angeles, and Chicago received the larger proportions of new arrivals. Cubans had had a presence in these metropolitan areas prior to the fall of the Batista regime. The relocation programs provided financial entitlements and assistance in obtaining housing and employment.

THE MARIEL BOAT LIFT

In an attempt to alleviate the costs of caring for the mentally ill and prisoners and to rid the island of those his regime believed to be undesirable, Castro made an unprecedented move. In 1980, Cubans were allowed to leave the island. Thousands took to the sea in fishing and charter boats, many in crafts not considered seaworthy. However, word had quickly come to Miami that anyone wishing to leave Cuba would be allowed to do so. Cuban-American exiles, eager to be reunited with their families, piloted their boats or hired boats to pick up those left behind. Fidel Castro responded by emptying prisons and mental institutions, forcing those he designated as undesirables to leave the island. Each boat attempting to pick up family members was forced to carry the "unwanted." The unexpected influx left Miami unprepared.

Immigration and Naturalization Service (INS) officials, aware of Castro's strategy, prepared a makeshift processing center, where the latest immigrants could be detained until their former status could be determined. Those with no prior history of mental illness or a criminal past began the application process toward residency and were released into the custody of their Miami relatives. Following approval for registration as legal aliens, some were selected by the Cuban Relocation Program for resettlement in other regions of the country. These regions were selected based on the availability of employment and housing. By this time, the Mariel boat lift had come to an end, and over 125,000 had migrated to Miami. This un-

precedented political response by Fidel Castro would change how Cuban Americans would be perceived in the media and affect policy relating to those from the Caribbean basin.

Miami residents had mixed responses to the influx of "undesirables." As the news hit Miami that Castro was opening prisons, Cubans and natives alike were ambivalent about how to react to the new arrivals. Due to the overwhelming number of new immigrants reaching the shores, county officials had difficulty in discerning the histories of the newest immigrants. Therefore, a possible threat to public safety became a concern. In response to questions and as a means of controlling the high volume of immigrants entering the United States from Cuba, a temporary detention area was set up.

Many were first housed in a makeshift camp at Orange Bowl Stadium as INS began to find a means to deal with the situation. Federal allocations to the INS were redistributed to the Miami office to assist in the processing and investigation of Cuban entrants. The slow processing of the individuals led to increased frustration within the camps and what many described as the premature release of many detainees before an investigation could be completed.

However, through the relocation of Cuban immigrants and the increasing willingness of the Cuban-American community to accept the latest arrivals, eventual absorption did proceed. Yet, as turbulent as this mass migration may have been, it seemed as though the end result were certain: All would become part of American society. This experience was not one shared by the immigrants from Haiti.

THE UNWANTED REFUGEES: THE HAITIAN MIGRATION

Haitians attempting to migrate to the United States would encounter a very different reception from the Miami-Dade community. Characterized as uneducated, poor, and likely to burden society, Haitian immigrants faced many challenges. They were confronted by racism and negative stereotypes associated with being from a less developed country, making acceptance into Miami's multiethnic community more difficult. Few in Miami were aware of the long relationship Haiti has had with the United States. The United States had long been an important trading partner to Haiti and had intervened in Haitian politics many times, sending troops there several times in the twentieth century.

In power since 1957, the dictator François "Papa Doc" Duvalier ruled Haiti tightly. Fearful of the dictator's reign, all sectors of Haitian society began emigrating to Miami-Dade, New York City, and Montreal, Canada. As with the Cuban migration, the first to leave Haiti were representative of Haiti's elite classes. The turmoil associated with the Duvalier regime devastated Haiti's market economy. Facing high unemployment and trade deficits, Haitian markets had difficulty repaying their increasing debts. Near economic collapse and with poverty permeating every sector of Haitian life, immigration seemed like the only option. Throughout Haiti, many sought to break away from the economic upheaval and repression in hopes of rebuilding their lives in the United States.

Duvalier's government was well known for the use of force and covert tactics by the secret police against those attempting to challenge the regime. The dictatorship was marked by an increase in the disparity between the affluent and the poor of Haitian society. Those fearful of losing all their possessions attempted to escape to Miami in hopes of rebuilding their lives. Their reception, however, was less than positive. Haitians were also seen as less desirable than other immigrant populations due to the stigma attached to their relatively high incidence of the human immunodeficiency virus (HIV). In the late 1970s, Haitian activists such as the Reverend Gerard Jean Juste, director of the Haitian Refugee Center, asserted that race also seemed to be a factor weighing against their immigration status, since most Haitians were of African descent.

Upon entering the United States, Haitians were quarantined in detention facilities such as Krome Detention in South Dade County. Rumors spread that Haitians were likely to be infected with various communicable diseases such as HIV and tuberculosis. During their confinement, they would be tested for HIV and given the opportunity to apply for temporary residency. Heightened resistance against the current Haitian immigration policy increased political participation within predominantly Haitian neighborhoods.

In Miami, they created a smaller enclave known as Little Haiti in the Edison/Little River neighborhoods. Within these areas, Haitian-style restaurants and small grocery marts began appearing. The culture was reproduced with the assistance of neighborhood churches and community organizations. Intertwined within the Haitian culture are the remnants of French rule under which the elites in the country were educated in French and the lesser-educated working class primarily spoke Creole.

Citing the human rights abuses of the Duvalier re-

gime and fearful of a mass exodus from Haiti, the United States sent a political envoy led by former president Jimmy Carter to force the removal of Duvalier from Haiti in 1986. With the threat of military action, he finally acquiesced to the demands of the United States. U.S. troops occupied Haiti as a means of stabilizing political institutions, limiting the looting of businesses, and preparing Haiti for its second try at democracy.

With the downfall of the Duvalier regime and the election of a democratic government, Haiti is continuing its struggle to stabilize its market economy and is still dependent on the United States for much of its trade. Haitian immigration continues to be a point of contention between Haiti and the United States. In an agreement with the elected president Jean-Bertrand Aristide, all Haitians found illegally entering the United States were supposed to be returned to Port-au-Prince, Haiti. This policy had done little in the 1990s to prevent Haitians from attempting the dangerous journey across the Florida Straits in an attempt to reach economic independence, especially as political unrest continued to grip the island nation.

IMMIGRATION POLICY IMPLICATIONS

With immigration policy shifts such as the Refugee Act of 1980 and Immigration Reform and Control Act of 1986, the net effect on migration to Miami has changed. The Refugee Act of 1980 granted refugee status to both Haitians and Cubans as a means of equalizing the burden of proof for asylum. The one-time status as Cuban-Haitian Special Entrant had the unexpected result of bringing thousands of Cubans and Haitians to South Florida. In an attempt to curb the high numbers emigrating from both countries, Congress responded by amending the legislation. The result was the Immigration Reform and Control Act of 1986.

The act granted amnesty to all illegal aliens who could demonstrate that they had lived in the United States since 1982 and imposed sanctions on all employers who had knowingly hired illegal workers. The effectiveness of these policies was short lived.

Cuban migration took a more political turn in 1994 with the migration of rafters known as "Balseros." With the disintegration of the former Soviet Union, the Cuban economy was in shambles. Out of desperation, many chose to take their chances on makeshift rafts in an attempt to reach the United States, where immigration policy had stood firm that any Cuban reaching its shore would be granted political asylum.

With this reception and the promise of jobs, a welcoming exile community, and other entitlements, hundreds of desperate Cubans built unseaworthy rafts in an attempt to reach American soil.

In a treaty signed with Cuba, the United States has agreed to grant 15,000 visas to Cuba immigrants each year through the United States/Cuban Interest Section in Havana. Additionally, there is also what is called the "wet feet, dry feet" policy. If a Cuban can reach American soil, he or she can apply for political asylum. However, Coast Guard patrols have been vigilant in picking up all immigrants attempting to flee the island. If found on the open seas, they are quickly repatriated according to the new policy. This marks a change to the former policy dating back to 1962.

Comparatively, the INS has continued to refuse asylum hearings for Haitians reaching American shores. If discovered and deemed not to have legal status in the United States, Haitians are quickly repatriated without the opportunity to file for a hearing.

CURRENT MIGRATION TRENDS

Current migration trends have been affected by both internal and external migration patterns. Although earlier waves of Cuban immigrants were resettled in other locations, Miami has been affected by internal migration that brought many former residents back to Miami over the years. The desire to be near other Cubans and to live in a tropical climate has motivated thousands to return to the largest Cuban community outside their homeland.

Cubans and Haitians have continued their attempts to emigrate to Miami, although current immigration policy focuses on the intervention at sea. Coast Guard cutters strategically patrol the Florida Straits and the Florida coastline looking to turn back Cubans and Haitians attempting to reach U.S. soil illegally.

Haitian immigration remains a contentious issue. As discussed above, the early migration of Haitians was marred by negative beliefs about their "desirability." With some believing that Haitians are coming to this country only for economic benefits, claims of political persecution and physical threat are left unheard. Negated are political activists, who despite voicing opposition to Haitian politicians and the remnants of the Duvalier administration that would seem to put them in political danger back home, are returned to Haiti unprotected to face possible danger. Few legal avenues are available through which to obtain entry, and there are many within the Haitian-

American community of Miami-Dade County who believe that U.S. immigration policies are based on racial biases and ignore the political asylum issues and status offered Cuban immigrants. Consequently, the debate continues as the two opposing sides persist in voicing their dissatisfaction with current policies.

The economic desperation experienced by Cuba, Haiti, and most countries of the Caribbean basin has contributed to the ongoing attempts to emigrate. Hundreds of Haitians continue to pay smugglers high fees in hopes of making it to American soil and finding work. Most are well aware of the dangers of crossing the Florida Straits or facing the interdiction by Coast Guard patrols, yet these émigrés favor the possibility of starting a new life in a new country.

Emigration from the Bahamas, Jamaica, and the Dominican Republic has also added to the frustration of the immigration debate. Although their labor has greatly contributed to the growth and vitality of the county, their presence has also been a source for criticism. Many fail to note the historical role these nations have played in creating the globally linked city which Miami is today.

WHAT THE FUTURE HOLDS FOR MIAMI

If the current migration patterns continue, projections indicate that Miami's relationship with Latin America will also continue to grow. The net effect on Miami will be a continued immigration stream, predominantly from the Caribbean basin, and a strengthening of economic ties with that same region. The attractions of Miami include the warm weather, economic opportunity, and a large Hispanic population, which reduces obstacles such as language and an unfamiliar culture. Moreover, the Caribbean basin will continue to play an important economic role in relationship to South Florida, from its tourism industry to a more active trade partner.

Ties to Latin America and particularly the Caribbean have played an integral part in the development of Miami. Through international migration and the creation of an import and export economy, Miami was well positioned to take advantage of a changing economy. The first great wave of Cuban migration provided an educated class with the language skills to develop trade routes throughout Latin America.

Cuban Americans were the new mediators for American businesses eager for additional trading partners. Latin America presented an opportunity for the sale of American domestic goods. As a lesser-developed region open to new products, Latin America is ready for the new Cuban entrepreneurs to create their niche in this market. Moreover, Miami, with greater human capital and resources, is also prepared to develop linkages to support these new ventures. With the construction of warehouses, a physical infrastructure adaptable to the information age, and transportation facilities, Miami-Dade County is becoming an active partner in the development of trade routes.

As trade began to flourish, transnational corporations found Miami to be an important location at which to build operation centers for their Latin American distributors. The strong Hispanic presence provided an ample workforce to service the new center. Furthermore, the large immigrant population of coethnics supplied an abundant low-wage labor pool eager for work to rebuild the lives they had left behind. These laborers would provide the support services needed for the trade center to thrive. Immigrant workers found employment in various supportive roles from custodial services to security to basic restaurant work and car repair. All are vital links that have provided the means for Miami-Dade County to reach out and take advantage of its global positioning.

Immigrants from the Caribbean also found plentiful work in the construction of new housing and the creation of a physical infrastructure to support the growing population of Miami-Dade County. In response to the growing population, Miami has needed to continue to develop both to the western and the southern regions of the county. With continued expansion, the next movement of immigrants may first be to the north to Broward County and then to Palm Beach County. Immigrant settlement will no longer be localized in Miami. This may result in a redistribution of the immigrant population to these areas to take advantage of better employment opportunities.

Previous movements of immigrants have initiated concerns from the Anglo population. Responding to the early large influx of immigrants, Anglos moved northward to Broward County and other parts of Florida. Some referred to themselves as nativists and expressed resentment over the changes occurring within their city. Many of these Anglos participating in "white flight" were fearful of the newcomers. Soon bumper stickers were circulated with such slogans as "Would the last American to leave remember the Flag?" Increasing movement of immigrants to northern counties may face a similar reception. For the time being, however, the focus has remained on Miami.

Projected population estimates for Miami-Dade County indicate that a positive increase due to continued migration and an expansion of developed areas will greatly affect Miami's economy as it moves into the new millennium. A housing shortage has focused attention on the limited availability of affordable housing. Yet affordable housing is only one indicator of the impact of a continued migration stream to Miami.

The large immigrant community is growing to the extent that Miami-Dade County is continually trying to keep up with the increased demand on its infrastructure. Overcrowding in schools, insufficient health care delivery, and additional use of transportation systems are some of the problems resulting from the rapid growth. The burdens of the increasingly conservative nature of immigration reform and of preparing for the increase in population are more likely to fall on local shoulders, possibly spurring on more contentious debate over immigration. Immigration reforms, such as limiting access to entitlement programs (e.g., Social Security, welfare, and Medicaid), have all been highlighted in the national press. However, these issues have done little to deter an international migration stream intent on experiencing the idyllic lifestyle dubbed the American Dream.

Sandra Dalis Alvarez

See also: Immigrant Politics III: The Home Country (Part II, Sec. 6); Central America, Cuba, English-Speaking Caribbean, Haiti and French-Speaking Caribbean (Part III, Sec. 2); President Carter's Announcement on the *Marielitos,* 1980, President Bush and Courts on Return of Haitian Refugees, 1992, District Court on Admissions of Haitians, 1993 (Part IV, Sec. 1).

BIBLIOGRAPHY

Bureau of the Census. *Statistical Abstract of the United States.* Washington, DC: Bureau of the Census, 1990.

Immigration and Naturalization Service. *Statistical Report.* Washington, DC: Department of Justice, 1996.

Miami-Dade County, Department of Planning. *Project 2000–2015.* Miami: Department of Planning, 1996.

Grenier, Guillermo, and Alex Stepick, eds. *Miami Now: Immigration, Ethnicity and Social Change.* Miami: University of Florida Press, 1992.

Portes, Alejandro. *City on the Edge: The Transformation of Miami.* Berkeley: University of California Press, 1993.

NEW JERSEY AND SUBURBAN AMERICA

*B*ecause of its varied topography and strategic location, New Jersey has always attracted people of various races, religions, and nationalities. Situated between New York City and Philadelphia—two major ports of entry for immigrants—and offering rich farmland, an extensive variety of industry, and many natural resources, New Jersey has been the place to live and work for millions of migrating people since its colonial beginnings.

The first census in 1790, as well as all that followed, showed New Jersey as the most diverse state in the nation. New Jersey's ethnic and racial composition more closely mirrors that of the nation than any other state. Moreover, its immigrant, racial, and ethnic history has always been a microcosm of the United States in terms of settlement patterns, adjustment, societal hostility, and acceptance. That smaller version begins with the indigenous Lenni Lenape and their encounters with the early Dutch, Swedish, and English settlers, through the large influx of Germans and Irish, the subsequent arrival of Italians, Jews, and other Central and Eastern Europeans, followed by the black and Puerto Rican northern migrations, and capped by recent African, Arabic, Asian, and Hispanic arrivals.

Within that context, New Jersey was the locale of Indian massacres (1643), one of the first reservations (Brotherton in Burlington County), public burnings at the stake (Hackensack, 1741), slavery and liberation (those born after July 4, 1804, were emancipated), the Underground Railroad, election of a governor, six state senators, and fifteen state assemblymen from the anti-immigrant Know-Nothing Party (1850s), violent labor strife (Paterson silk strike, 1913), and Ku Klux Klan marches in Long Branch and Red Bank (1920s). Similarly, the post–World War II suburban housing boom emptied New Jersey cities, both large and small, of a great bulk of their European-American populace, making room for people of color who often found themselves the new residents of financially troubled, physically decaying central cities that only now are mostly recovering. And the more recent, notable presence of first-generation ethnicity in suburbia also mirrors the national pattern.

EARLY IMMIGRATION

New Jersey's immigrant diversity began during its colonial era. Swedesboro was founded in the 1640s, as part of the colony of New Sweden at the mouth of the Delaware River. Finns and Swedes who settled there brought with them the knowledge of log cabin structure and thus built some of the New World's first log cabins in New Jersey. Conquered by the Dutch in 1655, then ceded to the English in 1664, the Swedish colony and its inhabitants were soon absorbed into the dominant English-American culture, though the still-named town of Swedesboro continues to this day.

Seventeenth-century Dutch settlers established farms in the Hackensack River valley and soon built other brownstone farmhouses and spacious barns in the fertile valleys of the Passaic, Ramapo, and Raritan rivers. Their cohesiveness and insularity enabled the Jersey Dutch to remain a persistent subculture into the twentieth century, although by the late nineteenth century English had gradually replaced Dutch at most worship services. The Dutch legacy remains in the abundance of original Dutch colonial architecture throughout the state, in its many Reformed churches, and in the Sunday "blue laws" that still prohibit the sale of merchandise in many communities, such as Paramus, home to several major shopping malls.

By the 1750s, German settlement of New Jersey extended from the Delaware Bay to Hackensack, as German immigrants heavily populated the present-day counties of Hunterdon, Warren, Somerset, Sussex, Bergen, Essex, and Morris. Two "pure" German towns were founded: Carlstadt, near the Meadowlands

In recent decades, New Jersey has become home to thousands of East Indian immigrants, including this family shown outside their Jersey City apartment building. *(Clark Jones/Impact Visuals)*

sus in 1790. At that time the state population of 184,139 broke down into the following percentages: English (47 percent), Dutch (16.6), German (9.2), Scottish (7.7), Black (7.7), Scotch-Irish (6.3), Swedish (3.9), Irish (3.2), French (2.4), and the remainder a mixture of Alsatians, Danes, Finns, Flemings, Walloons, Welsh, Lenape, and a smattering of other European groups.

CONTINUING IMMIGRATION

When oppression and famine drove the Irish out of their homeland and into the United States from 1830 onward, New Jersey was a major beneficiary. Often recruited in New York City, work gangs of "Paddies" labored from sunrise to sunset building dikes in the Newark Meadows, the Morris Canal, the Delaware and Raritan Canal, the Camden and Amboy Railroad, as well as roads and other railroad spur lines. Undernourished, overworked, exposed to sickness and disease, hundreds died and were buried in unmarked graves beside the canal or railroad line that destroyed them.

Irish migration peaked in the 1850s, and by 1860 the Irish were the largest foreign-born group in the state, as they were in the nation. Outnumbering the British by three to one, they comprised more than 50 percent of New Jersey's foreign-born residents. The largest concentration of Irish was in the Horseshoe District of Jersey City, an unsanitary slum bordering marshes and railroad yards. Out of this area would evolve the state's best example of Irish machine politics, easily rivaling those in Boston or New York City. Paterson's Dublin District and other Irish neighborhoods in Newark, Elizabeth, New Brunswick, and Trenton also offered vivid testimony to the Irish immigrant presence.

Germans continued to settle in New Jersey throughout the nineteenth century. These newcomers varied in their religions, occupations, and backgrounds. Some settled in the northwestern and southern rural areas, continuing the farm life they knew. Most, however, settled in urban regions, becoming storekeepers, merchants (such as Louis Bamberger, founder of a department store chain), and industrialists (such as George Merck, of the giant pharmaceutical company). Hoboken became the most German city in the state; it was definitively a bilingual city until the patriotic hysteria of World War I effectively ended its German visibility in street names, store signs, German-language newspapers, and other manifestations of ethnicity. Elsewhere, the "Hill" section

Sports Complex; and Egg Harbor, near Atlantic City. Germans planned Egg Harbor for Germans only, with its streets bearing German names, the city charter written in German, and overseas advertisements recruiting new immigrants. Hamburg in Sussex County and Guttenberg in Hudson County are other New Jersey towns whose names give testimony to their German origins. Several New Jersey German Americans left their mark on today's society: engineer John A. Roebling, who designed the Brooklyn Bridge, and Thomas Nast, the nation's first prominent political cartoonist, who popularized the political symbols of Uncle Sam, the donkey, and the elephant.

The English eventually dominated the colony, both numerically and politically, but they were simply the largest minority group, not a majority. Widespread immigration to New Jersey resulted in a pluralistic population, as documented by the nation's first cen-

of Newark and parts of its "Ironbound" section endured a similar fate.

By 1860 the Germans were the second-largest foreign-born group in New Jersey, comprising 27 percent of the total. In fact, beginning with the 1890 census and thereafter, the German-born population of New Jersey surpassed the Irish-born by an increasing proportion.

THE GREAT MIGRATION

When the state became a major destination between 1880 and 1920 for a large share of the 23 million immigrants who came to the United States, New Jersey developed what historian Rudolph Vecoli called "a split personality." There was the "old" New Jersey of rolling farmlands and small country towns, both populated by light-haired and fair-complexioned immigrants and their descendants from northern and western Europe. The "new" New Jersey was densely populated with prisonlike factories and belching smokestacks. Here the dark-haired, dark-complexioned newcomers began their personal quest for fulfillment of the American Dream.

By the turn of the century, the six primary immigrant-receiving counties—Bergen, Essex, Hudson, Middlesex, Passaic, and Union—contained two-thirds of the state's population, three-fourths of whom were foreign-born. In 1900, 74.2 percent of Paterson's population was either foreign-born or of foreign stock, while Newark's proportion was 74.7 percent. These figures were comparable to all other cities throughout the New England, Middle Atlantic, and Midwestern states.

The presence of so many "different" people precipitated a fierce reaction. Nativists spoke out and wrote about the "contamination of America" that they were witnessing in "their" state. In his multivolume study, *A History of the American People* (1902), Woodrow Wilson, then president of Princeton University, wrote the following words, which would come back to haunt him in his subsequent political campaigns:

> [N]ow there came multitudes of men of the lowest class from the south of Italy and men of the meaner sort out of Hungary and Poland, men out of ranks where there was neither skill nor energy nor any initiative of quick intelligence; and they came in numbers which increased from year to year, as if the countries of the south of Europe were disburdening themselves of the more sordid and hapless elements of their population, the men

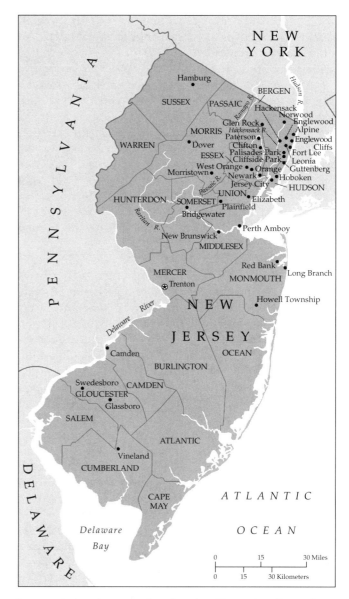

In recent decades, new immigrant settlement patterns have emerged. Increasingly, the suburbs—such as those in New Jersey—represent destinations for both first- and second-generation immigrants. *(CARTO-GRAPHICS)*

whose standards of life and of work were such as American workmen had never dreamed of hitherto.

Despite such negative reaction, Italian immigrants flocked to New Jersey: from Abruzzi to Newark and Paterson; from Avellino to Newark; from Naples and Santa Croce to Paterson; from Villalba to Trenton; from Potenza to Orange; from Bagnara to Cliffside Park; and from Riberato to Elizabeth. First, to aid the struggling immigrant families, came the formation of mutual aid societies. When death or illness struck the breadwinner, the society would step in and care for the widow and orphans. As families became more affluent, the societies expanded into social clubs named after the old hometown or a patron saint identified with a particular region in Italy.

Affluence came later. First there was the grinding poverty in the factories and mills—and the prejudice in the streets. For example, Italian laborers built the ornate Hamilton Club for the city's elite on Paterson's Church Street. Once it was completed, neither the workmen nor their children could step inside the club, except as employees. Years later, when men of Italian extraction had risen to the top of New Jersey's professions and industries, they still were frozen out of the majority of the country clubs that dotted Bergen and Passaic counties.

In Haledon, a suburb of Paterson settled by weavers from the Italian Piedmont area, stands the Pietro Botto House, now on the register of National Historic Sites and site of the American Labor Museum. Once, it was the meetinghouse for textile strikers forbidden to assemble in Paterson. The Botto House was headquarters for the likes of William Dudley "Big Bill" Haywood, leader of the Industrial Workers of the World, the feared Wobblies who led the great silk strikes that involved 25,000 immigrant workers of many nationalities and shut down virtually every mill and dye house in Passaic County. From its balcony, author Upton Sinclair harangued thousands of workers, urging them to stand fast in the face of threats. After months of turmoil and arrests, the strike finally ended with neither side the victor: the workers were destitute and the mill owners nearly bankrupt.

Various areas became known by names reflecting the concentration of immigrants from specific areas. Now, however, instead of a New Sweden, a Dublin District, a Hamburg, or a Guttenberg, another part of Europe was represented. Little Italys, as elsewhere in the nation, sprang up in most of the state's cities. The east side of the city of Passaic, known as the "Dundee" section, had a mixed population of Poles, Magyars, Slovaks, Ukrainians, Lithuanians, Italians, and Russian Jews. Perth Amboy's "Budapest" section was home to Poles, Czechs, and Hungarians. The many Armenians, Syrians, and Turks who lived in West Hoboken brought the appellation "The Dardenelles" to that section. Paterson's Fourth Ward came to be known as "Jewtown," and Newark's Central Ward became known as "Greek Town," as did the area in West Orange near the Edison Laboratories by Main Street. Wallington's nicknames were "Poletown" and "Poland on the Passaic [River]."

Wallington today is a collection of modest, two-story houses set on small lots and placed close to narrow, tree-lined streets. The glassed-in porches and the pastel colors—pinks, mints, lemons, and creams—give the town the air of a seaside village. No architect designed these houses; they were carpenter-built for men with a few thousand dollars to spend and large families to house. On Shohank Hill, where the land rises to the east, the houses are newer and the yards more spacious, and old-timers refer jokingly to the area as "billionaires' row." Many of Wallington's children have bought homes in this section upon returning to the community.

From the top of Shoshank Hill, on a clear night, you can see the shimmering towers of the World Trade Center, but Wallington itself has remained insulated from the world about it. To understand Wallington, one must understand the heritage that has shaped its people and set them apart from their neighbors. About two-thirds of the community is Polish, and many others are also Slavic. Polish immigrants still come to Wallington, and the Polish People's Home still serves as a magnet for many of the newcomers. Hundreds of newly arrived Poles flock to the home for its Saturday night dances—noisy, often boisterous affairs where the air is thick with the music of Polish bands, which alternate American rock and roll with traditional polkas and mazurkas.

A small number of Sephardic Jews had lived in New Jersey at least since the early eighteenth century. The mid-nineteenth-century German migration, however, made the Jewish presence in the state truly felt, as noted by the establishment of synagogues in Paterson (1847), Newark (1848), Trenton (1858), New Brunswick (1859), and Jersey City (1864). The East European Jewish migration dramatically increased the state's Jewish population, from 5,600 in 1880 to 84,000 in 1910, and 219,000 in 1930. Some worked in factories, while others engaged in mercantile trades. The oft-cited upward mobility among Jews within two generations is well illustrated in New Jersey. For example, in 1937 they comprised 16 percent of the population in Passaic, but 50 percent of its doctors and 84 percent of its lawyers and judges. In Trenton at that time, 12 percent of the Jewish labor force was in the professions, compared to 5 percent of the general population, and two-thirds of the state capital's doctors, lawyers, and judges were Jewish.

Newark's Ironbound—a Portuguese village about 20–30 minutes by car or train from Manhattan—got its name because it is enclosed by railroad tracks and major roadways. Before the 1970s, German, Italian, Irish, Polish, and other European immigrants mostly populated the neighborhood, but they yielded slowly to the Portuguese in a typical invasion–succession process that began in the 1950s and 1960s. Brazilians, drawn by the language they share with the Portuguese, have also settled here in recent years, opening restaurants, bakeries, and bars. Indeed, on walks down Congress, Ferry, Madison, or Pacific streets, one encounters today an enticing array of the Portuguese culinary landscape: bakeries, cafes, restaurants, and fresh fish markets.

PRESENT-DAY IMMIGRATION

According to a 1999 report by the Bureau of the Census, more than 15 percent of New Jersey's residents were foreign immigrants in 1997. The majority of the state's foreign-born population migrated to the nation during the 1980s (414,000, or 34.3 percent) and 1990s (356,000, or 29.5 percent), a proportion comparable to national statistics. By including the native population with foreign parentage (either or both parents are foreign immigrants), the entire foreign stock in New Jersey was about 2.5 million in 1997. That means almost one in every three New Jerseyans was either born abroad or has a foreign or mixed parentage.

According to the most recent data from the Immigration and Naturalization Service, the leading countries of origin of legal immigrants admitted to New Jersey in the late 1990s were India, the Dominican Republic, the Philippines, Colombia, and Peru. The Census Bureau reports that the foreign immigrants' labor-force participation, income levels, educational attainment, and proportion of managerial and professional jobholders were higher in New Jersey than in the nation as a whole. These findings are partly reflected in the fact that immigrant physicians from many countries have set up shop throughout New Jersey. In Bergen County, almost 40 percent of Hispanic households have incomes in excess of $50,000 annually, while the percentage of upper-income Hispanic families in Morris County is the highest in the nation.

The most recent wave of immigration to New Jersey actually began in the late 1970s, drawing large numbers of people from troubled countries such as Colombia, El Salvador, Nicaragua, Peru, the former Soviet Union, Vietnam, and the former Yugoslavia, as well as from other parts of the Developing World. Some settle immediately in the state's older suburbs, or its newer ones, but others settle in cities such as Jersey City, which is home to the state's largest Asian Indian and Coptic Christian Egyptian populations. In South Paterson, Arabic and Turkish are the languages of commerce in many stores. The Arab presence in Paterson continues a settlement pattern dating back to the Great Silk Strike of 1913, when labor agents recruited Syrian and Lebanese at Ellis Island to work in the area's factories and mills. Joining them in recent years have been Jordanians, Palestinians, Turks, Circassians, and immigrants from North Africa.

Caribbean immigrants also are also settling in the state's cities in large numbers. Most numerous are those from the Dominican Republic and Jamaica. Stores specializing in West Indian foods and other recognizable aspects of a growing Caribbean presence can be found in all of New Jersey's larger cities.

Although New Jersey is the nation's fifth smallest state in area, today it is the fifth most common destination of immigrants, behind California, Texas, Florida, and New York, and ahead of Illinois. In some of the most popular county destinations, the changes are significant. One in three Hudson County residents is foreign born, while in Bergen and Passaic counties the figure is one in five. Among foreign immigrants in the nation's six major states, according to the Census Bureau, New Jersey had the lowest proportion of Latin American-born residents (42.5 percent), while Texas had the highest proportion (75.9 percent) in 1997. On the other hand, New Jersey had the second highest proportion of Asian-born population (28.5 percent), behind California (33.5 percent).

Contributing to the state's unique multiethnic role is the fact that New Jersey is the most urban state in the nation: it has a greater population density than all the other states. The number of people per square mile in New Jersey is dramatically high. The "Garden State" has a 28 percent greater population density than India and three times the population density of China. It is precisely this population density, coupled with the extensive racial and ethnic diversity throughout the state's history, that makes New Jersey the most multiethnic state in the nation.

The immigrant groups currently living in New Jersey range from large groups such as the more than 50,000 Peruvians to small groups such as the 200 families in suburban Howell Township known as Kalmuks—Mongolian people whose ancestors rode with Genghis Khan across Asia eight centuries ago. After the fall of the Mongol empire, they settled in czarist Russia, moved on to Europe during the Russian Revolution, and then, after World War II, emigrated in small groups to the United States. A small Tibetan Buddhist temple marks the spiritual base of the community, and many of the children take Russian lessons at a local Russian Orthodox Church, but the fast-paced U.S. culture and the assimilation process lead many Kalmuks to fear that their traditions are fading rapidly.

Peruvians live throughout most of New Jersey, but their largest concentrations are in Bergen, Hudson, and Passaic counties. The Peruvian community was thriving so much by the 1980s that the Peruvian government opened a consulate in Paterson in 1987. By 2000, nearly 100 Peruvian restaurants were operating in North Jersey, and about two dozen civic and social organizations were functioning throughout the state, as well as over 100 Peruvian-owned businesses specializing in travel and insurance.

Since 1986, Peruvians have been streaming in by the tens of thousands from Connecticut, New York, and from everywhere within New Jersey to march in the four-hour, five-mile, annual Peruvian parade from Main Avenue in Passaic through Clifton and into Paterson, which is followed by several festivals. The Passaic County Peruvian community is the only one nationwide with a parade to commemorate Peru's July 28th Independence Day. So well known is this event in Peru that prominent officials fly in to participate, and that nation's television stations and newspapers send correspondents to cover it.

About 100,000 Colombians live in New Jersey. Their ranks include mostly college-educated entrepreneurs and professionals who officially arrive as tourists but who stay when their visas expire rather than go back to the chaos in their homeland. They head to the existing Colombian enclaves—such as Dover, Elizabeth, Englewood, Hackensack, and Morristown—to begin life anew. The plunge from middle-class comfort to immigrant struggle is the price they are willing to pay as, off the radar, they drive taxis, sweep office buildings, lay tiles, or work as other types of laborers as they build new lives.

Among their ranks, as with all immigrant groups, are the "fixers," established immigrants who are part of the community infrastructure providing advice, assistance, and referrals to their newly arrived compatriots. Maria Galvez, a waitress at El Prado restaurant in Englewood, is one such person. Now in her mid-thirties, she arrived from her native Colombia at age 20. With the blessing of her boss, another Colombian native, she often sits with her customers, goes over and fills out forms with them, helps them find apartments, jobs, or service providers, and even lends the indigent or unemployed a few dollars. She is representative of a long-standing immigrant ritual: immigrants who have moved ahead serving as points of light in what is the darkness, the maze, of the first few days or months of building a new life in a foreign country. They help sustain people during transition, acculturating others into a society that they have already negotiated. "I'm a referral center," she says. "I could set up an office right now and keep busy doing this twenty-four hours a day. There's that much need in the community for this type of help."

SUBURBAN ETHNICITY

For much of the twentieth century, everyday ethnicity existed in the recognizable territories of urban neighborhoods. Suburbia was the domain of homogenized, middle-class Americans whose ethnicity lay hidden in multigenerational layers and surfaced symbolically only on special occasions, if at all. Some of today's immigrants are still like those of the past: unskilled poor or working-class people, who typically settle in urban ethnic communities and may later move outward. Many others, however, possess an education and job skills that provide an income enabling them to choose suburban homes as their first place of residence in the United States. They are either the first of their family to do so or else they join relatives already in suburbia. As a result, ethnicity now peppers suburbia, as hundreds of thousands of foreign-born Americans put down roots and raise families away from cities. This change in socioeconomic profile has in turn altered both New Jersey's and the nation's suburban landscape.

As a result, an age-old urban American story is now being played out in suburbia. Striving immigrants from Colombia, India, Korea, Lebanon, Pakistan, Syria, and dozens of other Asian and Latin American countries are staking their claims to suburban life in New Jersey. With their arrival comes a diversity of benefits and a litany of conflicts. New businesses, cultural centers, shopkeepers, and laborers are changing the makeup of the suburban landscape and shoring up the flagging main streets of older suburbs. Yet tensions sometimes arise also, because of the newcomers' cultural or racial differences and, from the viewpoint of other suburbanites, their seeming reluctance to "merge."

These new Americans may be *in* the suburban community but they are not *of* it. Typically living in a scattered residential pattern, their primary relations will less likely be with next-door neighbors than with nearby compatriots sharing their language, customs, and values. Although immigrants have always sought out others like themselves, today's suburban ethnics lack a territorial neighborhood that fosters social interaction. Instead, theirs is an interactional network, connected by the car, telephone, and e-mail. Life-cycle events (births, weddings, funerals), special holidays, and events provide other opportunities, as do mothers meeting one another while walking their children to and from school. Unlike native-born Americans, who typically join various organizations and participate in group activities, suburban ethnics typically do not, except within the confines of their own ethnic organizations. Scouting leadership, organized sports coaching, PTA initiatives, and similar suburban endeavors often hold little allure for the foreign-born, adding to the social distance between them and the rest of the community.

New Jersey's 15,000 Sikhs offer a good example of many of today's suburban ethnics. In the suburbs of Bridgewater, Deptford, and Glen Rock, women in bright silk dresses trimmed with gold, and men in suits and turbans, their beards and mustaches carefully combed, enter dome-topped temples to attend worship services. Unlike past immigrant groups, who lived in close proximity to their religious edifice, however, most Sikhs live in a dispersed pattern and travel as much as 10–15 miles from their residences to worship. They hold a variety of jobs, but many are doctors, scientists, and engineers with advanced degrees. Others work in construction and manufacturing, own restaurants, or are owners or attendants at gasoline stations.

While some immigrants arrive and settle immediately in a suburban locale, other first-generation Americans move there from urban ethnic enclaves. Despite their relocation, they usually keep their business and social ties to the community that originally welcomed them. They may have friendly relations with their neighbors, but their lives unfold mainly within the confines of their ethnic world, and suburbia becomes a place to sleep and rest, not to work and socialize. For this generation at least, such a pattern maintains a social distance between the newcomers and the native-born suburbanites. It is a classic example of what Georg Simmel (1858–1918) once described: the physical nearness of strangers who are socially remote because they have different values and ways of doing things.

Some Hispanics who, two or more decades earlier came to New Jersey cities from Puerto Rico and Cuba, illustrate this migration trail from the region's cities into its suburbs. Replacing them in cities are new immigrants from such countries as Chile, Colombia, Guatemala, El Salvador, Peru, and the Dominican Republic. Hudson County (at 41 percent) and Passaic County (at 29 percent) have the highest proportions of Hispanic residents, accounting for 36.5 percent of the state's total Hispanic population in 1998. Seven New Jersey counties are in the nation's top 100 in Hispanic population: Hudson (24th), Passaic (39th), Essex (44th), Union (54th), Middlesex (59th), Bergen (64th), and Camden (90th). Hispanics make up major voting blocs in Camden, Jersey City, Newark, and Paterson, but they also have clout in Glassboro, Hackettstown, Hackensack, Perth Amboy, Plainfield, and Vineland, and an increasing presence in such suburban communities as Secaucus and Toms River.

In sheer numbers, the state's Hispanic population increased more than any other group and now exceeds 1 million people. Their 34.4 percent growth between 1990 and 1998 constituted 70 percent of New Jersey's population growth during this period. They now account for nearly 13 percent of the total state population.

Nowhere in the United States is the per-capita growth of Asians greater than in New Jersey, according to the Census Bureau. New Jersey's Asian population grew by 63.4 percent between 1990 and 1998, making them the fastest-growing racial group in the state and continuing a trend begun in the 1980s. New Jersey, with 5.6 percent of its residents Asians or Pacific Islanders, now has the highest proportion of any state outside the nation's West Coast. Although one of two Asians and Pacific Islanders lived in just three counties (Bergen, Middlesex, and Hudson) in 1998, ten counties were in the nation's top 100 in Asian and Pacific Islander population: Bergen (19th), Middlesex (26th), Hudson (35th), Essex (52nd), Morris (56th), Monmouth (65), Union (77th), Somerset (81st), Camden (85th), and Passaic (86th).

According to the Census Bureau, Asians moved more rapidly into New Jersey suburban areas than any other group in both the 1980s and 1990s. In Hudson County, Asian Indians are the largest single group of Asians, while about 20 percent of all New Jersey Asians live in Bergen County, making them the single largest minority group there. Large concentrations of Chinese, Japanese, Korean, and Southeast Asian immigrants live in such older suburban communities as Englewood Cliffs, Fort Lee, Leonia, and Palisades Park, as well as in more affluent communities such as Alpine and Norwood.

Particularly prominent is the Korean community, particularly in Fort Lee, Leonia, and Palisades Park. Now numbering over 50,000, they have reinvigorated the business areas in older adjoining towns and buoyed real estate markets. Throughout North Jersey, Koreans have at least 130 churches, 30 restaurants, 270 dry cleaners, nail salons, groceries, 30 fraternal and business groups, 5 newspapers, and the U.S. headquarters for at least 50 Korean corporations. Indicative of the general pattern of assimilation in recent years is the trend of second-generation Korean Americans leaving to form their own congregations or else insisting on worshiping separately at English-language services.

Despite an average 60,000 new immigrants settling in New Jersey each year and its continued ranking as the state with the greatest population diversity, it nevertheless continues to rank ninth nationally in its white population and thirteenth in its black population. New Jersey immigrants, a 1997 Urban Institute study reported, are more diverse, better educated, better skilled, and more attached to the United States than their counterparts elsewhere in the nation (New Jersey has the highest percentage of naturalized-citizen residents among the nation's six states with substantial numbers of foreign-born). Those qualities—along with the state's ethnic history, solid economy,

small undocumented population, and progressive political leadership—make for a place where immigrants find more acceptance and less hostility than those in other states, the study said.

Vincent Parrillo

See also: Settlement Patterns (Part II, Sec. 3); Cuba (Part III, Sec. 2); South Asia (Part III, Sec. 3).

BIBLIOGRAPHY

Espenshade, Thomas J., ed. *The New Jersey Experience: Keys to Successful Immigration.* Washington, DC: Urban Institute, 1997.

Cohen, David Steven, ed. *America, The Dream of My Life: Selections from the Federal Writers' Project's New Jersey Ethnic Survey.* New Brunswick: Rutgers University Press, 1990.

NEW YORK CITY

Unlike other urban magnets for contemporary population flows from abroad, New York City has a long history of immigration. Perhaps no other city is as aware of the part that immigrants have played in the development of the local environment. Although the "nation of immigrants" narrative is a familiar one to most Americans, New York City is the symbolic center for the production and re-production of this legend. The Statue of Liberty and Ellis Island are constant reminders of this glorified past, and New Yorkers are encouraged to celebrate their immigrant roots through these and other elements of the social landscape.

Recent scholarship on immigration to New York City has made a habit of referring to this area as an "immigrant city" or a "city of immigrants." This label has formed over the many years that New York has been a primary destination for immigrants to America. New York has always had a larger percentage of the foreign-born population than the national average, and this tendency peaked in the 1850s and again around 1910, when immigrants accounted for over 40 percent of the New York City population. New York is also the nation's oldest and largest continuing port of entry for immigrants. Furthermore, immigrants who come to New York State overwhelmingly decide to live and work in New York City—currently, over 80 percent of New York State's foreign-born population is concentrated in the New York metropolitan area. All these factors combine to make New York City the quintessential immigrant city.

But the fact that New York City has a long history with immigration does not *necessarily* guarantee a positive identification with immigrants, past or present. In fact, native New Yorkers' cultural perceptions of the foreign-born during the "great waves" of European immigration were quite negative. However, these past immigrants have left their mark on the city by attaining material success and respectability *despite* prejudice and discrimination. In the process, Euro-

pean groups have facilitated a rather positive identification with immigrants, as a very broad category of people. But the "huddled masses" that have arrived over the past few decades once again challenge native attitudes toward immigrants.

Most scholars studying immigration are quick to point out differences between contemporary flows and those which peaked almost one hundred years ago. One frequently noted difference is the geographic origins of contemporary immigrants: The foreign-born population arriving in the United States since 1965 has been predominantly from "third world" countries rather than Europe, as was previously the case. Although this is also the case in New York, the tradition of European immigration continues here, albeit on a lesser scale, while a variety of Latin and Asian newcomers add further complexity to the ethnic and racial mosaic.

IMMIGRANT SUCCESSION IN NEW YORK CITY

One way of making sense of the history of immigration to the United States as a whole and to New York City specifically is by looking at the peaks and lulls of immigrant flows and the primary sending regions. If approached in this manner, there are three distinct phases of U.S. immigration: The first phase, or "wave," was from western Europe during the mid-nineteenth century, followed by a second wave from eastern and southern Europe around the turn of the twentieth century. The second phase continued until a sharp decline during the later part of the 1920s and the onset of the Great Depression. After a considerable lull well into the post–World War II period, the third phase began in the 1960s, with New York again emerging as one of the main destinations for persons from abroad. New York's international linkages, a de-

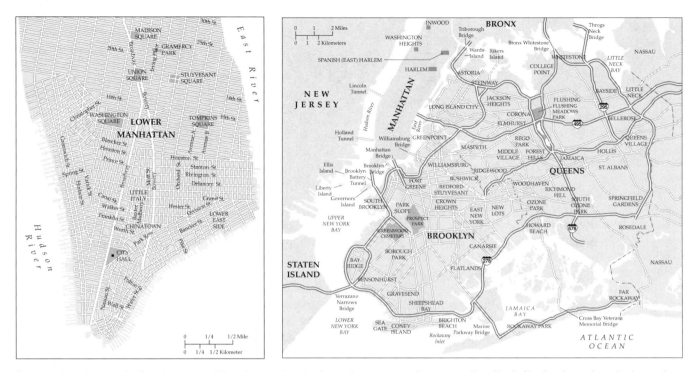

Since its founding as the Dutch colony of New Amsterdam in the early seventeenth century, New York City has been America's number-one destination for immigrants from a variety of countries. *(CARTO-GRAPHICS)*

cline in European flows, and the abolition of a national-origin quota system brought about an unintentional change in the direction of immigration since 1965. As a result, contemporary immigrants to New York City now come primarily from Latin American, Caribbean, and Asian countries.

The more recent Latino and Asian immigrants have been rather gradually added to New York City's ethnic mix as Europeans slowly fade in prominence. Table 1 details the top ten immigrant-ethnic groups in New York City, according to "specified nationalities" reported by the 1990 census. The immigrant-ethnic origins of New York's population are quite diverse, with the "older" immigrant groups from Europe still making their presence felt. In fact, because Puerto Ricans are not an official immigrant group due to the commonwealth status of their homeland, and the West Indian category is a pan-ethnic grouping, the highest non-European, immigrant-ethnic group from a specific country are the Dominicans, ranking sixth with just 5.4 percent of the total. Moreover, European-origin ethnics still account for well over half of the total for the top ten immigrant-ethnic groups in 1990.

Just as the predominance of Irish and German immigrants during the mid-nineteenth century was eventually overshadowed by the large influx of Italians and eastern Europeans at the turn of the twentieth century, now it is people from countries such as

the Dominican Republic, Jamaica, and China (to name a few of the more prominent ones) that are redefining the face of the immigrant city. But the defining characteristic of New York's contemporary immigrant population is its diversity, especially as compared with other urban areas with large foreign-born communities. More important, there is no single national-origin group that dominates the ranks of the more recent arrivals, and New York continues to attract a fair share of foreign nationals from traditional sending countries in Europe such as the former Soviet Union, Poland, Italy, and Ireland. Overall though, it is a rather diverse group of Latin American/Caribbean and Asian immigrants that are now emerging as the most prominent segment of New York's contemporary foreign-born population. Table 2 charts the relative numbers for the major national-origin groups in 1960 and 1980.

At first glance, the "old" European groups appear to be evenly mixed with the "new" immigrant groups among the top ten source countries, as in the previous table. However, when we look at the *change in rankings* and the *percentage change* over the twenty-year period, the eventual predominance of Caribbean and Asian immigrants seems to be the obvious trend. There is a clear pattern of European-origin decline and non-European ascendancy, especially among the Caribbean countries of origin. The only European immi-

Table 1
The Top Ten Ethnic Groups in the New York Metropolitan Area, 1990

Ethnic Group	Number (000s)	Percentage
Total specified nationalities	6,364	100.0
Italian	996	15.7
Puerto Rican	898	14.1
Irish	553	8.7
West Indian (non-Hispanic)	403	6.3
German	389	6.1
Dominican	343	5.4
Russian	290	4.6
Polish	259	4.1
Chinese	249	3.9
U.S./American	193	3.0
Total for top ten	4,573	71.9

Source: Bureau of the Census, *Census CD v. 1.1*, 1990.
Note: The census reports these ethnic groups according to "specified nationalities," although some of these groups do not represent official nation-states.

grant group that did not fall in the ranks are the Italians, who continued to maintain their hold on the top spot as of 1980. Table 2 also shows Jamaicans as the main national-origin group for the "West Indian" category, and the Caribbean nations of Cuba and Haiti are likewise specifically identified as main countries of origin. Puerto Ricans are not included in this table because they are not officially considered immigrants, although they are one of the earliest and most important non-European ethnic groups in New York City.

By 1980, Dominicans seemed well on their way to overtaking Italy as the premier country of origin, since it is the top sending country for much of the contemporary period. In fact, all the non-European countries in the table continued to make gains until at least 1990, with the exception of Cuba. Conversely, there were no European countries among the top ten during the 1980s and only two among the top twenty: the Soviet Union (twelfth) and Poland (eighteenth). Due to the 1990 "diversity program" and refugee flows, European immigrants to New York City more than doubled in the first four years of the 1990s, and the former Soviet Union and Poland broke into the top ten during this same period.

If we compare the data from the two tables, we see a considerable discrepancy between the rankings for specific ethnic groups (Table 1) and immigrants by country of origin (Table 2). For instance, although the Irish are the third most numerous ethnic group in 1990, by 1980 Ireland is tenth among the immigrant

population, and appears to be descending rather rapidly. Furthermore, Ireland was not among the top twenty sending countries to the New York City area during the 1980s. While a fair share of Irish immigrants, both legal and illegal, have continued to arrive in New York, the discrepancy between the two tables is largely explained by the intergenerational nature of ethnic identity: Although an official "immigrant" status is reserved for the foreign-born (i.e., the first generation), many people continue to identify with their immigrant-ethnic origins for multiple generations.

As the sociologist Richard Alba has observed: "Generally speaking, ethnic differences appear to be strongest among the generations closest to the immigrant experience and grow fainter among those further away." Although this is a fair generalization, the scholars Stanley Lieberson and Mary Waters have also noted that immigrant-ethnics who arrive directly from their homeland and concentrate in a specific urban area for a number of generations may have a lasting impact on the culture and traditions of a city long after the first generation. Therefore, although their numbers may be declining among the foreign-born population, many European-origin ethnics—especially Italians, Irish, and Jews—continue to maintain their ethnic identity, at least symbolically. Furthermore, many of these ethnics still celebrate their immigrant origins through parades, festivals, and visits to sacred sites such as Ellis Island and the Statue of Liberty. Exactly how more recent arrivals from non-European countries will be perceived in relation to earlier waves is not yet clear. However, the diversity of the foreign-born population, New York's profound sense of its immigrant roots, and the gradual pace of immigrant-ethnic succession make an inclusive orientation toward newcomers in New York City more likely.

MAJOR IMMIGRANT GROUPS, PAST TO PRESENT

We will now look at the particular experiences for *some* of New York City's more prominent immigrant groups. Because most arrived during a specific historical period and encountered a variety of obstacles to advancement, it is important to understand the uniqueness of each group's experience. There are also many common themes among these various national-origin groups. I will simply focus on the most noted groups since the mid-nineteenth century. Of course,

Table 2
Sources of Top Ten Immigrant Groups in New York City, 1960 and 1980, and Percentage Change, 1960–1980

Country	1980 Rank	1960 Rank	Percentage Change
Italy	1	1	−44
Dominican Republic	2	26	+1,208
Jamaica	3	24	+734
USSR	4	2	−57
China/Taiwan/Hong Kong	5	15	+330
Poland	6	3	−54
Germany	7	4	−60
Haiti	8	42	+1,571
Cuba	9	11	+74
Ireland	10	5	−62

Source: Elizabeth Bogen, *Immigration in New York* (New York: Praeger Publishers, 1987), p. 38.

this does not do justice to the great diversity of immigrants who have made New York City their home over the years. But it is precisely the diversity of New York's foreign-born population, especially in the present, that makes a complete account impossible.

THE FIRST GREAT WAVE OF IMMIGRANTS

New York City's foreign-born have been a significant portion of the population for as long as official figures on nativity have been collected. In the mid-nineteenth century, the census recorded the foreign-born at about 42 percent of the total New York City population, a mark not to be reached again until 1910. The first half of the nineteenth century saw over 5 million people emigrate from Europe, and it was those from Germany and Ireland who were most numerous and made the biggest impact on the United States in general and on New York City in particular. Both German and Irish immigrants came primarily as a result of changing material conditions in their place of origin, but the Irish were much more uniformly destitute at the time of emigration. Changes in traditional agricultural methods, the onset and spread of industrialization, and political and religious motives all contributed to encourage a more varied flow of German people to America.

A mostly native-born commercial class, as well as the earlier, more experienced immigrants, set in motion various mechanisms for the recruitment and articulation of newcomers to American society. By the 1850s, there was a network of immigrant "societies"

and labor contractors in place that helped immigrants both get in touch with others "of their kind" and find work. Most Germans moved through New York City to points west upon arrival in America. While many did stay in the city, Germans were much more likely than the Irish to gravitate toward more rural settings. The historian Robert Ernst estimates that over half of Manhattan's population was foreign-born by 1855, 54 percent of which came from Ireland and another 29 percent from various German states. Not only were the Germans less numerous than the Irish in New York City, they were also much more diverse in terms of their occupational niches and religious faith. A good share of Germans brought a marketable skill with them from Europe, and were thus able to concentrate in trades as furniture and cabinet makers, machinists, tailors, and so on. While New York Germans were much more likely than the Irish to be skilled workers, they were much less likely to be Catholic. Although there was a sizable German Catholic constituency, German Protestants—themselves a diverse lot—were most numerous. There was also a rather small but influential group of German Jews in New York City during this period, who preceded the much larger group of eastern European Jews who would start to arrive en masse in the late nineteenth century.

There was a large concentration of German immigrants between Canal and 14th Streets, to the east of the Bowery, and New York City was the center for a small but influential group of German radicals who played a crucial role in the U.S. labor movement. Through labor struggles and high rates of employment in skilled trades, Germans managed to gain some economic security and stability. Although their material situation may have facilitated the process, German-American assimilation was greatly hastened due to fierce anti-German sentiment during World War I. Although the extent of their assimilation is open to debate, few traces of a once vibrant and distinct German ethnic community remain in the New York City area.

The Irish immigrants of New York were less fortunate than the Germans, at least initially. Their large numbers, high rates of poverty, and slum dwelling made them a highly visible and disdained ethnic group. Most were too poor to venture to the interior of the country to find work, especially those who emigrated with dependent family members. The vast majority of Irish immigrants during this period were also unskilled and Catholic, traits that further hindered their incorporation into the American mainstream. The young, unmarried women from Ireland were perhaps the most fortunate of the lot. They were

Some of New York City's new immigrants. Korean youngsters celebrate their native and adopted lands with costumes and American flags at the Korean Day parade. *(Clark Jones/Impact Visuals)*

often able to find work as live-in domestic workers among New York City's more affluent families. Many of the older and less fortunate Irish women worked as seamstresses, both inside and outside the home. While a modest proportion of Irish men in New York City did find jobs as semiskilled workers or in the trades, the vast majority were relegated to hard, physical labor.

The tenements that were hastily converted or built during this period to house the large numbers of German and Irish immigrants were laboratories for disease and despair. The unsanitary and crowded conditions of tenement life, coupled with inadequate health care and the ravaging effects of abject poverty, forced many onto the rolls of the increasingly overwhelmed public hospitals in New York City. Aside from their high incidence of poverty and poor health (both physical and mental), immigrants became highly associated with the criminal element in New York City. Furthermore, the appalling living conditions, coupled with economic competition and a precarious future, brought out the worst among some of

the more desperate and hardened of the burgeoning underclass. For instance, many Irish workers saw blacks and other immigrant groups as competitors, a perception encouraged by employers who used other groups as strikebreakers to counter the Irish struggle for higher wages and shorter hours. The Irish were frequently the main aggressors in the mob violence that was rather commonplace in New York City during the latter half of the nineteenth century. One of the worst examples was the 1863 Draft Riots in which the black population of New York City was indiscriminately targeted by a large mob of mostly Irish men.

The Irish were often criticized for their dependence on the very organizations that provided them with economic mobility and spiritual strength. They pragmatically used the Democratic political machine to make inroads into such municipal jobs as police officer, firefighter, and teacher. While ward politics enabled the Irish to gain prominence among the ranks of the more respectable occupations, the Catholic Church provided them with a source of collective faith and identity (as well as economic assistance dur-

Some of New York City's earlier immigrants. The San Genarro Festival in the Little Italy section of Manhattan attracts thousands of descendants of Italian immigrants from the New York City metropolitan area. *(Ned Sublette)*

ing hard times). Despite the symbiotic situation between the Irish and these social organizations, many of the more established New Yorkers simply understood these Irish-dominated institutions as corrupt and dangerous.

THE SECOND WAVE ARRIVES

As the Germans and Irish made their gradual ascent up the socioeconomic ladder, southern and eastern Europeans were increasingly present to shore up the base of the hierarchy. But just as the first wave of Europeans differed in terms of occupational patterns and rates of assimilation (among other things), so too did the wave around the turn of the twentieth century. Italians were the largest of the southern and eastern European immigrant groups that made their way to the United States, especially after 1890; as many as 3 million arrived between 1900 and 1914. Although most were agrarian laborers from southern Italy, the tendency was to settle in urban America, with New York hosting the largest contingent. According to the 1910 census, there were then over 700,000 Italians liv-

ing in New York City, which accounted for roughly 15 percent of the population. However, any estimate of the Italian population during this period must be made with some caution due to the large number of Italians who repatriated. According to some estimates, as many as 1.5 million Italians returned to their country of origin during the first fifteen years of the twentieth century.

Italian men were much like the Irish before them in terms of their concentration within the manual labor force. Italians provided the bulk of the physical labor that was necessary to accomplish various public works projects in the city, such as the subways, aqueducts, and sewer system. Both Italian and Jewish women were prominent as garment workers, although most of this work was done in the home after marriage. Eastern European Jews brought with them valuable skills, as did many of the midcentury German immigrants. Moreover, the earlier German Jews are credited with smoothing the transition for many of the later eastern European Jews, channeling them into the garment industry and other prominent occupations of the time.

Like previous immigrants, Italians and Jews were crowded into the many tenement slums of lower Manhattan. Despite such humble beginnings and widespread prejudice, intergenerational struggles have now put the Italians and Jews squarely into the ranks of the American middle class, and beyond. Perhaps as a result of their rising affluence, Italian Americans are currently exhibiting a decidedly less Italian, more American ethnic character. But it is the eastern European Jews who have exhibited the most rapid economic success. Some of the more common reasons given to explain their unparalleled advances are that they were better educated, possessed more appropriate skills, and were more accustomed to an urban lifestyle than other immigrants. Despite their economic gains, some Jews continue to maintain a distinct ethnic identity. Their social and economic advances, however, were not earned without resistance. Prejudice, discrimination, and ethnic conflict were common characteristics of relations between Jews and other ethnic groups, and the desecration of Jewish sites of congregation and worship can still be evidenced today.

NEW YORK'S NEW IMMIGRANTS

Although there are many similarities among the various national-origin groups that have settled in New York City over the years, the latest flow is distinct in a number of ways. First, they are predominantly from the Caribbean basin and Asian countries—most notably the Dominican Republic, Jamaica, China, Haiti, and Korea. Second, they enter a very different society, one that has been transformed as a result of economic restructuring as well as various struggles over equal rights and opportunities. Throughout history, some groups have been more successful than others, and the new immigrants further complicate this picture.

Prior to 1965, New York's ethnic and racial mosaic was broadened by the "internal migration" of southern blacks and Puerto Ricans. The more established African-American and Hispanic populations of New York City were then themselves diversified by immigration from various Latin American/Caribbean and Asian nations. The Spanish-speaking population is no longer dominated by Puerto Ricans, as many newcomers from the Dominican Republic, Cuba, Colombia, and Ecuador (among many others) have made New York City their home. Also, immigrants from Afro-Caribbean nations such as Jamaica and Haiti have further complicated what it means to be "black" in New York City. And a rather small but long established Chinatown in Manhattan has seen significant expansion—spreading well into what was previously

considered Little Italy. The Asian component is also bolstered by immigrants from other countries, most notably Korea.

Although countries of origin have changed considerably, the newer immigrants have much in common with previous flows from Europe. For example, profound changes taking place in the increasingly global economy make the motives for contemporary immigration from the "third world" similar to those for immigrants from countries such as Ireland and Italy during the nineteenth and early twentieth century. Moreover, the new immigrants have concentrated within and rejuvenated specific neighborhoods and sectors of the local economy, such as the garment industry, that have long been dependent on immigrants. Of course, much has changed over the years, and some argue that the "hourglass" shape of the new economy will make upward social mobility difficult for these newcomers and even their children. However, as the sociologist Nancy Foner has argued, immigrants are not only shaped by American society but also reshape it in the process of their adaptation. Let us now look at the particular experience for some of the more prominent immigrant groups in New York City today.

THE CARIBBEAN CONNECTION

By far the largest sending region to New York City since the postwar period has been the Caribbean, and especially prominent have been immigrants from the Dominican Republic, Jamaica, and Haiti. But each of these national-origin groups have distinct histories and represent diverse populations. Therefore, I will briefly look at the particulars for each of these groups, attempting to point out both similarities and differences with other immigrants, past to present.

Caribbean nations were intimately involved in the slave trade and European colonialism, developing a rather complex cultural understanding of race. Caribbean immigrants are more sensitive to variations within the more simplistic black/white racial categories dominant in American society. Although many white Americans tend to see darker-skinned Caribbean immigrants as "black," these immigrants resist homogenization with the African-American population, often stressing their unique ethnic characteristics. The scholars Frederick Binder and David Reimers claim that by 1990, one-quarter of the black population of New York City was foreign-born.

Advances in air transportation and communications, the social networks provided by earlier arrivals, and the removal of national-origin quotas promoted a surge in Caribbean immigration since 1965. The Dominicans are the largest and perhaps most important of the new immigrant groups in New York City. Although the independent status of this Western Hemisphere nation has long allowed for unrestricted entry into the United States, the Trujillo dictatorship in the Dominican Republic curtailed emigration up until 1961. Since then the flow has increased steadily. Although not one of the largest immigrant groups to the United States, it is the concentration of Dominicans in the New York City area that makes them highly visible. The largest concentration of Dominicans can be found in the Washington Heights/Inwood section of Upper Manhattan.

Although their African origins are less pronounced than immigrants from some other Caribbean nations, 75 percent of Dominicans identify as either mulatto or black. Those who do leave the Dominican Republic are not the poorest or least skilled, as compared with the U.S. population as a whole and even many other immigrant groups, yet Dominicans have rather low educational levels, high rates of poverty, and a propensity for low-wage labor. Their poor economic performance is partially due to race and gender discrimination: Black and mulatto Dominicans have nearly twice the poverty rate as Dominicans that identify as white, and Dominican women are especially vulnerable to low wages and poverty.

Dominican women have an experience decidedly different from that of Dominican men within the United States, as the experience of immigration has changed traditional gender roles. Dominican women are more likely to work outside the home while living in the United States. They are highly concentrated in the garment industry, perpetuating a long tradition of immigrant and minority workers in this occupation. Dominican males tend to be concentrated in the low-wage service sector, although their specific occupations are more heterogeneous than that of their female counterparts. While it is not clear how much economic advantage Dominican women gain from paid labor, it does appear that they have increased their domestic position vis-à-vis men.

Jamaicans are another prominent Caribbean group in the New York area, especially in Brooklyn. Due to restrictive quotas, few Jamaicans entered the United States between 1952 and 1965. Since then, employment opportunities and economic aspirations have brought many Jamaicans to New York City. In 1980, there were 98,000 foreign-born Jamaicans living in New York, 85 percent of these arriving since 1965. Like other Afro-Caribbean people, the Jamaicans had to adjust to the dichotomous black/white racial system in the United States. In Jamaica, most of the population is nonwhite, and there is far less of an asso-

ciation between skin color and social status—this is reflected in the racial diversity within the middle class and more affluent segments of Jamaican society. Many believe that a high social class position in Jamaica effectively "erases" racial distinctions. Therefore, it is understandable that Jamaicans of relatively high social status in their country of origin resist being lumped into the relatively homogeneous American "black" population.

Most Jamaicans came to this country because of job opportunities they learned about through coethnic networks, and they were often "sponsored" by kin already in residence. These social networks were crucial to the migration process, both stimulating a "snowball" effect for further immigration and providing recent arrivals with economic assistance and information on job and housing availability. Like the mid-nineteenth-century Irish women before them, Jamaican females have found an employment niche as domestic servants. Due to a high demand for "domestics" among the more affluent in New York City, Jamaican women outnumbered male immigrants by as much as three to one in the late 1960s. Although there is a smaller, albeit significant professional/technical component within the ranks of the Jamaican community, most men and women concentrate in the lower ranks of the service economy and manufacturing.

On average, Jamaicans tend to do better economically than native-born blacks. This results from a number of factors, including a higher percentage of skilled workers and a willingness to accept low wages and poor working conditions with the expectation that they can improve their lot over time. Because they are doing relatively well economically and are ethnically distinct from other blacks, Jamaicans (as well as other Afro-Caribbeans) tend to display group pride that sometimes borders on ethnic chauvinism. This naturally raises the potential for group tension and conflict among these newcomers and the more Americanized blacks. Yet the potential also exists for alliances among black New Yorkers, especially around common causes such as combating racial discrimination and prejudice.

As Foner points out, while race unites all blacks in this country, ethnicity tends to divide them into distinct communities. The Haitians exemplify this tendency due to their rather unique history and ethnic background. Unlike pan-ethnic identities such as Latino or West Indian, Haitians are the only major immigrant group that has a French colonial history, which tends to make them distinct among New York's many immigrant-ethnic groups. Haitians emigrate for both economic and political reasons—the nation's history has been plagued by repressive government and extreme poverty. According to the 1980 census, there were 52,700 Haitians living in the New York–New Jersey metropolitan area, constituting over half of all Haitians in the United States at the time; nearly 90 percent had arrived since 1965. Like most other immigrants, Haitians are mostly unskilled or semiskilled workers in the manufacturing and service sector, although there is a small but growing professional, white-collar segment among this group. Because many come to the United States in response to political repression at home, there are some Haitian refugees, as well as others awaiting a decision on applications for political asylum.

THE "NEW" ASIANS

Although less numerous than the Caribbean component of new arrivals, Asians constitute a large and growing proportion of New York's immigrants. Chinese are by far the largest of the recent Asian immigrants, further expanding the ethnic base established by the "old" Chinese in Manhattan's Chinatown. Koreans are a much smaller Asian group but are highly visible because of their predominance in small business pursuits, especially as owners of the many small markets for fresh fruit and vegetables in the city.

New York's Chinatown was previously a male "bachelor" society of people from rural areas in China. The more recent arrivals from China are much more likely to emigrate as a family group from urban areas. Contemporary Chinese also exhibit both a higher level of formal education and a more open attitude toward American institutions than the older generations. However, there are similarities among the Chinese: the new arrivals, like those before them, tend to concentrate in coethnic neighborhoods, relying on social networks for necessary information (e.g., jobs and housing) and other forms of social support. Likewise, the "new" Chinese are similar to both older Chinese and other immigrant groups in terms of their concentration in low-paying jobs in manufacturing (e.g., garment industry) and the service sector (e.g., ethnic restaurants).

Many Asians, especially the Koreans, have started small family businesses in their attempts at socioeconomic mobility. Family members are a source of relatively cheap, flexible, and reliable workers that enable such enterprises to survive, especially during the crucial start-up phase of a business. The Koreans are most widely recognized for their entrepreneurial spirit, accounting for an estimated 9,000 small businesses in 1985. The number of small businesses is especially impressive given the relatively small size of the Korean population in the New York City area.

Some explanations for Koreans' strong propensity for small business include their middle-class background and relatively high levels of education and professional experience before emigration. Furthermore, the demographic and economic changes that New York City experienced during the 1970s–80s created a ripe situation for many of the Koreans' small business pursuits.

IMMIGRANT ADAPTATIONS IN NEW YORK CITY

Recent immigrants will adapt to New York City as the city itself adapts to these newcomers. This is an established process in New York, newer immigrants taking up where previous groups left off. For instance, the foreign-born have filled many of the labor and housing gaps created by "white flight" from the city to the suburbs. But immigrants have not simply occupied spots previously held by the native-born; they have also generated new demands within various social institutions. Thus, there is a process of mutual adaptation under way in New York between immigrants and the social institutions that they increasingly confront in their daily lives.

One main factor influencing the adaptive process for the foreign-born is their immigration status. Immigrants are sorted according to established categories such as "refugee" and "illegal alien." Although some negotiation is possible, the status associated with such labels can have a lasting impact on the foreign-born, as well as their children. For instance, a refugee status enables some immigrants to obtain federal assistance that is not available to others. New York City has become a haven for refugees escaping war and political persecution. New York is the largest receiver of refugees from Europe and is second overall only to Los Angeles. In addition to the federal assistance designed specifically for refugees, New York City also has an established network of agencies that provide social services to this segment of the foreign-born population.

On the other hand, immigrants who are labeled as "illegal" are the least privileged, effectively excluded from full membership in this society. The size of New York City's illegal immigrant population is second only to that of Los Angeles. California has exhibited a decidedly hostile and exclusive orientation toward this segment of its population, passing legislation to deny social services and all but emergency health care to illegal immigrants and their children (Proposition

187). While New York City has sought reimbursement from the federal government for services to undocumented immigrants, the orientation toward such immigrants was not one of active exclusion or alarm. For instance, the mayor of New York City, Rudolph Giuliani, passed an executive order that instructed the city's public servants not to check the legal status of immigrants requesting social services, as federal law now requires.

Other factors that influence the process of adaptation are personal knowledge and training, such as education and work skills. In general, the more educated and skilled immigrant groups have adjusted better than those lacking these traits. But the vast majority of immigrants have been and continue to be concentrated in low-wage sectors of the economy. This brings up the related issue of how immigrants affect the job market in urban areas where they concentrate. Immigrants appear to have little effect on unemployment rates at the national level, and they may actually create more jobs than they fill. The evidence is more mixed when the level of analysis is specific urban areas or specific occupations. As we have seen, immigrants do tend to cluster within specific industries such as garments and the service sector. There is general agreement that a high proportion of immigrant labor in these areas does suppress wages, although the overall effect that this has on the economy is open to debate. Although some native workers certainly are negatively influenced, both directly through job displacement and indirectly through wage depression, whether or not such effects are significant is simply not clear.

Another important labor market issue is that of economic mobility. In general, immigrants take the least desirable jobs and are willing to work long hours in substandard conditions for lower wages than are native workers. Many in the first generation are willing to make sacrifices in the hope of a better future. Although the first generation may compare their situation favorably with that of compatriots back in the country of origin, the second generation will judge their situation in relation to a decidedly American standard of living, thus increasing the likelihood for contempt of an economic system that lacks opportunities for upward mobility. But the fact that immigrants concentrate in the many low-wage jobs of today's economy does not *necessarily* relegate them to the ranks of the poor. Historically, New York's immigrants were able to improve their collective lot through collective labor struggles, garnering more respectable wages and benefits as a result. The traditional link between New York City unions and immigrant labor makes it all the more likely that labor

organizers will look to recruit these newcomers into their ranks.

Immigrants tend to cluster together in specific geographic areas. This presents special challenges for organizations based in these neighborhoods, such as schools and churches. Pastors and school administrators must find ways to effectively incorporate these culturally distinct groups into their membership. Catholic parishes in New York City have adopted new practices to meet the needs of their increasingly non-European parishioners. For instance, religious services are now often performed in Spanish or Creole to accommodate the influx of many Caribbean Catholics. Also, the church has now become a trusted broker between the city's social services and many recent immigrants who are unaware of the procedures necessary for obtaining social services. Of course, the Catholic Church and other religious organizations still provide much in the way of direct assistance to the poor. In many ways, New York City's religious organizations have become an important bridge in the acculturation process for immigrants.

Although New York City's parochial schools have certainly increased their rolls as a result of the new immigration, it is the public schools that must deal with the sharp increase in the number of immigrant children and children of immigrants. Immigrants and their children played a decisive role in the foundation and development of New York City's public education system. As the sociologists Robert Dentler and Anne Hafner have found in their research within the southwest United States, school districts benefit from having a history of adaptation to demographic and economic changes. New York's public schools are once again challenged with the very difficult task of educating a student body that is increasingly diverse in its racial and ethnic background. But despite the linguistic and other cultural difficulties that immigrant children face in New York's public schools, they seem to be adjusting quite well, at least academically. But it is far from certain that a public education will afford these children much advantage in an economy that lacks stable, well-paying jobs and still exhibits racial and ethnic discrimination. Schools will definitely help to "Americanize" immigrant students, but the lesson learned might be that effort and attitude count less than who you know, where you live, or racial/ethnic attributes.

Perhaps the most important aspect of the new immigrants' adaptation will be in the political realm. Due to advances in communication and transportation, contemporary immigrants are much more likely to have knowledge of political activities in their country of origin. Moreover, many Latin American and Caribbean nations, including the Dominican Republic, Mexico, and Colombia, have made it possible to maintain dual citizenship, even permitting emigrants to cast votes in political contests from abroad. However, it will be political participation in local politics that will most directly affect New York City's new ethnic groups. One promising domestic development is that immigrants are now applying for citizenship in record numbers, increasing the pool of potential voters. There were two immigrants on the New York City Council in 1997, Una Clarke from Jamaica and Guillermo Linares from the Dominican Republic. Furthermore, the creation of a Dominican-dominated electoral district in the Washington Heights section of Manhattan, as well as participation in local school and community boards, makes Dominicans an increasingly significant political group. However, because of the diversity of the immigrant population and the wider racial/ethnic composition of New York City, future political power will necessitate building cross-cultural coalitions and interracial alliances around important issues and salient political causes.

As we start the new millennium, immigrants and their children are estimated to account for over half of New York City's total population, and in many neighborhoods, the foreign-born and their families have been in the majority for quite some time. Although immigrant-ethnic group succession has been rather gradual in the city as a whole, certain areas have experienced a rapid influx of immigrants, and native groups have not always welcomed such changes. Although New York may be more hospitable toward contemporary immigrants than other cities, the process of mutual adaptation will no doubt create the potential for future conflict. The main question is whether or not the new immigrant groups in New York City will be able to repeat the experiences of European groups, attaining some moderate upward mobility by the second generation. Of course, as in the past, some groups will make gains more rapidly than others. In many ways, the legacy of the immigrant city will hinge on the experiences of contemporary immigrant groups and how they are incorporated into New York City's social institutions.

Kevin Keogan

See also: Dominican Republic, English-Speaking Caribbean, Haiti and French-Speaking Caribbean, Puerto Rico (Part III, Sec. 2); China, Korea, Middle East, South Asia (Part III, Sec. 3); Eastern Europe, Former Soviet Union, Ireland, Western and Southern Europe (Part III, Sec. 4); New York State Report on Multicultural Textbooks, 1991 (Part IV, Sec. 2).

BIBLIOGRAPHY

Alba, Richard. *Ethnic Identity: The Transformation of White America.* New Haven: Yale University Press, 1990.

———. "Italian Americans: A Century of Ethnic Change." In *Origins and Destinies,* ed. Pedraza and Rumbaut. New York: Wadsworth, 1996.

Binder, Frederick, and David Reimers. "New York as an Immigrant City." In *Origins and Destinies,* ed. Pedraza and Rumbaut. New York: Wadsworth, 1996.

Bogen, Elizabeth. *Immigration in New York.* New York: Praeger Publishers, 1987.

Brown, Mary Elizabeth. "The Adaptation of the Tactics of the Enemy: The Case of Italian Immigrant Youth in the Archdiocese of New York during the Progressive Era." In *Immigration to New York,* ed. Pencak, Berrol, and Miller. London: Associated University Presses, 1991.

Buchanan-Stafford, Susan. "The Haitians: The Cultural Meaning of Race and Ethnicity." In *New Immigrants in New York,* ed. Foner. New York: Columbia University Press, 1987.

Bureau of the Census. *Census CD v. 1.1.* 1990.

Corcoran, Mary. *Irish Illegals: Transients between Two Societies.* Westport, CT: Greenwood Press, 1993.

Crahan, Margaret, and Alberto Vourvoulias-Bush, eds. *The City and the World: New York's Global Future.* New York: Council on Foreign Relations, 1997.

Dentler, Robert, and Anne L. Hafner. *Hosting Newcomers: Structuring Educational Opportunities for Immigrant Children.* New York: Teachers College Press, 1997.

DeWind, Josh. "Educating the Children of Immigrants in New York's Restructured Economy." In *The City and the World,* ed. Crahan and Vourvoulias-Bush. New York: Council on Foreign Relations, 1997.

Diner, Hasia. "The Most Irish City in the Union: Overview of the Era of the Great Migration, 1844–1877." In *The New York Irish,* ed. Ronald Baylor and Timothy Meagher. Baltimore: Johns Hopkins University Press, 1996.

Ernst, Robert. *Immigrant Life in New York City, 1825–1863.* 1949. Reprint, New York: Octagon Books, 1979.

Federal Writer's Project. *The Italians of New York.* New York: Arno Press, 1969.

Firestone, David. "Mayoral Order on Immigrants Is Struck Down." *New York Times,* July 19, 1997, p. A21.

Foner, Nancy. "The Jamaicans: Race and Ethnicity among Migrants in New York City." In *New Immigrants in New York,* ed. Foner. New York: Columbia University Press, 1987.

———. ed. *New Immigrants in New York.* New York: Columbia University Press, 1987.

Friedman-Kasaba, Kathie. *Memories of Migration: Gender, Ethnicity, and Work in New York, 1870–1924.* Albany: State University of New York Press, 1996.

Gold, Steven, and Bruce Phillips. "Mobility and Continuity among Eastern European Jews." In *Origins and Destinies,* ed. Pedraza and Rumbaut. New York: Wadsworth, 1996.

Grasmuck, Sheri, and Patricia Pessar. "Dominicans in the United States: First- and Second-Generation Settlement, 1960–1990." In *Origins and Destinies*, ed. Pedraza and Rumbaut. New York: Wadsworth, 1996.

Kamphoefner, Walter. "German Americans: Paradoxes of a 'Model Minority.'" In *Origins and Destinies*, ed. Pedraza and Rumbaut. New York: Wadsworth, 1996.

Kim, Illsoo. "The Koreans: Small Business in an Urban Frontier." In *New Immigrants in New York*, ed. Foner. New York: Columbia University Press, 1987.

Lieberson, Stanley, and Mary Waters. *From Many Strands: Ethnic and Racial Groups in America*. New York: Russell Sage, 1988.

Nadel, Stanley. "From the Barricades of Paris to the Sidewalks of New York: German Artisans and the European Roots of American Labor Radicalism." In *Immigration to New York*, ed. Pencak, Berrol, and Miller. London: Associated University Presses, 1991.

New York City Department of Planning. *The Newest New Yorkers: An Analysis of Immigration into New York City during the 1980s*. New York: Department of Planning, 1992.

Pedraza, Silvia, and Ruben Rumbaut, eds. *Origins and Destinies: Immigration, Race, and Ethnicity in America*. New York: Wadsworth Publishing, 1996.

Pencak, William, Selma Berrol, and Randall Miller, eds. *Immigration to New York*. London: Associated University Presses, 1991.

Pessar, Patricia. "The Dominicans: Women in the Household and Garment Industry." In *New Immigrants in New York*, ed. Foner. New York: Columbia University Press, 1987.

Ravitch, Dianne. *The Great School Wars: A History of the New York City Public Schools*. New York: Basic Books, 1988.

Reimers, David. "Recent Third World Immigration to New York City, 1945–1986: An Overview." In *Immigration to New York*, ed. Pencak, Berrol, and Miller. London: Associated University Presses, 1991.

Rumbaut, Rubén. "Origins and Destinies: Immigration, Race, and Ethnicity in Contemporary America." In *Origins and Destinies*, ed. Pedraza and Rumbaut. New York: Wadsworth, 1996.

Salvo, Joseph, and Arun Peter Lobo. "Immigration and the Changing Demographic Profile of New York." In *The City and the World*, ed. Crahan and Vourvoulias-Bush. New York: Council on Foreign Relations, 1997.

Sanjek, Roger. *The Future of Us All: Race and Neighborhood Politics in New York City*. Ithaca: Cornell University Press, 1998.

Smith, Robert. "Transnational Migration, Assimilation, and Political Community." In *The City and the World*, ed. Crahan and Vourvoulias-Bush. New York: Council on Foreign Relations, 1997.

Stevens-Arroyo, Anthony. "Building a New Public Realm: Moral Responsibility and Religious Commitment in the City." In *The City and the World*, ed. Crahan and Vourvoulias-Bush. New York: Council on Foreign Relations, 1997.

Wong, Bernard. "The Chinese: New Immigrants in New York's Chinatown." In *New Immigrants in New York*, ed. Foner. New York: Columbia University Press, 1987.

Youseff, Nadia. *The Demographics of Immigration: A Socio-Demographic Profile of the Foreign-Born Population in New York State*. New York: Center for Migration Studies, 1992.

RURAL AMERICA

For much of American history, the vast majority of Americans lived in rural areas. Not surprisingly, then, most immigrants in the eighteenth and early nineteenth centuries—whether free or indentured—settled in rural areas. After the 1820s, however, most immigrants were urban. Still, differences existed among different immigrant groups, with most Scandinavians, Japanese, and Germans settling in rural areas, while most Irish, Chinese, and Italian immigrants settled in urban areas. But as the United States changed from a rural to urban country in the late-nineteenth and early-twentieth centuries, so, too, did the patterns of immigration. Thus, an overall decrease in immigration to rural areas occurred after 1920.

HISTORICAL IMMIGRATION PATTERNS OF EUROPEAN IMMIGRANTS

In the 1830s, many Irish settled in New England and many worked in timber. Most Irish immigrants could not afford to purchase farms, and their farming experience in Ireland did not prepare them to work in American agriculture, which is why they worked primarily in the timber industry.

The majority of German immigrants settled in rural areas. A cluster of German settlements lies between the cities of St. Louis, Cincinnati, and Milwaukee. This area is known as "the German triangle." In 1870, one in four Germans worked in agriculture, and more than one-third of all foreign-born farmers were German. German immigrants remained longer where they settled than other ethnic groups, and as a result tended to invest more in things such as buildings and improvements. Thus, the German language is still spoken today into fourth and fifth generations. There is also a continued contemporary presence of German Americans in agriculture.

Many immigrants from Norway, Sweden, and Denmark settled in rural areas, especially in the far Midwest and the Great Plains. Over half of all Norwegian immigrants settled in Wisconsin, Minnesota, or North Dakota. Among Danish immigrants were many who were Moravian and who settled in Pennsylvania with their coreligionists. One of the first large immigrant groups from Denmark was composed of converted Mormons, who settled largely in the valley of the Great Salt Lake in Utah. From 1868 to 1900, approximately 3.4 percent of Danish immigrants were independent farmers, and 43.2 percent were rural laborers. The largest population of Danes lived in Iowa, and many others lived in Wisconsin, Minnesota, and Nebraska.

Many Italian immigrants were looking for rural economic opportunities. Although the majority of Italians lived in urban areas, there were also rural colonies. For example, there was a substantial Italian agricultural presence in Bryan, Texas, and other areas in the Far West. There was a particularly strong Italian presence in California, and many Italian Americans worked in the grape-growing wine industry.

HISTORICAL IMMIGRATION PATTERNS OF ASIAN AND HISPANIC IMMIGRANTS

Most Chinese Americans were concentrated in the West, particularly in California. Hundreds of Chinese owned or operated farms, and they greatly contributed to California agriculture by introducing new crops and developing methods of distribution. A substantial number of Chinese immigrants also worked in Hawaii on sugar plantations. It should also be noted that as Japanese immigrants' prosperity grew, Chinese immigrants replaced their presence in agricultural labor, and, likewise, as Chinese workers ob-

While the classic image of the immigrant is that of a city dweller, many newcomers find their way to rural areas of the United States, like these Salvadoran farmworkers in a Michigan cornfield. *(Donna DeCesare/Impact Visuals)*

tained nonfarm jobs, Mexican immigrants filled the agricultural job vacancies. This same phenomenon also occurred in railroad labor. The building of railroads in the West was difficult, low-paid work, and as a result it was not uncommon for immigrants to perform such labor in these rural areas.

A large number of Japanese immigrants also worked on Hawaiian sugar plantations. By 1900, many Japanese immigrants were working in agriculture in California. Soon, however, the Japanese began to acquire farmland. By 1904, Japanese were farming more than fifty thousand acres in California alone; by 1909, more than one hundred fifty thousand acres, and by 1919, more than four hundred fifty thousand acres.

The initial large group of Mexican immigrants entered the United States around 1909. Many of these immigrants left because of the Mexican Revolution, which made it dangerous for them to remain in their homeland. Additionally, the economies of California and the Southwest were booming, creating an entice-

ment for emigration from Mexico. Most of these immigrants found jobs in agriculture.

One of the first major influxes of Mexican immigrants to the United States occurred from 1942 to 1964, during the Bracero Program. World War II created a labor shortage in the United States, triggering a deliberate move by the United States government to stimulate immigration of Mexican laborers to the American Southwest and West, mostly to perform agricultural work. The temporary worker program was called *bracero*, which means "arm" in Spanish, indicative of the nature of the labor program. The Bracero Program brought in many workers to the United States, in addition to several million illegal immigrants. As many critics of the Bracero Program, including sociologists Sandra L. Martin, Todd E. Gordon, and Janis B. Kupersmidt, have noted, "there is nothing more permanent than temporary workers."

In general, guest-worker programs seem to initially benefit both growers and farmworkers, but in the long term, they carve out a rather permanent class dichotomy, which is both financially and socially detrimental to farm workers. Sociologist Philip L. Martin points out the ramifications that the Bracero Program left on Mexican farmworkers when he writes that the program "laid the groundwork" for the large number of illegal immigrants who cross the United States–Mexican border on a regular basis. In fact, illegal Mexican workers are caught by the Immigration and Naturalization Service (INS) so often that a "revolving door" phenomenon exists. Illegal Mexican workers stay in the United States as long as they can, until they are caught and sent back across the border to Mexico, but they return to the United States, sometimes even on the same day. This occurs because INS officers report only the number of illegals they catch, but on paper it makes no difference to them if the same people are caught on a regular basis. Alternately, the Mexican farmworkers know that if caught, they will be sent back across the border, but that they can return as soon as INS officials have left.

Another circular phenomenon that occurs in immigrant farm labor has to do with the number of farm jobs available to immigrant workers. Growers support a large number of jobs for farmworkers but want to pay them low wages. Due to the greater number of farm jobs, more immigration occurs to fill the jobs (whether legal or not). This then leads to more poverty in the rural areas of America where the immigrants are headed. One cannot examine Mexican immigration without considering farm labor and its effects on rural poverty.

The Bracero Program left a legacy of an oversupply of labor due to Mexicans' willingness to work for low wages and in poor working conditions. Some farm workers (rightly) believe that growers prefer Mexican laborers due to their tolerance of poor treatment. There is, of course, an element of racism to the growers' treatment of farmworkers. They do not have a problem providing substandard housing and low wages to Mexicans, Filipinos, Haitians, Guatemalans, or Ecuadorans, for example, but non-Hispanic whites are perceived differently. It is interesting to note that Mexico and the rest of Latin America was not put under a quota system until after 1965, suggesting that race played a different role for Spanish-speaking immigrants than it did for Asian immigrants. Growers were more willing to hire Mexican workers because they were perceived to be more likely to return home. Due to easy accessibility of labor and acceptable low wages, growers have not had much incentive to mechanize harvesting. Consumers have increasingly shown a demand for labor-intensive fruits and vegetables, and growers have simply employed laborers when needed.

This topic lends itself to the distinction between seasonal farmworkers and migrant farmworkers. Seasonal farmworkers are employed during specific times in the year, depending on the timing of harvests. Migrant farmworkers follow crops, constantly moving depending on where jobs are available. There are three main agricultural migration patterns in the United States: the Western stream, consisting of California, Oregon, Washington, and other Western states; the Central stream, consisting of the Midwest, including Minnesota, Illinois, Wisconsin, and Michigan (among others); and the Eastern stream, made up of Florida, Delaware, Maryland, Virginia, and continuing up to Maine and Vermont where workers travel during the summer harvests.

One especially important area to Mexican migrant workers is the San Joaquin Valley in California. It is estimated that about 50 percent of immigrants who arrived from 1980 to 1990 to the San Joaquin area were from Mexico, while another 25 percent arrived from Southeast Asia. Logically, such an influx of cheap labor from Mexico tends to suppress real wages for farmworkers, and thus encourages the increase of labor-intensive crop production. This, then, discourages the adoption of labor-saving production methods, and ultimately has a great impact on the economies of towns in rural America. It becomes easy to recognize that immigration, farm employment, and income are all dependent upon one another, and that new patterns of poverty in rural America are the result.

The *Rural Migration News* reports that the number of poor residents in an area increases at the same time that farm sales are increasing. This phenomenon is ubiquitous throughout the United States. One reason for the poverty experienced by immigrant farmworkers is the new and prominent role of farm labor contractors. Both farm workers and growers are dependent upon farm labor contractors, who are also known as "crew leaders." Contractors link workers and growers, thereby providing growers with necessary labor, and likewise providing workers with jobs. Contractors sometimes have assistants, called *mayordomos* or *contratistas*, who are field walkers, and *riteros*, who are crew bosses. Contractors are in charge of laborers, keep track of the time they work and their production, and additionally sometimes transport laborers to the field. Contractors are in charge of labor camps, thus bypassing any direct communication between growers and laborers. Some critics have attributed this lack of contact between farmworkers and growers as contributing to low wages and substandard housing and working conditions for laborers. Farm labor contractors are not known to be kind people, and have a reputation for making false promises to farmworkers during recruitment, intimidating and threatening them, and transporting them in dangerous vehicles.

It is not uncommon for farm labor contractors to take advantage of immigrant farmworkers' alcohol and/or drug addictions. Robert Wilson, a farm laborer in Pahokee, Florida, emphasized the prevalence of alcohol in the migrant community when he said, "The first thing a crewleader's got to have is something for the workers to drink," notes sociologist Daniel Rothenberg. Drug-addicted farm laborers oftentimes are paid in the currency of drugs and/or alcohol. There have also been accounts of contractors paying workers in the form of sex from a coerced or forced fellow laborer, thus taking rape as a form of currency. Thus, it is not surprising that high levels of HIV infection have been found among migrant farmworkers in Florida. HIV is prevalent among migrant farmworkers due to the mobile nature of their work, as well as a high tendency of drug usage and participation in the commercial sex industry.

One of the most alarming conditions of farm labor is exposure to pesticides. Many cases have been documented of workers becoming ill, the appearance of skin rashes, nausea, vomiting, coughing, and so on. There have also been documented cases of babies being born with serious birth defects, for example, missing limbs. Growers are required to post signs after fields are sprayed with pesticides, but laborers often ignore the signs because they need their wages so badly.

Housing conditions vary depending on geographic locations. Farmworkers live in a variety of habitats, including tents, cardboard boxes, apartments, holes in the ground, or parts of houses. In Georgetown, Delaware, for example, many Guatemalan immigrants work in the poultry industry and share houses with two to four other immigrant families. Such living accommodations are illegal, but nonetheless occur and are even prevalent. There have also been reports of substandard conditions of living among immigrants who work in the meatpacking industry. The labor supply in the meatpacking industry is similar to that in agriculture. Immigrant workers are recruited from Mexico to work in dangerous meatpacking plants where pay is low.

Although not prevalent, it is shocking to observe some farmworkers living under debt peonage—a form of slavery. One can observe forms of debt peonage in southern areas of the United States, even today. Debt peonage occurs when workers agree to pay back recruiters for the costs of their transportation to the United States, and for food and shelter. They agree to work until they earn enough money to pay back

the contractors. Sometimes, however, it is virtually impossible for farmworkers to earn enough money to pay back the contractors because they come to the United States with nothing. If they become dependent upon drugs and/or alcohol, the system of debt peonage takes full effect, because oftentimes the contractors supply the workers with drugs.

Another factor contributing to the immigrant farmworker's situation is lack of education, and the difficulty of continuing education. This is especially a problem for the children of immigrant farmworkers. Studies have also shown that children of immigrant farmworkers are exposed to a lot of violence; as a result, these children oftentimes experience emotional and/or behavioral problems.

After their initial arrival into the United States, most Mexican immigrants do not speak English, and overcoming the linguistic obstacle is not an easy task, especially because most immigrant farmworkers have no time to spend learning English. Additionally, it is difficult, if not impossible, for the children of immigrant farm laborers to stay in school because of the nomadic living patterns of their families. In order to make enough money for survival, many families follow crop harvests, which prevents children from being in school at all when they work in the fields, and makes it more difficult to continue their education due to temporal factors. Many migrant parents do not think it is worth placing their children in a school for only a few months (until a harvest is over), so they end up not attending school at all.

Lack of health care is another problem for immigrant farm laborers. Agricultural jobs are dangerous, not only due to ever-present pesticides, but also because of constant bending necessary for picking crops, and working under the hot sun all day long. Only recently were growers obligated by law to provide drinking water and toilet facilities for their workers. Medical professionals who have treated farmworkers have reported seeing the same types of ailments in farmworkers living in the United States as they have observed in developing countries. This comes as no surprise considering that they live under similar conditions.

IMMIGRATION POLICY AND RURAL AMERICA

After the Bracero Program ended, growers had become accustomed to an abundance of cheap farm labor. The agricultural industry has managed to escape many labor laws that other industries must abide by. Many people, like Rothenberg, attribute this phenomenon to the power of "ruthless, unscrupulous special-interest groups." One of the most powerful strategies of the agricultural lobby is to keep in place "an oversupply of workers, low wages, and antiunion conditions." By 1980, there were an estimated 3 million undocumented immigrants in the United States. As a result, the Immigration Reform and Control Act (IRCA) of 1986 came about in an effort to combat the large presence of undocumented workers. The goal of IRCA was to discourage and prevent employers from hiring illegal immigrants. IRCA allowed undocumented workers who had lived continuously in the United States for five years to apply for permanent residency through a special amnesty program. However, by the year 2000, there were an estimated 5 million undocumented workers in the United States.

There were three main provisions included in IRCA. The first was deferred sanctions enforcement and search warrants. Growers convinced Congress that during the legalization program for farm workers, INS officials should be required to obtain search warrants before raiding any fields. Growers also lobbied successfully that farms were "extraordinarily dependent" upon undocumented workers for labor, and that sanctions against growers should not be enforced while the legalization program for farmworkers was taking place. Second, IRCA created two legalization programs. The first was a general program known as I-687, which "granted legal status to illegal aliens if they had continuously resided in the United States since January 1, 1982," says Philip L. Martin. The second legalization program was the Special Agriculture Worker (SAW) program, which "granted legal status to aliens" who worked at least ninety days in farm work during the period 1985–86. Third, IRCA revised the H-2A nonimmigrant worker program and established the new Replenishment Agricultural Worker (RAW) program. These last two programs enabled United States farmers to import foreign (cheap) labor. H-2A is a contractual program whereby a farmer must have the government certify that a genuine labor shortage exists. In return, the farmer is allowed to recruit foreign workers "wherever and however [s/]he pleases." Under the RAW program, the United States government could admit replenishment agricultural workers if it believes that a labor shortage will occur.

According to Martin, neither the RAW program nor the H-2A program "admitted any additional legal foreign worker since the mid-1980s," primarily due to a surge in illegal immigration as a result of the rampant production of falsified documents. Since IRCA,

many illegal workers simply acquire false documents and do not get caught. Both INS officials and growers are aware of the great number of illegal workers possessing false documents, but there is not yet a method for controlling the problem.

Martin points out one of the most explanatory elements of the farm system and its workers when he writes, "IRCA imposed penalties on employers who knowingly hire illegal aliens, but it did not change the structure of industries that had become dependent on such workers." Thus, more illegal immigrants were working and living in the United States after IRCA than prior to its enactment. The government attempted to enact two opposing policies simultaneously, with the result that the goals of IRCA were not achieved. IRCA was an attempt to slow and prevent illegal immigration, especially from Mexico. By allowing farmers to attach clauses onto the act allowing for RAWs and SAWs, the United States government pleased participants of both sides of the issue. Legally, the government had acted to prevent illegal immigration, yet in reality, the undocumented workers simply obtained falsified documents, and farmers still had access to cheap labor. Immigration opponents, growers, and farmworkers were all content with IRCA because the workers got their wages and the farmers got their cheap labor. In the long run, however, the economy will suffer as a whole as Mexican poverty simply is relocated to pockets of rural poverty in the United States. Ultimately, IRCA has had a negative effect on the economy of Mexico as well as that of the United States. In addition, growers' historic dependence and expectation of abundant and cheap labor has hindered investment in mechanization.

Mechanization, however, is not the only possibility for improving the agricultural labor system. Increasing workers' wages would give farmers the incentive to find substitutes for farmworkers. Labor costs are much more important to farmers than they are to consumers. Past experience shows that an increase in farmworker wages leads to a reduced demand for laborers, not an influx of American workers into the farm workforce. In fact, agricultural economists have shown that charging consumers $1.13/pound for grapes instead of $1.00/pound, for example, would actually double the wages of farmworkers from $6 to $12/hour.

By attempting to give farmworkers the jobs they so desperately want, as well as allow farmers an ample supply of cheap labor, the government actually imposes contradictory policies that enable many immigrants to join the workforce, while simultaneously treating agricultural workers differently than any other laborers in the United States. Such separate treatment of farmworkers induces them into long-lasting poverty and marginalization from the rest of society. Immigrant farmworkers come into the United States linguistically and financially marginalized; they frequently find themselves racially marginalized in the United States; and because the rural areas involved in farm work are often remote, they are often geographically marginalized as well. At the same time, farmers across the country are making requests to their congressional representative to keep the labor laws as they are, and due to the efforts of their powerful farm lobby, their political goals are frequently met. Immigrant farmworkers, on the other hand, have virtually no political voice, especially when they do not speak English, and after working ten to twelve hours in the fields there is not a lot of time for learning another language.

The American farm system has contributed to silencing migrant workers' voices. It is in the interests of growers that the workers do not, for example, unionize. The leading figure of farmworker unionization was Cesar Chavez, who, in 1965, organized a grape boycott in order for farmworkers to have the right to unionize, and in an attempt to get growers to sign contracts. Although the grape boycott was a success, the group he and Dolores Huerta founded, United Farm Workers of America (UFW), has not experienced a lot of success in its fight for higher wages and better housing and working conditions. One of the group's main goals was to empower farmworkers and farmworker unions. However, the conservative state government in California during the 1980s, as well as the large number of undocumented workers following IRCA, made the UFW's goals virtually impossible to meet. In addition, "the arrival of desperate workers . . . made it hard for unions to negotiate ever higher wages and benefit improvements," says Philip Martin. The temporary nature of farmwork has also contributed to difficulties in union organization, and "farmworker unions have [thus] rarely had enough economic and political power to maintain union organizations and to effectuate lasting structural changes in the farm labor market."

IRCA's failed attempt at slowing illegal immigration from Mexico, as well as its unintended contribution to an increase in undocumented workers in the United States, has contributed to the transferring of rural poverty from Mexico to the United States. Agricultural immigration scholars refer to this transfer of poverty as the "Latinization of rural America." Eventually this transfer of rural poverty becomes urban poverty as migration toward urban areas occurs.

POLICY OPTIONS RELATED TO IMMIGRANTS IN RURAL AMERICA

There are three principal options available to the United States and Mexico in dealing with the influx of workers from Mexico to the United States. First, the United States could develop better border patrols, which would be successful in deterring Mexican and other illegal immigrants from entering the United States. This could be achieved by using a computer system capable of detecting fraudulent documents, for example. Second, the United States could legalize undocumented workers by converting them into legal guest workers. Third, the United States could make a greater effort at inducing the Mexican government into cooperating to reduce illegal immigration. The Mexican government could implement policies geared at reducing the great domestic income inequalities that contribute to emigration. Also, both Mexico and the United States could cooperate to reduce development at the border. By focusing on development located in the interior of Mexico, fewer Mexicans would see the incentive to emigrate. Last, Mexico could cooperate with the United States to reduce illegal immigration. Mexican citizens are not legally allowed to leave Mexico except at authorized ports. Thus, Mexicans entering the United States illegally are breaking laws in both countries.

Gretchen S. Carnes

See also: West Africa (Part III, Sec. 1); Dominican Republic, Haiti and French-Speaking Caribbean, Puerto Rico (Part III, Sec. 2).

BIBLIOGRAPHY

Daniels, Roger. *Coming to America—A History of Immigration and Ethnicity in American Life.* New York: Harper Perennial, 1990.

Escobar, Gabriel. "Immigration Transforms a Community." *Washington Post,* November 29, 1999: A1.

Hedges, Stephen J., Dana Hawkins, and Penny Loeb. "The New Jungle." Updated September 23, 1996. *U.S. News Online.* http://www.usnews.com/usnews/issue/23/htm. Cited February 3, 2000.

Martin, Philip L. "The Endless Debate: Immigration and U.S. Agriculture." http://www.agecon.ucdavis.edu/Faculty/Phil.M/endless/endless.htm. Cited January 30, 2000.

———. "The Mexican Crisis and Mexico–U.S. Migration." http://www.agecon.davis.edu/Faculty/Phil.M/crisis/crisis.htm. Cited January 1, 2000.

————. "Promises to Keep: Collective Bargaining in California Agriculture." http://agecon.ucdavis.edu/Faculty/Phil.M/promises/promises1.htm. Cited January 30, 2000.

Martin, Philip L., and Edward J. Taylor. "Poverty Amid Prosperity: Farm Employment, Immigration, and Poverty in California." *American Journal of Agricultural Economics* 80 (1998): 1008–14.

Martin, Sandra L., Todd E. Gordon, and Janis B. Kupersmidt. "Survey of Exposure to Violence Among the Children of Migrant and Seasonal Farm Workers." *Public Health Reports* 110 (May/June 1995): 268–76.

Rothenberg, Daniel. *With These Hands—The Hidden World of Migrant Farmworkers Today.* New York: Harcourt Brace, 1998.

Rural Migration News. "California: Welfare, Development, and Options." http://migration.ucdavis.edu/Rural-Migration-News/Oct98RMN.html. Cited January 29, 2000.

Sanchez, George J. "Race and Immigration History." *American Behavioral Scientist* 42 (June/July 1999): 1271–75.

Taylor, J. E., and P. L. Martin. "The Immigrant Subsidy in California Agriculture: Farm Employment, Poverty, and Welfare." *Population and Development Review* 23 (December 1997): 855–74.

Weatherby, Norman L., Virginia H. McCoy, and Keith V. Bletzer. "Immigration and HIV Among Migrant Workers in Rural Southern Florida." *Journal of Drug Issues* 27 (Winter 1997): 155–72.

SAN FRANCISCO

$\mathcal{P}$icturesque hills, bridges, and islands shape the beautiful geographic landscape of San Francisco, California. Located on a peninsula, San Francisco cleanses itself mornings and evenings with the majestic fog from the Pacific Ocean. One of the city's natural features, the thick fog enters the San Francisco Bay through the magnificent Golden Gate Bridge. It then rolls over more than forty hills, which allow the city's population splendid views of the bay and surrounding cities and countryside.

Yet San Francisco's natural and architectural beauty only begins to tell the larger, more painful history of a city that has been home to more than fifty Native American communities and immigrant populations. It is indeed a history that Native Americans, immigrants, and migrants have built together. Whether it was colonizers destroying Native American societies in the eighteenth and nineteenth centuries or refugees fleeing economic and political exploitation in their homelands in the 1980s, newcomers have made San Francisco the city it is today. This history of the city and its immigrants has not been one of open arms and cheerful welcome. More often, San Francisco's immigrants have encountered outright attacks and violence, the racial hatred targeting the latest arrivals to the city, which is often heralded as the bastion of openness and liberal attitudes.

BEFORE THERE WAS A CITY

Long before the arrival of the first missionaries and soldiers sent by Spain to establish the Mission of Saint Francis of Assisi in 1776, dozens of small, independent tribes populated the San Francisco Bay Area. Speaking about twelve different languages, these Native American communities have been collectively referred to as the Ohlone Indians, but they include numerous groups such as the Karkin, the Huchiun, the Salson, and the Tuibun. These were societies whose livelihood depended primarily on the region's abundant game and water sources and, to a lesser extent, annual acorn harvests.

As Spanish soldiers began to build their fort, the Presidio, the friars set to build their mission. To do so, they forcibly baptized and enslaved the Ohlone of the region. Life for the Native American populations changed dramatically as they became indentured workers for the Spanish Crown. Yet the Ohlone fought against their harsh conditions in different ways. They never altogether accepted Spanish at the cost of their native languages, and despite close scrutiny from the friars, many native women and men were able to maintain some sort of social life among themselves. Often, the Ohlone Indians also deserted the mission to go to the East Bay, the region now known as the city of Oakland in Alameda County. Such actions were necessary for their basic survival, because native communities were not immune to European diseases. In April 1806, a measles epidemic killed over two hundred Indians within two days, one-fourth of the Native American population.

With Mexican independence from Spain secured in 1821, numerous Mexican ranchers called Californios settled in an area to the south of Yerba Buena. Spanish for "good herb" and descriptive of the aromatic shrub growing there, Yerba Buena was the name given to the small settlement off the San Francisco Bay. Throughout the 1830s and 1840s, Yerba Buena remained a frontier village with growing but small commercial activity based on trading goods.

The Mexican ranchers had less than three decades of regional stability for themselves. Located far from Mexico City's control, California became a tempting prize for colonial empires of the period, including England, France, and Russia. But the United States's geographic proximity would allow it to beat all others to the land. The rhetoric of manifest destiny, to ex-

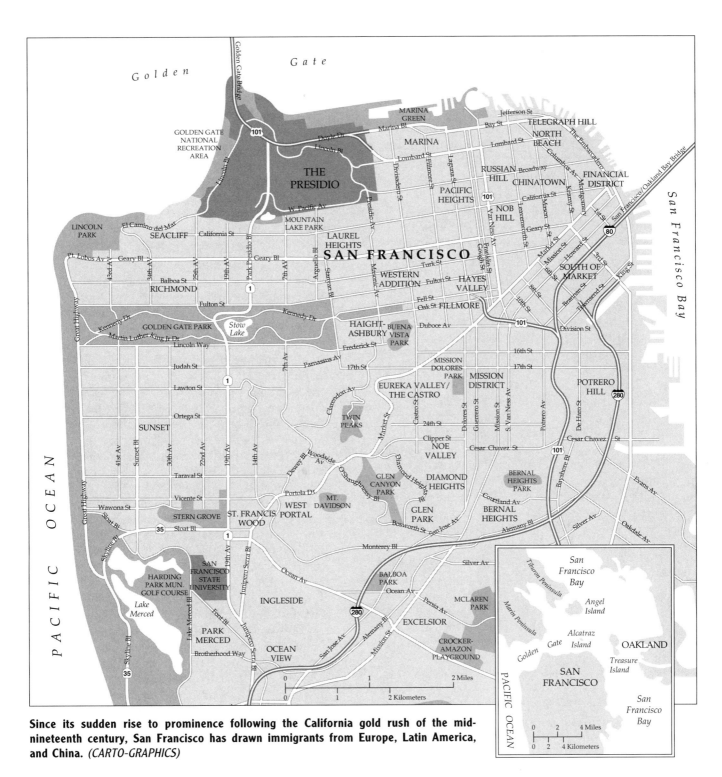

Since its sudden rise to prominence following the California gold rush of the mid-nineteenth century, San Francisco has drawn immigrants from Europe, Latin America, and China. *(CARTO-GRAPHICS)*

pand westward at any cost, was in full force in the country by the mid-1840s. With its invasion of Mexico in 1846 and eventual defeat of that country's armed forces in 1847, the United States acquired over half of Mexico's territory, including the much coveted California. In 1847, as California passed from Mexican possession into that of the United States, Yerba Buena became San Francisco. Soon the quiet settlement would be overwhelmed by adventurers seeking fortunes of gold in California.

GOLD, GREED, AND RACISM

No other single event transformed the San Francisco Bay Area more than the gold rush. Discovered on January 24, 1848, near the Native American village of Cullomah, gold created an intense fever nationally and internationally. First found at the sawmill of Captain John Sutter, a native of Switzerland, gold promised quick riches in a region with still relatively few inhabitants.

Although the gold rush did not truly occur until President James Polk delivered the news to Congress on December 2, 1848, in which he confirmed the abundance of gold in California, the flow of immigrants was overwhelming. By 1849, the city's population was doubling every ten days, with San Francisco constantly receiving ships. A small, quiet village was being transformed into a burgeoning city. In this year, more than twenty thousand arrived by sea, with an additional one hundred thousand making the trek by land. The overwhelmingly male immigrant wave included Chileans, Filipinos, Italians, Hawaiians, Australians, Irish, blacks, and Chinese. By 1852, California had more than 250,000 residents, the majority arriving in the midst of the promises of the gold rush.

The search for gold had a devastating effect on the region's native peoples. During the first two years of the California gold rush, more than one hundred thousand Indians lost their lives. Despite killing some miners to drive them off native lands and seizing livestock and goods to fight against further encroachment into their territories, Native Americans were soon overwhelmed. In addition, the federal government continued to enforce its policy of placing Indians in reservations, by force if necessary. By 1857, just before the eventual, gradual decline of reservations in California, nearly one-fifth of the state's surviving Native American population of fifty thousand lived in dismal conditions on reservations.

Those who had arrived in California for the first time during the gold rush did not encounter a city of civility or order. San Francisco in the 1850s was a lawless town still enmeshed in a frontier mentality, one with an anti-immigrant focus. Chileans, for example, were targets of the violent Hounds in 1849. Recruited in New York at the start of the Mexican–American War (1846–1848) for Colonel Jonathan Drake Stevenson's regiment, the Hounds were a group of white men who began to intimidate Chilean immigrants. On one particular night, the Hounds invaded Chiletown, a group of tents and shanties where the growing Chilean population had settled, attacking anyone who spoke what they believed was Spanish. Self-described

as the "San Francisco Regulators" who wanted to make the city "safe" for white Americans, the Hounds had become a violent group of fifty to sixty men, divided in bands that raped, killed, and stole from the Chileans. After being successfully tried in court and found guilty, they were banished from California soon after.

The violent record of anti-immigrant activity started by the Hounds slowed Chilean immigration significantly. But other national groups made the venture toward California, including Australians. In a matter of few months in 1851, more than two thousand had arrived in San Francisco. Noticing that a few Australian criminals had joined this immigrant wave, newspapers such as the *Alta California* and San Franciscans of the period began to argue that all arriving "Sydney men" were dangerous. In June 1851, the first Committee of Vigilance was formed under the pretense of securing life and property for the citizens of San Francisco. Working outside legal authority, the committee, primarily businessmen, took the law into its own hands. They hanged people without trial and turned back ships of immigrants from the bay.

With an economic depression hitting the city hard in 1854, it would be only two years before the second Committee of Vigilance was formed, reacting against economic hardship by once again scapegoating and targeting immigrants. Now, the one-thousand-man-strong committee targeted Irish political leaders, among other newcomers. Attracted by the gold rush and escaping Ireland's disastrous potato famine, the Irish in San Francisco had entered every possible area of life in the city. In the mid-1850s, an anti-Catholic movement focusing on the "threat" of Irish and German political power coalesced as the Know-Nothings. As a nativist, anti-immigrant political party challenging the Democratic Party of the period, the Know-Nothings were able to elect their own governor, Neely Johnson, in 1854.

By 1860, San Francisco no longer offered the same intense promises that the short-lived, five-year excitement with gold had produced. But the lure of gold had been strong enough to turn the city into the most important one in the West, with over one hundred thousand inhabitants. To connect this growing urban center with the East Coast, a prominent civil engineer named Theodore D. Judah sought to build the stretch of a transcontinental railroad from Sacramento to the Missouri River. Four Sacramento merchants and former gold seekers joined forces to form the Central Pacific Railroad Company. Winning the lucrative bid to build the western half of the railroad, Collis P. Huntington, Mark Hopkins, Charles Crocker, and Leland Stanford required the labor of thousands of workers to begin the project in 1863; the Chinese would be among those most sought for this lucrative business venture. Having become millionaires, the four businessmen, known as the Big Four, would eventually build palatial homes in the Nob Hill district of San Francisco. Their influence on California's economy and politics remains to this day.

THE PROMISE OF GOLD MOUNTAIN AND THE THREAT OF THE "CELESTIALS"

The Chinese had been barely tolerated in California since their first arrival during the gold rush. Future anti-Chinese, antimiscegenation, and antifamily legislation would reinforce an early pattern of mostly male immigration. Seeking prosperity in the place they called "Gold Mountain," these first Chinese in California numbered over four thousand in 1850, whereas there were only seven Chinese women. Throughout the 1850s, anti-Chinese laws were enacted to keep them from enjoying most benefits of civil society. Chinese could not vote, own land, attend school with whites, or testify in state court against whites, which restricted their ability to defend themselves legally against white assaults. Racist legislation even attempted to control their bodies. A "pig-tail" ordinance in the 1850s, for example, forbade them to wear their traditional long braid down their back.

General contempt for the Chinese did not prevent Charles Crocker from seeking them for railroad construction. Having already proved themselves a strong workforce of gold miners, migrant laborers, successful businessmen, and fishermen, the Chinese were contracted at low wages to lay the rails. Known as "Crocker's pets," thousands of Chinese railroad workers died in the process. Working in harsh conditions and terrain, Chinese laborers laid as much as ten miles of rails per day. The faster they worked, the greater the profits would be for the investors. In the infamous winter of 1866, forced to work in tunnels under the snow, Chinese laborers were buried alive by avalanches. Chinese attempts to get better working wages were also forcefully crushed. In 1866, five thousand laborers went on strike. To coerce them back to work, Crocker stopped their food supply. In addition, the Central Pacific Railroad was more than ready to "divide and conquer," considering the transporting of replacement black workers. The strike failed, and by 1867, more than twelve thousand Chinese had worked on building the railroad.

With the completion of the transcontinental railroad on May 10, 1869, the Chinese were no longer a desired immigrant group. In the 1870s, with the United States experiencing its worst economic depression to date, unemployed white workers in San Francisco and other western cities strengthened ideas of white supremacy based on unity against the latest immigrants. Contending neither Irish nor German immigration could be compared with that of the dangerous "Celestials" or the "Chinese problem," the tide against immigrants had turned forcefully against Chinese. In 1877, vicious racism against them culminated in anti-Chinese riots. Drawing on working-class frustration at unemployment and low wages, Denis Kearney, an Irish-born teamster, began spouting vicious, inflammatory rhetoric that culminated in his famous call, "The Chinese must go!" Under this banner, his Workingmen's Party built the false perception that immigrants were the direct cause of the economic downturn.

As Chinese men faced discrimination in the Bay Area's labor force, the comparatively fewer Chinese women of San Francisco also met uncertainty in their lives. Like many Latin American women arriving from Mexico, Chile, Peru, and Colombia, a significant number of Chinese women had arrived in San Francisco as indentured or even enslaved sex workers. As prostitutes, they were at risk of exploitation and abuse from their patrons. As early as 1865, they were also specifically targeted by the San Francisco Board of Supervisors as the group in greatest need to be removed from city premises. Both Chinese women and men remained under close vigilance, finding themselves ghettoized in their own Chinatown.

By 1870, United States–born San Franciscans numbered seventy-six thousand, compared with seventy-four thousand who had been born abroad. Irish, Chinese, Germans, and Italians remained the dominant immigrant groups, but as the experiences of the Chinese testify, these groups did not all enjoy equal access to the city's resources. Sentiments against Chinese would soon reach national proportions, having devastating effects on the formation of families and communities.

In 1882, Congress passed the Chinese Exclusion Act, banning all Chinese laborers from the United States for ten years. Reenacted in 1892 and later made permanent, the act signaled that race and nationality had become valid bases for restricting immigration to the United States. Its passage had a clear-cut impact on Chinese immigration to the country. In 1881, forty thousand Chinese had immigrated. In 1887, a mere ten Chinese entered the United States. In 1884, a federal court ruling had confirmed that the 1882 act

The oldest and arguably the largest Chinatown in the United States, San Francisco's Chinatown has become as much a haven for tourists as a home to Chinese immigrants. *(SFCUB Photo Library)*

banned entry to the wives of those Chinese men already in the United States. Nationwide, antimiscegenation laws prevented these same men from marrying white women.

In San Francisco, Angel Island, a large and historically rich island, tells the story of the city's discrimination against Chinese immigrants. Built to enforce the 1882 exclusion act, the island's immigration compound opened in 1910 and remained in operation for thirty years. It was the main entry point for many immigrants coming to the western United States. Off San Francisco's mainland and inside the bay, Angel Island became the destination for those coming by sea to San Francisco who did not pass immigration officials' inspections. Detainees there faced a difficult and purposefully confusing interrogation process, remaining there until their cases were settled. Life on Angel Island was difficult, and some individuals were isolated for almost two years from family and friends. Although only about 5 percent of the detainees were eventually not admitted to the United States, life in

the island's barracks was a harrowing and uniquely Chinese immigrant experience.

EARTHQUAKE, FIRES, AND WHITE SUPREMACY

By 1900, San Francisco had over three hundred thousand residents. As the city approached the turn of the century, distinct neighborhoods could be discerned, a pattern that would remain largely unchanged for decades to come. African Americans still remained a relatively small population, numbering less than two thousand by 1900. Also drawn to the city by labor opportunities brought by the gold rush, blacks had hoped that San Francisco would be less segregationist and discriminatory than the South. Their encounters with residential segregation in part led to their concentration in the Western Addition section of the city, as well as in the South of Market and North Beach enclaves.

Italians had already concentrated themselves in three primary areas: North Beach, which remains to this day the city's historical connection to its Italian heritage; the Mission District; and Potrero Hill. The Irish had the strongest presence in the Mission District, but many other foreign-born lived there as well.

In 1905, powerful labor leaders formed an organization to extend the Chinese Exclusion Act to Korean and Japanese immigrants. Exaggerating white fears of an "Asiatic Coolie invasion," San Francisco's Japanese and Korean Exclusion League argued that California could remain a prosperous state as long as it remained "white man's country." The term "coolie" made reference to the 250,000 Chinese who were shipped as labor to different countries between 1847 and 1874. For the league, there were no national and ethnic differences between the Koreans, the Japanese, and the Chinese. To them, these immigrant groups represented the eventual racial decay of "their" city. In close connection with the growing organized labor movement, white supremacy remained as San Franciscan as the city's fog, paralleling a national trend against nonwhite immigrants.

San Francisco's April 18, 1906, earthquake and the accompanying fires on the three succeeding days destroyed more than twenty-eight thousand buildings, with an estimated damage at $500 million. Nearly five hundred people lost their lives, and four square miles of the city lay in ruins. The flames stopped short of engulfing the Western Addition,

Mission, and Potrero Hill districts, which remained largely in good condition. As refugees of the disaster, thousands of the city's survivors flowed into the Mission District. Although many Mission homes had sunk during the earthquake, fire had not affected this sunny side of the city. Survivors found a Mexican population, dating from before California's accession to the Union, which would increase with those fleeing their country's revolutionary period after 1910. They were joined by Central Americans in the 1920s and 1930s who also were escaping political turmoil.

Ironically, the disaster did bring indirect relief to thousands of Chinese immigrants still in legal limbo in the city. With city hall destroyed, its registries could no longer be used to determine the immigrant status of the city's population. Without these records, men could claim or apply for citizenship and travel to China to get their wives. But Chinese also lost dearly in 1906. The fires resulting from the earthquake destroyed Chinatown. It took the ingenuity and quick action of the United States–born Tin Eli to plan the rebuilding of Chinatown, using a loan from Hong Kong. Like him, other "American Born Chinese," or ABCs, would soon make up the majority of Chinese in San Francisco. Between 1900 and 1940, the American-born Chinese population quadrupled, while the wave of new Chinese immigrants was reduced by half.

The city's multicultural and multiracial character had survived the earthquake. It could be observed especially among its dozens of newspapers and the languages, cultures, and nationalities they represented: French, Spanish, German, Greek, Chinese, Swedish, Italian, African American, Japanese. Yet, whereas the quake and fires had altered the city's physical geography, racial and labor antagonisms remained unchanged. The Roaring Twenties in San Francisco held little to celebrate for its immigrant communities.

Pointing to the number of Asian immigrants who had become the majority of Hawaii's population, white workers, farmers, and politicians argued for alien land laws to prohibit ownership to those ineligible for citizenship. Reference to the Japanese was not direct, but given their citizenship ineligibility, the results were obvious. First discussing them in 1907, the California Senate and Assembly passed alien land laws by an overwhelming majority in 1913. To those advocating their passage, the laws were a step toward keeping California white.

The fear of an immigrant presence in San Francisco remained consistent from the nineteenth century into the twentieth. Such fears were particularly strong when white supremacy was challenged. In 1922, Stanford University psychologist Lewis M. Terman conducted intelligence testing with Japanese and white children. His results, suggesting that white and Japanese children were equal in mental capacities, caused an uproar among whites. Despite his desire not to make his results public, individuals and such organizations as San Francisco's Japanese Association of America quickly realized the importance of his work to challenge popular eugenic ideas of the period.

In 1924, Congress passed the National Origins Act, barring immigration for all those ineligible for citizenship. With Asian immigration virtually stopped from then on, Asian American family and community formations were under attack as well. For those men wishing to marry white women, a 1907 federal law implied that white women marrying immigrants would lose their citizenship. The 1922 Cable Act modified the 1907 law so that citizenship loss applied only to those women marrying immigrant men not eligible for citizenship. Across the bay in the town of Corte Madera, Japanese Gunjiro Aoki met and eventually married Helen Gladys Emery. Emery's family could trace its roots to the *Mayflower*, yet she still lost her citizenship. Harassed for their interracial union, Gunjiro and Helen remained outcasts in San Francisco, and Helen did not regain her U.S. citizenship until Gunjiro died in 1932.

For less stigmatized immigrant communities, San Francisco offered more peaceful opportunities. Yet not all immigrants who came to San Francisco remained there for good. Italians, for example, often returned to their homeland within a few years. Still, despite a strong pattern of return migration for thousands of Italian immigrants, enough remained behind that San Francisco had the second largest Italian population in the United States by 1930, following New York. By that year, there were approximately twenty-seven thousand Italian immigrants and an additional thirty thousand Italian Americans who had made the city their permanent home.

WORLD WAR II AND THE TRANSFORMATION OF THE SAN FRANCISCO BAY AREA

With the demand for shipbuilding during World War II, San Francisco became not only the Western passageway to the warfront but also a leading industrial center. African Americans in particular arrived by the thousands, seeking employment opportunities and the sense of equality denied them in the Jim Crow South. Their arrival changed the cultural, political, and economic life of the Bay Area, as they formed vibrant communities in San Francisco, Alameda, Oakland, and Richmond.

The war industry afforded both skilled and semiskilled workers opportunities for employment. Among the tens of thousands of African Americans who escaped racial segregation in Texas, Alabama, Mississippi, Arkansas, Oklahoma, and the Carolinas, women in particular were faced with challenging white employers' and workers' assumptions about their abilities. White women were the first to be hired by such defense industries as the Kaiser shipyards in Richmond. Once hired, they kept the best jobs, leaving what was left to other women, including African Americans. Whereas African-American women could be expected to fill domestic service jobs easily, white employers did not accept the idea that African-American women could succeed as easily in managerial, clerical, or professional positions.

African-American men too found clear limits to the war industry's opportunities. For most of them, advancement beyond entry-level positions was nearly impossible. Supervisory positions were even less likely given racial attitudes and policies similar to those curtailing African-American women's employment opportunities. White men had a hard time accepting the idea that an African-American man could supervise them. Both African-American women and men in San Francisco experienced such everyday forms of racism as racial slurs and insults. When they attempted to move into several of the city's neighborhoods, African Americans met vocal resistance from real estate agents, property owners, and neighborhood improvement associations. Left with few choices, San Francisco's black residents in the Western Addition occupied a disproportionate amount of substandard housing. Thus, at a time when the United States was fighting a war against worldwide fascism, African Americans, now a significant demographic force in the city, found themselves experiencing some of its racist traditions.

Still, despite these challenges, African-American women and men came and settled in the Bay Area. Before the war, only 2 percent of the area's population of 1.5 million were African American. By the war's end, more than two hundred thousand had arrived. Immediately following the war, African-American women and men once again faced uncertainty. Though challenged in the courts, housing and employment discrimination remained. Like others before

them, blacks in San Francisco did not find the city's Golden Gate wide open.

World War II brought contradictions for U.S. immigration policies. On the one hand, more than twelve thousand Chinese Americans had joined U.S. forces to fight the war. China was also on the side of the Allies, fighting Japan, while the United States and European powers concentrated their efforts against Germany and Italy. Although the United States had repealed the Chinese Exclusion Act on December 17, 1943, this move proved to be only a political act to save face given wartime alliances. Chinese immigration quotas were set at 105 annually, and citizenship applicants were required to pass difficult English competency and U.S. history examinations.

But it was President Franklin D. Roosevelt's signing of Executive Order 9066 in 1942 which brought U.S. racial contradictions to the forefront. Billed as a military necessity, the order targeted the Japanese as a potential internal threat during the war and required that young and old alike be relocated to internment camps. From the San Francisco Bay Area alone, more than eighteen thousand Japanese and Japanese Americans, both citizens and noncitizens, were relocated to barracks in Oregon, California, and Washington. Believed to be less patriotic than their German and Italian immigrant counterparts, neither of which faced internment, the Japanese paid a personal price on behalf of the fight against fascism abroad.

One less obvious but still significant transformation in San Francisco's population also traces its roots to the World War II period. Unlike perhaps any other city in the world, San Francisco became the destination for gay women and men following the war. Given the massive mobilization of women and men for the war, military and psychiatric personnel sought to remove lesbians and gay men from all military forces. Believed to be incompetent for armed battle, many were discharged. San Francisco's Treasure Island, built in the 1930s to hold the city's 1939 Golden Gate International Exposition, held many gay sailors to be discharged from its naval hospital. Many of these sailors as well as those returning from the war made their way back to San Francisco, having heard rumors that the city offered a social and nightlife for gay women and men. North Beach's bohemian and gay culture in particular, made famous by such writers as Allen Ginsberg and Jack Kerouac, attracted gays escaping intolerance across the nation. In 1964, a *Life* magazine article added some power to the rumors, declaring San Francisco the gay capital of the United States. By the late 1970s, a growing gay male population turned the formerly Irish, working-class Eureka Valley into the Castro, a hub for gay social, cultural, and political activity.

INTO THE 1960s AND 1970s: IMMIGRANT STRUGGLES FOR VISIBILITY, SPACE, AND RIGHTS

More than one hundred years after changing its name from Yerba Buena, San Francisco in the 1960s would gain national notoriety for its hosting of several countercultural and race-based movements. Throughout the 1950s, civil rights advocates built a foundation for eventual battles that would enmesh United States–born and immigrant communities of color with the white establishment in city hall in the 1960s. Earlier struggles over land rights reemerged as well.

On November 20, 1969, nearly two hundred years after the first European settlement on their lands in San Francisco, seventy-eight Native Americans landed on Alcatraz Island. The occupants argued that because the federal government had abandoned the prison facility in 1963, they had the right to claim it as unused federal land. They cited the Fort Laramie Treaty of 1868, which granted surplus federal land to the Sioux. Given their communities' historical experiences with genocide, unemployment, poverty, and alcoholism, the Native American occupation of Alcatraz caught local, national, and international attention. Over the next few months, more than ten thousand Native Americans from every state visited the occupied island. The San Francisco Board of Supervisors considered supporting the occupation through legislation, and San Francisco mayor Joseph Alioto was asked about it during his trip to Europe.

In the late 1960s, Chicano students from several Bay Area campuses protested discriminatory educational policies, low enrollment of Mexican-American students across higher education, and curricula which rarely mentioned their contributions to the United States. In June 1968, several graduating Mexican-American seniors at San Jose State College (later renamed San Jose State University) walked out during commencement. Joined by several audience members, the students called attention to low minority student enrollment and the poor training received by those working with the Mexican-American community.

Other students of color were similarly engaged in protesting educational conditions in San Francisco. In November 1968, these student forces coalesced into the organized Third World Strike at the San Francisco State College (later renamed San Francisco State University) campus. Lasting until March 1969 and engaged in confrontations with the police, the strike leaders called for the creation of the School of Ethnic Studies. Originally begun over issues raised by black students, the strike brought national attention to the dismal enrollment and graduation rates of students of color.

In 1969, San Francisco's Mission District also evidenced the racial struggles of its community. That year, seven young men, all sons of immigrants from Central America, were accused of killing a police officer. Their defense became a community struggle that highlighted police brutality in their district and the deterioration of their neighborhood, the second largely a result of the middle-class flight beginning in the 1940s. With their acquittal, the case of *los siete de la raza* (seven of the race) brought more attention to the district's conditions and the plight of its immigrants. With the majority of Italians and Irish having moved out following World War II, Nicaraguans, Salvadorans, Mexicans, Cubans, Samoans, Filipinos, Puerto Ricans, Native Americans, and many South Americans slowly but consistently transformed the culture and politics of the Mission District. With the arrival of young, white professionals in the 1980s and 1990s, gentrification would once again cause frictions in one of the most diverse areas of the city.

San Francisco's Filipino community came into full political view in the late 1960s as well. First arriving in California in the 1920s and 1930s, Filipinos eventually gave birth to San Francisco's Manilatown, a mostly male migrant labor community next to Chinatown. In the center of this community of ten thousand was the International Hotel (known as the I-Hotel), long recognized as the most famous residence for Filipinos in the city. In 1968, as a response to corporate desire to tear down the building and increase the city's financial district, I-Hotel tenants organized themselves into the United Filipino Association to fight evictions, including those of many elderly persons. The struggle to save the hotel eventually involved thousands of Asians, African Americans, Latinos, Native Americans, and local whites, as well as students and activists. San Francisco garnered bad national publicity when a force of three hundred riot police and sheriffs deputies forcibly evicted all tenants in the early morning of August 4, 1977.

THE 1990s AND BEYOND: THE RISING PRICE FOR THE CITY BY THE BAY

At the dawn of the twenty-first century, the City by the Bay has increasingly become a center of immigrant labor, culture, and entrepreneurship. As many whites have left the city for its suburbs, racial minorities have quickly formed a base majority of the city's population. San Francisco retains its immigrant character, discerned in every facet of the city. A series of anti-immigrant statewide propositions have found significant challenge in San Francisco. In 1994, Proposition 187, the "Save Our State" initiative, was passed by California voters and made it impossible for immigrants to seek public health care and education without the fear of being questioned about their legal status. Throughout the state, only San Francisco rejected the measure by a significant margin. Reminiscent of earlier anti-Chinese and anti-Asian immigration, citizenship, and land laws in the state, Proposition 187 gave San Francisco the opportunity to reject overtly anti-immigrant legislation.

Proposition 209, which banned affirmative action policies in the state, has also found resistance in San Francisco. The city's mayor, Willie Brown, has publicly condemned the measure and guaranteed that the city would not comply with some of its features. In addition, Bay Area civil rights organizations, such as the Chinese for Affirmative Action, have challenged the measures and the anti-immigrant attitudes that came with it. In 1998, yet one more state measure, Proposition 227, played on fears of an immigrant takeover of the state; bilingual education now came under attack with the proposition's passage. Immigrant advocates, though, remain strong. Since 1986, the Northern California Coalition for Immigrant Rights has defended the rights of all immigrants and refugees in the city. Members continue to work against anti-immigrant legislation, for women's and workers' rights, and against Immigration and Naturalization Service raids on workplaces where Hispanic immigrants are employed.

San Francisco remains a diverse city as well as one of contradictions. In 1999, one of the city's most well-known gay politicians, Board of Supervisors president Tom Ammiano, of Italian descent, captured 40 percent of the vote against the winner, Willie Brown, the city's first African-American mayor who was originally elected in 1995. African Americans in the city, however, have their most visible representation among the increasing homeless population, estimated to be at fif-

teen thousand. And high rates of infection with the human immunodeficiency virus (HIV) continue to affect disproportionate numbers of African Americans and Latinos, especially women and young gay men in those ethnic groups.

In this context, neighborhoods still strive to mark their presence. The predominantly immigrant Mission District remains alive with such Latino cultural institutions as the Galería de la Raza; political advocacy organizations such as the Coalition for Immigrant Rights; and health and education agencies such as Proyecto ContraSIDA Por Vida, which offers services to those with acquired immunodeficiency syndrome (AIDS) and is located at one of the most dynamic intersections of the city, 16th Street and Mission Boulevard. Famed local legend and transgender *ranchera* singer Teresita la Campesina also marks the cultural boundaries of the city, making her artistic rounds between restaurants, bars, and homes. (Ranchera is a style of popular music from northern Mexico.) In January 2000, Mission-raised, Mexican-born singer Carlos Santana led all artists with ten Grammy Award nominations. After thirty years and dozens of albums, his success represents part of the strength of immigrant San Francisco which continues today.

Class struggles have not subsided in the city. As more young, white, middle-class professionals find employment opportunities in the booming computer and multimedia industries of Silicon Valley and the Bay Area, housing becomes one of the most expensive and least available human resources. Perhaps the 2000 census will indicate the first reversal in the city's demographic changes, with middle-class whites slowly but surely displacing poor and working-class natives and immigrants alike from areas they once inhabited. With the average cost for a home in San Francisco rising to more than $400,000 in the year 2000, working-class families are finding it difficult, if not impossible, to remain in the city. Ironically, the more wealthy newcomers may displace the artists, performers, and activists who built the cultures that have made the city and its neighborhoods so attractive in the first place. In 2000, San Francisco's 750,000 residents have profound questions to answer and social problems to address.

Horacio N. Roque Ramírez

See also: Central America, Mexico (Part III, Sec. 2); China, Japan, Oceania, Philippines, Southeast Asia, Taiwan and Hong Kong (Part III, Sec. 3); Western and Southern Europe (Part III, Sec. 4); *Lau v. Nichols*, 1974, California Proposition 187, 1994, California Proposition 227, 1998 (Part IV, Sec. 1).

BIBLIOGRAPHY

Berchell, Robert A. *The San Francisco Irish, 1848–1880*. Berkeley: University of California Press, 1980.

Bérubé, Allan. *Coming Out under Fire: The History of Gay Men and Women in World War Two*. New York: Free Press, 1990.

Brook, J., Chris Carlsson, and N. J. Peters, eds. *Reclaiming San Francisco: History, Politics, Culture*. San Francisco: City Lights, 1998.

Broussard, Albert S. *Black San Francisco: The Struggle for Racial Equality in the West, 1900–1954*. Lawrence: University Press of Kansas, 1993.

Cinel, Dino. *From Italy to San Francisco: The Immigrant Experience*. Stanford: Stanford University Press, 1982.

Daniels, Douglas H. *Pioneer Urbanites: A Social and Cultural History of Black San Francisco*. Berkeley: University of California Press, 1990.

Darsie, M. L. "The Mental Capacity of American-Born Japanese Children." In *Comparative Psychology Monographs*, vol. 3. Serial no. 15. Baltimore: Williams and Wilkins, 1926.

Drescher, T. W. *San Francisco Bay Area Murals: Communities Create Their Muses, 1904–1997*. 3d ed. St. Paul: Pogo Press, 1998.

Godfrey, Brian J. *Neighborhoods in Transition: The Making of San Francisco's Ethnic and Nonconformist Communities*. Berkeley: University of California Press, 1988.

Heins, Marjorie. *Strictly Ghetto Property: The Story of Los Siete de la Raza*. Berkeley: Ramparts Press, 1972.

Kazin, Michael. *Barons of Labor: The San Francisco Building Trades and Union Down in the Progressive Era*. Urbana: University of Illinois Press, 1987.

Lai, H. M., Genny Lim, and Judy Yung. *Island: Poetry and History of Chinese Immigrants on Angel Island, 1910–1940*. Seattle: University of Washington Press, 1991.

Lemke-Santangelo, Gretchen. *Abiding Courage: African American Migrant Women and the East Bay Community*. Chapel Hill: University of North Carolina Press, 1996.

Margolin, Malcolm. *The Ohlone Way: Indian Life in the San Francisco–Monterey Bay Area*. Berkeley: Heyday Books, 1978.

Nee, Victor G., and Brett B. Nee. *Longtime Californ': A Documentary Study of an American Chinatown*. Stanford: Stanford University Press, 1972.

Quinn, Arthur. *The Rivals: William Gwin, David Broderick, and the Birth of California*. New York: Crown, 1994.

Smith, Paul C., and Robert A. Warrior. *Like a Hurricane: The Indian Movement from Alcatraz to Wounded Knee*. New York: New Press, 1996.

Trafzer, Clifford E., and Joel R. Hyer, eds. *Exterminate Them! Written Accounts of the Murder, Rape, and Slavery of Native Americans during the California Gold Rush*. East Lansing: Michigan State University Press, 1999.

Yung, Judy. *Unbound Feet: A Social History of Chinese Women in San Francisco*. Berkeley: University of California Press, 1995.

WASHINGTON, D.C.

In the popular imagination, Washington, D.C., is most famously viewed as the nation's capital. The White House, the Capitol, the Washington Monument, the Lincoln Memorial, the National Mall, and its museums and other monuments have long been the city's dominant images. From the perspective of the everyday life of its inhabitants, however, Washington offers a different image. It is a diverse metropolitan area where people live and work and whose reach extends well beyond the urban center into the suburbs of Maryland and Virginia.

During the latter half of the twentieth century, the area has experienced rapid population growth, particularly in the suburban areas, as well as significant changes to its population composition. In the process, Washington transformed itself from a "bi-racial provincial 'Southern town' into a multicultural, international metropolis," in the words of sociologist Robert Manning. The influx of immigrants who have come to Washington in great numbers since the 1970s has been a major factor driving this process.

As of 1997, the Washington, D.C., metropolitan area, which encompasses multiple jurisdictions spanning the District of Columbia and parts of Maryland, Virginia, and West Virginia, has a total population of 6.5 million people, of whom 800,000 are immigrants. This makes Washington the nation's sixth largest city of immigrant settlement. Although immigrant populations in the metropolitan areas of Los Angeles (4.8 million) and New York (4.6 million) are larger, Washington is not far behind third-ranked San Francisco (1.4 million) and fourth-ranked Chicago (1.1 million). Between 1990 and 1997, the Washington metropolitan area grew by 9 percent, nearly half of its growth due to net international migration. The Washington metropolitan area has expanded and changed boundaries many times over, which has made tracking changes difficult.

URBAN GROWTH AND CHANGE

Despite the high volume of immigration that Washington has experienced in recent decades, its history distinguishes it from traditional cities of immigration in the United States. Historians have long emphasized the contributions that immigrants have made to the building of the nation's industrial economy and the role of cities as centers of production and commerce. In contrast to such other cities in the eastern United States as New York, Philadelphia, Baltimore, and Boston, Washington never developed an industrial base in the late nineteenth and early twentieth centuries. Without a commercial or manufacturing nucleus, Washington did not draw immigrants in the same high numbers as other cities that could offer more economic opportunities.

Indeed, until late in the nineteenth century, newcomers to Washington resulted largely from domestic migration, particularly of southern blacks. The low wages of black workers discouraged European immigrants from competing in the D.C. labor market. Thus, whereas the foreign-born populations of other cities increased dramatically, Washington's immigrant population remained small. By the advent of the twentieth century, Washington's black population had established itself as the largest African-American community in the nation. In 1900, Washington's population was 31 percent black and 7 percent foreign-born, a sharp contrast to most major cities, such as New York (2 percent African American and 37 percent immigrant); Philadelphia (5 percent and 23 percent); Boston (2 percent and 35 percent); and Chicago (2 percent and 35 percent).

The federal government, Washington's main industry, expanded during the period leading up to World War I, opening up job opportunities for white-collar workers, craftworkers, and laborers. This labor demand was filled, again, largely by the migration of

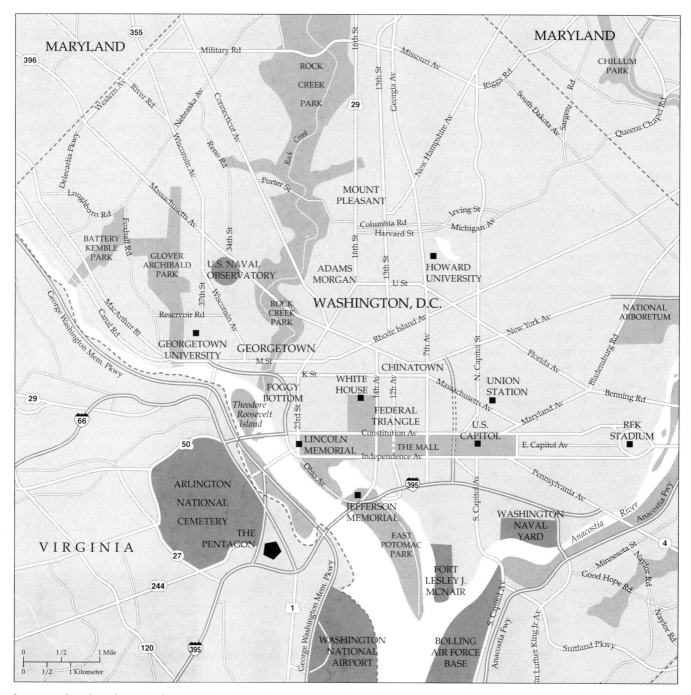

In recent decades, the nation's capital has drawn increasing numbers of immigrants, particularly from Central America, the Middle East, and Africa. *(CARTO-GRAPHICS)*

native workers, both white and black, from other parts of the country. By 1920, Washington's population of 436,112 was still relatively small in comparison with that of other cities in the East, although it grew by more than half between 1900 and 1920. Immigration consisted of the small numbers of European and Chinese immigrants who made their way to Washington at this time; the percentage of the resident population who were foreign-born stayed at around 7 percent during this period.

As the United States approached World War II, its expanded federal bureaucracies created numerous new job opportunities in Washington, and by 1940 the city had more than 660,000 residents, nearly 34,000, or about 5 percent, of them immigrants. Housing needs grew as a result, and new neighborhoods within the

District of Columbia developed. Residential expansion into the suburbs followed, and such places as Arlington, Virginia, and Silver Spring and Bethesda, Maryland, increased in size.

After World War II, Washington moved into a new period of growth spurred on by the postwar economic boom, continued high employment by the federal government, and the accretion of thousands of private-industry jobs. The capital city also took on a new role as an emergent international capital, with many global agencies establishing headquarters in the District. For example, the World Bank (1944), the Organization of American States (1949), and the International Monetary Fund (1945) all located their operations in Washington. As Washington became a center for international affairs, private organizations focusing on security and defense issues and economic and social concerns also gravitated to the area. The "internationalization" of Washington continued as diplomatic missions settled in and as foreign students were attracted to area universities. Subsequent waves of immigration resulted from family and chain migration as well as the settlement of various refugee groups from Latin America, Asia, and Africa.

In 1947, the population of the District of Columbia peaked at more than 870,000 residents. As the population growth in Washington's suburban regions accelerated, the city's resident population declined steadily to 519,000 in 1999. Between 1950 and 1970, the population of suburban Washington swelled by more than 200 percent. In 1970, the city's population of approximately 756,000 residents was only 25 percent of the entire metropolitan area's nearly 3 million residents.

These changing patterns of metropolitan growth coincided with the beginning of the new wave of post-1965 immigration. Immigrants were increasingly drawn to the suburbs: more than seven times as many immigrants lived in the Maryland and Virginia suburbs (425,562) than in the city (58,887) in 1990. Nonetheless, the foreign-born population of the city of Washington has risen from 4.4 percent of the total population in 1970 to 6.4 percent in 1980 to 9.7 percent in 1990, while the proportion of foreign-born in the suburbs has increased from 4.5 percent to 8.7 percent to 12.8 percent over the same period.

HISTORICAL SOURCES OF IMMIGRATION TO WASHINGTON, D.C.

The national origins of the early immigrants who settled in Washington, D.C., were consistent with the origins of immigrants to other cities. The Irish were among the first immigrant groups to arrive, and by 1850, they represented the largest foreign-born group in Washington, with 2,373 persons of Irish nationality recorded. The earliest Irish immigrants came at the beginning of the 1800s to work in the construction of the city. As a group, they constituted a majority of the white construction workforce. These newcomers worked mostly as unskilled laborers, but a few, such as James Hoban, architect of the White House in the 1790s, were skilled artisans. After federal construction slowed in the 1830s, Irish immigrants helped to build the Chesapeake and Ohio Canal that ran from Washington to Cumberland, Maryland. Unlike the majority of Irish immigrants who came to D.C. after having lived in other American cities, most of the unskilled canal workers were recruited directly from Ireland by the canal company. Other Irish immigrants worked in Washington's industrial operations, like the Gas Light Company gasworks (begun in 1856) in Foggy Bottom, a neighborhood of the city near the Potomac. Irish immigrants also operated saloons, groceries, and other small businesses throughout the city. The Irish tended to settle near their places of employment and lived all over the city. Many, especially single men, lived in workers' barracks or boardinghouses. The neighborhood then known as Swampoodle, located on low, damp land north of the Capitol, was home to a large concentration of Irish.

Germany was another important source of immigration to Washington, D.C. Like the Irish, most early German immigrants worked in the construction of the Capitol and later helped to build canals and railroads. The U.S. government actively recruited German skilled laborers for construction at the beginning of the 1800s because they were seen as serious and hardworking. By 1850, Germans made up 30 percent of the foreign-born population in Washington, or 1,415 people. The German population increased substantially after 1850, more than doubling to 3,222 in the decade of the 1850s. Most of these later German immigrants came to Washington, D.C., with a specific trade or profession. Many opened small businesses as jewelers, butchers, and bakers and provided other service as well. A few established large businesses such as breweries or department stores. For example, Hecht's Department Store, still in operation today, was founded by a German immigrant in 1896.

German immigrants settled in many different parts of the city. In 1768, a German immigrant named Jacob Funk bought 500 acres of land in present-day Foggy Bottom and divided part of the land into lots. He named the settlement Hamburgh and hoped to attract German settlers. Few people settled in the area—although a German Protestant church was established there in 1833. Most early Germans lived in Georgetown, a neighborhood that existed before Washington was built, but eventually, some Germans settled in the Foggy Bottom area to work in the neighborhood breweries. After the Civil War, many Germans lived along Seventh Street in the commercial district or in southwest D.C.

Washington has also been home to a Jewish community of mixed national origins over the years. The earliest Jews to settle in Washington were of German heritage and had close connections to the larger German community. Many of these early German Jewish immigrants were shopkeepers, operating businesses in Georgetown, the Seventh Street shopping corridor, and southwest D.C. Beginning in the 1880s, eastern European Jews from Russia, Poland, and Romania began arriving in the District of Columbia in significant numbers. Many of these newcomers worked as street peddlers—one of the only occupations open to them in Europe—until they were able to obtain the capital to open their own small businesses.

Jews mostly lived near commercial districts where they had their shops or where they worked as peddlers. Therefore, Georgetown, Seventh Street, and southwest D.C. were all major areas of eastern European Jewish settlement. In the 1950s and 1960s many Jews moved to the Maryland suburbs, and many Jewish organizations and institutions also relocated, making suburban Maryland the new center of the area's Jewish community. A considerable number of Jews and Jewish institutions, however, actively chose not to leave the city. Activists in the upper northwest neighborhood of Shepherd Park, including the civil rights activist Marvin Caplan, for example, founded Neighbors, Inc., which fought against real estate "blockbusting" and worked to maintain racial integration.

Italians have also been an important part of D.C.'s social fabric. Among the first Italians to immigrate to D.C. were musicians that President Thomas Jefferson recruited from Italy for the U.S. Marine band. Most Italian immigrants to D.C. arrived in the late 1800s under more humble pretenses and labored in construction or service trades. Many were skilled artisans, working, for instance, as stone carvers in the construction of the Library of Congress in the 1890s. Italian labor, particularly unskilled workers from southern Italy, was also instrumental in the building of Union Station from 1905 to 1907. At the turn of the century, Italians also operated a variety of small businesses and were especially prominent in shoe repair.

Like other groups, early Italian immigrants tended

to settle near their work. Workers building Union Station lived in controlled labor camps near the building site, a move by the more established Italian community and native-born citizens to exert social control over the newly arriving unskilled laborers from southern Italy. Many other Italians lived in the Swampoodle neighborhood, replacing Irish immigrants who began leaving the neighborhood in the 1920s for the suburbs. By the post–World War II years, the Italian community had become well established, and like other immigrant groups and native-born whites, the majority moved to the suburbs.

Greek immigrants began arriving in Washington, D.C., in the 1890s. New arrivals mainly worked in unskilled jobs as peddlers and railroad laborers and in other trades, while more established Greeks ran small businesses such as barbershops, shoeshine parlors, and restaurants. Some operated larger businesses as candymakers or produce wholesalers. The earliest Greek immigrants were mostly men and lived together in group rowhouses in downtown areas previously occupied by German immigrants. By 1903, Greek women began arriving, and the community became more established. The downtown community remained vibrant until after World War II, when Greeks joined their Italian counterparts in moving to the suburbs.

Chinese immigration, which continues today, began in the late 1800s. The first documented Chinese resident in the District appeared in 1851, but it was not until the 1880s that a Chinatown began to develop on Pennsylvania Avenue. Although Chinese immigrants lived throughout the District, Chinatown served as the commercial and cultural heart of the community. By 1903, Chinatown had become home to numerous laundries, drugstores, restaurants, and other Chinese businesses. The community remained almost exclusively male through the 1920s due to the low number of Chinese immigrant women and the Chinese Exclusion Act of 1882 that barred the entry of all Chinese laborers. In 1929, the federal government evacuated almost four hundred residents from Chinatown to allow for the construction of Federal Triangle, where the Federal Bureau of Investigation and the Ronald Reagan International Trade Center, among other government buildings, are located today. With the help of Chinese business interests locally and in New York, Chinatown was subsequently moved to its present-day location near H Street between Fifth and Seventh Streets, NW, in 1931. By the 1960s, the old Chinese community had begun to move to the suburbs, but a new wave of immigrants from Asia have helped to maintain Chinatown.

978 ENCYCLOPEDIA OF AMERICAN IMMIGRATION

CHARACTERISTICS OF HISTORICAL MIGRATION TO D.C.

In many ways, immigrant life in D.C. was similar to that in more traditional cities of immigration. For example, immigrants in the capital played an active role in forming their own local networks and community organizations. Likewise, immigrant settlement in Washington followed the traditional pattern of city center to suburban movement. As immigrant groups became more established, they moved to more suburban parts of the city, leaving their old neighborhoods to newer arrivals.

Immigration to Washington, D.C., also had many unique characteristics. First, for the vast majority of immigrants, Washington was historically not their first destination in the United States because of its limited employment opportunities. Rather, many immigrant workers came to D.C. to fill prearranged jobs. For example, construction companies recruited many, while others came to participate in business ventures with friends or family already in the District.

Second, different immigrant populations interacted with each other more often and with fewer conflicts than in many other cities. For example, German Jews and eastern European Jews worked together to found community organizations, such as the Hebrew Home for the Aged. This kind of cooperation was rare in other cities. Group interaction may have been more harmonious in Washington than in other areas because of the small numbers of immigrants, which prompted newcomers to pool their resources and depend on each other's skills and services. Small numbers also meant less competition for jobs, which made for more peaceful interactions. Furthermore, because Washington lacked factories, it was also without the concentrated settlement patterns that usually result from industrialization. Therefore, immigrants of different national origins could be found living throughout the city. In many cases, distinct immigrant groups shared the same neighborhoods, shopped in one another's stores, and worshiped together.

Immigrants' relations with the native white population were also more congenial than in other cities. Washington did have its own anti-immigrant organizations and in 1854 even elected a mayor of the Know-Nothing Party, a nativist, anti-Catholic party. However, anti-immigrant hostility never reached the intensity that it did in such cities as New York or Boston. Several factors prevented immigration from attracting white attention in the same ways that it did in other cities. The low numbers of foreigners gave immigration a low profile and meant that immigrant competition with native white workers was less of an issue. Furthermore, because immigrant enclaves were not extensive in D.C., some evidence suggests that immigrants assimilated faster into mainstream Washington society. In addition, tensions between whites and D.C.'s large black community drew whites' attention away from immigration.

Black-immigrant relations were somewhat more contentious. Immigrants and blacks often competed for jobs, and in the early 1800s, white immigrant laborers succeeded in gaining restrictions on black labor. Overall, however, again due to their relatively small numbers, immigrants in Washington did not have the same negative effect on black employment that they did in other cities. Immigrants and blacks often worked together and lived in the same neighborhoods. The Greek-American historian Christine Warnke quotes the son of Greek immigrants in Washington, D.C., as he recalls his father's produce business: "The Greeks would organize a system on Market Street where the blacks and young Greek men would dump the celery in large wooden buckets of water and use brushes to scrub off the debris. . . . Greek was spoken to such an extent that some of the blacks became proficient in it."

Third, Washington, D.C.'s unique political status also shaped immigrant life in the city. Washington was a city where local and national politics were closely intertwined. In 1874, D.C. residents lost the power of home rule. Without elected local government, immigrant groups could not turn to local political machines to address their interests as they often did in other cities. Instead, immigrants in Washington had to look to the federal government to deal with local matters. The historians Hasia and Steven Diner note that Congress was involved on several occasions in deciding rules for the sale of kosher meats in the District, for example. Washington's status as a capital city also attracted national immigrant group involvement in local immigrant affairs. For instance, to establish a national symbol of a strong American Jewry, national Jewish leaders helped to fund the construction of the Jewish Community Center on Eleventh Street and Pennsylvania Avenue, NW, in 1925.

WASHINGTON, D.C.'s NEW IMMIGRATION

Washington, D.C., today is a thriving metropolis that ranks as the fifth most common destination for immigrants to the United States. The area's foreign-born residents account for an estimated 12 percent of the total population, a stunning contrast to 1970, when only 4.5 percent of the metropolitan area were foreign-born. Nine out of ten new immigrants are destined for the suburban areas, and many formerly white-ethnic neighborhoods have become communities of mixed white and non-white national origins. For example, suburban Wheaton, Maryland, saw immigrants from eighty-five countries settle within its boundaries in 1996 alone. Immigration and Naturalization Service (INS) records show more than three hundred thousand legal immigrants chose to live in the metropolitan area during the period of 1983–96, about half of them from the following ten countries: El Salvador, Vietnam, South Korea, India, Philippines, China, Iran, Ethiopia, Jamaica, and Pakistan.

The scope of these changes is all the more striking when we recall that for most of its history Washington attracted few immigrants. How did this dramatic transition come about? As described previously, Washington shifted from a national capital to an international capital after World War II. Many international organizations established themselves in Washington, foreign embassies expanded their presence, and the number of overseas students in area universities rose. In addition, legislative changes to immigration law in 1965 broadened admittance categories. It opened up immigration, particularly initially for well-educated and high-skilled individuals from the developing countries of Asia and Africa. The law also favored family reunification, which provided for the continuation of immigration from nations where immigration, once begun, became a self-supporting process. In part due to these changes, Washington by the 1980s and 1990s had emerged as a major immigrant destination.

To better understand Washington's transformation into a major immigrant receiving area, it is necessary to look at the particular groups of immigrants who have come to the area in more recent years. Obtaining estimates of specific nationality groups residing in Washington in the late 1990s is difficult. The most current Census Bureau estimates are from the 1990 census, but much has changed in the decade of the 1990s that cannot be accounted for with available data estimates.

Today's immigrants in the Washington metropolitan area are of heterogeneous national origins, and unlike in many other contemporary receiving cities, no single group dominates. Of those newcomers settling in the region over the past fifteen years, slightly more than half are women, more than half are married, and approximately two-thirds are of working age. Immigrants to the capital city are also diverse in

The many Ethiopian restaurants in the Adams Morgan district of Washington, D.C., reflect the city's attraction as a destination for African immigrants. *(Rick Reinhard, Impact Visuals)*

their legal status—the mix includes legal permanent residents, naturalized citizens, undocumented migrants, and refugees. Immigrants with differing backgrounds and legal statuses present challenges that contrast markedly with respect to social, political, and economic integration.

Immigrants from El Salvador form the largest national origin group in Washington, and it is believed to be the second largest concentration of Salvadorans in the United States, after Los Angeles. Social scientist Terry A. Repak explains that the origin of Central American immigration to D.C. was a consequence of the recruitment of domestic workers, largely women, by Washington's international and diplomatic staff from the region in the 1960s and 1970s. The population grew and became more gender-balanced as family members and friends joined these early migrants. Early Central and South American immigrants settled in the Adams Morgan

In recent decades, the Washington, D.C., metropolitan area has become home to an increasingly diverse array of immigrants, including these Brazilians parading down Pennsylvania Avenue during the city's annual Latin-American festival. *(Donna DeCesare, Impact Visuals)*

and Mount Pleasant neighborhoods, which were located near the embassies. In the 1980s, with civil wars in Central America intensifying, thousands of Central Americans fled to Washington, D.C. Because of the established community, many of these newcomers moved into the Adams Morgan–Mount Pleasant neighborhood, but many others settled in D.C.'s suburbs, especially in northern Virginia.

Other Latin American groups have also chosen to reside in Washington, D.C. Earlier waves included immigrants from the Dominican Republic, Cuba, and Puerto Rico, whereas in recent years, Washington has seen an influx of Peruvians, Bolivians, Ecuadoreans, and Mexicans. Early arrivals, as in most immigration streams, tended to be educated professionals seeking employment opportunities. Subsequent immigrants are more likely to come from lower-status backgrounds and to have found work in Washington's vast service sector, many working in restaurants, cleaning, or domestic service. Some have opened their own small businesses, such as restaurants or groceries catering to Latin American clientele.

Immigration from Asia is much more diverse today than the modest inflow of Chinese immigrants to the District in the late 1800s. Although Chinese immigration continues, immigrants from Vietnam, Korea, Thailand, the Philippines, India, and Pakistan have also settled in the Washington metropolitan region. There were few Southeast Asians residing in Washington prior to 1975—mostly students and personnel working in international organizations. The flow of refugees began when the war in Vietnam ended. Since then, they have entered the United States in various waves that correspond to military and political events in the region. Many Vietnamese, Cambodians, and Laotians were settled in northern Virginia by refugee resettlement organizations due to the availability of housing, social services, and employment. Today, an estimated fifty thousand Vietnamese live in the Washington metropolitan area. Many Vietnamese restaurants and stores can be found in the region, and the largest Vietnamese marketplace on the East Coast, known as Eden Center, is located in northern Virginia. The Clarendon neighborhood in Arlington County, Virginia, housed the earliest concentration of Washington's Vietnamese community. The Adams Morgan-Mount Pleasant area in the District is home to the city's Southeast Asian community, and others have settled in various neighborhoods in both Virginia and Maryland.

Koreans constitute another large immigrant group in Washington, an estimated forty-four thousand in the early 1990s. The majority of Korean immigrants came for the economic opportunities that the region offers, particularly entrepreneurial ventures. Koreans are very likely to own businesses, even though few were merchants in Korea before their arrival in the United States. They are especially active in the dry-cleaning business, convenience stores, shoe repair, carryout restaurants, liquor stores, and groceries. Most live in the Maryland and Virginia suburbs, commuting to shops and other jobs in the District.

Although smaller in absolute numbers than other regional groups, immigrants from Africa are a significant presence in Washington, where they make up the largest concentration of African immigrants in the United States. Drawn-out civil wars and political oppression have driven many to leave their home countries. It is estimated that more than fifty thousand immigrants from the African continent reside in the area. They come from many countries, the greatest numbers from Ethiopia, Eritrea, and Somalia, as well as from Nigeria, Ghana, Sierra Leone, Senegal, and Cameroon.

While the first African immigrants to the Washington area arrived as slaves in the 1600s, contemporary African migration happens under very different circumstances. Like Latin American migration, contemporary African migration can be traced back to the arrival of embassy staff and other international workers to Washington, D.C., in the 1950s and 1960s, after many African nations gained independence. The presence of a large native-born, African American community is also part of the draw. Howard University, in particular, has served an important role in attracting and organizing the African immigrant community. Early immigrant arrivals laid the foundation for the chain migration that followed, as other African immigrants came to Washington in the last three decades of the century, and as Ethiopian and Somali refugees were settled in the area.

African immigrant settlement was originally centered in Adams Morgan–Mount Pleasant, but Virginia and Maryland now house most of the community. Although many Africans who live in Washington hold graduate degrees, underemployment is common.

Many Africans operate restaurants, drive cabs, and work in other service jobs, particularly in hotels and hospitals.

Washington, D.C., is home to immigrants from many other parts of the world, most notably Eastern Europe, the former Soviet Union, the Caribbean, and the Middle East. Immigration and Naturalization Service records show that in 1996, more than thirty-four thousand immigrants arrived in the Washington metropolitan area from 182 countries. The city's most recent newcomers have been a major source of the social and cultural change occurring in the area. Washington, D.C., offers an important example of how people adapt economically, socially, culturally, linguistically, and politically in a "new" city of immigration.

Audrey Singer and Amelia Brown

See also: East Africa, North Africa, West Africa (Part III, Sec. 1); Central America (Part III, Sec. 2).

BIBLIOGRAPHY

Bureau of the Census. *State and Metropolitan Area Data Book, 1997–98.* 5th ed. Washington, DC: Government Printing Office, 1998.

Cary, Francine Curro, ed. *Urban Odyssey: A Multicultural History of Washington, DC.* Washington, DC: Smithsonian Institution Press, 1996.

Cohn, D'Vera, and Pamela Constable. "Culture Clashes Put Immigrant Women on the Front Lines." *Washington Post,* September 1, 1998, A01.

———. "Lives Transplanted, a Region Transformed: Steady Immigration Changes Face of the Region; Schools Add Up Immigrant Costs." *Washington Post,* August 30, 1998, A01.

Diner, Hasia, and Steven Diner. *Fifty Years of Jewish Self-Governance: The Jewish Community of Greater Washington, 1938–1988.* Washington, DC: The Council, 1989.

Gibson, Campbell J., and Emily Lennon. "Historical Census Statistics on the Foreign-Born Population of the United States: 1850–1990." Population Division Working Paper no. 29. Washington, DC: Bureau of the Census, Population Division, February 1999.

Immigration and Naturalization Service. *Statistical Yearbook of the Immigration and Naturalization Service, 1996.* Washington, DC: Government Printing Office, 1997.

———. *Statistical Yearbook of the Immigration and Naturalization Service, 1997.* Washington, DC: Government Printing Office, 1999.

Manning, Robert. "Multicultural Washington, DC: The Changing Social and Economic Landscape of a Post-Industrial Metropolis." *Ethnic and Racial Studies* 21: 2 (1998).

Melder, Keith, with Melinda Young Stuart. *City of Magnificent Intentions: A History of Washington, District of Columbia.* 2d ed. Washington, DC: Intac, 1997.

Repak, Terry A. *Waiting on Washington: Central American Workers in the Nation's Capital.* Philadelphia: Temple University Press, 1995.

Smith, Kathryn Schneider, ed. *Washington at Home: An Illustrated History of Neighborhoods in the Nation's Capital.* Northridge, CA: Windsor Publications, 1988.

Warnke, Christine. "Greek Immigrants in Washington, 1890–1945." In *Urban Odyssey: A Multicultural History of Washington, D.C.,* ed. Francine Curro Cary, pp. 173–89. Washington, DC: Smithsonian Institution Press, 1996.

Wood, Joseph. "Vietnamese American Place Making in Northern Virginia." *Geographical Review* 87:1 (1997): 58–72.

INTERNATIONAL PERSPECTIVES

*I*NTRODUCTION

Section 13 of Part II of the *Encyclopedia of American Immigration* is devoted to the international perspective on immigration. The section is divided into two types of entries. The first set includes entries that cover the causes and effects of international migration, including globalization and world politics. The second set of entries focuses on immigration to other major immigrant destination countries and regions, including Australia, Canada, Israel, and Western Europe. In addition, the entry on Japan describes a country that—though industrialized—does little to encourage immigration and has a relatively small foreign national population.

In her entry on immigration and the global economy, Patricia Landolt opens with an examination of the structural link between capital and population flows before putting international migration in historical perspective. She then goes on to look at capitalist expansion and global migration, as well as the segmented labor markets globalization creates. In addition, Landolt discusses the new modalities of industrial production and its effect on global migration, as well as citizenship and the global economy. She closes with an exploration of transnational settlement within the context of the global economy.

Ulf Haeussler's entry on immigration and international law provides a detailed look at the body of international law as it pertains to emigration, immigration, admission, integration (of both immigrants and refugees) into labor markets and host societies, and repatriation.

In his entry on international politics and immigration, Marc Rosenblum begins by discussing how global politics affects the making of U.S. immigration policy, starting with a history of the subject and then discussing the contemporary situation. He then details U.S.–Mexican immigration relations and the guest-worker programs established between the two countries from 1917 to 1964. Rosenblum also covers Western Hemispheric politics and their effect on immigration before

focusing on U.S. relations with Haiti, Cuba, Mexico, and Central America over the past forty years.

The entries on individual countries and their immigration situation begins with a discussion of Australia by Christine Inglis. The author begins by describing the European-oriented immigration that prevailed in the country until the 1970s, and how this has changed to an immigration population that largely hails from Asia. Inglis then discusses the country's settlement policies and the way immigrant incorporation takes place. In addition, she takes a look at the growing criticism of Australia's relatively open immigration policy and the country's emphasis on multiculturalism. She concludes with a discussion of immigration's future in Australia.

In his entry on Canada, K. Bruce Newbold begins with a discussion of the immigration history of the country, including changing immigration politics and policies. Next, the author explores the economic and demographic issues accompanying contemporary immigration to Canada, as well as the geographic distribution of the nation's newcomers.

The entry on Israel by Caitlin Killian opens by focusing on the Jewish presence in Palestine before the arrival of Zionist settlers in the late nineteenth century. The author then discusses Zionist ideas and immigration prior to the establishment of the British mandate at the end of the World War I. After recounting Jewish immigration to Palestine under the British Mandate from 1917 to 1948, Killian examines the immigration policy of the Jewish government since independence, as well as the history of immigration since 1948, including a detailed breakdown of the various Jewish arrivals from the different parts of the diaspora. Finally, the author closes with a discussion of the future of immigration and immigrant life in Israel.

Ayumi Takenaka's entry on Japan begins with a discussion of the changing state of immigration in the country during the boom years of the 1980s, when an unprecedented number of new arrivals came to the country, largely from Asia. The author then discusses the revisions in immigration law that occurred in the late 1980s and early 1990s, including rules concerning company trainee programs and the *nikkejin* policy (for children of Japanese living abroad). Finally, Takenaka concludes with a discussion of the future of immigration to Japan and whether the country will further open its doors to newcomers.

In his entry on Western Europe, Daniel James focuses on the three major immigrant destination countries in the region: France, Germany, and Great Britain. The author points out that while all three have seen vast influxes of immigrants in recent years, both the pattern and history of immigration in each of the three countries differs enormously. France and Britain, both with long traditions of immigration, are seeing many newcomers from their former empires in Africa, Asia, and the Caribbean. Germany, with more of a tradition of emigration than immigration, is forced to cope with large numbers of people coming from the Middle East and, more recently, Eastern Europe and the former Soviet Union in the wake of communism's collapse.

GLOBAL ECONOMY AND IMMIGRATION

Since the late twentieth century, a sea change has taken place in the way world society is organized. Now, with the click of a mouse, transatlantic business mergers, stock trades, product dumping, and million-dollar acquisitions are made on a daily basis. Not a month has passed before the latest fashions of New York, Paris, and Tokyo are hanging in the closets of men and women in Guayaquil, Calcutta, and San Salvador. A toxic spill in Alaska is linked to the death of hundreds of sea whales off the coast of Mexico. In effect, the change that has taken place, commonly understood as the process of globalization, has involved a widening, deepening, and speeding up of worldwide interconnectedness in all aspects of contemporary life.

Globalization, rather than being a completely novel process, involves a monumental increase in the cross-border flows of everything—finances, trade, ideas, cultural norms, pollution, products, and people. One of the motor forces behind this speed-up in international circuits of contact and exchange is the global economy, which can simply be understood as the latest incarnation of the international capitalist system. A central feature of this system is the age-old process of capital going abroad in search of investment opportunities and profits. It is the unparalleled intensity, scope, and volume of international capital flows that distinguishes early-twenty-first-century capitalism.

Generally, flows of money, goods, and services have been welcome by the holders of economic and political power. In contrast, the movement of people and the cultural differences they introduce are seen as a threat to national sovereignty and identity. Yet these two flows—of products and people—are now, as they have always been, inextricably bound together. The ups and downs of the international capitalist system steadily shape the size and direction of international population flows.

Three aspects of the structural relationship between the capitalist system and international migration deserve consideration. The first section below focuses on the theoretical link between capital and population flows. It also presents a historical example of this relationship. The following section explores the new features of the global economy and their impact on international migration flows. The final section focuses on the ways in which immigrant populations have adjusted to the globalization of the capitalist economy. In particular, it examines the new strategies of transnational settlement developed by immigrant populations in the United States.

THE STRUCTURAL LINK BETWEEN CAPITAL AND POPULATION FLOWS

In the course of the last five hundred years, the capitalist market economy has grown outward from Europe and North America through an ever-expanding cycle of investment, production, and profit. Such expansiveness is an inherent feature of the profit-seeking capitalist system of production. Capital must steadily incorporate new regions, greater numbers of people, a wider variety of activities, and more resources into its sphere of market activities to ensure the constant accumulation of profit.

As the capitalist economy expands, it penetrates into regions in which nonmarket social and economic structures prevail. The incorporation of nonmarket societies into the capitalist system of production displaces people from secure livelihoods and creates a footloose population prone to migration. Population movements, whether local or international, are thus driven by twin structural forces that have their roots in economic production: labor market dislocations in sending regions and labor market demand in receiving areas.

Globalization has disrupted economies around the world and has sent many immigrants to America. It has also triggered protests among American workers. Demonstrators forced these Taiwanese delegates to the 1999 World Trade Organization in Seattle to find alternative routes to the conference. *(Associated Press)*

INTERNATIONAL MIGRATION IN HISTORICAL PERSPECTIVE

A classical example helps demonstrate the way in which the expansion of the capitalism system of production is linked to the ebb and flow of population movements. In the late nineteenth century, Europeans migrated en masse to the Americas and Australia. Europe's rapid process of industrialization displaced peasants from their lands and led to an acute problem of overpopulation in urban areas. In spite of rapid growth, the regional economy could not absorb the local labor surplus. Landless rural workers and redundant urban workers were thus encouraged, if not forced, to migrate. The European labor surplus coincided with a dramatic labor shortage in the former

colonies, young countries such as the United States and Argentina, which were also undergoing a phase of rapid capitalist expansion. For European emigrants, the economies of North America, Australia, and Argentina thus held the promise of wage work in the city and abundant arable land in the countryside.

Changes in the economies of both Europe and the Americas therefore resulted in a massive international migration flow that lasted fifty years. Yet the process by which European labor was tied to American jobs was by no means automatic. No invisible hand of the market eased the transatlantic adjustment of labor demand and supply. Instead, an entire industry of labor recruiters, travel agents, and sea merchants emerged to link European workers to wage work in the New World. While statesmen promised newcomers land

and freedom, industrialists promised a decent wage for a day's work. As has been amply documented, the realities of European immigration to the Americas involved a great deal of hardship, loss, and adjustment.

With the outbreak of World War I, large-scale European emigration came to an abrupt end. In the 1920s, immigrant-receiving countries passed restrictive admissions policies. Later, the onset of the Great Depression, followed by World War II, stifled practically all international migration. Global economic stagnation and regional political turmoil effectively halted large-scale international labor migrations for four decades.

CAPITAL AND POPULATION FLOWS IN THE LATE TWENTIETH CENTURY

In the post–World War II era, immigration became a truly global phenomenon as the number and variety of sending and receiving countries increased. European migration declined, and emigration from Africa, Asia, and Latin America increased dramatically. The variety of destination countries grew to encompass not only Canada and the United States, Australia, Argentina, and New Zealand, but also the countries of Western Europe. Self-contained, regional international migration regimes emerged in Asia and the Gulf countries.

Changes in the character of postwar international migration flows are linked to transformations that have taken place in the international capitalist economy. Late-twentieth-century capitalism is distinguished by two features: the emergence of new sites of autonomous capitalist production and the development of new strategies for organizing industrial production systems. Together, these two factors have produced new forms of labor dislocation in the third world and a restructuring of labor markets in advanced nations. The result is the construction of new circuits of international labor migration and the emergence of novel patterns of immigrant settlement.

CAPITALIST EXPANSION AND GLOBAL MIGRATION

Beginning in the 1950s, capitalism experienced a period of rapid growth and global expansion that led to the construction of three new circuits of international labor migration. First, the post–World War II reconstruction of Europe prompted vigorous economic activity and an increased demand for labor. Germany and Switzerland in particular faced serious labor shortages and initiated immigrant recruitment programs to import workers from abroad. Demand was first met by southern European labor, and later by workers from the Mediterranean Basin and North Africa, who eventually came to dominate the flow. By the 1970s, even Europe's traditional migrant-sending countries, such as Spain and Italy, had become countries of net immigration.

Second, after 1973 the rapid escalation of oil prices placed the oil-rich countries of the Middle East Gulf region in the distinct situation of generating industrialization through wealth. The oil-producing nations of the Middle East had amassed huge reserves of capital, which state officials deployed to construct an industrial infrastructure. A fundamental problem in this project for national development was the absence of skilled workers. The fastest solution to this structural imbalance was the importation of labor. Regional leaders designed temporary recruitment programs that enabled them to import labor without having to grant workers the costly rights of citizenship. Some of the principal countries providing labor to the Gulf region have been Egypt and Iran in the Middle East, and India, Bangladesh, and Pakistan in South Asia. In 1990, 68 percent of the labor force in the oil-producing Gulf countries was foreign-born.

Asia was the third region to experience rapid capitalist expansion and the simultaneous construction of a new, regionally self-contained system of international migration. In the 1970s, following a period of political and economic withdrawal from the international arena, Japan emerged as a center of advanced capitalist activity, on a par with the United States and Europe. In order to meet industrial demand, the government struggled to develop a labor importation strategy that would not violate Japanese preferences for racial uniformity and cultural homogeneity. Temporary workers from the Japanese diaspora in the Americas—Peru, Brazil, and Colombia—were recruited. Large numbers of Asians were also allowed to enter Japan as "trainees" in "exchange programs." In reality, these programs function like thinly veiled guest-worker systems very similar to those of Europe. Thus, in spite of a national discourse of cultural homogeneity, in 1993 Japan's legal foreign population was estimated at 1.3 million and its unauthorized migrant population at more than three hundred thousand.

In the 1980s, the newly industrializing nations of Asia, including Singapore, Malaysia, Hong Kong, Taiwan, and Korea, also became net labor importers. The most important migrant worker source countries for the "Asian tigers" are the nations of the Philippines, Thailand, Indonesia, Malaysia, Sri Lanka, Bangladesh, and India.

INTERNATIONAL MIGRATION TO THE UNITED STATES

It is indisputable that the emergence of multiple new sites of capitalist expansion has led to a dramatic diversification of immigrant sending and receiving countries. Many nations across the globe now take in large numbers of immigrants. Nonetheless, the United States continues to absorb the lion's share of the world's immigrants. Between 1980 and 1989, the United States received roughly one-third of all of the world's international immigrants. By the 1980s, the flow of immigrants to North America exceeded the record levels observed during the great European migration at the turn of the century. The net increase has been accompanied by a pronounced shift in immigrant origins away from the historical source countries of Europe and toward new sources in Asia, Latin America, and the Caribbean. Together, these regions now contribute 85 percent of immigrants to the United States.

The changes evidenced by international migration flows to the United States result from the country's hegemonic presence in economic and political world affairs. The United States's ubiquitous global presence has the often unintended consequence of linking foot-loose populations of the third world to the country. Two central agents of this relationship are transnational corporations (TNCs) and the government's military complex.

It has been established that foreign investment by an industrially advanced nation is closely associated with the onset of immigration from the affected region to that country. In the 1960s, U.S. transnational corporations penetrated deep into third-world countries in search of natural resources and to take advantage of the region's reservoir of cheap labor. In particular, U.S. investment was concentrated in Latin America and the Caribbean. The presence of these TNCs in less developed countries has had a dual effect.

First, capitalist investment in the region has dislocated populations from secure livelihoods. The displaced first migrated to the city in search of wage work, where they joined the ranks of the informal sector, eking out a living as street peddlers, market women, gardeners, or domestic servants. The growing

population of redundant workers also began to migrate north. Indeed, research has established a strong relationship between direct foreign investment by U.S. TNCs and immigration. In a study of eighteen Caribbean source countries, sociologist Erol Rickets found that the annual rate of outmigration to the United States from 1970 to 1979 was strongly related to the growth in U.S. investment from 1966 to 1977.

Second, the presence of TNCs in the third world prompts the formation of ideological and material links to the investing nation that also encourage immigration. The globalization of the American lifestyle has remolded local cultural forms. New consumption standards have been introduced that bear little relation to local wage levels. As a result, future immigrants are presocialized into what to expect of their lives abroad, although this may only be an illusion. The foreign cultural presence increases individuals' desire to break through the gap between local realities—poverty, low wages, instability—and first world consumption aspirations. The result is a tendency for the middle and working class to emigrate. Ironically, globalization means that immigrants are acculturated to American culture long before they leave home.

The United States foreign policy initiatives and its direct military involvement in third world regions have also been linked to the initiation of international migration flows to the country. For instance, with the withdrawal of U.S. armed forces from Vietnam and the subsequent collapse of U.S.-backed governments in South Vietnam, Laos, and Cambodia, Southeast Asia in the late 1970s and 1980s emerged as a major source of refugees. Logically, the largest number of refugees ended up in the United States and created the links that have facilitated subsequent economic migration from the region. In effect, the United States's rise to world domination, sown through foreign investment and diplomacy as well as by military intervention, has transformed the nation into a magnet for international migrants.

SEGMENTED LABOR MARKETS, IMMIGRANT JOBS

The equation is simple: Capitalist expansion simultaneously displaces labor in the third world and creates new types of labor demands in advanced nations. This relationship suggests that immigration is caused first and foremost by the structural economic demands of advanced nations. The built-in demand for immigrant workers stems from the labor market structure of advanced capitalist economies, which is segmented into primary and secondary sectors. While the primary sector is characterized by stable, well-remunerated employment, the secondary sector is characterized by low wages, unstable conditions, and the lack of any prospects for mobility.

In this structural context, immigrant labor is imported to fill positions in the secondary segment, positions that native workers will not accept either because they are poorly remunerated or because they are culturally stigmatized. In the United States newly arrived immigrants toil at culturally stigmatized jobs such as agricultural stoop labor, domestic services, restaurant kitchen work, and garment production in sweatshops.

THE NEW MODALITIES OF INDUSTRIAL PRODUCTION

The second distinctive feature of late-twentieth-century capitalism is the new modes that have been developed to organize transnational production activities. In the 1970s, the entry of Japan as a global economic competitor fundamentally altered the way in which advanced countries thought about managing their economies and third world countries sought to develop theirs. The basis of the Japanese challenge focused on the efficient application of known technologies to the production of manufactured goods with an increasing value-added component. The response of the established economic players—namely, U.S. transnational corporations—was a strategic restructuring of industry referred to as a "spatial fix." The result was a reorganization of the international capitalist economy into a system of flexible accumulation.

The spatial fix involves a spatial fragmentation of the production process into distinct components. Labor-intensive aspects of the production process—stitching together clothing, assembling computer chips, processing data—are shifted to the third world, where labor is cheap and abundant. Planning, product design, and marketing strategies are centralized in strategic urban centers of the advanced world. Improvements in long-distance transportation and real-time communications technologies have facilitated this fragmentation, intensification, and acceleration of the transnational production process. Today, a garment design conceived in New York can be transmitted electronically to a factory in Haiti and the first batches of the product received in San Francisco in a week's time.

Flexible accumulation has had a troubling impact on labor markets in both the first and third worlds. Hardest hit in the restructuring of the international economy has been the industrial working class. In advanced countries, the state and private sector aligned to jettison the social pact on which the primary labor force had been built. Industries were shut down and workers laid off. Unions were weakened or broken. Subcontracting, temporary and part-time work, and a general deskilling of labor were the order of the day. Workers had to submit to the new dictates of transnational corporations or face the flight of industry.

As a result of the restructuring of industry, labor markets in the advanced countries became increasingly polarized by skill and wage differentials. The middle segment of skilled, unionized, and well-paid blue-collar workers shrank. The large majority of expelled blue-collar workers moved downward to a relatively low-skill, low-wage reservoir for manufacturing production and service jobs. Finally, extensive job losses, deepening poverty, and unemployment also led to the growth of the informal economy. By the 1980s, the labor market of the United States industrial centers had been bifurcated. The previous distribution of the labor market—a large middle-wage sector, and small upper- and lower-wage sectors—had changed to an hourglass shape consisting of large upper- and lower-wage sectors and a tiny middle-wage sector.

In the third world, the incipient working class, created behind barriers of import substitution, suffered a similar fate. Seeking to emulate the economic success of the "Asian tigers" and facing pressures from international finance organizations, the countries of Latin America and the Caribbean opened up their economies. Third world countries developed two strategies in order to attract the labor-intensive segments of the transnational production process. Some countries opted to curtail local labor standards and the minimum wage. Other governments created export-processing zones, literally islands of impunity for transnational capital, that allowed foreign investors to simply bypass the country's labor legislation.

Sociologist Saskia Sassen has argued that the establishment of export-processing zones contributes to international migration. Export-processing zones contribute to outmigration by producing goods that compete with those made locally, by feminizing the workforce without providing factory-based employment for men, and by socializing women for industrial work and modern consumption without providing a lifetime income capable of meeting these needs. The result is a population that is socially and economically uprooted and prone to migration.

RESTRUCTURING LABOR IN THE GLOBAL CITY

The expansion of the capitalist market economy into ever-farther reaches of the globe is directed and coordinated from a relatively small number of "global cities." Global cities, such as New York, London, Los Angeles, and Tokyo, manage the increasingly decentralized and scattered production processes of the global economy. The distinguishing feature of such urban centers is that they concentrate the technical and information systems required to manage fragmented transnational industries—telecommunications, banking, finance, insurance, legal systems, and sciences.

Global cities generate a very distinct type of labor market. On one hand, the management of the global economy creates a strong demand for highly educated workers with expertise in the high-tech services industry. On the other hand, the congregation of high-income workers and wealthy capitalists in global cities generates a demand for ancillary workers in restaurants, hotels, construction, maintenance, and personal services. Native workers are reluctant to accept such onerous jobs at low pay in the secondary segment of the labor market. Since these service jobs cannot be easily shifted overseas, employers recruit immigrants into these positions. In effect, the structure of late-twentieth-century capitalism, now orchestrated in global cities, has a built-in demand for immigrant workers.

A case in point is Los Angeles, which has been one of the world economy's dynamic industrial growth poles throughout the twentieth century. In the 1970s, the emergence of Los Angeles as a world city involved a dual process of economic growth and decline in the region. Branch plants shut down and were replaced by manufacturing industries in the high-tech aerospace industry and the garment, furniture, and leather manufacturing sectors. Thus, blue-collar jobs in unionized sectors were replaced with low-wage jobs in sectors with low rates of unionization. The concentration of advanced, global finance and management processes in Los Angeles also prompted the expansion of a white, male-dominated sector of top-level professionals and a low-wage sector of workers to service their high-income lifestyles.

Massive immigration into the Los Angeles region shadowed this transformation of the local economy. The magnitude and diversity of immigration to Los Angeles since the 1960s is comparable only to the immigration experienced by New York City at the turn of the century.

In 1900, 40 percent of the population of New York City was foreign-born. Between 1960 and 1990, the immigrant population of the Los Angeles region leaped from 8 to 27 percent. In 1990, 27 percent of the population in the Los Angeles region, 33 percent of the population in Los Angeles County, and 37 percent of the population in the metropolitan area were foreign-born.

CITIZENSHIP AND THE GLOBAL ECONOMY

Immigrant-receiving nations such as the United States face a growing political and economic contradiction. On one hand, the global economy, particularly its global cities, has an enduring structural demand for immigrant labor. Competitive segments of the economy require newcomers willing to accept menial, low-wage work. On the other hand, the process of deindustrialization, prompted by the capitalist system's spatial fix, has given rise to high native worker unemployment and a growing underclass of socially, politically, and economically marginal citizens. This structural tension has prompted a social and political response from both native workers and immigrant newcomers.

First, there is a growing demand from native workers to restrict immigrant admissions and to limit the citizenship rights granted to newcomers. The state has willingly complied with this demand. It has retrenched from its social obligations, allowing immigrants to participate in the economy but not in the nation. Increasingly, even legal immigrants are being excluded from social benefits, such as access to means-tested health benefits and income transfers. New antiterrorist legislation now authorizes the deportation of legal immigrants ever convicted of a felony. Finally, states with high rates of immigration, such as California and Florida, have sought to assert the primacy of English, legitimizing the growing xenophobia of civil society.

The new dynamics of the global economy means that a larger proportion of newcomers are destined to fill only the most marginal niches in highly segmented labor markets and have little hope of ever finding more-stable and better-remunerated jobs. Politically, labor migrants are unlikely to gain full citizenship rights, and they face a host society that is becoming more hostile and xenophobic. Facing increasingly limited opportunities for economic mobility and political participation in the host society, immigrants have begun to develop a variety of novel, transnational strategies of settlement.

GLOBAL ECONOMICS, TRANSNATIONAL SETTLEMENT

Availing themselves of the space-time-compressing technologies that have proliferated in the global economy—relatively affordable long-distance travel and real-time communications by phone, fax, or E-mail—immigrants are now forging dense and complex ties with their places of origin. These transnational ties have been developed by immigrants as part of a strategy of economic insertion, social mobility, and political participation.

Salvadoran immigrants in the United States are exemplary of this transnational settlement strategy. The clearest expression of Salvadorans' continued engagement in the social life of their places of origin is the sending of cash remittances to friends and family in El Salvador. In 1996, total remittances, estimated at $1.26 billion, were greater than the country's export earnings. Households that receive remittances demonstrate tangible improvement in their standard of living. Remittance dollars grant greater access to health and education for young people, or the ability to purchase a house or make improvements on an existing property.

In the three decades that Salvadorans have been immigrating to the United States, the majority of them have toiled in dead-end, low-wage jobs in the secondary labor market. While this path of labor incorporation is still common, there is also a growing trend toward new forms of transnational entrepreneurship. In the course of the last two decades, Salvadoran immigrants have created hundreds of small and medium-size transnational enterprises in the United States and El Salvador.

Several factors distinguish transnational enterprises both from traditional return-immigrant businesses and from the types of ethnic enterprises typically created to serve the immigrant market. First, the startup and expansion capital for such firms is commonly pooled by a group of business partners who labor as wage workers in the United States. Second, the types of enterprises established cater to families

whose members live in El Salvador and the United States. Living across borders, families require such things as real estate agencies, remittance agencies, and legal services that enable them to contribute to the nonimmigrant household. For transnational enterprises, the key to turning a profit are the price and information differentials between the sending and receiving countries.

Salvadorans have also maintained a social and political presence in El Salvador. One of the most distinctive and ubiquitous Salvadoran transnational formations is the hometown association or *comité del pueblo*. *Comités* are typically formed by immigrants from the same place of origin who organize social and cultural events in the Salvadoran immigrant community to raise funds for improvement projects in the members' place of origin. The status and recognition granted immigrants who undertake such projects often help offset the hardships and vagaries of being a marginal citizen in the host society.

The Salvadoran case is hardly anomalous. A growing number of immigrants now establish these types of transnational connections to their places of origin. The majority of immigrants from the Caribbean basin engage in transnational settlement strategies. South Asian immigrants in England and Canada, Kurdish workers in Germany and Holland, and Hong Kong Chinese and Filipinos worldwide are also among the groups that sustain economic and political relations with their countries of origin.

The trend toward transnational settlement breaks with the traditional dynamics of immigrant incorporation in the sending country. Prior to the rise of the global economy, the decision to exit one's country of origin and settle in a host country was identified with two distinct ways of life—one left behind and another just beginning. Transnational settlement strategies imply that the immigrant experience is no longer as sharply segmented between home and host society. This popular response to globalization, specifically to the economic and political limits imposed by the global economy in the host society, has effectively transformed the immigrant experience.

Patricia Landolt

See also: Economics II: Push Factors (Part II, Sec. 1); Legal and Illegal Immigration: A Statistical Overview, Transnationalism: Immigration from a Global Perspective (Part II, Sec. 2); Report on the Shortage of Technology Workers, 1997 (Part IV, Sec. 2).

BIBLIOGRAPHY

Alba, Francisco. "Mexico's International Migration as a Manifestation of Its Development Pattern." *International Migration Review* 12 (1978): 502–51.

Ardittis, Solon. "Labour Migration and the Single European Market: A Synthetic and Prospective Note." *International Sociology* 5 (1990): 461–74.

Arnold, Fred, and Nasra M. Shah, eds. *Asian Labor Migration: Pipeline to the Middle East.* Boulder, CO: Westview Press, 1986.

Basch, Linda, Nina Glick Schiller, and Cristina Szanton-Blanc. *Nations Unbound: Transnational Projects, Postcolonial Predicaments and Deterritorialized Nation-States.* Amsterdam: Gordon and Breach, 1994.

Castells, Manuel. *The Rise of the Network Society.* Oxford: Basil Blackwell, 1996.

———. *The Informational City: Information, Technology, Economic Restructuring and the Urban-Regional Process.* Oxford: Basil Blackwell, 1989.

———. "Multinational Capital, National States, and Local Communities." IURD Working Paper. Berkeley: University of California Press, 1980.

Castells, Manuel, and Alejandro Portes. "World Underneath: The Origins, Dynamics, and Effects of the Informal Economy." In *The Informal Economy: Studies in Advanced and Less Developed Countries,* ed. A. Portes, M. Castells, and L. A. Benton, pp. 11–37. Baltimore: Johns Hopkins University Press, 1989.

Davis, Mike. "The Internationalization of Downtown Los Angeles." *New Left Review* 164 (1987): 61–86.

de Janvry, Alain. *The Agrarian Question and Reformism in Latin America.* Baltimore: Johns Hopkins University Press, 1982.

Edwards, Richard. "The Social Relations of Production in the Firm and Labour Market Structure." In *Labour Market Segmentation,* ed. R. C. Edwards, M. Reich, and D. M. Gordon, pp. 341–67. Lexington, MA: D. C. Heath, 1975.

Harvey, David. *The Condition of Postmodernity.* Oxford: Basil Blackwell, 1990.

———. *Limits to Capital.* Chicago: University of Chicago Press, 1982.

Held, D., A. McGrew, D. Goldblatt, and J. Perraton. *Global Transformations: Politics, Economics and Culture.* Cambridge: Polity Press, 1999.

Ibrahim, S. E. *The New Arab Social Order: A Study of the Impact of the Oil Wealth.* Boulder, CO: Westview Press, 1982.

Landolt, Patricia, Lilian Autler, and Sonia Baires. "From Hermano Lejando to Hermano Mayor." *Ethnic and Racial Studies* 22:2 (1999): 290–315.

Massey, Douglas, J. Arango, G. Hugo, A. Kouaouci, A. Pellegrino, and J. E. Taylor. *Worlds in Motion: Understanding International Migration at the End of the Millennium.* Oxford: Clarendon Press, 1998.

Mingot, Michel. "Refugees from Cambodia, Laos and Vietnam." In *The Cambridge Survey of World Migration,* ed. Robin Cohen, pp. 452–57. Cambridge: Cambridge University Press, 1995.

Piore, Michael J. *Birds of Passage: Migrant Labor in Industrial Societies.* New York: Cambridge University Press, 1979.

Portes, Alejandro. "Globalization from Below: The Rise of Transnational Communities." In *The Ends of Globalization: Bringing Society Back In,* ed. Don Kalb et al., pp. 253–70. Lanham, MD: Rowman and Littlefield, 2000.

———. "Neoliberalism and the Sociology of Development: Emerging Trends and Unanticipated Facts." *Population and Development Review* 23 (1997): 229–59.

Portes, Alejandro, Luis Eduardo Guarnizo, and Patricia Landolt, eds. Special issue on transnational migrant communities. *Ethnic and Racial Studies* 22:2 (1999).

Portes, Alejandro, and Rubén G. Rumbaut. *Immigrant America: A Portrait.* Berkeley and Los Angeles: University of California Press, 1990.

Portes, Alejandro, and John Walton. *Labor, Class, and the International System.* New York: Academic Press, 1981.

Raijman, Rebeca, and Marta Tienda. "Immigrants' Socioeconomic Progress Post-1965: Forging Mobility of Survival?" Center for Migration and Development working paper, Princeton University, 1998.

Rickets, Erol. "U.S. Investment and Immigration from the Caribbean." *Social Problems* 34 (1987): 374–87.

Sassen, Saskia. "Economic Internationalization: The New Migration in Japan and the United States." *International Migration Review* 31 (1993): 43–72.

———. *The Global City: New York, London, Tokyo.* Princeton, NJ: Princeton University Press, 1991.

———. *The Mobility of Labor and Capital: A Study in International Investment and Labor Flow.* Cambridge: Cambridge University Press, 1988.

Seccombe, Ian J. "Foreign Worker Dependence in the Gulf and the International Oil Companies." *International Migration Review* 20 (1986): 548–74.

Soja, Edward W. *Postmodern Geographies: The Reassertion of Space in Critical Social Theory.* London: Verso, 1989.

Smith, M. P., and Luis E. Guarnizo, eds. *Transnationalism from Below.* New Brunswick, NJ: Transaction Publishers, 1998.

Waldinger, Roger, and Mehdi Bozorgmehr. *Ethnic Los Angeles.* New York: Russell Sage Foundation, 1996.

Williamson, John, ed. *The Political Economy of Policy Reform.* Washington, DC: Institute for International Economics, 1994.

Zegeye, Abebe, and Julia Maxted. "Race, Class and Polarization in Los Angeles." In *Exploitation and Exclusion: Race and Class in Contemporary U.S. Society,* ed. Abebe Zegeye, Leonard Harris, and Julia Maxted, pp. 224–44. London: Hans Zell Publishers, 1991.

Zlotnik, Hania. "South-to-North Migration Since 1960: The View from the South." Paper presented at the International Population Conference, Montreal, 1993.

INTERNATIONAL LAW AND IMMIGRATION

The rules governing global immigration can be derived from all sources of international law—treaty, custom, and general principles—and in particular from the principles of state sovereignty and individual free movement. Everyone has the right to emigrate, but at the same time, states may control and administer immigration. In short, sovereignty takes precedence over freedom of movement.

Each aspect of immigration is governed by distinct rules. There are rules of admission to state territories and rules of sojourn of immigrants in their capacities as aliens (foreign nationals), members of society, and economic subjects. Moreover, special rules govern termination of immigrant status by either repatriation or granting membership in the host polity (naturalization). Frequently, however, international law merely respects domestic policy decisions provided they are congruent with fundamental human rights standards.

EMIGRATION

Article 13 of the United Nations Universal Declaration of Human Rights adopted in 1948 and Article 12(2) of the UN International Covenant on Civil and Political Rights (CCPR) provide for the right of emigration. This right has laid the legal basis for flight from persecution.

IMMIGRATION

Both international and domestic law classify people entering states as immigrants or nonimmigrants. Aliens are generally regarded as tourists if they do not sojourn for a period exceeding three months or ninety days and do not seek employment. In turn, aliens are treated as immigrants if they seek entry for the purpose of establishing their habitual residence, taking up permanent gainful employment, or engaging permanently in self-employed business. In addition, states have introduced nonimmigrant categories in order to administer sojourns for fixed periods and for purposes specified before entry. However, relevant provisions of law frequently envisage or even encourage adjustment to immigrant status where nonimmigrants are deemed able to contribute to respective states' common good.

Many bilateral and multilateral treaties adopted at both the universal and the regional levels put a special focus on global immigration, some of them within a multi-issue policy framework. Many international agreements have been designed to administer immigration in its relation to other influential factors. Usually, these factors are categorized as push and pull factors. Push-migration is predominantly motivated by conditions of life at the place of departure, and includes such factors as international and internal armed conflicts, political persecution by totalitarian regimes and other violations of human rights, forced resettlement ("ethnic cleansing"), discrimination against vulnerable groups, terrorism, poverty and hunger, bad working conditions, natural disasters, and ecological devastation. Pull-migration is motivated by expectations of living conditions at the point of destination, such as availability of public assistance, the prospect of success in education, training and the labor market, political stability, constitutional democracy, pluralism, and effective protection of human rights.

Usually multiple factors lead to decisions in favor of emigration. However, existing legal regimes for managing immigration address only a few factors. The key sources of global immigration dealt with in relevant agreements are flight from persecution (international refugee law, which puts a special focus on certain push factors), emigration in the context of global or regional economic cooperation, and family reunification (today's main source of pull-migration in

Various United Nations treaties—including one on refugees—that have been adopted by the United States bind this country to the terms of those international agreements. *(Christopher Smith/Impact Visuals)*

both the United States and Europe). Recently, other factors, including trafficking in human beings, have become increasingly important and have jeopardized the effectiveness of existing regimes.

ADMISSION

As early as Immanuel Kant's *Metaphysics of Morals* (1797), it has been pointed out that the recognition, by general international law, of the human right of emigration does not imply a right of entry into any particular foreign state. International law respects states' sovereignty over their borders. Thus, they may grant or deny entry on a discretionary basis. Usually states require persons seeking admission to hold valid passports or surrogate passports and necessary visas. International law does not provide for judicial review of admission decisions, leaving it to domestic law whether such decisions are reviewable and which standards of review apply. Hence the U.S. Supreme Court's plenary power doctrine, which bestows more or less unfettered discretion upon the administration

in admission matters, does not violate international law.

Special rules apply to refugees under the nonrefoulement principle. This principle, embodied in Article 33(1) of the Convention Relating to the Status of Refugees, merely prohibits repatriation by host states of recognized refugees present in their respective territories. However, nonrefoulement would be an empty nutshell if states could evade the obligation thereunder simply by keeping persons claiming to be refugees out of their territories. Hence states must not only offer refugee determination proceedings but also grant entry on a provisional basis (parole) where necessary for that purpose. But they need not accord a right of entry or otherwise permit definitive entry. Moreover, states may deny entry of refugees where they have reached respective territories from safe third countries or where their cases are manifestly unfounded.

There is only one exception to admission discretion. Under Article 13 of the Universal Declaration on Human Rights and Article 12(4) of the CCPR, "No one shall be arbitrarily deprived of the right to enter his own country." The Human Rights Committee has applied this right to immigrant members of host states' society, that is, lawful permanent residents who have maintained their habitual residence for a significant period.

Human rights law does not outlaw restrictive immigration policies. The European Agreement on Regulations Governing the Movement of Persons Between Member States of the Council of Europe (ETS no. 25) expresses the state of international law by limiting facilitated movement of persons (Article 5) by the right of every signatory state "to forbid nationals of another Party whom it considers undesirable to enter or stay in its territory" (Article 6). Only supranational European Community law provides for freedom of movement as a right. Community law is, therefore, the only legal order that has almost removed internal border sovereignty. Workers, providers and recipients of services, and self-employed persons have the right to migration within European Union (EU) nations in relation to their respective participation in the common market. Other EU citizens enjoy freedom of movement subject to the measures adopted to give it effect. To date, such measures cover pensioners, students, and other persons provided that they have sufficient health insurance and means of living without dependency on public assistance.

INTEGRATION

The notion of integration covers such subject matters as security of residence status, social and political rights, and membership in host polities. Except for refugee law, relevant instruments cover only parts of the integration issue. Many standards of integration can be derived from instruments that do not focus on immigration as such, in particular, international human rights. As far as specialized instruments are concerned, the more ambitious they are, the less states have ratified them.

INTEGRATION OF REFUGEES AND STATELESS PERSONS

Under the Convention Relating to the Status of Refugees, refugees are entitled to national treatment in respect of freedom of religion (Article 4), protection of industrial and intellectual property (Article 14), elementary education (Article 22[1]), public assistance (Article 23), and labor market and social security rights (Article 24). Additionally, states shall respect acquired rights dependent on personal status (Article 12[2]). Moreover, refugees are entitled to treatment no less favorable than that accorded to aliens generally,

as regards free movement (Article 26), the acquisition of property and related rights or contracts (Article 13), membership in nonpolitical and nonprofit associations and trade unions (Article 15), access to the labor market free from restrictions imposed on other aliens (Article 17), housing (Article 21), and advanced education (Article 22[2]). Self-employment shall be open to refugees (Article 18). Refugees may be expelled only on grounds of national security or public order and in pursuance of a decision reached in accordance with due process of law (Article 32). States shall as far as possible facilitate the assimilation and naturalization of refugees (Article 34). The UN Convention Relating to the Status of Stateless Persons contains similar rights. Moreover, Article 1 of the UN Convention on the Reduction of Statelessness provides that signatories shall grant their nationality to persons born in their territory who would otherwise be stateless if relevant domestic conditions, as allowed for in the convention, are met. Many instruments provide for a right to acquire a nationality upon birth (e.g., Article 15[1] of the Universal Declaration; Article 24[3] of the CCPR; Article 7[1] of the UN Convention on the Rights of the Child; Article 4[a] of the Council of Europe's European Convention on Nationality).

IMMIGRANT INTEGRATION INTO THE LABOR MARKET AND HOST SOCIETIES

Policy concepts regarding integration of immigrants into the labor market and into host societies reflect fundamental concepts of the interaction between state and societies that differ significantly throughout the world. For instance, in its present shape, the notion of the "melting pot" in the United States would require "Americanization." Canada and Australia, in turn, have adopted multiculturalism policies that leave to immigrants the determination of the way and extent of integration. European nations are now redefining their long-held notions as nonimmigration countries.

Regardless of the different concepts, integration has turned out to be an issue predominantly governed by human rights. International human rights as enshrined in the UN International Covenant on Economic, Social and Cultural Rights function as the basis of immigrant integration into the labor market and host societies. Thus, everyone is entitled to just and favorable working conditions (Article 7), social security (Article 9), protection of the family (Article 10[1]), an adequate standard of living (Article 11), the highest attainable health standards (Article 12[1]), and education (Article 13[1]).

There is an ongoing dispute over whether immigrant communities qualify for state protection of their cultural, religious, or linguistic peculiarities as minorities under Article 27 of the CCPR. European Union law prohibits discrimination on the ground of nationality. EU citizens enjoy national treatment in all member states with respect to almost all social rights. Comprehensive rules govern transborder social security with a view to protecting health care and pension rights.

The revised Council of Europe's European Social Charter (ETS no. 163, nine ratifications) provides for workers' rights subject to domestic implementation. In particular, Article 19 is dedicated to the right of immigrant workers and their families to protection and assistance. Both this provision and the Council's European Convention on the Legal Status of Migrant Workers (European Treaty Series), which was ratified by eight countries, are guided by international human rights.

To date, neither domestic nor international jurisprudence has upheld claims for family reunification based on family protection clauses contained in relevant bills of rights. Only European Union law provides for almost comprehensive family reunification of intra-EU immigrants. From a policy point of view, the effects of family reunification on integration are ambiguous. For one, family reunification may facilitate integration because it enables immigrants to maintain networks that are needed to settle. However, it may equally contribute to segregation of growing immigrant communities.

Integration of immigrants has been also addressed by the UN International Convention on the Protection of the Rights of All Migrant Workers and Members of Their Families. This convention is not yet in force, and it appears that no major receiving country has signed it.

INTERNATIONAL ECONOMIC COOPERATION

European economic integration might become the blueprint of increasingly dense international economic cooperation. Existing international and regional arrangements accord freedoms similar to those enshrined in the treaty establishing the European Community. Economic cooperation is not limited to transfrontier movement of goods and capital. Rather, it also implies transfrontier movement of human resources. In particular, international trade in services frequently involves provision of services abroad ("posted work") or transfrontier loan employment. States have agreed in principle to facilitate access to their country by foreign service providers, in the General Agreement on Trade in Services. Regional agreements include supplementary provisions. For instance, Canadian and Mexican nationals may be admitted to the United States under the North American Free Trade Agreement for the purpose of temporary employment provided that they have a baccalaureate degree or appropriate professional credentials.

European market freedoms include the freedom of movement for workers and the freedoms to provide services and to establish a business. The European Court of Justice has extended the freedom to provide services as entailing a right to receive services in other EU member states and has assimilated the legal position of Turkish workers to that of EU workers under the association agreement with Turkey.

INTEGRATION INTO HOST POLITIES

International law recognizes states' sovereign right to determine the criteria for acquisition of membership in their polities. However, states need not treat a person as a national of another state where no genuine link between the person and the state in question exists.

State practice knows different ways of acquisition of nationality at birth and at later stages in life. Most states have introduced rules that combine acquisition of one's parents' nationality or nationalities and acquisition of the nationality of the place of birth. International law does not give preference to either principle. Ius Soli (the legal concept whereby a person acquires, upon birth, the nationality of the state where he/she was born) leads to automatic integration of children of immigrants into host polities, be it unlimited, such as in the United States—where even children of illegal immigrants are born as Americans—or dependent on parents' or grandparents' lawful residence, as in many European states. As to naturalization upon application, states usually require clean criminal records, extended periods of lawful permanent residency, and a certain degree of acculturation or assimilation. The European Convention on Nationality (ECN) (ETS no. 166, three ratifications) binds states to provide for the possibility of naturalization of persons lawfully and habitually resident on respective territories (Article 6[3]), and in particular for spouses and children of their nationals (Article 6[4]). Loss of nationality is limited to cases of conduct seriously prejudicial to the vital interests of the state in question or voluntary acts of renunciation (Articles 7 and 8). Dual or multiple nationals may be treated as nationals of the state they live in (effective nationality). Special rules apply with respect to military obligations in cases of multiple nationality under ECN and the "Convention on the reduction of cases of multiple nationality and military obligations in cases of multiple nationality."

International law does not either guarantee or deny a right of political participation in host polities (immigrant franchise). However, there is a trend toward granting local franchise to immigrants. In particular, citizens of the member states of the European Union may vote in and stand for local elections throughout the union. The Council of Europe Convention on the Participation of Foreigners in Public Life at Local Level (ETS no. 144; five ratifications) extends this right to all immigrants, regardless of their nationality, after five years of lawful residence.

REPATRIATION

Standards for repatriation of both legal and illegal immigrants have been developed under international law to different extents at universal and regional levels. Article 13 of the CCPR guarantees due process in expulsion cases. Although this provision does not limit grounds of expulsion, the individual or collective expulsion of aliens on grounds of race, color, religion, culture, descent, or national or ethnic origin is prohibited (Article 7 of the UN Declaration on the Human Rights of Individuals Who Are Not Nationals of the Country in Which They Live). Article 4 of Protocol no. 4 to the 1950 European Convention for the Protection of Human Rights and Fundamental Freedoms outlaws collective expulsion of aliens regardless of the motive. Moreover, under relevant European Community law and Council of Europe conventions, repatriation is justified only on grounds of public policy, public security, or public health or on grounds of national security, public order, public health, or morals, respectively.

Article 3(1) of the Convention for the Protection of Human Rights and Fundamental Freedoms prohibits repatriation of aliens who would be exposed to torture or to inhuman or degrading treatment or punishment. According to the European Court of Human Rights, even the absence of medical assistance in home states of deportees qualifies as a threat of inhuman treatment where this would cause a real risk of death. However, deciding on extradition, the court has thus far left open whether it regards capital punishment as inhuman.

States are not presently obliged under customary international law to readmit persons who emigrated from their respective territories to other states of destination. However, there is a strong tendency toward the emergence of such an obligation. European states in particular have concluded readmission agreements with many home and transit countries, and they press for inclusion of readmission clauses in agreements concluded by the EU alone or by its member states with third states on economic or development cooperation. In addition, the recently concluded Cotonou Agreement between the European Union and seventy-six African, Caribbean, and Pacific (ACP) states provides for return of and readmission of any national illegally present in respective territories, at request and without further formalities (Article 13[5][c][i]). Cotonou also creates mutual obligations to combat illegal immigration.

REFUGEES

International refugee law flows from the Convention Relating to the Status of Refugees and the 1967 Protocol on the convention's worldwide application. One hundred thirty-nine states have acceded to the convention or the protocol, resulting in an opting out from global refugee protection of states representing more than one-sixth of world population (including India).

Refugees are persons who have fled their home country "owing to a well-founded fear of being persecuted for reasons of race, religion, nationality, membership of a particular social group, or political opinion" (Article 1). Refugees may neither be treated as illegal immigrants (Article 31[1]) nor expelled or returned to states where they would be threatened with persecution (Article 33[1], the nonrefoulement principle). The convention has established the United Nations High Commission for Refugees (UNHCR), an independent institution entrusted with surveillance of states' adherence to their obligations. The institution may participate in individual refugee determination proceedings, but is not competent to issue binding decisions. The Convention on the Rights of the Child envisages appropriate protection of and humanitarian assistance for refugee children in the enjoyment of their rights (Article 22[1]).

There is a tendency to apply the Refugee Convention to almost all forms of push-migration. However, states prefer to grant temporary protected rather than refugee status to persons who have fled from armed conflicts and ecological disasters in order to facilitate return. Recent United States and European experiences in such places as Cuba, Haiti, Bosnia, and Kosovo witness the effectiveness of this policy approach.

Ulf Haeussler

See also: Economics II: Push Factors, Political, Ethnic, Religious, and Gender Persecution, Wars and Civil Unrest (Part II, Sec. 1); Amnesty, Civil Rights, Legislation I: Immigration (Part II, Sec. 5); U.S. Report Under the International Covenant on Civil and Political Rights, 1994 (Part IV, Sec. 2).

BIBLIOGRAPHY

Goodwin-Gill, Guy S. *The Refugee in International Law.* 2d ed. Oxford: Clarendon Press, 1996.

Hailbronner, Kay. *Immigration Law and Policy of the European Union.* Dordrecht, Netherlands: Kluwer Academic Publishers, 2000.

Hailbronner, Kay, David A. Martin, and Hiroshi Motomura, eds. *Immigration Controls.* Oxford: Berghahn Books, 1997.

———. *Immigration Admissions.* Oxford: Berghahn Books, 1998.

Hathaway, James C. *Reconceiving International Refugee Law.* The Hague, Netherlands: Nijhoff, 1997.

Joppke, Christian. *Immigration and the Nation State: The United States, Germany, and Great Britain.* Oxford: Oxford University Press, 1999.

Koslowski, Rey. *Migrants and Citizens: Demographic Change in the European State System.* Ithaca: Cornell University Press, 2000.

Legomsky, Stephen H. *Immigration and Refugee Law and Policy.* 2d ed. Westbury, NY: Foundation Press, 1997.

INTERNATIONAL TREATIES AND DECLARATIONS

The instruments referred to are available on the Web sites of the UN High Commissioner for Human Rights and the Council of Europe: http://www.unhchr.ch and http://conventions.coe.int

GOVERNMENT AND NONGOVERNMENT ORGANIZATION WEB SITES

Australian Department of Immigration and Multicultural Affairs	www.immi.gov.au
Citizenship and Immigration Canada	www.cic.gc.ca
Commission on Immigration Reform (U.S.)	www.utexas.edu/lbj/uscir
European Union	www.europa.eu.int/eur-lex/en/ and www.europa.eu.int/comm/development/politique_en.htm
Immigration and Naturalization Service (U.S.)	www.ins.usdoj.gov
International Organization for Migration	www.iom.int
UNHCR	www.unhcr.ch

INTERNATIONAL POLITICS AND IMMIGRATION

Although immigration is obviously an international phenomenon, immigration policy is typically considered a domestic political process in which economic and ethnic interest groups lobby national legislatures, such as Congress, to demand policies that serve their particular interests. But international migration has effects in both immigrant-receiving and emigrant-sending states, and the latter often have strong preferences about immigration flows and policies. As a result, U.S. immigration and international politics are related in two important ways.

First, even when immigration policy responds strictly to domestic political demands, the effects of policy decisions are also felt abroad, thus immigration policymaking often has foreign policy consequences and may cause international political responses. For example, presidents have frequently been forced to renegotiate treaties or otherwise exercise diplomacy in response to domestically driven immigration policies that have negative symbolic or material effects on other countries. When presidents have been unwilling or unable to respond to immigration policy demands in this way or when immigration flows or the preferences of migrant-sending states about immigration conflict sharply with U.S. concerns, international migration may create foreign policy crises that are difficult to resolve. On the other hand, in some cases, diplomacy has been successfully employed to persuade migrant-sending states to support domestically defined U.S. immigration policy goals.

A second general type of interaction between immigration and international politics occurs when foreign policy implications are so important that foreign policy concerns *cause* immigration policy decisions, such that immigration policy fails to reflect domestic political demands. The most obvious example of this phenomenon is the making of refugee policy explicitly to advance the president's foreign policy agenda during the Cold War, but it is neither the case that Congress always defers to the president on refugee issues nor that refugee policy uniquely reflects foreign policy concerns. For as long as the United States has regulated immigration, migrant-sending states have periodically bargained with the executive branch or lobbied Congress to influence immigration policy. The influence of migrant-sending states over U.S. immigration policymaking has been greatest in the post–World War II period because interdependence between the United States and its migration partners has increased and the president has become more powerful relative to Congress. Since the 1980s, however, immigration to the United States has increasingly been characterized by large-scale flows that have raised the domestic stakes of immigration policymaking, and domestic-international conflicts have intensified.

THE MAKING OF U.S. IMMIGRATION POLICY

Whether domestic or foreign policy concerns influence immigration depends on the dynamics of the immigration policymaking process. On the one hand, Congress has often dominated immigration policymaking and tends to be more concerned with its domestic constituents than with international issues. This is especially true because immigration laws have been handled by the judiciary committees and (to a limited extent) by agriculture and labor committees. The Foreign Relations and Foreign Affairs Committees of the Senate and the House, respectively—which *are* interested in international politics—have generally not made immigration policy. Congressional dominance of immigration dates back to 1882, when Congress enacted the first general immigration statutes, barring Chinese laborers and various types of "undesirables." Congress's authority over immigration was confirmed seven years later by the Supreme

1001

Court in the so-called Chinese Exclusion Case (*Chae Chan Ping v. United States*, 130 U.S. 581) in which the Court ruled that Congress had plenary (i.e., constitutionally based) power to override international treaties by passing legislation to regulate immigration.

But the president is not powerless to influence immigration. In 1893, the Supreme Court revisited immigration policy in *Fong Yue Ting v. United States*: "The power to exclude or to expel aliens, being a power *affecting international relations*, is vested in the political *departments* of the government, and is to be regulated by *treaty or by act of Congress*, and then to be *executed by the executive authority* according to regulations so established" (149 U.S. 698; emphasis added). Thus the Court recognized that international politics are inherently related to immigration policy-making and identified both political branches of government as having power to make immigration policy. Indeed, even if immigration policy was a purely legislative process, the president's veto power guarantees him some influence over outcome, and since 1896, presidents have vetoed at least eleven significant immigration bills. The Court also recognized the other tool available to executive branch actors: the power of enforcement. Presidents have often taken advantage of this power, even without congressional approval, to ensure that immigration policy enforcement is consistent with the president's foreign policy agenda. More recently, two 1999 Court decisions, *Reno v. American-Arab Anti-Discrimination Committee* (525 U.S. 471) and *I.N.S. v. Aguirre-Aguirre* (526 U.S. 415) reaffirmed the president's ability to employ immigration as a tool of foreign policy, including by the selective enforcement of policy.

CONGRESSIONAL DOMINANCE, 1868–1940

At the turn of the century, the battle between Congress and the president over immigration policy centered on immigration from Asia. In 1868, the United States and China signed the Burlingame Treaty, which established the right of free migration between the two countries. In 1879, however, Congress passed the Fifteen Passenger Bill, a measure designed to restrict Chinese immigration by limiting to fifteen the number of Chinese passengers on each ship coming to the United States. President Rutherford B. Hayes vetoed the bill because it violated the Burlingame Treaty. But he then authorized a delegation to visit China and renegotiate the treaty. In November 1880, the United

States and China signed a new treaty in which they recognized the right of the United States to regulate, limit, or suspend—but not prohibit outright—the immigration of Chinese laborers. In 1882, Congress disregarded even the revised treaty by passing the Chinese Exclusion Act, which suspended the immigration of *all* Chinese laborers for ten years. The act was renewed twice and then made permanent in 1904, remaining on the books until 1943.

A similar chain of events unfolded in the early 1900s when Californians protested Japanese immigration. The first diplomatic solution was announced in 1900 when Japan agreed to stop issuing passports to Japanese workers heading for the United States, but many continued to come by passing through Hawaii. Then, in 1907, the United States and Japan negotiated the Gentlemen's Agreement, which prohibited new migration to the United States by Japanese workers and which was backed up by congressional action to block immigration by Japanese from Hawaii to the United States. In 1924, Congress disregarded the Gentlemen's Agreement, as well as lobbying by the president, the State Department, and the Japanese ambassador, by including a Japanese exclusion clause in the 1924 Immigration Act. Thirty years later, in its report *Whom We Shall Welcome* (1953), the President's Commission on Immigration and Naturalization concluded that the legislation "contributed to the growth of the nationalistic, militaristic, and anti-American movement in Japan which culminated in war against the United States."

Congress and the president also clashed at this time over literacy provisions designed to exclude immigrants from eastern Europe. Between 1896 and 1915, Presidents Grover Cleveland, William H. Taft, and Woodrow Wilson vetoed three immigration bills because of their disregard for America's "traditional . . . belief in the right of political asylum," as Wilson explained in his 1915 veto message. Nonetheless, domestic restrictionist sentiment was strong enough in 1917 that Congress passed the Immigration Act of that year over Wilson's veto, implementing a literacy requirement that discriminated against eastern Europe, as well as an Asiatic Barred Zone, which discriminated against one-third of the world. Similarly, so strong was congressional opposition to unlimited immigration from the U.S. colony of the Philippines that Congress passed a law in 1934 over President Franklin D. Roosevelt's veto granting eventual independence to the country. In these cases, domestic politics dominated presidents' foreign policy agendas.

Although domestic restrictionism gained in intensity during the 1920s and, especially, following the onset of the depression in 1929, the executive branch was successful in some efforts to inject foreign policy concerns into the debate. In particular, when Congress passed the 1924 Immigration Act, which established permanent by-country quotas limiting Eastern Hemisphere immigration, the rationale was explicitly to support "Anglo-Saxon superiority." Thus, many strong proponents of the bill advocated additional quotas to limit the immigration not just of "inferior" Asians and eastern Europeans but also of Mexicans and other Latin Americans. In this case, however, international politics prevailed. The State Department made strong appeals that the Western Hemisphere should be excluded from the quota system *for diplomatic reasons,* and Congress deferred. Additional bills were debated by Congress to limit Western Hemisphere (1928) and Mexican (1930) immigration. The executive branch blocked these efforts on the grounds that such restrictions "would adversely affect the present good relations of the United States with Latin America," according to Secretary of State Frank Kellogg's 1928 congressional testimony.

UNITED STATES–MEXICAN IMMIGRATION RELATIONS AND GUEST-WORKER PROGRAMS, 1917–1964

United States–Mexican relations prior to World War II exemplify conflict between domestic immigration politics and foreign policy. With U.S. entrance into World War I in 1917, domestic interest group demands and internationally based U.S. demands for labor coincided, and the U.S. attorney general waived immigration controls along the southwest border. Agricultural employers recruited Mexicans to labor in the Southwest without any government regulation, a practice that was extended throughout the 1920s, during which time 500,000 Mexicans migrated to the United States. When the depression began in 1929, Mexican workers were the first to be laid off by agricultural employers, were often denied wages and welfare benefits due them, and were generally harassed by U.S. citizens and immigration authorities. Thus, although the depression hit Mexico—which was still recovering from ten years of civil war ending in 1920—much harder than the United States, the Mexican government expended enormous resources to help Mexican nationals escape brutal conditions in the United States and resettle in Mexico. The unwillingness to deal fairly with Mexican immigrants in the early 1930s had

foreign policy implications later in the decade when it contributed to the Mexican government's support for striking oil workers and the naturalization of U.S. oil interests in 1938 and, subsequently, to a short-term crisis in bilateral relations exactly when the United States needed Mexico's support for the U.S. war effort.

If the initial experiment with guest-worker flows was a foreign policy disaster, however, the following period illustrated how immigration can be made harmonious with foreign policy and how migrant-sending states may influence U.S. immigration policy decisions. During and after World War II, U.S.-Mexican relations were dominated by a series of bilateral international agreements regulating the importation of guest workers, or *braceros.* (In addition to Mexicans, bracero agreements also regulated the importation of workers from Canada, Jamaica, and the Bahamas, but the vast majority, 4.6 million out of about 5 million, came from Mexico.) In 1942, with the United States experiencing a significant demand for agricultural labor *and* acutely concerned about strengthening the U.S.-Mexican relationship in trade, military cooperation, and other areas, the United States requested a bilateral guest-worker agreement on Mexico's terms. As a result, on August 28, 1942, the United States and Mexico signed the most generous guest-worker agreement between any two countries ever. Mexican workers were guaranteed higher wages and better benefits than their U.S. counterparts, and their packages were backed up by the U.S. and Mexican governments. In addition, the United States paid all transportation costs to and from recruiting stations inside Mexico, and Mexico was allowed to select which Mexican regions would participate. There is no question that Mexico was able to extract these generous concessions—in spite of strong opposition by U.S. business and labor groups—because of executive branch foreign policy concerns.

The evolution of U.S.-Mexican bracero agreements after World War II further illustrates the interaction between foreign and domestic sources of immigration policy. Immediately after the war, U.S. growers pressed Congress to exert its influence over what had been an executive branch program and thereby to extend the program beyond its original wartime mandate while overturning most of the pro-worker regulations Mexico achieved in 1942. Mexico and President Harry S. Truman objected to the program's failure to deter undocumented immigration or protect wages. But when the United States entered the Korean War in 1950 and U.S. unemployment fell to 3.3 percent, Mexico insisted on renegotiating the treaty and reestablished many of its original terms. International factors reversed themselves in 1953 with the end of the Korean War, and presidential elections in both countries resulted in a short-term but severe worsening of U.S.-Mexican relations. In this case, foreign policy problems allowed domestic politics to dominate; and in January 1954, the United States forced Mexico's hand with an undesirable take-it-or-leave-it offer that sharply reduced Mexico's influence over future bracero flows and working conditions. Finally, in 1961, President John F. Kennedy and his Democratic congressional supporters were ready to abandon guest-worker recruitment for domestic reasons to raise U.S. wages, but given the Kennedy administration's foreign policy emphasis on strong U.S.–Latin American relations, Mexico convinced the president to extend the program until 1964.

THE POSTWAR BATTLE OVER IMMIGRATION AND REFUGEE POLICY, 1948–1980

Following World War II, U.S. immigration policymaking was otherwise dominated by the conflict between Congress, which supported domestic demands for restrictionist policies, and the executive branch, which wanted increased flexibility to employ immigration as an inclusive tool of foreign policy. Eventually this conflict was only *partly* resolved by creating separate policies to govern "immigration" and "refugee" flows, though there is continued interbranch and domestic-international conflict in each area.

Between 1948 and 1952, Congress and President Truman sharply disagreed about the relationship between immigration and foreign policy, with Congress passing restrictionist bills in 1948 (Displaced Persons Act), 1950 (Internal Security Act), and 1952 (McCarran-Walter Immigration and Nationality Act, the INA), all of which Truman considered harmful to U.S. strategic interests. (The 1950 and 1952 acts both passed over the president's vetoes.) Truman had two broad objections to these three bills. First, he argued that they hurt U.S. foreign policy interests by making it too difficult for European refugees and opponents of communism to enter the United States, and he contended that a number of visas should be reserved for the president to distribute for foreign policy reasons. Second, Truman objected to the INA because it institutionalized discriminatory policies that damaged the United States's credibility as the leader of the free world.

As the Cold War intensified in the 1950s, the president's ability to frame immigration as a foreign policy issue increased. In 1953, Congress approved the Emergency Migration Act, which reserved 209,000 nonquota visas for escapees from communist countries. A secret National Security Council memorandum described the 1953 act as being designed to "encourage defection of USSR [Union of Soviet Socialist Republics] nationals and key personnel from the satellite countries in order to inflict a psychological blow on Communism." Following the Soviet invasion of Hungary in November 1956 and the flight of tens of thousands of Hungarians to Austria and Yugoslavia, U.S. policy reached a critical turning point. President Dwight D. Eisenhower considered it a foreign policy priority that the Hungarian refugees be allowed to resettle in the United States, but existing immigration policy limited Hungarian immigration in 1956 to 865 people. In December, with Congress out of session, Eisenhower used a procedure, which Congress had explicitly intended to be applied only to *individuals*, to waive background checks for 6,200 Hungarians and "parole" them into the United States. Congress might have approved of the act—there was substantial national sympathy for the Hungarians—but by *informally* meeting with members of Congress and then *unilaterally assuming* the power to expand immigration policy in response to a political situation, Eisenhower set a precedent of applying foreign policy considerations to refugee decisions which affected all future refugee policymaking.

Nonetheless, the tension between immigration and foreign policy mounted, especially as U.S. foreign policy became increasingly focused on the developing world, making the pro–Western European bias of the 1952 INA more damaging. In 1965, Congress finally approved the amendments to the INA originally proposed by Kennedy in 1962 which resolved the two most pressing conflicts between immigration and foreign policy. First, the 1965 amendments to the INA abolished the race-based national origins quota system and replaced it with a flat quota of 20,000 per country for the Eastern Hemisphere. Within those limitations, the legislation established that visas would be allocated based on a seven-category preference system that gave highest priority to family reunification, followed by occupational demands. The second major change established by the 1965 amendments was that, within the preference system, the "seventh preference" was set aside for those fleeing a "Communist or Communist-dominated country or area, or . . . any country within the Middle East." Thus, the seventh preference officially established that some immigrant visas should always be reserved for refugees and that refugee visas were to be allocated in pursuit of U.S. foreign policy (Cold War) priorities.

With the issue of *whether* visas should be set aside for refugees resolved by the 1965 amendments, the conflict between Congress and the executive branch shifted to the question of *how* refugees should be defined and visas allocated. Congress sought to insure that the United States adopt and apply the United Nations (UN) definition of refugees as "those who have fled their countries because of a well-founded fear of persecution for reasons of their race, religion, nationality, political opinion or membership in a particular social group, and who cannot or do not want to return." Although legislation passed in 1967 inserted this definition into the amended INA, the president still retained discretion about when to request refugee status. Thus, over the next decade the United States applied a Cold War rationale to its refugee policies, and 97 percent of all refugees admitted by the United States came from communist countries. The tension between congressional advocates of a need-based refugee policy enforcement and executive branch advocates of refugee policy as a foreign policy tool came to a head in 1980 following the admission of 250,000 Indo-Chinese refugees in 1975–76 at the end of the Vietnam War. In response, President Jimmy Carter and Congress agreed on the 1980 Refugee Act, which completely "delinked" refugee and other immigration policies, accepted the UN definition of refugees, and established a formal consultation procedure between Congress and the president to regulate the admission of a flexible number of refugees, starting at 50,000 per year. Despite these efforts to "depoliticize" refugee policy, however, the Cold War continued to dominate U.S. refugee policy, and 95 percent of all refugees admitted in the 1980s still came from communist countries.

U.S. REGIONAL RELATIONS SINCE THE 1970s

The decision to apply Cold War reasoning to the enforcement of refugee policy toward the Eastern Hemisphere was always controversial, but these policy decisions never exhibited the passions that had characterized earlier immigration debates. The same cannot be said of immigration controversies within the Western Hemisphere. Conflicts between domestic and international sources of Western Hemisphere immigration policy have tended to be greater for two broad reasons. First, on the domestic side, immigration from the Western Hemisphere appears more threatening to those concerned about too much im-

migration because a larger number of people from the Western Hemisphere want to migrate to the United States and because geographic proximity makes it easy for them to do so. Second, on the international side, there is more to be gained from linking immigration to foreign policy because immigration to the United States plays a large role in the economies of Western Hemisphere, migrant-sending states and because, since the 1960s, the migrant-sending states of the Western Hemisphere have been at the center of the overall U.S. foreign policy agenda. In these cases, many of the most important decisions have been the decisions *not* to grant refugee and asylum status to migrants from repressive right-wing regimes deemed "friendly" by the United States.

U.S. RELATIONS WITH HAITI AND CUBA

The most glaring example of foreign policy domination of U.S. immigration policymaking toward the Western Hemisphere between the 1970s and 1990s is the contrasting treatment offered immigrants from Haiti and Cuba. During the 1950s and 1960s, Cubans and Haitians both fled to the United States in large numbers. Cubans were usually granted refugee status, and they often became naturalized as U.S. citizens. But Haitians usually entered on short-term tourist visas and then failed to return to Haiti, so they were undocumented immigrants whom the Immigration and Naturalization Service (INS) chose not to pursue in recognition of their quasi-refugee status. When Haitian outflows increased following the 1971 rise to power of the repressive Jean-Claude "Baby Doc" Duvalier regime, however, the visibility of the flows forced the INS to act, and it began excluding would-be Haitian migrants. Thirty thousand Haitians applied for political asylum in the first years of Duvalier's rule, and less than fifty were granted asylum status. Congressional hearings held by the Senate Immigration Subcommittee in 1975–76 concluded that the State Department had played an inappropriate role by preventing fair asylum hearings so as to avoid embarrassing the Duvalier regime. Nonetheless, discrimination against Haitians continued and was institutionalized in 1978 through the INS's "Haitian Program," which expressed unconditional support for the Duvalier government by prejudging Haitian asylum claims as unfounded.

Although the Haitian Program was ruled illegal (and the inappropriate foreign policy rationale exposed) by the U.S. Fifth Circuit Court in *Haitian Refugee Center v. Civiletti* (614 F.2d 92), discrimination against Haitian migrants (in favor of the Duvalier regime) and in favor of Cuban migrants (against the government of Cuban president Fidel Castro) accelerated in 1980–81 when 125,000 Cubans and 20,000 Haitians made their way by boat to Florida. Many of the Cubans who came as part of the so-called Mariel Boatlift (named for the harbor from which they departed) admitted coming for economic reasons, and most Haitians described human rights abuses they sought to escape. Yet the former were granted refugee status, and the latter were not. Finally, in response to massive protests by Haitians in the United States, President Carter partially reversed the policy by creating a temporary "Cuban-Haitian entrant" status that legalized some Haitian migrants. In the wake of these massive flows in the early 1980s, domestic demands for immigration control have often overwhelmed foreign policy concerns in the Caribbean: a 1981 treaty with Haiti enlists Haiti's assistance for immigration control in exchange for increased financial aid; a 1984 agreement with Cuba briefly normalized flows from that country, and a similar deal in 1995 reinstated normal flows in exchange for Cuba's promise to prevent refugee flows to the United States; and President George Bush's so-called Kennebunkport Order mandated that Haitians be interdicted at sea and immediately returned to Haiti. It was only following the return to power of the United States–supported Haitian president Jean-Bertrand Aristide that President Bill Clinton reversed this policy and, in a concession to international human rights concerns, began screening Haitians asking for asylum and placing them in third-country safe havens.

U.S. RELATIONS WITH MEXICO AND CENTRAL AMERICA

In the wake of the Indo-Chinese "boat people" of the mid-1970s and the Mariel and Haitian boatlifts of 1980–81, the threat that civil wars in Central America would cause massive refugee flows prompted President Ronald Reagan in 1982 to warn of a possible invasion of "feet people" from Central America. Reagan's appeal for increased military and economic aid to Central America linked immigration and foreign policy by citing the desire to influence immigration as a rationale for implementing certain foreign policy goals. Similarly, in 1983, the Reagan administration cited the need to reduce migration "push factors" as a primary motivation for supporting the Caribbean Basin Initiative trade agreement, and the Bush and Clinton administrations similarly noted a reduction in immigration as one of the main benefits to follow from Mexico's inclusion in the North American Free Trade Agreement, signed in 1992. The foreign policy politicization of immigra-

tion issues was also reflected in the so-called sanctuary movement, in which opponents of U.S. policy in Central America expressed their opposition by providing housing and support to undocumented Central American immigrants who were denied refugee status for political reasons.

While domestic immigration concerns influenced the making of U.S. foreign policy during the 1980s, however, the large-scale influx of undocumented immigrants in the 1970s and 1980s guaranteed that the domestic salience of immigration was high in the 1980s; foreign policy, therefore, was not decisive in shaping immigration policymaking. On the contrary, migrant-sending states were usually unsuccessful in their attempts to influence U.S. policymakers at this time. In particular, although Mexico was strongly opposed to the unilateral U.S. attempt to reduce undocumented immigration from Mexico and Central America in the 1980s (the issue received extensive attention by Mexico's legislature in the first years of the decade), Mexico refused an invitation to testify at congressional hearings prior to the passage of the 1986 Immigration Reform and Control Act (IRCA). Mexico understood that the United States was unwilling to take account of Mexico's concern; Mexico also believed that participation would give undue credibility to the proceedings. Following passage of the act, which increased border enforcement and made it illegal for U.S. employers to hire undocumented immigrants, Mexico and Central American countries that were home to many of the undocumented feared mass deportations. Mexico responded in the following years by expanding its United States–based lobbying efforts and by encouraging Mexican Americans to become more involved in U.S. politics. The five migrant-sending states of Central America (El Salvador, Guatemala, Honduras, Nicaragua, and Panama) issued a joint declaration in May 1987 opposing IRCA enforcement. United States ally El Salvador was most aggressive in seeking immigration relief; its president, José Napoleón Duarte, appealed unsuccessfully to President Reagan and to the U.S. Senate in April 1987 for the granting of extended voluntary departure status for El Salvadorans, which would have exempted them from deportation. A year later, the Congress responded to additional El Salvadoran appeals by granting temporary protected status to some El Salvadoran immigrants.

In the 1990s, the tension between domestic and international sources of immigration has again been high; domestic demands for immigration control—climaxing with the increased border enforcement through Operation Gatekeeper and related programs and with the passage of the 1996 Illegal Immigration

Reform and Immigrant Responsibility Act (IIRIRA)—have clashed with President Clinton's strong foreign policy interest in regional integration and cooperation. While electoral politics and high domestic political controversy prevented the Clinton administration from opposing the harshly restrictionist IIRIRA, the administration has responded in various ways to mitigate the damage to U.S. regional relationships. First, with respect to Mexico, the Clinton administration has invested unprecedented resources in the U.S.-Mexican Binational Commission, especially in its Working Group on Immigration and Consular Affairs. The commission has responded to the escalation of border enforcement by devising a number of locally based institutions that have encouraged cooperation between U.S. immigration enforcement officials and Mexican consuls and citizens. Second, with respect to Central America, the Clinton administration helped pass in 1997 the Nicaraguan Adjustment and Central American Relief Act (NACARA) to reverse the most discriminatory aspects of the IIRIRA by effectively granting amnesty to a large number of Central Americans whose refugee status had been in limbo since the 1980s. Although the bill originally introduced by Clinton was amended by congressional conservatives to reinforce the old Cold War patterns that Clinton had sought to avoid, the president expanded the scope of the NACARA during its implementation and through later legislation, and in so doing, he satisfied most Central American demands for immigration relief.

Marc Rosenblum

See also: Political, Ethnic, Religious, and Gender Persecution (Part II, Sec. 1); Anti-Immigrant Politics, Immigrant Politics I: Activism, Immigrant Politics II: Electoral Politics, Immigrant Politics III: The Home Country, Public Opinion and Immigration (Part II, Sec. 6); U.S. Report Under the International Covenant on Civil and Political Rights, 1994 (Part IV, Sec. 2).

BIBILOGRAPHY

Craig, Richard. *The Bracero Program: Interest Groups and Foreign Policy.* Austin: University of Texas Press, 1971.

Green, Rosario, and Peter H. Smith, eds. *Foreign Policy in US-Mexican Relations.* La Jolla: University of California at San Diego Center for US-Mexican Studies, 1989.

Joppke, Christian, ed. *Challenge to the Nation-State: Immigration in Western Europe and the United States.* New York: Oxford University Press, 1998.

Kritz, Mary, ed. *U.S. Immigration and Refugee Policy: Global and Domestic Issues.* Lexington, MA: D.C. Heath, 1983.

Loescher, Gil, and John Scanlan. *Calculated Kindness: Refugees and America's Half-Open Door, 1945 to the Present.* New York: Free Press, 1986.

Mitchell, Christian, ed. *Western Hemisphere Immigration and United States Foreign Policy.* College Park: Pennsylvania State University Press, 1992.

Morris, Milton. *Immigration—the Beleaguered Bureaucracy.* Washington, DC: Brookings Institution, 1985.

Pastor, Robert. "U.S. Immigration Policy and Latin America: In Search of the 'Special Relationship.'" *Latin American Research Review* 19 (1984): 35–56.

President's Commission on Immigration and Naturalization. *Whom We Shall Welcome.* Washington, DC: Government Printing Office, 1953.

Rosenblum, Marc. "Abroad and at Home: The Foreign and Domestic Sources of U.S. Migration Policy." Ph.D. diss., University of California, San Diego, 2000.

Teitelbaum, Michael S., and Myron Weiner, eds. *Threatened Peoples, Threatened Borders: World Migration and U.S. Policy.* New York: W. W. Norton, 1995.

Tucker, Robert W., Charles B. Keely, and Linda Wrigley, eds. *Immigration and U.S. Foreign Policy.* Boulder, CO: Westview Press, 1990.

Vernez, Georges, ed. *Immigration and International Relations: Proceedings of a Conference on the International Effects of the 1986 Immigration Reform and Control Act (IRCA).* Washington, DC: Urban Institute, 1989.

IMMIGRATION TO AUSTRALIA

Since its settlement by Britain in 1788, immigration has played a vital role in Australian national development. By 2000, one-quarter of the population of nearly 20 million people were born overseas while some 40 percent were either immigrants or the children of immigrants. With the exception of Israel, this proportion of immigrants is far greater than in other traditional countries of immigration such as Canada (17.4 percent) or the United States (9.7 percent).

Australia's distance from Europe ensured that the government has always played the major role in the promotion and management of Australian immigration. For the first half of the nineteenth century, convict transportation supplemented a range of British government initiatives, including travel assistance and offers of land, to attract settlers to the British colonies. With the end of transportation, pastoralists explored the possibilities of importing labor from Asian countries. Before extensive recruitment occurred, the discovery of gold in 1851 attracted fortune hunters from the Americas, Europe, and China. The Chinese miners encountered the same hostility in Australia as they had experienced in North America. Also similar was the construction of the "Great White Walls" of anti-Chinese and Asian legislation enacted to protect European miners and workers from competition. The desire to control immigration, and especially Asian immigration, was one of the major factors spurring the six former British colonies to federate as the independent Commonwealth of Australia in 1901. Until the 1970s, the twin objectives of successive Australian governments remained the attraction of desirable groups of immigration (especially those with a British background) and the exclusion of Asians and other non-Europeans. However, exclusion was never complete, as the White Australia Policy allowed temporary entry to certain categories of migrants, including workers for the pearling industry, Chinese restaurants, and trading companies. Economic recession and war slowed immigration in the 1930s and 1940s. By 1947, Australia's population of 7.6 million included a historical low of only 9.8 percent of immigrants, most of them from the United Kingdom and Ireland.

MASS IMMIGRATION AND THE GROWTH OF DIVERSITY

The need to increase the population became an important priority for future security and for the restructuring and growth of the economy toward industrial self-reliance. Mass migration to increase the population by 1 percent per year was the ambitious strategy adopted to achieve these objectives. In announcing the program, the minister for immigration, Arthur Calwell, assured the population that priority would be given to ensuring that the British roots of the population would not be diminished.

The task of attracting such large numbers of British immigrants was unrealistic and, from the earliest years of the postwar immigration program, the government made bilateral agreements with other governments and international organizations to meet the target of a hundred thousand immigrants per year. Among the first arrivals were refugees from Eastern Europe, followed by settlers from Germany and the Netherlands, then by immigrants recruited from Italy, Greece, and Yugoslavia and, finally, in the late 1960s, settlers from Turkey and Lebanon. During this period there was a gradual relaxation of the White Australia Policy to allow entry for the spouses of Australian citizens, those of part-European background, and highly skilled non-Europeans. The White Australia Policy was finally abandoned in 1973 when the incoming Australian Labor Party government announced its replacement by a nondiscriminatory immigration selection program similar to Canada's.

At the same time the preferential treatment for British immigrants was removed, with all foreign-

Long a destination for British and European immigrants, Australia is increasingly finding itself home to many Asian immigrants, like this family at a Sydney fast-food restaurant. *(Associated Press)*

born individuals required to wait two years before becoming eligible for Australian citizenship. Driving these changes was the Australian government's desire to establish good relations with newly independent countries nearby in Asia. The first large group of Asian immigrants came from Vietnam following the end of the Vietnam War. By the mid-1980s, growing numbers of immigrants were arriving from Malaysia, Hong Kong, and the Philippines. By the end of the 1990s, there was also a growing number of migrants from India and the rest of the Asian subcontinent. In 1968–69, 45.7 percent of all immigrants had arrived from the United Kingdom and Ireland, and the only major Asian source country was India (the 2 percent of arrivals it provided were mainly of Anglo-Indian background). Thirty years later, in 1998–99, the United Kingdom was the source of only 10.4 percent of all immigrants, with another 22.2 percent from New Zealand. Major Asian source countries included China (7.3 percent), the Philippines (3.9 percent), India, Indonesia, Vietnam, and Hong Kong. In the twelve years between 1985–86 and 1997–98, 39.3 percent of the 1.3 million immigrants who arrived to settle in

Australia came from Asia, 15 percent from the United Kingdom, and 13.7 percent from the rest of Europe, with 12.1 percent from New Zealand. Among the Asian-born, 19.3 percent were from Southeast Asia, 13.4 percent from northeast Asia, and 6.6 percent from southern Asia. The major Asian birthplaces were Vietnam, Hong Kong, the Philippines, and China.

Australian immigration selection policy does not operate with quotas for specific countries. Instead, each year the government, after community consultation, announces the number of immigrants to be admitted in each of the three main entry categories: family reunion, skilled migration, and refugee/humanitarian. The only group of immigrants who do not require entry visas and are not subject to these selection criteria are New Zealanders, who can enter Australia without any restrictions as part of the close integration that exists between the two countries. In addition to making annual adjustments to the total numbers of immigrants to be admitted, the government also decides the numbers for each entry category. The family-reunion and skilled-entry categories have always been much larger than the refugee and humanitarian program, which has allowed entry for some twelve thousand persons over many years. Family-reunion immigration has always been important, but the recruitment of skilled immigrants became increasingly important in the 1980s as part of a government policy to restructure the Australian economy to meet the challenges of globalization and international economic developments by developing the service sector and the knowledge-based areas of the economy. In contrast to family-reunion entrants, knowledge of English is an important criterion for entry in the skilled migration categories. In 1998–99, almost two-thirds of immigrants who had been employed prior to migration were in skilled occupations, with almost one-third having worked in the professions.

The increasing diversity in the birthplaces of the immigrants has been associated with growing linguistic and religious diversity. In 1996, although the United Kingdom (6.0 percent) and New Zealand (1.6 percent) were still the two most important foreign birthplaces, they were followed by Italy (1.3 percent), Vietnam (0.8 percent), Greece (0.7 percent), China (0.6 percent), and Germany (0.6 percent). By 1996, 18.8 percent of the population spoke a language other than English in the home. Italian (2.2 percent) was the most common language, closely followed by various Chinese languages, which accounted for 2 percent of all language speakers. Then came Greek (1.6 percent) and Arabic (1.0 percent). In Sydney, which has displaced Melbourne as the major destination for immigrants, the two major languages spoken after English are Chinese and Arabic. In contrast, in Melbourne, which was the major destination until the 1980s, Italian and Greek remain the major languages. In the 1980s, with increased immigration from continental Europe, Catholics had displaced Anglicans as the largest religious group. The more recent growth in non-European immigration has been associated with growth in non-Christian religions. Muslims are now 1.1 percent of the population, as are Buddhists. Hindus, with 0.4 percent of the population, are the fastest-growing religious group.

SETTLEMENT POLICIES AND INCORPORATION

By comparison with the United States, Australian governments have played a far more active and interventionist role in immigration and social policy. The preference for British immigrants was associated with a long-standing emphasis on assimilation as the socially and politically required mode of incorporation. Successful assimilation, it was believed, would prevent the development of social conflict. Immigrants were expected to speak English and adopt Australian customs and practices soon after arrival. Such a policy was accompanied by what Jean Martin has referred to as a "policy of denial," since the assumption that assimilation inevitably would occur freed governments from instituting special programs or policies to assist settlers or members of ethnic minorities. By the late 1960s, the failure of assimilation to take place as quickly as expected encouraged academics, professionals working in education, health, and social services, and members of ethnic minority groups to campaign for greater assistance for immigrants to overcome their social disadvantage. The government therefore announced that a policy of integration was to replace the official policy of assimilation. Although never fully articulated, the main characteristic of integration policy was that while individuals were still expected to accommodate to Australian institutions in the public sphere, it was accepted that in private they could retain their traditional customs and culture. The partial acceptance of diversity involved in the policy was unsatisfactory and did little to overcome the difficulties encountered in schools, hospitals, and the workplace. Moves to adopt a more radical approach to immigrant incorporation began soon after the election of the Whitlam Labor government in 1972, with a strong commitment to social reform to overcome social disadvantage. The minister for immigration, Al Grasby, began to speak about the need for change that would reflect the multicultural nature of Australian society at the same time that changes began to be made in school curricula and translation services began to be provided. The 1978 Galbally Report, adopted by the conservative Liberal National Party government of Prime Minister Malcolm Fraser, was a major turning point in the institutionalization of multiculturalism as official government policy. For the first time funds were given to ethnic community organizations so that they could provide a range of welfare and educational services for members of their communities in what was considered to be a culturally appropriate manner. The importance of cultural, and particularly linguistic, dimensions of ethnic minority status were made explicit in the term "non-English-speaking background" (NESB), which was adopted to describe the ethnic minorities targeted for assistance in a variety of special government programs.

Australia shares with Canada the distinction of having a policy of multiculturalism as the official ba-

Table 1
Australian Settler Arrivals by Region and Selected Birthplaces, 1985–86 to 1997–98

Birthplace	1985/86	1985/86 %	1986/87	1986/87 %	1987/88	1987/88 %
Oceania	15,610	16.9	16,564	14.6	25,564	17.8
New Zealand	13,191	14.3	13,561	12.0	20,910	14.6
Bosnia-Herzogovina		0.0		0.0		0.0
Croatia		0.0		0.0		0.0
Europe & the former Soviet Union	28,020	30.3	36,434	32.2	43,566	30.4
United Kingdom	14,671	15.9	20,177	17.8	24,591	17.1
Middle East & North Africa	6,499	7.0	7,484	6.6	10,021	7.0
Southeast Asia	17,907	19.4	23,004	20.3	29,491	20.6
Brunei	62	0.1	127	0.1	343	0.2
Burma/Myanmar	148	0.2	236	0.2	298	0.2
Cambodia	866	0.9	1,366	1.2	1,224	0.9
Indonesia	1,083	1.2	1,384	1.2	1,241	0.9
Laos	521	0.6	526	0.5	703	0.5
Malaysia	2,285	2.5	3,941	3.5	6,265	4.4
Philippines	4,128	4.5	6,406	5.7	10,427	7.3
Singapore	869	0.9	1,527	1.3	2,077	1.4
Thailand	776	0.8	863	0.8	929	0.6
Vietnam	7,169	7.8	6,628	5.8	5,981	4.2
Other	521	0.6	526	0.5	3	0.0
Northeast Asia	8,190	8.9	8,926	7.9	12,679	8.8
China excl. HK & Taiwan	3,138	3.4	2,690	2.4	3,282	2.3
Hong Kong	3,117	3.4	3,398	3.0	5,577	3.9
Japan	250	0.3	390	0.3	720	0.5
Korea	1,212	1.3	1,550	1.4	1,811	1.3
Macau	91	0.1	94	0.1	142	0.1
Mongolia	1	0.0	0	0.0	1	0.0
Taiwan	381	0.4	804	0.7	1,146	0.8
Southern Asia	4,486	4.9	6,253	5.5	6,719	4.7
Afghanistan	332	0.4	518	0.5	279	0.2
Bangladesh	71	0.1	66	0.1	116	0.1
Bhutan	0	0.0	0	0.0	0	0.0
India	2,135	2.3	2,537	2.2	3,039	2.1
Maldives	0	0.0	1	0.0	0	0.0
Nepal	13	0.0	11	0.0	25	0.0
Pakistan	287	0.3	325	0.3	366	0.3
Sri Lanka	1,648	1.8	2,795	2.5	2,894	2.0
North America	2,651	2.9	2,854	2.5	3,069	2.1
S & Central Amer & Caribbean	4,068	4.4	4,268	3.8	4,630	3.2
Africa excl. North Africa	4,977	5.4	7,517	6.6	7,635	5.3
South Africa	3,132	3.4	4,669	4.1	3,792	2.6
Not Stated	2	0.0	5	0.0	26	0.0
Total All Countries	92,410	100.0	113,309	100.0	143,490	100.0

(continued)

Table 1
Australian Settler Arrivals by Region and Selected Birthplaces, 1985–86 to 1997–98 *(continued)*

1988/89	1988/89 %	1989/90	1989/90 %	1990/91	1990/91 %	1991/92	1991/92 %
27,998	19.3	15,270	12.6	10,970	9.0	10,362	9.6
23,539	16.2	11,178	9.2	7,467	6.1	7,242	6.7
	0.0		0.0	NA	NA	NA	NA
	0.0		0.0	NA	NA	NA	NA
42,438	29.2	38,386	31.7	32,333	26.6	26,870	25.0
23,933	16.5	23,521	19.4	20,746	17.0	14,465	13.5
8,044	5.5	5,754	4.7	7,154	5.9	7,021	6.5
31,702	21.8	28,201	23.3	29,417	24.2	22,325	20.8
333	0.2	109	0.1	88	0.1	98	0.1
220	0.2	148	0.1	116	0.1	162	0.2
1,480	1.0	309	0.3	193	0.2	322	0.3
1,422	1.0	1,252	1.0	1,071	0.9	1,145	1.1
426	0.3	280	0.2	349	0.3	236	0.2
7,681	5.3	6,417	5.3	5,744	4.7	3,123	2.9
9,204	6.3	6,080	5.0	6,388	5.2	5,917	5.5
1,946	1.3	1,567	1.3	1,275	1.0	867	0.8
1,017	0.7	889	0.7	945	0.8	863	0.8
7,971	5.5	11,156	9.2	13,248	10.9	9,592	8.9
2	0.0	1	0.0	0	0.0	0	0.0
15,874	10.9	16,395	13.5	22,100	18.2	21,473	20.0
3,819	2.6	3,069	2.5	3,256	2.7	3,388	3.2
7,307	5.0	8,054	6.6	13,541	11.1	12,913	12.0
806	0.6	634	0.5	574	0.5	536	0.5
1,666	1.1	1,378	1.1	982	0.8	1,224	1.1
176	0.1	205	0.2	256	0.2	240	0.2
0	0.0	0	0.0	00.0	0	0.0	0
2,100	1.4	3,055	2.5	3,491	2.9	3,172	3.0
7,025	4.8	6,011	5.0	9,389	7.7	10,594	9.9
338	0.2	239	0.2	324	0.3	949	0.9
219	0.2	167	0.1	358	0.3	605	0.6
1	0.0	0	0.0	0	0.0	0	0.0
3,109	2.1	3,016	2.5	5,081	4.2	5,608	5.2
1	0.0	1	0.0	10.0	0	0.0	0
35	0.0	32	0.0	54	0.0	54	0.1
385	0.3	311	0.3	300	0.2	601	0.6
2,937	2.0	2,245	1.9	3,271	2.7	2,777	2.6
3,068	2.1	3,015	2.5	2,811	2.3	2,570	2.4
4,322	3.0	4,125	3.4	3,745	3.1	3,308	3.1
4,830	3.3	4,061	3.3	3,728	3.1	2,823	2.6
3,024	2.1	2,424	2.0	2,084	1.7	1,274	1.2
14	0.0	9	0.0	41	0.0	45	0.0
145,315	100.0	121,227	100.0	121,688	100.0	107,391	100.0

Birthplace	1992/93	1992/93 %	1993/94	1993/94 %	1994/95	1994/95 %	1995/96	1995/96 %
Oceania	9,517	12.5	10,196	14.6	13,592	15.5	16,225	16.4
New Zealand	6,694	8.8	7,772	11.1	10,498	12.0	12,265	12.4
Bosnia-Herzogovina	NA	NA	NA	NA	NA	NA	3,405	3.4
Croatia	NA	NA	NA	NA	NA	NA	710	0.7
Europe & the former Soviet Union	22,200	29.1	20,473	29.3	25,523	29.2	26,463	26.7
United Kingdom	9,484	12.4	8,963	12.8	10,689	12.2	11,268	11.4
Middle East & North Africa	5,417	7.1	4,826	6.9	7,146	8.2	7,608	7.7
Southeast Asia	13,853	18.1	14,239	20.4	14,861	17.0	13,147	13.3
Brunei	51	0.1	38	0.1	38	0.0	29	0.0
Burma/Myanmar	116	0.2	489	0.7	598	0.7	448	0.5
Cambodia	343	0.4	927	1.3	1,356	1.6	1,357	1.4
Indonesia	1,184	1.6	622	0.9	1,013	1.2	1,793	1.8
Laos	63	0.1	61	0.1	87	0.1	63	0.1
Malaysia	1,555	2.0	1,252	1.8	1,107	1.3	1,081	1.1
Philippines	3,731	4.9	4,179	6.0	4,116	4.7	3,232	3.3
Singapore	472	0.6	502	0.7	650	0.7	841	0.8
Thailand	686	0.9	735	1.1	799	0.9	736	0.7
Vietnam	5,651	7.4	5,434	7.8	5,097	5.8	3,567	3.6
Other	1	0.0	0	0.0	0	0.0	0	0.0
Northeast Asia	12,504	16.4	8,045	11.5	9,899	11.3	18,668	18.8
China excl. HK & Taiwan	3,046	4.0	2,740	3.9	3,708	4.2	11,247	11.3
Hong Kong	6,520	8.5	3,333	4.8	4,135	4.7	4,361	4.4
Japan	435	0.6	409	0.6	527	0.6	593	0.6
Korea	929	1.2	673	1.0	666	0.8	704	0.7
Macau	140	0.2	105	0.2	68	0.1	124	0.1
Mongolia	0.0	0	0.0	1	0.0	1	0.0	1
Taiwan	1,434	1.9	785	1.1	794	0.9	1,638	1.7
Southern Asia	6,632	8.7	5,482	7.9	7,616	8.7	7,709	7.8
Afghanistan	764	1.0	660	0.9	392	0.4	636	0.6
Bangladesh	344	0.5	300	0.4	709	0.8	759	0.8
Bhutan	0	0.0	1	0.0	0	0.0	0	0.0
India	3,553	4.7	2,643	3.8	3,908	4.5	3,700	3.7
Maldives	0.0	0	0.0	2	0.0	0	0.0	2
Nepal	47	0.1	32	0.0	54	0.1	60	0.1
Pakistan	346	0.5	415	0.6	598	0.7	603	0.6
Sri Lanka	1,578	2.1	1,431	2.1	1,953	2.2	1,951	2.0
North America	2,021	2.6	2,002	2.9	2,576	2.9	2,499	2.5
S & Central Amer & Caribbean	1,557	2.0	1,153	1.7	1,329	1.5	1,324	1.3
Africa excl. North Africa	2,570	3.4	3,249	4.7	4,857	5.6	5,444	5.5
South Africa	1,021	1.3	1,654	2.4	2,792	3.2	3,190	3.2
Not Stated	59	0.1	103	0.1	29	0.0	52	0.1
Total All Countries	76,330	100.0	69,768	100.0	87,428	100.0	99,139	100.0

(continued)

Table 1
Australian Settler Arrivals by Region and Selected Birthplaces, 1985–86 to 1997–98 (continued)

1996/97	1996/97 %	1997/98	1997/98 %	1985/86–1997/98 % Total Arrivals	1985/86–1997/98 Total Arrivals
16,761	19.5	17,792	23.0	15.4	20,6421
13,072	15.2	14,723	19.0	12.1	162,112
2,059	2.4	2,135	2.8	NA	NA
667	0.8	1,024	1.3	NA	NA
22,167	25.9	19,501	25.2	28.7	384,374
9,674	11.3	9,193	11.9	15.0	201,375
6,225	7.3	5,790	7.5	6.6	88,989
11,357	13.2	9,700	12.5	19.3	259,204
44	0.1	270.0	0.1	1,387	
394	0.5	170	0.2	0.3	3,543
800	0.9	505	0.7	0.8	11,048
1,750	2.0	1,917	2.5	1.3	16,877
43	0.1	30	0.0	0.3	3,388
1,056	1.2	931	1.2	3.2	42,438
2,808	3.3	2,769	3.6	5.2	69,385
925	1.1	694	0.9	1.1	14,212
571	0.7	346	0.4	0.8	10,155
2,966	3.5	2,311	3.0	6.5	86,771
0	0.0	0	0.0	0.1	1,054
15,125	17.6	10,214	13.2	13.4	180,092
7,761	9.1	4,338	5.6	4.1	55,482
3,894	4.5	3,194	4.1	5.9	79,344
485	0.6	508	0.7	0.5	6,867
707	0.8	596	0.8	1.1	14,098
97	0.1	970.1	0.1	1,835	
0.0	30.0	0.0	8		
2,180	2.5	1,518	2.0	1.7	22,498
5,602	6.5	5,333	6.9	6.6	88,851
350	0.4	524	0.7	0.5	6,305
481	0.6	282	0.4	0.3	4,477
0	0.0	80.0	0.0	10	
2,681	3.1	2,786	3.6	3.3	43,796
0.0	10.0	0.0	9		
50	0.1	360.0	0.0	503	
623	0.7	435	0.6	0.4	5,595
1,415	1.7	1,261	1.6	2.1	28,156
2,417	2.8	2,049	2.6	2.5	33,602
1,040	1.2	667	0.9	2.7	35,536
5,014	5.8	6,256	8.1	4.7	62,961
3,211	3.7	4,281	5.5	2.7	36,548
44	0.1	25	0.0	0.0	454
85,752	100.0	77,327	100.0	100.0	1,340,574

Source: DIMA 1998 Settler Arrivals 1997–98, DIMA 1997 Settler Arrivals 1995–96.

sis for incorporating ethnic minority groups. This policy has evolved over three decades in response to changes in Australian society. Since the early 1970s, when the initial focus was on overcoming social disadvantage, there have been shifts in the extent to which policy has emphasized social disadvantage and cultural maintenance. The shifts reflect the preferences of the political leadership as well as the changing nature of Australian society. Under the conservative Fraser government (1975–83), the emphasis shifted toward cultural maintenance and included the introduction of a large number of school-based community-language programs as well as the setting up of the government's Special Broadcasting Service, which broadcasts radio and television programs in a wide range of languages. The election of the Hawke Labor government in 1983 in the midst of a major recession saw a reemphasis on policies to ensure social equity, especially in terms of access to a wide range of government services. The 1989 National Agenda for a Multicultural Australia, a report to the Australian Parliament, distilled the major developments and direction of government multicultural policies. It made clear that multiculturalism was to be a policy for *all* Australians, including the indigenous Aboriginal population and those of English-speaking backgrounds as well as the "migrant" or NESB population. The agenda identified three dimensions of rights: cultural identity, which was the right to express and share cultural heritage; social justice, which was the right to equality of treatment and opportunity; and economic efficiency. This last, innovative element in the policy was a key element in legitimizing the policy, inasmuch as it promoted that policy as being of benefit to all Australians and emphasized the need to "maintain, develop and utilize effectively the skills and talents of all Australians." It signaled a major thrust of government policy during the 1990s: that the cultural resources of immigrants constituted a major economic resource for Australia in the new globalized economy. Especially with the economic growth of the Asian countries that were Australia's major trading partners, immigrants from those countries were seen as a valuable asset in the development of Australia's international trade. Immigrants were now no longer viewed simply as a source of labor; they were also being depicted as important sources of human capital, derived from their technical and cultural knowledge. A further emphasis in the national agenda, which was designed to allay concerns among Anglo-Celtic Australians about the potential for the development of divisiveness, was that it also defined the limits of multiculturalism. These included the premise that all Australians should have a commitment to Australia, and that there should be an acceptance of the basic institutional structures, including the constitution and rule of law, tolerance and equality, freedom of speech and religion, English as the national language, and equality of the sexes. Also emphasized was that the right to freedom of expression included the obligation to recognize others' similar right.

CRITICS OF IMMIGRATION AND MULTICULTURAL POLICIES

Government commitment to multicultural policy has always attracted criticism from sections of the population concerned about perceived threats to the Australian way of life and the costs of government policies directed to specific sections of the population. These criticisms are also closely linked to critiques of immigration policy. Until the 1980s, there was bipartisan political support for immigration as a valuable contribution to Australian society, but in the face of often vocal popular opposition to immigration, this unanimity was lost. In the 1970s, environmental groups began to complain that immigration's contribution to population growth was a threat to Australia's fragile physical environment. In 1984, a growth in immigration, especially from Asia, at a time of high unemployment was the background for what became known as the Asian immigration debate. This debate, which recalled nineteenth-century hostility to Asian immigrants, was condemned by political party leaders. A short-lived return to this anti-Asian-immigrant theme occurred in public debate in the late 1980s when it was supported by John Howard, whose conservative Liberal National Party government gained power in 1996, when Howard became prime minister. Although neither multiculturalism nor immigration was a major factor in his electoral success, Howard's well-known opposition to multiculturalism was soon evidenced in the closure of the Office of Multicultural Affairs and the Bureau of Immigration, Multiculturalism, and Population Research. While the previous Labor government, under Prime Minister Paul Keating, had also pursued policies to reduce welfare spending, these increased under the Howard government. Howard's commitment to conservative economic and social policies also ensured that benefits that previously had been available to all permanent residents were now restricted to those resident in Australia for two years, the minimum period of time to qualify for Australian citizenship. Funding was also cut to ethnic organizations and community groups.

Also elected in the 1996 federal elections was an independent, Pauline Hanson, who pursued an aggressively populist policy which included hostility to spending on Aboriginal and multicultural programs. The Hanson debate, as it was called, lasted from 1996 to 1999, a period during which the One Nation Party she founded gained significant electoral support from country voters in the Queensland and New South Wales state elections. Subsequently, internal party fighting led to its demise as a political force. Significantly, the prime minister, John Howard, was extremely reluctant to take a stand against the racist statements of Hanson and the One Nation Party, a position that confirmed observers' perception that he was in sympathy with many of her views. Despite his reluctance to criticize Hanson, in 1999 he was persuaded to launch the latest report from the government's National Multicultural Advisory Council. While this report still operates within the basic framework of the 1989 National Agenda, its title, *Australian Multiculturalism for a New Century: Towards Inclusiveness,* indicates a renewed focus on the need to overcome vocal, albeit minority, hostility to multiculturalism. Despite the official launch of the report, its various recommendations have been largely ignored by a government whose commitment to multiculturalism remains questioned.

THE FUTURE OF IMMIGRATION

While active government commitment to multiculturalism has waned, the size of the immigration intake is increasing as the Australian economic recovery continues in spite of the Asian economic crisis. The government also has relaxed restrictions on temporary entry for businesspeople and skilled workers, so long-term temporary entrants now outnumber those admitted as permanent immigrants. In the early 1980s, the economic disparity between immigrants and native-born in Australia was already less than in the United States or Canada. The economic recovery of the late 1990s and the decline in unemployment to less than 7 percent has reduced the economic disparity that had increased during the early 1990s between NESB immigrants and others. Nevertheless, considerable differences remain in the economic experiences

of immigrants, with those who arrive as refugees experiencing the greatest difficulty reestablishing themselves economically. Despite such disparity and the lingering racist hostility to immigrants, there is little evidence that the hitherto remarkably conflict-free and nonviolent diversification of the Australian population that began after World War II will change in the foreseeable future.

Christine Inglis

See also: China, Oceania, Philippines, Southeast Asia, Taiwan and Hong Kong (Part III, Sec. 3); Great Britain, Ireland, Western and Southern Europe (Part III, Sec. 4).

BIBLIOGRAPHY

Castles, S. "Australian Multiculturalism: Social Policy and Identity in a Changing Society." In *Nations of Immigrants: Australia, the United States and International Migration,* ed. G. Freeman and J. Jupp. Melbourne: Oxford University Press, 1992.

Department of Immigration and Multicultural Affairs. *Population Flows: Immigration Aspects.* Canberra, 1999.

———. *Settler Arrivals, 1998–99.* Canberra, 1999.

Galbally, F. *Review of Post-Arrival Programmes and Services for Migrants.* Canberra: Australian Government Publishing Service, 1978.

Inglis, C. "Asians and Race Relations in Australia." In *The State of Asian Pacific America: Transforming Race Relations: A Public Policy Document,* ed. P. Ong. Los Angeles: LEAP Asian Pacific American Public Policy Institute and UCLA Asian American Studies Center, 2000.

Jones, F. L. "The Sources and Limits of Popular Support for a Multicultural Australia." In *The Future of Australian Multiculturalism* ed. G. Hage and R. Couch, pp. 21–30. Sydney: Research Institute for Humanities and Social Sciences.

Jupp, J. *Immigration.* Melbourne: Oxford University Press, 1998.

Martin, J. *The Migrant Presence.* Sydney: Allen and Unwin, 1978.

National Multicultural Advisory Council. *Australian Multiculturalism for a New Century: Towards Inclusiveness.* Canberra, 1999.

Office of Multicultural Affairs. *National Agenda for a Multicultural Australia.* Canberra: Australian Government Publishing Service, 1989.

Price, C. *The Great White Walls Are Built.* Canberra: Australian National University Press, 1974.

Reitz, J. *Warmth of the Welcome: The Social Causes of Economic Success for Immigrants in Different Nations and Cities.* Boulder, CO: Westview Press, 1997.

IMMIGRATION TO CANADA

Like the United States, Canada's immigration policy embodies a similar progression from exclusionary policies favoring people of northern European origins toward more liberal policies that opened the door to people of diverse origins. Enacted in the 1960s in both cases, these new policies had profound effects on the population structures of both Canada and the United States in terms of the diversity of immigrants as measured in cultural, linguistic, and religious terms. At the turn of the millennium, large proportions of immigrants in both countries are now from either Asia or Latin America.

Although the experiences of Canada and the United States with respect to immigration are similar, there are subtle yet important differences between the two. Immigration has been important in the evolution of Canadian society and the economy, helping it move from a resource-based to an industrial economy via the importation of immigrants who settled and farmed the western provinces. Later immigrants held skills that were in short supply in the domestic labor force. Since World War II, immigration policies have been designed to promote economic development and demographic stability over fears associated with an aging population and its economic consequences. While politicians and academics alike debate the success, logic, and coherence of immigration policies, Canada has attempted to create a more specific agenda that focuses on economic growth, while U.S. policy has fluctuated among humanitarian, economic, and social agendas.

IMMIGRATION HISTORY

First explored and settled by the French in the sixteenth and seventeenth centuries and bolstered by the arrival of United Empire Loyalists—American colonists loyal to Great Britain—during and immediately after the American Revolution, Canada became an independent confederation in 1867. The nation's initial population growth was slow and unsteady. Immigrants came from England, Ireland, and Scotland, but not until the early years of the twentieth century did immigration to Canada experience a sustained increase. Roderic Beaujot, a population geographer at the University of Western Ontario, describes four periods of immigration to Canada: 1861–1895, 1896–1913, 1914–1945, and 1946 to the present. The first decades following confederation in 1867 saw a net emigration from Canada, with more people leaving the country than entering it. Even as the federal government actively encouraged immigration and settlement, international depression and the prospect of employment in the newly industrializing United States sparked this departure. Immigration rebounded in the period from 1896 to 1913, driven in part by policies that actively encouraged immigration, along with industrialization and the opening of the western provinces of Manitoba, Saskatchewan, and Alberta for agriculture. The years immediately preceding World War I saw the arrival of 300,000 to 400,000 immigrants per year, numbers that still represent the nation's highest annual immigration levels, with the majority of these immigrants tracing their origins to the British Isles or to central and southern Europe. The period from World War I to the end of World War II saw a decline in immigrant arrivals, as the government curtailed immigration in the face of a postwar depression and labor unrest. Much of this period again saw a net departure from the country, and annual arrivals dropped to less than 20,000 between 1933 and 1944. From 1946 to the present day marks the fourth and relatively sustained period of immigration. Peaks in the late 1950s, late 1960s, and mid-1970s corresponded to events such as the Suez crisis and the Hungarian revolt, along with periods of economic expansion within the Canadian economy.

In recent years, federal legislation has meant that

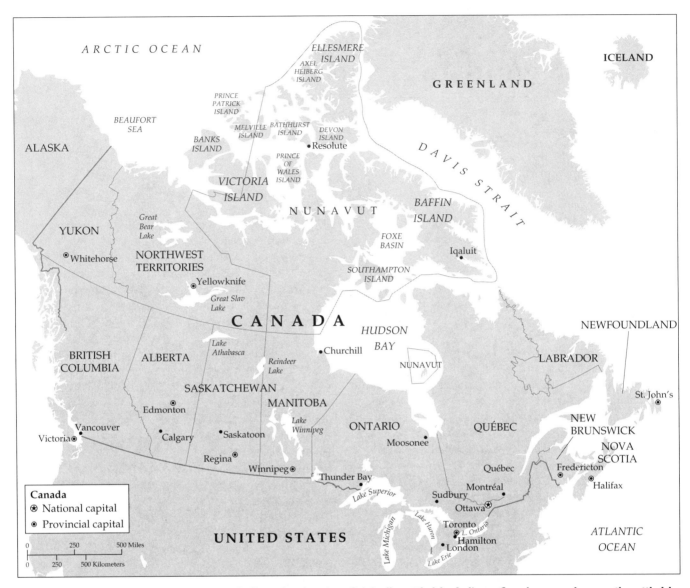

Like the United States, Canada is a nation built on immigration. Originally settled by Indians, Canada was subsequently settled by immigrants from the British Isles and France, and later from southern and eastern Europe. Today, the country is home to increasing numbers of people from Asia and the Caribbean. *(CARTO-GRAPHICS)*

the Canadian government has taken a short-term approach to managing the annual number of immigrant arrivals. Immigration can best be described as a series of ups and downs in the number of immigrants admitted to Canada on a yearly basis. Immigration levels were allowed to drop in the 1980s, reaching a low of 84,000 in 1985, but increased to 220,000 per year in the 1990s. Most recently, the government has reduced its yearly target levels to between 190,000 and 215,000 immigrants (including refugees), with the actual number of entrants echoing this trend, dropping to 174,100 in 1998 according to Citizenship and Immigration

Canada (CIC), the federal agency responsible for shaping immigration policy.

Source countries have also changed significantly since confederation. Statistics Canada, Canada's national statistical agency, notes that northern and western Europe have traditionally been the largest source of immigrants. In 1957, 95 percent of all immigrants were from Europe or the United States, with the largest single group represented by the United Kingdom. This trend was evident as recently as 1961 to 1971, when 75 percent of all immigrants came from these areas, even as revisions to immigration law in the

Like its neighbor to the south, Canada has welcomed immigrants since its inception. Many, like these East Indian women celebrating the Krishna festival in Toronto, come from other nations within the former British Empire. *(Richard Renaldi/Impact Visuals)*

1960s changed the focus of immigration. By the mid-1990s, only about one-fifth of all yearly arrivals were from Europe and the United States, compared with nearly half from Asia, with the largest origins including Hong Kong, Philippines, India, and China.

IMMIGRATION POLICY SINCE CONFEDERATION

In their book, *Twentieth Century Canada*, Jack Granatstein and his colleagues illustrate these changes, with the evolving source countries and number of immigrants corresponding largely to changes in immigration policy. As early as 1868, the Canadian government became involved in immigration through its Free Grants and Homestead Act. With the lure of free land, the act encouraged agricultural workers to emigrate to Canada and aid in the settlement of the western terri-

tories, although this agenda did not achieve success until the turn of the century. Immigration in the period immediately after confederation served two purposes. First, it was seen as a sovereignty tool, allowing the Canadian government control over its western territories and keeping them away from the orbit of American control. Second, the government of Prime Minister Wilfrid Laurier viewed immigration as a nation-building tool, laying the infrastructure for Canada's development in the twentieth century, with mining, lumber, and railway interests requiring laborers. The policies of Cliford Sifton, Minister of the Interior under Laurier, particularly encouraged the immigration of agricultural workers from countries that had not traditionally supplied Canada with immigrants, leading to immigration from Russia, Italy, and Austria-Hungary. Most of these either settled in the western provinces or went to work in the mining and timber camps in remote areas, where they were acceptable as immigrants as long as they were out of sight. Sifton's policies were so successful that Canada saw its population grow by 40 percent between 1900 and 1914, with approximately 25 percent of the Canadian population in 1914 being foreign born. Not surprisingly, it also led to concerns as to whether or not these new arrivals could be assimilated, articulated by James S. Woodsworth, a Methodist minister and politician, in his 1909 book, *Strangers within our Gates*.

While Canada encouraged European immigration, nonwhite immigration was restricted or severely limited. Deeming the Chinese unable to assimilate into Canadian society, the government passed the Chinese Immigration Act in 1885, which imposed a "head tax" on Chinese immigrants. Further restrictions in 1907 and 1908 limited immigration from Japan and India as well. Laws enacted in 1906 and 1910 placed diseased persons and those advocating violent political change on the restricted list.

The post–World War II era saw a general continuation of these immigration policies. Under the leadership of Prime Minister William Lyon Mackenzie King, the government charted a careful course between concerns over too many immigrants, the need to integrate returning soldiers, increasing immigration for domestic economic development, and assistance to Europeans displaced by the war. In particular, King's vision of immigration policy was to encourage immigration from traditional sources, so as not to alter the character of the population. Ever the consummate politician, King steered a path through the potentially unpopular policy of allowing entry to Jewish survivors of the Holocaust, along with Ukrainians, Russians, and Poles, through the auspices of family reunification. By 1953, however, with concerns over immigration again surfacing, revisions to the Immigration Act allowed the government to prohibit the entry of immigrants based on nationality, national security, and ethnicity. Preference was again given to those of British or French birth, representing Canada's two founding countries, along with those from the United States, and with a secondary preference for those from Western European countries.

It was not until 1962 that national-origin restrictions were finally lifted, followed by the establishment of a "points system" for selecting immigrants in 1967. This system became an important tool in shaping immigration to Canada in the late twentieth century. Whereas the United States has favored family reunification, the points system encourages economic immigration by outlining the education, age, training, skills, and language ability required for admission. Immigrants are evaluated on ten factors and admitted only if they score a minimum of seventy points. Multicultural policies initiated under the leadership of Prime Minister Pierre Trudeau in 1971 underlined Canada's open attitude toward the arrival of immigrants.

Although immigration policy has been revised numerous times since its most dramatic reorientation in 1962, the policies of nondiscrimination, family reunion, humanitarian assistance, and the promotion of its economic and social goals have remained at its core. Amendments to the Immigration Act in 1976 introduced yearly target levels for immigrants, determined after federal consultation with provinces and other organizations concerning demographic and labor needs along with social and cultural considerations. Other recent revisions to immigration policy include immigration agreements with the provinces. The most far-reaching of these is the Canada-Quebec Accord of 1991, which allows Quebec, Canada's largest French-speaking province, greater control over its immigrant intake. Although the federal government continues to set national standards and objectives and has control over family-class entrants and refugees, the government of Quebec has exclusive control over the selection of economic immigrants along with their linguistic and cultural integration.

ECONOMIC AND DEMOGRAPHIC ISSUES

Although attempts at crafting immigration policy have sometimes met with ambivalence and critics have argued whether Canada's immigration policy is clearly articulated, Canada has pursued the twin goals of population growth and economic development as the underlying components of its immigration policy. Since 1981, Statistics Canada has reported that the total fertility rate has been 1.6, indicating that not enough children are being born to "replace" the Canadian population. Freda Hawkins, a critic of government immigration policy, has called for increasing immigration to counter this impending population decline. Demographically, immigration has little impact on the age structure of the population, although it counters the trend toward a slowing of the growth rate of the population.

With a declining population growth rate over the past four decades and an increasing elderly population, demographic concerns have been linked with economic concerns. The economic emphasis is illustrated by the distinctions made among immigrant groups, with immigrant arrivals divided into three major classes—family, refugee, and independent classes. Representing only 29 percent of all entrants in

1998 (down from a high of approximately 45 percent in the 1980s), the family class includes spouses, dependent children, parents, and grandparents who join relatives already settled in Canada. Refugees include those who come to Canada and apply for safe haven, reflecting approximately 10 percent of all arrivals. Admitted under the points system, the independent class includes skilled workers and business immigrants and their families, as well as "investor" and "entrepreneur" immigrants. Investor immigrants are required to invest a minimum amount within Canada to generate economic growth and provide employment opportunities. Entrepreneurs must establish or buy a business within Canada sufficient to support the entrepreneur and his or her family while creating one or more jobs beyond family needs.

The government has recently reaffirmed the importance of the independent class by strengthening the economic component of immigration policy. Although family reunification remains an important component of immigration policy, the government has placed a greater emphasis on independent immigrants, with the latter class now representing over 50 percent of admittances. A new "right of landing fee" of $975 is assessed on all permanent residents age 19 and over. Federal immigration policy has also shifted, and now focuses more on language, education, work experience, and the adaptability of immigrants to a changing labor market.

In spite of the economic focus of Canadian immigration policy, the economic impacts of immigration are debatable and difficult to delineate. The findings of the Macdonald Commission of 1985 and critics such as Shirley Seward promoted immigration as a demographic and economic policy tool. Traditional viewpoints equate population growth with economic growth, while an aging population implies the need for economic adaptation and redirection of financial resources. Increased immigration levels should permit greater economies of scale, greater technological change, and a labor force better able to adapt to structural changes within an increasingly competitive environment. Despite these apparent claims, the relationship between immigration and economic growth is relatively weak, even as immigration has been regarded as a potent short-term policy tool allowing particular skill shortages to be alleviated quickly.

GEOGRAPHIC DISTRIBUTION

Immigration has important impacts on the distribution of the Canadian population. Although settlement of the western provinces benefited greatly from immigration at the turn of the century, most of the newcomers in the post–World War II era have settled in Ontario, Canada's most populous province. With its large labor markets and immigrant communities, Statistics Canada and Citizenship and Immigration Canada (CIC) documents show that Ontario typically attracts 50 percent or more of annual arrivals, followed by British Columbia (20 percent) Quebec (12 percent), and Alberta (6 percent). The four eastern provinces of Newfoundland, Nova Scotia, New Brunswick, and Prince Edward Island, and the interior prairie provinces of Saskatchewan and Manitoba, receive relatively small numbers of immigrants, reflecting their more remote locations, lack of employment opportunities, or small existing immigrant populations. Since World War II, immigrants have also shown a strong preference for urban locations, particularly Toronto, Montreal, and Vancouver, such that immigration has been referred to as a city-building process. Toronto has been the most important destination, attracting over ninety thousand immigrants annually, or approximately one-third of all new arrivals from 1995 to 1997. This concentration of immigrants in urban areas has had profound effects on the diversity and visual appearance of the urban environment, creating ethnic neighborhoods and "visible minorities" (people of non-European or non-Aboriginal descent) for the first time in Canadian history. In 1991, for example, the visible minority population made up 24 percent of metropolitan Toronto's population. These urban areas provide contact with other members of the immigrant group and assistance in terms of housing, employment, or language, reflecting kin networks that link origins and destinations.

Despite some similarities, Canadian immigration policy and experiences have diverged markedly from those of the United States. To be sure, the two countries have simultaneously engaged in restrictive immigration policy, and both countries revised their immigration policy in the 1960s to encompass a nondiscriminatory agenda. However, important differences between Canada and the United States exist, particularly with respect to their attempts and success with immigration policy. In contrast to other countries, Canada has a long history of policies and programs related to economic immigration, with newcomers continuing to play an important role in population growth. Immigration to Canada has not been without tension and racism, but major problems have been relatively infrequent, and cities have been enriched by the cultural diversity and pluralism that immigration brings.

K. Bruce Newbold

See also: American Emigration Abroad (Part II, Sec. 2); English-Speaking Caribbean, Haiti and French-Speaking Caribbean (Part III, Sec. 2); China, South Asia, Taiwan and Hong Kong (Part III, Sec. 3); Eastern Europe, Former Soviet Union; Great Britain, Ireland, Western and Southern Europe (Part III, Sec. 4).

BIBLIOGRAPHY

Beaujot, Roderic. *Population Change in Canada.* Toronto: McClelland and Stewart, 1991.

Citizenship and Immigration Canada. www.cicnet.ci.gc.ca

Granatstein, Jack L., I. M. Abella, D. J. Bercuson, R. C. Brown, and H. B Neatby. *Twentieth Century Canada.* 2d ed. Toronto: McGraw-Hill–Ryerson, 1986.

Hawkins, Freda. *Canada and Immigration: Public Policy and Public Concern.* 2d ed. Montreal and Kingston, ON: McGill–Queen's University Press, 1988.

Royal Commission on the Economic Union and Development Prospects for Canada. Report, 3 vols. Ottawa: Supply and Services, 1985.

Seward, Shirley. "Demographic Change and the Canadian Economy: An Overview." *Canadian Studies in Population,* 14:2 (1987): 279–99.

Statistics Canada. *Canada Year Book, 1997.* Ottawa: Statistics Canada, 1996.

Woodsworth, James S. *Strangers within Our Gates.* Toronto: University of Toronto Press, 1972 (originally published in 1909).

IMMIGRATION TO ISRAEL

THE JEWISH PRESENCE IN PALESTINE BEFORE THE MODERN PERIOD

Since the defeat of the Jews by the Romans in 135 C.E., the majority of Jews in the world have lived outside of what is today called Israel. The Jews of the Diaspora founded flourishing communities throughout Europe, Asia, and North Africa, but were subject to attacks and expulsion by the native populations. Despite the exile, *galut* of most, Jews maintained a small but continuous presence in Palestine throughout the centuries of Byzantine, Arab, and Ottoman rule, their numbers augmented from time to time by immigrants from other areas of the Diaspora. After the Spanish Inquisition and the forced conversions and expulsions in Portugal at the end of the fifteenth century, groups of Jews fled to Palestine, and more joined them after 1517 when the Ottomans wrested control of the area from the Egyptian Mamelukes. After the influx of Sephardic Jews (Jews from the Iberian peninsula, North Africa, and the Balkans), Jewish migration to Israel dwindled until the middle of the 1700s. Both Sephardim and Ashkenazim (Jews from northern and eastern Europe) settled in Palestine in the late 1700s and throughout the 1800s, including Hassidim, particularly religious Jews from Poland and Russia. At the end of the nineteenth century, the Ottoman government began requiring passports and visas for those trying to enter Palestine.

ZIONISM AND IMMIGRATION BEFORE WORLD WAR I

The *Yishuv*, the community of Jews in Palestine, changed greatly at the end of the nineteenth century with the aid of benefactors, such as Adolphe Crémieux and Sir Moses Montefiore, who created medical and educational institutions and expanded the Jewish quarters beyond the walls of the old city in Jerusalem. In 1862, Moses Hess published *Rome and Jerusalem*, in which he argued that Jews are not just united by religion but also constitute a distinct nation. Hess rejected the idea of assimilation into European society, insisting that Jews needed a natural homeland. This was followed in 1882 by Leo Pinsker's book, *Autoemancipation*, which called for Jewish regroupment in Israel. The belief in Zionism—the creation of a state for Jews—attracted numerous European settlers, including largely assimilated students, Orthodox Jews led by rabbis, and political revolutionaries. These immigrants came as organized groups centered around ideological motives, such as the Bilu, whose name comes from the initials of the biblical phrase, "House of Jacob, Arise and Go," and the Hovevei Zion, "lovers of Zion." While many Jews believed that they would eventually attain equal rights in Europe, others argued that continued anti-Semitism throughout the continent necessitated a Jewish homeland, and Russian Jews escaping pogroms in the early 1880s added to the size of Palestine's Jewish population. In 1880, Palestine had a Jewish population of only 30,000 people; between 1881 and 1903, 25,000 *haloutsim,* or pioneers, making their *aliya,* or ascension to Israel, founded several new villages. With many of these villages failing due to poor agricultural yields, disease, and problems with Ottoman rulers and Yishuv Jews alike, Baron Edmond de Rothschild stepped in with financial aid to keep the settlements afloat. Although some Arab Palestinians opposed the sale of land to Jews, there was little organized resistance, and large landowners continued to sell plots to Zionist organizations.

In 1896, Theodor Herzl, a Hungarian Jew, wrote *The Jewish State.* This pamphlet, which presented the case for a Jewish state, was quickly translated into several languages and published across Europe. In 1897, the first Zionist Congress met in Switzerland to discuss the

Like America, Israel is a land of immigrants from around the world, but with one important exception. In Israel, immigrants must be of the Jewish faith. *(Jeff Greenberg)*

political reality of creating a Jewish state. Many Jews rejected Zionism altogether, believing that a return to the Jewish homeland of Israel should occur only with the arrival of the Messiah. Most Russian Jews who supported the creation of Israel disliked Herzl, whom they considered too culturally assimilated. Herzl gained more enemies in 1903 when he advocated the British proposal of giving Uganda to the Zionist Congress as a haven for Jews. In 1904, after Herzl's death, the Zionist Congress rejected Great Britain's offer.

Between 1904 and 1914, 40,000 haloutsim, including many Russian socialists, constituted the Second Aliya. They launched the first *kibbutzim,* lands held and worked as a collective, and *moshavim,* communal land allotted in plots to individual families. Agriculture remained the primary economic sector, but industry became more prevalent. The building of Tel Aviv began in 1909. The rapid progress was put on hold during World War I. The Jewish population of

Palestine declined from over 80,000 to 56,000 between 1914 and 1918 due to the expulsion and harassment of Russian Jews by the Ottoman authorities, severed supply lines, closed banks, and general duress brought on by the war, as well as famine and disease after a poor harvest in 1915.

IMMIGRATION TO PALESTINE UNDER THE BRITISH MANDATE

In 1917, Lord Arthur James Balfour, the British foreign minister, wrote to Lord Lionel Walter Rothschild: "His Majesty's Government view[s] with favor the establishment in Palestine of a national home for the Jewish people, and will use their best endeavors to facilitate the achievement of this object." With the Balfour Declaration, Jews regained hope that if the Allies won, they would be granted autonomy. However, the declaration was purposely ambiguous, and when the British took control of Palestine after World War I, pressured by contradictory promises to Arabs and Jews, they were slow to move on Jewish self-rule. Nevertheless, Jewish immigrants continued to flock to Palestine: 35,000 people settled between 1915 and 1923, the majority arriving after the war. The members of the Third Aliya were even more radical and militant socialists than those of the previous aliya. Many fled Russia after the October Revolution and subsequent attacks on Jews in the Ukraine. In spite of the growth in the number of kibbutzim and progress in industry, the Jews in Palestine were plagued by economic instability, poor wages, and unemployment. Out of the 8,093 *olim,* immigrants who arrived in 1923, approximately 3,500 later left Palestine.

The new arrivals during the Fourth Aliya, from 1924 to 1929, were different from their predecessors. Many were Poles leaving behind increased taxation and anti-Semitism in Eastern Europe, and many of them chose Israel simply because the United States had restricted immigration in 1924. These immigrants were less likely to work the land and more likely to bring substantial capital with them to invest in businesses and workshops. Others joined the growing numbers of Jews doing construction work in cities such as Haifa and Tel Aviv, or they operated citrus plantations. These olim held fairly conservative political views, which generated tension with the earlier left-wing immigrants. Although the Fourth Aliya contributed more than 80,000 people and substantial capital to the Jewish community, in 1927 more Jews emigrated from Palestine than immigrated to it.

During the 1920s, Arab–Jewish conflict escalated. Violence broke out in Jerusalem and the north of the country in 1920, in Jaffa in 1921, and in Jerusalem and Hebron in 1929, where the Jewish community was decimated. Trying to calm the situation, the British resolved to stand by the Balfour Declaration, yet at the same time they rejected the idea of turning all of Palestine into a Jewish state, and they decided that future Jewish immigration should be limited. The British announced the Passfield White Paper in 1930, which restricted Jewish labor immigration and granted the development of an autonomous Arab government. These decrees were largely revoked a few months later, once Arab violence had subsided.

IMMIGRATION ON THE EVE OF WORLD WAR II

As Hitler rose to power and attacks against Jews spread across Europe, immigrants continued to arrive but increasingly came illegally. During the Fifth Aliya, from 1929 to 1939, between 180,000 and 200,000 olim entered Palestine by legal means, and another 17,000 to 20,000 arrived clandestinely. They came primarily from Germany, Austria, Czechoslovakia, and Poland. The first to arrive were teenagers sponsored by Zionist organizations, but as violence in Europe intensified, families with little Zionist affiliation came not to build Israel, but rather to escape the anti-Jewish policies and physical attacks in what they still viewed as their homelands. Many chose Palestine because the United States and European countries had closed their doors to Jewish immigrants. In 1933, German officials agreed to allow Jews who wanted to leave to take part of their capital with them. These 20,000 *Haavara,* transfer immigrants, escaped the Holocaust, but given the British restrictions on immigration to Palestine, for each person accepted, another was rejected. No matter which country they came from, and the hardships they had escaped, these mainly urban, well-off immigrants had great difficulties adjusting to the climate, language, and way of life in Palestine. Many wished to leave for the United States or return to their countries of origin once the situations there returned to normal.

During the 1930s, Jews circumvented obstacles to immigration by arranging marriages to obtain fiancé(e) visas and by overstaying their tourist visas. Of the 25,000 people who were granted tourist visas to attend the 1932 Maccabian athletic competition, approximately 20,000 failed to leave the country. In 1933, ever more alarmed at the tide of immigrants from Eu-

Israel was created in 1948 as a homeland for the Jews of the world. Although its Zionist founders initially envisioned a nation of European Jews, Israel's Jewish population today is divided roughly in half between Jews from Europe and Jews from the Middle East. *(CARTO-GRAPHICS)*

rope, Arabs held massive demonstrations across Palestine and attacked Jews and British soldiers alike. Illegal immigrants continued to cross the borders. Organized illegal immigration by sea, "Aliya Bet," as opposed to legal immigration "Aliya Aleph," began in 1934. Arab Palestinians held a six-month general strike in 1936—which lasted intermittently until 1939—and the mufti of Jerusalem called for a halt to Jewish immigration, laws against selling land to Jews, and an increase in Arab participation in the government. The British decided to divide Palestine into three sections: one for Jews, one for Muslims, and British-controlled Jerusalem. In addition, in 1939 they issued the McDonald White Paper, in which they reduced Jewish immigration to 10,000 arrivals a year for five years, plus 25,000 visas for refugees, for a total of 75,000 people allowed legal entry.

ILLEGAL IMMIGRATION DURING AND AFTER WORLD WAR II

With the situation stalemated, relatively few Jews reached and remained in Palestine during World War II. British soldiers searched for illegal immigrants hiding in the countryside and intercepted ships fleeing Europe. Those arrested were no longer imprisoned in Palestine but rather were sent to Mauritius and later to Cyprus. Several ships carrying refugees sank. The British were so strict in preventing Jewish immigration that during the war the original 1939 quotas were never met: only 54,000 immigrants arrived legally or were legalized after illegal entry between 1939 and 1945; another 20,000 to 40,000 may have reached Palestine illegally and remained hidden during the war. Some Jews in Palestine wanted to attack the British for preventing immigration, but most remained ambivalent because the British were fighting the Germans. After the Allied victory and the discovery of the extent of Nazi genocide in concentration camps, Jews increased their resistance to the British authorities by sabotaging railways and bridges. Illegal immigrants arriving after the war included many Jews who had survived the Holocaust. Over 70,000 *Haapala* immigrants, those who had overcome obstacles to reach Palestine, managed to bypass the British between 1945 and 1948. For those who were successful, many others were caught and interned in camps in Cyprus. Jews protested with arms, explosions, and the slogan, "Open the gates of Zion!" With growing international pressure and the destruction of a government building, the British submitted the question of Palestine to the United Nations. On November 29, 1947, the United Nations voted to divide Palestine into two states, with Jerusalem under international jurisdiction. When the British left Palestine on May 14, 1948, the Jewish population of Israel was approximately six hundred thousand.

MASS IMMIGRATION AND IMMIGRATION POLICY AFTER INDEPENDENCE

The Declaration of Independence on May 14, 1948, affirmed that "the State of Israel is open to Jewish immigration and the Ingathering of Exiles (*Kibboutz Galuyot*)." On July 5, 1950, the Knesset, the Israeli parliament, passed the "Law of Return." Every Jew in the world now had the legal right to immigrate to Israel and automatically become a citizen. Between 1948 and 1951, almost 700,000 new immigrants settled in Israel, elevating the number of the Jewish citizens to over 1,300,000. Yet the total population remained the same, because of the emigration of hundreds of thousands of Arabs between 1947 and 1949. In 1952, the remaining Arabs were granted Israeli citizenship but exempted from military service, which was universal for Jews. The problem of Palestinian refugees and troubled relations with neighboring Arab countries contributed to instability in Israel.

A crucial issue since independence has been the lack of separation between religion and the state in Israel. Religious affiliation is stamped in official documents, and the question of who is truly Jewish remains a divisive question. The Law of Return did not define who was a Jew, and when it was amended in 1970, religious leaders were able to exclude those who were not born of a Jewish mother or had not converted according to Orthodox specifications. Yet many immigrants without proof of their religion and that of their parents have been allowed to immigrate if their papers were destroyed or they came from a Communist country where religion was discouraged. Potential immigrants from Western Europe and the United States, on the other hand, are routinely called upon to substantiate their claims of having a Jewish mother.

Absorption centers were established in the 1960s and run by the Jewish Agency that housed immigrants and tried to facilitate their adaptation to Israel. After 1967, the Jewish Agency remained in charge of the initial absorption of immigrants, but the Ministry of Immigrant Absorption (MIA) was given responsibility for permanent absorption. Much of the funding for the MIA comes from money raised outside of Israel by the Jewish Agency. Power struggles between the Jewish Agency and the MIA leads to confusion and increased bureaucratic red tape for immigrants. Upon arrival, immigrants receive a small sum of money at the airport ($50). Immigrants from wealthier countries receive between $375 and $660 for settlement expenses, whereas those from underdeveloped countries receive at least $660. Immigrants are given aid for three years, and their health insurance is provided for their first six months in Israel. They are also given Hebrew language classes for six months.

Although material aid is an asset, bureaucratic control over immigrants, especially non-Western immigrants, is not always in their best interest. Many critics argue that it fosters discrimination, excessive intervention, and the fostering of long-term dependence. This furthers weakens those in a vulnerable position, particularly women and older people, and impedes immigrants' integration into Israeli society. Despite strides toward cultural pluralism, the term "absorption," which implies eventual assimilation to the dominant culture, is still in use today. The increasing acceptance of ethnic differences in the face of melting-pot ideology has been hard won, and the adaption of immigrants of various backgrounds remains a subject of conflict in Israel.

Communities of Jews with different religious beliefs, traditions, and ways of life had always lived in Palestine with more or less friction. Although non-European Jews were less likely to be counted in British immigration statistics because they entered primarily by land (those from Africa crossed through Egypt and those from Asia and Turkey entered by way of Syria or Lebanon), their numbers were relatively small. Between 1919 and 1948, 87.7 percent of immigrants were from Europe, 1.9 percent came from the Americas and Oceania, 1.0 percent arrived from Africa, and 9.7 percent immigrated from Asia. While Jews from Europe continued to stream into Israel after 1948, much larger numbers of Jews also began to arrive from Africa and Asia. The immigration and installation of these various groups continued to overlap throughout the next four decades.

One of the largest divisions among Jewish citizens has been between Ashkenazim and Sephardim. Many Jews from Muslim countries fled anti-Jewish violence and insecurity born of the Arab–Israeli conflict. In 1949 and 1950, 50,000 Jews were transported from Yemen; in 1950 and 1951, 120,000 Jews left Iraq and 27,000 left Iran; and by 1952, 33,000 Turkish Jews had arrived in Israel. More than 15,000 Libyans, 28,000 Tunisians, and 197,000 Moroccans fled the threat of Arab nationalism in 1952, and 15,000 Egyptians arrived in 1956 after the Suez crisis. A total of nearly 700,000 Jews from Africa and Asia arrived between independence and the end of the 1950s. By the late 1950s, 36 percent of the population were Israeli born, 36 percent were Ashkenazim, and 28 percent were Sephardim. Overall, between 1948 and 1981, 1,707,703 immigrants came to Israel; of these, 46 percent were from Europe, 24 percent were from Africa, 20 percent were from Asia, and 8 percent were from America and Oceania. With their larger community in Palestine during British rule, and their growing numbers of World War II survivors, Ashkenazim had the upper hand politically and financially in the early days of Israeli statehood. They were more likely to be members of the middle class and were typically less religious than the poorer Sephardim, who faced housing and employment problems in Israel.

Many Sephardic Jews spent years living in temporary transit camps; others were sent to development zones, areas far from large cities and often located in the desert or near the northern borders. In 1959, Moroccan Jews in Haifa began a demonstration that spread nationally. They protested discriminatory practices by Ashkenazi officials that kept them out of work, in overcrowded housing, and limited the educational opportunities for their children. The government responded by implementing programs designed to provide scholarships to students, education and job training for adults, improved housing for immigrants, and encouragement of Sephardic cultural traditions. Throughout the 1960s and 1970s there was a revival of ethnic festivals and an emphasis on ethnic pride. Protests continued, including those by a group of young Sephardim, the Black Panthers, but many second-generation Sephardim achieved social mobility and began entering the political realm. In 1985, 58 percent of Jews in Israel were of Sephardic origin.

The ideal of *mizug galuyot,* mixing of the exiles, was recognized as meaning assimilation into Ashkenazi culture, and insistence on this goal of immigrant incorporation has diminished. Since the 1960s, Israelis have been increasingly aware of the diversity of their society and the need to deal with the realities of cultural pluralism. This diversity exists not only between Ashkenazim and Sephardim, but also within these groups. Jews from around the world continue to arrive, bringing with them particular cultural practices and regional loyalties. Thus Israelis face the difficult task of fostering various traditions while at the same time developing a unified nationalism. Each new group of arrivals faces different conditions of reception given the political and social climate, the percentage of their group in Israel, and the reasons for their migration.

EXAMPLES OF IMMIGRANT GROUPS

NORTH AFRICANS

In ancient times, Jewish settlements were established in North Africa by Jews who came with Phoenician colonizers. Other Jews arrived after the destruction of the Second Temple in 70 C.E. After expulsion from Spain in the fifteenth century, many Jews went to Morocco, where Jewish culture experienced a renaissance. Then, until the beginning of the twentieth century, North African Jews experienced severe discrimination and ghettoization, and a decline in learning. French control of North Africa improved their lot, and Algerian and other North African Jews were granted French citizenship. After the French left North Africa in 1962, the majority of Algerian Jews immigrated to France. Middle-class Moroccan and Tunisian Jews also chose France, so immigrants to Israel were comprised primarily of the poor.

By 1971, the Jewish population in North Africa had dwindled to less than 10 percent of its original size, and there were 400,000 North Africans in Israel, including 230,000 from Morocco and 70,000 from Tunisia. Although the original policy of assimilation separated them upon arrival, extended families and even small towns managed to regroup in Israel. Most North African immigrants had little or no exposure to the Zionist movement prior to emigration. Jews from North Africa, where the social and physical space between men and women was highly controlled, had to adjust to Israel, where women were expected to work in the fields and factories. In the past few decades, Israelis have witnessed the revival of the North African cult of saints and the institutionalization of the Moroccan festival Mimouna following Passover.

YEMENITES

Yemenite Jews believe that they arrived in Yemen during the rule of King Solomon, and archeological evidence proves that there were Yemenite Jews as early as 70 C.E. Jews of North and South Yemen practiced Sephardic rituals, while the Jews of Central Yemen had their own particular traditions. The majority of Jewish men in Yemen worked as artisans and craftsmen, merchants, and peddlers. Women in villages had vegetable gardens, but men were prohibited from farming.

Small groups of Yemenite Jews settled in Palestine during the First Aliya, and more Yemenites and North Africans came during the Second Aliya. By 1948, there were 28,000 Jews of Yemenite descent living in Israel. After the establishment of Israel, Yemenites flocked to a refugee camp in Aden, where they awaited transfer to Israel. Conditions in the camp were dire, and almost one-third of emigrants died en route. During "Operation Magic Carpet" between 1948 and 1950, 50,000 Yemenite Jews were airlifted to Israel. An estimated 3,000 to 5,000 remained in Yemen. While many Yemenites ended up on moshavim, those with ties to the earlier Yemenite communities in Israel went to live in cities. Yemenite Jews were particularly religious, often with Messianic beliefs about their return to Israel, and their traditional worldviews led to culture shock upon arrival.

INDIANS

Indian Jews lived in the state of Kerala in southwestern India, many in the town of Cochin, and those known as the Beni-Israel lived in Bombay. Alternative theories exist to explain their arrival in India. Some claim descendance from sailors of King Solomon's fleet of merchant ships; others trace their arrival to dispersions from the Holy Land by the Assyrians, Babylonians, and Romans. The Jews of Cochin were primarily members of the black caste and did not intermarry with white Jews who arrived from Spain in the sixteenth century. The majority were involved in commerce or peddling. They had several synagogues, prayed in Hebrew, and kept Kosher. With the creation of the state of Israel, Indian Jews wished to leave *en masse*, but Israeli officials spread their immigration over several years, often encouraging adolescent children to come first. Indians balked at the separation of families, and between 1953 and 1955 most of the community of 2,000 migrated together. By 1968 there were only a few hundred Jews left in Kerala, most of them white Jews. In Israel, they were not settled in cities; some families spent years in transit camps and others were sent directly to moshavim, where they found farming difficult due to their lack of agricultural experience.

IRAQIS

Jews have lived in Iraq since the destruction of the First Temple in 586 B.C. Many Iraqi Jews were traders and merchants; some of the wealthiest installed branches of their families all over the world, particularly in India, China, Burma, and England, to capitalize on trade. Jews were fairly well integrated into Iraqi society until Iraq became an independent state in 1932, but the Jewish community experienced attacks, including bombings, throughout the 1930s. Influenced by the Nazis, Iraqis conducted a pogrom in 1941 and killed 180 Jews. The Iraqi government tried to protect Jews, punishing many Nazi sympathizers, but many Jews abandoned their hopes of assimilation and turned toward Zionism. Other Jews remained loyal to Iraq until Israel's independence resulted in more discrimination. Members of Zionist organizations were jailed and tortured, but the underground in Iraq continued to work with the Mossad (the Israeli intelligence service). In 1950, the Iraqi government permitted emigration of Jews who gave up citizenship, and by 1952, 121,500 people had arrived on airlifts named "Operation Ezra and Nehemiah." Only a few thousand Jews chose to remain in Iraq. In 1969, young Jews were seized and hanged and others imprisoned. Another 4,000 Jews fled Iraq, and very few, mostly elderly Jews remain in Iraq today.

ETHIOPIANS

Jews were a small minority in Ethiopia, where most of the population is either Muslim or Coptic Christian. In the early 1980s, there were fewer than 30,000 Jews in Ethiopia. Ethiopian Jews contend that they are the descendants of the servants sent to Ethiopia with Menelik, the son of King Solomon and the Ethiopian Queen of Sheba, and refer to themselves as the Beta Israel (house of Israel). When urging Israelis to accept them as Jews, the Sephardic Chief Rabbi of Israel advanced the belief that Ethiopian Jews are descendants of the lost tribe of Dan. Neither of these theories can be confirmed, but in April 1975, the Ministry of the Interior recognized Ethiopian Jews as eligible to become citizens under the Law of Return. Ethiopians, however, were not allowed to emigrate, and the Ethiopian government had severed diplomatic relations with Israel in 1973 during the Yom Kippur War. The Ethiopian Revolution in the 1970s and the droughts of the 1980s made Jews more eager to find a way to Israel, despite the threat of imprisonment and torture if caught escaping and the perils of the trip itself. An estimated 4,000 Jews died from dehydration and disease during their trek or in Sudanese refugee camps.

Fewer than 400 Jews migrated from Ethiopia to Israel before 1979. Between 1979 and 1984, over 6,000 Ethiopian Jews reached Israel, but Ethiopian Jews were dying in refugee camps faster than they were being transported to their new land. Israeli officials decided to act. During Operation Moshe, 7,000 Ethiopian Jews were evacuated between November 21, 1984, and January 6, 1985. After a leak to the press, the operation was halted. Operation Joshua, with the help of the United States, transported another 800 people a few months later. Emigration was then slowed until 1989, when the Ethiopian government agreed to allow the exodus of Jews in two years. Due to political instability in Ethiopia, a decision was made to engage in another massive airlift, this time from the capital, Addis Ababa. Over 14,000 Ethiopian Jews were airlifted to Israel in thirty-six hours on March 24 and 25, 1991, during Operation Solomon.

Despite the ruling in 1975, some question remained as to whether the Beta Israel were really Jewish even though they self-identified as Jewish and kept Kosher. Rabbis allowed them to migrate as Jews if they agreed to submit to a compromised conversion: after arrival in Israel, women went to the *Mikveh,* the ritual baths, and men were symbolically re-circumcised. These forced rituals were abandoned due

to public outcry by Ethiopians, although they are still required before marriage to non-Ethiopians. Although this community was particularly religious, their children were obligated to go to religious schools in Israel instead of having the choice between religious and secular education that other immigrants were given. In addition, Ethiopian Jews face discrimination as blacks. They were settled in development areas usually without being consulted, and the Ministry of Absorption deemed that Ethiopian immigrants should continue being monitored even after they had found permanent housing and work.

LATIN AMERICANS

A few Jews arrived in Latin America from Europe during the colonial period, but immigration increased substantially after these countries gained independence from Spain and Portugal in the nineteenth century. Most immigration occurred between 1900 and 1945 and has dwindled since. Jews in Latin America were typically members of the middle class, but political instability has created larger numbers of poor Jews in Argentina, Chile, and Uruguay. In 1984, there were over 495,000 Jews living in Latin America, the majority in Argentina, Brazil, and Mexico. Nationalist movements and anti-Semitic sentiment keep South and Central American Jews in a vulnerable position, and in many countries they are excluded from politics. Very few Jewish families remain in Cuba, El Salvador, and Nicaragua, and Jews have been the target of multiple attacks throughout the twentieth century in Argentina.

There are over 100,000 Latin-American Jews in Israel. Early immigration, until 1958, was composed of Zionists who primarily joined kibbutzim. After this period, increasing numbers of businesspeople and professionals came, and they migrated to cities. Post-1975 arrivals included political refugees and those migrating because of political and economic instability. About half of Latin-American Jews were born in Europe. Although the majority chose to immigrate because of Zionist ideology or a strong feeling of Jewishness, only half had received any formal Jewish education in their countries of origin. Most came from an Orthodox background even if they themselves were no longer as religious. Although many Latin-American immigrants assess their standard of living in Israel as poorer than that in their countries of origin, the majority still claim satisfaction with life in Israel, and over three-fourths plan to remain in Israel. However, between 1970 and 1974, 18 percent of Latin-American Jews left Israel within three years of immigrating.

BULGARIANS

A small group of Bulgarians immigrated to Israel in 1898. Over 45,000 of Bulgaria's 50,000 Jews emigrated to Israel between 1948 and 1949. Although Bulgarian Jews are a part of the larger Balkan Sephardic community, Bulgarian Jews are comprised of both Sephardim and Ashkenazim. Jews have lived in Bulgaria since the Roman period, but many are descendants of Iberian Jews who fled Spain and Portugal in the fifteenth century for the more tolerant Ottoman Empire. Until the early part of the nineteenth century, Bulgarian Jews spoke Ladino, or Judeo-Spanish, but later generations grew up speaking Bulgarian. Bulgarian Jews were not particularly religious, but they were committed Zionists well before World War II. From the 1920s, Bulgarian Jews sent their children to Hebrew schools and enrolled them in Zionist youth organizations. During World War II, the Bulgarian government did not deport Jews beyond its borders, but all Jews were forced out of Sofia. Men were compelled into forced labor and all Jewish property was confiscated. In 1945, the government passed the Law of Restitution, but little Jewish property was actually returned, leaving the majority of Bulgarian Jews in dire poverty. Given the strength of Zionist sentiment before World War II, and the economic deprivation during and after the war, it is not surprising that as soon as emigration was allowed, most of Bulgaria's Jews left for Israel. Over 7,000 Bulgarian Jews were smuggled in illegally before Israel's independence. As soon as the gates were open, young people were sent, and within a few years, their parents and grandparents joined them. The majority settled in Jaffa, where they recreated a community choir and championed a soccer team comprised of Bulgarian Jews. After the fall of Communism in Eastern Europe, between 1,000 and 2,000 more Jews left Bulgaria for Israel. Many of these Jews had intermarried, and some chose not to remain in Israel. Although many Bulgarian Jews are Sephardic, they are from Europe, and thus escape much negative stereotyping in Israel.

SOVIETS

Between 1968 and 1988, 297,000 Jews left the Soviet Union; 169,000 of them went to Israel. Another 500,000 arrived in Israel between 1989 and 1993. These emigrants left for several reasons: anti-Semitism, rejection of the Soviet system, relative attractiveness of life in the United States and Israel compared to the Soviet Union, and the wish to join family members already abroad. Few Jews left for religious reasons, and Soviet Jews had a particularly high rate of marriage to non-Jews: between one-third and one-half had intermarried. Between the Russian Revolution and World War II, Soviet Jews had become largely assimilated and were very well represented in the Communist Party. During and after World War II, conditions for Jews deteriorated, and expressions of Yiddish culture were officially forbidden.

Emigration during the 1970s and 1980s was not stable, but rather varied from year to year based on U.S.–Soviet relations, developments in the Arab–Israeli conflict, and the work of Soviet emigration activists and human rights organizations. After receiving an invitation from a relative abroad, Jews had to petition to leave, and if permission was granted, they were forced to renounce Soviet citizenship. Many Jews were refused permission to leave on the grounds that they knew military or economic state secrets, had military expertise, or were highly trained, and Jewish professionals leaving in 1972 were forced to pay a "diploma tax" to reimburse the government for their education. Those who were denied the right to leave were called "refuseniks."

Although close to half of Soviet emigrants went to the United States, all left the Soviet Union with visas for Israel; those who chose the United States instead were referred to as "dropouts." Through the early 1970s the majority of Jews leaving the Soviet Union did settle in Israel, but by 1979, two-thirds of emigrants elected to go to another country, usually the United States, Canada, Australia, or New Zealand. Jews from Russia and the Ukraine, comprising 57 percent of immigrants, were more assimilated into Russian culture than Jews from other republics, who had more traditional Jewish backgrounds. Russian and Ukrainian Jews were more likely to choose the United States, whereas Uzbekistani, Georgian, Latvian, and Moldavian Jews were more likely to make Aliya. Since emigrants of this period had the choice to go to the United States, those who went to Israel were those motivated to do so, either for Zionist/Jewish identity or family reasons; however, they do not report being more religious than immigrants to the United States. After 1989, U.S. officials decided to accept only those Soviets who had U.S. visas; thus Soviet Jews could no longer drop out to the United States. Consequently, these immigrants to Israel were less likely to wish to be there. The Perestroika period in Russia saw a relaxation of exit requirements from the Soviet Union, and 480,075 Jews arrived in Israel between 1989 and 1993, 69 percent of them in 1990–1991.

The majority of pre-1989 Soviet Jews have been successful in terms of structural incorporation into Israel. Relative to other immigrants, Soviets have high levels of education. They found better housing more quickly than other groups, and most settled in urban centers. Over 90 percent immigrated as families. In addition, they learned Hebrew more quickly than American immigrants, and those with a higher education were granted six months in an immigrant hostel, where they received daily intensive Hebrew classes. In the 1980s, almost all of those who had been employed in the Soviet Union were currently working three years after immigration, although 15 percent of those with university training had changed careers. Also, one-third of people 55 or older had failed to find a job. In a 1981 study, while 29.8 percent of Soviet Jews in Israel thought their standard of living had gone up, and 26.6 percent believed it had remained the same, 36.9 percent felt it had gone down; and although 54.2 percent reported being satisfied with life in Israel, 38.6 percent were dissatisfied. Central Asian Jews were the most likely to be dissatisfied, and many feel that they are discriminated against compared to Ashkenazim. However, the majority of Soviet Jews said they would leave the Soviet Union if they had to do it all again, and three-fourths said they would still choose Israel over another destination. Post-1989 immigrants, on the other hand, are taking longer to find full-time employment, and many have experienced extreme downward socioeconomic mobility. In 1992, only half of recent Soviet immigrants had found work, and of those, only 20 percent were employed in their chosen profession.

AMERICANS

Over 2,000 Americans settled in Israel between 1880 and 1914, primarily for religious reasons. Another 6,600 to 11,000 arrived during the British Mandate, but these Jews were less religious and more motivated by Zionism; the majority were second-generation Americans from New York City. American Aliya increased steadily after Israel's independence: 3,610 in the 1950s, 12,227 in the 1960s, and 41,234 in the 1970s. Immigration diminished in the 1980s, but 19,140 American Jews arrived in Israel between 1980 and 1987. While over two-thirds of pre-state immigrants chose to live on kibbutzim, the majority of American immigrants after independence went directly to cities. These later immigrants were more religious, had more knowledge of Hebrew and more education in general, and immigrated as families and individuals, not as members of Zionist organizations; 77 percent of them had been born in the United States.

American Jews who have immigrated to Israel since the Six Day War in 1967 are increasingly religious. Approximately 40 percent of olim who migrated between 1967 and 1971 self-identified as Orthodox, compared to the Orthodox population among U.S. Jews of 11 percent. There is a small overrepresentation of nonaffiliated Jews, 20 percent compared to 14 percent in the United States, but Conservative and Reform American Jews are underrepresented: 27 percent compared to 42 percent in the United States for Conservative and 13 percent compared to 33 percent in the United States for Reform. By 1986, almost two-thirds of emigrating Americans were Orthodox.

Realizing that Jews from Western countries had little material incentive to come to Israel, the government provided for tax breaks, import privileges, and loans for housing and small businesses that were more advantageous than those provided to other immigrants. These benefits were greatly reduced in the mid-1970s due to public dissatisfaction and tougher financial times in Israel. Nevertheless, American Jews in Israel have better housing and jobs than Israelis. While they complain about bureaucracy and politics, a study conducted in 1967 revealed that 95 percent of American immigrants were comfortable and felt at home in Israel. In addition, a 1975 study found that the expectations of 55 percent of American olim were either completely or mostly fulfilled, those of 18 percent were somewhat fulfilled, and those of 26 percent were not at all fulfilled. Despite the positive experiences of many, around 38 percent of American immigrants to Israel return to the United States within five years of their aliya.

A small group of black Jews from the United States established itself in the south of Israel in the 1970s. Numbering over 700 in 1975, these black Americans assert that they are the real descendants of Abraham and that true Jews were originally black. Their claim of Judaism is not accepted in Israel, and they have refused to convert. The majority arrived as tourists and remained in the country illegally; some have renounced their American citizenship. Israeli officials are unwilling to deport them as a group for fear of being charged with racism, and although many have been deported as individuals, the policy has generally been to ignore them.

CHALLENGES FOR IMMIGRANTS— CHALLENGES FOR ISRAEL

Immigrant adjustment is helped or hindered by many factors. Those leaving behind poor social and economic conditions in their countries of origin experience less relative deprivation in Israel. This is one of the reasons why poorer Sephardic immigrants tended to be less disappointed in Israel than European immigrants. Ideology plays a role in further distinguishing between immigrants; a traditional religious worldview buffered Eastern and North African immigrants from frustration, while among European immigrants, those with Zionist ideology were more receptive and less disappointed in Israel than those who did not adhere to Zionist ideology. Timing is also important. Ethiopian Jews arrived at a time when religious minorities in Israel were gaining power, and thus have not experienced the devaluation of religious acts and beliefs that met immigrants just after statehood. Soviet Jews who arrived during the 1970s and 1980s had more socioeconomic success than the more numerous post-1989 arrivals. In addition, older immigrants in general feel more deeply the loss of social networks and are less likely to learn the new language fluently; they report lower levels of satisfaction in the new country than younger immigrants, who feel they have time to start over.

Immigrant groups vary greatly in their socioeconomic status and their ability to maintain cultural traditions in Israel. Some groups are viewed more positively than others. A 1978 survey of *sabras* (native-born Israelis) revealed that 95 percent liked North Americans, 94 percent liked Latin Americans, 83 percent liked North Africans, and 70 percent liked Russians. Ethiopians, because of their skin color, are especially likely to face discrimination. While the children of Sephardic immigrants are much closer to their Ashkenazi peers in terms of educational level and occupational opportunities than were their parents, they have not reached parity. Although the majority of Israelis consider immigration as very important to Israel, in a 1992 poll many voiced the opinion that immigrants created competition for jobs and housing.

Israel faces many challenges relating to immigration. Nearly half of the growth of the Jewish population in Israel between 1948 and 1990 was due to immigration. In 1995, 39 percent of the Jewish population were born outside of Israel, and another 40 percent were the children of immigrants. Since the 1980s, over 20 percent of Jewish marriages in Israel have been between members of different ethnic groups. The Palestinians view immigration as a direct threat, since it changes the balance of population and jeopardizes their geographic, economic, and political aspirations. They particularly fear that new immigrants will be settled outside the "green line," or pre-1967 borders. Arabs inside and outside Israel have put pressure on various nations to curtail Jewish immigration to Israel. The Likud, the conservative political party, used continued immigration as a reason to justify not turning over more territory to Palestinians. In the 1992 elections, however, almost 60 percent of immigrants voted for the Labour Party. A growing political development is the influence of religious parties. Although only 30 percent of Israeli Jews are Orthodox, coalitions between established parties and religious parties have contributed to an overrepresentation of the very religious in the political arena. Hassidic, and other Orthodox immigrants, swell their ranks and lobby against returning land to Arabs.

Another much discussed problem for Israel is the number of emigrants. Between 1948 and 1979, 340,000 people emigrated from Israel. Of these, 318,000 were Jews. While immigrants from Africa and Asia rarely return to their countries of origin, they sometimes migrate west, and Western European and American immigrants are particularly likely to return home. Approximately 38 percent of American olim left Israel within five years of their arrival. Estimates vary widely because it is hard to determine who has left permanently, but in the early 1980s there were between 130,000 and 300,000 Israelis in the United States. Reasons cited for emigration are the ongoing climate of war and tension, changes in economic conditions, and the strong draw of economic opportunity in the United States.

While Israelis continue to struggle with religious and political differences and the repercussions of cultural pluralism, there is much to unite them. Despite their diverse origins, Israeli Jews share a sense of peoplehood, a common history, and a profound attachment to the land of Israel. Immigration has been a key component of nation building and will continue to shape Israel in the twenty-first century.

Caitlin Killian

See also: American Emigration Abroad (Part II, Sec. 2); Islam, Judaism (Part II, Sec. 11); Middle East (Part III, Sec. 3); Eastern Europe, Former Soviet Union, Western and Southern Europe (Part III, Sec. 4).

BIBLIOGRAPHY

Ben-Porot, Mordechai. *To Baghdad and Back: The Miraculous 2,000 Year Homecoming of the Iraqi Jews.* New York: Gefen, 1998.

Datan, Nancy, Aaron Antonovsky, and Benjamin Maoz. *A Time to Reap: The Middle Age of Women in Five Israeli Subcultures.* Baltimore: Johns Hopkins University Press, 1981.

Deshen, Schlomo, and Moshe Shokeid. *The Predicament of Homecoming: Cultural and Social Life of North African Immigrants in Israel.* Ithaca, NY: Cornell University Press, 1974.

Eisenstadt, Shmuel Noah. *The Transformation of Israeli Society.* London: Weidenfeld and Nicolson, 1985.

Galper, Allan S. *From Bolshoi to Be'er Sheva, Scientists to Streetsweepers: Cultural Dislocation among Soviet Immigants in Israel.* New York: University Press of America, 1995.

Gat, Moshe. *The Jewish Exodus from Iraq: 1948–1951.* London: Frank Cass, 1997.

Gerber, Israel J. *The Heritage Seekers: American Blacks in Search of Jewish Identity.* Middle Village, NY: Jonathan David Publishers, 1977.

Gilad, Lisa. *Ginger and Salt: Yemeni Jewish Women in an Israeli Town.* Boulder, CO: Westview Press, 1989.

Gitelman, Zvi. *Becoming Israelis: Political Resocialization of Soviet and American Immigrants.* New York: Praeger, 1982.

Grynberg, Anne. *Vers la terre d'Israel.* Paris: Gallimard, 1998.

Goldscheider, Calvin. *Israel's Changing Society: Population, Ethnicity, and Development.* Boulder, CO: Westview Press, 1996.

Haskell, Guy H. *From Sophia to Jaffa: The Jews of Bulgaria and Israel.* Detroit: Wayne State University Press, 1994.

Hermaan, Donald L. *The Latin-American Community of Israel.* New York: Praeger, 1984.

Hertzog, Esther. *Immigrants and Bureaucrats: Ethiopians in an Israeli Absorption Center.* New York: Berghahn Books, 1999.

Jones, Clive. *Soviet Jewish Aliyah 1989–1992: Impact and Implications for Israel and the Middle East.* London: Frank Cass, 1996.

Kessler, David, and Tudor Parfitt. "The Falashas: The Jews of Ethiopia." *The Minority Rights Group*, Report No. 67, 1985.

Kushner, Gilbert. *Immigrants from India to Israel: Planned Change in an Administered Community.* Tucson: University of Arizona Press, 1973.

Leshem, Elazar, and Judith T. Shuval, eds. *Immigration to Israel: Sociological Perspectives. Studies of Israeli Society*, Vol. 8. New Brunswick, NJ: Transaction Books, 1998.

Lewis, Herbert S. *After the Eagles Landed: The Yemenites of Israel.* Boulder, CO: Westview Press, 1989.

Litwin, Howard. *Uprooted in Old Age: Soviet Jews and Their Social Networks in Israel.* Westport, CT: Greenwood Press, 1995.

Naor, Mordechai. *Haapala: Clandestine Immigration 1931–1948.* Tel Aviv: State of Israel Ministry of Defense Publishing House, 1987.

Ofer, Dalia. *Escaping the Holocaust: Illegal Immigration to the Land of Israel 1939–1944.* New York: Oxford University Press, 1990.

Shuvall, Judith. T. *Immigrants on the Threshold.* London: Prentice-Hall International, 1963.

Sicron, Moshe. *Immigration to Israel: 1948–1953.* Jerusalem: Falk Project and the Central Bureau of Statistics, 1957.

Simon, Rita J. *New Lives: The Adjustment of Soviet Jewish Immigrants in the United States and Israel.* Lexington, MA: Lexington Books, 1985.

Sobel, Zvi. *Migrants from the Promised Land.* New Brunswick, NJ: Transaction Books, 1986.

Wagaw, Teshome G. *For Our Souls: Ethiopian Jews in Israel.* Detroit: Wayne State University Press, 1993.

Waxman, Chaim I. *American Aliya: Portrait of an Innovative Migration Movement.* Detroit: Wayne State University Press, 1989.

IMMIGRATION TO JAPAN

$\mathcal{U}$ntil recently, Japan was an exception among the major industrialized countries because it achieved economic growth without relying heavily on foreign migrants. Instead of foreign workers, Japan long relied on internal rural migrants and part-time female workers, and dealt with labor shortages by automating manufacturing and relocating production offshore. During the 1970s and 1980s, numerous Japanese firms moved production to lower-cost areas such as China, Thailand, Malaysia, and Mexico.

THE INCREASE IN FOREIGN IN-MIGRATION

In the late 1980s, however, an increasing number of foreign immigrants began to enter Japan. They were mostly from Asia (China, Philippines) and South America (Brazil, Peru) and they engaged in manual work to fill labor shortages. Domestic sources of cheap labor had plummeted due to economic growth and urbanization, while the economic boom increased total employment by 4.4 million workers during 1986–1991. The Ministry of Labor reported in 1989 that the ratio of advertised employment to job seekers reached 1.35; labor shortages were particularly acute in smaller firms in manufacturing and construction. The increase in foreign in-migration was induced by labor recruitment by these firms, and was further prompted by wide income differentials between Japan and the major immigrant-sending countries. The appreciation of the Japanese yen, following the 1985 Plaza Agreement, led to increasing disparities in gross national product (GNP) per capita; in comparison to Japan's $23,810 in 1989, that of China was $350, $710 for the Philippines, $1,220 for Thailand, $370 for Pakistan, and $180 for Bangladesh.

Since the late 1980s, the number of immigrants has steadily increased (see Table 1, Figure 1). Although the majority of foreign residents are long-term Korean residents (63 percent in 1990), they have declined both in number and proportion (42 percent in 1998), due to their tendency to be naturalized and the growing inflow from other countries, particularly China, Brazil, and the Philippines (see Table 1). Although the presence of foreign nationals in Japan is still relatively negligible, it has grown at a faster rate than in most other industrialized countries: from 1 million in 1990 to 1.5 million in 1998. Currently, foreign nationals constitute 1.18 percent of the total population, up from 0.6 percent in 1973 and 0.8 percent in 1989 (Ministry of Justice, 1999) (see Tables 2 and 3).

The rapid increase in foreign in-migratory flows spurred heated public debates over the "foreign worker problem" in a country widely believed to be racially and culturally homogeneous: Should Japan continue to accept foreign workers or close its doors?

Figure 1
The Increase in Foreign In-Migration

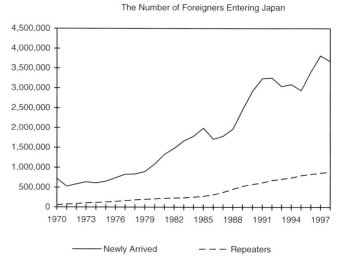

Source: Ministry of Justice. "Press Release: Statistics of Foreigners Resident in Japan and Entering Japan." Tokyo: Ministry of Justice, 1999.

Table 1
Trends and Characteristics of Immigration to Japan (in thousands)

	1990	1994	1996	1998
Inflow of foreign nationals[1]		237.5	225.4	265.4
Stock of foreign nationals	1,075.3	1,354.0	1,415.1	1,512.1
By country of origin				
Korea	678.9	676.8	657.2	638.8
China	150.3	218.6	234.3	272.2
Brazil	56.4	159.6	201.8	222.2
Philippines	49.0	86.0	84.5	105.3
United States	38.3	43.3	44.2	42.8
Peru	10.3	35.4	37.1	41.3
By region (percent of total registered foreigners)				
Asia		77.6%	74.9%	74.3%
South America		15.1%	17.6%	18.1%
North America		0.4%	0.4%	0.4%
Europe		0.2%	0.2%	0.3%
Other[2]		0.1%	0.1%	0.1%
By status				
Permanent residents		631.5	626.0	626.8
Long-term residents[3]		375.4	438.2	482.3
Foreign workers with permission for employment		105.6	98.3	119.0
Specialist in humanities or international services		24.8	27.4	31.3
Entertainer		34.8	20.1	28.9
Engineer		10.1	11.1	15.2
Skilled labor		6.8	8.8	10.0
Instructor		6.8	7.5	7.9
Intracompany transferee		5.8	5.9	6.6
Professor		3.8	4.6	5.4
Investor and business manager		4.5	5.0	5.1
Religious activities		5.6	5.0	4.9
Researcher		1.7	2.0	2.8
Journalist		0.4	0.5	0.4
Artist		0.2	0.3	0.3
Medical services		0.2	0.1	0.1
Legal and accounting services		0.1	0.1	0.1
Estimates of Japanese descendants[4]		181.5	211.2	
Estimates of illegal workers[5]	290	280		
Number of foreign nationals deported		65.6		54.3

Sources: Ministry of Justice; Organization for Economic Cooperation and Development (OECD), 1999.
[1]Excluding temporary visitors and reentries.
[2]Oceania, Africa, those without nationality.
[3]Including spouse or child of Japanese national; spouse or child of permanent resident.
[4]Estimates made by the Ministry of Foreign Affairs.
[5]Estimates made by the Ministry of Justice on the basis of the number of overstayers.

Table 2
Foreign or Foreign-Born Population and Labor Force in Selected Countries

| | Foreign Population | | | | | Foreign Labor Force | | | |
| | Thousands | | Percent of Total Population | | | Thousands | | Percent of Total Labor Force | |
	1987[1]	1997[2]	1987	1997	Percent Increase	1987[3]	1997[4]	1987	1997
Japan	884	1,483	0.7	1.2	1.7		660[5]		1.0
France	3,714	3,597	6.8	6.3	0.9	1,525	1,570	6.3	6.1
Germany	4,241	7,366	6.9	9.0	1.3	1,866	2,522	6.9	9.1
Italy	572	1,241	1.0	2.2	2.2	285	332	1.3	1.7
Spain	335	610	0.9	1.5	1.7	58	176	0.4	1.1
Sweden	401	522	4.8	6.0	1.3	215	220	4.9	5.2
United States[6]	14,080	24,600	6.2	9.3	1.5	7,077	14,300	6.7	10.8

Source: SOPEMI, Organization for Economic Cooperation and Development, (OECD), 1999.
[1]1982 for France.
[2]1990 for France.
[3]1988 for Spain, 1991 for Italy.
[4]1995 for Italy.
[5]No data available for 1987.
[6]Foreign-born population and labor force (census data): figures are for 1986 and 1996.

It was a "problem," as depicted by the media, policy makers, and academics alike, because the increasing presence of foreigners would pose a threat to Japan's national cultural integrity as well as to social and moral order in association with the fear of rising crime rates and the bifurcation of the labor market. Particularly "problematic" were undocumented workers (mostly visa overstayers). Thus, the debates arose out of two contradictory needs: (1) the need to rely on foreign unskilled laborers while preserving the country's social and national integrity; and (2) the need to selectively discriminate immigrants in a manner nationally and internationally acceptable within the framework of multilateral conventions and diplomatic relations.

THE REVISION OF THE IMMIGRATION LAW

In this context, Japan's immigration law was revised in 1989 (enforced in 1990). In response to the growing inflows of illegal migration, the Immigration Control and Refugee Recognition Act was amended in order to "control foreign migrants more effectively." To do so, the government stipulated its fundamental principles: although Japan readily accepts foreigners pos-

sessing technological expertise, specialized skills, or cultural knowledge not possessed by Japanese nationals, unskilled laborers and illegal immigrants shall not, under any circumstance, be admitted. To enforce these principles, occupational and status categories, under which foreigners were admitted, were reorganized and expanded from 18 to 27, and

Figure 2
The Increase in South American In-Migrants

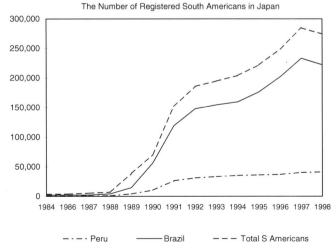

The Number of Registered South Americans in Japan

Source: Ministry of Justice. "Press Release: Statistics of Foreigners Resident in Japan and Entering Japan." Tokyo: Ministry of Justice, 1999.

Table 3
Percent Increase in Foreign Migrants

Year	Total Number of Registered Foreigners	Percent Increase from Previous Year	Index (1973 = 100)	Percent of Total Population
1973	738,410		100	0.68
1978	766,894	3.9	104	0.67
1983	817,129	6.6	111	0.68
1988	947,005	15.2	127	0.77
1990	1,075,317	9.2	146	0.87
1992	1,281,644	5.1	174	1.03
1994	1,354,011	2.5	183	1.08
1996	1,415,136	3.9	192	1.12
1998	1,512,116	2.0	205	1.20

Source: Ministry of Justice. "Press Release: Statistics of Foreigners Resident in Japan and Entering Japan." Tokyo: Ministry of Justice, 1999.

punishment was introduced for the first time for both illegal immigrants and their employers (fines of 2 million yen per alien or up to three years in prison).

THE COMPANY TRAINEE PROGRAM

Simultaneously, however, two channels were introduced as "side-door" mechanisms to allow in unskilled foreign immigrants. One was "on-the-job training," under which foreigners worked in a Japanese sponsoring firm for two years. Originally initiated in the 1960s to train foreigners employed by Japanese overseas affiliate companies, the program was extended to smaller firms without an overseas affiliate in 1990 and expanded thereafter. The Japanese government officially justifies the program as a vehicle of technology transfer to poorer countries; in reality, however, most "company trainees" engage in unskilled work.

THE NIKKEIJIN POLICY

The other mechanism for admitting unskilled immigrants was the policy that accommodated the entry of ethnic Japanese (the children and grandchildren of Japanese emigrants), known collectively as *Nikkeijin*

(foreign nationals of Japanese descent). Under this law, those who can claim Japanese ancestry within three generations (i.e., who have one Japanese grandparent) are granted a special visa without any work restrictions. Visas are renewable in perpetuity, and no numerical ceilings were set. Second-generation descendants, who are admitted as "the spouse or child of Japanese nationals," are eligible for a three-year visa, while third-generation descendants can obtain only a one-year visa, entering under the distinct and newly introduced category of "long-term resident." Since the implementation of the law, the number of Nikkeijin has steadily and dramatically increased: from 6,872 in 1988 to 70,500 in 1990, 195,000 in 1993, and further to 274,000 in 1998 (see Figures 2 and 3). Despite their middle-class backgrounds at home, most of the Nikkeijin engage in manual factory work as contract laborers. Moreover, regardless of their pledged ethnic ties, they remain largely unassimilated and are treated as an "ethnic minority" in Japan.

The ethnicity-based immigration policy was a particularly effective mechanism to cope with Japan's aforementioned contradictory needs, namely, the need simultaneously to incorporate and control unskilled foreign labor. In addition to the limited size of the Japanese-ancestry population (estimated at 2.5 million around the globe by the Ministry of Foreign Affairs), Nikkeijin were admitted not as "unskilled foreign workers" but under "special familial ties" justified by their descent. Moreover, this preferential policy was consistent with Japan's descent-based nationality law and acceptable in a country where a sense of "blood ties" is fundamental to nationhood.

Figure 3
The Increase in South American Migrants in Japan

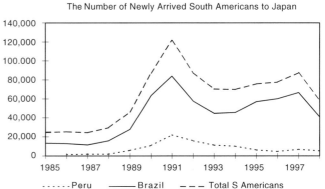

The Number of Newly Arrived South Americans to Japan

······ Peru   ———— Brazil   – – – Total S Americans

Source: Ministry of Justice. "Press Release: Statistics of Foreigners Resident in Japan and Entering Japan." Tokyo: Ministry of Justice, 1999.

TOWARD A MORE OPEN COUNTRY?

Faced with its rapidly aging population and a shrinking labor force, Japan continues to debate its immigration policies. Meanwhile, the number and proportion of foreign residents has steadily increased. Despite the country's persistent recession, the inflow of skilled foreign workers increased by almost 20 percent in 1997. Contrary to the government's intention, the number of estimated illegal immigrants has not declined. Contrary to the government's original prediction, Nikkeijin workers, too, have remained in Japan. Just like many Western European countries, Japan, once an emigrant country, is slowly and reluctantly becoming an "immigrant" country.

Ayumi Takenaka

See also: China, Korea, Philippines, Southeast Asia, Taiwan and Hong Kong (Part III, Sec. 3).

BIBLIOGRAPHY

Cornelius, Wayne A. "Japan: The Illusion of Immigration Control." In *Controlling Immigration: A Global Perspective*, ed. Wayne A. Cornelius, Philip L. Martin, and James F. Hollifield. Stanford, CA: Stanford University Press, 1994.

French, Howard W. "Still Wary of Outsiders, Japan Expects Immigration Boom." *New York Times*, March 14, 2000, A1.

Lie, John. "The 'Problem' of Foreign Workers in Contemporary Japan." *Bulletin of Concerned Asian Scholars* 26:3 (1994): 3–11.

Ministry of Justice. "Press Release: Statistics of Foreigners Resident in Japan and Entering Japan." Tokyo: Ministry of Justice, 1999.

Ministry of Labor. "Foreign Workers and the Labour Market in Japan." *International Migration Quarterly Review* 31:2/3 (1993): 442–62.

Mori, Hiromi. *Immigration Policy and Foreign Workers in Japan*. New York: St. Martin's Press, 1997.

Organisation for Economic Co-operation and Development (OECD). *Trends in International Migration: Continuous Reporting System on Migration*. Paris: SOPEMI, 1999.

Sekai Minzoku Mondai Jiten. *The World Encyclopedia of Race and Ethnicity*. Tokyo: Heibonsha, 1995.

Shimada, Haruo. *Japan's "Guest Workers": Issues and Public Policies*. Tokyo: University of Tokyo Press, 1994.

IMMIGRATION TO WESTERN EUROPE

Recent immigration to Western Europe is the largely the product of three major geopolitical trends of the second half of the twentieth century: the region's extraordinarily rapid and substantial economic recovery from World War II; the collapse of European empires in much of Africa, Asia, and the Caribbean from the late 1940s to the mid-1970s; and the collapse of communism, which began with the fall of the Berlin Wall in 1989. While all Western European countries—defined as those outside the Cold War–era Soviet bloc—have received varying numbers of immigrants, largely from the developing world, most of these immigrants have headed for three nations: France, Germany, and Great Britain.

FRANCE

Almost unique in Western Europe, France has been a major destination for immigrants since the early nineteenth century. While some earlier immigrants may have been drawn to France for economic reasons, many of those who came to the country did so for political reasons. The outward expansion of French revolutionary ideas about universal human rights after 1789 gained France a reputation as a nation where immigrants—and particularly political refugees—would be welcome. Following the failed continent-wide revolutions of 1848, tens of thousands of refugees from Central and Eastern Europe poured into France. This reputation continued to pull other religious and political refugees—including many Eastern European Jews—into the country up through the Second World War, albeit with a significant slowdown after the outbreak of World War I.

These refugees were joined by even larger numbers of regular immigrants seeking economic opportunities as France's industrialization process began to accelerate in the late nineteenth and early twentieth

centuries. With many French unwilling to leave the countryside—a large proportion owned real estate thanks to the land reforms of the revolutionary era—French industrialists looked elsewhere for laborers to fill their factories and workshops. While some of these workers came from impoverished regions in the eastern half of the continent, most arrived from neighboring countries, generally with smaller industrial bases. Italians were the largest group of pre–World War I immigrants, followed by Spaniards, Belgians, and Swiss. Altogether, between 1850 and 1914, about 4.3 million foreigners entered France.

The interwar period saw a continuation of the trends from the pre–World War I era, though with a somewhat larger contingent coming from the eastern part of Europe. While French law had put few restrictions on immigration before World War I, the government actively encouraged newcomers in the interwar period. During the First World War, France had seen much of its industrial base in the northeastern part of the country destroyed by fighting and needed to rebuild. More importantly, the Great War had decimated France's population, with nearly one-fourth of all young males having been killed in the slaughter of trench warfare. Thus, with economic instability and growing political turmoil engulfing the central and eastern parts of the continent in the 1920s and 1930s—and with laws encouraging newcomers—France saw its immigrant population soar in the interwar period. Between 1918 and 1940, some 3 million foreigners poured into the country, constituting by the latter year some 6 percent of the total population. Again, most came from neighboring countries of Italy (35 percent), Spain (15 percent), and Belgium (10 percent). But now there was also a major contingent from Poland (20 percent).

The postwar economic "miracle" that came to France after 1945 further encouraged immigration. The vast economic expansion of the years between 1945 and the great energy crisis of the early 1970s cre-

In recent decades, Western Europe has become home to increasing numbers of immigrants from former European colonies and, since the collapse of communism in the late 1980s and early 1990s, from Eastern Europe and the former Soviet Union as well. *(CARTO-GRAPHICS)*

ated a nearly insatiable appetite for immigrant workers. Many of these continued to come from France's traditional sources, the poorer nearby states of Italy, Spain, and Portugal. But now they were superseded by immigrants from France's former colonies, particularly those in North Africa. (In addition, some 1 million immigrants of European background—known as *colons*, or settlers—poured into France from Algeria, after the latter won its independence from France in a long and brutal war of liberation in 1962. Most of these refugees settled in the south of France, where they earned the nickname *pieds noirs*, or "black feet," because they were believed to be so poor that they had to go barefoot.) By the 1980s, approximately 4 million foreigners lived in France, about 7 percent of the population.

While the French generally welcomed European immigrants throughout their history, the new immigrants received an altogether different reception. Even when they were desperately needed in French factories—greater educational and economic opportunities, combined with a declining birth rate, created an exodus by native-born French nationals from industrial work—the new immigrants were shunned, rarely being able to integrate into French life and housed in massive and quickly decaying housing projects on the periphery of major cities. The causes were both cultural and economic. Unlike European immigrants, the new entrants from North Africa were darker-skinned and Muslim. Many refused to give up their Muslim culture in order to adopt the Western ways of France, making them seem ungrateful to their new hosts.

At the same time, the French turned increasingly hostile to the immigrants after the economic downturn of the mid-1970s. With unemployment rising, many French began to resent the immigrants in their midst, seeing them as competitors for coveted jobs. By the latter part of the decade, increasing numbers of native-born French were willing to accept factory work, thereby displacing immigrant laborers. The economic downturn had an even more devastating effect on immigrant populations. With rising levels of poverty and unemployment, some turned to crime; greater numbers went on welfare. Both trends seemed to convince native-born French citizens that the immigrants were a threat to their way of life. In the 1980s, a number of politicians—including Jean-Marie Le Pen—rose up to denounce immigrants and call for their deportation or, at least, a halt to any further immigration.

GERMANY

Unlike France, Germany has little in the way of an immigrant tradition. Indeed, before the Second World War, the country—and the various German-speaking states of central Europe that preceded its formation in the late nineteenth century—was more likely to be a source of immigrants than a destination for them.

The aftermath of World War II saw a massive relocation of German-speaking immigrants from regions to the east. This trend, along with the readjustment of German borders westward, drew no less than 12 million refugees into the country in the immediate postwar period. These ethnic German refugees were joined by millions of other displaced persons who chose not to live under the Soviet-dominated communist regimes that came to power in the eastern half of the European continent in the late 1940s. Meanwhile, between the end of World War II and the erection of the Berlin Wall in 1961, West Germany saw the inmigration of some 2 million refugees from East Germany. Most of these German and Eastern European refugees were welcome. Germany, until quite recently, was the only major European nation that had an ethnically based concept of citizenship. That is to say, citizenship was—and still largely is—reserved for persons of German ethnic background.

Nevertheless, since at least the mid-1950s, Germany has welcomed millions of immigrants of non-German and non-European background. With much of its industrial and urban infrastructure destroyed in World War II, the country needed vast numbers of laborers for reconstruction. This reconstruction enterprise was at the core of what has come to be known

Table 1
Number of Foreign Nationals in France: 1990

Country of Citizenship	Population	Percentage
Portugal	645,578	1.14
Algeria*	619,923	1.09
Morocco*	584,708	1.03
Italy	253,679	0.45
Spain	216,015	0.38
Tunisia*	207,496	0.37
Turkey	201,480	0.36
Others	878,711	1.55
French	53,026,709	93.68
Total	56,634,299	100.0

*Former French colonies
Source: Europa Publications. "France." In *Europa Yearbook*. London: Europa Publications, 1995.

Since the end of World War II, Western European countries have played host to ever-growing numbers of immigrants. Many come from former colonies, like this Cape Verdean tile worker in Portugal. *(Tom Benton/Impact Visuals)*

as the German "economic miracle," the rise from the ashes of one of the wealthiest and most economically productive nations in the world. Invited in as so-called *Gastarbeiten*, or guest-workers, millions of Turks, Italians, Spaniards, Greeks, Poles, and Yugoslavs came to Germany to seek unskilled and semi-skilled work in factories, leaving the higher-paying skilled and management positions to German nationals.

Under German immigration law and policy, they were supposed to come for only a short time, but soon many of them were settling into life in West Germany and bringing their families to live with them. By 1989, and despite an economic downturn following the energy crisis of the mid-1970s, which led to high rates of unemployment and general economic stagnation into the 1980s and 1990s, the foreign-born population constituted some 6.4 percent of Germany's total population. Because of low birth rates among German nationals, immigrants—with their larger families—have

come to contribute about 65 percent of the nation's population growth in the 1980s and 1990s.

Although strict antiracism laws have been written into the West German lawbooks in the post-Nazi era, immigrants and foreign nationals remain on the margins of national life. There is little ethnic mixing in the country, and most of the immigrants earn incomes far below that of their German colleagues; they tend to live in poor and underserviced immigrant ghettos in and around major German cities.

Meanwhile, the same trend—on a significantly smaller scale—occurred in East Germany. There, the communist government welcomed nationals from poorer communist states such as Angola, Cuba, Mozambique, and Vietnam. Invited in for both political reasons and to provide laborers for East German factories, these non-European immigrants were also shunned by locals and forced to live in the poorer housing projects of East German cities, largely outside mainstream East German culture and life.

Since the collapse of the Berlin Wall in 1989, Western Europe has seen an inrush of immigrants from the eastern half of the continent, including this Russian man in an Austrian train station. *(Hias)*

With the collapse of communism in Eastern Europe and the former Soviet Union in the late 1980s and early 1990s—including the unification of the two Germanys in 1990—the country has seen a vast influx of economic and political refugees. The late 1980s and early 1990s saw a wave of some 377,000 ethnically German refugees who had lived in Russia and the Soviet Union for generations. Generally poorer than East Germans, and often not even German-speaking, they have had a much harder time adjusting to life in the capitalist West. In addition, the fall of the Berlin Wall in 1989 created a flow of some 250,000 migrants annually from the former East Germany that persisted into the 1990s.

Finally, Germany has also become the most popular destination for non-German ethnic refugees from Eastern Europe and the Soviet Union in the 1990s. Some of these people were fleeing the rapidly deteriorating economic conditions in the former communist bloc. Others—specifically those from the former Yugoslavia—came because of the various wars that

engulfed their native lands in the 1990s. Indeed, no country in Europe or the world has accepted more Yugoslav refugees than Germany. But the collapse of the former communist bloc also created the conditions for another kind of immigrant. Economic refugees from the Middle East and South Asia have taken advantage of the increasingly porous borders of the states that once made up the Soviet Union and communist Eastern Europe to make their way to Western Europe. Germany, being on the edge of this region—and being the largest economy in Europe—has attracted more of these immigrants than any other country. By 1995, just over 1 million immigrants were coming to Germany annually.

The increasing flow of non-German refugees has produced a political reaction among many German nationals, particularly those in the more economically hard-pressed eastern part of the country. Since the early 1990s, racist gangs have attacked immigrants and immigrant hostels in both western and eastern German cities. This has produced stricter immigration

Table 2
Immigrants to and Emigrants from Britain: 1995

Country	Immigrants	Emigrants
Former British Colonies	86,000	64,000
Australia	21,000	27,000
New Zealand	10,000	10,000
Canada	8,000	6,000
South Africa	4,000	4,000
Other African nations	9,000	4,000
Bangladesh, India, Sri Lanka	11,000	2,000
Pakistan	5,000	2,000
Caribbean	2,000	2,000
European Union	33,000	39,000
United States	13,000	19,000
Other foreign countries	55,000	41,000

Source: Europa Publications. "United Kingdom." *Europa Yearbook.* London: Europa Publications, 1995.

laws, but also a vast outpouring of pro-immigrant sentiment, as demonstrated in massive antiracist marches in several German cities.

GREAT BRITAIN

With its immigration history more resembling that of France than Germany, Great Britain has long served as a refuge for political, religious, and economic immigrants from the European continent. Since at least the mid-nineteenth century, Britain—with its tradition of political liberalism and relative tolerance, as well as its early industrialization—has long been a draw for people fleeing persecution, poverty, and war. In the wake of the French Revolution, for example, numerous aristocrats fled to Britain, joined by thousands of others fleeing the Napoleonic wars on the continent. Others fled the failed revolutions of 1848. During the latter half of the nineteenth century, Britain served as a major immigrant destination for hundreds of thousands of economic refugees from Eastern Europe, as well as a refuge for many Jews fleeing the persecutions in late czarist Russia.

At the same time, of course, the country has arguably had Europe's longest and greatest tradition of emigration. More than any other country, Britain has established numerous settler colonies around the world that have served as safety valves for overpopulation and unemployment. In the seventeenth and eighteenth centuries, the main destinations were the colonies in North America. While the independent United States remained an important destination for British immigrants in the nineteenth century, new lands—including Australia, Canada, New Zealand, and South Africa—opened up as well.

In the post–World War II era, Britain has seen a new and far greater immigration from the world outside of Europe. This new wave of immigrants has been caused by several factors: economic expansion, liberalized immigration laws, and, most important, the end of empire. Depite its older and less dynamic industrial base—vis-à-vis continental Western Europe—Britain has seen the need to encourage low-wage factory and service workers from the developing world and has modified its laws and policies to bring them in.

Still, more than any other nation, Britain has borne, in its expanding immigrant numbers, the legacy of empire. By the mid-1950s, immigration from the Commonwealth countries—that is, most of the newly founded states that once were the colonies of the British Empire—had become significant. Between the late 1950s and the early 1960s, Britain saw a net influx of persons from the Commonwealth for the first time, with the bulk coming from South Asia—including Bangladesh (independent from Pakistan since 1971), India, Pakistan, and Sri Lanka—and the West Indies. In the early 1960s, these immigrants were joined by smaller numbers from the newly independent British colonies in Africa. Moreover, during these years, immigration from the Commonwealth was free and open. But even the restrictions put into place in 1962 barely stemmed the tide, with hundreds of thousands of newcomers taking advantage of laws encouraging family reunification to join those immigrants already in Britain.

Even today, Britain remains a net importer of people from the Commonwealth. In 1995, approximately eighty-six thousand persons immigrated from the Commonwealth, while Britain saw sixty-four thousand of its own nationals—including many nationalized immigrants and their offspring—leaving for Commonwealth countries. In total, some 257,000 foreigners emigrated to Britain in that year, while some 220,000 British nationals left the country.

Somewhat separated from Europe, Britain has been a bit less affected by the flood of refugees from Eastern Europe and the former Soviet Union in the wake of the collapse of communism. At the same time, immigrants from its former colonies—particularly those in the West Indies—have increasingly seen the more economically dynamic United States as a destination with better educational and economic opportunities, leading to a shift in immigration patterns from those Commonwealth countries. In addition, Canada, with its relative dearth of people, has actively encouraged Commonwealth immigration.

Yet, despite these trends that go somewhat against the general Western European current, Britain has been hit by the same political reaction. The formation of xenophobic and racist anti-immigrant groups has been accompanied by a rising level of anti-immigrant violence in Britain. At the same time, however, it has not reached the levels that eastern Germany saw, nor has it resulted in the formation of a major anti-immigrant political party, as has been the case in France.

With the possible exception of France, western Europe has had a much longer and richer tradition of out-migration than inmigration. Indeed, peoples from western Europe became the dominant settler populations in the Americas, Australasia, and southern Africa between the sixteenth and early twentieth centuries. But since World War II, that trend has been reversed, as this part of Europe collectively has become the most important destination for immigrants in the world, even outstripping the historically immigrant-welcoming United States. Inevitably, that has produced a backlash on the Continent, which has included racist violence, anti-immigrant politics, and stricter immigration law.

Daniel James

See also: East Africa, North Africa, Southern Africa, West Africa (Part III, Sec. 1); English-Speaking Caribbean, Haiti and French-Speaking Caribbean (Part III, Sec. 2); Middle East, South Asia, Southeast Asia (Part III, Sec. 3); Great Britain, Eastern Europe, Former Soviet Union, Ireland, Western and Southern Europe (Part III, Sec. 4).

BIBLIOGRAPHY

Feldblum, Miriam. *Reconstructing Citizenship: The Politics of Nationality Reform and Immigration in Contemporary France*. Albany: State University of New York Press, 1999.

Horowitz, Donald L., and Gérard Noiriel. *Immigrants in Two Democracies: French and American Experience*. New York: New York University Press, 1992.

James, Winston, and Clive Harris, eds. *Inside Babylon: The Caribbean Diaspora in Britain*. London; New York: Verso, 1993.

Layton-Henry, Zig. *The Politics of Immigration: Immigration, "Race" and "Race" Relations in Post-war Britain*. Cambridge, MA: Blackwell Publishers, 1992.

Schuck, Peter H., and Rainer Münz. *Paths to Inclusion: The Integration of Migrants in the United States and Germany*. New York: Berghahn Books, 1998.

Part III

IMMIGRANT GROUPS IN AMERICA

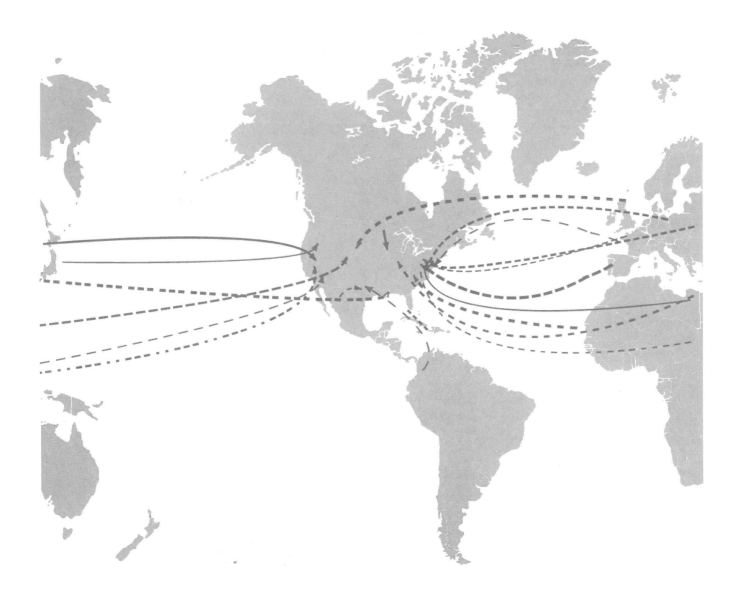

$\mathscr{I}$NTRODUCTION

$\mathscr{P}$art III of the *Encyclopedia of American Immigration* is devoted to discussions of immigration and immigrants from various countries and regions around the world. It is divided into four sections, corresponding to major regions of the world: Section 1 covers Africa, Section 2 focuses on the Americas, Section 3 examines immigration and immigrants from Asia (including the Middle East) and the Pacific, and Section 4 is devoted to Europe and the former Soviet Union. Within each section, individual entries generally focus on regions. However, in some cases, individual countries with unusual or particularly important roles in American immigration receive entries of their own.

For much of American history, immigrants largely came from Europe, with a few major exceptions. Through much of the seventeenth and eighteenth centuries—and continuing through the ban on the international slave trade in 1808—some six hundred thousand persons were brought to these shores as slaves. Some came directly from Africa; many others had been slaves in the Caribbean first. Another significant exception has been Hispanics, and specifically Mexicans. Under the 1848 Treaty of Guadalupe Hidalgo, which ended the Mexican-American War, Mexico ceded millions of square miles of its northern frontier, and with that territory came several tens of thousands of Mexican nationals. In a sense, then, these Mexicans did not come to the United States; the United States came to them. Throughout the late nineteenth century and particularly in the early part of the twentieth, significant numbers of Mexicans continued to move northward in search of work, followed by smaller numbers of Central and South Americans. Under the immigrant restriction acts of 1921 and 1924, persons from the Western Hemisphere were exempted from the quotas. Shortly after World War II, these mainland Hispanic immigrants were joined by a new wave of Puerto Rican immigration. Although technically residents of a U.S. colony, the Puerto Ricans who came largely to New York City beginning in the late 1940s experienced much of the same prejudice that met other early Hispanic groups in the United States.

Still more exceptions to the European dominance of immigration came from East Asia, specifically China, Japan, and the Philippines. Since the California gold rush days of the mid-nineteenth century, Chinese immigrants had been making their way to the western United States in the thousands, drawn first by mining opportunities and later work on the railroads. But this first wave of Asian immigration met stiff opposition among certain working-class elements on the West Coast, who were able to win a federal exclusion bill against the Chinese by the 1880s. A similar story marked Japanese immigration. Rising numbers led to increased reaction, which resulted in an effort, at the federal level, to exclude Japanese immigrants. But because Japan was a growing military and economic power in the world—as opposed to China, which was increasingly coming under foreign occupation in the late nineteenth century—the agreement between Japan and the United States on immigration was covered with the fig leaves of diplomacy and voluntarism. The Philippines also sent large numbers of immigrants to the agricultural fields of California and the Far West in the decades following that archipelago's absorption as a U.S. colony in 1900.

Still, for all of these exceptions, the vast majority of immigrants in the more than 350 years of colonization of and immigration to the United States between the founding of Jamestown in 1607 and passage of the 1965 immigration reform act came from Europe. But even here, there were significant shifts in the source of immigrants. The first European settlers to the North American mainland largely came from England, with a smattering of Spanish settlers and French traders and trappers. By the early eighteenth century, however, the variety of immigrants had expanded to include Scotch Irish (from what is now Ulster, or Northern Ireland), people from the German-speaking states of central Europe, and French Huguenots, or Protestants.

By the mid-nineteenth century, the source of European immigration had shifted once again, though it is important to remember that even as new countries sent large numbers of immigrants, the old sources hardly dried up. Indeed, throughout the nineteenth century, for example, large numbers of immigrants from England, Northern Ireland, and Germany continued to arrive in the United States. But in the 1840s and 1850s, there was a huge and highly noticeable influx of Irish. These were not the much-admired Scotch-Irish Protestant yeomen who often settled on the frontier, but desperately poor Catholic Irish from the south of the island, what is now the Republic of Ireland. The Catholic Irish of the mid-nineteenth century were also the first major immigrant group to attract widespread prejudice—no doubt a product of their desperate poverty and their Catholicism, then considered an alien religion that rendered its followers subject to the dictates of Rome and therefore citizens with questionable loyalties. The power of this anti-Irish, anti-Catholic prejudice can be measured by its longevity. As late as 1960, presidential candidate John Kennedy—a descendant of Catholic Irish immigrants—was forced to defend himself against charges that his loyalties would be divided between Washington and the Vatican.

Around the turn of the twentieth century, the source of immigration had once again shifted, this time to the southern and eastern reaches of the European continent. Whereas roughly 70 percent of the 5 million immigrants who arrived during the 1880s came from northern and western Europe, nearly 60 percent of immigrants in the first decade of the 1900s arrived from southern and eastern Europe. Meanwhile, immigration from western and northern Europe had fallen in absolute as well as relative terms, amounting to less than 2 million in the decade of the 1900s. Various explanations have been offered for this shift, but perhaps the most convincing are the economic ones. Specifically, it has been argued that the gradual spread of the market-driven economy to the rural areas of countries such as Russia, Italy, and Poland disrupted peasant-based production. Landholdings were consolidated and modernized, which rendered many peasant farmers economically redundant. First, they moved to nearby urban centers, which were insufficiently developed economically to absorb such numbers, and then to immigrant-host countries— especially, but not exclusively, the United States. (Other major destinations included Argentina, Australia, Brazil, Canada, France, and Great Britain.)

In the United States, once again, the influx of im-

migrants from new and alien European cultures produced a predictable backlash among native-born citizens, fearful that the newcomers were incapable of becoming democratic, capitalistic Americans. The ultimate result of this nativist sentiment was highly restrictive pieces of legislation passed in 1917, 1921, and 1924. The first act—known informally as the Literacy Act—was meant to keep out not specific nationalities, but all those immigrants who were seen as potential wards of the states. That is to say, those who could not read and write either in their native language or in English were viewed as persons incapable of understanding American democracy, absorbing American culture, or succeeding in the American economy. The acts of 1921 and 1924, respectively, tightened the screws on immigration from the so-called new sending countries of eastern and southern Europe. This was done by establishing quotas based on the number of persons from that country living in the United States in a given year. The first act established a limit of 3 percent and used the base year of 1910. When that did not prove restrictive enough, the quota was dropped to 2 percent and the base year was set in 1890, safely before most of the new immigration had occurred. The result was exactly what the authors of the bill hoped for: By the 1930s, immigration had dropped to a fraction of what it had been in the 1900s (although this decline can partly be attributed to the Great Depression).

And while European immigration climbed once again in the immediate post–World War II decades— to about 1 million in the 1950s, of which about half came from the eastern and southern parts of the Continent—it remained small by comparison to the turn-of-the-century period. Meanwhile, immigration from the Western Hemisphere—free, as noted above, from the quotas—rose dramatically, to some 1 million, in the 1950s. Still, it was the 1965 Immigration and Nationality Act, ending national quotas and prioritizing family reunions as an acceptable reason for being allowed into the United States legally, that changed the face of immigration for the remainder of the twentieth century. By the 1980s, nearly 90 percent of the over 7 million immigrants legally entering the United States were natives of countries in Latin America, the Caribbean, and Asia.

There are several explanations for this shift offered by sociologists and other immigrant experts. First, as in the case of southern and eastern Europe nearly a century before, intensification of market economies— particularly in rural areas—saw the displacement of millions of impoverished persons, particularly in Latin America. At the same time, the rising expectations of the newly literate masses of the Western

Hemisphere and Asia were running up against the rock of undeveloped economies. Higher expectations and a broader view of the world combined with easier transport led to a vast increase of immigrants to the United States and other traditional host countries for immigrants in Australia, Western Europe, and other locales. (In addition, a far smaller number of immigrants—refugees, really—were sent flowing into the United States and elsewhere by the endless conflicts that marked the Cold War and post–Cold War eras, particularly those in Southeast Asia, the Middle East, and Central America.) At the same time, the 1965 legislation's emphasis on reuniting families had a snowball effect. As increasing numbers of immigrants flowed into the United States from Asia and Latin America, the number of persons who could claim legitimate family ties grew exponentially. The result has been an explosion of immigration and, again, a backlash of nativist sentiment expressed in efforts to restrict social services to both legal and illegal immi-

grants and to make English the country's official language.

Today, America has become the most ethnically heterodox country in the history of the planet. Particularly in large urban areas such as New York and Los Angeles, governments are forced to cope with people speaking literally dozens of languages, while the predominance of Latino immigrants has made some American cities—again, Los Angeles, but also San Antonio, Miami, and elsewhere—essentially bilingual communities, with radio stations, newspapers, advertising, and other media offering their wares in both Spanish and English. As early as the 1700s, a visitor to New York commented on the babel of tongues spoken in that city's streets. A visitor in the twenty-first century could not help but notice that the pattern remains the same, even if the particulars—specifically, that the languages now are not just European and African ones—have changed.

AFRICA

Introduction

East Africa
Rogaia Mustafa Abusharaf

North Africa
Daniel James

Southern Africa
Grace Ebron

West Africa
Zain A. Abdullah

$\mathscr{I}$NTRODUCTION

$\mathscr{S}$ection 1 of Part III of the *Encyclopedia of American Immigration* is devoted to immigration and immigrants from the African continent. The section includes four regional entries: East Africa, North Africa, Southern Africa, and West Africa.

Africans, of course, were among the first outsiders to visit and settle in the Americas after permanent contact was established between the Western and Eastern Hemispheres in the late fifteenth century. There were Africans in Columbus's crew and Africans among the many expeditions launched by Spain and other European countries to explore and conquer the Americas. The first Africans to arrive in what is now the United States came with the Spaniards to Florida and the Southwest in the early sixteenth century. In the English colonies, the initial date for the arrival of Africans is 1619, in Jamestown, Virginia.

But while Africans have lived in the Americas for centuries, the vast majority came involuntarily as slaves. Free African immigration to the United States on a significant scale is a much more recent phenomenon, dating back but a few decades. The four articles in this section generally focus on this recent history.

In his entry on immigrants from East Africa, Rogaia Mustafa Abusharaf focuses primarily on the four countries of the region that have sent the largest number of people to the United States: Somalia, Eritrea, Ethiopia, and the Sudan, particularly the latter. The author begins with a study of the Sudanese in the Americas before focusing on the post–Gulf War period. He analyzes the Christian Copts among the newcomers from the Sudan and the phenomenon of female Sudanese immigration.

In the article on North Africa—which includes Egypt, Libya, Tunisia, Algeria, and Morocco—Daniel James begins with a discussion of the region's history. He then goes on to point out how the vast majority

of immigrants to the United States from this region are from Egypt. Examining immigration from that country, he begins with a discussion of the Christian Copts, who generally came to this country earlier than Muslim Egyptians. Finally, James explores the recent wave of Muslim Egyptian immigrants to the United States.

The entry on Southern Africa by Grace Ebron begins with an exploration of the forced migrations and slave trade in the region up through the period of European colonization. She then goes on to discuss the process of decolonization and how that led to the current—albeit modest—wave of immigration to the United States. Finally, she explores the settlement patterns and cultural adaptations made by Southern African immigrants once they settle in the United States.

In the last entry in this section, "West Africa," Zain A. Abdullah divides immigration from the region into three phases. On the first phase, Abdullah largely focuses on the massive importation of West African slaves into the United States in the seventeenth and eighteenth centuries. (For a more thorough discussion of the slave trade, see "Enslaved Africans" in Part I, Section 1 of the encyclopedia.) The second phase of West African immigration to the United States, according to Abdullah, covers the period from America's outlawing of the international slave trade in 1808 to the 1965 Immigration and Nationality Act, which liberalized immigration law and opened the gates to more African immigration. The third phase covers the period since 1965 and represents the fullest part of the entry. Here, the author explores both the causes and the phenomenon of female immigration, among other things. Finally, Abdullah looks at the two main West African immigrant groups in America—Nigerians and Ghanaians—before discussing some of the minor groups.

EAST AFRICA

Population mobility has been a defining aspect of human society. It has not only shaped demographic landscapes but has also defined international politics, history, and cultures around the world. Today, the number of contemporary international migrants is increasing, due in part to socioeconomic and political discontent and displacement in the developing world, and includes many whom sociologist Reginald Appleyard describes as being "at the deprivation end of the income, political freedom and human rights spectrum." For more than a century, most new arrivals to the United States were Europeans, the "arbiters of the core national culture." Now, immigrants are coming from Asia, Africa, and Latin America.

Since independence, the African continent has witnessed recurrent internal ethnic conflict leading to massive human dislocations. By mid-1980, most observers regarded the refugee crisis in Africa to be the world's worst. In East Africa, during the 1980s, the problems deepened, as millions of people deserted their homes in search of refuge in neighboring countries and elsewhere. Although environmental degradation, famine, and political repression were the main reasons behind large-scale refugee movements, such other forces as ethnic strife and wars in Ethiopia, Somalia, Eritrea, and Sudan were more important in forcing people to migrate en masse. The basic premise, however, is that these population movements should be understood as a combination of historical factors connected to economic, demographic, and political conditions in both sending as well as receiving countries. Historically, East Africa and the Horn have suffered from natural disasters, political repression, and economic crisis that prompted large numbers of people to flee. The scholar Aderanti Adepoju, has distinguished four regimes for understanding the mass migration of people from African countries: the economic, the political, the demographic, and the cultural regimes. This distinction is exceptionally relevant to East Africa, in

which all these factors have combined to force individuals and households to emigrate. Harsh socioeconomic realities, political repression, ethnic strife, and demographic pressures generated large-scale exodus in Somalia, Ethiopia, and Sudan in recent years and forced many to come to the United States.

While this entry will focus on the migratory experience of Sudanese, who represent the greatest proportionate rise in United States immigration in the 1990s, it will provide a brief background on other examples in East Africa: Ethiopia, Eritrea, and Somalia. Drawing from the insight of macrostructural migration theory, which treats migration as a process generated by structural inequalities around the world and within nation-states, the entry describes the forces that shape most of the migration movements from Africa to the United States. This diversity, as we shall see below, manifested itself in the increased variation within the African migrant communities in the United States.

SOMALIA

Somalia occupies an area of 246,550 square miles with a coastline of 2,000 miles running along the Indian Ocean and the Gulf of Aden. Although Somalia is often regarded as the most ethnically, religiously, and linguistically homogeneous African society, it is divided along clan lines: the dominant Samaale constitute 75 percent, while the Sab constituency is estimated at 25 percent. These clans are known to have exhibited independence, clan consciousness, and resistance to foreign rule. Like the majority of East African countries, Somalia is a labor- and refugee-sending country. The main causes of refugee exodus can be attributed to the 1977–78 Ogaden War, which prompted many to flee. For example, the

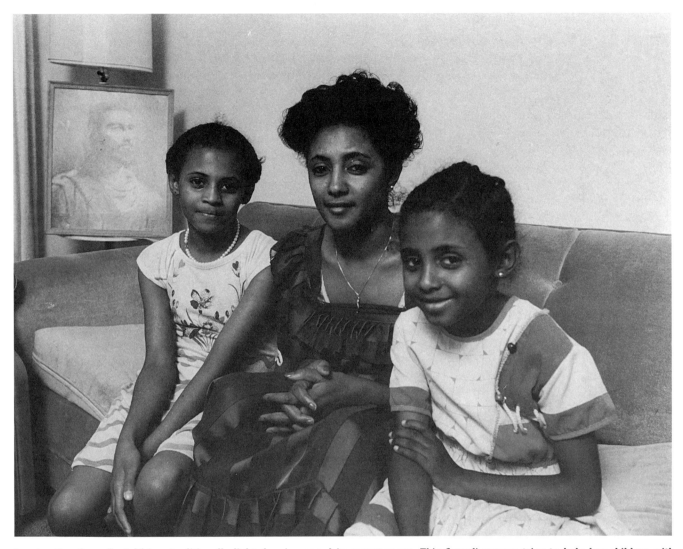

Immigration from East Africa, traditionally light, has increased in recent years. This Somali woman tries to help her children with their homework, though she speaks little English. *(AP/Wide World Photos)*

United Nations High Commissioner for Refugees (UNHCR) has estimated the numbers in early 1981 to be 1.3 million in camps in eastern Ethiopia in addition to another 1 million who were displaced. Moreover, internal instability, political repression, and economic decay have forced people to seek better lives away from the homeland. Political disintegration, which resulted in mass exodus, erupted when insurgent movements demanded political reforms during Mohamed Siad Barre's government. Siad Barre departed Mogadishu under massive pressure, and his flight led to further clan antagonism. Significant numbers of the Somali population have emigrated to Sweden, Denmark, Canada, and the United States, where they now form part of the new African diaspora.

ETHIOPIA AND ERITREA

Like Somalia, Ethiopia has been one of the largest refugee-producing countries in Africa. According to the sociologist Lucia McSpadden, out of an estimated population of 30 to 38 million, at least 1.25 million Ethiopians are refugees, approximately one out of every twenty Ethiopians. The forces prompting Ethiopian migration to the United States are similar to those shaping the experiences of other Africans from the Horn. Repression, war, and insecurity pushed many to seek asylum. One of the main observations regarding these migrations is that refugees apply for resettlement while in the country of first asylum. Although the number of East African refugees in the United States is generally small, it is rising. According to the United States Office of Refugee Resettlement, Ethiopians represented 2.75 percent of admissions to the United States in 1983–92.

The involuntary migration of the Eritrean population resulted from the long-standing war with Ethiopia. According to the scholars Atsuko Matsuoka and John Sorenson, Ethiopia annexed the Italian colony in 1962, a decade after a federation of the two entities was implemented by the United Nations. The annexation was opposed by much of the Eritrean population. After long periods of strife and war, Eritrea gained its political independence in 1993. However, the war continues, and large numbers of the civilian population were impelled to leave. While the majority crossed the borders to Sudan and Somalia, thousands have found refuge in Europe, the United States, and Canada. According to McSpadden, nearly 1.25 million Ethiopians and Eritreans were refugees in 1991, and of these, 23,500 had been granted asylum in the United States since 1980.

THE SUDAN

The Sudan is the largest country by territory in Africa. It occupies 965,000 million square miles, an area as vast as that of Italy, France, Belgium, Norway, Denmark, Sweden, Spain, and the United Kingdom combined. The Sudanese land and its location at the crossroads of Africa influenced the course of its politics and history, and the Sudanese people have written themselves in multilayered identities across it. The characteristics of the land have deeply influenced the life and social organization of its inhabitants, defining in a dramatic way the socioeconomic and political organization of its people. The Sudanese people are ethnically diverse. Though characterized by a high degree of ethnic heterogeneity, observers have often classified them in binary social categories on the basis of religion (Islam versus Christianity), region (north versus south), and ethnicity (Arabs versus Africans). Yet, a wide variety of ethnolinguistic and religious groups do not necessarily fall into this opposition.

Since independence in 1956, political turmoil has been a permanent aspect of Sudanese sociopolitical life. The country has experienced two forms of government: civilian and military. Parliamentary governments were forced out by coups, and military dictatorships have ruled the country for nearly thirty-one years. Under military regimes, substantial migration and refugee movements, especially to the United States, took place—and continue to take place.

A HISTORY OF SUDANESE IN THE NEW WORLD

Sudanese peoples have been arriving in the New World since the early 1800s. A pattern of Sudanese soldiers and marines being drafted into military service in the armies of European and American armed forces had been established at different moments in Euro-American historical trajectories. In 1863, Sudanese military units crossed the Atlantic en route to Veracruz, Mexico, in response to Emperor Napoléon's request for Sudanese troops in the French war against Mexico. This request was justified by the high rates of morbidity and mortality of the French soldiers in Mexico and the alleged immunity of Sudanese to tropical diseases.

But what appeared at the outset to be an isolated, rare historical incident is part of a pattern of Sudanese wartime service in the New World. Eighty years after the service of the conscript battalion in Mexico, a distinctive Sudanese migratory wave was ushered in as a response to the insistent demand by the United States for navy officers during World War II. Those were the Sudanese seamen, the merchant marines whose migration constituted the inaugural wave of an African migration to the United States. When they arrived at American ports, they were recruited into the American navy. Under similar circumstances, more Sudanese seamen were recruited during the Korean War. So, it is reasonable to suggest that the migration of Sudanese to the United States falls into three distinctive waves. The first wave began when these seamen joined the navy as early as 1940. The second wave consisted of a small-scale, voluntary but temporary migration of students that began after the country's attainment of independence from the British in 1956. Last, the largest wave of migration began after the advent of the military regime of Lieutenant General Omar Ahmed al-Bashir in 1989. This larger migration stems from political unrest, economic stringency, religious factors, and a perceived lack of choice in migratory destinations.

Today, Sudanese migrants are in the United States as refugees, asylum-seekers, Diversity Visa Lottery winners, and holders of temporary protection status, among others. Their migration to the United States will be treated below under four categories: those who were forced out of Kuwait after the Gulf War, those who came to the United States as refugees fleeing the war in Southern Sudan, Christian Copts fleeing a Muslim fundamentalist regime, and an increasing number of women who have migrated by themselves, a completely new thread in the Sudanese migratory tapestry.

BEYOND DESERT STORM

Prior to the Iraqi invasion of Kuwait in 1990, Sudanese nationals dominated migration to oil-rich Arab countries, which were major attractions of migrant labor throughout the region and beyond. Studies undertaken on Sudanese migration to oil-rich countries have noted that since 1969, the movement of highly qualified skilled workers had reached such an extent that the Sudan, which in the 1960s trailed all other labor-exporting countries in Africa, emerged as the largest exporter of migrant labor in Northeast Africa. This loss was associated with a locally rising cost of living, a deteriorating economy, and reduced civil service benefits. One of the attractions of the Persian Gulf was its geographic proximity. At the level of individuals, families, and communities, working in the gulf was an economically advantageous experience as the local economy slowly deteriorated. How, then, did the gulf crisis undermine the sizable Sudanese worker and expatriate community that had been employed there for decades? And why were these new migrants directed to North America?

As a result of political alignments during the war, Sudanese migrants were forced to leave. According to J. Addelton, "For expatriate communities in Kuwait, the invasion represented the worst scenario, the single event which put into jeopardy employment and remittance relationships developed over the preceding decade." This led in part to the redirection of migration to the United States, where most people perceived expulsion as the primary reason behind their move. It is reasonable to suggest that this particular pattern was an attempt to overcome increasing constraints arising from the political crisis in the Sudan as well as from wider events in the Middle East that altered the established migration pattern from the Sudan to the gulf. In a comprehensive ethnographic survey conducted by the author, nearly 40 percent of the sampled Sudanese respondents indicated having held jobs in Kuwait, Saudi Arabia, or Iraq.

SOUTHERN SUDANESE

The migration of southerners from Sudan can be seen as a forced migration resulting from violence associated with the longest running civil war on the African continent. Southerners are therefore considered to be refugees insofar that a refugee is defined as "any person who is outside his or her country of nationality and is unable or unwilling to return to that country because of persecution or a well-founded fear of persecution." Claims of persecution may be based on race, religion, nationality, membership in a particular social group, or political opinion.

Responses obtained from the survey and in-depth key informant interviewing demonstrated that policies of Islamization, added to the sociopolitical marginalization, have combined to prompt southerners to leave. Concomitantly, factors such as political and religious freedom in the United States, assistance provided by churches and refugee resettlement organizations, as well as encouragement by family members were all offered as objective forces that shaped their migration to the United States. Southerners are mainly young and middle-age individuals who started arriving in the United States in the 1980s and continue to arrive as a result of the ongoing civil war. They are mostly Christians, and overall, those arriving are educated, having completed college or at least a high secondary education at the time of arrival.

Most respondents stated that they would go back to the Sudan if the country returns to a secular constitution and if democracy prevails or if secession of the South takes place. According to the sociologist Augustino Lado, "The time to let our people go is long overdue. We cannot continue to be a nation of masters and slaves; pursuing peace in the context of a united Sudan sustains Arab hegemony over Africans in Sudan. Partitioning the country would deliver African Sudanese from centuries of bondage at the hands of the Arabs."

THE COPTS

The migrations of the Sudanese Copts, past and present, are illustrative of the power of the state over religious minorities. The present migration of the Copts to the United States is related to experiences of religious oppression that reaches back in history. A migrant in the United States remarks, "Traditionally the Copts have always been attached to their homeland; emigration was something new to them, an adventure into the unknown. Our friends and relatives looked at us in surprise, mixed with pity. Most of the church leaders were reluctant to bless such movement, if they were not totally against it." Around 1969–70, a small Coptic migration from the Sudan occurred, due in part to the confiscation by President Jaafar Nimeiri's government of businesses owned by Copts. Today, religious factors are cited by Copts as the primary forces behind their migration to the United States, Canada, Australia, and Western Europe. Three interconnected issues linked to the Coptic migration are the Islamization of the country, citizenship, and militarism. First, in 1983, the Nimeiri government declared its goal of transforming the country into an Islamic state, stressing unequivocally that Islam is the state's guiding religion and that its binding code directs the laws, regulations, and policies of the state (Article 1 of Sudan's constitutional decree). An Islamic constitution based on historic jurisprudence, known as *sharia*, was adopted. Under the Islamic state, the Copts became more aware of their ethnoreligious identity as a non-Muslim religious minority. The volume of the new Coptic migratory phenomenon touched a high point in the period between 1989 and 1999. As far as citizenship is concerned, one has to point out at the outset that the Copts used to live in equanimity and peace with other groups and were fully integrated in the Sudanese society. The situation has changed due to measures which were seen as restrictive to civil liberties and which denied non-Muslims the full range of rights given to a citizen. For instance, non-Muslim religious education was banned from the schools. According to an Africa Watch report of 1992, practices that are seen as discriminatory manifested themselves in the sphere of the compulsory conscription into paramilitary training camps where young people and students are forced to take part in military training in preparation for Jihad, holy war. This concern has forced many to seek safe haven for their children and families.

Driven by the abiding conviction that to survive in foreign lands, they must preserve their forms of worship, Coptic migrants in the United States have re-created in revealing terms what they had left behind: their churches. Religion continues to play a pivotal role in adapting to life in the United States.

WOMEN

The migration of African women in general and Sudanese in particular has received scant attention in most studies of migrancy. Even when they receive such attention, they are relegated to a subsidiary position as dependents, who move only as part of family units. Appalling as this neglect may seem, it is to be expected. As a result of prevailing attitudes in Sudanese society toward the migration of single women, few have ventured to migrate.

One of the most recent trends I encountered in the course of researching Sudanese migration to the United States is the migration of single women. Over the last decades, circumstances at home and abroad have intersected to transform widely held conventions and traditions, resulting in the feminization of international migration. The increased presence of single women is attributed to the Islamization of the country, which posed restrictions on women's participation in public life and on their mobility. The adoption of the sharia figured prominently in the migratory decisions of these women. Coming to the United States is seen as an attempt to circumvent new obstacles imposed on them by the military regime.

This entry attempted to describe some trends of East African migration to the United States, with a special focus on major waves of Sudanese migration. As becomes clear, the political regime seems to have the most impact on migratory decisions. There are at least two implications for the receiving society. First, the migrants are highly skilled and are in the prime of their productive years. Hence, they are capable of making positive contributions. On the other hand, migrants increase the ethnic, cultural, and religious diversity of American society, with all the pressures and tensions that such diversity creates.

Rogaia Mustafa Abusharaf

See also: Natural Disasters, Environmental Crises, and Overpopulation, Political, Ethnic, Religious, and Gender Persecution, Wars and Civil Unrest (Part II, Sec. 1); Houston, Washington, D.C. (Part II, Sec. 12); Immigration to Western Europe (Part II, Sec. 13); Refugee Act of 1980 (Part IV, Sec. 1); U.S. Report Under the International Covenant on Civil and Political Rights, 1994, New U.S. Rules on Asylum for Women, 1995 (Part IV, Sec. 2).

BIBLIOGRAPHY

Abusharaf, Rogaia. "Sudanese Migration to the New World: Socioeconomic Characteristics." *International Migration* 35:4 (1997): 513–37.

Addelton, J. "The Impact of the Gulf War on Migration and Remittances in Asia and the Middle East." *International Migration* 29:4 (1991): 509–27.

Adepoju, Aderanti. "Preliminary Analysis of Emigration Dynamics in Sub-Saharan Africa." *International Migration* 32:2 (1994): 197–217.

Africa Watch. *The Copts: Passive Survivors Under Threat.* New York: Human Rights Watch Publications, 1992.

Appleyard, Reginald. *International Migration: Challenge for the Nineties.* Geneva, Switzerland: International Organization of Migration, 1991.

———. 1994. "IOM/UNFPA Project on Emigration Dynamics in Developing Countries." *International Migration* 32:2 (1994): 179–97.

Apraku, Kofi. *African Emigrés in the United States.* Westport, CT: Praeger, 1991.

Bariagaber, Assefaw. "Linking Political Violence and Refugee Situations in the Horn of Africa: An Empirical Approach." *International Migration* 33:2 (1995): 209–29.

Delancy, Mark, et al. *Somalia*. World Bibliographic Series. Oxford: Clio Press, 1988.

Hill, Richard, and Peter Hogg. *A Black Corps d'Elite*. East Lansing: Michigan State University Press, 1995.

Lado, Augustino. *Arab Slavery in Southern Sudan*. London: Pax Sudani Organization, 1994.

Matsuoka, Atsuko, and John Sorenson. "Eritrean Canadian Refugee Households as Sites of Gender Renegotiation." In *Engendering Forced Migration,* ed. D. Indra, pp. 218–41. New York: Berghahn Books, 1999.

McSpadden, Lucia. "Ethiopian Refugee Resettlement in the Western United States." *International Migration Review* 21:3 (1987): 796–819.

———. "Negotiating Masculinity in the Reconstruction of Social Place." In *Engendering Forced Migration,* ed. D. Indra, pp. 242–60. New York: Berghahn Books, 1999.

McSpadden, Lucia, and H. Moussa. "I Have a Name." *Journal of Refugee Studies* 6:3 (1993): 203–25.

U.S. Department of State. *Somalia: A Country Study*. Area Handbook Series. Washington, DC: Government Printing Office, 1993.

Yanney, Rudolph. "Aspects in the Life of the Copts and Their Church in the U.S." *Coptologia* 10 (1989): 65–70.

NORTH AFRICA

For the purposes of this entry, North Africa is defined as these countries (from east to west): Egypt, Libya, Tunisia, Algeria, and Morocco. There are both great similarities and great differences among these five countries. Most importantly, all five countries are overwhelmingly Muslim, although Egypt has a significant minority (roughly 6 percent of the population) of Christians, who are also known as Copts. In addition, all of the countries of the region share Arabic as their official language, though significant minorities in Algeria and Morocco, in particular, speak Berber. Culturally, too, these countries consider themselves part of the Arab world. All five were invaded by Arab armies in the seventh and eighth centuries C.E., which brought the Muslim faith and the Arabic language to indigenous populations.

NORTH AFRICAN HISTORY

Still, there are significant differences between these five countries, and these differences begin with history. Egypt, of course, is one of the cradles of civilization, with a written history that goes back at least 5,000 years. In contrast, the four countries to the west were largely made up of decentralized tribes through much of their history. At the same time, these four always had strong cultural divisions between their coastal and interior regions. The former were largely part of the Mediterranean world since at least the first millennium B.C.E., having been colonized by the Phoenicians, the Romans, the Arabs and finally the Ottoman Turks in the sixteenth century C.E. The latter mostly consisted of Berber tribes in the near interior and Tuareg and other nomadic tribal peoples in the Saharan desert to the south. With the exception of Egypt, the populations of the North African countries are ethnically divided between Arabs and Berbers, the difference between the two mainly being linguistic.

During the period of European imperialist expansion, the five countries underwent varied historical experiences. Algeria, Morocco, and Tunisia were colonized by the French. Algeria, in particular, became an integral part of the French empire as colonists from France and Europe settled there in large numbers. By the 1950s, there were approximately 1 million *colons*, or European colonists, in Algeria out of a total population of 10 million. The consequence of this was that while Morocco and Tunisia won their independence from France peacefully, Algerians were forced to fight a long and bloody war of national liberation from 1954 to 1962. Libya was settled late, by the Italians, while Egypt was briefly a British colony. In 1922, Egypt was granted nominal independence under a king selected by the British. Thirty years later, however, King Farouk was overthrown in a coup led by the nationalist military officer Maj. Gen. Mohammed Naguib, commander in chief of the Society of Free Officers. Lt. Col. Gamal Abdel Nasser removed Naguib, who became the republic's first premier, and became premier himself in 1954.

In the postindependence period, the five countries have followed very different paths. Morocco and Tunisia have followed a pro-Western course, with the former organized as a monarchy and the latter as a republic, though most powers were concentrated in the hands of long-serving president Habib Bourguiba (1957 to 1987). Libya's monarchy was overthrown in a coup led by the Arab socialist and nationalist Col. Muammar Khadafi, who has made Libya a self-contained, anti-Western country.

Climatically, all five countries are quite similar. All have a coastal region that enjoys a Mediterranean climate of long, dry summers and short, cool, winters. Morocco, Algeria, and Tunisia also have mountains in the near interior, though the extent of these mountains varies. Finally, all five countries of North Africa are dominated by the Sahara Desert, which covers between 50 percent (Tunisia) and 95 percent

numbers of people to the United States, this essay focuses on the immigrants from that country.

COPTIC EGYPTIAN IMMIGRANTS

Following a similar pattern in the rest of the Arab Middle East, most of the early Egyptian immigrants to the United States were Christians, or Copts. The word *Copt* is believed to be derived from the ancient Egyptian word for spirit, *ka*, and the term was Arabized to Qipt in the seventh century C.E. Like Christian minorities in other Arab countries, many Copts were landowners and merchants. When Nasser became premier in 1954 and instituted land reform and other socialist measures, many wealthier Copts fled, some to Britain and some to the United States. Most of these 1950s-era Copt immigrants settled in the New York City metropolitan area or California. A new wave of Coptic immigration followed the 1967 Six Day War between Egypt and Israel, when Arab nationalism and Muslim fundamentalism swept Egyptian society. Many Muslim Egyptians saw Copts as a dissenting minority who could not be trusted, and popular persecution—although officially frowned upon—created fear in the Coptic community. By 1970, it was estimated that approximately 25,000 of the 30,000 Egyptians living in the United States were of Coptic background. Maintaining a rather high birthrate in the United States, it is estimated that the population of Coptic immigrants and their descendants numbered some 265,000 by the end of the twentieth century.

Many Copts in the United States are economically successful, with a high proportion of professionals in their numbers. Tight families and a church-centered cultural life also mark the Coptic American community. For the most part, Copts have kept themselves separate from Muslim Egyptians in the United States, the latter constituting the bulk of that country's immigration to the United States in recent decades.

MUSLIM EGYPTIAN IMMIGRANTS

Egypt is a very crowded country. Although larger than Texas, its settled area—largely the Nile River valley and delta—comprises just 4 percent of the land mass, or an area just twice the size of New Jersey. Over 95 percent of the country's 67 million people live in this area, with the Cairo metropolitan area accounting for about a fifth of this total. While advances in

The vast majority of North African immigrants come from Egypt, like this elderly man and his granddaughter. *(Hias)*

(Libya) of their respective territories. With the exception of Egypt and its great Nile River valley, all suffer from a lack of fresh water.

Relative to other parts of the Middle East and the Arab world, North Africa has sent few immigrants to the United States. With the exception of Egypt, less than 30,000 immigrants from the region immigrated to the United States in the 1990s, with about half of these coming from Morocco. There are several explanations for this dearth of North African immigrants, depending on the country of origin. The three countries of Maghreb (Arabic for "land of the setting sun"), or the Arab West—that is, Morocco, Algeria, and Tunisia—were, as noted earlier, colonized by the French. Thus, most of their émigré populations have chosen France as their destination of choice, with smaller numbers settling in other Western European countries. Libya, of course, has had a long and stormy relationship with the United States. This—and the country's relative, oil-fed prosperity—has meant that few of the nation's people leave and, when they do, almost none make it to the United States. As Egypt is the only North African country that sends significant

medicine and the "green revolution"—which introduced scientifically developed, high-yield crops—have contributed to a population explosion since the end of World War II, Egypt has always been extremely crowded. Yet for all its population density, immigration was relatively rare until recent decades. Government policy aimed at dissuading emigration and a highly diversified economy were two reasons for this phenomenon. In addition, Egyptians have traditionally seen themselves as the economic, political, and cultural capital of the Arab world; non-Egyptian Arabs move to their country, many Egyptians felt, not the other way around.

Several events in the 1960s and 1970s conspired to change this pattern. First, of course, was the exploding population. Despite the enormous fertility of the Nile valley and the land reform policies of the Nasser government, young people increasingly found it impossible to support themselves on the land. At the same time, increased educational levels created higher expectations for many Egyptians, leading them to seek their fortunes overseas. Finally, there were geopolitical factors behind the change in immigration patterns. The 1967 and 1973 wars with Israel created enormous disruptions in the Egyptian economy, including the loss of lucrative shipping revenues when the Suez Canal was shut down in 1967. Moreover, between these two conflicts, Israel and Egypt fought the "war of attrition," a tit-for-tat struggle in which both sides shelled and bombed the other. Egypt got the worst of it as Israeli warplanes routinely destroyed factories, utilities, and other pieces of infrastructure. The wars also had a detrimental effect on Egyptian national pride, leading to a feeling that the country was no longer the center of the Arab world.

Finally, the enormous wealth accruing to the Persian Gulf states after the oil embargo of 1973–74 enticed many Egyptians who were looking for higher-paying jobs. For the first time, large numbers of Egyptian nationals were seeking work abroad, creating a growing sense that immigration was an acceptable way of improving one's lot in life. With shrinking oil revenues in the 1980s, many Persian Gulf countries began to limit immigration, forcing many outward-looking Egyptians to look elsewhere. Both Western Europe and the United States took up the slack. Between 1961 and 1991, approximately eighty thousand Egyptians immigrated to the United States, though this number remained a fraction of the hundreds of thousands who continued to live in or move to the Persian Gulf oil states.

Most Egyptian immigrants to the United States settled in Washington, D.C., Chicago, New York, New Jersey, and Southern California. Muslim Egyptian immigrants vary widely in their background. There are both highly trained professionals and unskilled workers among the immigrant population. Like other Arab immigrants, Muslim Egyptians are ambivalent about assimilating into American life. Many dislike the secularism, crass commercialism, and sexual license. At the same time, they sense a distinct anti-Muslim bias, especially whenever U.S. foreign policy clashes with the interests of the Arab world. In particular, the 1993 bombing of the World Trade Center—in which an Egyptian-born cleric and terrorists were involved—created an anti-Arab backlash in the U.S. that caused consternation in the Egyptian-American community, many members of which further withdrew into their own mosques and cultural centers.

North African immigration is unlikely to change markedly in the next few years. Morocco, Algeria, and Tunisia will no doubt maintain their close ties with France and Western Europe, sending most of their emigrants there. With its small population, great oil wealth, and inward-looking politics, Libya is unlikely to send large numbers of emigrants to the United States in the near future. Egypt is, therefore, the most likely source of most North African emigration to the United States in the next few years. Thus far, the country has not sent enough immigrants to create a critical base for a distinct community. In addition, as part of a wider Arab world, Egyptian Americans tend to see themselves as part of that larger ethnic group once they arrive in the United States. Thus, while the number of Egyptian Americans will no doubt continue to climb in the twenty-first century, it is not clear when a distinct and noticeable Egyptian-American culture will emerge.

Daniel James

See also: Washington, D.C. (Part II, Sec. 12); Immigration to Western Europe (Part II, Sec. 13).

BIBLIOGRAPHY

Araby, Kadri, et al. "Egyptian Muslims." In *The New Jersey Ethnic Experience,* ed. B. Cunningham. Union City, NJ: William H. Wise, 1977.

Haddad, Y. *The Muslims of America.* New York: Oxford University Press, 1991.

McCarus, E., ed. *The Development of Arab-American Identity.* Ann Arbor, MI: University of Michigan Press, 1994.

Metz, H. C. *Egypt: A Country Study.* Washington, DC: Federal Research Division, Library of Congress, 1991.

Patrick, T. H. *Traditional Egyptian Christianity: A History of the Coptic Orthodox Church.* St. Cloud, MN: North Star Press, 1996.

SOUTHERN AFRICA

While present-day immigration from Africa has risen in recent years, the southern African region accounts for a small percentage of immigrants to the United States. Immigrants from this region (Angola, Botswana, Lesotho, Malawi, Mozambique, Namibia, South Africa, Swaziland, Zambia, and Zimbabwe) represent less than 10 percent of African immigrants admitted into the United States each year; more than two-thirds of all African immigrants hail from Nigeria, Ghana, and Ethiopia. The vast geographic distance and the effects of colonialism in the region have not resulted in much movement of southern Africans to the United States. While political and economic conditions have served as factors to encourage immigration, most southern Africans have been limited in their migratory choices and have settled for movement within the region itself, with many being pulled southward to the stronger economy in South Africa. Like other immigrants to the United States, southern Africans immigrated for greater economic opportunity and for increased personal freedom.

FORCED MIGRATIONS AND THE COLONIAL PERIOD

Prior to 1800, the largest movement in history was the forced migration of approximately 20 million Africans to the Americas as slaves. At the end of the nineteenth century, immigration of free blacks into the United States was low. With the passage of the Naturalization Law in 1870, aliens of "African descent or African nativity" could apply for citizenship. African immigrants who responded to this legislation were mostly from the British West Indies. Between 1916 and 1932, 1,609 black immigrants came to the United States, including some South Africans, but the majority of the group were from the Caribbean countries. The presence of southern Africans in the United States during this period was almost nonexistent due to the cost and difficulty of arranging passage over the great distance between the two continents as well as the strict colonial rule, which ended in the 1960s and 1970s. Various schemes such as forced military and labor recruitment soon followed. In response to external pressures to end slavery in the 1850s, Portugal introduced a forced-labor scheme in its colonies of Angola and Mozambique. Mozambicans were needed to sustain the plantation economy in the French colony of Réunion, and to support mining in South Africa and Zimbabwe, while Angolans were taken to the Portuguese colony of São Tomé and Príncipe. To escape indentured servitude, Angolans and Mozambicans fled to neighboring countries until they won independence in 1975. Zimbabweans, Zambians, and other southern Africans were also forcibly recruited for the burgeoning mining industry in South Africa.

END OF COLONIALISM AND THE BEGINNING OF SOUTHERN AFRICAN IMMIGRATION

The end of colonialism in the southern African region and the passage of the Immigration and Nationality Act in the United States in 1965 increased the number of southern African immigrants to America; however, the numbers were small and remain so in comparison with other countries. While the average southern African did not qualify under either provision of the 1965 law—unlikely to have skills needed by the United States or to have close relatives already in the country—those from the relatively industrialized South Africa easily met these requirements, as did those highly educated immigrants from the former British colonies of Zimbabwe, Zambia, and Malawi. The majority of immigrants from southern

The vast majority of southern African immigrants find their way to former colonial powers like Britain and Portugal. An exception is this Angolan family in Queens, New York. *(Mel Rosenthal)*

Africa were of European descent or from English-speaking nations. Highly skilled professionals, they easily met the preferences of the Immigration and Naturalization Service, and the common language assured them of easier integration into American society.

During the ten-year period from 1971 to 1980, 80,779 Africans were admitted into the United States, representing a mere 2 percent of all immigrants in the decade. Of these, only 16,242, or 20 percent, hailed from southern Africa. Of this group from southern Africa, 11,151, or 69 percent, were from South Africa. The number of African immigrants as a whole has steadily increased, so that during the period from 1987 to 1997, southern Africans totaled 32,474, or a little less than 9 percent of the 358,561 African immigrants admitted to the United States. Of these, South Africans numbered 23,792, or 73 percent of total southern African immigrants over the same period. The apartheid government in South Africa was a factor in the large number of South African citizens seeking to immigrate to the United States. Scholars, physicians, and other professionals easily gained

immigrant status, while others secured entry with temporary visas, as skilled workers and tourists. Those who were deemed government dissidents applied for and were granted political asylum in the United States.

During the 1980s, economic and political conditions in southern Africa worsened. Led by civil wars in Zimbabwe, Mozambique, and Angola, massive migration movements occurred within the region, and to some extent, to Europe and the United States. The Refugee Act of 1980 did not significantly increase the number of southern Africans in the United States. During a six-year period from 1980 through 1985, the United States granted 517,411 admissions to refugees, but admitted only about 81 refugees from South Africa and were not favorable to the region overall. In 1987, regional ceilings for the continent were set at 3,500, while those for East Asia were 40,500 and Eastern Europe and the Soviet Union, 10,000. Refugees from the region resettled in the area and poured into neighboring countries with varied results. While Malawi received the greatest number of Mozambicans,

South Africa erected electric fences around its borders to prevent the refugees from moving onto its land. Drought conditions from 1982 to 1986 in southern Africa were also responsible for displacement and again in 1992, when water shortages led to mass starvation.

Representation of southern African people in the United States is considerably less than other groups due in part to the great geographical distance between the two continents and the costs involved in migration. The average southern African simply did not have the means nor the resources to migrate over such a vast distance and found Europe to be an easier and more convenient destination. Additionally, the legacy of colonialism formed a historical link between southern African countries and their colonizers in the United Kingdom, Germany, and Portugal. The strong cultural ties between Europe and the southern African region meant a larger social and professional network for southern Africans in these countries. Often, the colonizing country instituted the same educational and social system in their colonies, installing expatriate instructors who trained students and personnel for foreign-oriented qualifications, without creating job opportunities that utilized such training. Even in the postcolonial period, educational and professional credentials continue to be regulated and patterned after Western institutions, offering southern Africans an easier transition and settlement in the country of their former colonizers. Many were offered a claim to residency or citizenship status in these countries because they were descendants of large European settler populations in the region. For instance, some South Africans held British passports or could claim family ties in the United Kingdom, so that at the height of political unrest, they were able to migrate to the United Kingdom.

The end of colonialism in the 1960s and 1970s ushered in an era of greater movements for many students in the region. Those who would have otherwise studied in Europe instead enrolled in American universities and quickly joined Pan-African movements. Church groups and other agencies provided assistance to southern African students who would not be eligible for refugee status until 1980. When political turmoil occurred in their native countries, most students opted to remain in the United States and married or secured jobs that would allow them to stay legally. Some let their visas lapse and remained in the country illegally. Those supported by government scholarships were required to return home as a condition of their studies, thus ensuring that the native country will profit from the students' newly acquired skills. Other students promptly returned because of

pressures from family members still residing at home. Students constitute a substantial proportion of Africans in the United States, and those who choose to stay after they complete their programs make up a percentage of the immigrants from southern Africa. While the contributions of these students and other professionals clearly benefit the United States, their absence from the southern African region is significant and hinders the development of economically and politically sustainable nations. One study showed that most students prefer to remain in the United States because of the higher standard of living, greater employment opportunities, and the level of personal freedom they experience. As the political and economic conditions worsen in the region of southern Africa, applications for immigration to the United States and other nations will continue to rise.

SETTLEMENT PATTERNS, ETHNICITY, AND CULTURAL ADAPTATIONS

Like other newly arrived immigrants, southern Africans joined organized black communities, quickly establishing small businesses and social clubs to serve the needs of their countrymen. Grocery stores, nightclubs, ethnic restaurants, and travel services thrived in the areas in which they settled: California, New York, Washington, D.C., and the eastern states. However, since most southern African immigrants held professional credentials, they often pursued employment opportunities regardless of location or the presence of an established immigrant enclave. Southern African immigrants work in a variety of sectors, including professional positions, such as college professors, engineers, and physicians. The technology industry in the Silicon Valley has drawn many immigrants to that area. Southern African immigrants, regardless of their ethnic or linguistic background, are quick to come together as a group due to their strong sense of cultural and tribal identities. Some have expressed concern that their identities will be lost as they are absorbed into the local culture and identified as native-born blacks by the white population. Linguistic differences, educational level, and skills background have played an important role in helping African immigrants maintain their cultural, national, and regional identities.

To most Americans, black southern African immigrants were indistinguishable from African Americans. Upon their arrival they were therefore subjected to the racism and discrimination that affected native-born African Americans. Tensions sometimes occurred between native-born African Americans and African immigrants as each group competed with the other for jobs and services. In other communities, interest in African immigration issues was perceived as an attempt to divide the black community or to dispel Pan-African movements. One study showed that African immigrants felt they could not advance in their careers, evidenced by only a few African immigrants in highly ranked jobs. Despite experiencing racial discrimination in the United States, southern Africans have remained, citing opportunities for professional development, job satisfaction, and the high level of compensation they receive as reasons to stay. Another reason cited is the deteriorating political and economic conditions in their respective home countries. Others simply have adapted to American culture, including marriage to an American spouse, raising American children, and enjoyment of personal freedom not available in their home countries. The southern African immigrant lists political freedom, civil liberties, and economic opportunities in the United States as major factors in immigrating to and remaining in the United States.

The rate of return migration of southern African immigrants is low. A thriving U.S. economy has not encouraged return migration to the region. Those who do return enjoy a relatively comfortable life because of the stronger American currency. Although they provide remittances to their friends and family still remaining at home, the economic impact of southern African immigration to the United States on their respective countries is significant. Because the immigrant group is highly educated, their departure is considered a brain drain for the southern African countries. Remittances represent a great financial benefit, but many advocate the return of skilled immigrants to the region so that their nation as a whole can benefit from their expertise. Remittances were meant to provide temporary relief from economic pressures, but in fact have created a situation of dependence on foreign funds. During the 1980s, remittances provided the primary source of income for over 40 percent of households in Lesotho and represented 80 percent of the account deficit in Botswana. While primarily used for immediate consumption, remittances are also beneficial on a long-term basis; once immediate subsistence needs are met, the funds are usually invested for educational and entrepreneurial purposes.

The brain drain phenomenon is deeply felt in the educational sector. In 1991, both the University of Zambia and the University of Zimbabwe reported extreme staff shortages, causing departments to close and a decline in the quality of teaching as inexperienced or less qualified staff was recruited. In the same year, the University of Zimbabwe reported that only twenty-three out of sixty-eight vacant posts were filled. Physicians, professors, and engineers are continuously lured not only to the United States but also southward in the region, as the promises of higher wages and living standards, and greater personal freedom in Botswana, Namibia, and South Africa attract highly qualified people.

Immigration statistics show that Africans, along with Asian immigrants, have the highest percentage of naturalization rates. The threat of political instability in their native lands plays a key role in the decision of many southern Africans to promptly become U.S. citizens. Studies by the Immigration and Naturalization Service show that immigrants from distant countries tended to have higher naturalization rates than those who come from countries geographically closer to the United States, such as Canada and Mexico. Attaining citizenship provides a sense of security for southern Africans, who have long suffered from political and economic turmoil and who have come from great distances to live in the United States. Citizenship also provides a chance for family members to join their immigrant relatives. Southern Africans come from close-knit family and tribal units, and reunification is important to them. Immigrants enable their friends and relatives to join them by providing assistance and guidance with employment and shelter when they arrive. As southern Africans continue to experience periods of political and economic instability, a very high rate of internal, regional, and international migration will continue to affect the region and will bring an increasing number of immigrants to the United States.

Grace Ebron

See also: Political, Ethnic, Religious, and Gender Persecution, Wars and Civil Unrest (Part II, Sec. 1); Western and Southern Europe (Part III, Sec. 4).

BIBLIOGRAPHY

Apraku, Kofi. *African Emigres in the United States.* New York: Praeger Publishers, 1991.

Bigman, Laura. "Contemporary Migration from Africa to the USA." In *The Cambridge Survey of World Migration,* ed. Robin Cohen, pp. 260–62. Cambridge: University of Cambridge Press, 1995.

Curtin, Philip. *Why People Move: Migration in African History.* Waco, TX: Baylor University Press, 1995.

Fuchs, Lawrence. "The Reactions of Black Americans to Immigration." In *Immigration Reconsidered*, ed. Virginia Yans-McLaughlin, pp. 293–314. Oxford: Oxford University Press, 1990.

Immigration and Naturalization Service. *1980 Statistical Yearbook of the Immigration and Naturalization Service.* Washington, DC: Government Printing Office, 1982.

———. *1997 Statistical Yearbook of the Immigration and Naturalization Service.* Washington, DC: Government Printing Office, 1999.

Reid, Ira De A. *The Negro Immigrant.* New York: Columbia University Press, 1939.

Ueda, Reed. "The Changing Face of Post-1965 Immigration." In *The Immigration Reader*, ed. David Jacobson, pp. 72–91. Oxford (UK): Blackwell Publishers, 1998.

Wortham, O. C. "Contemporary Black Immigration to the United States." In *Contemporary American Immigration: Interpretive Essays*, ed. D. L. Cuddy, pp. 200–219. Boston: G. K. Hall & Co., 1982.

WEST AFRICA

$\mathcal{A}$ long history of migrations spurred by religious pilgrimages, commercial trade routes, political rivalries, and natural disasters have long defined West Africans as "a people on the move." Prior to the late nineteenth century, the region of West Africa was widely known as the Western Sudan. It stretched from the coast of the African bulge in the west to the great bend of the Niger River in the east, including the lands from the southern Sahara in the north to the gulf coast of Guinea in the south. By today's standards, its size was comparable to the entire land mass of the continental United States. Despite an active period of West African migration dating back to the seventh century B.C.E. (Before the Common Era), the partition, colonization, and decolonization of West Africa have had the greatest impact on population movement in and out of the region.

A "scramble for Africa" began when delegates from Great Britain, France, Portugal, and eleven other Western nations, which also included the United States, met at the Berlin Conference between November 1884 and February 1885 to settle disputes over the control of African lands. Without the attendance or approval of any African representatives, European nations agreed to partition Africa into "spheres of influence" to meet their industrial needs for natural resources, expanding markets, and new investment sites. By 1900, 90 percent of Africa was colonized, and West Africa fell primarily under British and French control, except for the German domination of Togoland and the Portuguese occupation of Guinea-Bissau and the Cape Verde Islands. Under colonial rule, West Africa was divided into two broad categories: Anglophone (English-speaking) and Francophone (French-speaking). French West Africa included the present-day countries of Mauritania, Mali, Niger, Senegal, Upper Volta (Burkina Faso), Guinea, Ivory Coast (Côte d'Ivoire), and Dahomey (Benin), while British

West Africa consisted of the Gold Coast (Ghana), Sierra Leone, Nigeria, and the Gambia. The only West African country to escape colonial rule was Liberia; still, it was heavily influenced by U.S. economic interests. These arbitrary partitions created new borders that changed the nature of West African migration.

Colonial partitions redrew preexisting political lines and altered the relationship between long-standing ethnic groups. Dividing the region without regard to ethnic politics, subsistence patterns, or seasonal differences changed the character of West African migration. During precolonial times, for example, movement throughout the region was relatively open and free, and an individual would maintain family and ethnic ties across long distances. During colonial times, however, the separation of groups redirected population movement, causing disharmony and even civil war. Ironically, another result of the partitioning was that it isolated rival groups and reduced interethnic conflict.

A period of relative peace among West African rivals enabled colonial governments and traditional authorities to enact compulsory cropping and forced-labor migration. Rural West Africans migrated freely to coastal cities in search of jobs and money. This movement was aided, in part, by improvements in rail and road transportation and by a change in the system of exchange from trade by barter to British and French currency. However, major inequalities and developmental imbalances were also created between rural and urban sectors. These and other colonial innovations changed the motivations of West African migrants and altered the volume, pattern, and direction of population movements throughout the region. To escape the French policy mandating the conscription of agricultural workers, for example, thousands of peasant laborers emigrated from such French colonies as the Ivory Coast, Dahomey, Upper

Many West African immigrants in New York have found an economic niche selling souvenirs without a permit on the city's sidewalks. This enterprise requires little capital but frequently lands the vendors in trouble with the police. *(Amy Zuckerman/Impact Visuals)*

Volta, and Mali to the British colonies of the Gold Coast and Nigeria. This long-distance travel during the colonial period was called "interterritorial" migration. Later, with the decolonization of West Africa and the creation of national borders, the context of population movements changed from interterritorial to international.

On March 6, 1957, the Gold Coast became the first West African nation to win independence from colonial rule and was renamed Ghana. As the rest of West Africa gained its freedom (which was completed only on July 5, 1975, with the independence of Cape Verde), independent states were carved out of vast colonial territories and new international borders were erected. Like the colonial borders, these boundaries divided major ethnic groups that were forced to live on either side of the frontier. The Yoruba, for example, who live along the borders of Nigeria and Benin, have been separated by these national boundaries. Other examples are the Fulani (or Fulbe), a nomadic people who roam the Sahel (grassy desert area) from Senegal and Guinea to Nigeria, and the Ewe people, who re-

side on both sides of the border shared by Togo and Ghana. In an effort to maintain family or group ties, a type of international migration emerged as West African migrants moved back and forth across national borders, usually crossing into neighboring countries with similar economies and cultural affinities. In recent decades, the historic migration of seasonal laborers, moving from their country of origin to another country of employment, has also contributed to a mode of international migration in West Africa.

To facilitate the free movement of migrant workers, goods, services, and capital throughout the region, fifteen West African states, which now include Cape Verde, met in Lagos, Nigeria, on May 28, 1975, and established ECOWAS (Economic Community of West African States). The formation of this regional organization has increased the ease with which migrants cross national boundaries. Some even claim that this economic union has contributed to what has been called a "floating population," a movement of West African laborers from one country to another that extends as far away as the United States.

A HISTORY OF WEST AFRICAN IMMIGRATION TO THE UNITED STATES

THE FIRST PHASE

West African immigration to the United States has been essentially divided into three phases. While a number of works attest to the presence of West African explorers in pre-Columbian America, including their later travels with early-sixteenth-century Spanish explorers, the first phase began with the transatlantic slave trade that forced 10 to 15 million Africans to the Americas from the seventeenth to the nineteenth centuries. Among the total population, however, approximately 7 percent or 700,000 to over 1 million were sent to the North American mainland. While these enslaved peoples were acquired at various points along the Atlantic coastline, a great number originated from the western part of Africa. While the first phase is important for the understanding of the presence of West Africans in America, the more recent periods directly explain the nature and quality of their voluntary migration to the United States.

THE SECOND PHASE

The second phase marks West African immigration from the Prohibition of the Slave Trade Act of 1808, a federal law abolishing the importation of enslaved Africans, to the period just before 1965. Although the act was widely ignored, it made the enslavement of Africans a prosecutable offense (as evidenced by the Amistad case of 1841). Because the Immigration and Naturalization Service (INS) did not record the country of origin for Africans until the 1960s, its records indicate that there was only one African immigrant in the country in 1820, which was the first year a count was taken.

Early West African immigration was also affected, in part, by the efforts of the controversial American Colonization Society. Ironically, while the society reached its goal by colonizing Liberia in 1822 and repatriating 2,638 free blacks by the next decade, the establishment of the new nation (independent since 1847) initiated a chain migration between West Africa and the United States. Between 1891 and 1900, for example, INS data estimate that there were a total of 350 African immigrants in America. During this period, many West Africans immigrated to the United States as religious students supported by Christian missionaries, who had hoped that they would return home following their studies to spread the Gospel.

By World War I, the average number of all Africans immigrating to America had reached nearly one thousand per year, with most classified as "African" coming from Egypt and South Africa. However, due to restrictive immigration laws of the 1920s and the Great Depression, these numbers began to decline drastically. After World War II, however, the INS reported that African immigration had doubled from 7,367 in the 1940s to 14,092 between 1951 and 1960. Although the U.S. census of 1910, 1930, and 1960 classified 89 percent of these African-born immigrants as "white," there is no indication of how many were whites of European descent fleeing the liberation struggles of emerging African states. Nonetheless, while most African immigrants in the 1960s were Egyptians and South Africans, a significant number were now from Ghana, Nigeria, Liberia, and Cape Verde. Because the INS records only legal immigration to America, the figures for Africans are generally higher in U.S. census data, which records both legal and illegal persons. In 1970, for example, census data estimated that out of a total of 80,143 Africans in the United States, 40,080 were from West Africa. In contrast, the INS recorded that for almost the entire decade between 1961 and 1970 there were a total of 28,954 immigrants in the country; even so, both figures are minuscule compared with other ethnic groups arriving in the United States. The small numbers of West African immigrants can be partly explained by the nature of U.S. immigration policy before 1965 and the colonial control of West African economies.

Prior to 1965, American anti-immigration sentiments brought about such mandates as the Chinese Exclusion Act (1882), which, unlike previous laws prohibiting the immigration of "undesirables" likely to be a public charge, was the first legislation barring immigration based on ethnicity. In 1921, 1924, and 1929, a host of other protective laws were enacted to restrict immigration according to specific traits and nationality. These efforts led to the establishment of a quota system, with some revisions over time, which granted entry to immigrants according to the proportion of their fellow nationals already living in the United States. For example, because the largest number of immigrants in the United States came from the British Isles, this group was given the highest quota and granted the greatest entry into the country. This national provision was one of the major obstacles to West African immigration prior to its eradication by the 1965 Immigration Act.

The poor condition of West African economies also impeded immigration. From World War I to the 1960s, colonial interests in the development of foreign exports, the expansion of urban sectors, and the exploitation of rural areas greatly devastated the natural and human resources of the region. Through a system of forced-labor migration, thousands of rural migrants were eventually driven to the urban coasts in search of cash income. Colonial officials argued that a balanced development would occur through a process of modernization, which meant that rural areas would eventually benefit from the "trickling down" effect of urban development. Instead, as West African urban centers grew increasingly dependent on European exports, massive unemployment and underemployment produced high levels of poverty. Those West Africans who were able to escape these harsh conditions traveled to neighboring African countries and parts of Europe.

THE THIRD PHASE

The third phase of West African immigration extends from 1965 to the present. Following World War I, members of the educated West African elite, such as Nnamdi Azikiwe, who became the first president of Nigeria in 1963, and Kwame Nkrumah, who was elected Ghana's first president in 1960, came to the United States as college students during the first half of the century. While Azikiwe began his studies in 1925 and Nkrumah followed ten years later, both attended black universities and both were inspired by the American black consciousness movement. Because Azikiwe and Nkrumah rose to the forefront of the nationalist and Pan-African movements that led to African independence, many younger West Africans undoubtedly saw their U.S. studies as a training ground for their activity. More important, their example inspired thousands of West Africans to come to the United States for higher education after World War II.

During the postwar period, West African students in the United States received support from the American government and a number of private U.S. foundations. Financial assistance from the African Scholarship Program of American Universities (ASPAU), for example, helped to increase the immigration of West African students, particularly from Anglophone countries, from 3.6 percent between 1954 and 1956 to 8.4 percent by the mid-1960s. This increase amounted to a total of 1,306 Africans in the United States on student visas in 1967. Much of this assistance was given as part of U.S. Cold War strategies to contain the spread of communism in Africa. Because these students were part of the newly emerging West African elite, it was believed that the United States would benefit upon their return home to occupy new leadership positions.

After 1965, however, West African returnees quickly discovered that while some benefited politically and economically from independence, many more faced the horror of repressive regimes, the massive bloodshed of successive military takeovers, and the specter of poor economic conditions. Seeking refuge, many who had completed their studies in the United States were forced to return. This dreadful turn of events also convinced a number of West African students to remain in the United States, at least temporarily. This period marks the beginning of massive African migration to the United States. To illustrate the point, the INS reported that during the 100-year period between 1861 and 1961, only 46,326 Africans immigrated to America. During the following twenty-eight years, however, that figure swelled to 232,631.

Causes of West African Immigration

After 1965, there were a number of major factors that contributed to the rapid growth of West African immigration. Beginning in 1962, British policies grew increasingly hostile toward African immigrants from its former colonies. By 1971, various pieces of legislation were enacted to deny Africans their citizenship rights, reduce the flow of immigration from developing nations, and actually promote repatriation. Even France, which in the early 1960s encouraged the immigration of its former African subjects as a source of cheap labor, had terminated legal immigration in 1974. At the same time, however, immigration policy in the United States was becoming more flexible with the passing of the Immigration Act of 1965. By shifting the criteria from a quota system favoring northern and western Europeans to a preference system supporting family reunification for permanent residents (74 percent), skilled workers needed by the economy (20 percent), and political refugees (6 percent), this act set the stage for a dramatic increase in West African immigration.

Because changes in immigration policies also favored skilled and educated immigrants, many professional, technical, and kindred workers (PTKs) from West Africa were attracted to the career opportunities that America offered. The average African immigrant, for example, has 15.7 years of education and holds more college degrees than white Americans and white immigrants. According to the 1980 census, Nigerian immigrants ranked among the four most educated groups in the United States, along with Egyptians,

Taiwanese, and Indians. Moreover, 94 percent of them were high school graduates and 49 percent had a four-year college degree. During the same period, only 68.6 percent of all Americans over twenty-five years old were high school graduates, and 17 percent had four-year college degrees. In 1990, the U.S. census reported that 64 percent of Nigerian immigrants over the age of twenty-five had obtained at least a four-year college degree. This is compared with 21.3 percent of Americans. Due to their high level of education, along with growing rates of West African unemployment and underemployment, PTKs are "pushed" from their countries and "pulled" into a postindustrial (service-based) American economy. West African women also have increasingly joined the pool of immigration to the United States.

Female Immigration

During the second phase of West African immigration, migrants were basically young adult males and single. Because most West African men came to the United States as temporary migrants (nonimmigrants) to work or study, few were allowed to bring family members without being naturalized citizens or permanent residents. Under the 1965 Immigration Act, however, West Africans could apply to become permanent residents and send for relatives under the family reunification provision. This change in the immigration laws helped to increase the number of West African women in the United States.

Another factor that expanded female immigration was the changing role of women in West Africa. By the 1970s, colonial changes in the West African economy made women into autonomous migrants (sole decision makers about their movement). Because male-dominated migration created an abundance of female-headed households, young mothers placed their children in the care of grandparents and migrated to cities for jobs, self-employment, and education. As opportunities to study and work in the United States increased, West African women began joining their male counterparts abroad and competing with them for jobs and college scholarships.

A third factor has been the dramatic increase of women and children as refugees of civil war, ethnic strife, famine, drought, and political unrest. As a response to these tragedies, many have fled to neighboring West African countries. However, because many poor, weak African nations are unable to protect these victims, rebels can easily pursue their targets across national borders. This problem has forced some to seek refuge in more powerful nations like the United States. In Liberia, for example, a recurring civil

war has been raging since December 1989. Because the bloodshed has shut down food production and trade, the country has been ravaged by widespread famine and hunger. Unfortunately, civilians have been the greatest victims. People have been tortured, women have been raped, and children, as young as eight years old, have been kidnapped and coerced to fight. Out of a total population of 2.9 million, over half are homeless and an estimated 150,000 to 250,000 have been killed or have died of starvation. Today, over 15,000 Liberian refugees, including thousands of women, have been granted U.S. residence under the Temporary Protected Status Program (initiated under the Immigration Act of 1990).

WEST AFRICAN IMMIGRANT GROUPS IN AMERICA

West African immigrants originate from sixteen different countries located in what is still a developing region. The area of West Africa today is defined by the member states that belong to ECOWAS, which fosters economic cooperation within the area. These states are Benin, Burkina Faso, Cape Verde, Côte d'Ivoire, the Gambia, Ghana, Guinea, Guinea-Bissau, Liberia, Mali, Mauritania, Niger, Nigeria, Senegal, Sierra Leone, and Togo. Some exclude the Sahelian countries of Mali, Mauritania, and Niger from West Africa, while others include Cameroon and Chad. In 1992, the total population in the region was estimated at 204 million. With such a vast and culturally diverse area, West African immigrants enter the United States speaking a great many languages and representing numerous ethnic identities.

The two largest West African immigrant groups are from Nigeria and Ghana. While the vast majority of West African groups identify most directly with their ethnic affiliation (including language, religion, tradition, and values), they are most commonly recognized by outsiders in terms of their nationality. The 1990 census reported that for foreign-born populations there were 55,350 Nigerians and 20,889 Ghanaians in the United States. By 1997, the Current Population Survey (CPS) of the U.S. census estimated that the Nigerian population had increased to 109,000 and the Ghanaian to 32,000. While both figures are conservative, informal estimates are much higher.

NIGERIAN GROUPS IN THE UNITED STATES

Considered the most populous country in Africa, a United Nations count in 1995 estimated that Nigeria had 126,929,000 inhabitants. While its size approximates the combined area of Arizona, New Mexico, and California, there are, amazingly, over 250 ethnic groups. Only four constitute 65 percent of the population: the Fulani and Hausa living mainly in the north, the Igbo (or Ibo, both pronounced "ee-bow") in the southeast, and the Yoruba in the southwest. Other groups such as the Edo, Ibibio, Kanuri, Nupe, Tiv, Chamba, Ekoi, and Ijaw are smaller in size. While English is the official language of the country, each group has its own language, and some of the larger ones may have 200 dialects. Besides standard English, a Pidgin English (a hybrid language used for communication) has become a common mode of speaking. Most Nigerians are at least bilingual and many are multilingual.

The religion of Islam is professed by the majority of Hausa, Fulani, Kanuri, and about 40 percent of Yoruba, who together constitute about 48 percent of the population. Another 34 percent are Christians, with mostly Roman Catholics among the Igbo and some Methodists and Anglicans among the Yoruba. While the remainder practice traditional religion, which involves some belief in a supreme being, a series of minor deities, and ancestor veneration, most West Africans syncretize the beliefs and practices of all three to a greater or lesser extent.

Among Nigerian immigrants, the Yoruba and Igbo (or, as they refer to themselves in the United States, Ndi Igbo) are the predominant ethnic groups among Nigerian immigrants. The term "Yoruba," which was first applied to a subgroup of the seventeenth-century Oyo kingdom, was supposedly used by the Hausa and others to describe the group as "cunning." The term later applied to the entire group partly due to its use in missionary schools; nevertheless, some refuse to recognize it and refer to themselves by one of many ethnic names, such as Awori, Ondo, Bunu, Ife, Ana, Ketu, Oyo, Shabe, Egba, Ijesha, Ekiti, Igbomina, Egbado, Yagba, Owo, Ilaje, Aworo, and Itsekiri. Under the constraints of British colonialism, the Igbo were also compelled to reinvent themselves into a larger cultural and political unit. Depending on the context, however, Nigerian immigrants organize themselves and re-create their identity along interethnic, ethnic, and national lines.

Like other African immigrants, Nigerians have settled mostly in urban and suburban areas throughout the United States. Their greatest concentration, however, has been in such large cities as New York, Newark (New Jersey), the Washington, D.C., area, Atlanta, Chicago, Los Angeles, Houston, and Dallas. For reasons described above, the vast majority came to the United States as PTKs. Many have advanced degrees

from Nigeria. However, because their academic credentials are rarely recognized by American institutions, many resort to menial jobs, staff positions in government or industry, entrepreneurial activities, or other jobs unrelated to their areas of specialization. In fact, it is not uncommon to find a Nigerian engineer or Ph.D. degree holder driving a taxicab in New York or Washington, D.C.

A great number of Nigerian immigrants participate in traditional ceremonies (e.g., baby naming events, weddings, funerals, and religious holidays) to promote their cultural values. As a result, numerous ethnic or hometown associations have been established in most of the urban areas where they settle. For example, the Akwa Ibom organization, which takes its name from a province in southeastern Nigeria, and the Nwannedinamba Association are among many that sponsor traditional dances, musical performances, forums, and celebrations to help Nigerians negotiate their identities and find their way in a foreign environment. To date, there are plans to build a $1 million center in Washington, D.C., to promote Igbo culture.

In addition to joining American religious groups, Nigerian immigrants are increasingly establishing their own churches, *masjids* (Muslim places of worship), and centers associated with traditional religion. Because these organizations play a vital role in helping them re-create and maintain an ethnic identity, many hold religious services and meetings in their indigenous languages. These ethnic and religious activities also help Nigerian immigrants to maintain traditional family values and obligations. During wedding ceremonies, for example, family elders are required to perform certain roles. Because these ceremonies take place so far away from the home country, the proper family member is not always available. In such cases, a member of the ethnic or religious association will fill in as a fictive family member. Also, because outsiders are often invited to these cultural events, Nigerian immigrants use these activities to bridge their communities with native-born American groups. All this activity in America does not mean that Nigerian immigrants are "uprooted" from their country of origin. Through their organizational efforts in the United States, they remain very active in Nigerian politics, and by sending millions of dollars in remittances, they build homes, run businesses, and engage in other development projects in Nigeria.

GHANAIAN GROUPS IN THE UNITED STATES

Ghanaian immigrants come from a country with about one hundred ethnic groups; each has its own language or dialect. In 1995, the population of Ghana was estimated at 17,453,000. The largest groups are the Akan (including the Asante, Fante, Akuapem, Nzima, Brong), who constitute about 44 percent of the population; the Moshi-Dagomba, 16 percent; the Ewe, 13 percent; and the Ga-Adangme, 8 percent. Although the urban centers are growing rapidly, two-thirds of the people are agricultural workers living on farms in rural villages. While English is the official language, the government sanctioned the use of nine indigenous languages: Akuapem-Twi, Asante-Twi, Fante, Ga, Ewe, Dagbani, Dangbe, Nzima, and Kasem. Although Ghana is divided into ten administrative districts, these languages are mutually intelligible among neighboring groups. Similar to the majority of West Africans, most Ghanaians can speak a number of languages.

While Ghanaians practice Christianity, Islam, and traditional African religion, estimates vary regarding their percentages. According to one count, Christians (mostly Protestant with about one-third Roman Catholic) constitute 63 percent of the population, practitioners of traditional religion are at 21 percent, and Muslims represent 16 percent. Other sources indicate that Muslims are 30 percent of the population, Christians are 24 percent, and indigenous African religion totals about 46 percent. Perhaps part of the reason for the inconsistency is because Ghanaians, along with many other West Africans, tend not to make rigid distinctions among the three faiths. In fact, it is not uncommon to find a Ghanaian household with family members sharing and combining elements from all three religions.

While there are many Ghanaian ethnic groups in the United States, some of the major ones are the Asante, Ga-Adangme, Ewe, and Moshi-Dagomba. There are also significant numbers among the multiethnic Islamic alliance called "Yankasa," which includes such ethnic groups as the Bako, Damale, Yoruba, Fulani, Nupe, Kanuri, Wangara, Kotokoli, Zabrama, and the predominant Hausa. Other members of Yankasa considered more indigenous to Ghana are the Ga, Dagomba, Frafra, Grunshie, Akan, Ewe, and Sempe. In Ghana, Muslims mostly live in the northern parts of the country. In major Ghanaian cities of the south, however, they form "Zongo" areas or "stranger quarters" that have a notably Islamic flavor. While Ghanaian immigrants in the United States maintain good ethnic relations among themselves, especially as compatriots in a foreign land, these linguistic, religious, or regional affiliations tend to mark a degree of distance.

In 1990, the U.S. census reported that there were 20,889 foreign-born Ghanaians residing in the United States. Among this total, almost half (40.3 percent) were in the mid-Atlantic states. New York State alone claimed 75 percent of this mid-Atlantic total. By 1997, their numbers increased to about 32,000, according to the CPS. While New York has been a primary point of entry, New Jersey, Connecticut, Massachusetts, and the District of Columbia area are increasingly becoming places of settlement. Like their Nigerian counterparts, many Ghanaian immigrants arrive in the United States as highly skilled workers and well-educated professionals. Others come to continue their education and remain in the country to work for various public and private agencies.

As the religion of Islam gains converts in the United States, particularly among African Americans, Islamic agencies such as the Muslim World League Office at the United Nations and Dar al-Ifta (Mission of Islamic Propagation) employ Ghanaians as Islamic clerics. The majority of these Muslim Ghanaians are graduates of Islamic universities in the Arab world and are recruited to teach in centers and masjids across America.

There are currently about forty-three Ghanaian ethnic and religious associations in the United States. There are also twelve Christian churches with Ghanaian ministers and a number of Islamic alliances led by Ghanaian *shaykhs* (scholars). Traditional African religion is generally promoted by many of the ethnic and cultural associations such as the Asanteman Kuo. This group is part of an umbrella organization called the Asanteman Council of North America, which links associations between such cities as New York, Newark, Hartford, Boston, Atlanta, Chicago, Dallas, Los Angeles, and Toronto and Montreal, Canada. Because part of their mission is to promote African culture through religious song, dance, and music, their efforts tend to attract African-American and Latino groups who practice African-based religions like Santeria, Shango, Candomblé, and voodoo. However, because the preservation of African culture in the United States is associated with these traditional practices, any strict adherence to Islam or Christianity is often a cause for conflict.

Although these associations were established in the United States, most of them have parent organizations in Ghana that foster a link between the two nations. The Asanteman Kuo, for example, operates transnationally by seeking recognition and other sanctions from the Asantehene (king of the Asante nation), who resides in Kumasi, the Asante capital. Disputes are resolved and officers in the United States are elected through a flow of networks that spans the two countries. As a result of this global relationship, bank transfers from Ghanaian immigrants to relatives or contacts in Ghana were estimated at $300 million in 1995. Their relationship with the home country also facilitates the return of a deceased family member for burial. According to African cosmology, a person who dies does not cease to exist but is transferred to the world of the ancestors. Funerals therefore can be expensive; however, many take out additional life insurance to pay for the extra burden or receive financial assistance from their associations.

OTHER WEST AFRICAN IMMIGRANT GROUPS

Due to the causes of immigration previously mentioned, West African immigration to the United States became much more diverse after 1980. During this period, groups from French-speaking West Africa began to join their English-speaking counterparts in America. Today, immigrants from each of the sixteen West African countries live in the United States. Like the Nigerians and Ghanaians, their communities are growing and becoming more visible. While most have settled in large cities across America, just about all West Africans come from countries that are still predominantly rural with rapidly expanding urban centers. One notable exception is Liberia, which has an urban population of over 50 percent.

Hundreds of languages are spoken throughout West Africa. Although most people speak a number of traditional African languages, European languages are still used by the government and for official business. In the Cape Verde Islands and Guinea-Bissau, for example, Portuguese is used for official matters, while its Creole version, Crioulo, is widely spoken. The Gambia, Ghana, Liberia, Nigeria, and Sierra Leone have all maintained English as their official language. With the exception of the former French colony of Mauritania, which has authorized the use of Arabic in schools and government, French has been retained in Benin, Burkina Faso, Guinea, Mali, Niger, Senegal, and Togo.

Religion is an integral part of West African life. In Benin, Burkina Faso, Côte d'Ivoire, Guinea-Bissau, Liberia, Sierra Leone, and Togo, traditional African religion is professed by more than 50 percent of the people. With the possible exception of Mauritania, there is a Christian minority, mostly Roman Catholics, living in every West African country. By some estimates, Ghana's Christian population is as high as 62 percent. While the majority of Cape Verdeans (which had a population size of nearly half a million in 1995) are Roman Catholics, Nigeria and Togo had Christian populations estimated at only about 35 percent. The Christian communities in both Benin and Côte d'Ivoire are 20 percent of the population, and those

living in Burkina Faso, the Gambia, Guinea, Guinea-Bissau, Liberia, Mali, Niger, Senegal, and Sierra Leone were estimated at 10 percent or below. Islam is widespread throughout West Africa as well. The Gambia, Guinea, Mali, Mauritania, Niger, and Senegal all have Muslim populations of well over 80 percent. Islam is professed by populations of about 30 percent and above in Guinea-Bissau, Nigeria, and Sierra Leone. The remaining countries, Benin, Burkina Faso, Côte d'Ivoire, Ghana, Liberia, and Togo, have Muslim populations ranging between 15 and 30 percent.

While West Africans arrive with various ethnic affiliations, the U.S. census ordinarily records their national identity under foreign-born populations. The 1990 U.S. census estimated that there were approximately 117,306 West Africans living in America. The census count for West African groups in the United States is as follows: Benin, 272; Burkina Faso, 126; Cape Verde, 14,368; Côte d'Ivoire, 1,388; the Gambia, 1,485; Ghana, 20,889; Guinea, 1,032; Guinea-Bissau, 114; Liberia, 11,455; Mali, 469; Mauritania, 82; Niger, 238; Nigeria, 55,350; Senegal, 2,287; Sierra Leone, 7,217; and Togo, 534. U.S. census population estimates for the year 2000 should reveal much higher numbers. While most of these groups will grow only incrementally, others will show dramatic increases.

An increasing number of academic institutions, museums, centers, and institutes are conducting research on African immigrants in America. To name a few, the African Immigrant Project at the University of California, Davis, is studying religious communities among African immigrants across America. The International Center for Migration, Ethnicity, and Citizenship at the New School for Social Research (New School University) is also researching religious communities among African and other immigrants in New York City. In Washington, D.C., the Smithsonian Institution's Center for Folklife and Cultural Heritage has sponsored the African Immigrant Folklife Study Project. Participants have documented the activities of African immigrants as performers, presenters, and researchers of their own communities. In Philadelphia, a project to create a directory of African immigrant activities is being compiled in cooperation with the immigrants themselves, the Balch Institute, and the African Studies Center of the University of Pennsylvania. These and other programs can be accessed through their Web sites.

Zain A. Abdullah

See also: Political, Ethnic, Religious, and Gender Persecution, Wars and Civil Unrest (Part II, Sec 1); Washington, D.C. (Part II, Sec. 12); Immigration to Western Europe (Part II, Sec. 13).

BIBLIOGRAPHY

Adepoju, Aderanti. "Migration in Africa: An Overview." In *The Migration Experience in Africa*, ed. Jonathan Baker and Tade A. Aina, pp. 87–108. Sweden: Nordiska Afrikainstitutet, 1995.

Apraku, Kofi K. *African Émigrés in the United States: A Missing Link in Africa's Social and Economic Development.* New York: Praeger, 1991.

Attah-Poku, Agyemang. *The Social-Cultural Adjustment Question: The Role of Ghanaian Immigrant Ethnic Associations in America.* Brookfield, VT: Avebury, 1996.

Bureau of the Census. *Characteristics of the Foreign-Born Population in the United States.* Washington, DC: Government Printing Office, 1990.

Bureau of the Census. *Current Population Survey.* Washington, DC: Government Printing Office, 1997.

Conniff, Michael L., and Thomas J. Davis. *Africans in the Americas: A History of the Black Diaspora.* New York: St. Martin's Press, 1994.

Frosch-Schröder, Joan. "Re-Creating Cultural Memory: The Notion of Tradition in Ghanaian-American Performance." *UCLA Journal of Dance Ethnology* 18 (1994): 17–23.

Gordon, April. "The New Diaspora—African Immigration to the United States." *Journal of Third World Studies* 15:1 (1998): 79–103.

Halter, Marilyn. *Between Race and Ethnicity: Cape Verdean American Immigrants, 1860–1965.* Urbana, University of Illinois Press, 1993.

Immigration and Naturalization Service. *Statistical Yearbook of the Immigration and Naturalization Service.* Washington, DC: Government Printing Office, 1997.

Kamya, Hugo A. 1997. "African Immigrants in the United States: The Challenge for Research and Practice." *Social Work* 42:2 (March 1997): 154–65.

Makinwa-Adebusoye, P. K. "Emigration Dynamics in West Africa." *International Migration* 33:3–4 (1995): 435–67.

N'Diaye, Diana B. "Public Folklore As Applied Folklore: Community Collaboration in Public Sector Folklore Practice at the Smithsonian." *Journal of Applied Folklore* 4 (1998): 91–114.

Nyang, Sulayman. *Islam in the United States of America.* Chicago: Kazi Publications, 1999.

Offoha, Marcellina U. *Educated Nigerian Settlers in the United States: The Phenomenon of Brain Drain.* Philadelphia: Temple University Press, 1989.

Pellow, Deborah, and Naomi Chazan. *Ghana: Coping with Uncertainty.* Boulder, CO: Westview Press, 1986.

Selassie, Bereket H. "Washington's New African Immigrants." In *Urban Odyssey: Migration to Washington, DC,* ed. Frances Carey. Washington, DC: Smithsonian Institution Press, 1996.

Speer, Tibbett. "The Newest African Americans Aren't Black." *American Demographics* 16:1 (January 1994): 9–10.

Takougang, Joseph. "Recent African Immigrants to the United States: A Historical Perspective." *Western Journal of Black Studies* 19:1 (Spring 1995), 50–57.

THE AMERICAS

Introduction

Andean Countries
Carol Moe

Brazil and the Southern Cone
Leticia Marteleto and Cristina Gomes

Canada
Aonghas Mac Thòmais St.-Hilaire

Central America
Cecilia Menjívar

Cuba
Sara Z. Poggio

Dominican Republic
Pamela Graham

English-Speaking Caribbean
Daniel James

Haiti and French-Speaking Caribbean
Regina Ostine

Mexico
Wayne J. Pitts

Puerto Rico
Héctor R. Cordero-Guzmán

*I*NTRODUCTION

The entries in Section 2 of Part III of the *Encyclopedia of American Immigration* are devoted to immigrant groups coming from the various countries and regions of the Western Hemisphere. Regional entries include the Andean countries (Bolivia, Colombia, Ecuador, Peru, and Venezuela), Brazil and the Southern Cone (the latter including Argentina, Chile, Paraguay, and Uruguay), Central America (Costa Rica, El Salvador, Guatemala, Honduras, Nicaragua, and Panama), the English-speaking Caribbean (Belize, Guyana, Jamaica, Trinidad, and the English-speaking countries of the Lesser Antilles; and Haiti and the French-speaking Caribbean (the latter including Guadeloupe and Martinique). Individual country entries include Canada, Cuba, the Dominican Republic, Mexico, and Puerto Rico.

In her entry on the Andean countries, Carol Moe begins with a discussion of immigration from the region during the nineteenth and early twentieth centuries, bringing the story up to the present. Next, she turns to the life Andean immigrants have made for themselves in the United States, as well as their contributions to the society of their adopted land. Letitia Marteleto and Cristina Gomes focus on immigration from Brazil and the Southern Cone in their entry. They open with an examination of economic immigrants from the region before looking at the current demographics. The authors close with a discussion of illegal immigration to the United States from the countries of that region.

Aonghas Mac Thòmais St.-Hilaire's entry on immigration from Canada begins by looking at what he calls the "old Canadian immigrant," that is, those who came up through World War II. Next, he turns to the "new Canadian immigrant" of the postwar era, examining their settlement patterns, ethnicity issues, and cultural adaptation.

In her entry on immigrants and immigration from Central America, Cecilia Menjívar starts off with a look at the demographics before going on to a dis-

cussion of U.S. law and immigration from the region. Next, the author turns to work and labor force incorporation, and then goes on to discuss the issue of female, child, and elderly immigrants from Central America. She concludes with a discussion of Central American immigrant life in America, including the reliance on social networks and the church. Finally, she examines the settlement patterns of Central American immigrants and the impact they have on American culture and the impact American culture has on them.

In her entry on Cuba, Sara Z. Poggio explores the history of immigration from the island both before the Castro revolution and after. In addition, the author explores the subject of *cubanidad*, or Cuban identity, and how it survives in the United States. Finally, she examines the controversial relationship between the exile Cuban community and U.S. foreign policy toward Cuba itself.

Pamela Graham's entry on the Dominican Republic opens with an exploration of the patterns and causes of Dominican immigration to the United States. The author then goes on to discuss the characteristics and settlement patterns of these immigrants in this country before exploring their political, economic, and social incorporation. Finally, she examines the political, social, and cultural incorporation of Dominican immigrants into U.S. life and society.

In the entry of immigrants and immigration from the English-speaking Caribbean, Daniel James examines the numbers of people coming from countries in that linguistic region, before exploring the reasons why they leave and the life they experience in the United States. He also offers a capsule history of the region as well as its history of emigration.

In her entry on Haiti and the French-speaking Caribbean, Regina Ostine begins by looking at the history of the French in the Caribbean before examining recent immigration trends from the region to the United States. Much of the entry later focuses on the case of Haitian immigration.

Wayne J. Pitts's entry on Mexico begins with a discussion of the Treaty of Guadalupe Hidalgo, ending the Mexican-American War and guaranteeing full citizenship rights to Mexicans living in territory that now belonged to the United States. The author then discusses the history of immigration in the period leading up the Mexican revolution in the early twentieth century. The author continues with a discussion of immigration during the Bracero Program years of the 1920s and the discontinuation of that policy in the Great Depression. A discussion of postwar immigration and the various U.S. immigration reform acts of the 1980s and 1990s follows. Finally, the entry concludes with an examination of the future of Mexican immigration to the United States.

Héctor R. Cordero-Guzmán's entry discusses the unique immigration of Puerto Ricans—who are, of course, U.S. citizens. He begins with an examination of the economic conditions on the island since the 1950s before discussing the situation of Puerto Ricans living within the continental United States as well as return migration to the island. He closes with an exploration of recent trends in Puerto Rican migration.

ANDEAN COUNTRIES

On the west side of South America are the five Andean countries of Argentina, Bolivia, Chile, Ecuador, and Peru. They are grouped because the Andes Mountain range runs through them. The main language of these five countries is Spanish, although significant proportions of the population speak a variation of an Indian family of languages called Quechua. The countries had large Indian populations but were conquered by Spain in the sixteenth century. They all won their independence from Spain during the 1800s. The countries have a vast range of climates and features including deserts, jungles, lakes, coastal regions, and mountains. The different regions are beautiful and have not yet been overwhelmed by industrialization. Travel around the countries remains difficult. Consequently, modernization has been slow, and traditional ways continue to be important.

Members of the Andean countries began coming to the United States in small numbers at the turn of the twentieth century. The 1900 census reported that 5,000 individuals then living in the United States listed South America as their place of birth. While small factions certainly entered before then, most notably the approximately three hundred Peruvians that came to participate and trade in the California gold rush of 1849, these people either returned to their country of origin or "melted" into the general population. Generally, South American immigration was low in the first part of the twentieth century. A small group of several hundred professionals (nurses, accountants, pharmacists, and so on) came from Colombia after World War I. Immigration from the Andean countries did not substantially increase until the 1960s, and during that decade immigration for Colombians and Ecuadorians was triple that of the 1950s. Also, at that time, the Census Bureau began counting people by particular country instead of as "South American" or "Other American." Andean immigration again grew significantly in the 1980s. Between 1971 and 1980, 77,347 immigrants from Colombia entered, for example; between 1981 and 1990, those entering numbered 122,849. Although immigration peaked in 1990–91 and has fallen somewhat since then, it still continues to be strong. In 1997, the United States received 13,004 Colombians, 7,780 Ecuadorians, 10,853 Peruvians, and 3,328 Venezuelans.

REASONS FOR IMMIGRATION

Starting around the 1960s, the Andean countries began experiencing economic problems and depressions. In Colombia, for example, unemployment was estimated at 20–25 percent in the 1970s. Whereas prior to this time the majority of the population had lived in rural areas, people were no longer able to eke out a living on the land they owned. Mechanization replaced the need for many workers. As a result, large numbers of country dwellers migrated to the cities, causing overcrowding and other difficulties. These problems drove the urban population to the suburbs, and those who could afford to do so moved to other countries. Many believed that in the United States they would be able to make enough money to buy land or a business in their country of origin. Those who were educated yet balanced tenuously on the edge of the middle class often availed themselves of this option. Throughout the 1970s and later, wages continued to fall, inflation soared, and immigration to the United States increased.

In addition to economic factors, political turmoil motivated emigration. In Colombia, the civil war (1946–1958) and series of dictatorships that lasted from 1946 to 1962 were so destructive that the period is known as La Violencia. Moreover, guerrilla warfare has continued since then. Peru has also suffered an intense civil war, the fiercest part lasting from 1980 to 1992. Typically in such periods of violence, peasants go to the city to escape the violence in the country-

Vilma and her three-year-old daughter—seen here celebrating at New York's annual Hispanic Day parade—are recent immigrants from Bolivia, an Andean country whose population is dominated by native people. *(H. L. Delgado/Impact Visuals)*

side. This, in turn, displaces city residents. The instability of these governments contributes to the economic problems.

As Western technology and medical treatment reached the inner regions of South America, the death rate, particularly infant mortality, sharply declined. This, along with other factors such as higher fertility rates, contributed to the rising population. In combination with increasing mechanization, competition from industrialized countries, and stifling inflation, the burden became overwhelming, and many people in the Andean countries chose to leave.

Andean immigrants choose the United States due to the family and friendship networks that exist here. Often, other members of the family have already immigrated and settled. Thus, immigrants are sure to have someone to receive them as well as a place to stay upon arrival. For all Andean countries, the fam-

ily—and very often the extended family—is a very important unit. Once they have acquired citizenship, individuals will try to bring in as many members of their family as they can. Immediate family members of U.S. citizens are not subject to quota regulations. In 1997, almost half as many parents of U.S. citizens as children were admitted. This statistic suggests a picture different from that of a hundred years ago, when parents usually brought their children with them as they immigrated. It also suggests that immigrants expect immediate gains from moving to the United States, for it is unlikely that the 7 percent of Andean immigrants age sixty and over (admitted in 1997) plan to work for another ten or twenty years.

As some unfortunately find out, however, family and friends protect their pride by perpetuating images of wealth and a high standard of living in the United States even if they themselves have not attained such status. In 1989, 16 percent of immigrant families from Andean countries earned below the poverty level. Statistics show, though, that the longer that immigrant groups reside in the United States, the more upwardly mobile they become. According to the 1990 census, while 27 percent of persons who had immigrated from Andean countries between 1980 and 1990 were below the poverty level, only 11 percent of those who had immigrated before 1980 were. Because many people who come from Andean countries have at least a high school diploma or the equivalent, they tend quickly to acclimate themselves to American or Latino economic life.

Theorists attribute the rise of Andean immigration in the 1960s to the affordability of air travel for people. Traveling by plane was also much faster and safer than the boat trips taken by earlier immigrants. In psychological terms, it made regular visits home feasible. It is estimated (unfortunately, no statistics are available) that many immigrants go back and forth between their country of origin and the United States.

In contrast to the political life of the Andean countries, the political and social structure of the United States appears sound. When political turmoil erupted in the Andean countries, professionals and skilled workers believed that they could find much better opportunities in the United States, in terms of both money and working conditions. Unfortunately, this caused Andean countries to experience a "brain drain" in the 1970s, in which professors, engineers, doctors, and other professional and skilled workers left the country in disproportionate numbers. Many immigrants also believed that their children would have better educational opportunities in the United States. In Colombia, for example, only a limited number of students are permitted to attend college (predominantly the wealthy). Even with a college education, the number of applicants far exceeds the number of jobs.

Andean countries also favor traditional family values such that women do not work outside the home. In the United States, it very often becomes a necessity for the wife to work full-time. Interviews with women often reveal that they are reluctant to cede their increased freedom when the family decides to return to the country of origin. Others find the social structure in Andean countries to be very set according to class, heritage, and education. They feel the United States offers an opportunity for social mobility.

Because immigrants from the Andean countries have come in the latter part of the twentieth century, they differ remarkably from groups that came earlier. Most are familiar with U.S. culture through television, movies, companies, and organizations (such as the Peace Corps) that exist in the home country. For example, in 1978, right before the wave of immigration in the 1980s, U.S. television shows accounted for 25 percent of the total programming in Colombia and 33 percent in Peru and Latin America generally. In 1991, studies indicated that Venezuelan television programming consisted of 60 percent imported programming, largely from North America, and approximately 10 percent advertising, most of which featured U.S. products. In terms of the role that U.S. business plays in representing the U.S. abroad, there are good stories and sad stories. Currently, Peru imports 40 percent of its goods from the United States and exports 33 percent of its goods to the United States. Certainly, this aspect gives a favorable impression of the United States. But Ecuadorians sued and won a judgment in U.S. courts in the 1990s against Texaco for its damaging oil spill in the Peruvian forest. Negative images of industrialization are not uncommon.

Most immigrants of today have visited the United States already. Some have even tried living here for a while as a student, intern, or illegal alien. Currently, about seven hundred thousand people from the Andean countries visit annually for pleasure, and about three hundred thousand come for business, school, and internships. Some of these use this time as a trial period before applying to immigrate. Some meet and marry U.S. citizens. Others stay even after the expiration of their visa, making them illegal aliens. Periodically, the Immigration and Naturalization Service offers a forgiveness period for those who have been living in the United States continuously for at least seven years. The United States is only beginning to see the arrival of peasants because the trip is still very expensive. Since unskilled laborers have lowest priority in the quotas, generally they must come illegally.

For undocumented persons to come to the United States from an Andean country costs an average of $3,000 by land and $6,000 by air—prices that are beyond the range of most peasants.

Even though Andean immigrants differ from prior immigrant groups in the above-mentioned ways, theorists are quick to point out that the way they choose to stay only temporarily in New York City contrasts with the immigration of the Irish, Italians, Jews, and Poles at the beginning of the twentieth century. Whereas the latter groups came with the intention of putting down roots and starting a new life in the United States, many immigrants from Andean countries expect to stay only long enough to work until they make enough money to establish themselves in their own country. While approximately forty thousand people legally immigrate from the Andean countries annually, the return rate for immigrants who have previously immigrated is estimated to be high. Life in the United States does not necessarily suit all those who come.

ANDEAN LIFE IN AMERICA

While immigrants from the Andean countries reside in all fifty states, the largest Andean communities can currently be found in the New York area (including New Jersey). Just under 50 percent of the Andean immigrant population lives in this area. Florida and California serve as the next points of destination. In fact, small numbers of Colombians and Venezuelans, along with Cubans, played an important role in the development of the Latino neighborhoods in Miami. The neighborhoods in Chicago also deserve mention. Predominantly urban dwellers in their country of origin, very few immigrants settle in rural areas.

Most of the people of the Andean countries have multiple ethnic backgrounds, including Native South American (indigenous), Spanish (from Spain), black (of African ancestry, having arrived during the slave trade), other European, and Asian (high levels of immigration in the early twentieth century). For example, thousands of Chinese Ecuadorians live in the United States. These background differences, along with class and geographic differentiation, affect the way immigrants from the same country interact with one another in their new country. People originally from the Andean countries' coast, for instance, will not always associate with people from the mountains, who they believe to be inferior.

While Andean immigrants of all ages come to the United States, most are adults and range between 20

Table 1
Employment of Andean Immigrants Age 16 and Up, 1995

Occupation Category	Colombia	Ecuador	Peru	Venezuela	Total	Percentage of Total Andean Workforce
Managerial/professional	29,970	12,699	16,928	6,342	65,939	18
Technical/sales/ administrative support	46,830	22,717	23,652	5,953	99,152	26
Service	39,037	17,259	21,794	2,802	80,892	22
Operators, fabricators, laborers	37,810	23,766	16,676	2,025	80,277	21
Total	176,696	88,540	90,337	18,912	326,260	100

Source: Immigration and Naturalization Service. *Statistical Yearbook of the Immigration and Naturalization Service*. Washington, DC: Government Printing Office, 1997.

and 64 years of age. Within that range, approximately one-third of the immigrants are between 25 and 34. The next largest group is 35 to 44. Approximately an equal number of men and women immigrate. About two-thirds of the immigrants are married, and a little over twice the number of housing units are rented versus owned.

Roman Catholicism is the most prominent religion in the Andean countries. In fact, several Catholic churches in the United States have made an effort to have services in Spanish for their immigrant members. Some even hire priests and nuns from Andean countries in an effort to reach their community. Protestantism also has its constituents, chiefly in Ecuador. Moreover, the familiarity that people in Ecuador have with Protestant missionaries may lead them to choose the United States over other countries when they decide to immigrate.

Immigrants from the Andean countries are fairly well educated. Over 70 percent have at least a high school diploma or equivalent. A high percentage of those who come are professionals and assimilate quickly into U.S. life. Others find uses for their skills and experience within the immigrant community.

Certain skills have been very valuable to the U.S. economy at various times. Western ranches have sought shepherds from Peru. Eastern textile factories have solicited Colombian workers. Most notably in 1969, twenty skilled loom fixers were recruited to revive a dying plant. Although that company did not survive, one of the workers set up an immigrant network that brought back four mills in Lowell, Massachusetts. There, Colombians made up only 11 percent of the workforce, but they held key positions in the four mills, which employed nearly one thousand people. This is one example of immigrant labor helping

"Americans" to keep their jobs, challenging the criticism of those who claim that immigrants take jobs away from U.S. citizens.

The growing Latino community in the United States has a need for restaurants, grocery stores, banks, money-wire services, and travel agencies. Immigrants have also found employment as mechanics, as well as in shoe repair and jewelry making. The 1990 census showed manufacturing and technical, sales, and administrative support occupations as the most widely performed among the foreign-born. The former uses 27 percent of employed persons age sixteen and older, and the latter accounts for 23 percent. Service occupations follow with about 20 percent. Upper-class Peruvians who have been able to transfer their capital and business experience to their new home own factories and stores, among other prestigious jobs.

CONTRIBUTIONS TO AMERICAN LIFE

Andean life centers around community. As first-generation immigrants still constitute a significant portion of the community in the United States, many of the traditional Andean values remain in place. In such cities as New York that maintain large numbers of immigrants from the various Andean countries, groups tend to congregate according to nationality. In the streets one can talk with people from one's area in the home country. Newsstands with papers from the home country proliferate. Someone, either through the newspaper, television, or ham radio, knows the latest scores from the soccer or baseball teams. The stores, particularly the bodegas (Latin

American grocery stores), are filled with the friendly faces of people who speak Spanish and who perhaps have heard of a company that needs workers, cheap apartments, or doctors and dentists that speak Spanish. While one generally does not find many organizations that help new arrivals, immigrants can count on their community for this information.

The Andean countries are known for their music. Traditional music consists of winds and percussion; string instruments are often used as well. Although some describe the music as monotonous, others find it hypnotic. One can see Ecuadorians in traditional Native South American garb performing this music in university concerts or even on the New York streets or in the subways. Such dances as the Colombian *cumbia* have gained popularity even outside the Hispanic community in the United States. The Joropo comes from Venezuela and is a lively couples dance that employs the accordion, harp, guitar, and maracas.

In addition to the fame they have received for carrying on Andean dance, Ecuadorians are also renowned for their volleyball teams. The sport of ecuavoley, as it is called, uses nine-foot-high nets and three-person teams. Among all the Andean groups, soccer is very popular. Of course, their children who are born and raised in the United States share an equal affinity for football and basketball. Among Venezuelans, the most popular sport is baseball, and many Venezuelans have come to play in the Major Leagues.

The groups all support newspapers and radio stations in cities where they number enough to do so. The newspapers advertise job and housing opportunities in the United States as well as report on the political and social life of the country of origin. Peruvians in New York and New Jersey find it feasible to produce a weekly cable program. While these communications serve predominantly to bring a little bit of "home" to the immigrants, they also allow all Spanish-speaking immigrants and Spanish-speaking natives easy access to world news.

Festivities provide an opportunity for Andean immigrants to show off their cultural heritage. Many depend on celebrations to rally their compatriots and to make the general American public aware of the positive aspects of their existence. The Andean countries each celebrate their own Independence Day, which is usually marked by a parade in cities with a substantial number of immigrants. Colombian Independence Day occurs on July 20, and Ecuador's, a few weeks later on August 10. Begun in 1984, the New York parade in celebration of Ecuador Day (Independence Day) follows 37th Avenue in Queens. Numerous other Ecuador Day celebrations, picnics, and get-togethers

are held in Flushing Meadows Park in Queens. Peruvian Independence Day falls on July 28. Other important Peruvian holidays include El Senor de Los Milagros (October 18), St. Martin of Porras (November 3), and St. Rose of Lima—patroness of Peru (August 30). Traditional Catholic holidays receive varying amounts of attention. Two religious holidays that have always been more widely celebrated in Latin America than in the United States are All Saints' Day (November 1) and All Souls' Day (November 2).

A fringe benefit of attending the parades and festivities is the opportunity to try Andean specialties. One's mouth waters at the thought of *arroz con pollo* (chicken and rice), tamales, meat or poultry seasoned with onions and hot peppers, *ceviche* (an Ecuadorian dish consisting of raw seafood marinated in citrus juice and served cold), and *caldo* (soup).

Another way that immigrants promote their home cultures is through clubs. New York is home to the Ecuadoran Club Social Salitre and the Club Peru de Nueva York. New Jersey hosts the Ecuadoran Confraternidad Ecuatoriana.

Immigrants from the Andean countries tend to organize according to nationality. A few groups serve primarily to help immigrants in the United States. (See list of organizations on p. 1089.) The rest coordinate dances and other social activities as fundraisers for the home country. These groups are supported by their members, donations from the community, and funds from businesses and banks. Since the mid-1980s, immigrants from each country have also hosted an annual national conference held in various cities throughout the United States as a means of encouraging contact and interaction with members of their community living in the United States. Frequently, organizations unite over a specific goal or project. For example, in 1990, the Colombian community came together to send aid to the victims' families after the Avianca flight 052 plane crash.

DISUNITY AND DISCRIMINATION

Even though various groups exist to help acclimate new arrivals to life in the United States, lack of information about life in the United States and resources available to immigrants are the chief complaints. Regardless of how much exposure they may have had in their countries of origin, many immigrants still find American culture perplexing and difficult to negotiate. Immigrants do not always realize what government services are available to them, nor do they know how to access these services. Sometimes these services are lacking. Many communities need more English classes, especially for working adults. Often, immigrants do not know where to turn in their community. Due to prejudice, they have poor relationships with whites and troublesome relationships with the police. Outside their own cultural group, they find little unity with other Hispanic groups.

Cultural differences between traditional Andean family values and those in U.S. society cause families to break apart as children and wives become more Americanized. Divorce is much more prevalent among immigrant couples than in the home countries. Children often expect more freedom in American society, while parents tend to clamp down harder in an effort to counteract what they consider "loose" American values. Teenage girls receive more educational freedom, but they resent the social freedom that is denied them by their parents. Men are often caught between a society in which they cannot be the sole provider for their family and a family that no longer seems to respect them as it once did.

Perhaps the largest problem Andean immigrants face is discrimination. While studies show that many European and Cuban immigrants feel that they suffer little or no prejudice in the United States, people from Andean countries differ in their perception. Examples of unfair treatment abound. During World War II, the United States forced 1,800 Peruvian-Japanese people into concentration camps. Later, some were exchanged for U.S. prisoners of war; the rest were deported to Japan. More current, due to the media and the Hollywood portrayal of the drug cartels in their country of origin, Colombians suffer prejudice because they are thought to be involved in the drug business. Even in places where their number is large, immigrants encounter discrimination. For example, in Jackson Heights in Queens, New York, Colombians believe that the community board does not welcome Colombian members and acts in a hostile manner to Colombian business leaders who request licenses or other services of the board. Recently, Andean immigrant organizations have strived to create positive images of their communities.

CULTURE AND CUSTOMS

Because many members of the Andean countries come for economic reasons and anticipate that they will return home after saving some money, they tend not to naturalize. Many still have close relatives in the country of origin. They send money to these individuals not only for subsistence or savings but also to contribute to organizations and charities much as they would if they still lived in the home country. Many are still very much a part of their home community and are reluctant to lose this position by naturalizing as U.S. citizens. Many feel that becoming a U.S. citizen betrays their strong ties to the home country in favor of a country in which they do not feel welcome.

Many myths and realities about the naturalization process also scare immigrants away. Rumors (such as one must stand and spit on the home country's flag) proliferate among migrants. If they become U.S. citizens, immigrants are afraid they will be treated badly by people in their home country when they come to visit. Moreover, naturalization involves copious amounts of paperwork, an English language test, and little-known historical questions about the colonies. Colombians especially are known for splitting their citizenship—one spouse will become American and one will remain Colombian. This enables immigrants to keep their options open between a country with an unstable economy and government and a country that can represent both opportunity and discrimination.

As long as they stay emigrants, the countries of origin allow them to vote in national elections. However, the percentage of Colombians (the Andean country that has allowed its nationals to vote abroad) that actually do vote has been decreasing. The home countries support these rights because their nationals frequently send home remittances to family members, thereby contributing to their country's economy; the nationals sometimes even contribute to political campaigns. Consequently, immigrants from the Andean countries tend to pay more attention to the politics of their home country over U.S. politics. Candidates for positions in Colombia will frequently campaign in New York. However, because most of these countries adopted policies (Colombia in 1991, Ecuador in 1995) to allow natives dual citizenship, including voting privileges in the home country, a greater percentage of immigrants from the Andean countries have naturalized.

Theorists speculate that it may become a problem for Andean immigrants not to use the American political system. Immigrants cannot vote until they become naturalized, which leaves them with little room to effect change. They cannot provide candidates from their own numbers until they become citizens. Even those candidates who do come from their communities may be less likely to take nonvoting constituents into account.

Carol Moe

See also: Catholicism, Evangelical Christianity (Part II, Sec. 11).

BIBLIOGRAPHY

Auerbach, Susan. *Encyclopedia of Multiculturalism.* 6 vols. New York: Marshall Cavendish, 1994.

Berrol, Selma Cantor. *Growing Up American: Immigrant Children in America Then and Now.* New York: Twayne, 1995.

Binder, Frederick M., and David M. Reimers. *All the Nations under Heaven: An Ethnic and Racial History of New York City.* New York: Columbia University Press, 1995.

Bureau of the Census. *Persons of Hispanic Origin in the United States.* Washington, DC: Government Printing Office, 1993.

Chaney, Elsa M. "Colombian Migration to the United States." In *The Dynamics of Migration, International Migration.* Investigators, Wayne A. Cornelius et al. Washington, DC: Interdisciplinary Communications Program, Smithsonian Institution, 1976.

Constructing the New York Area Hispanic Mosaic: A Demographic Portrait of Colombians and Dominicans in New York. Claremont, CA: Tomas Rivera Policy Institute and NALEO Educational Fund, 1997.

Diversifying the New York Area Hispanic Mosaic: Colombian and Dominican Leaders' Assessments of Community Public Policy Needs. Claremont, CA: Tomas Rivera Policy Institute and NALEO Educational Fund, 1997.

Ferguson, James. *Venezuela: A Guide to the People, Politics, and Culture.* London: Latin America Bureau, 1994.

Galens, Judy, Anna Sheets, and Robyn V. Young, eds. *Gale Encyclopedia of Multicultural America.* 2 vols. Contrib. ed. Rudolph J. Vecoli. Detroit: Gale Research, 1995.

Immigration and Naturalization Service. *Statistical Yearbook of the Immigration and Naturalization Service.* Washington, DC: Government Printing Office, 1997.

Jones-Correa, Michael. *Between Two Nations: The Political Predicament of Latinos in New York City.* Ithaca: Cornell University Press, 1998.

Levinson, David, and Melvin Ember, eds., *American Immigrant Cultures: Builders of a Nation.* 2 vols. New York: Simon and Schuster Macmillan, 1997.

Mahler, Sarah J. *American Dreaming: Immigrant Life on the Margins.* Princeton: Princeton University Press, 1995.

Meltzer, Milton. *The Hispanic Americans.* New York: Thomas Y. Crowell, 1982.

Monaghan, Jay. *Chile, Peru, and the California Gold Rush of 1849.* Berkeley: University of California Press, 1973.

Redden, Charlotte Ann. *A Comparative Study of Colombian and Costa Rican Emigrants to the United States.* New York: Arno Press, 1980.

Reimers, David M. *Still the Golden Door: The Third World Comes to America, 1943–1983.* New York: Columbia University Press, 1985.

Thernstrom, Stephan, ed. "Central and South Americans" in *Harvard Encyclopedia of American Ethnic Groups.* Cambridge: Harvard University Press, Belknap Press, 1980.

Weyr, Thomas. *Hispanic U.S.A.: Breaking the Melting Pot.* New York: Harper and Row, 1988.

Professional Organizations

Colombian American Bar Association

Cartagena Medical Alumni Association—A Colombian medical association established in the late 1960s which primarily hosts fund-raisers for Cartagena Medical School and helps newcomers in Chicago. It now includes other professionals.

FEDECOP—Colombian professional association.

Peruvian-American Medical Society—Coordinates fund-raisers to support Peruvian hospitals.

PROECUA—Ecuadorian professional association.

Sports Organizations

Liga Colombiana de Bolos (LICOBOL)—Coordinates thirty-four bowling teams that participate in local, national, and international championships.

Football Women's Soccer League (FWSL)—Consists of eight soccer teams; 75 percent of its members are Colombians, and the rest are other Latin Americans.

Political/Social Organizations

Casa Peru—Transmits Peruvian culture and produces the weekly cable program *Peru Aqui.*

Centro Civico Colombiano—Among other services, offers English classes.

Centro Juvenil Colombiano (CEJUCOL)—Counters negative stereotypes of Colombians through educational, cultural, and recreational opportunities for youth.

Colombian Charities of America—Designed originally to give relief to victims of natural disaster in Armero, it now focuses on Colombians in New York; it offers assistance for immigrants and organizes citizenship campaigns.

Colombianos Unidos para Labor Activista—A political club of students and permanent residents which hosts social activities as well.

Comite Civico Ecuatoriano—Among other activities, hosts fund-raisers for Ecuador.

Ecuadorian Cultural Brotherhood—Located in Virginia, it hosts a celebration of Ecuadorian independence, among other activities

Federacion de Organizaciones Colombianas (FEDOCOL)—Sponsors citizenship drives and encourages involvement in U.S. politics.

Federation of Ecuadoran Organizations in the Exterior (FEDEE)—Maintains strong ties to Ecuador. Fought for dual citizenship of Ecuadorian emigrants (achieved in 1995).

Political/Social Organizations *(continued)*

Fundación Gran Mariscal de Ayacucho (FUNDAY ACUCHO)—Supports the development of human resources necessary for the economic, social, and cultural advancement of Venezuela. Founded in 1975. Coordinated in the United States by Latin American Scholarship Program of American Universities (LASPAU).

International Lions Club—In cities where there is a substantial Andean population, Colombian or Ecuadorian Lions Clubs will form. They send money, supplies, and medicine to Latin American countries in times of trouble.

Peruvian-American Association for Cultural Promotion—Hosts fund-raisers and then donates the money for humanitarian projects in Peru.

Solidaridad Peruana—Hosts fund-raisers for projects in Peru.

Various political groups for American politics

Various political groups for Colombian politics

Venezuelan American Chamber of Commerce of Florida (CUCIVA)

$\mathscr{B}$RAZIL AND THE SOUTHERN CONE

$\mathscr{A}$fter the restrictive policies of the 1920s, there are three relevant characteristics of immigration in the United States: expanded immigration after World War II, increased refugee numbers, and increasing immigration from Asia and Latin America after 1970. The movement of immigrants from South America to the United States is rather new. While there have always been South Americans living in the United States, their rate of immigration increased sharply in the mid-1980s as most countries on the South American continent suffered from severe economic conditions: hyperinflation, unemployment and underemployment, low wages, and pervasive economic uncertainty. The experiences of Latin Americans and those of Latin American descent residing in the United States are extremely diverse. Despite existing contrasts, there are a number of similarities in the characteristics and experiences of South Americans living in the United States.

ECONOMIC IMMIGRANTS

The majority of immigrants from South America living in the United States are economic immigrants, the so-called target earners. This distinctive migration due to economic cause is important, because individuals who migrate for political reasons tend to be permanent, in contrast with individuals who migrate due to economic restrictions. Those who migrate for economic reasons have a higher rate of return, while those who migrate for political reasons have a lower rate of return.

Many immigrants from Brazil and the Southern Cone are undocumented. (The Southern Cone consists of Argentina, Chile, Paraguay, and Uruguay.) However, Brazilian and Southern Cone immigrants are in general *visa overstayers* and *settlers*, in opposition to Mexicans, for example, who are mainly *without visa*

and *sojourners*. This difference exists because Mexican immigrants can cross the United States–Mexico border on a daily or almost daily basis to work in the United States, whereas immigrants from Brazil and the Southern Cone cannot.

RECENT FIGURES

There are different data sources for estimating the number of immigrants in the United States. However, census data offer information only about legal immigrants. Current Population Survey (CPS) data are more useful for estimating Mexicans immigrants, but other countries' estimates are unreliable, because these immigrants are spread over so many different countries of origin. Data on immigrant apprehensions are often used to assess changes in flow of immigrants. However, this is valuable information only on flows from Mexico, because the vast majority of immigrant apprehensions in the United States are of Mexicans. Estimates of stocks and flows from individual non-Mexican countries must therefore rely on other data sources. Illegal aliens from Brazil and Southern Cone countries differ from Mexicans, because they generally come to the United States legally and then overstay their visas. As such, data on visa overstays provide one way to estimate changes in illegal flows from Brazil and the Southern Cone. According to the 1999 *Triennial Comprehensive Report on Immigration*, in 1994, 5.9 percent of all immigrants to the United States were from South America (47,377 individuals).

BRAZIL

According to the 1980 U.S. census, approximately fifty thousand Brazilian-born individuals were present in

In recent decades, the West Side of midtown Manhattan has become home to many Brazilian businesses and restaurants. *(Kirk Condyles/ Impact Visuals)*

the United States between 1965 and 1980. Their presence was directly related to the Immigration and Nationality Act of 1965, which opened the United States to immigrants from South America and other places for the first time. According to the 1999 *Triennial Comprehensive Report on Immigration*, in 1994, Brazil was ranked sixth in terms of number of visas issued for all classes.

Brazilians began immigrating at higher rates to the United States in the mid-1980s, mostly as a consequence of the poor economic conditions during this so-called lost decade in Brazil. State Department data from 1991 show that in 1981, approximately 110,000 Brazilians were issued U.S. nonimmigrant visas, which ranked Brazilians tenth among recipients of U.S. nonimmigrant visas. By 1991, that number had risen to approximately 260,000 visas, ranking Brazilians fourth among recipients of U.S. nonimmigrant visas.

Attracted by higher wages, Brazilian immigrants tend to be younger, more educated, and more often of European ancestry than the average Brazilian population. Most settle in urban areas. Among Brazilian

immigrants, there is a predominance of migrants from the state of Minas Gerais and, specifically, from the city of Governador Valadares.

The uniqueness of Brazilian immigrants is often not recognized, because most wrongly consider them to be Hispanics, a term that does not exist in Brazil. There is no apt census category for Brazilians in the 1990 census, which makes it difficult to estimate the precise number of Brazilian migrants in the United

Table 1
Number of Legal Immigrants to the United States Born in Brazil and the Southern Cone

Country	1988	1989	1990	1991
Argentina	2,371	3,301	5,437	3,889
Brazil	2,699	3,332	4,191	8,133
Chile	2,137	3,037	4,049	2,842
Uruguay	612	948	1,457	1,161

Source: United Nations. *Demographic Yearbook, 1997.* United Nations, 1998.

States. Studies estimate that at least 350,000 to 400,000 Brazilians live in the United States, of which some 80,000 to 100,000 reside in New York City. According with the Brazilian census, the most important migratory movement occurred in the 1980s: the net migration between 1980 and 1990 was 631,000 individuals (415,000 men and 216,000 women). Most individuals, whether male or female, are between twenty and twenty-nine years of age.

SOUTHERN CONE

Immigrants from the Southern Cone in general have significantly higher rates of educational attainment in comparison with those who migrate from the Caribbean and other Latin American countries. Immigrants from the Southern Cone also tend to be younger and more educated than the Southern Cone population overall.

The number of immigrants from Argentina has increased from 13,000 in 1960 to 44,803 in 1970 and to 68,887 in 1980. The main increase in the 1970s is due to economic difficulties and the authoritarian government, violence, and political persecution. The majority of Argentineans in the United States are males of economically active ages, with a high level of education (60 percent of them have more than ten years in school). They are mainly married (71 percent), and the majority work (82 percent of men and 46 percent of women), especially in the service sector (nearly 60 percent). Between 1970 and 1980 there was a change in the characteristics of Argentinean immigrants: the proportion of unmarried males with high levels of education has increased.

The out-migration of Uruguayans to the United States has also increased since 1974. Most emigrate to Argentina, but a small number emigrate to the United States: the more educated group, mainly individuals who work in the public sector, include university students or professors. In the case of Uruguay, the determinant factor of this migratory flow was the difficulty to assess the labor market and the higher salaries in the countries of destination. Migration owing to political concerns was also an important cause of emigration when the military government began in 1973, but overall the most important cause has been economic.

Using data on "expected departure" from the Nonimmigrant Information System, Frank Bean, Barry Edmonston, and Jeffrey S. Passel estimate the rates of system error for different modes of arrival and

Table 2
Long-Term Immigrants to the United States by Country of Last Permanent Residence, 1958–1970

	1959	1963	1967	1970
Brazil	2,378	NA	3,249	2,500
Argentina	3,042	7,627	3,248	3,616
Chile	854	1,496	952	996
Uruguay	152	347	376	874

Source: Frank Bean, Barry Edmonston, and Jeffrey S. Passel. *Undocumented Migration to the United States: IRCA and the Experience of the 1980s.* Washington, DC: Urban Institute, 1990.

broad classes of admission of aliens in the United States, as well as the number of overstays. For example, the proportion of individuals who entered the United States as tourists by air between October 1986 and March 1987 was 7.5 percent of Argentineans, 9.0 percent of Brazilians, 11.3 percent of Chileans, and 9.8 percent of Uruguayans.

WORK

Occupational earnings of male immigrants from South America show the second highest average among immigrants. This demonstrates the high level of education and of human capital of this group, especially of male immigrants from the Southern Cone. If the statistics excluded Colombians and Ecuadorians, the educational level of the majority of immigrants from South America would be even higher. Immigrant women from South America often work in domestic service employment in the United States.

Leticia Marteleto and Cristina Gomes

See also: New York City, San Francisco, Washington, D.C. (Part II, Sec. 12).

BIBLIOGRAPHY

Bean, Frank, Barry Edmonston, and Jeffrey S. Passel, *Undocumented Migration to the United States: IRCA and the Experience of the 1980s.* Washington, D.C.: Urban Institute, 1990.

———. *Report of the Visa Office, 1991.* Washington, DC: Bureau of Consular Affairs, 1992.

Department of State. *Report of the Visa Office, 1990.* Washington, DC: Bureau of Consular Affairs, 1990.

Fortuna, Juan C., Nelly Niedworok, and Adela Pellegrino. *Uruguay y la emigracion de los 70*. Geneva: United Nations and CENEP, 1988.

Goza, Franklin. *Brazilian Immigration to North America, 1994*. New York: International Migration Review, Spring 1994.

Hakkert, R., and Franklin Goza. "Demographic Consequences of the Austerity Crisis in Latin America." In *Lost Promises: Debt, Austerity, and Development in Latin America*, ed. W. L. Canak. Boulder, CO: Westview Press, 1989.

Hofstetter, Richard R, ed. *U.S. Immigration Policy*. Duke Press Policy Studies. Durham: Duke University Press, 1984.

Jasso, Guillermina. "Have the Occupational Skills of New Immigrants to the United States Declined over Time? Evidence from the Immigrant Cohorts of 1977, 1982, and 1994." Paper presented at the IUSSP Conference, Barcelona, 1997.

Lattes, Alfredo E., and Enrique Oteiza. *Dinamica Migratoria Argentina (1955–1984): Democratizacion y retorno de expatriados*. Geneva: United Nations and CENEP, 1986.

Pinal, Jorge del, and Audrey Singer. "Generations of Diversity: Latinos in the United States." *Population Reference Bureau Bulletin* 52: 3 (1997): 1–44.

Portes, Alejandro, and R. Rumbaut. *Immigrant America: A Portrait*. Berkeley: University of California Press, 1990.

Taylor, J. Edward. "International-Migrant Remittances, Savings, and Development in Migrant-Sending Areas." Paper presented at the IUSSP Conference, Barcelona, 1997.

The Triennial Comprehensive Report on Immigration. Washington, DC: Department of Justice, Immigration and Naturalization Service, and Department of Labor, Bureau of International Labor Affairs, 1999.

CANADA

Canadians have a long history of immigration to the United States, and for more than a century and a half have been a strong demographic presence in the United States. The geographic proximity and the many shared cultural traits of the two countries are among the most important factors that work in favor of the movement of Canadians to the United States and of their integration into American society. Changing political and economic conditions in Canada and the United States have also strongly influenced the pattern of Canadian immigration to the United States. Since the end of the American Civil War in 1865, Canadian immigration to the United States has outpaced American immigration to Canada. Relatively limited economic growth and opportunities in Canada have served as push factors encouraging many Canadians to look to the United States for their economic future. Conversely, the relatively prosperous U.S. economy has served as a pull factor attracting Canadian immigrants southward.

However, post–World War II economic transformations in both countries and recent U.S.–Canadian political agreements designed to further continental economic integration have changed the magnitude and nature of Canadian immigration to the United States. Nevertheless, large numbers of Canadians continue to seek and find work and take up residence in the United States. As a result of a long tradition of immigration, Canadians and their descendants are now well represented in the U.S. population as a whole, although important regional variations continue to exist. The settlement patterns of Canadians in the United States vary by period of immigration and by the ethnicity and language of the immigrants. Historically, differences in immigration and settlement patterns exist between English-speaking and French-speaking Canadians, the two largest cultural subgroups of Canada, as well as among the many non-British and non-French ethnic peoples that compose the Canadian population migrating to the United States. However, recent trends point to a convergence of patterns of settlement across the different Canadian ethnic groups immigrating to the United States.

THE OLD CANADIAN IMMIGRANT

Migration between Canada and the United States is older than the two countries themselves. Initially, political concerns motivated the large-scale movement of people from the north to the south and vice versa. In 1717, the British, using their North American colonies as a military base and source of provisions, conquered Acadia (present-day Nova Scotia) from the French. In 1755, as part of an effort to clear land for loyal English-speaking colonists, the British expelled the French-speaking and Catholic Acadians from the territory, forcing many of them into exile in small, scattered communities throughout the American colonies of the Eastern seaboard in the hope that they would quickly assimilate to the dominant Anglo-Saxon cultural and linguistic norms. Other Acadians migrated to Louisiana, where they and their descendants evolved into the unique Cajun French people, with a language and culture distinct from the rest of the United States and from the rest of the French-speaking world. (The word "Cajun" derives from the term "Acadian.") In 1759, the British conquered New France (present-day Quebec), but allowed the French Canadians to maintain their religion, language, and culture. For the next two hundred years, the French Canadians of Quebec guarded a distinct identity in relation to the English-speaking Canadians, who tended toward greater identification with Great Britain and stronger loyalty to the British Crown.

During the American Revolution for independence from Great Britain from 1775 to 1783, large numbers of English-speaking loyalists from the American colonies emigrated to Canada, settling in the Maritime provinces of Eastern Canada, the township region of Quebec, and Ontario. After 1783 the border between the newly independent United States of America and the still British-controlled Canada became increasingly politicized, as did the differences between the emerging American and nascent Canadian national identities. Great Britain did not accept defeat by the Americans well. The War of 1812, once again pitting the United States and Great Britain against each other, further complicated relations in North America and intensified the political importance of the U.S.–Canadian border. After 1815, however, relations between the United States, on the one hand, and Great Britain and Canada, on the other, steadily normalized. Nevertheless, for the first half of the nineteenth century, Canadian immigration to the United States remained on a small scale. Canadians still had access to tracts of arable land from which to make a living. During the second half of the nineteenth century, however, population growth in Canada resulted in a shortage of land for children of large farming families. Also during this period, industry grew rapidly in the United States, providing jobs for millions of immigrants. With relaxed or nonexistent border restrictions and a prosperous U.S. economy, Canadians began to head south in search of a better life.

Canada, like the United States, is a nation of immigrants. However, despite moderate European immigration prior to 1900, the total population of Canada barely grew until the twentieth century. A large percentage of European immigrants used Canada as a launching pad to the United States. At the time, Canada offered relatively little in the way of urban, industrial employment, and many European immigrants found homesteading in Canada's West unattractive. After 1860, emigration from Canada to the United States surpassed European and U.S. immigration to Canada for the first time. Canadian immigration to the United States was particularly heavy before 1900. Between 1861 and 1901, Canada experienced a net outflow of people, both Canadian-born and European immigrant, to the United States. The net outflow from Canada was greatest in the 1880s. During that decade alone, approximately 390,000 Canadians immigrated to the United States.

Until recently, the political border delineating the two countries has rarely been enforced as a means to control population flows. Therefore, pre-1900 Canadian immigration is difficult to enumerate. Canadians and Americans alike, if they so desired, could pass the border with relative ease, taking up residence and working in their newly adopted country. Many Canadians simply crossed the border undetected. While border crossings typically were not counted, census figures from both sides of the border indicated 1,180,000 Canadian-born people in the United States and only 128,000 U.S.-born people living in Canada in 1901. The United States typically attracted Canada's youngest, brightest, and most ambitious, providing the labor and skills that helped fuel U.S. growth. Furthermore, an estimated two million Canadian-born and six million people born outside of Canada emigrated from Canada to the United States between 1891 and 1931. With the Great Depression, however, the employment opportunities of the boom period vanished. Nevertheless, between the 1920s and the 1950s a further 1.4 million Canadians came to the United States in continuation of a trend of nearly a century in duration.

Approximately three-quarters of all Canadian immigrants were from British Canada, with the remaining one-quarter from French Canada. High levels of natural increase and a limited supply of affordable arable land encouraged Canadian emigration, primarily from the provinces of Ontario and Quebec. However, Canada's Maritime provinces, long the poorest of Canada, also contributed large numbers of immigrants to the United States. A chronic depression beginning in 1871 sent many young French- and English-speaking Canadians from Prince Edward Island, New Brunswick, and Nova Scotia to New England. Patterns of immigration differ somewhat between French-speaking and English-speaking Canadians. Most French-speaking Canadians went to the various mill towns of New England, while the majority of English-speaking Canadians joined the California gold rush, went to the industrial cities of New York State, or took up farming in the plains states. French-speaking Quebecers, whose population had skyrocketed due to a phenomenally high birthrate, migrated individually or as families to contiguous parts of the United States. In 1890, two-thirds of the 302,000 French Canadians in the United States lived in New England, 15 percent in Michigan, and 12 percent in upper New York State. Initially, French Canadians from Quebec and New Brunswick came to the United States seasonally to work in the brickyards, construction sites, logging camps, railroads, and canals, often leaving their families back in Canada. Later, however, they tended to settle more permanently in the United States, bringing their families with them and maintaining community life apart from their English-speaking Yankee neighbors. Despite the farming origins of most early Canadian immigrants to the United States, these migrants were primarily wage seeking rather than land seeking.

THE NEW CANADIAN IMMIGRANT

After World War II, Canada witnessed rapid economic and industrial growth. The number of Canadians immigrating to the United States diminished as opportunities in Canada abounded. Similarly, Canada retained a large proportion of immigrants coming to Canadian soil. The United States lost some of its relative economic attractiveness. Nonetheless, Canadians did continue to migrate southward, though in smaller numbers. Whereas during the peak decade from 1881 to 1890 some 390,000 Canadians immigrated to the United States, a full century later, during the decade from 1981 to 1990, only 160,000 Canadians immigrated. The reduction in the number of immigrants is even more striking given the fact that Canada's total population in 1980 exceeded the 1880 population by more than fivefold. Hence, in relative terms, even fewer Canadians chose to immigrate to the United States in the 1980s than absolute numbers suggest. The post–World War II Canadian immigrants share wage-seeking migratory patterns with their prewar counterparts. Canada's population urbanized rapidly after 1945, reducing that country's reliance on agriculture. In many respects, the Canadian economy came to take on many of the characteristics of the American economy, being marked first by a high level of manufacturing activity until the 1970s and then by service-oriented activity after the 1970s.

Whereas Canadians immigrating to the United States before the 1950s tended to have relatively low levels of education and to enter the working class, immigrants arriving after the 1950s were better educated and possessed increasingly specialized and marketable job skills. Particularly since the 1980s, Canadian immigrants have differed considerably from both earlier Canadian immigrants and from contemporary immigrants from other countries in terms of professional background and levels of education. Canadians immigrating to the United States after 1980 have been primarily white-collar and highly educated workers. Among contemporary Canadian immigrants, the male–female sex ratio is close to even and the median age is near 30. In 1987, of the 5,605 economically active Canadian immigrants in the United States, 2,910, or 53 percent, were professionals and managers. Only Indian and Taiwanese immigrants have higher rates of professional and managerial employment. Of all immigrant groups, however, Canadians are situated in the middle in terms of self-employment. Most Canadian immigrants hold educational and professional credentials and possess the language skills that allow them to enter the U.S. workforce with relative ease.

Hence, the motivation for self-employment is less among Canadians than among many other immigrant groups.

The trend of professional and highly educated Canadian immigration received further impetus with ratification of the North American Free Trade Agreement (NAFTA) in 1994. NAFTA is designed to reduce barriers to trade. NAFTA has had the effect of increasing the volume of commerce between the United States and Canada and deepening Canada's dependence on the U.S. economy. The great majority of Canadian exports enter the United States. Canada is also the United States's largest trading partner. The historical bond between the two countries, as reflected by the flow of goods and the historical movement of people across the border, was formalized through NAFTA. The trade agreement stipulates that Canada, the United States, and Mexico, the three members of the common market, must ease restrictions on the movement of business executives and professionals. Canadians with highly sought-after professional skills have steadily increased their proportion among all Canadian immigrants. Due to the cultural proximity of the two countries, educational and professional credentials from Canada are widely recognized in the United States. This unique sociocultural status sets Canadians apart from most other immigrant groups. Because of the economic, social, and cultural similarities between Canada and the United States, Canadian immigrants are at a distinct advantage in relation to non-Canadian immigrants. NAFTA further entrenches the relative privileged status of Canadian immigrants in the United States by facilitating the movement of educated, skilled people across the border and by tying the two national economies more closely with each other.

SETTLEMENT PATTERNS, ETHNICITY, AND CULTURAL ADAPTATION

The old Canadian immigrant and the new Canadian immigrant differ in terms of patterns of settlement. Before 1945, English-speaking and French-speaking Canadian immigrants followed distinct settlement patterns. Recent Canadian immigrants, however, show less divergence by linguistic and ethnic background. Today's Canadian immigrant, typically professional and highly educated, no longer relies on networks of family and compatriot acquaintances to adapt to U.S. life. The contemporary Canadian immigrant follows employment opportunities independent of established immigrant communities in the United States. Modern communications and transportation technologies and the complementarity of the Canadian and U.S. economies enable professional Canadian immigrants to dispense with the immigrant enclave so crucial to other immigrant groups. Typical of all professional and managerial immigrants, Canadians are dispersed throughout the United States. Many are attracted to the economic opportunities of the information and computer industries of Silicon Valley and the West Coast. Others gravitate to the service industries of the Northeast and the South. Canadian immigrants today are a diverse group, maintaining no cohesive and easily distinguishable community within the United States.

The impact of Canadian immigration to the United States on Canadian society is substantial. The United States attracts some of the best-educated and most qualified of Canada's young adults. The flow of this highly productive group to the United States has been deemed a "brain drain" for Canada. Canada maintains high-quality undergraduate and graduate education through a network of publicly supported universities. Canada in essence subsidizes the education of its young adults. Many of these, the talent of Canada, immigrate to the United States in search of more lucrative careers than what they could find if they stayed in Canada. NAFTA's easing of restrictions on the movement of professionals has made it easier for well-educated Canadians to leave their country of origin and take up careers in the United States. The growing interdependence of the two national economies also facilitates this movement. In certain aspects, the national societies of Canada and the United States are converging. English-speaking Canadians are particularly drawn to the United States. The lack of a strong, discernible independent national culture does little to prevent English-speaking Canadians from immigrating southward, where they blend imperceptibly into American society. French speakers of Quebec, however, tend to show greater attachment to Quebec than English speakers do to the rest of Canada. The French language and unique *Québécois* culture serve to reinforce an identification among young French speakers with Quebec. However, the emigration rates of young English-speaking Jews in Quebec to the United States is among the highest of all Canadian ethnic groups.

Canadian immigrants, old and new, regardless of their linguistic or ethnic background, tend to maintain their Canadian citizenship, even after years of residence in the United States. Canadian rates of U.S. naturalization are among the lowest of all immigrant groups in the United States. Canadians in the United States, like the Mexicans, display a marked indifference to naturalization, adopting U.S. citizenship very slowly, if at all. Low transportation costs facilitate frequent return visits to Canada. The geographic proximity of Canada is one factor that reduces the attractiveness of naturalization. Many Canadians migrate circularly, moving across the border on several occasions in consonance with changing career opportunities. Furthermore, with each year of education before immigrating to the United States, the naturalization rate of Canadians decreases by 21 percent. Professional and highly educated Canadian immigrants, now dominant within the immigrant group, are less likely to abandon their Canadian citizenship for an American passport. In addition to the geographic proximity of Canada to the United States, a major reason for the reticence of Canadians to seek U.S. naturalization may be the superior social infrastructure of Canada. Canada offers greater social support to retired people and in health care and suffers from less crime and violence. Quality-of-life factors are likely determinant in the decision of many Canadian immigrants not to become U.S. citizens.

Aonghas Mac Thòmais St.-Hilaire

See also: Immigration to Canada (Part II, Sec. 13).

BIBLIOGRAPHY

Bryce-Laporte, Roy. "Voluntary Immigration and Continuing Encounters between Blacks." In *The Immigration Reader*, ed. David Jacobson, 183–99. Oxford: Blackwell, 1998.

Hansen, Marcus, and John Brebner. *The Mingling of the Canadian and American Peoples.* New Haven, CT: Yale University Press, 1940.

Lavoie, Yolande. *L'émigration des Canadiens aux États-Unis avant 1930: mésure du phénomène.* Montreal: Les Presses de l'Université de Montréal, 1972.

Nugent, Walter. *Crossings.* Bloomington: Indiana University Press, 1992.

Portes, Alejandro, and Ruben Rumbaut. *Immigrant America.* Berkeley: University of California Press, 1990.

Ueda, Reed. *Postwar Immigrant America.* Boston: Bedford Books of St. Martin's Press, 1994.

———. "The Changing Face of Post-1965 Immigration." In *The Immigration Reader*, ed. David Jacobson, 72–91. Oxford: Blackwell, 1998.

CENTRAL AMERICA

Central Americans have been migrating to the United States for more than a century. In the early 1900s, Salvadoran and Nicaraguan coffee growers traveled to and from the United States for business and pleasure. Through the commercial ships that transported bananas from Honduras to the United States, Hondurans became acquainted with new opportunities and then traveled north in the search of them. But the presence of Central Americans (Guatemalans, Hondurans, Salvadorans, Nicaraguans, Costa Ricans, Belizeans, and Panamanians) in the United States did not receive major attention until the late 1970s, when a political and economic crisis destabilized several countries in the region and many of their citizens were forced to abandon their homes. Many (mostly Guatemalans, Nicaraguans, and Salvadorans) went to adjacent Central American countries, others (mostly Guatemalan Maya) settled in refugee camps in southern Mexico and have since returned to their homeland, and still others made their way farther up north to the United States and Canada, where they have established vibrant communities. Central Americans now constitute one of the fastest-growing Latino groups in the United States.

The causes for contemporary Central American immigration can be linked in one way or another to political crises that have roots deep in the history of Central America. A civil war in El Salvador that lasted approximately twelve years, an armed conflict in Guatemala that lasted three times as long, and another one in Nicaragua that went on for several years contributed to tripling and sometimes more than quintupling (as in the case of the Salvadorans) the number of these immigrants in the United States. This surge in Central American immigration has contributed to a dramatic change in the U.S. Latino population. In contrast to the Mexican immigrants who have dominated U.S.-bound Latin American immigration, Central Americans, who come from dissimilar contexts, comprise groups that are socioculturally and economically very different and have been received dissimilarly by the U.S. government as well. As professors Nestor Rodriguez and Jacqueline Hagan observe, the U.S. Latin American population now includes well-educated and unskilled immigrants, political refugees, wealthy landowners, and peasants, as well as a variety of ethnic groups such as Garifuna (Black Caribs) from Belize and Honduras, and Maya groups from Guatemala.

It is worth noting that circumstances associated with the crisis in Central America shaped the immigrants' decision to leave their countries, but did not influence their eventual arrival in the United States. The reason why so many of these immigrants crossed several international borders to reach their destination has to do with the informal links they had already established in the United States, which had been forged over a long history of U.S. political, military, economic, and cultural influence in Central America. Thus, when the conditions in Central America deteriorated to the point where many sought refuge elsewhere, the United States emerged as a logical destination. The families and friends already in the United States provided the conduit through which these immigrants arrived.

DEMOGRAPHICS

According to the 1990 census, the most numerous group from Central America living in the United States is the Salvadorans, who account for 43 percent of all Central American immigrants, followed by Guatemalans with 20 percent and Nicaraguans with 15 percent of the total. As a whole, women comprise slightly more than half of these immigrants, a pattern consistent within all groups (with a high of 58 percent among Panamanians), except among Guatemalans, where men account for slightly more than half of

These Costa Rican immigrant children celebrate their native country's independence day in a New York City parade. *(Donna DeCesare/ Impact Visuals)*

these immigrants, and Salvadorans, among whom men and women have almost equal representation. With respect to age, Central Americans fall somewhere in between the two other large Latin American immigrant groups: They are slightly older than the Mexicans—with a median age of 28 years (Nicaraguans and Salvadorans are a bit younger than the rest) compared to 24 years for Mexicans—but younger than the Cubans, who have a median age of 43.

In terms of educational attainment, Panamanians and Costa Ricans stand out as the most educated, with approximately one-fourth of those over twenty-five having a high school diploma, one-third of those over twenty-five having some college education, and slightly over 10 percent of those over twenty-five having completed bachelor's degrees. At the other end of the spectrum, about 16 percent of Guatemalans and Salvadorans over twenty-five have a high school diploma, approximately 15 percent have some college, and fewer than 4 percent over twenty-five have bachelor's degrees. Approximately two-thirds of Guatemalans and Salvadorans do not speak English well,

whereas close to three-fourths of Panamanians speak English well or very well. Costa Ricans, Hondurans, and Nicaraguans fall somewhere in between. This group is linguistically diverse. Although Spanish is the first (and sometimes only) language for the majority of Central American immigrants, it is often not the only tongue they speak. For instance, Guatemalans who are of Mayan descent also speak K'anjob'al, Kaqchikel, or K'iche. Hondurans who come from the Caribbean coast of their country and some Belizeans may also speak Garifuna, and Nicaraguans who come from the Atlantic coast of Nicaragua may speak English or Mesquito at home instead of Spanish.

Central Americans are diverse in terms of their family composition and living arrangements as well. For instance, whereas under 10 percent of Panamanian households include people who are not related, more than one-fourth of Nicaraguan and Guatemalan and almost one-third of Salvadoran households include nonfamily members. Approximately two-thirds of Central American households include children under the age of eighteen, and the average size of these households ranges from three members among Costa Ricans and Panamanians to slightly over four members among Guatemalans, Salvadorans, and Nicaraguans. Even though Central American households often have several family members in the labor force, and their labor force participation rates are high, ranging from 70.5 percent among Panamanians to 76 percent among Salvadorans, their family incomes are not high. The mean family income of Guatemalans, Salvadorans, and Hondurans in the United States is about $27,600, of Nicaraguans $31,277, and of Costa Ricans $38,409, and Panamanians $38,934. Per capita income of Guatemalans, Hondurans, Salvadorans, and Nicaraguans is about $7,500, of Costa Ricans $11,019, and of Panamanians $12,223. Approximately one-fifth of Guatemalan, Salvadoran, and Nicaraguan families live below poverty, whereas this percentage is 13.4 percent among Costa Ricans and 13.1 percent among Panamanians. Women head approximately one-fifth of Central American households; however, in the Panamanian case, this proportion is approximately one-fourth.

LAW AND CENTRAL AMERICAN IMMIGRANTS

Although the number of Central American immigrants increased at a time when U.S. immigration policies stiffened, the immigration law has been applied unevenly to these immigrants, contributing to discrepancies among them. The increasingly rigid immigration laws make obtaining even a simple tourist visa very difficult. People are required to show proof of hefty bank accounts, land and property titles, and letters from employers to guarantee that they would have a reason to return to their country—making a visa beyond the reach of many potential immigrants. Thus, many Central Americans have been traveling without a U.S. visa, which means that they have had to enter the United States clandestinely and travel by land at least part of the way. Traveling by land from Central America to the United States often involves complicated arrangements with *coyotes* (smugglers), as well as robberies, assaults, and extortion by local authorities—mostly in Mexico.

Although many Central Americans left their countries for reasons linked to the political conflicts in that region, they were not officially recognized as refugees by the U.S. government due to U.S. foreign policy toward the region. During the civil conflicts in Guatemala and El Salvador, for instance, both the Salva-

doran and Guatemalan governments fought the opposition with substantial U.S. support; thus the U.S. government could not legally recognize the refugees generated by the conflict. Notwithstanding legal barriers, however, many Central Americans entered the United States. Once on U.S. soil, they could apply individually for political asylum. (Refugees are those who apply for protection outside the United States, whereas political asylees do so on U.S. soil.)

Salvadorans and Guatemalans did not fare well. Throughout the 1980s, less than 3 percent of these applicants were granted political asylum. Immigrants' rights groups lobbied on the Guatemalans' and Salvadorans' behalf, and eventually Congress granted temporary protection from deportation to all Salvadorans who arrived prior to September 19, 1990. This temporary amnesty was not extended to Guatemalans. The special dispensation, Temporary Protected Status (TPS), allowed Salvadorans to live and work in the United States for a period of eighteen months beginning January 1, 1991. Given the intractable nature of the Salvadoran conflict, this provision was extended a couple of times, and it finally expired in December 1994. To ensure a smooth transition, these Salvadorans' work permits were extended for an additional nine months. Although originally close to two hundred thousand Salvadorans applied for this dispensation, fewer submitted applications for the successive extensions. (Some changed their status to permanent residents, but others found the application procedure for the extensions confusing and reliable information hard to obtain.) Temporary Protected Status was only temporary. It was neither asylum nor refugee status; the only privilege bestowed was the conferral of a work permit. The approximately sixty thousand Salvadorans who continued reapplying and maintaining their TPS until this dispensation expired were given the opportunity to submit asylum applications. In 1991, as a result of a settlement of a class action suit (*American Baptist Churches v. Thornburgh*) that alleged discrimination against Guatemalans and Salvadorans on the part of the Immigration and Naturalization Service, immigrants from these countries were allowed to resubmit asylum applications. Initially, in fiscal year 1992, the success rate of Salvadoran applications increased to 28 percent and those of Guatemalans to 18 percent, but has since leveled off and declined.

Some Salvadorans and Guatemalans were included as beneficiaries of the 1997 Nicaraguan Adjustment and Central American Relief Act (NACARA). Designed for Nicaraguans, it also included Cubans and nationals of former Soviet-bloc countries. Salvadorans who entered the country before September 19, 1990, and Guatemalans who entered on or before October 1, 1990, and registered under the settlement, or who had filed an asylum application before April 1, 1990, could be granted a "cancellation of removal" (cancellation of deportation). This is a special discretionary relief, which, if granted, permits an individual who is subject to deportation or removal to remain in the United States. Salvadorans who are already faced with deportation procedures, and are therefore required to appear before an immigration judge, can request a cancellation of removal. If an individual is granted cancellation of removal, his or her immigration status will then be readjusted to that of a permanent resident. Immigrant rights groups have been lobbying on behalf of the Salvadorans and Guatemalans so that the benefits that NACARA confers to Nicaraguans and to other nationals included in this act—adjustment to permanent residence without a hearing on a case-by-case basis—would also be extended to Salvadorans. However, in October 1998, Congress once again denied Salvadorans and Guatemalans such benefits.

Nicaraguan asylum seekers during the 1980s were given an ambivalent reception. In the aggregate during this decade, about one-quarter of the Nicaraguan applicants were successful. The U.S. government had been reluctant to grant Nicaraguans any special dispensation, but under pressure from the Cuban-American constituency in Miami—where the majority of the Nicaraguans lived—it stopped deporting Nicaraguans for a short period of time between 1987 and 1988. Nicaraguans were invited to apply for asylum; they were given work permits but not access to the resettlement aid similar to that given to lawfully recognized refugees. When Congress froze military support for the Contras in 1988, the number of Nicaraguans entering the United States increased substantially. To stem this flow, the U.S. government reversed its policy, and Nicaraguans—now without work permits or protection from deportation—once again were treated as undocumented immigrants. Currently, the Nicaraguans are the intended beneficiaries of NACARA. Unlike Salvadorans or Guatemalans, Nicaraguans are not required to appear before an immigration judge in order to be granted the benefits. Nicaraguans who can prove that they have continuously resided in the United States since December 1, 1995, can be considered for adjustment of status to permanent residency. This act, signed into law in November 1997, gave Nicaraguans until March 31, 2000, to submit their applications. Another group of Central Americans that has been granted a temporary special dispensation is Hondurans. After Hurricane Mitch devastated many towns in Honduras in 1998 and left

thousands of people homeless, many Hondurans made their way to the United States to join relatives and friends already here. To alleviate the plight of these displaced people, Hondurans were granted TPS for a period of nine months; they had until July 1999 to submit their applications.

Many Central Americans who arrived in the United States prior to January 1, 1982—the cutoff point to apply for amnesty under the Immigration Reform Control Act (IRCA)—applied for this benefit. However, the thousands who arrived at the height of the political conflict in their countries (approximately three-quarters of the Salvadoran-, Guatemalan-, and Nicaraguan-born population arrived between 1980 and 1990) were ineligible for this provision. All of this means that a large proportion of these immigrants have been and remain in the country undocumented. The Immigration and Naturalization Service has estimated that close to 60 percent of Salvadorans and Guatemalans and approximately 40 percent of Nicaraguans in the country are undocumented. Professors David Lopez, Eric Popkin, and Edward Telles depict Salvadorans and Guatemalans as constituting "the most vulnerable national-origin group in the United States because they are among the most undocumented.... Their claim to refugee status has never been recognized, and they are about to lose what temporary protection against deportation they had." The legal instability of the situation of many Central Americans has had repercussions in all aspects of their lives.

WORK AND LABOR-FORCE INCORPORATION

Central Americans have high rates of labor-force participation, but they are likely to be concentrated in a few occupations and industries. Those with relatively higher levels of education and English language skills (Costa Ricans and Panamanians, and to a lesser degree Nicaraguans) tend to be employed in technical and administrative support occupations, whereas those with lower educational levels and less English-language proficiency (Guatemalans, Salvadorans, and Hondurans) are more likely to work in service occupations and in manufacturing, as operators and laborers. Central American men with skills find white-collar jobs, whereas those with fewer or no skills work in construction, landscaping, in restaurants and hotels, and in janitorial services. Skilled Central American women find clerical and administrative jobs, whereas the unskilled or semi-skilled ones work as housekeepers, baby-sitters, hotel chambermaids, or janitors. These are not always clear-cut distinctions. It is noteworthy that the legal status of many Central American men and women has affected greatly their options in the labor force; those who are undocumented, even though they have attained higher educational levels (some are even college graduates) and have substantial work experience, are found in positions that require few, if any, skills. Some Central Americans have opened businesses that cater mostly to compatriots and other Latino clientele, and there is a growing proportion who are self-employed, many as street vendors. The street vendors in Los Angeles (mainly Central Americans) have even formed the Association of Street Vendors to lobby for the legalization of street vending in that city.

The employment that Central American immigrants find does not depend solely on their individual characteristics and human capital levels but on the jobs that are available both at the time they arrive in the United States and in the places of their destination. During recessionary times, for instance, jobs—albeit low-paid—in the occupations and industries where Central Americans usually are found are scarce, and therefore these immigrants resort to whatever work may be available. This was the case of California during the latest recession. Many undocumented as well as documented Guatemalan and Salvadoran men, for instance, were unable to find work in the usual niches, and many had to resort to day labor, congregating on street corners waiting for a potential employer to hire them. The recession also forced many Central Americans (men and women) into the "informal economy," selling products and services out of their homes or in the streets of the cities in which they concentrate.

Job opportunities also vary by location. For instance, Professor Terry Repak found that jobs in construction were plentiful in Washington, D.C., for Central American men—mostly Salvadorans. Wages in this sector in Washington also were higher than in comparable jobs elsewhere—particularly in Los Angeles, where the majority of Central American immigrants live. In fact, Repak reports that one immigrant man traveled to Washington every spring for the construction season and then returned to Los Angeles during the winter. Central American men (mostly Guatemalans, Hondurans, and Salvadorans) also labor in restaurants as dishwashers and busboys in Washington, a pattern also found among Salvadoran men in New Jersey and in San Francisco. Although Central American men often congregate on corners of the cities in which they live, scholar Sarah Mahler

found that in New Jersey these men found jobs in construction in suburban areas, and they therefore congregated on corners of suburbia, not in the inner cities or downtown of major cities. Central American men have located similar jobs in other states, such as Arizona, where they can be found on some city corners waiting for a potential employer to drive by, but these sights are not as commonplace as they are in cities of other states, such as California.

These immigrants' gender influences in important ways their labor-force participation. The jobs that women perform, such as baby-sitting, tend to be available even during recessionary times. Also, women are likely to work unregulated jobs away from the public eye, which makes it easier for employers to hire them on informal terms, often not accounting for them to immigration authorities. For these reasons women (even when undocumented) often are able to find jobs more easily than men, and in some cities, such as Los Angeles, Salvadorans and other Central American women seem to have taken over the housekeeping niche. For instance, Salvadoran women in Los Angeles are twelve times more likely than the general population to work as private servants, as cleaners and childcare workers; for Mexican women this factor is only 2.3. An indigenous Guatemalan woman in Los Angeles had been able to locate jobs as a baby-sitter almost since she arrived, but her husband was not always successful in finding day jobs at the corner he frequented, which meant that she had to shoulder the financial responsibility for her family. So intense was the pressure to generate an income, albeit meager, that she had to resume baby-sitting two days after she gave birth. Interestingly, however, in spite of the relative ease with which these immigrant women find jobs (a situation observed in different settings, from San Francisco to Los Angeles to New Jersey), when men and women both work, men earn more than the women do. And in spite of sometimes more human capital advantages and extensive social networks, Central American women have been found to experience less success and occupational mobility than their male counterparts.

WOMEN AND GENDER RELATIONS

Central American women figure prominently in this migration, sometimes as pioneers. For instance, Repak found that it was primarily women who initiated Central American, mostly Salvadoran, migration to Washington, D.C. U.S. diplomats working in El Salvador and other Central American regions in the 1960s brought their housekeepers back to the United States. Once in the United States, these women petitioned for their relatives, who in turn brought other family members, thus initiating an enduring pattern of chain migration. In the 1980s, when Central American migration increased exponentially, women took part in this migration in great numbers. Some moved to reunite with or accompany husbands, parents, or other relatives, but many migrated on their own. In fact, Repak found that two-thirds of the Central American women in her sample had made the decision to migrate on their own, without the collaboration or assistance of male partners or fathers, demonstrating an "unusual degree of autonomy." These women migrated mostly to seek a better future for themselves or their children or to avoid the consequences of the political conflicts occurring in Central America in that period.

Some Central American women have come to the United States single and have established families here; others have arrived alone but have left their families back home. Many women came undocumented, meaning that their journeys had to be undertaken by land, which would put accompanying children in much danger. Most are resolute to come and work hard, and knew beforehand that they would have little, if any, time to supervise their children. Some have brought their children, but given the high crime rates and ubiquity of drugs in the neighborhoods where many of these immigrants live, the parents send the children back to their countries to shield them from such dangers. Many of these children have been either sent back or left in the care of other relatives while their mothers labor in the United States to send them money for school supplies and for the necessities of life. Although the material and financial lot of these children (as well as of their relatives) improves when the mothers send money and goods from the United States, this betterment does not come without a price. Many Central American women suffer the painful consequences of these separations and often find themselves squeezed between competing demands. If the children remain back home, the women worry about their well-being; if the children are with them in the United States, these mothers are concerned about the neighborhoods in which the children must live, the schools they attend, and ultimately wonder about the ever more tenuous benefits of living in the United States.

In some cases the women (as have their male counterparts) have established new families in the United States, rearrangements that do not always work out smoothly. These new family arrangements coupled with the increased economic contributions of these women (although Central American women have long histories of labor-force participation in their countries), have had important repercussions for gender relations among this group, though not always in the expected direction. For instance, as these women acquire more status within their families as a result of their increased economic contributions, sometimes gender relations become more egalitarian; other times the result is comparatively more unbalanced gender relations in favor of men because the women do not want to upset delicate arrangements in the home that would threaten the men's position. And yet, in other cases, most notably among indigenous Guatemalans who start out from relatively more egalitarian gender relations, there is not much change in such relations with women's increased economic participation as a result of immigration.

The type of jobs that Central American women perform has been found to affect their social networks in important ways. For instance, Hagan found that Guatemalan indigenous women who worked as live-in domestics had more reduced and weaker social networks than the men, who had more extensive contacts in the community. A study of Salvadorans and Guatemalans lends support to this finding. Women who work as domestics but do not live in their employers' homes were found to have wide-reaching networks in the community. In fact, this study found that because women actively sought resources in community organizations—since they were in charge of those family needs for which these organizations could provide assistance—their networks ended up being farther reaching than those of men. Spending time in community organizations gave women opportunities to forge networks independent of those of men, learning about (and later on sharing with other women) crucial information about their rights and other important things such as U.S. laws that protect women against domestic violence.

CHILDREN AND THE ELDERLY

Central American children generally confront the triple burden of simultaneously entering adolescence, a new society, and reconstituted families with little resemblance to those they knew before, which indubitably puts great pressure on the children as well as on the rest of their family members. Many of these children have been exposed to the ravages of war, witnessing the abduction or murder of family members, tortured bodies in the streets, bombings, cross fires, and other instances of violence. In addition, many of them, some as young as twelve years old, were forcefully recruited by combatant groups. The considerable trauma with which many of these children have arrived in the United States sometimes has been manifested in learning inhibitions and delinquent behavior during adolescence. And many Central American children can be diagnosed with post–traumatic stress disorder, which leads to educational delays that curtail their capacity to adapt.

This issue gets compounded because once in the United States, many of these children become overburdened with adult duties that sometimes interfere with their schooling and emotional development. One of the most important transformations for these children is linked to their increased contact with the wider society. Children often acquire knowledge of English before others in their families, and they also become more familiar with the culture of their immediate environment. Very often they translate for their parents and interpret the culture and world around them for adult family members. In this way, the children acquire considerable authority and status within their families—which previously was granted mainly to adults—a situation that often spurs conflict between the parents and children.

It must be noted that many of these youngsters acquire a great deal of knowledge of their immediate neighborhood, not of the wider society or of American culture at large. Many come to live in inner-city neighborhoods, where they attend troubled schools. Thus these children do not always learn to speak standard English, but rather the version that they learn with their peers, a problem that afflicts several Central American communities, as the case of Nicaraguans in Florida, Salvadorans in San Francisco, and Guatemalans in Los Angeles may attest. This problem has immediate consequences, as these youngsters do not always perform well their duties of interpreters for their families. Also, and perhaps more importantly, in the long run these children's futures may be hampered by a faulty education and lack of language skills needed to function in the professional world.

When the children of Central American immigrants remain in the care of relatives back home, the parents sometimes send for them eventually. But the lengthy separations between parents and children create tension when they are finally together, as they feel like strangers and ultimately find little to share as a family. For instance, Professor Leigh Leslie observes that family reunification for Central Americans is often problematic because of the unrealistic expectations that the parents have of their children. Sometimes, the children feel abandoned and reproach the parents for having left them for too long. Other times, the children, accustomed to the material goods financed by the parents' labor in the United States, demand the same when they join the parents, who are usually unable to provide these material goods because having the children in the United States often entails significant additional expenses. Other times, family reunifications do not work out smoothly because new families have been formed in the United States, particularly when step- and half-sibling combinations have been created. These problems are exacerbated when newcomers have to join U.S. relatives in overcrowded homes, living conditions that are common among many poor Central Americans.

Older Central Americans also go through their share of change in the United States. Often they are not able to find the kinds of jobs that the younger immigrants locate, and they seldom master the English language; thus many must depend on their relatives. And even though cultural dictates among these immigrants call for the children to support parents in old age, in the United States older immigrants become dependent on their children for all forms of support, such as financial, material, informational, and emotional comfort. And not all older immigrants (or their children) welcome this situation, particularly because older immigrants enjoyed a higher status and a measure of respect in their home communities that is absent in the contexts in which they now reside. There are also other issues that concern this group, such as the high cost of health care, which becomes a primary concern among older Central American immigrants who lack access to health benefits or other means to treat themselves; even though they might have labored hard in their home countries, they are not guaranteed old age security either there or in the United States.

Older Central Americans, however, contribute in many important ways to their communities and families. For instance, they often care for their children's children, a welcome relief for the often financially overburdened younger immigrants. They are also important transmitters of culture and provide key emotional and moral support, advising and comforting the younger members of their families. Though these older immigrants are not always heard and their grandchildren often reject their admonishments and rebel against them, their presence is key. In a study of Nicaraguan elderly in San Francisco, scholar Stephen Wallace identified them as making very important contributions not only to their families but also to building the community.

SOCIAL NETWORKS AND THE CHURCH

Central Americans leave their places of residence for reasons that often are linked directly or indirectly to the conflicts in that region in the past decade. But they arrive in the United States because of the dense networks of family and friends that most have here. Generally, through their relatives, Central American immigrants obtain financial and informational help for the journey; they locate jobs and places to live upon arrival and also receive a measure of emotional and moral support that is often indispensable for survival. But this pattern, though common among most immigrants, sometimes is not found when the conditions in the places where immigrants arrive make it difficult for them to accumulate enough resources to help others. It is noteworthy, however, that even though the relatives who await the newcomers do not always rally to support their arriving relatives, the newly arrived manage to procure assistance from others around them, either other family, friends, or compatriots.

An important aspect of these immigrants' social networks is their secondary migration patterns. For instance, in a recent study of Latino immigration to the Phoenix metropolitan area that included Guatemalans, Salvadorans, and Hondurans, it was revealed that although the majority of these immigrants had initially settled in other areas of the United States—mainly in California—they had relocated to the Phoenix area because they had either a relative or a friend who informed them of the different opportunities that Phoenix had to offer. In some cases, the relatives or friends even put a job within reach of the person who planned to resettle even before the person physically moved to Phoenix.

One of the most important places for Central Americans to connect with others and to obtain varied forms of assistance is the church. They frequently attend Catholic and other mainline Protestant parishes as well as evangelical and pentecostal churches, often traveling substantial distances to get to their places of worship. Importantly, the church not only connects immigrants with others and facilitates the exchange of assistance among them but it often has in place a range of services that help the immigrants with their settlement. Additionally, through the church, these immigrants are often able to remain connected to their communities of origin, as churches create institutional spaces that connect the immigrants with people back home. Thus, for many Central American immigrants their church-based networks are vital, as they help

them establish important links in the communities where they now live and with the ones back home—both of major importance for these immigrants' physical and emotional survival.

DESTINATIONS AND CULTURAL IMPACT AT BOTH ENDS

Central Americans have settled throughout the United States, mostly in cities and metropolitan areas, but there are some salient concentrations. With the exception of Panamanians (only half of whom live in urban conglomerates), the overwhelming majority of these immigrants have concentrated in large metropolitan areas. California received more than half of them, followed by Florida, Texas, New York, New Jersey, and the Washington, D.C., area. Within these locations, there are some important concentrations. Los Angeles, for instance, is home to half of all Central Americans in the United States, with more than half of the top two most numerous groups (Salvadorans and Guatemalans) residing there. More than half of all Nicaraguans in the country call Miami their home, while New York is the more popular destination for Panamanians, and the rest are geographically more dispersed.

These concentrations have created bustling communities and neighborhoods in those destination points in which these Central Americans have re-created important aspects of their culture. Existing institutions, like churches, in places where Central Americans concentrate, have expanded, and they have created a host of new institutions and hundreds of small businesses to service a growing number of fellow immigrants. These immigrants build communities in their daily lives—patronizing restaurants and commercial establishments, expanding church activities and the like—but also through their contributions to the arts. Many Central American writers, painters, and poets—some born and raised in their countries of origin, some in the United States, and others having arrived at young ages—are actively contributing to the ever-growing diversity of Latino cultural expressions in the United States. Undoubtedly, their presence will alter the sociocultural landscape of those sites.

The presence of Central Americans in the United States has also changed decisively their communities of origin, as sizable numbers of Central Americans (20 percent of Salvadorans) left their countries. Initially, many Central Americans planned to return to their native land when the turmoil there subsided. However, as they reared children in the United States and spent more time here, those plans got further and further postponed. However, the temporary nature of Central American migration, coupled with an unfavorable context of reception for most Central Americans in the United States and poverty and turmoil still reigning back home, has greatly influenced these immigrants' fervent desire to remain closely connected to their homelands. Many send large amounts of money and goods to their families, sometimes remitting as much as or more than those countries' national budgets, which at times has served to keep the recovering Central American economies afloat. The immigrants also play a key role in other aspects of the national affairs of their countries, such as in their political and cultural life. Some have formed hometown associations through which they not only remain connected to their hometowns but influence community projects, elections, and most of those towns' everyday life, and invest their savings in houses and businesses back home.

These strong links between the immigrants and their hometowns have not always led to positive outcomes. One concern is the alarming growth of gang activity in the Central American countries with heavy emigration to the United States. In even the remotest areas of Guatemala, Belize, and El Salvador, for instance, one can find evidence of gang activity in walls covered with graffiti and in adults' comments lamenting the "loss" of their youths to gangs. The gangs in those countries bear the same names of gangs in U.S. cities, such as Los Angeles, and the youths who belong to them have adopted the same clothing style, slang, and musical tastes, even though they have never left their native villages or towns. A possible explanation for this disturbing phenomenon may be found in the practice of sending back to their hometowns youths that got into trouble in the United States. Sometimes a desperate parent would ship a troubled kid back home to a relative, but just as often the U.S. government has deported them. Once back in their homeland, these youths find fertile soil to continue their activities and restructure their gangs.

Many former combatants in the Central American conflicts and unemployed (and still heavily armed) young males have become prime candidates for gang membership. Also, as Professors Miller Matthei and David Smith observe, as long as trends of uneven development continue, there will be incentives for people from countries such as those in Central America to seek employment abroad. The problems facing Central American families—in the United States and

in the countries of origin—may therefore continue for as long as deep inequalities between and within these societies exist.

Cecilia Menjívar

See also: Wars and Civil Unrest (Part II, Sec. 1); Houston, Los Angeles, Mex-America, Miami, Rural America, San Francisco, Washington, D.C. (Part II, Sec. 12).

BIBLIOGRAPHY

Bureau of the Census. *Census of Population. Persons of Hispanic Origin in the United States.* U.S. Department of Commerce, Economics and Statistics Administration. CP-3-3 Washington, DC: Government Printing Office, 1990.

Chinchilla, Norma Stoltz, and Nora Hamilton. "Seeking Refuge in the City of Angels." In *City of Angels*, ed. Gerry Riposa and Carolyn Deusch, pp. 84–100. Dubuque, IA: Kendall/Hunt, 1992.

Chinchilla, Norma, Nora Hamilton, and James Loucky. "Central Americans in Los Angeles: An Immigrant Community in Transition." In *In the Barrios: Latinos and the Underclass Debate*, ed. Joan Moore and Raquel Pinderhughes, pp. 51–78. New York: Russell Sage Foundation, 1993.

DeCesare, Donna. *The Children of War: Street Gangs in El Salvador.* NACLA Report on the Americas. 22:1 (1998): 21–43.

Espino, Conchita M. "Trauma and Adaptation: The Case of Central American Children." In *Refugee Children: Theory, Research, and Services*, ed. Frederick L. Ahearn, Jr., and Jean L. Athey, pp. 106–24. Baltimore: The Johns Hopkins University Press, 1991.

Fernández-Kelly, M. Patricia, and Richard Schauffler. "Divided Fates: Immigrant Children in a Restructured U.S. Economy." *International Migration Review* 28:4 (1994): 662–89.

Funkhouser, Edward. "Mass Emigration, Remittances, and Economic Adjustment: The Case of El Salvador in the 1980s." In *Immigration and the Workforce: Economic Consequences for the United States and Source Areas*, ed. George Borjas and Richard B. Freeman, pp. 135–75. Chicago: University of Chicago Press, 1992.

Immigration and Naturalization Service. *Nicaraguan Adjustment and Central American Relief Act, 1997.* Department of Justice. Washington, DC: Government Printing Office, 1998.

———. *INS Releases Updated Estimates of U.S. Illegal Population.* Department of Justice. News Release. February 7, 1997.

Hagan, Jacqueline Maria. Social Networks, Gender, and Immigrant Incorporation: Resources and Constraints. *American Sociological Review* 63:1 (1998): 55–67.

Hondagneu-Sotelo, Pierrette, and Ernestine Avila. "I'm Here, but I'm There: The Meanings of Latina Transnational Motherhood." *Gender & Society* 11:5 (1997): 548–71.

Leslie, Leigh A. "Families Fleeing War: The Case of Central Americans." *Marriage and Family Review* 19:1–2 (1993): 193–205.

Lopez, David E., Eric Popkin, and Edward Telles. "Central Americans: At the Bottom, Struggling to Get Ahead." In *Ethnic Los An-*

geles, ed. Roger Waldinger and Mehdi Bozorgmehr, pp. 279–304. New York: Russell Sage Foundation, 1996.

Mahler, Sarah J. *Salvadorans in Suburbia: Symbiosis and Conflict.* Boston: Allyn and Bacon, 1995.

Menjívar, Cecilia. *Fragmented Ties: Salvadoran Immigrant Networks in America.* Berkeley, CA: University of California Press, 2000.

———. "Immigrant Kinship Networks and the Impact of the Receiving Context: Salvadorans in San Francisco in the Early 1990s." *Social Problems* 44:1 (1997): 104–23.

———. "The Intersection of Work and Gender: Central American Immigrant Women and Employment in California." *American Behavioral Scientist* 42:4 (1999): 595–621.

———. "Living in two worlds? Guatemalan-origin children and emerging transnationalism." Paper presented at the Conference on Transnationalism and Second-Generation Immigrants, Harvard University, April 1998.

———. "Religious Institutions and Transnationalism: A Case Study of Catholic and Evangelical Salvadoran Immigrants." *International Journal of Politics, Culture and Society* 12:4 (1999): 589–612.

———. "Salvadorans and Nicaraguans: Refugees Become Workers." In *Illegal Immigration in America: A Reference Handbook*, ed. David Haines and Karen E. Rosenblum, pp. 232–53. Westport, CT.: Greenwood Press, 1999.

Menjívar, Cecilia, Eugenio Arene, Cindy Bejarano, Michelle Moran-Taylor, Edwardo Portillos, and Emily Skop. "Contemporary Latino Migration to the Phoenix Metropolitan Area." Report presented to the Center for Urban Inquiry, Arizona State University, May 1999.

Menjívar, Cecilia, Julie DaVanzo, Lisa Greenwell, and R. Burciaga Valdez. "Remittance Behavior of Filipino and Salvadoran Immigrants in Los Angeles." *International Migration Review* 32:1 (1998): 99–128.

Miller Matthei, Linda, and David A. Smith. "Belizean 'Boyz 'n the 'Hood'? Garifuna Labor Migration and Transnational Identity." In *Transnationalism from Below*, ed. Michael Peter Smith and Luis Eduardo Guarnizo, pp. 270–90. Vol. 6 in *Comparative Urban and Community Research Series.* New Brunswick, NJ: Transaction Publishers, 1998.

National Asylum Study Project. "An interim assessment of the asylum process of the Immigration and Naturalization Service." Immigration and Refugee Program, Program of the Legal Profession, Harvard Law School. Harvard University, Cambridge, MA, 1992.

Popkin, Eric. "Guatemalan Mayan Migration to Los Angeles: Constructing Transnational Linkages in the Context of the Settlement Process." *Ethnic and Racial Studies.* 22:2 (1999): 267–89.

Portes, Alejandro, and Alex Stepick. *City on the Edge: The Transformation of Miami.* Berkeley: University of California Press, 1993.

Repak, Terry A. *Waiting on Washington: Central American Workers in the Nation's Capital.* Philadelphia: Temple University Press, 1995.

Rodriguez, Nestor P., and Jacqueline Hagan. "Central Americans." In *The Minority Report: An Introduction to Racial, Ethnic, and Gender Relations*, 3d ed., ed. Anthony Gary Dworkin and Rosalind J. Dworkin, Dallas, TX: Harcourt Brace Jovanovich, 1999.

Urrutia-Rojas, Ximena, and Néstor P. Rodríguez. "Unaccompanied Migrant Children from Central America: Sociodemographic Characteristics and Experiences with Potentially Traumatic Events." In *Health and Social Services Among International Labor Migrants: A Comparative Perspective*, ed. Antonio Ugalde and Gilberto Cárdenas, pp. 151–66. Austin: University of Texas Press, Center for Mexican American Studies, 1997.

Wallace, Stephen P. "Community Formation as an Activity of Daily Living: The Case of Nicaraguan Elderly in San Francisco." *Journal of Aging Studies* 6:4 (1992): 365–83.

CUBA

Cubans, by and large, are considered the most successful of the Hispanic immigrants in the United States. There are more than 1 million people of Cuban origin in the United States, of which 65 percent live in Florida, largely in the Miami metropolitan area. About 20 percent of Cuban-Americans have at least four years of college, which is more than double that of other Hispanics. Different from the rest of the Hispanic population, the Cuban-American profile approximates that of the rest of the United States population. Another important aspect in which Cubans are similar to the total United States population and different from other Latin-origin groups is the Cuban poverty rate of 15.2 percent. Like their non-Hispanic white counterpart, a quarter of employed Cuban-American males are professionals or hold managerial positions. Differences with other Hispanics are in part the consequences of age. The average age for Cuban Americans is 39 years, that of the other Hispanics is 26 years, and for the United States population as a whole, it is 33 years. Higher educational levels and work experience associated with age also translate into higher income. In 1989, the median household income for Cuban Americans was $27,890 as compared with $28,905 nationwide and $21,922 for other Hispanics. Furthermore, 21 percent of Cuban-American households and 24 percent of all households nationally had annual incomes of more than $50,000. The rate of ethnically owned enterprises, one per every sixteen persons for Cuban Americans, compares favorably with those of most other groups and with the population at large. Self-employed Cuban Americans are also more numerous and earn higher incomes, $26,253, than those who are not, $15,389.

The economic success of the Cuban immigrant population in the United States is often related to their higher level of adaptation to American society. However, a careful analysis of the Cuban economic, social, and cultural patterns of adjustment to American society reveals an unusual adaptation to their new society, accomplished by keeping close ties to their culture and dreaming about returning to their country. Cubans did not leave Cuba looking for a better economic future, a main motivation for most migrants; they left their country out of political necessity. They have kept alive their dream of a return to Cuba and it seems that this is precisely what allowed them to adjust easily to their life in the United States.

Their success in adapting to life in American society is a function of several factors including upper-class origin and level of education of pre-Castro immigrants who were thus more resourceful than the migrants from other Hispanic countries; familiarity with the United States's culture and language; the economic resources that Cubans had established in the United States before Castro's revolution; the fact that early post-Castro immigrants were viewed as political exiles rather than as economic migrants; and the bilingual education that was provided for their children as a result of federal law that authorized and provided funding for bilingual education.

Cubans are also the most demanding immigrants as they expect the United States to be their ally in the struggle against Fidel Castro and the communist revolution. Cubans feel entitled to request and receive American support against the communist regime installed in their country in 1959. Cubans perceive themselves and their status as exiles as different from the status of other immigrants, even from that of other refugees from Latin America. This perception is based in the close connections between the United States and the Cuban ruling class after Cuba became independent from Spain in 1902; the fact that Cuba's economy has been highly interpenetrated by the U.S. economy; and by the long history of American interventions in Cuban political life in which politicians and economic groups went back and forth from Cuba to the United States and vice versa.

This long history of Cuban-American relations and the characteristics of early immigrants laid the

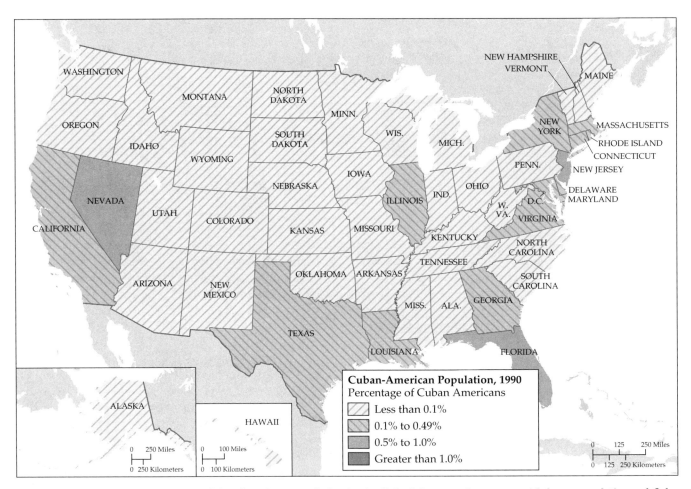

While Florida is home to the largest Cuban-American population in the United States, other states with large populations of Cuban Americans include New Jersey and New York. *(CARTO-GRAPHICS)*

groundwork for the post-Castro Cuban community which developed in Miami after 1959 and has contributed to this community both keeping its culture and contributing a Cuban flavor to America, especially to Miami. The Cuban-American community is not homogeneous in terms of social class nor in its perspective on the Castro regime. In addition to immigrants being of different social strata, they arrived at different economic and political times with some of them having spent a number of years under Castro and his communist government. Though both Cubans and Americans first welcomed Castro's revolution against the regime of Fulgencio Batista, Cubans shared with Americans the sense of betrayal when Castro changed his revolutionary movement from democratic to communist. When Castro oriented the revolution toward the left, expropriated American properties, and nationalized privately owned companies as well as individual properties, middle- and upper-middle-class Cuban immigrants who moved to the United States, especially to Miami, were confident

that, as had been true in the past, Americans would help them to reestablish the old order.

The first post-Castro immigrants assumed that they would not live the rest of their lives in the United States, but that they would move back to Cuba at some time. That oriented their lives to short-term plans. Many professionals took nonprofessional jobs because they thought that they would be working in these jobs for only a short time. Cubans wanted and obtained bilingual education for their children. They figured that they and their children would be going back to Cuba in a short time, so their children needed to be educated in Spanish.

However, what was true for the first post-Castro years of the Cuban immigration was not necessarily true in subsequent years. In analyzing Cuban immigration, it is possible to distinguish at least four different waves for the post-Castro arrivals. These immigration waves brought Cubans from different social classes, different levels of education, and Cubans with different long-term objectives. The earliest migrants

The first major wave of Cuban immigrants made their way to the United States during and shortly after the Castro revolution of 1959. *(National Archives)*

were distinguished by being perceived as exiles, not immigrants. The last two waves, the Marielitos and the *balseros* (Spanish for "rafters"), are not only immigrants but many could be considered illegal immigrants.

HISTORY OF PRE-CASTRO CUBAN IMMIGRATION TO THE UNITED STATES

Cubans have been regularly exiled to the United States since the economic ties between Cuba, then owned by Spain, and the United States became very close. Cubans began migrating to the United States and Europe at the outbreak of the war for independence from Spain in October 1868. More than 100,000 Cubans sought refuge abroad in 1869. Among them,

a small number went to Europe, a larger group of professionals went to New York, Boston, and Philadelphia, and the largest group of workers settled in south Florida. Even after the Cuban Republic was established, the periods of exile did not end. From 1902 to 1928 economic and political difficulties increased the number of people that moved to Miami from all sectors of Cuban society. The repressive regime of dictator Gerardo Machado forced Cubans to continue to escape to Miami, which had become the center for Cuban expatriates. In 1952, a coup d'etat directed by Batista brought on a new wave of political exiles. Between 1952 and 1959 10,276 Cubans became naturalized American citizens. However, it was not until the Fidel Castro revolution in 1959, that the main flow of Cubans, the largest group of Cuban exiles arriving in the United States (approximately 1 million by 1979, roughly 10 percent of the population), left their country and established themselves in Miami.

In 1980, when Cuban leader Fidel Castro created a brief opening for people to leave the country, tens of thousands made their way to the United States from the port of Mariel, earning themselves the nickname "Marielitos." *(United States Coast Guard)*

POST-CASTRO IMMIGRATION

The main factors determining why Cubans departed from Cuba were fear of execution, loss of properties, losses of individual freedoms, ideological indoctrination, shortages of basic foods, and the harassment of the clergy.

FIRST WAVE (1959–1965)

The first wave of Cuban exiles after the Castro revolution—numbering more than 200,000 by 1962—settled in Miami. The Cuban economy and culture was permeated by the American way of life, which made Miami a very familiar place for Cubans. It was the ideal location for them because it was close, had a climate similar to Cuba and because of the existing Cuban community. For most Cubans, periods of dictatorship and exile were common, thus exiles from Castro's revolutionary regime did not believe that

they would stay in the United States for a long time, so they chose not to explore other parts of the country and stayed in Miami, close to their friends and relatives.

The first to leave were those who were a part of the corrupt Fulgencio Batista government, many of whom were industrialists, bankers, aristocrats, land owners, and government officials. Some had amassed large fortunes, and by emigrating they escaped the consequences of their positions, often including the risk of execution and loss of properties. Others, not associated with Batista, leaving Cuba were the upper-class followed by the upper-middle and middle class, merchants, professionals, and businessmen. In 1962, the working class, skilled and semiskilled workers as well as artisans, started to leave Cuba to settle in the United States.

In general, Cubans arriving in the United States in this period enjoyed the sympathy of the American government and population, which made their experience unique in the history of immigrants to the United States; however, they also encountered some resistance to their settlement in Miami. Miami residents were very supportive of these educated immigrants, but due to the economic recession they feared the loss of jobs to Cubans willing to accept lower wages and downward mobility, especially in the case of the middle-class Cuban professionals.

Commercial air traffic from Cuba to the United States was not interrupted after the Bay of Pigs invasion, but it did end with the Cuban Missile Crisis in October 1962. The United States confronted the Soviet Union when the presence of nuclear missiles in Cuba became known, and Castro closed the Havana airports. The political arrangement between John F. Kennedy and Nikita Khrushchev, including the non-intervention clause, disappointed Cuban émigrés who expected America to invade the island and overthrow Castro. Cuban exiles were also disappointed by the interruption of the Freedom Flights that had made the arrival of new exiles possible. Despite the lack of communication between Cuba and United States, approximately sixteen thousand Cubans arrived in the United States between 1962 and 1965, most of them via third countries. Many were given visas because they were relatives of Cubans already in the United States; 5,000 arrived in the ships and planes of the Red Cross that carried the ransom for Bay of Pigs prisoners; and others sailed to the United States clandestinely in small boats or on rafts.

Cubans who arrived during the early 1960s settled primarily within the four-square-mile area that became known as "Little Havana." The area that at-

In the Little Havana section of Miami, Cuban immigrants have recreated some of the sights and tastes of their homeland. *(Anne Burns)*

tracted the second largest percentage of Cubans was Union City ("Havana of the Hudson") and the West New York area of New Jersey. By 1975, Cubans comprised more than two-thirds of Union City's residents and almost half of the residents of the neighboring city of West New York.

Cubans were attracted to Little Havana because it already had a small Cuban neighborhood; there were low-rent houses and apartment buildings available; there was good public transportation to the central business district and to the Centro Católico Hispano (Spanish Catholic Center) and the Cuban Refugee Center; and Cuban-owned drugstores and grocery stores were available to serve the Cuban community. Cubans renovated this area, and although non-Cuban residents were at first worried that the area would become a ghetto, Cubans turned an economically depressed area into a lucrative and prosperous commercial and residential area. By 1970, 14 percent of

the total Cuban population in the United States resided in Little Havana. Changed by Cubans, the local economy grew and diversified as they purchased homes, set up businesses such as restaurants, groceries, supermarkets, gas stations, drugstores, photography studios, department stores, factories, theaters, bars, and nightclubs. Major banks would not lend money to Cuban entrepreneurs without collateral, but the smaller banks, mostly Cuban or Latino owned, lent Cubans money for their business. Women entrepreneurs made it possible for other women to enter the labor force. The needs of women entering the workforce for services such as day care, housekeeping, delivery services, laundries, and dry cleaners were satisfied by other women who offered these services. One of the most successful of these businesses was the Cantinas, subscription home delivery food services that delivered hot meals every evening throughout the city.

SECOND WAVE (1965–1973)

In 1965, Castro surprised the international community by saying that Cubans who had relatives in the United States and wished to leave Cuba would be able to do so. To induce them to go to the Cuban port of Camarioca to meet their relatives and return with them to the United States, Cuban exiles were given guarantees—they would not be killed, would not be prosecuted, and would be allowed to return to the United States. Negotiations between Cuba and the United States were conducted through the Swiss embassy in Havana to facilitate the entry of this new group of Cubans to the United States. In keeping with the spirit of the Immigration Act of 1965, the United States government gave priority to political prisoners and Cubans with relatives in the country. In December 1965, daily chartered planes went to Baradero to bring Cubans to temporary barracks at the Miami airport. This second wave, different from the first wave, was constituted mostly of women, because many men who were skilled workers were not allowed to leave Cuba. Still, half of Cuba's professional class—which included doctors, lawyers, engineers, and professors—managed to arrive. The second wave was more racially diverse than the first wave, which was mostly white. Though this group had the support of Americans, as with the first wave, there was concern in Miami that they would depress the labor market by accepting low salaries. Some of these exiles were settled in other parts of the United States. The Cuban black population was not represented in the second emigration wave because the United States's history of discrimination against blacks was not an incentive for a population that was at the low end of pre-Castro society but was one of the most favored by the revolution. Additionally, Castro's propaganda was oriented toward discouraging black emigration because such emigration would damage the image of the socialist revolution. On April 6, 1973, Castro ended the Freedom Flights, which by this time had carried more than 260,000 refugees to the United States.

The end of the Freedom Flights did not stop Cubans from leaving Cuba for the United States. Several thousand Cubans arrived in the United States, mostly via a third country (primarily Mexico). There was a constant clandestine migration of desperate Cubans who risked their lives boating to the United States.

THIRD WAVE: THE MARIEL BOAT LIFT (1980)

In 1978, Castro offered to discuss several matters with the exile community. These were, mainly, the release of political prisoners in Cuba, family visits to and from Cuba, and the permanent return of older exiles, as well as visas for those who desired to leave Cuba. The Cuban government's dialogue offer produced tensions within the exile community. The extreme anti-Castro militants were opposed to the dialogue, while others, those who were interested in being reunited with family living in Cuba and those who had not really suffered under Castro and thus had a different point of view on the Castro revolution, supported Castro's proposition.

In this climate of Cuba–United States relations, the third wave of Cuban immigration, the Marielitos, occurred as one of the events following an incident at the Peruvian embassy in Havana, in 1980, in which six Cubans crashed through the embassy's gate, killing one Cuban guard. After the incident, the gate-crashers solicited and obtained political asylum from the Peruvian government. The Peruvian government refused repeated requests by Cuban authorities to surrender the gate-crashers. Cuba responded by withdrawing all guards and barricades from the embassy and announcing by radio that anyone who wanted to leave the country should go to the Peruvian embassy. In less than seventy-two hours, more than 10,000 people had crowded onto the embassy grounds. Castro characterized those who rushed to the embassy as criminals, lumpen parasites, and antisocial elements, claiming that because none of them were subject to political persecution, none were in need of political asylum. They were economic not political émigrés.

The Mariel Boat Lift, beginning in 1980 when Castro opened the port of Mariel to a "freedom flotilla" of American boats, was the subject of innumerable press articles and stories of the heroism and determination of the more than 125,000 Cubans who made the perilous crossing from Mariel to Key West. This group differed in many ways from the earliest waves, and were perceived differently by Americans partly due to Castro's characterization of those who gathered at the Peruvian embassy. The earlier perceptions of Cuban immigrants as desirable were changed by Marielito horror stories to perceptions of these immigrants as undesirables. Stories characterized them as Cuban misfits; homosexuals; criminals that Castro had sent as a means to both rid Cuba of undesirables and to make trouble in the United States; as being without relatives or friends in the United States; and as having left Cuba simply to try their luck in the United States, rather than to escape political persecution or to reunite with family. This characterization mobilized public opinion, even among Cuban exiles, against the Marielitos who, in Miami, were blamed for increasing rates of crime. The new refugees resented this stigmatization and also felt betrayed by family and friends who had told them how life would be wonderful in the United States.

Marielitos was initially a negative term used by the older waves of Cubans to refer to the new ones. Later, this term became a term of pride used by the Marielitos to distinguish themselves from the older émigrés. The Marielitos had a profound, healthy impact on the cultural life of the émigré community. The Marielitos' impact was due to their different experiences and their more open political perspective enabling them to assess the accomplishments and failures of the revolution and also those of the capitalist system. At first the oldest exile waves feared and resented the new arrivals for the negative attention they attracted. Because the Marielitos had, in general, done as well as the earliest émigrés, over time the older waves developed a profound respect for their compatriots, but did not like the openness of the Marielitos on topics such as abortion.

On December 14, 1984, the United States and Cuba reached an agreement that ensured that Cuba would take back 2,746 mental patients and criminals who had come to the United States with the Mariel Boat Lift, and the United States would issue visas, in 1985, to 3,000 political prisoners and their families, and to as many as 20,000 (increased to 27,845 in 1990) other Cubans. However, the United States has generally granted far fewer visas than the number agreed to. Many Cubans have taken the risk of traveling to Florida from the island by boat in order to take advantage of the provisions of the Cuban Adjustment Act. The auspicious and hopeful beginnings of the immigration agreement between Cuba and the United States were abruptly interrupted on May 20, 1985, by the commencing of broadcasting by Radio Marti (Voice of America) which had the mission of portraying the real situation in Cuba to Cubans. To show his displeasure with Radio Marti, Castro discontinued the terms of the agreement on migratory issues, repatriation of the mentally ill and criminal, and suspended all visits from Cubans living in the United States.

BALSEROS (FOURTH WAVE), AND THE REFUGEE CRISIS

As the interruption of the migratory agreement and the economic crisis faced by Cuba began to be felt within Cuba, and as the difficulties of leaving the country legally increased, the number of Cuban balseros increased. These difficulties also led many to attempt to steal or hijack state-owned boats to escape the deteriorating economic conditions. These attempts were faced with harsher treatment by the Cuban au-

thorities. In June 1994, coastal authorities from the port of La Fé shot and killed José Inesio Pedraza Izquierdo when he attempted to set to sea for the United States. Several incidents in which Castro did not allow asylum-seekers to leave the country resulted in a massive demonstration against the government. The day after the demonstration, Castro stated that Cuba was not opposed to letting those leave who wanted to leave. In the weeks that followed, more than 35,000 Cubans left the island on boats, the largest exodus since the Mariel Boat Lift. What had been a Cuban crisis suddenly became a crisis in United States policy toward Cuba, as the Clinton administration was caught in a dilemma of how to respond to the large numbers of arriving refugees. The dilemma was that allowing the new refugees to gain residency would alienate non-Cuban-Americans concerned about immigration, while returning the refugees to Cuba would alienate the Cuban-American community.

On August 19, 1994, under pressure from Florida politicians, President Bill Clinton stated that illegal refugees from Cuba would not be allowed to enter the United States. He declared that those who were picked up at sea would be taken to the United States Naval Base at Guantánamo, while those who reached the United States would be apprehended and treated like any other refugee. In an attempt to anticipate the angry reaction of the Miami exiles, Clinton met the same day with Cuban American National Foundation (CANF) president Jorge Mas Canosa, who publicly supported the plan in return for a tightening of sanctions against Cuba. Flights from Miami were restricted, cash remittances from Miami were cut back, and media broadcasts to Cuba were increased.

Initially, the policy changes had little effect as émigrés were convinced that they would be allowed into the United States. Talks with Cuba about migration issues resulted in a new agreement, signed by both governments. The United States government agreed to grant visas to a minimum of 20,000 Cubans without relatives who were citizens of the United States, and to grant additional visas to Cubans already on a waiting list. In return, the Cuban government agreed to prevent illegal departures by restoring the illegal exit provisions of the penal code. Even though the new agreement had the effect of ending the massive refugee flows, the problem of how to process the refugees who had been intercepted at sea following the policy shift remained for the United States government.

These political moves put the United States government under pressure from the Cuban exiles and attracted criticism from the human rights groups Amnesty International and Human Rights Watch, who accused the United States of violating Article 33 of the 1951 UN Convention Relating to the Status of Refugees by refusing to allow Cubans to seek asylum in the United States. In addition, the United States government was accused of complicity with the Cuban government's violation of Articles 12 and 19 of the UN's International Covenant on Civil and Political Rights by curtailing the flow of people and ideas between Cuba and the United States, and by insisting that the Cuban government prevent people from leaving Cuba.

Continuing talks between Cuban and American officials failed to solve the problem until a secret meeting was held in Toronto on April 17, 1995, between Ricardo Alarcón, president of Cuba's National Assembly, and Peter Tarnoff, United States undersecretary of state. The two produced a bilateral agreement under which the United States would admit most of the refugees at Guantánamo and subsequently rafters would be intercepted at sea and repatriated to Havana if they did not qualify for political asylum, thus treating Cuban refugees in the same way as those from other countries in the region. The agreement was made public May 2, 1995, provoking Miami exile organizations to call a general strike on May 16, which led to the closure of offices and shops and was followed by an evening rally of 10,000 people.

Despite the protests, the Cuban-American community was clearly split. Polls taken in Miami in May showed majority support for Clinton's new immigration policy. A poll of Cuban Americans taken by Florida International University found that while support for sanctions against Cuba, and even military invasion, remained high, a majority saw dialogue as an acceptable tactic to advance Cuban reform and 46 percent favored "the establishment of a national dialogue between Cuban exiles, Cuban dissidents, and representatives of the Cuban government."

CULTURAL IDENTITY AND *CUBANIDAD*

Cubans, especially those who arrived in the early 1960s, were concerned with preserving their *Cubanidad* or their Cuban identity as expressed by their customs, values, and culture. For them, preserving their *Cubanidad* was not a nostalgic attempt to live in the past. Defining themselves as exiles, *Cubanidad* implied a political responsibility, a commitment to remove Castro from governing Cuba. The efforts to keep their *Cubanidad* eased their adaptation to the United States by giving a larger meaning to their hardship; the effort psychologically empowered them and put them in better condition to deal with exile. In order to preserve their *Cubanidad* it was necessary to stay in Miami, where they could reproduce aspects of their *Cubanidad*. By doing so, they transformed Miami in many ways, of which the use of Spanish is only one. Miami became bilingual. Most exiles realized the importance of learning English in order to succeed in the United States, but some Cubans refused to speak English, and for them life was not difficult because there were so many Cubans working throughout Miami that they could survive speaking only Spanish. By the mid 1980s one study reported that more than half of Cubans spoke Spanish at work and over 70 percent used it in social situations.

Cultural organization had a very important role in the Cuban exiles' efforts to keep their identity. During the 1960s and 1970s Cubans created many cultural organizations; Cruzada Educativa Cubana fostered the study of Cuban history and traditions through literary contests and awards; Cuban-owned bookstores organized "Peñas Literarias"—literary circles for artists, poets, writers; local colleges and universities also sponsored art exhibits, theatrical productions, and lectures by distinguish émigré artists, writers, and scholars. Schools and churches established after-school programs to help parents educate their children in the essentials of *Cubanidad*, such as Cuban geography, history, and culture.

Also active in the cultural mission to preserve *Cubanidad* were the *municipios* (townships) named after Cuban townships, the first of which were founded in 1962. The municipios-in-exile were social organizations that provided cultural and recreational activities, and served as clearinghouses of information on local residents and on practical matters such as housing and employment. Through the municipio named after their township in Cuba, recent Cuban arrivals could get information on the whereabouts of friends, family, or neighbors. The principal objective of the municipio was to give comradeship and guidance to its members, to create a sense of brotherhood to overcome the political differences among exiles by appealing to cultural bonds that would be retained once a return to the homeland was possible. Cuban exiles realized that their identity was dependent upon a continuity between past and present, and between Cuba and the United States, so they tried to duplicate the past so exactly that Cubans who arrived in Miami during the Mariel Boat Lift joked about stepping back into the Cuba of the 1950s.

The exile media—Spanish-language periodicals

and radio and television stations—kept Cubans informed on issues important to them. The Nicaraguan-owned *Diario Las Americas* provided news in Spanish to Dade County, but hundreds of newspapers, tabloids, and magazines were published by the exiles, mostly in Miami. The most popular and most controversial of the periodicals were the *periodiquitos* (little newspapers). Hundreds of periodiquitos were published in south Florida and all of them were vehicles of propaganda for the different political organizations.

Although Cubans were concerned about *Cubanidad*, some began to perceive themselves as more than exiles. They were on the whole economically successful, some of them sought naturalization and gradually became involved in domestic civic and political affairs. Their concern about keeping their culture did not preclude their economic and social success in Miami, nor did it preclude their concern and interest in the local and national political and economic affairs.

Non-Cuban residents of Miami had mixed feelings about *Cubanidad*, particularly they were concerned with the refusal of Cubans to speak English and on several occasions asked for the relocation of Cubans to other parts of the country, but the various attempts at relocations were not very successful.

THE CUBAN EXILE COMMUNITY AND THE UNITED STATES GOVERNMENT

Although on the whole the U.S. government has been supportive of the Cuban exile community, there have been several periods of severe strain. The 1960s witnessed the rise of many groups within the exile community that explicitly aimed at overthrowing Castro, using violence if necessary. The exile community, then and now, has been based in Miami, along with various anti-Castro opposition groups. Among these are Omega 7 and Alpha 66. These groups gained not only rhetorical but financial support from the U.S. government, starting with President Dwight D. Eisenhower's approval in 1960 of funding for a Cuban "paramilitary organization." His efforts were abetted by the involvement of the Central Intelligence Agency in providing the groups with training and weapons. The best-known of them is Alpha 66, which was organized after the failed Bay of Pigs invasion in 1961. Alpha 66 leaders claim that their organization has made four attempts on Castro's life, staged military raids into Cuba, and set up illegal radio broadcasts to Cuba. The

U.S. government has, however, diminished support for groups advocating violence to achieve their aims.

In recent years, the CANF has become the most politically important Cuban exile organization. Founded in 1980, the CANF aims to bring down the Castro regime through political means, including unrelenting support of the U.S. embargo of Cuba and the use of propaganda. Because the CANF has been the chief voice representing the exile community in Washington, it has dominated the U.S. policy debate on Cuba.

The Mariel exiles brought with them their own perspectives, which have at times clashed with the prevailing CANF positions. In particular, the Mariel arrivals disagreed with the CANF's unwavering support of the U.S. embargo because they had firsthand knowledge of its effects on relatives. But they found the CANF inhospitable to differences of opinion, in some cases reportedly experiencing harassment and intimidation by CANF stalwarts.

Recently, the well-known case of Elian Gonzales, a six-year-old boy who survived the drowning death of his mother while trying to reach Florida by boat, created one of the more critical moments in the relationship between the United States government and the Cuban exile community. Relatives of Elian Gonzalez, supported by a large part of the Cuban exile community, pressured the United States government to allow Elian to remain in America, regardless of the fact that his father was waiting for him in Cuba. After months of negotiation, on Easter Sunday 2000 Elian was taken by force from his relative's home in Miami and returned to his father. For the Cuban community, the American government's behavior in this incident is a betrayal of the cause against communism and Castro, their principal enemy. For the first time, the Cuban community did not receive preferential treatment and had to confront the United States government.

Sara Z. Poggio

See also: Political, Ethnic, Religious, and Gender Persecution (Part II, Sec. 1); Politics III: The Home Country (Part II, Sec. 6); Miami, New Jersey and Suburban America (Part II, Sec. 12); President Carter's Announcement on the *Marielitos,* 1980 (Part IV, Sec. 1).

BIBLIOGRAPHY

Bach, Robert L. "The New Cuban Immigration: Their Background and Prospect." *Monthly Labor Review* 103 (1980): 39–46.

Bureau of the Census. *Census of the General Population, 1970, 1980, and 1990*. Washington, DC.

Cuban Committee for Democracy, The. Online http://www.us.net/cuban/portrait.htm.

Garcia, Maria Cristina. *Havana USA: Cuban Exiles and Cuban Americans in South Florida, 1959–1994*. Berkeley: University of California Press, 1996.

Gonzalez-Pando, Miguel. *The Cuban Americans*. Westport, CT: Greenwood Press, 1998.

Grenier, Guillermo J., and Alex Stepick. *Miami Now! Immigration, Ethnicity, and Social Change*. Gainesville, FL: University Press of Florida, 1992.

Masud-Piloto, Felix. *With Opens Arms: Cuban Immigration to the United States*. New York: Rowman and Littlefield, 1988.

Portes, Alejandro. "Los Angeles in the Context of the New Immigration." *Newsletter of the Section on International Migration* 4:1 (1997): 1–4.

———, and Robert L. Bach. *Latin Journey: Cuban and Mexican Immigrants in the United States*. Berkeley, CA: University of California Press, 1985.

———, and Alex Stepick. *City on the Edge: The Transformation of Miami*. Berkeley, CA: University of California Press, 1993.

Rodriguez, Richard. "Elian, the First Cause That Could Unify Hispanics." *Jinn: the Online Magazine of the Pacific News Service*, n.d., 2000. http://www.ssc.msu.edu/~intermis/womv4nol/porte_1.htm.

Suro, Roberto. *Strangers Among Us: How Latino Immigration Is Transforming America*. New York: Alfred A. Knopf, 1998.

DOMINICAN REPUBLIC

People from the Caribbean nation of the Dominican Republic comprise the third largest Latin American immigrant group in the United States, after Mexicans and Cubans, and the fourth largest Latino group (which includes nonimmigrant Puerto Ricans). Since the late 1960s, the Dominican Republic has ranked within the top ten source nations for immigration into the United States, and since the early twentieth century, approximately 810,000 people have entered the United States as legal immigrants from the Dominican Republic. There has also been a sizable flow of undocumented immigration. While it is difficult to obtain precise figures due to problems with undercount, 1990 census results and more recent population surveys indicate that at least 632,000 Dominican-born individuals live in the United States and 153,000 others of Dominican parentage. Dominicans and Dominican Americans live throughout the United States, but the most concentrated settlements are in New York City, where the Dominican Republic has been the top source country of immigration for most years in the 1980s and 1990s. Other northeastern states, such as New Jersey, Massachusetts, Rhode Island, and Connecticut, have seen the growth of Dominican-born populations in the last several decades. Florida and Puerto Rico also contain large numbers of Dominican immigrants.

Although a relatively new immigrant group, during the last forty years Dominicans have established strong communities, developed an important presence in local and state politics, and influenced cultural and educational arenas in areas of settlement. They have also played important roles in the economic development of the communities in which they live. Dominicans continue to have an important influence on the political and economic life of their home country as well—a fact reflected in the election in 1996 of a president who had grown up in New York City.

PATTERNS AND CAUSES OF DOMINICAN IMMIGRATION TO THE UNITED STATES

The search for a better life has undoubtedly characterized much of Dominican immigration from the mid-1960s to the present, although there have been episodes of politically motivated emigration in the Dominican Republic's recent history. Prior to the 1960s, a very limited amount of immigration from the Dominican Republic to the United States took place, with fewer than 17,000 persons admitted as legal immigrants between 1932 and 1960. The 1960 census counted a population of almost twelve thousand Dominican-born persons living in the United States. During the regime of General Rafaél Trujillo Molina (1930–61), tight restrictions on travel and emigration out of the Dominican Republic existed, and only those well-connected to the government could secure the necessary permission to leave. A limited number of opponents of the Trujillo regime fled the country, however, and in exile they maintained a visible campaign of protest against the Dominican government by establishing political parties and holding regular demonstrations in Washington, D.C., and at the United Nations headquarters in New York City.

Dominican immigrant admissions into the United States increased by a factor of ten between the 1950s and the 1960s. Several events taking place during the 1960s led to this dramatic increase. First, the assassination of General Trujillo in 1961 led to the relaxation of emigration restrictions. The politically turbulent years that followed the end of the Trujillo regime, including a civil conflict and intervention and occupation by U.S.-led international peacekeeping forces, prompted new waves of politically motivated emigration. By 1966, many of those opposed to the new government of the former Trujillo protégé Joaquín Balaguer had left the country. Finally, the 1965 amend-

Dominican immigrant children in the New York City neighborhood of Washington Heights play in an open fire hydrant to beat the heat of a humid summer afternoon. *(Dan Steiger, Impact Visuals)*

ments to the Immigration and Nationality Act of 1952 abolished the decades-old formula that gave preference to individuals of northern European national origin. The reforms established a new preference system and increased quotas of immigrant visas available to those from other regions of the world. Dominicans formed part of the wave of "new immigrants" from Latin America and Asia whose admissions were facilitated by these changes in U.S. immigration policies.

During the 1960s and 1970s, the average number of Dominicans admitted annually was 9,300 and 14,800, respectively. Political motivations for immigration continued to exist during this time. President Balaguer held office throughout this period, although his reelections in 1970 and 1974 were subject to controversy and charges of fraud by his opponents. Repression and human rights abuses directed at the opposition prompted the emigration of many of those associated with other political parties and movements. However, most Dominican immigrants came to the United States during this time with the hope of

finding better work opportunities and to join family members already living abroad.

The dramatic economic and social changes taking place in the Dominican Republic during the 1960s and 1970s fostered economically motivated immigration. The country underwent a shift from a predominantly agricultural economy that had been heavily controlled by Trujillo and relatively isolated internationally, to a more diversified economy with a greater emphasis on the manufacturing and service sectors. Increasing trade with other countries and the receipt of aid and foreign loans integrated the Dominican Republic more deeply into the world economy, with mixed results for the country's development, as it became increasingly dependent on the United States.

These changes led to the displacement of large portions of the workforce. The Dominican Republic registered the highest urban population growth rate in all Latin America between 1966 and 1970. Increases in urban unemployment and stagnation in wages fueled the increasing desire of many Dominicans to seek work abroad. Surveys done in the Dominican Republic in the mid-1970s indicated that three-fourths of those leaving the country were from urban areas and that the desire to find employment and obtain higher income were the primary reasons for migrating. The outflows of labor taking place during the 1960s and 1970s undoubtedly eased the economic, social, and political pressures produced by the dramatic changes taking place in the Dominican Republic.

At the same time, transformations in the northeastern cities of the United States attracted a growing pool of foreign immigrant labor. The decline of manufacturing industries in urban areas, population decline caused by flight to the suburbs, and the growth of service economies relying on unskilled labor characterized many urban areas in this region of the United States. New waves of immigration supplied a labor force for these emerging service economies, helped to reverse population decline, and revitalized declining inner cities. These changing economic and demographic conditions in the Northeast formed a complement to the many factors within the Dominican Republic that had been fostering the immigration process.

By the 1980s, a steady immigrant stream had become established between the United States and the Dominican Republic, and admission levels continued to increase to an annual average of about twenty-five thousand. In addition to documented immigration, a growing amount of undocumented immigration took place, usually through overstaying tourist visas or clandestine and dangerous boat trips to Puerto Rico, from which entry into the United States could more easily be made with false documentation. By the mid-1990s, an estimated fifty thousand undocumented Dominicans were living in the United States.

Economic and political conditions continued to foster the desire and need for emigration out of the Dominican Republic in the 1980s. The presidency shifted to one of the major opposition political parties, the Dominican Revolutionary Party, between 1978 and 1986, but the country continued to grapple with economic crises, including heavy foreign debt, stagnant or falling export prices, and overall low rates of growth. The lack of economic improvement dampened hopes of permanent return and resettlement for many immigrants who had viewed their sojourn in the United States as temporary.

During the last decade of the century, annual immigrant admissions continued to be at the maximum allowable amount, averaging nearly thirty thousand. While both temporary and more permanent return migration have taken place, strong economic and social networks between the Dominican Republic and the United States have become well-established and

have helped to perpetuate the immigration process. Dominican governments have promoted further diversification of the economy away from agricultural production and toward tourism, services, and manufacturing for export. However, remittances sent from immigrants living abroad have become a vital source of income for many Dominicans, and reliance on emigration to seek employment abroad has become a structural feature of the country's development and an ingrained aspect of Dominican culture.

CHARACTERISTICS OF DOMINICAN IMMIGRANTS AND SETTLEMENT IN THE UNITED STATES

Between 1960 and 1970, the number of Dominican-born persons in the United States increased by over 400 percent, according to conservative estimates. The Dominican-born population in the United States and in New York City more than doubled between 1970 and 1980, and by 1990, over half a million individuals of Dominican birth or parentage were living in the United States. Population surveys from 1996 estimated the Dominican-born population at 632,000. The actual population may be much higher given problems of census undercount and the difficulty of tracking undocumented immigration. The number of Dominican-born persons in the United States represented about 8 percent of the 1997 population of the Dominican Republic.

Traditionally, most Dominicans immigrating into the United States have settled in the New York metropolitan area. This trend peaked in the 1970s, when almost 84 percent of Dominican-born individuals in the United States were living in New York City. By the 1980s and 1990s, more dispersed patterns of settlement were emerging, with only about 65 percent of the Dominican foreign-born in New York City by 1990. Dominican populations in such northeastern states as New Jersey, Massachusetts, Rhode Island, and Connecticut have been increasing since the 1980s, totaling about sixty-four thousand Dominicans by 1990. In addition, Florida has been the destination of an increasing number of Dominican immigrants.

Within New York City, most Dominicans live in the Borough of Manhattan, which contained 41 percent of all Dominican-origin persons living in the city in 1990. The Lower East Side and parts of the Upper West Side attracted Dominican residents in earlier years, but most Dominicans have settled in the northern neighborhoods of Hamilton Heights (or West Harlem), Washington Heights, and Inwood. During the 1980s, these neighborhoods were the intended place of residence for over forty thousand Dominican immigrants admitted to the United States. Significant numbers of Dominicans have also settled in other boroughs; the Bronx was the site of residence of about one-fourth of Dominican-origin persons in the city in 1990, and the Dominican population of the Bronx has grown rapidly as a result of housing shortages and rising rents in northern Manhattan. In Queens, the neighborhoods of Jackson Heights/Corona have also been common areas of residence, although the entire borough contained only about 16 percent of Dominican-origin persons by 1990.

The Dominican immigrant population in the United States is relatively young, with a median age of twenty-eight in 1990 and almost 50 percent of the Dominican-born population between the ages of twenty-five to forty-four years. The average age of Dominican immigrants upon entry has been thirty-one in recent years. Recent population surveys indicate that most Dominican-origin persons were born abroad (71 percent), and native-born persons of Dominican parentage consist mostly of children—the median age for this group is about ten years. Within New York City, Dominican children make up an estimated 10 percent of the student body of the public school system.

Women have been strongly represented in the immigration process, making up 53 percent of Dominican immigrants admitted to the United States in 1997 and frequently accounting for over half of the annual admissions over the last four decades. By the mid-1990s, almost 59 percent of Dominican-born persons in the United States were women. Research on gender and immigration indicates that Dominican immigrant women experience significantly higher labor-force participation in the United States than do those who remain in the Dominican Republic, and women may be less likely than men to want to return to the country of origin. In the United States, female-headed households are more common among Dominicans than in other immigrant and nonimmigrant groups. In New York City, half of the Dominican immigrant population were living in a female-headed household in 1997, compared with an average of 26 percent for the city's population generally, or 41 percent for the overall Hispanic population.

Education and employment data from the 1990s reflect how the Dominican-origin population has been incorporated into U.S. social and labor market structures. Dominicans have a lower percentage of the population who have obtained a high school diploma or beyond (42 percent) among those aged twenty-five and older than either the non-Hispanic or Puerto Rican populations. The vast majority of Dominicans speak a language other than English at home, and among those who speak English, 60 percent said that they do not speak English "very well." About 16 percent of the Dominican-origin labor force (sixteen years and older) was unemployed at the time of the 1990 census, compared with about 6 percent for the non-Hispanic population. The manufacturing industry employed most of those of Dominican origin, followed by the retail trade and service sectors.

Income and poverty data reveal gaps in economic status that exist between Dominicans and other Hispanic-origin groups, as well as between the former and the non-Hispanic population. Census and survey data from the 1990s indicate that per capita income among the Dominican-origin population is about half that of the non-Hispanic population and lower than that of Puerto Ricans and Mexicans. In addition, Dominican families show a greater tendency to have incomes below the poverty level, with 33 percent of families at this status. Again, this figure is higher than those for Puerto Ricans, Mexicans, and Cubans and contrasts sharply with that for the non-Hispanic population, which has only 9 percent of families with incomes below the poverty level.

Many of these trends are repeated in the data for Dominicans in New York City. Figures on employment by industry show that in New York City, Dominicans tend to be more evenly divided between the manufacturing and retail trade sectors than is the case for the national population as a whole. Poverty rates for Dominican-origin families are higher in New York City; in 1989, almost 39 percent of such families had incomes below the poverty level. This figure exceeded that for Puerto Ricans and was higher than that for any Hispanic-origin group in New York City. Figures for median household income followed the same trend, with Dominican households earning an average of $24,000 per year in the mid-1990s.

Although poverty and unemployment have been a central aspect of the Dominican immigrant experience, many Dominicans have emerged as small-business owners, especially within communities of concentrated settlement. Small grocery stores or bodegas, travel and shipping agencies, and livery cab services are the most common businesses owned by Dominican immigrants. Researchers have identified the important role of entrepreneurs in revitalizing neighborhoods and in supporting small-scale enterprise in the Dominican Republic.

POLITICAL, SOCIAL, AND CULTURAL INCORPORATION OF DOMINICAN IMMIGRANTS

Over the decades, Dominicans and Dominican Americans have become increasingly visible as a distinct national immigrant group and have worked to direct political and economic resources into needed areas within their communities. But the process of incorporation has been inhibited by slow recognition of the growing populations of Dominican immigrants within communities of settlement. In the 1960s and 1970s, Dominicans in New York were often referred to as "invisible" immigrants, mistaken by Anglos at times for Puerto Ricans or Cubans. Within the Dominican communities, the persistent desire to return to the country of origin and the effort to maintain political and cultural ties to the Dominican Republic led many to place a lesser emphasis on incorporation into American society and politics. The common use of the term *dominicanos ausentes* (absent Dominicans) set the home country as the central point of reference in the lives of many.

As with other immigrant groups, early organizing among Dominicans centered around social, professional, civic, and recreational clubs. By the end of the 1970s, several dozen voluntary organizations were in existence in New York City. These organizations were often associated with towns and cities of origin within the Dominican Republic and were often used as vehicles to provide economic aid to the home country. Branches of Dominican political parties were other prominent immigrant organizations. These branches continue to play a very visible role in Dominican communities, engaging in campaigning and fund-raising for elections taking place in the Dominican Republic.

During the mid to late 1980s, a shift toward a greater participation in local politics occurred, especially within New York City. Dreams of return to the Dominican Republic faded for many immigrants, as the country faced continued economic crisis and stagnation. Dominican-born activists reared primarily within the United States began taking a more prominent role in forming organizations and participating in U.S. politics. Activists pursued links with the Democratic Party and, to a lesser extent, the Republican Party. New York governor Mario Cuomo and New York City mayors Edward Koch and David Dinkins appointed Dominicans to advisory positions on Latino affairs at both state and city levels in New York.

In New York City, the District Six school board, covering much of Washington Heights, has been an important stepping stone on the path to greater political representation within city politics. A Dominican-born immigrant was first elected to the board for District Six in the 1970s, and in the 1980s, Dominican-born educator Guillermo Linares and other Dominican activists engaged in campaigns to mobilize Dominican voters to participate in school board elections. (City rules permit noncitizens with children registered in the school system to vote.) Linares and other activists succeeded in bringing over ten thousand Dominicans into the electoral process, and Linares became head of the school board for District Six in 1986.

During the 1990s, the political visibility of Dominicans increased through the elections of Linares and Adriano Espaillat to the New York City Council and New York State Assembly, respectively. Both these seats are based in districts that were reformed in the early 1990s under mandate of the Federal Voting Rights Act to increase the likelihood of election of candidates from underrepresented groups. Dominicans have also run for local office in New Jersey, Rhode Island, and Florida. By the late 1990s in New York City, new, younger candidates were emerging to challenge the first generation of Dominican-origin politicians.

Despite these political gains, most Dominicans remain outside the arenas of conventional electoral politics due to low naturalization and citizenship rates. By 1997, only half of the Dominican foreign-born population over age eighteen had naturalized, although this figure reflected an increase from 1980, when only 25 percent had naturalized. The availability of dual nationality and the growth in U.S.-born populations of Dominican-origin persons may change this pattern of retaining Dominican nationality and thus may alter the patterns of participation in more formal political processes.

Other areas of public life have seen the participation of Dominicans. Such community-based organizations as Alianza Dominicana in New York provide social and economic assistance to those living in predominantly Dominican neighborhoods. In 1994, the Dominican Studies Institute, located on the campus of the City College of New York, was founded as a research unit of the City University of New York. The institute has promoted the greater visibility of Dominican studies within the curricula of colleges and universities throughout the region and has received national funding to support the research and documentation of the Dominican experience at home and abroad. New generations of Dominicans have formed student and youth groups at schools and universities throughout the United States, and they have also organized national forums to discuss present and future issues confronting Dominicans and Dominican Americans. In addition, Dominicans have joined with other groups in New York to mobilize against police brutality and to combat negative stereotyping within the mainstream media.

The experience of immigration has consistently informed the cultural and artistic production of Dominican immigrant communities. Although authors of Dominican origins have lived in the United States for decades, many were not well known beyond Dominican and Dominican-American circles. In recent years, writers such as Julia Alvarez and Junot Díaz have reached wide audiences through their novels, poetry, and short stories. Dominican music in the form of *merengue* and *bachata* have been popularized abroad, and the lyrics of many songs have served as vehicles for expressing immigrants' experiences on both sides of the border. These experiences have also been depicted on the screen in such films as *Nueba Yol* (Spanish slang for New York), written and directed by Angel Muñiz.

Few Dominican-American newspapers or magazines have appeared with regularity in the United States, although publications from the Dominican Republic are widely available and devote significant coverage to immigrant communities living abroad. Dominican papers are also widely available via the Internet. Many Dominican-born journalists work in the Spanish- and English-language media, including local cable television in New York City, where news and entertainment programming focusing on the Dominican Republic and the Dominican communities can be found. Dominican Day parades, in existence for decades in New York, are now held in many cities and operate as visible forums for promoting Dominican culture and pride. In sports, many Dominicans have achieved fame through careers in major league baseball, the best-known being Sammy Sosa, the Chicago Cubs slugger who hit more than sixty home runs in both 1998 and 1999.

TRANSNATIONAL TIES TO THE DOMINICAN REPUBLIC

After four decades of extensive immigration into the United States, Dominicans and Dominican Americans are becoming increasingly settled and more visible as an important national group within the American mosaic. But a persistent and major aspect of Dominican immigration has been the maintenance of important social, economic, and political ties to the country of origin.

The economic influence of Dominican immigrants on the Dominican Republic has been significant. While it has been difficult to track the amount of money that is sent back to the Dominican Republic by immigrants, many researchers estimate that such remittances make up the second largest source of foreign exchange for the country, amounting to hundreds of millions of dollars per year by the 1990s. The sending of money to family members and investment in housing and businesses in the Dominican Republic have been a continuing subsidy to the Dominican economy. Social clubs and organizations continue to assist towns and localities of origin, contributing to the building and equipping of schools, hospitals, and other infrastructure. Dominican immigrants have also stepped forward to organize and offer assistance to their home country in the aftermath of hurricanes and other natural disasters.

In the political area, Dominicans have retained and built strong ties to the country of origin. Dominican political parties operate extensively in immigrant communities, relying heavily on campaign donations to fund increasingly expensive campaigns at home. All major presidential candidates now appear regularly in American communities to mobilize support among immigrants. Dominican immigrants have lobbied for citizenship and voting rights, seeking to retain a direct role in the political system of their country of origin. As of 1996, Dominicans who naturalized as U.S. citizens have been allowed to recover Dominican nationality. More recently, Dominicans were granted permission to vote in Dominican elections from abroad, although as of early 2000, the Dominican government had not yet implemented a system for such a practice. The Dominican government has also supported the creation of representation in its legislature for Dominicans living abroad.

United States politicians have recognized the importance of these political ties. It is not uncommon for candidates running in heavily Dominican districts for local and state offices in the United States to pay a visit to the Dominican Republic at some point in their campaigns. This trend has occurred with candidates for recent New York City mayoral elections.

Many other areas of life reflect the close connections between the Dominican immigrant communities and the country of origin. The high volume of flights between commonly traveled routes and the prevalence of such services as money transfer and travel and shipping agencies have all facilitated ongoing connections between countries. The growth of the Internet has also facilitated communication across borders, with several discussion groups and Web sites serving as forums in which Dominicans around the world can interact. While only a small minority of Dominicans in the Dominican Republic or abroad have access to such technologies, there is the potential for greater use of the Internet in the future to forge economic, political, and cultural ties across borders such as e-mail communication.

Scholars of immigration have debated the lasting significance of these transnational ties, characterizing them as common in newer immigrant groups but likely to fade over time. The connections have not yet weakened with deeper integration of Dominicans into the United States, however. The ongoing dependence of the country of origin on its immigrant populations and the interest of the Dominican government in including immigrants in the political, economic, and social life of the nation will serve to encourage an ongoing relationship across borders. The effects and consequences of these transnational ties on Dominican immigrants and their future development within the United States remain open questions. For the foreseeable future, transnational ties will be an important and interesting component of the Dominican immigrant experience.

Pamela Graham

See also: Miami, New York City (Part II, Sec. 12).

BIBLIOGRAPHY

Aponte, Sarah. *Dominican Migration to the United States, 1970–1997: An Annotated Bibliography.* New York: CUNY Dominican Studies Institute, 1999.

Georges, Eugenia. *The Making of a Transnational Community: Migration, Development, and Cultural Change in the Dominican Republic.* New York: Columbia University Press, 1990.

Graham, Pamela M. "An Overview of the Political Incorporation of Dominican Migrants in New York City." *Latino Studies Journal* 9 (Fall 1998): 39–64.

Grasmuck, Sherri, and Patricia R. Pessar. *Between Two Islands: Dominican International Migration.* Berkeley: University of California Press, 1991.

Guarnizo, Luis E. "Los Dominicanyorks: The Making of a Binational Society." *Annals of the American Academy of Political and Social Science* 533 (May 1994): 70–86.

Hernández, Ramona, and Francisco Rivera-Batiz. *Dominican New Yorkers: A Socioeconomic Profile, 1997.* New York: CUNY Dominican Studies Institute, 1997.

Pessar, Patricia R. *A Visa for a Dream: Dominicans in the United States.* Boston: Allyn and Bacon, 1995.

Torres-Saillant, Silvio, and Ramona Hernández. *The Dominican Americans.* Westport, CT: Greenwood Press, 1998.

ENGLISH-SPEAKING CARIBBEAN

The English-speaking Caribbean consists of nineteen different nations and colonies. These include nine independent island states: Antigua and Barbuda; Barbados; Dominica (not to be confused with the Dominican Republic); Grenada; Jamaica; St. Kitts and Nevis; St. Lucia; St. Vincent and the Grenadines; and Trinidad and Tobago. In addition, there are two mainland nations that—for reasons of culture, language, and history—are generally included in the list of English-speaking Caribbean states. These are Belize in Central America and Guyana on the northern coast of South America. And while technically not in the Caribbean—but close to it—the independent nation of the Bahamas is usually placed in the category of English-speaking Caribbean nations for the same reasons that Belize and Guyana are.

Moreover, the region also includes a number of islands that remain under the jurisdiction of the United Kingdom and the United States. For the United Kingdom, these include Anguilla; the British Virgin Islands; the Cayman Islands; Montserrat; and the Turks and Caicos (the latter just north of the Caribbean). And while it is situated far out in the Atlantic Ocean, the British colony of Bermuda is also included for cultural and linguistic reasons. The U.S. Virgin Islands, as its name implies, is a possession of the United States. The Garifuna, another English-speaking Caribbean people, do not have a nation of their own, but live on the eastern littoral of the predominantly Spanish-speaking Central American nations of Honduras, Guatemala, Nicaragua, Costa Rica, and Panama.

Collectively, the English-speaking Caribbean has a population of approximately 6,179,000 people, plus an estimated 300,000 to 400,000 English-speaking Garifuna (estimated because Central American countries do not keep exact records of the first language of their citizens). Most of the English-speaking Caribbean nations—and particularly the colonies—have tiny land areas and very small populations. In fact, the three nations that predominate in the region include roughly 75 percent of the total population (minus the Garifunas). These are Jamaica (with a population of about 2.6 million), Trinidad and Tobago (1.3 million), and Guyana (700,000).

IMMIGRATION TO THE UNITED STATES

People from the English-speaking Caribbean have been coming to what is today the United States since the very beginnings of North American colonization. Indeed, the very first shipment of blacks to the Virginia colony in 1619 consisted largely of persons of African descent who were born or had lived in the Caribbean. In fact, during the entire history of slave importation to the United States—from 1619 until the trade was outlawed in the United States in 1808—the vast majority of slaves coming into the United States came from the Caribbean, not directly from Africa. In addition, in the very early years of colonization, numerous poor whites and wealthier planters moved to the American southern colonies from the Caribbean. Many residents of Charleston, the cultural capital of the antebellum South, were immigrants or the descendants of immigrants from Barbados. With the end of slavery in the United States after 1865, Caribbean immigrants continued to move to the United States in small numbers. In the early twentieth century, there was a brief upturn in the flow—an estimated 50,000 Jamaicans and another 50,000 persons from the rest of the Caribbean (including non-English-speaking lands) made their way to the United States between 1900 and the passage of restrictive immigration laws in the 1920s.

With the passage of the Immigration and Nationality Act of 1965—which ended national quotas—the inflow of Caribbean peoples began to climb again, soon surpassing the numbers from the early twentieth century. In 1966, for example, just 2,743 Jamaicans em-

Table 1
English-Speaking Caribbean Immigration to the United States, 1980–1997

Region/Nation	1981–1990	1991–1995	1996	1997
English-speaking Caribbean*	341,500	155,600	32,900	29,500
Jamaica	213,800	90,700	19,100	17,800
Trinidad and Tobago	39,500	33,700	7,300	NA

*Antigua and Barbuda; Barbados; Dominica; Grenada; Jamaica; St. Kitts and Nevis; St. Lucia; St. Vincent and the Grenadines; and Trinidad and Tobago.
Source: Bureau of the Census. *Statistical Abstract of the United States.* Washington, DC: Government Printing Office, 1999.

igrated to the United States; in 1967, the number jumped to 10,483. For Barbadians, or Bajans as they are informally called, the growth was equally dramatic. Whereas the number of islanders coming to the United States in the 1950s could be counted in the hundreds, over 16,000 came between 1967 and 1976. Similarly, only about 3,500 Guyanese came to the United States between 1925 and the early 1960s, while fully 100,000 emigrated between the mid-1960s and 1990. Also, there were few Trinidadian immigrants before 1965, but there have been about 275,000 since then. All of these numbers and those in the table concern legal immigrants, but, according to the Immigration and Naturalization Service, there is also a large population of English-speaking Caribbean people who live in this country illegally. These include about 50,000 people each from Jamaica and Trinidad, ranking both nations in the top fifteen sources of illegal immigrant populations in the United States.

A BRIEF HISTORY OF THE ENGLISH-SPEAKING CARIBBEAN

The islands of the English-speaking Caribbean were settled in pre-Columbian times by groups the Europeans called the Carib and Arawak Indians. With the arrival of the Spanish after 1492, virtually all of the native Caribbean population was wiped out by European-borne disease, slavery, and massacre. Small pockets of the original population survived on the larger islands like Trinidad or on islands—such as Dominica—that, for reasons of climate or topography, had little appeal to European colonists seeking to establish plantation economies. On other islands, the remaining natives mixed with and married whites and Africans.

While the Spanish claimed sovereignty over all of the Caribbean in the late fifteenth and early sixteenth centuries, they focused their colonization efforts on the larger islands such as Cuba and Hispaniola (now Haiti and the Dominican Republic). Most of the smaller islands remained sparsely settled until they were seized by the Dutch, the English, and the French, who then established flourishing plantation economies in the seventeenth, eighteenth, and nineteenth centuries. To work these labor-intensive operations—first in Barbados and then Jamaica—the English brought indentured servants from Britain. The death rate among them was appalling, however, and the English workers soon insisted on better living conditions and a say in their governance. As a result, English indentured servants were replaced by African slaves, and by the eighteenth century, the population of Barbados, Jamaica, and other English-controlled islands was predominantly of African descent, with a minority of whites of whom most worked as plantation supervisors, civil servants, soldiers, and the like. (Many of the landowners themselves were absent and lived in their home country.) While Africans had a lower mortality rate than whites, they too died with great frequency, and their numbers were maintained only through the continued importation of large numbers of slaves, until the British banned the trade in 1807. Slave rebellions were also a frequent problem for the English, particularly in Jamaica where runaways—called "maroons"—fought off the British army and maintained autonomous communities in the interior mountains of the large island.

In 1833, Britain outlawed slavery in all of its possessions, which led to a decline in the sugar and other commercial agricultural crops in the Caribbean, as newly freed slaves drifted from the plantations. In some of their possessions, including Trinidad (which the British took from the Spanish in 1797) and Guyana (which the British took from the Dutch in 1796), the colonizers tried to overcome this labor shortage by importing indentured servants from colonies in India. This colonial and labor history is reflected in the ethnic profile of these two nations. Guyana's population in 1995 consisted of 51 percent persons of East Indian origin, 43 percent of African origin, and the rest a mix

While immigrants from the English-speaking Caribbean—like this Trinidadian-born New Yorker—traditionally made their way to Britain, more and more choose the United States, as a by-product of geographic proximity, a vibrant economy, and American cultural influence. *(Wanderlan P. Silva/Impact Visuals)*

of whites, Chinese, and Native Americans. In Trinidad and Tobago, people of African descent represented 43 percent of the population in 1995, while persons of East Indian descent constituted 41 percent, with 16 percent largely consisting of people of mixed origin. In Jamaica and Barbados, on the other hand, the population in 1995 was largely of African origin—roughly 90 percent in the former and 80 percent in the latter. Between 1960 and 1970, all of the larger and more populous English-speaking Caribbean colonies gained their independence: Jamaica (1962); Trinidad and Tobago (1962); Barbados (1966); and Guyana (1970).

REASONS FOR IMMIGRATION

Because of their size and population, educational and economic opportunities have always been lim-

ited in the English-speaking Caribbean, even on the larger islands like Jamaica and Trinidad. This has led to a long history of out-migration. Until independence, most of these immigrants went to Britain for school and work. Even today, there remains a large flow of persons moving from the English-speaking Caribbean to the United Kingdom, and there are large West Indian neighborhoods in virtually all British cities. At the same time, there has always been a significant number of English-speaking West Indians who have chosen to emigrate to the United States. Indeed, it is estimated that in the 1920s roughly one-third of the population of Harlem—the largest and most influential black community in the United States—were West Indian–born or the children of West Indian immigrants.

Beginning with independence in the 1960s, a large-scale shift in immigration away from Britain and toward the United States occurred. Several factors were behind this change. First has been the sheer power of the United States economy and its ability to absorb large numbers of immigrant workers. Indeed, in 2000, the United States had a gross national product over six times that of Britain. In addition, the United States has far more opportunities for a college or university education—always a draw for West Indian immigrants—than the United Kingdom. The United States is closer geographically to the Caribbean, and there are far more low-cost flights to North America than to the United Kingdom. Geographic proximity also makes it easier for immigrants to travel back and forth to visit hometowns and loved ones. A less tangible, but still potent, draw of the United States is its culture. Over the past forty years, the English-speaking Caribbean has become increasingly less influenced culturally by Britain and ever more so by U.S. mass media.

Economic factors remain the dominant spur for immigration from these countries to the United States, as opposed to Cuba or various Central American countries where political oppression and war have sent people fleeing to the United States in large numbers. While Trinidad and Tobago has a natural gas and an oil industry and Jamaica has a small manufacturing sector, most of the rest of the English-speaking Caribbean has depended on tourism and agriculture for economic survival, as the small-scale farming necessitated by the geographical limitations of the islands makes it very difficult to produce crops that are economically competitive on the international market. Indeed, there is an ongoing trade dispute between the United States and the European Union (EU) over Caribbean-grown bananas. Special agreements between the European Union and the former colonies of EU countries permit higher prices for Caribbean-grown bananas, which U.S. banana companies, such as Chiquita, complain is an unfair trade practice. Tourism, then, remains the only viable industry in much of the English-speaking Caribbean. For those who cannot find jobs in this sector—or who aspire to other occupations and trades—there is very little option but to emigrate.

Education, as noted earlier, is also a major draw of the United States. While the English-speaking Caribbean has some of the best primary and secondary school systems in the developing world (partly, a legacy of British colonialism), it lacks an adequate university system. Except for the University of the West Indies in Jamaica, the English-speaking Caribbean has few major institutions of higher education.

EXPERIENCES IN THE UNITED STATES

People of the English-speaking Caribbean who emigrate to the United States face all of the problems that other newcomers have to deal with: finding a job and decent housing, getting used to the fast pace of American life, and adjusting to urban culture. Indeed, the vast majority of English-speaking Caribbean immigrants have settled in the major metropolitan areas of the Northeast, with nearly 75 percent in the New York–New Jersey area alone. A small minority of very impoverished Jamaicans have become migrant farmworkers, often coming into this country under special immigrant visas that allow them to work in agriculture only. Many of these migrate up and down the East Coast with the harvest.

But West Indian immigrants, particularly those of African descent, must also confront racial issues. Having grown up in societies where there are few whites, they are often unfamiliar with the more subtle and debilitating aspects of American racism. Not surprisingly, a number of West Indian black immigrants have been central to the history of civil rights in the United States, including Jamaican Marcus Garvey in the 1920s and Trinidadian Stokely Carmichael in the 1960s. In addition, relations between American-born blacks and black West Indian immigrants have often been strained. While the two groups often live together in the same neighborhoods, socialize together, and frequently intermarry, stereotypes abound. Some West Indians say that American-born blacks are unwilling to work hard and use racism as a too-easy rationalization for failure. American blacks—echoing the stereotypes many white Americans have about immigrants from the developing world—say that West Indians are too willing to work for poverty-level wages, thereby taking jobs away from native-born Americans.

Caribbean persons of Indian background also can have a difficult time adjusting to American culture. As Hindus and Muslims, they must adjust to life in a largely Christian society, whereas the largely Protestant and Catholic population of Caribbean blacks share a common religious and ethical heritage with the majority of Americans.

In sum, immigrants from the English-speaking Caribbean have exhibited patterns similar to those of other immigrants from the developing world. Most have come here because of the availability of jobs and education, which are lacking at home. But because of their color, most of them face the additional hurdle of

American racism. Still, many have managed to do quite well. Jamaican and Trinidadian immigrants, for example, have a much lower poverty rate than American blacks or Hispanics, perhaps reflecting the fact that the most skilled, educated, and ambitious persons from those islands are often the ones to emigrate, a pattern common to many immigrants from the developing world. The main difference between black Caribbean immigrants and immigrants from other parts of the globe, however, is that the former often find themselves caught between two American cultures. Seen as blacks by American whites, they are viewed as immigrants by black Americans. Many find it a struggle to maintain their cultural identity as they are whipsawed by age-old American attitudes about race.

Daniel James

See also: Alternative Faiths, Catholicism, Evangelical Christianity, Hinduism and Sikhism (Part II, Sec. 11); Miami, New York City (Part II, Sec. 12); Immigration to Canada, Immigration to Western Europe (Part II, Sec. 13).

BIBLIOGRAPHY

Bureau of the Census. *Statistical Abstract of the United States*. Washington, DC: Government Printing Office, 1999.

Gosine, Mahin. *Caribbean East Indians in America: Assimilation, Adaptation, and Group Experience*. New York: Windsor Press, 1990.

Immigration and Naturalization Service. "Illegal Alien Resident Population." Published June 22, 1998. www.ins.usdoj.gov/stats/illegalalien/index.html.

Kasinitz, Philip. *Caribbean New York: Black Immigrants and the Politics of Race*. Ithaca, NY: Cornell University Press, 1992.

Palmer, P. W. *Pilgrims from the Sun: West Indian Migration to America*. New York: Twayne, 1995.

HAITI AND FRENCH-SPEAKING CARIBBEAN

The practice of dividing the Caribbean into language groups can be somewhat misleading and imprecise. The French-speaking Caribbean, for example, is not a self-designated confederation of Caribbean nation-states. Rather, it is made up of distinct islands that vary not only in size, demographics, geography, and political organization but also in the specifics of their colonial history with France. In fact, while the official language of these islands is French, most of the residents speak Creole—the two are neither interchangeable nor mutually intelligible. Nevertheless, language and colonial legacies are significant common denominators particularly in their effect on emigration to the United States and the experiences of the immigrants once they arrive.

THE FRENCH IN THE CARIBBEAN

The French began to establish holdings in the Caribbean as early as 1635. Settlements in Martinique and Guadeloupe gave France a permanent interest in the region and served as a base for expansion to St. Barthélemy, St. Martin, and the western part of Hispaniola, which was ceded by the Spanish in the Treaty of Ryswick 1697. In its official status, Guadeloupe is still an archipelago of French possessions. This island group, located in the eastern part of the Caribbean Sea called the Lesser Antilles, includes Basse-Terre or Guadeloupe proper, Grande-Terre, Marie Galante, Désirade, Iles des Saintes, St. Barthélemy (St. Barts), and part of St. Martin. The Republic of Haiti, part of a group of larger islands in the northern Caribbean known as the Greater Antilles, is the former French colony of St. Domingue. However, Haiti has been an independent nation since 1804. And Martinique, like Guadeloupe, is currently an overseas French department whose residents are citizens of France and can vote in French elections.

Some accounts of the French-speaking Caribbean include French Guiana, located in northern South America between Brazil and Suriname, because its history and social structure are so similar to those of the islands in the Caribbean region. Yet, people from French Guiana identify themselves as South American rather than Caribbean—stressing that their country is not a Caribbean island. There are also the islands that make up Saint-Pierre and Miquelon, a self-governing territory of France in the Caribbean. At 1.5 times the size of Washington, D.C., and a population of less than ten thousand people, Saint-Pierre and Miquelon is seen more as an inviting vacation destination than a source of immigrants. For these reasons, only Guadeloupe, Haiti, and Martinique will be discussed here. Table 1 provides some basic population characteristics about these islands.

The Caribbean region, as a whole, contained 32.5 million people at the beginning of the 1990s. Of those, only 20 percent lived in the French-speaking countries. Relative to the United States, these islands are small and poor, with high unemployment rates and scarce resources. The overwhelming majority of the inhabitants of Guadeloupe, Haiti, and Martinique are nonwhite, 95 percent or more in all the islands. The racial demographics of the islands represent a mix of African- and European-origin people as a result of the legacy of slavery. In the 400 years of slavery in the West Indies, an estimated 4.6 million slaves were brought to the region—1.6 million to the French colonies alone.

Yet, there are unmistakable differences between them. Guadeloupe and Martinique are both significantly smaller than Haiti, with lower unemployment rates and much lower rates of out-migration. Haiti is further distinguished by its racial homogeneity. French planters began to import Asian Indians, Chinese, and Javanese to the Caribbean as indentured workers to augment labor shortages on the plantations after the emancipation of slavery in the nine-

This marketplace in the Little Haiti section of Miami is a replica of the famous Iron Market in the Haitian capital of Port-au-Prince. *(Jack Kurtz/Impact Visuals)*

teenth century. Accordingly, there is no minority community of East Indian, Javanese, or Chinese in Haiti, as in Guadeloupe and Martinique.

IMMIGRATION TRENDS

The geographic proximity of these small and economically limited islands to the United States, the world's richest nation, is usually sufficient as an explanation for the levels of immigration. Due to its political and economic power in the twentieth century, the United States is seen as a natural destination for Caribbean people seeking a better life. Indeed, workers from all the Caribbean islands use emigration as a means of improving their lives.

Nearly one-third of all newcomers to the United States are from the Caribbean region. Table 2 provides data from the Immigration and Naturalization Service (INS) on the number of legal immigrants from the Caribbean, in general, and from Guadeloupe, Haiti, and

Martinique, in particular. The limitations of the statistical data are clear. First, no exact figures are available for Guadeloupe and Martinique entrants prior to 1971. For most of the twentieth century, the INS lumped all Caribbean countries together (with the exception of Cuba) under the heading of West Indies. In addition, these figures are known to be gross undercounts because of the large undocumented population and high rates of interisland migration. Even the most conservative estimates conclude that at least half a million people have migrated from the French-speaking Caribbean to the United States since the turn of the century.

Although most arrived after World War II, in the early 1900s, the routes of U.S. commercial vessels trading between Caribbean and U.S. port cities established the patterns and destinations of the immigrants. Made up of both unmarried male workers and upper-class urban families, these early immigrants settled among black Americans in Harlem and are said to have assimilated into the mainstream of American society.

Table 1
Population Characteristics, French-Speaking Caribbean

Nation/Territory	Population (1999)	Area (Sq. Mi/Sq. Km)	Racial/Ethnic Composition	Net Migration Rate	Unemployment Rate
Guadeloupe	420,943	327/1,848	90% African/mixed, 5% white, 5% other	16 per 1,000	29.5% (1997)
Haiti	6,884,264	10,714/27,750	95% African, 5% mixed, white	3.26 per 1,000	60% (1996)
Martinique	411,539	436/1,128	90% African/mixed, 5% white, 5% other	−0.9 per 1,000	24% (1997)

Source: Central Intelligence Agency, *The World Factbook 1999.* Washington, DC: Brassey's, 1994.

Ira de Augustine Reid, a pioneer in the study of immigrant blacks, provides the best account of the lives of the prewar immigrants. He described the early French-speaking *émigrés* as "more bourgeois" than native-born blacks, "sharing the Frenchman's taste for good food and wine." Reid argues that few became naturalized citizens. Coming from self-governing colonies that elected representatives to the French parliament in Paris, they were proud to remain French citizens. They resented, even ridiculed, the "American way" of disenfranchising African Americans in the South.

According to Reid, of the 98,620 black immigrants residing in the United States in 1930, 73 percent (87,478) were born in the West Indies. By contrast, the 1990 census counted 1,455,294 foreign-born blacks living in the United States—the vast majority of them from the Caribbean. However, it was not until 1965, with the passage of the Hart-Celler Act, that migration from the Caribbean swelled. The 1965 immigration law repealed the national-origins quota system; removed discrimination based on race or ancestry; and altered the basis of selection to use criteria such as family ties and skills on a first-come, first-served basis. As a result, the Caribbean Basin has replaced Europe as the largest source of immigrants into the United States.

The majority of immigrants from the French-speaking Caribbean come to the United States from Haiti. Guadeloupe and Martinique have never been among the top sending countries from the Caribbean region. Given their relationship to France and the language barrier that exists for non-English speakers in the United States, the majority of emigrants head to their European mother county where they enjoy the full range of citizenship rights, or to the Francophone Canadian province of Quebec. Circumstances on the islands themselves—such as population density, the strength of the tourist industry, and the unemployment rate—are also important variables in explaining differences in immigration from these islands.

The various dependency statuses mentioned above are also important here since U.S. immigration policy has had a differential impact on emigration from Guadeloupe, Haiti, and Martinique. For example, Haiti was one of the few Caribbean countries that was unaffected by the McCarran-Walter Immigration and Nationality Act of 1952. This legislation exempted the independent nations of the Western Hemisphere

Table 2
Caribbean Immigrants Admitted by Country of Birth Since 1960

Country	1961–1970	1971–1980	1981–1990	1991–1997	Total
Guadeloupe	n/a	591	425	326	1,342
Haiti	37,537	58,705	140,163	129,420	365,825
Martinique	n/a	336	290	141	767
Total Caribbean	519,499	760,099	892,703	760,682	2,932,983

Source: Department of Justice, *Statistical Yearbook of the Immigration and Naturalization Service.* Washington, DC: Department of Justice, 1998.

from any limits on the number of immigrants entering the United States, while emigration from Guadeloupe and Martinique, or other colonies in the Caribbean, was limited to 100 per colony (as compared with 2,500 before the act).

THE CASE OF HAITI

Despite its enormous differences from the rest of the islands referred to as the French-speaking Caribbean, Haiti is significant in a number of ways. First, after Jamaica, Haiti is the largest source of Afro-Caribbean immigrants in this country. The cities of New York, Miami, and Boston each have more Haitians living in them than Cap Haitien, the second largest city in Haiti. The Haitian population is distributed, although unevenly, in almost all of the states, possessions, and territories of the United States. New York and Florida are by far the preferred locations; New Jersey, Massachusetts, and Washington, D.C., round out the largest Haitian settlements in the United States. More than half of this population consists of children born in the United States to Haitian parents.

Haitians have a long and rich history in this country. Though not significant in numbers, Haitian immigrants have been settling in the United States since the eighteenth century. Refugees from the Haitian revolution of 1791–1803 included colonists, free people of color, and slaves. They settled primarily in New Orleans, New York, Boston, Norfolk, Philadelphia, and Charleston. At this point the door was wide open for Haitians to emigrate to the United States; they did not need a passport or visa to make the journey. However, the numbers remained small because the United States was a young country and because of the prevalence of racial discrimination and segregation.

It wasn't until the American occupation of Haiti from 1915 to 1934 that the first sizable group of Haitian immigrants came to the United States. Haitian women were recruited by tourists to go to various American cities to work as live-in maids in white American homes. A number of Haitian students came to the United States to study, and a few Haitian professionals also came in search of work. Having migrated legally from Haiti's cities, their education and sophistication qualified them for a diversity of white-collar jobs. What separates this early trickle of Haitian immigrants from the massive waves who would come later is a sojourner mentality. Most had no intention of staying; their aim was to make enough money to enable them to return and live comfortably in Haiti.

However, the political situation on the island not only prevented their return migration, it stimulated a mass exodus.

The population of Haitian immigrants that has attracted the most scholarly attention came to the United States in three distinct waves. The first wave consisted of the educated, urban elite, and middle-class professionals of Haiti. They arrived after the hardening of the Duvalier regime in the late 1950s. François "Papa Doc" Duvalier became president of Haiti in 1957, and in 1963 he named himself president for life. Many opposition politicians and professionals left Haiti during that period, as did the families of earlier middle-class Haitians (which peaked between 1965 and 1971) and the less privileged urban working class. The second phase began with the transfer of power from Papa Doc to his son, Jean-Claude "Baby Doc" Duvalier. At this time, the United States was the final destination for itinerant laborers participating in the mass rural-to-urban migration in Haiti. These migrants were typically urban peasants fleeing a failing Haitian economy. The ousting of Baby Doc in 1986 triggered the third and current wave. This phase has been dominated by the massive influx of boat people—rural peasants and Haitians who previously worked in the Bahamas coming to the United States in leaky wooden sailboats. These boatloads of Haitians continually challenge U.S. government policies toward asylum-seekers and its distinction between economic immigrants and political refugees.

TRIPLE MINORITIES

It would be a mistake to ignore the many similarities in the experiences of French-speaking Caribbean immigrants in the United States. Notwithstanding the powerful differences, being in the subordinate position of foreign-born blacks in a white-dominated society has nurtured a common consciousness among them. They share, among other things, experiences of racial, political, and sociocultural alienation.

As foreigners, nonwhites, and non-English speakers, these immigrants are triple minorities. In many ways, the history of immigration from the French-speaking Caribbean undermines many of the generalizations made about West Indians or Caribbean blacks in the United States, which take as their reference point immigrants from the English-speaking Caribbean (i.e., Jamaica, Trinidad, etc.). Despite a few notable exceptions, the story of French-speaking immigrants in this country is largely untold, and as a result, the picture of American immigration remains incomplete.

Regina Ostine

See also: Political, Ethnic, Religious, and Gender Persecution (Part II, Sec. 1); Miami, New York City (Part II, Sec. 12); Immigration to Canada, Immigration to Western Europe (Part II, Sec. 13); President Bush and Courts on Return of Haitian Refugees, 1992, District Court on Admissions of Haitians, 1993 (Part IV, Sec. 1).

BIBLIOGRAPHY

Knight, Franklin W. *The Caribbean: The Genesis of a Fragmented Nationalism.* New York: Oxford University Press, 1990.

Laguerre, Michel. *Diasporic Citizenship: Haitian Americans in Transnational America.* New York: St. Martin's Press, 1998.

Pastor, Robert. "The Impact of US Immigration Policy on Caribbean Emigration: Does it Matter?" In *The Caribbean Exodus*, ed. Barry B. Levine. New York: Praeger, 1987.

Reid, Ira de Augustine. *The Negro Immigrant: His Background, Characteristics and Social Adjustment, 1899–1937.* New York: Columbia University Press, 1939.

Woldemikael, Tekle. *Becoming Black American: Haitians and American Institutions in Evanston, IL.* New York: AMS Press, 1989.

MEXICO

The historical and future trajectories of Mexico and the United States are intimately interwoven, especially in regard to international migration. Migration between Mexico and the United States represents the largest sustained current of migrant workers in the contemporary world. Between 1820 and 1996, some 5.5 million Mexicans were admitted into the United States as legal immigrants. During the Bracero Program years (1942–64), possibly 4 million came temporarily as contracted workers. Some scholars believe that an estimated 4 million Mexicans entered without documents between 1942 and 1992 as well. Under the stipulations of the 1986 Immigration Reform and Control Act (IRCA), about 2 million previously undocumented immigrants were legalized. Despite these measures, the Immigration and Naturalization Service (INS) estimated that undocumented Mexicans in the United States numbered 2.7 million in 1996, and is growing at a rate of 275,000 each year. However, understanding Mexican immigration to the United States goes beyond statistical trends and requires an awareness of the historical and structural factors that have shaped the modern reality of this phenomenon.

Some important events have served to shape the current situation of the two countries. The United States has initiated military action against Mexico three times. In 1848, following the Mexican-American War, the United States annexed nearly one-third of Mexico's national territory, and as a result an estimated seventy-five thousand to one hundred thousand Mexican citizens found themselves living as foreigners in their own land. Migratory flows over the past 150 years have been a product of political interventions, economic penetration, dependency, and curious immigration policies. Contrary to the conventional portrayal of Mexican immigration as an independent movement of foreigners across a well-defined border, the process had its origins in political and economic interests of the United States that had the effect of shaping Mexico so that dependable labor could be accessed, thus serving U.S. interests. Since the initiation of the North American Free Trade Agreement (NAFTA) in 1994, economic interdependence of the two countries has grown even more pronounced. Currently, the United States is Mexico's largest trading partner and a primary source of capital for Mexican investments, while Mexico is the second most important trading partner for the United States. Retracing the past 150 years of Mexican immigration history to the United States will allow a more thorough and organized explanation of some of the structural factors that have shaped Mexican immigration.

THE TREATY OF GUADALUPE HIDALGO

The Mexican-American War (1846–48) had a major impact on the expansion of the United States. On February 2, 1848, after nearly two months of negotiations between delegates from Mexico and the United States in the small town of Guadalupe Hidalgo, just outside Mexico City, the Treaty of Guadalupe Hidalgo was signed to end the war. The treaty recognized the previous annexation of Texas and ceded to the United States one-third of Mexico's northern territory which now comprises all or part of California, Arizona, Nevada, Utah, Wyoming, Colorado, Kansas, Oklahoma, Texas, and New Mexico. The United States paid $15 million to Mexico in exchange for the former northern provinces. Besides creating new political boundaries, the pact forever transformed the fate of the estimated seventy-five thousand to one hundred thousand Mexicans who remained in what had become the American Southwest. The memory of the war and the consequences of the treaty, which was largely dictated by the Americans, set the stage for what would become a critical intersection between the construction and

Many of Mexico's poorest and least educated immigrants end up doing the back-breaking labor of crop harvesting, like these workers in a Texas cauliflower field. *(Wim Van Cappellen/Impact Visuals)*

cultural perception of racial and social hierarchies in the United States and Mexico.

The terms of the Treaty of Guadalupe Hidalgo, and amendments made by the Querétaro Protocol in May 1848, had significant consequences for former Mexican citizens. Mexicans remaining in the U.S. territory were to have three basic citizenship alternatives according to Article IX of the treaty. They could relocate south of the new international border or retain their Mexican citizenship in the United States, with the status of permanent resident alien. Any former Mexican citizen who did not move south of the border or publicly announce his or her intention to become a permanent resident alien within one year of the effective date of the treaty was considered to have opted to become an American citizen. The Treaty of Guadalupe Hidalgo made Mexican Americans the first large group of non-Anglo-Saxons to have the full

privilege of U.S. citizenship, including the rights to appeal to intervention by the courts and private ownership of property, which clearly differentiated their situation from African Americans or other racial groups.

Many of the conflicts between the former Mexican citizens and U.S. interests arose over issues of land ownership. While Article IX granted displaced Mexicans access to American citizenship, Article X would have allowed for Mexicans to retain ownership of their lands granted prior to the annexation, but the U.S. Senate refused to ratify the measure. Secretary of State (and future president) James Buchanan attempted to soothe the concerns of Mexican diplomats by arguing that the rights to private property were assured under other articles in the treaty. Many Mexicans who elected to stay in the United States as American citizens appealed to the courts to uphold

Immigrants, like these young men from Mexico, have helped bring the world's most popular sport—soccer or *fútbol*—to the United States. *(Donna DeCesare/Impact Visuals)*

their property rights. While the courts frequently supported claims to land, numerous Mexicans lost their land and were ultimately displaced. Reasons for this displacement included unfair judicial processes, the lack of suitable counsel because of expensive legal fees, confusion about legitimate claims to land, the imposition of property taxes, and the unrelenting pressures of squatters on Mexican Americans to relinquish their holdings. Another factor that had an impact on new laws affecting Mexican ownership was the California gold rush.

The 1848 discovery of gold in California quickly reduced the resident Spanish-speaking population to a small minority as almost two hundred thousand immigrants streamed into California within just two years. Amid this influx of migrants were about five thousand South Americans and more than ten thousand well-trained miners from Sonora, Mexico, who introduced their methods to American prospectors. As gold fever spread and competition intensified, the California legislature passed the Foreign Miners Tax

in 1850 to discourage immigrant miners by charging a $20 per month tax for any person not native to the United States. By the early 1850s, Mexicans, Mexican Americans, and other Latin Americans were increasingly under violent threat from American Anglo-Saxon prospectors. Vagrancy laws were aimed at immigrants, and the Greaser Act of 1855 targeted people of mixed Spanish or Indian blood.

During the years following the Treaty of Guadalupe Hidalgo and the gold rush in California, Mexican immigrants continued a pattern that had been established in the eighteenth and nineteenth centuries when trade between New Spain and Mexico's northern frontier had provided economic incentive for migration. During this period, there were no official federal policies or quotas affecting Mexican immigrants, and immigration figures are notoriously inaccurate. However, an important trend of labor recruitment in Mexico emerged as railroad companies and agricultural employers began searching for workers as social, economic, and political conditions in both Mexico and

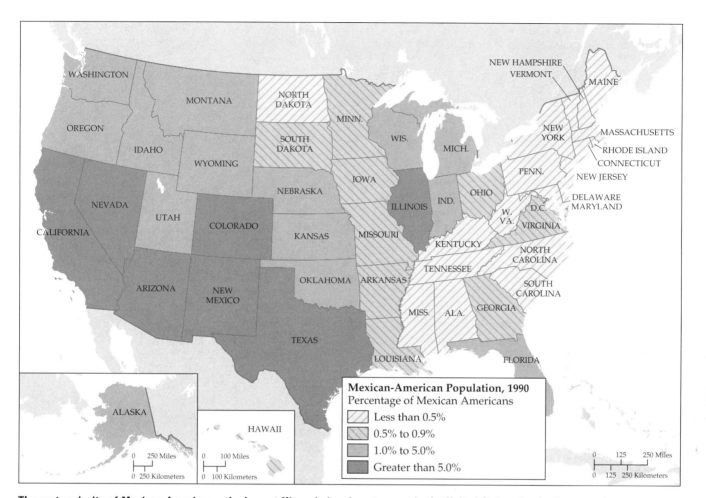

Mexican-American Population, 1990
Percentage of Mexican Americans

- Less than 0.5%
- 0.5% to 0.9%
- 1.0% to 5.0%
- Greater than 5.0%

The vast majority of Mexican Americans, the largest Hispanic immigrant group in the United States, live in those southwestern states that, until the Mexican-American War of the 1840s, were part of Mexico. *(CARTO-GRAPHICS)*

the United States set the stage for immigration. In the last half of the nineteenth century, growers and railroad developers sent paid recruiters into Mexico with offers of free rail travel and advances on wages as incentives for Mexican workers to come north. American-owned businesses in Mexico also became very effective in transporting Mexican workers across the border to work in American plants and facilities. Thus, Mexican immigration was not the result of wanton immigrants searching for economic livelihood, but instead had its direct origins in premeditated recruitment by U.S. business interests.

As U.S. companies continued to actively recruit foreign workers, some American workers complained about competition and lobbied to limit imported labor. As a result, the 1885 Contract Labor Law was created, which outlawed labor recruitment in foreign countries. However, due to a lack of enforcement, the law had little effect on labor recruitment practices in Mexico. Around 1900, authorities began enforcing

compliance of the law, initially in El Paso, Texas, and as a result brought an end to labor recruitment of Mexican workers in the interior of Mexico. Recruiters continued to work along the border, locating migrants and directing them to employers. Ordinarily, they made profits by charging the employer a fee but also by exacting inflated fares for transportation to job sites.

As mentioned above, relatively little is known about Mexican immigration during the last half of the nineteenth century since the Bureau of Immigration (the predecessor to the INS) primarily monitored immigration by sea, which likely included only the wealthiest Mexicans, and not those entering by land routes. Official statistics gathered by the Immigration Bureau from 1894 to 1900 show that only 970 Mexicans entered the United States. The Bureau of the Census noted an increase of 25,540 Mexican-born immigrants in the period from 1890 to 1900, increasing the Mexican-born population in the United States from about 78,000 to about 100,000. By the first decade of the twentieth century, the population in Mexico grew to 15.2 million, increasing by more than 50 percent from 1877 to 1910, while available land for settlement and farming decreased by nearly 30 percent. While population pressures and limited available land may have governed the decision of many Mexicans to emigrate, rising food prices and low wages influenced others. However, probably the most important factor affecting migratory patterns during this period was the dictatorship of Porfirio Díaz.

THE DÍAZ ERA (1876–1911)

After a failed attempt to be elected president in 1876, Porfirio Díaz (1830–1915) seized control of the country and harshly ruled Mexico for the next thirty-five years, until his overthrow during the Mexican Revolution. Under his reign, Mexico experienced an expanding land monopoly controlled by a few rich agriculturists, commonly referred to as *hacendados*. Aided by favorable government legislation and a sympathetic legal system perpetuated by Díaz, these primarily foreign and absentee owners acquired substantial tracts of Mexico's territory as well as control of *ejidos,* lands formerly farmed collectively. Over 5 million families lost their small farms or plots of land as a result of this accumulation of acreage. During the span of the dictatorship, wages for rural peasants never rose above 15 cents per day, while the costs of basic commodities and food increased significantly. The price of corn, the staple of the poor working class, rose by more than 50 percent from 1877 to 1903.

The dissonant land policies and harsh human rights abuses instituted and supported by Díaz propelled Mexican citizens toward the United States. They were also attracted by the rapidly diversifying and vigorous southwestern economy. For these reasons, the number of Mexican immigrants entering the United States climbed steadily after 1890. With the beginning of the Mexican Revolution in 1910, Mexican immigration to the United States increased steadily until their influx matched the earlier European migrations of the late 1800s. The increase was reflected in the official statistics of the INS as well as in reports from Mexico's *Secretaría de Relaciones Exteriores,* the Department of Foreign Relations. While the two governments varied in their reporting procedures, the assessments by both indicated at least half a million Mexicans entered the United States legally between 1899 and 1928.

The Mexican Revolution was a tumultuous period,

forcing many people to flee to the United States in search of asylum. After years of violent conflict, the newly emerging Mexican government produced the Constitution of 1917, the cornerstone of the revolution. The document included key provisions preserving many of the social goals of the revolution, although certainly these were imperfectly carried out in practice. The revolutionary government was concerned about emigration from their country, and the constitution included articles that attempted to reinforce the rights of Mexicans emigrants.

Despite changes made by the 1885 Contract Labor Law, in the early twentieth century, recruitment agents, sometimes called *contratistas* or *enganchistas,* continued to work for railroad companies, agricultural cooperatives, mining operations, and other employers of Mexican immigrants. Because there was a ready supply of Mexican immigrants at the border, recruiters rarely ventured into Mexico in search of labor. Now, their main job was not to locate workers, but to distribute them to employers who needed them. Troublesome accounts of maltreatment of Mexican immigrants by labor recruiters and American employers were not uncommon. One of the most well-documented situations was the essential enslavement of Mexican workers on salmon fishing boats in Alaska. Labor recruiters paid workers in advance for work contracts, usually written in English, requiring them to waive any rights to request better conditions, and forced them to work daily with unsatisfactory rations. The Mexican embassy appealed to the U.S. State Department, but conditions for Mexican workers did not improve.

In response to these abuses, the newly created Mexican constitution included legislation that attempted to protect its citizens working in the United States. Article 123 stipulated that Mexican emigrants were required to have a valid, signed contract indicating hours, wages, and conditions of employment prior to emigrating to the United States. Although the measure was meant to curb exploitation of Mexican workers by U.S. employers, the law was largely ignored by the United States, and of course the Mexican government had no jurisdiction in the United States to enforce the law.

During the same period, important legislation was introduced in the United States that had a major impact on Mexican immigration. Specifically, the Immigration Act of 1917 was passed as an attempt to limit foreign immigration by expanding the list of non-white foreigners who were barred from entry. The Immigration Act primarily affected Asian immigrants, the main target of the legislation, but it also imposed an $8 head tax and a literacy test for Mexican immigrants. However, enforcement of the law was generally lax against Mexicans, as the demand for Mexican labor grew dramatically with the beginning of World War I.

WORLD WAR I

Although Mexican immigration had steadily increased since the beginning of the Mexican Revolution, that rate grew exponentially with American entry into World War I in 1917. The involvement of the United States created a shortage of agricultural labor as low-wage American workers concentrated their work in war-related industries or entered military service. In the presence of the potential threat of the 1917 Immigration Act and growing concerns over the lack of available labor, growers were able to persuade the U.S. secretary of labor to exempt Mexican immigrants from the head tax and literacy restrictions of the act. Employers could thus recruit Mexican workers under a temporary-worker program to satisfy their need for sufficient labor to harvest crops. Between 1917 and 1921, drawn by agricultural labor shortages in the Southwest, more than seventy-two thousand Mexican workers participated in this program, along with significant numbers of undocumented immigrants also seeking employment. With the end of World War I in 1921 came the end of the temporary-worker program, as the secretary of labor rescinded his earlier decision and ordered the return of all temporary workers to Mexico.

Throughout the 1920s, Mexican immigrants continued to enter the United States, with large numbers traveling to California, whose Mexican-born population doubled during this period. Despite the end of the military phase of the revolution in 1921, violent upheavals and political discord continued in Mexico. The Cristero Revolt (1926–29), a rebellion against the anticlerical provisions of the 1917 constitution, resulted in an estimated ninety thousand Mexican deaths. More than two decades of political instability and civil war coupled with high inflation and low wages prompted many Mexicans to seek their fortunes just across the northern border. During the 1920s, Mexican workers established themselves as the backbone of large-scale, specialty-crop agriculture in California, and before long, they formed the largest single ethnic group of farm workers in the state.

Besides the push factors associated with the revolution, a number of related economic factors unfolded in the United States during the last quarter of

the nineteenth century and contributed to the swift growth of the ethnic Mexican population. Prior to 1900, the economy of the Southwest had been largely dependent on the surges and sudden drops of sporadic mining discoveries, real estate speculation, and bonanza farming. However, the early decades of the twentieth century witnessed the rapid expansion of railways and agricultural irrigation. These two developments laid the foundations for one of the most explosive periods of economic growth in American history.

In 1902, Congress passed the Newlands Federal Reclamation Act, which allowed millions of additional acres to be brought under cultivation through the use of modern irrigation techniques. By 1909, close to 14 million acres were under irrigation in the Southwest, compared to only slightly more than 1.5 million less than twenty years prior. The railroads, including the Southern Pacific, Topeka & Santa Fe, the Union Pacific, and the Atchison, linked the Southwest to important consumer markets in the East and consequently allowed western businesses to transport and sell their products in unparalleled quantities. The introduction of the refrigerated boxcar allowed agricultural foodstuffs to be shipped to eager eastern consumers. From 1880 to 1920, the amount of rail track laid had increased sixfold. By 1930, California produced one-third of the United States's fresh fruit, one-fourth of its vegetables, four-fifths of its wine, and nearly the entire American output of almonds, artichokes, figs, nectarines, olives, dates, and lemons.

After World War I, the unfulfilled need for labor began to decline as the United States returned to a peacetime economy. In the early 1920s, a severe but relatively short recession occurred, but the official response of the U.S. government set the stage for future relations with Mexican labor. Because of high unemployment, the United States adopted a strategy of repatriation to get rid of unwelcome competition for American jobs. Repatriation was popular politically among U.S. citizens and was an effective and cheap way for the government to regulate unemployment. Although the recession in the early 1920s was short lived and soon replaced by a robust economy, complemented by rapid growth and economic expansion, it was a portent of things to come, as the stock market crashed in October 1929.

THE GREAT DEPRESSION

The Great Depression of the 1930s was an important event in shaping the future of Mexican immigration to the United States. Thousands of Mexican workers were denied entry into the country, and more still were denied access to available jobs because of hiring preferences for U.S. citizens. Between 1929 and 1942, Mexican immigration to the United States was almost completely eliminated. The U.S. government forcefully repatriated many Mexicans, although state and local agencies often took the lead in ousting Mexican workers. Estimates of the actual number of Mexicans repatriated range from four hundred and fifteen thousand to as many as 2 million, but it seems reasonable to think that the actual number of repatriates was approximately 1 million. An unknown number of Mexicans (some have estimated the figure to be close to one hundred thousand) voluntarily participated in the exodus. As the depression worsened, repatriation, deportation, and voluntary or induced departures spread throughout the United States.

The beginning of the American involvement in World War II in 1941 initiated a new era for Mexican labor. Demand mushroomed, especially in the Southwest. The Bracero Accord, a contract-labor agreement allowing Mexicans to work in the United States on temporary visas, was established in 1942 between the governments of Mexico and the United States and lasted until December 1964. By the end of the program, some 4 million Mexicans had worked as braceros, or agricultural laborers, in the United States, and at its height in the late 1950s, more than four hundred thousand workers migrated each year. At the same time, undocumented immigration became a very serious concern for the U.S. government. In 1954, following U.S. involvement in the Korean War, the INS began a new deportation program known as Operation Wetback, during which over 1 million undocumented workers were detained. Despite the growing concern about undocumented workers and efforts to regulate the inflow, Bracero Program visas did not meet the labor demand and undocumented migration increased throughout the 1950s. From 1942 to 1964, an estimated 5 million Mexicans were apprehended in the United States for working without proper documentation.

The end of the Bracero Program in 1964 coincided with the Civil Rights Act of 1964 and with the amendments made to the Immigration and Nationality Act of 1952. These legislative modifications were influenced by the civil rights movement of the 1950s and 1960s and were implemented in an attempt to curb discrimination. The 1965 amendments made to the Immigration and Nationality Act were supposed to limit further immigration while simultaneously changing racist national-origin quotas. The result was the implementation of legislation that created an an-

nual quota of 120,000 from the Western Hemisphere. Besides abolishing the national-origin quotas, the amendments gave preferences to close relatives of American citizens and special status to individuals who possessed job skills in short supply in the United States. Ironically, the policy did not limit further immigration, as immigration from Latin America and Asia increased dramatically. By 1980, almost 80 percent of all immigrants to the United States were from these areas.

Although the Bracero Program ended in 1964, both legal and undocumented Mexican immigration continued to grow, resulting in a number of important changes. During the Bracero Program, the majority of immigrants were male. In the years following, however, women and families began to emigrate. Furthermore, Mexican workers began to settle in a broader geographic area, and Mexican labor diversified outside the traditional agricultural realm. One important area of change that occurred, resulting from increased enforcement and significant changes in the law, was the increasing number of undocumented Mexicans who were apprehended. The INS recorded about 1 million apprehensions in the 1960s, but the number increased sevenfold in the 1970s to over 7 million. Almost four hundred and fifty thousand Mexicans entered the country legally (not counting braceros, who numbered almost nine hundred thousand) from 1961 to 1970. During the following decade, about six hundred and forty thousand people legally entered from Mexico.

As a result of the 1965 amendments, many Mexicans rushed to legalize and many also sought documentation for their relatives. Within ten years, the number of Mexicans seeking legalization led Congress to impose annual limitations on the number of Mexicans who could be granted legal status. In 1976, the United States imposed quota restrictions of only 20,000 Mexican immigrants per year, excluding close family relatives. The changes had the similar effect of the earlier attempts to restrict immigration in 1965, resulting in an expansion of undocumented Mexican immigration.

THE IMMIGRATION REFORM AND CONTROL ACT OF 1986

The most dramatic change in U.S. legislation was the ratification of the Immigration Reform and Control Act (IRCA) of 1986, a measure that had been debated by the U.S. government for almost fifteen years. Proponents of IRCA sought to reduce illegal immigration by turning undocumented immigrants into legal immigrants by granting them amnesty and using employer sanctions to close the labor markets to additional illegal entrants. As a result, Mexican immigrants who could prove residency since January 1, 1982, were able to apply for amnesty. The law was also extended to agricultural workers who could prove they had worked for ninety days during specific periods. As a result of IRCA, the overall budget of the border patrol was increased by 50 percent, which in turn increased the number of border patrol agents. The Systematic Alien Verification for Entitlements (SAVE) computer system was also implemented to enable states and cities to verify the legal status of applicants for welfare benefits, although the use of the system has been limited. Finally, the IRCA legislation imposed harsh penalties on employers who knowingly hired illegal aliens, including fines ranging from $250 to $10,000 for each undocumented worker. Any employer found guilty of persistently hiring undocumented workers was subject to a maximum six months' prison sentence. The INS responded by initiating a campaign to educate employers about changes in the law and did not focus on aggressively enforcing sanctions. Several compounding factors complicated enforcement, including the enlargement of the fraudulent documents industry in the immigrant community and the tendency of employers to escape sanctions by appealing fines.

However, some caveats were created in the IRCA legislation. Specifically, agricultural employers considered producers of perishable agricultural crops, as determined by the secretary of agriculture, were exempt from the employer sanctions provisions of IRCA until December 1988. This exemption is known as the Special Agricultural Worker (SAW) program of IRCA and was designed to give agricultural employers time to adjust their recruiting and hiring practices. A second provision of the IRCA law was the creation of the H2A program, which allows agricultural employers to anticipate labor shortages and to apply for permission to bring nonresident workers into the United States for temporary or seasonal work.

In 1996, Congress passed the Illegal Immigration and Immigrant Responsibility Act (IIRIRA) in an attempt to further restrict legal immigration and to make it easier to deport immigrants attempting to enter without proper documentation. Under the provisions of the act, a person applying to sponsor a family member in an application for citizenship must prove an income at least 125 percent of the poverty threshold, the minimum annual income required to meet an acceptable standard of living in the United States. De-

portation regulations were also modified, increasing the reasons why an immigrant could be deported, such as situations in which the immigrant had been convicted of certain crimes. Rights to appeal were also limited by the act. Finally, the IIRIRA set restrictions on legal immigrants regarding Social Security benefits and other social welfare programs including food stamps.

THE OUTLOOK FOR MEXICAN IMMIGRATION

The number of Americans of Latin American descent grew from just below 7 million persons in 1960 to around 10.5 million in 1970, 14.6 million in 1980, and an estimated 20 million in 1990, a growth rate that far exceeds any other minority group. Citizens of Mexican descent, who historically have made up the majority of this population, have increased at a similar rate and currently represent about 60 percent of all Americans of Latin American descent. During the same thirty years, the number of Mexican Americans and Mexican immigrants residing in the United States increased from approximately 3.5 million in 1960 to 4.5 million in 1970, to 8.7 million in 1980 and an estimated 13.4 million in 1990.

In the face of such dramatic increases and the continued influx of thousands of undocumented Mexican immigrants each year, the U.S. border control policies already point in the direction of martial law. In the 1990s, several U.S.–Mexico border initiatives have been undertaken in an attempt to restrict immigration, including Operation Blockade (later named Operation Hold the Line) in El Paso, Texas, Operation Gatekeeper in San Diego, and Operation Safeguard in Arizona. Neither IRCA nor IIRIRA have been able to effectively regulate immigration flows from Mexico, and, in fact, the number of illegal crossings may have increased to levels present prior to 1986. The border patrol more than doubled in size in the 1980s, and under the Clinton administration, the INS has grown by 122 percent between 1993 and 1999, reaching a current staff level of 9,000 employees, including 7,000 border agents. The INS has requested $4.8 billion to fund its activities for the 2001 fiscal year—an 11 percent increase over its 2000 budget, and a 219 percent increase since 1993.

The INS has upgraded the quality of resident alien cards and reduced the number that it issues to aliens who are authorized to work in the United States. There have also been recent plans to expand and upgrade the SAVE computer tracking system that permits employers to verify the right to work of newly hired workers. The Clinton administration has advocated increasing fines against employers who knowingly employ undocumented workers and has argued to increase labor and immigration inspectors to check U.S. workplaces. Also, the INS has radically expanded its surveillance capabilities, including its Integrated Surveillance Intelligence System (ISIS), which assists in monitoring activity along the Mexico border.

Migration between Mexico and the United States is ultimately rooted in the structural economic transformation of both countries that occurred during the last 150 years. The conditions of the 1848 Treaty of Guadalupe Hidalgo, which allowed the annexation of nearly one-third of Mexico's national territory, set the stage for the cultural perception of racial and social hierarchies. The dictatorship of Porfirio Díaz created an abundant supply of Mexican labor in search of economic opportunities and refugees in search of asylum. A rapidly growing economy that emerged in the Southwest, particularly in mining and agriculture, created an urgent need for available inexpensive labor. The reliance on migrant labor was equally dependent on the ability to regulate its flow through repatriation and deportation in times of labor surplus. Technological developments, including the expansion of the railways and irrigation, led to the rise of industrial agriculture. The expansion of the national economy also spurred dependence on foreign labor. Several critical points in legislative history were affected by these structural factors, including the waivers allowed by the secretary of labor from 1917–21 and again during the Bracero years. Since 1964, several attempts to regulate and reduce Mexican immigration have in essence had the contrary effect. The IRCA legislation failed to reduce undocumented Mexicans living and working in the United States, as it appears that undocumented immigrants have reached pre-IRCA figures. Attempts to bolster enforcement and deny immigrants access have also been limited in their success. Mexican immigration must be understood and approached from a historical perspective, which takes into consideration the political, economic, and social factors that have interacted during the past 150 years.

Wayne J. Pitts

See also: Houston, Los Angeles, Mex-America, Rural America, San Francisco (Part II, Sec. 12); Treaty of Guadalupe Hidalgo, 1848, "Bracero Program" Act, 1949, California's Farm Labor Law, 1975 (Part IV, Sec. 1).

BIBLIOGRAPHY

Balderrama, Francisco, and Raymond Rodríguez. *Decade of Betrayal: Mexican Repatriation in the 1930s.* Albuquerque: University of New Mexico Press, 1995.

Cardoso, Lawrence. "Labor Emigration to the Southwest, 1916–1920." In *Mexican Workers in the United States,* ed. George C. Kiser and Martha Woody. Albuquerque: University of New Mexico Press, 1979.

———. *Mexican Emigration to the United States, 1897–1931: Socio-Economic Patterns.* Tucson: University of Arizona Press, 1980.

Cornelius, Wayne A. *Mexican Migration to the United States: Causes, Consequences, and U.S. Responses.* Migration and Development Monograph C/78–9. Cambridge, MA: MIT Center for International Studies, 1978.

———. "From Sojourners to Settlers: The Changing Profile of Mexican Labor Migration to California in the 1980s." In *US-Mexico Relations: Labor Market Interdependence,* ed. Jorge Bustamante, Raul Hinojosa, and Clark Reynolds, pp. 155–95. Stanford: Stanford University Press, 1992.

Griswold del Castillo, Richard. *The Treaty of Guadalupe Hidalgo: A Legacy of Conflict.* Norman: University of Oklahoma Press, 1990.

Guerin-Gonzales, Camille. *Mexican Workers and American Dreams: Immigration, Repatriation, and California Farm Labor, 1900–1939.* New Brunswick, NJ: Rutgers University Press, 1994.

Gutiérrez, David G. *Walls and Mirrors: Mexican Americans, Mexican Immigrants, and the Politics of Ethnicity.* Berkeley: University of California Press, 1995.

Hoffman, Abraham. *Unwanted Mexican Americans in the Great Depression: Repatriation Pressures 1929–39.* Tucson: University of Arizona Press, 1974.

Hondagneu-Sotelo, Pierrette. "The History of Mexican Undocumented Settlement in the United States." In *Challenging Fronteras: Structuring Latina and Latino Lives in the US,* ed. Mary Romero, Pierrette Hondagneu-Sotelo, and Vilma Ortiz. New York: Routledge Press, 1997.

Massey, Douglas, Joaquín Arango, Graeme Hugo, Ali Kouaouci, Adela Pellegrino, and J. Edward Taylor. *Worlds in Motion: Understanding International Migration at the End of the Millennium.* Oxford: Oxford University Press, 1998.

Passel, Jeffrey S. "Undocumented Immigrants: How Many?" *Proceedings of the Social Statistics Section,* Meetings of the American Statistical Association 1985, American Statistical Association, Washington, DC, 1985, pp. 65–72.

Piore, Michael J. *Birds of Passage: Migrant Labor in Industrial Societies.* New York: Cambridge University Press, 1979.

Oboler, Suzanne. "So Far from God, So Close to the United States: The Roots of Hispanic Homogenization." In *Challenging Fronteras: Structuring Latina and Latino Lives in the US,* ed. Mary Romero, Pierrette Hondagneu-Sotelo, and Vilma Ortiz. New York: Routledge Press, 1997.

Pitt, Leonard. *The Decline of the Californios: A Social History of the Spanish-Speaking Californians, 1846–1890.* Berkeley: University of California Press, 1966.

Reichert, Joshua, and Douglas Massey. "Guestworker Programs: Evidence from Europe and the United States and Some Implications for U.S. Policy." *Population Research and Policy Review,* 1 (1982): 1–17.

PUERTO RICO

Originally inhabited by Taino tribes, Puerto Rico was colonized by Spain after 1492, and received a steady stream of immigrants from Europe, Latin American, and the rest of the Caribbean. In 1898, as a result of the Spanish-American War, Puerto Rico became a territory of the United States. Puerto Ricans became U.S. citizens in 1917, but the island was ruled by U.S.-appointed governors until 1948, when the first elected governor, Luis Munoz Marin, took office. In 1952, a new constitution was adopted making Puerto Rico a Commonwealth of the United States under the authority of the United States Congress.

Over the last century, Puerto Rico has undergone a dramatic economic and social transformation that has included a significant out-migration of the population to the continental United States. Its economy, which was based primarily on agriculture and small commerce, became increasingly integrated with that of the United States and Puerto Rico developed over decades into a haven for multinational manufacturing and high-technology corporations, particularly in the pharmaceutical, electronic, chemical, commerce, and tourism industries. Puerto Rico's economic development involved the interplay of several factors, mainly investments of U.S. capital, the creation of the Commonwealth, a political arrangement that secured such investments, and the continued out-migration of large numbers of workers and their families to the continental United States.

PUERTO RICAN MIGRATION TO THE UNITED STATES

Puerto Rican migration to the United States had its origins in labor recruitment drives for work in agricultural fields throughout the Northeast, Southwest, and Hawaii. The migration flows accelerated significantly over time, and since the 1940s the movement of population between Puerto Rico and the United States—especially the Northeast—has been immense. In 1960, for example, the Puerto Rican population residing on the island numbered 2.3 million persons. The population sixteen years of age and older residing on the U.S. mainland was approximately 1.6 million of which 90,000 had migrated after 1955 and 364,000 prior to that date (the remainder are Puerto Ricans born in the U.S. mainland). By 1980, there were about 3.1 million Puerto Ricans on the island and 2.5 million on the mainland. Of the latter, close to 100,000 had migrated after 1975, while 732,000 were island-born persons who had immigrated earlier. The figures from the 1990 census indicate that there were 3.5 million people on the island and 2.7 million Puerto Ricans on the mainland. By 1998, the Puerto Rico population was estimated to be 3.8 million, and the number of Puerto Ricans in the United States was estimated to be 3.1 million persons. The flows that constitute Puerto Rico's migration history have varied over time, often increasing and decreasing under particular economic conditions, and are linked to differences in unemployment rates, wage rates, and incomes between the northeastern United States and the island.

Table 1 includes the decennial census estimates for the total population of Puerto Rico (column A), the percent of the island population born outside of Puerto Rico (column B), the total number of Puerto Ricans living in the United States (column C), the percent of Puerto Ricans living in the United States that were born on the island (column D), and the proportion of Puerto Ricans in the United States (column E). The figures indicate that the rate of increase for the Puerto Rican population in the United States is higher than the rate of increase on the island. The population of Puerto Rico increased by approximately 300,000 persons between 1980 and 1990, and the percentage of the population born outside of Puerto Rico increased from 6.7 percent to 10.3 percent. The Puerto Rican population living in the fifty states increased by more than 700,000 persons over the decade to 2,727,754 by 1990, but the percentage born on the island remained at 41.6 percent. This suggests that the

Table 1
Puerto Rican Population: Puerto Rico and the Mainland United States

Year	(A) Population in Puerto Rico	(B) Percentage of Puerto Rican population born outside Puerto Rico	(C) Puerto Ricans living in the U.S.	(D) Percentage of U.S. residents born on the island	(E) Proportion of Puerto Ricans in the U.S. (C)/(A)
1960	2,350,000	n/a	892,513	n/a	.379
1970	2,712,000	n/a	1,429,396	48.3	.527
1980	3,197,000	6.7	2,013,945	41.4	.629
1990	3,522,000	10.3	2,727,754	41.6	.774

Source: U.S. Census Bureau, Decennial Census, 1960, 1970, 1980, and 1990.

number of births to Puerto Ricans on the mainland was similar to the number of island-born immigrants during the decade. This was not the case in the previous decade between 1970 and 1980 in which a significant share of the increase in the Puerto Rican population on the mainland was due to mainland births (natural growth) rather than immigration from the island. Increased immigration from the island during the 1980s, and the relatively higher birth rates for the Puerto Rican population on the mainland, have resulted in an increase in the proportion of the Puerto Rican population residing on the mainland from .38 in 1960 to .77 by 1990. If the current trends continue, over the next twenty years there will be more Puerto Ricans residing on the mainland than on the island.

PUERTO RICAN MIGRATION AND ECONOMIC CONDITIONS IN PUERTO RICO

In Puerto Rico, the period from 1959 to 1974 was characterized by rapid growth in the GNP at a rate of 6.5 percent per year. Income per capita also increased at a steady 4.9 percent per year. More important, however, were the increases in real GDP by 7.2 percent per year and its per capita value at the rate of 5.6 percent. The gap between the growth rates of GNP and GDP point to the fact that the Puerto Rican economy was generating a substantial amount of goods and services whose gains were remitted to the United States as profits and interest to the island's creditors. Before 1974, the Puerto Rican economy generated a substantial number of jobs due to the predominance of labor-intensive industries producing apparel, leather and leather products, machinery, and other products. New jobs in combination with high out-

migration rates and declining fertility, led to small reductions in unemployment, and to increases in labor-force participation. In addition, the construction boom that turned Puerto Rico into a mostly urban country also employed a substantial number of people. Those who did not find jobs, or who wanted to seek better opportunities, considered the alternative of migrating to the U.S. mainland.

Puerto Rico's economic expansion did not last and the structural nature of the economic crisis began to manifest itself in the early 1970s, with the sharp decrease in domestic investment and its replacement by federal transfers and increased public debt, which subsidized the consumption of mostly imported products and did not stimulate local production. Additional external developments also affected the Puerto Rican economy, particularly the U.S. recession and the increases in the price of oil. Management inconsistencies also created additional problems for Puerto Rico, and there were concrete limitations imposed by U.S. lenders on further use of public debt to finance growth.

By 1974, the industrial composition of the island's economy had shifted toward more capital-intensive enterprises that involved manufactured chemicals, heavy equipment, precision instruments, and rubber, plastic, petrochemical, and metal products. Most of these industries, aside from the fact that they are major pollutants, were heavily automated and hence did not contribute substantially to generate new employment. The island's economic crisis had its biggest effect on employment (and unemployment) rather than on incomes or wages. As sociologists Ricardo Campos and Frank Bonilla point out, at this juncture Puerto Rico had two key structural problems: on the one hand, what was once the goal of economic development, mainly parity with the United States in terms of income and wages, began to be seen as one of the main obstacles to the creation of more jobs in the is-

A Puerto Rican man sells ices and oranges beneath the Brooklyn-Queens Expressway in New York City. *(Catherine Smith/Impact Visuals)*

land; while, on the other hand, federal and local government officials were creating policies that resulted in transfer structures that maintained a level of income and wages in the midst of increasing unemployment and fomented the consumption of imports rather than local production.

The economic structure that characterized Puerto Rico in the late 1970s and early 1980s is one in which a number of high-technology corporations obtained substantial tax-exempt profits by employing a relatively constant number of individuals. But because bottom-end labor costs in Puerto Rico are set by federal legislation, wages do not decline below a certain point with increased unemployment. Incomes in Puerto Rico, rather than growing, were kept from declining by influxes of federal transfer payments. The transfer structure, which contributed to 25 percent of personal consumption expenditures in 1978, allowed the economy to maintain constant wage rates and per capita incomes amid rapidly soaring unemployment.

Social indicators suggest that there have been some improvements over the last few decades but there are still significant gaps in socioeconomic indicators between Puerto Rico and the United States. In terms of educational attainment, the proportion of the population age twenty-five years and over with less than a ninth grade education decreased steadily from 62 percent in 1970, to 47.8 percent in 1980, to 35.4 percent by 1990. The proportion with a high school diploma was 27 percent in 1970, 39.5 percent in 1980, and 49.7 percent in 1990, while the proportion with a bachelor's degree or higher was 6.0 percent in 1970, 9.4 percent in 1980, and 14.3 percent in 1990. These figures suggest that during the last quarter century, educational attainment in Puerto Rico has continued to increase, but there are still significant proportions of the population with relatively low levels of education.

The main issue facing the Puerto Rican economy is the relatively high structural unemployment. Labor-force participation and unemployment statistics from the census show some stability in labor-force participation rates for males sixteen and over (58.1 percent in 1970, 54.1 percent in 1980, and 58.1 percent in 1990) and an increase for females (24.5 percent in 1970, 29 percent in 1980, and 37.1 percent in 1990). These figures suggest that most of the increase in labor-force participation on the island between 1970 and 1990 was due to the increasing involvement of women in the formal labor market. In addition, the figures sug-

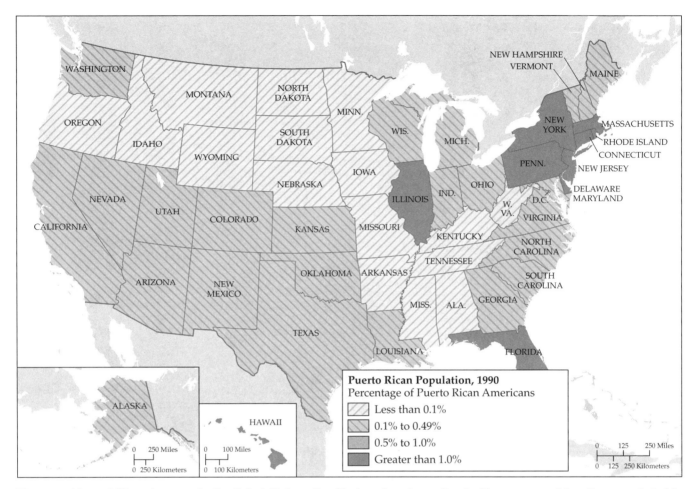

Puerto Rican Population, 1990
Percentage of Puerto Rican Americans
- Less than 0.1%
- 0.1% to 0.49%
- 0.5% to 1.0%
- Greater than 1.0%

The second-largest Hispanic group in the United States, after Mexican Americans, Puerto Ricans are most heavily concentrated in New York, New Jersey, and Florida. *(CARTO-GRAPHICS)*

gest that a large portion of the adult population (41 percent of males and 62 percent of women) were not working in the formal labor market. Problems of entry into stable jobs in Puerto Rico are acute. Unemployment rates increased significantly over the last two decades for both males (4.9 percent in 1970, 14.5 percent in 1980, and 18.9 percent in 1990) and females (7.1 percent in 1970, 16.5 percent in 1980, and 22.5 percent in 1990). The unemployment rate varies considerably by education from a high of 25 percent for those without a high school degree to a low of 9 percent for those with some college. The unemployment rate for high school graduates was at the same level as the total unemployment rate, around 16 percent. Not all persons over sixteen years of age are expected to work at all times, but the figures indicate that less than half of the adult population was working and that a significant number of those looking for work in the formal labor market (200,000 persons) could not find employment. This suggests that the island is far from generating the positions necessary to sustain its

population and to absorb new entrants into its labor force.

The effects of a weak labor market in Puerto Rico are further evidenced by the stagnation of family incomes between 1969 and 1989. According to census figures, household incomes in constant 1989 dollars were $8,604 in 1969, $8,962 in 1979, and $8,895 in 1989. This is a very small change in real terms over the decade. Levels of family poverty in Puerto Rico decreased from 64.3 percent in 1969 to 62 percent in 1979 to 55.3 percent by 1989. This is a decline of nine percentage points in two decades. More than half of the families in Puerto Rico fall below the federal poverty level, and this figure is much higher than the 25 percent rate for Hispanics and 31 percent for Puerto Ricans, or the 9 percent rate for all families living in the United States. The prevalence of high unemployment and poverty continue to create the conditions that lead to sustained migration between Puerto Rico and the United States.

CONSEQUENCES: PUERTO RICANS IN THE CONTINENTAL UNITED STATES

For Puerto Rican migrants from the working classes, life in the United States turned out to be full of opportunities as well as challenging, and many were faced with discrimination and exclusion in many communities, schools, and labor markets. Scholar Clara Rodriguez, for example, shows that several structural factors affected the economic position of Puerto Ricans. She argues that "automation, sectoral decline, blue-collar structural unemployment, racial and ethnic prejudice, restrictive union policies, inadequate educational opportunities, and the restriction of Puerto Ricans from government employment" combined to make living conditions difficult in New York and the Northeast, where most Puerto Ricans in the mainland settled. Rodriguez shows how a number of key changes in the macroeconomic structure, such as declines in manufacturing employment, technological changes in the forces of production, changes in the location of firms, and blue-collar structural unemployment, had a particular impact on the Puerto Rican labor force. She argues that the effects of these macroeconomic changes were exacerbated by persisting racial and ethnic discrimination, restrictive union practices, the adverse role of state employment, and the structure of welfare policies and programs to disproportionately affect Puerto Ricans. In addition, Rodriguez argues that New York's fiscal crisis and the evolving (more global) structure of the economy have combined with the entry of new immigrant groups, the evolution of the informal sectors of the economy, and the increasing importance of credentialism and networks for employment to increased levels of polarization in the economy and in the social structure. The middle segments of the economy were eroded through a combination of upgrading in some sectors (which implies the need for more credentials and contacts to obtain employment) and the downgrading and informalization of other sectors of the labor market. The net result of these changes is that working-class Puerto Ricans are increasingly competing in segments of the labor market in which wages have been stagnant, or declining, in which opportunities for mobility are limited, and in which working conditions are continually downgraded.

Rodriguez assigns central importance to the increasing fragmentation and segmentation of the labor market in explaining patterns of Puerto Rican exclusion from the labor force. But she also focuses attention on housing and community change, and on educational dynamics, as contributing to the reproduction of poverty and inequality. The negative effects of job losses, precipitated by broad changes in New York City's economic structure, are exacerbated by community decay (burned buildings, lack of maintenance, reductions in city services), planned shrinkage (policies that directly or indirectly induced the poor to leave New York City), and political neglect (through centralized and corrupt political party machines) combine to prevent the redevelopment of the areas where Puerto Ricans are concentrated.

RETURN MIGRATION TO PUERTO RICO

A main feature of Puerto Rican migration is that it has not been unidirectional. Beginning in the late 1950s, a significant counterstream of return migrants began to resettle in Puerto Rico. These individuals were primarily repelled by economic restructuring and increased automation in northeastern central cities, where most Puerto Ricans had moved, and were also attracted by the continual growth in the island's economy and the opportunities it offered for bilingual workers with experience in manufacturing and other growing service sectors. According to the study by sociologist Jose Hernandez Alvarez, there were close to 35,000 return migrants in Puerto Rico in 1960.

An estimated 16 percent of Puerto Rico's population in 1970 were either Puerto Rico-born recent migrants (13.8 percent), U.S.-born prior migrants (1.8 percent) or U.S.-born recent migrants (.5 percent). Close to 85 percent of all migrants to Puerto Rico were born on the island and presumably had networks of family and friends there. In 1980, a significant proportion of Puerto Rico's population were either Puerto Rico-born recent migrants (8.1 percent) or Puerto Rico-born prior migrants (6.3 percent). The number of U.S.-born migrants increased, reflecting the aging of the offspring of Puerto Ricans who moved to the United States after the 1940s. U.S.-born recent migrants constituted .9 percent of the island's population, while U.S.-born prior migrants, that is, those who moved before 1974, were 3.8 percent of the male population age sixteen to sixty-four years. Two things are interesting to note. First, substantively, by 1980, U.S.-born migrants to Puerto Rico constituted almost one-fifth of the migrant group and most are sons or other relatives, rather than household heads. Second, the inclusion in 1970 of a continuous-period measure rather than a question on residence five years ago, allowed researchers to identify 65.7 percent of Puerto

Rico-born return migrants between 1965 and 1970. In the 1980 census, the question on residence was extended to a ten-year period, which allowed researchers to identify the Puerto Rico-born prior category (those who migrated to the mainland before 1970). Together, the prior category accounted for 32.9 percent of the return migrants, and 54.4 percent of Puerto Rico-born recent (the latter being 23.1 percent of the total return migrants). Essentially, 56 percent of the total of return migrants, or 10 percent of the population, would have been classified as nonmigrants without the inclusion of a special question on migration on the Puerto Rico census schedules. This finding yields strong evidence that the standard residence questions used in the U.S. census for the study of mobility underestimates Puerto Rican migration in particular, and presumably other segments of the population that are equally mobile.

In the decade of the 1970s, it is estimated that 286,000 persons returned to Puerto Rico while census data for the 1980s indicates that 232,000 persons had lived in the United States for six months or more and returned to Puerto Rico at some point during the 1980s. This means that of the total population of Puerto Rico in 1990, close to 11 percent were island-born persons who returned during the decade, 6.3 percent were U.S. born of Puerto Rican parents, .6 percent were U.S. born of non-Puerto Rican parents, and 3.4 percent were foreign born. Most return migrants came from New York (43.8 percent), followed by New Jersey (11.3 percent), Illinois (6.0 percent), Pennsylvania (5.9 percent), Florida (5.8 percent), Massachusetts (4.5 percent), Connecticut (3.5 percent), and a few from Texas and Ohio.

Essentially, on the mainland side of the migration circuit, Puerto Ricans face prejudice and other obstacles to their educational, economic, and social mobility. Under these conditions, the island becomes an alternative that offers the possibility of a better living. Sociologist Barry Levine has summarized succinctly some of the reasons why Puerto Ricans returned to the island: "Life in New York was unpleasant. The problems of the city were overwhelming: drugs, discrimination, language, the persistent hassle of everyday life—all made it difficult for one to create a meaningful life. For some Puerto Ricans it [return migration] meant that they could rejoin family and friends; for others, that they could bring up their children properly; for still others, that they could satisfactorily deal with health problems. For many, return meant that they could start to think in terms of building a better life in their own country." High levels of return migration are seen as a potential problem for Puerto Rico's fragile economy and labor market.

Scholars Francisco Rivera-Batiz and Carlos Santiago, for example, argued that if deprived of the migration "escape valve," Puerto Rico will continue to face serious economic problems in absorbing new entrants into the labor force.

RECENT TRENDS IN PUERTO RICAN MIGRATION

Many of the same urban problems that were impacting Puerto Ricans in the United States were also present on the island after the economic crisis of the 1970s, and large-scale out-migration to the United States again became an option for many who were limited on the island and wanted to pursue other educational and employment options in the United States. Between 1982 and 1988, Puerto Rico experienced a renewal of the high migratory flows that characterized previous periods. According to a study conducted by Edwin Melendez, net out-migration between 1980 and 1988 was about 150,000 for persons sixteen years of age and older. According to Melendez's estimates, 285,787 Puerto Ricans sixteen years of age or older left the island between 1982 and 1998, and approximately 134,587 returned to Puerto Rico, for a net out-migration balance of 151,200 persons. Considering that only Puerto Ricans sixteen years of age and older are included in the estimates, the 25,200 average net outflow per fiscal year represents a substantial population movement. It is clear from these levels that migration continues to be a significant experience for many Puerto Rican families.

In a recent paper reviewing the voluminous literature on migration to and from Puerto Rico, Professor Jorge Duany of the University of Puerto Rico argues that "the bibliography on the return migration [of Puerto Ricans] has serious theoretical and methodological limitations." According to Professor Duany there are four main problems with recent studies of return migration to Puerto Rico. The first problem is that "the definition of a migrant is most problematic. . . . It is difficult to distinguish return migrants from permanent residents in the United States and temporary visitors to Puerto Rico, including tourists, as well as from those constantly circulating between the two countries." The second limitation of the literature on return migration is that "the socioeconomic profile of Puerto Ricans returning to the island is not clear, and much less is their impact on the local job market at differing historical junctures." The third limitation is that the process of integration of returnees is understudied. Professor Duany argues that "It is imperative to study more deeply the problems of sociocultural adaptation for Nuyoricans [sic] and to recommend practical solutions." The fourth problem that Professor Duany sees in the literature is that "most studies lose sight of the underlying unity of migration processes in Puerto Rico, conceptualizing Puerto Ricans' return as a discrete and definitive movement."

Puerto Rican migration is complex, varied, and involves many sectors of the society and social classes. Recent studies of Puerto Rican migration suggest a number of trends. First, Puerto Rican migration is becoming geographically more dispersed throughout the United States. New York is an important destination, but other areas in New Jersey, Connecticut, Pennsylvania, Massachusetts, Florida, and California have also become important destinations. Also, increasing numbers of Puerto Ricans have been settling in small towns throughout the Northeast and have become less concentrated in the central cities. Second, migration affects an increasing cross-section of Puerto Rico's population—from agricultural laborers and displaced workers to individuals that move to better job offers, to students moving to attend college or pursue advanced training, to individuals moving to reunite with relatives, to retirees. There are some general trends in the population, but broad averages conceal the richness in the diversity and types of Puerto Rican migrants. Third, there is no evidence of a massive exodus of professionals out of Puerto Rico. In fact, there is some evidence that Puerto Rico has problems absorbing a significant proportion of its college-educated population. Fourth, high levels of poverty are associated with the incidence of migration, but it cannot be said that Puerto Rican poverty is the result of high migration levels. Puerto Ricans do not have high poverty rates because they migrate in large numbers but, rather, they migrate because of high poverty rates. Fifth, in recent years the size of the flows and the levels of migration seem to have increased. These changes are intimately associated with the location of Puerto Ricans in the changing occupational/industrial structure and the relatively high unemployment levels that persistently affect Puerto Ricans in the United States and in Puerto Rico.

Puerto Ricans have relatively high poverty rates because (as a colonial population) they have been subjected to a systematic and sustained process of expropriation and proletarization perpetuated by detrimental material and institutional conditions in schools, by persisting discrimination in the labor market, and by a deterioration of the social and material infrastructure in many communities. Fiscal and social policies at the federal, state, and local level have a direct role

on perpetuating and reproducing Puerto Rican inequality and poverty. Puerto Ricans are increasingly forced to operate in more complex social, economic, and political spaces that they do not control and that are not organized to promote their individual and collective development. The result is that a significant proportion of the population continues to be trapped at the low end of the socioeconomic structure and, in the absence of intervening social investments, will continue to experience high levels of poverty, inequality, displacement, and migration.

The sustained penetration of Puerto Rico's economy by U.S. interests continues to force many Puerto Ricans to sell their labor power in increasingly unfavorable conditions, both on the island and on the mainland. This is evidenced by the fact that during the 1980s, poverty rates in Puerto Rico were around 55 percent, while the rate for Puerto Ricans on the mainland was close to 35 percent. Migration has been and continues to be an important survival strategy for many who live in difficult economic conditions, and has become an integral part of a complex sociohistorical process. The migration experience shows how Puerto Ricans are willing to make sacrifices and relocate in geographically distant and culturally distinct areas of the United States in an attempt to secure employment and a better living for their families and children. When unsuccessful in securing employment in an increasingly competitive and discriminating U.S. labor market, or when they are resistant to the process of "ghettoization" in cities such as New York, Hartford, Connecticut, Newark, NJ, Boston, or Chicago, some return to the island where the impact of unemployment is higher but somewhat cushioned by the presence of family, friends, and other support networks. High levels of Puerto Rican migration are the result of a fragile economy on the island and of mechanisms of exclusion and discrimination against Puerto Ricans on the mainland. Many Puerto Ricans are part of a mobile population that responds to relative changes in conditions and opportunities on the island and the mainland. At any point in time, there are multiple flows back and forth, and those with better education or with some market experience are more likely to find employment in either of the locations and remain there for some time. But for an increasingly larger segment of the working-class population, their lives, horizons, and experiences are shaped by an extended network of family, kin, and friends in the United States and in Puerto Rico that is often used to find employment, opportunities, and resources in both places.

Héctor R. Cordero-Guzmán

See also: Immigrant Politics III: The Home Country (Part II, Sec. 6); Miami, New Jersey and Suburban America, New York City (Part II, Sec. 12); Puerto Rico Citizenship Act, 1917 (Part IV, Sec. 1).

BIBLIOGRAPHY

Bonilla, Frank, and Ricardo Campos. "A Wealth of Poor: Puerto Ricans in the New Economic Order." *Daedalus* (Spring 1981): 133–176.

Cordero-Guzmán, Hector R. "The Socio-Demographic Characteristics of Return Migrants to Puerto Rico and their Participation in the Labor Market: 1965–1980." M.A. thesis, Department of Sociology, University of Chicago, 1989.

Department of City Planning. *Puerto Rican New Yorkers in the 1990s.* New York: Author, 1994.

Duany, Jorge. "Common Threads or Disparate Agendas? Recent Research on Migration from and to Puerto Rico." *Centro* 7:1 (1995): 67–77.

Hernandez-Alvarez, Jose. *Return Migration to Puerto Rico.* Population Monograph Series no. 1. Berkeley, CA: University of California, 1967.

History and Migration Task Force, Center for Puerto Rican Studies. *Labor Migration Under Capitalism: The Puerto Rican Experience.* New York: Monthly Review Press, 1979.

Levine, Barry B., ed. *The Caribbean Exodus.* New York: Praeger, 1987.

Melendez, Edwin. *Los que se van y los que regresan: Puerto Rican Migration to and from the United States, 1982–1988.* New York: Center for Puerto Rican Studies, 1993.

———, and Clara Rodriguez. "Puerto Rican Poverty and Labor Markets: An Introduction." *Hispanic Journal of Behavioral Science* 14:1 (1992): 4–16.

Ortiz, Vilma. "Changes in the Characteristics of Puerto Rican Migrants from 1955 to 1980." *International Migration Review* 20 (1986): 612–28.

Rivera-Batiz, Francisco, and Carlos Santiago. *Puerto Ricans in the United States: A Changing Reality.* Washington, DC: National Puerto Rican Coalition, 1994.

———. *Island Paradox: Puerto Rico in the 1990s.* New York: Russell Sage Foundation, 1996.

Rodriguez, Clara. *Puerto Ricans: Born in the USA.* Boston: Unwin Hyman, 1989.

Torres, Andres. *Between the Melting Pot and the Mosaic: African Americans and Puerto Ricans in the New York Political Economy.* Philadelphia: Temple University Press, 1995.

Weisskoff, Richard. *Factories and Food Stamps: The Puerto Rico Model of Development.* Baltimore, MD: Johns Hopkins University Press, 1985.

ASIA, THE PACIFIC, AND THE MIDDLE EAST

INTRODUCTION

Section 3 of Part III of the *Encyclopedia of American Immigration* is devoted to immigration and immigrants from Asia and the Pacific. The section includes ten entries, some focusing on key countries and others on regions: China, Iran, Japan, Korea, the Middle East, Oceania, the Philippines, South Asia, Southeast Asia, and Taiwan and Hong Kong.

The entry on China by Lawrence K. Hong examines the history and contemporary situation of the 1.65 million persons of Chinese ancestry living in the United States today. In his entry, Hong briefly goes into the history of legislation affecting Chinese immigrants before examining the development of various Chinatowns around the United States and the move of many Chinese immigrants and their descendants from urban enclaves to the suburbs. He also looks at the shift from a predominantly male immigrant culture to one where women predominate, and he offers an examination of the immigrant Chinese family. In other sections of his entry, Hong looks at marriage among Chinese immigrants and between Chinese immigrants and other ethnic groups. Finally, the author provides a portrait of Chinese immigrant educational and professional attainment, as well as religious life among immigrant and American-born Chinese.

In his entry on Iran, Mehdi Bozorgmehr looks into the reasons Iranians have immigrated to the United States over the years as well as the demographic trends in that immigration picture. In addition, there are sections in the entry on Iranian immigrant incorporation into the American economy and American society. The entry on Japan by Nobuko Adachi begins with a brief history of Japanese immigration before World War II, then turns to the phenomenon of the Japanese war brides of the World War II and post–World War II eras. In addition, Adachi looks at long-term economic and social trends among Japanese Americans that explain why that community has been so singularly successful.

In the entry on Korea, Yoonies Park begins with a brief history of Korean immigration to the United States prior to World War II, before examining what she calls the "interim" immigrant period from 1945 to 1964. A third section of the entry covers the period since 1965. In addition, Park discusses the whys and hows of Korean immigrant entrepreneurialism, as well as the consequences of immigration for Korean families and social customs.

Faedah Totah's entry on the Middle East covers all the Arab countries of the region (excluding North Africa, which is covered in its own entry in Part III, Section 1), as well as Israel and non-Arab and non-Muslim minorities in the region such as Armenians, Assyrians, and Kurds. He begins with a brief discussion of immigration from the pre–World War I Ottoman Empire before moving on to an examination of contemporary immigration from the Middle East. In this latter discussion, Totah looks at the causes, demographics, and social effects of immigration.

In her entry on Oceania, Grace Ebron looks at immigrants coming from the very different parts of the Pacific basin, including those from Australia and New Zealand, Melanesia, Micronesia, and Polynesia. After presenting a history of immigration from the region, she examines recent demographic trends as well as settlement patterns and acculturation among immigrants from Oceania. The entry on the Philippines by Carl Bankston III begins with a discussion of the history of immigration from the Philippines, especially in the years 1900 to 1946 when it was controlled by the United States. The last half of the entry is devoted to Filipino immigrants and immigration in the post-1965 immigration reform era.

Ann Morning's entry on South Asia covers the story of immigrants and immigration from India, Pakistan, Afghanistan, and Bangladesh. Much of the entry focuses on the three main countries of the subcontinent—India, Pakistan, and Bangladesh—and offers a history of immigration from the region under the

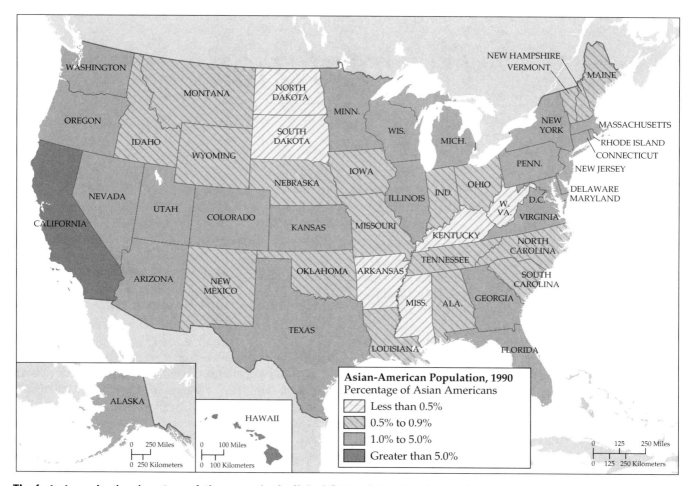

Asian-American Population, 1990
Percentage of Asian Americans
- Less than 0.5%
- 0.5% to 0.9%
- 1.0% to 5.0%
- Greater than 5.0%

The fastest-growing immigrant population group in the United States, Asian Americans, who once usually settled on the West Coast, are now making their homes across the country. *(CARTO-GRAPHICS)*

British Raj in the immediate postindependence period and over the past few decades, when the number of newcomers from South Asia has skyrocketed. She also offers a socioeconomic portrait of South Asian immigrants in the United States today.

The entry on Southeast Asia by N. Mark Shelley is divided into several sections that cover what the author calls "low immigrant inflow countries," that is, those with small numbers of immigrants in the United

States (Brunei, Singapore, Malaysia, Indonesia, and Burma); the "moderate immigrant inflow country" of Thailand; and those countries which have sent numerous immigrants and refugees to the United States, specifically those most impacted by the American war in Southeast Asia: Vietnam, Cambodia, and Laos. Finally, Lawrence K. Hong's second entry covers the experiences of largely Chinese-speaking immigrants from Taiwan and Hong Kong.

CHINA

According to the 1990 census, there are 1.65 million Chinese in the United States, of which about 69 percent are foreign-born and 31 percent born in the United States. Almost all the foreign-born Chinese came from mainland China, Taiwan, Hong Kong, and Southeast Asia. Between 1987 and 1997, a total of 653,522 Chinese emigrated to the United States from the first three places. For this cohort, 66 percent were born in mainland China, 20 percent in Taiwan, and 14 percent in Hong Kong. Even though there were more born in China, a significant number of those were residents of Taiwan and Hong Kong before emigration. The four states with the highest Chinese population are California, New York, Hawaii, and Texas. California has by far the most, accounting for more than 43 percent of the Chinese-American population, followed by New York with about 17 percent, Hawaii 4.2 percent, and Texas 3.8 percent. While the repeal of the Chinese Exclusion Act in 1943 had contributed to some increase in the Chinese population, other legislative actions in the post–World War II years had a much greater impact on its growth in the second half of the twentieth century.

With the end of World War II, Congress passed legislation, notably the Displaced Persons Act of 1948 and the Refugee Relief Act of 1953, designed primarily for the purpose of relieving the refugee situation in Europe. Chinese, however, also became beneficiaries of some of these congressional actions. In 1949, the Chinese Communists took control over mainland China after a bitter civil war with the Nationalist (Kuomintang) government. Unsure about their future, many Chinese nationals in the United States were fearful of returning to their homeland. In China, political and economic hardships caused many to flee to neighboring territories, especially Hong Kong, which was under British control until 1997. Many Chinese took advantage of the legislation to become permanent residents in the United States.

The 1965 Immigration and Nationality Act made sweeping changes in U.S. immigration policy by replacing national quotas with a seven-category preference system for the reunification of families and for persons with skills needed in the United States. A large number of Chinese came under those provisions of the new law. The end of the Vietnam War brought about the Indochina Migration and Refugee Assistance Act of 1975 and its amendment in 1976 which established a program to resettle refugees who had fled from Cambodia, Laos, and Vietnam. Among the many Southeast Asian refugees were ethnic Chinese who once lived in those countries. In response to the aftermath of the 1989 Tiananmen Democracy Movement in China, President George Bush issued Executive Order 12711 in 1990, granting permission for visiting Chinese students and scholars to adjust their status in the United States to that of permanent residents. More than fifty thousand Chinese qualified under this special authorization. In 1992, the Chinese Student Protection Act reaffirmed the provisions of the order.

FROM CHINATOWNS TO THE SUBURBS

In the nineteenth and early twentieth centuries, most Chinese lived in enclaves known as Chinatowns. In 1940, there were Chinatowns in twenty-eight cities from coast to coast. On the Pacific side, the largest and best known was in San Francisco, and on the Atlantic side, in New York. In the early days, Chinatowns were primarily bachelors' societies because most of the immigrants were either single or had left their wives in China thinking that they would not stay permanently in the United States. The Page Act of 1875 hindered immigration of Chinese women, and legislation enacted later in the century prohibited male laborers from bringing their families into the country, thus ag-

Chinese Population by States, 1990 Census

States	Total	American-born	Foreign-born	States	Total	American-born	Foreign-born
Alabama	4,415	999	3,416	Montana	688	228	460
Alaska	1,210	503	707	Nebraska	1,981	500	1,481
Arizona	13,163	5,153	8,010	Nevada	6,850	2,228	4,622
Arkansas	1,621	478	1,143	New Hampshire	2,128	856	1,272
California	713,423	220,464	492,959	New Jersey	58,080	17,978	40,102
Colorado	8,810	3,239	5,571	New Mexico	2,365	794	1,571
Connecticut	10,472	3,200	7,272	New York	285,332	68,478	216,854
Delaware	2,149	631	1,518	North Carolina	8,907	2,211	6,696
District of Columbia	3,028	779	2,249	North Dakota	421	77	344
Florida	30,352	7,014	23,338	Ohio	18,467	5,117	13,350
Georgia	13,180	2,922	10,258	Oklahoma	5,234	1,101	4,133
Hawaii	68,769	49,127	19,642	Oregon	13,746	5,074	8,672
Idaho	1,275	331	944	Pennsylvania	29,469	8,162	21,307
Illinois	49,773	14,249	35,524	Rhode Island	3,146	928	2,218
Indiana	6,572	1,422	5,150	South Carolina	2,819	792	2,027
Iowa	4,172	761	3,411	South Dakota	461	121	340
Kansas	4,952	1,079	3,873	Tennessee	5,415	1,467	3,948
Kentucky	2,960	681	2,279	Texas	63,227	16,869	46,358
Louisiana	5,718	1,687	4,031	Utah	5,137	1,628	3,509
Maine	1,103	371	732	Vermont	591	213	378
Maryland	30,596	8,947	21,649	Virginia	22,102	6,114	15,988
Massachusetts	53,545	16,137	37,408	Washington	34,114	10,952	23,162
Michigan	18,658	5,804	12,854	West Virginia	1,188	297	891
Minnesota	8,283	2,509	5,774	Wisconsin	7,397	2,103	5,294
Mississippi	2,462	948	1,514	Wyoming	513	198	315
Missouri	8,257	2,195	6,062	Grand Total	1,648,696	506,116	1,142,580

Source: Bureau of the Census. *We, the American Asians.* Washington, DC: Department of Commerce, September 1993.

gravating the imbalance in the sex ratio in the Chinese population in the United States.

By 1955, the number of Chinatowns had declined to twelve, and those that remained were shrinking in size and economic vitality. Their continued existence was sustained by the tourist trade and by the old-timers who lived there. In the late twentieth century, however, there has been a renaissance in many of the nation's Chinatowns, including those in Hawaii, San Francisco, Los Angeles, Chicago, and New York. New immigrants from Southeast Asia and mainland China have reinvigorated these communities. Still, Chinatowns have ceased to represent the Chinese community in the United States as they had done in the past, due to two developments that began in the late 1960s.

First, American-born Chinese and many new immigrants, especially those from Taiwan and Hong Kong, are settling outside of Chinatowns. Second, the emergence of Chinese middle-class suburbs has diminished the importance of traditional Chinatowns as cultural and commercial centers. Los Angeles's historic Chinatown, established in 1870, is one of the oldest in America. In the 1930s, it was moved to the present location from its original site about half a mile away to make room for a train station. Because of the relocation, it was officially called the New Chinatown. The name has now become a misnomer because of the many newer Chinese communities that have risen in the suburbs.

The San Gabriel Valley, east of Los Angeles, has become the home to 158,000 Chinese. The city of Monterey Park, on the western edge of the valley, is the first suburb in America with a majority of Chinese residents. The largest Chinese shopping mall in the United States is located in the city of San Gabriel. More than 70 percent of the Chinese doctors and nearly 60 percent of the Chinese attorneys and restaurants do business in the many cities within the valley, such as Alhambra, Rosemead, Hacienda Heights, Industry, and Rowland Heights in addition to the ones already mentioned. Many affluent Chinese from Tai-

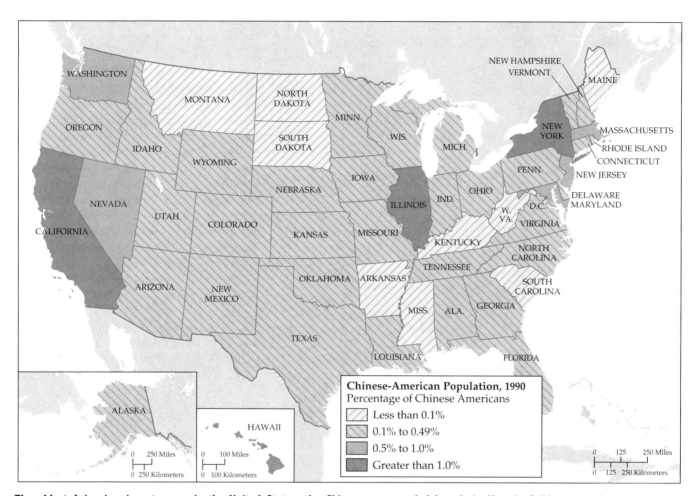

The oldest Asian immigrant group in the United States, the Chinese once settled largely in Hawaii, California, and other western states. Today, there are also large Asian-American populations in Illinois and New York. *(CARTO-GRAPHICS)*

wan and Hong Kong have bought homes in San Marino, one of the most prestigious communities in California. In a 1997 *Los Angeles Times* poll, the majority of the Chinese in all of southern California considered the San Gabriel Valley more important than Chinatown as their place of choice for social and economic activities. As for Los Angeles's first Chinatown, after years of stagnant development, it too has become a bustling community with the infusion of Chinese from Southeast Asia.

New York City's Chinatown, with an estimated population of seventy thousand to one hundred and fifty thousand, is the largest Chinese enclave in the United States. It also has the distinction of having the largest Fujianese-speaking population outside of Asia. Since the 1980s, a Little Fuzhou has coexisted within the larger Chinatown in lower Manhattan, which is dominated by Cantonese-speaking Chinese. Fujianese Chinese came from the province of Fujian, adjacent to Guangdong where Cantonese is spoken, but the two dialects are almost incomprehensible to each other.

While New York City's Chinatown continues to grow in size and importance as a cultural and commercial district, a large number of Chinese are residing outside the Lower East Side and Mott Street neighborhood where it is located. Today Chinese can be found in every borough in the city. Those who reside in other parts of Manhattan are sometimes referred to as "uptown Chinese" by the media, in contrast with the "downtown Chinese" who live in the Lower East Side. Since the late 1960s another Chinese community has flourished in Flushing, Queens, across the East River from Manhattan. By 1990, it had grown to 70,000. The more than six hundred Chinese businesses and services in Flushing mirror those found in Manhattan's Chinatown. The development in Queens bears resemblance to the suburbanization of Chinese elsewhere in the country. Queens County has become a popular residential area for many new Asian immigrants, including those from Korea, India, and the Philippines.

In San Francisco, too, the vast majority of Chinese have moved beyond the nation's oldest and most famous Chinatown. They have made homes in the more upscale Richmond District and in the Sunset District south of Golden Gate Park. Today, Chinese are among the largest groups in those neighborhoods. Large numbers of Chinese in the computer industry live in the Silicon Valley in the San Jose area, fifty miles south of San Francisco. In San Jose, a city of 800,000 people, individuals of Chinese and other Asian ancestry exceed those of European descent.

While San Francisco's Chinatown has ceased to be a place of residence for the majority of the Chinese, it still attracts elderly Chinese and new immigrants with limited income and English-speaking ability. It has its own hospital and banks, Chinese schools, produce and live fish markets, herbal doctors, and folk medicinal shops as well as restaurants and specialty shops. Some of the shops and many of the restaurants cater mainly to the tourist trade. The others serve the needs of the local population in Chinatown and Chinese who live in other parts of the city and in the suburbs.

Hawaii is the only state in the nation where Americans of Asian descent comprise the majority. Among them, Chinese are the third largest group, totaling more than 68,000 in 1990, behind Japanese and Filipino Americans. Historians officially recognize 1789 as the year of the arrival of the first Chinese in Hawaii. As early as 1880, Chinese owned 62 percent of the retail and 24 percent of the wholesale business in Hawaii. At the turn of the nineteenth century, nearly half of the Chinese businesses were located in a twenty-five-acre area known as Chinatown in downtown Honolulu. Today, most Chinese live outside Chinatown. Even though Honolulu's Chinatown has lost its status as an exclusive sanctuary for the Chinese, it has gained a Pan-Asian aura where Vietnamese, Thai, Filipino, Japanese, Korean, and other Asian groups do business as neighbors. It is also a place known for its lei market, where women of Chinese and Hawaiian descents make and sell the flower garlands that symbolize the beauty of Hawaii.

Houston, Texas, has a growing Chinese population. Like the trend in other cities, most of the Chinese in Houston do not live in the old Chinatown, which is located in downtown; they reside in other parts of the city. In recent years, a new commercial district has emerged in the southwest of Houston for the convenience of the Chinese population. Five Buddhist temples have been built in Houston in the past decade. These houses of worship serve the spiritual needs of the many Buddhists among the Chinese, especially those from Taiwan. Houston's Chinese population is relatively new, with many arriving in the 1980s.

FROM BACHELORS' SOCIETY TO FEMALE MAJORITY

In the nineteenth century, the sex ratio (number of males per 100 females) was as high as 2,679 and never lower than 1,284 among Chinese in the United States. In those days, the Chinese community was essentially a society of singles, where lives could be empty and lonely for many of the men. While natural increases have moderated the imbalance, as recently as 1960, Chinese men still outnumbered women by 135 to 100. The sex ratio did not approach parity until after the passage of the Immigration and Nationality Act in 1965 when Chinese Americans were able to sponsor family members to come to the United States. Others, both males and females, also came under the occupation provision of the new law. By 1990, the excess of males had disappeared, and today, in a reversal, Chinese women have emerged as the majority, with a slight advantage of 100 females to 99 males. Immigration was responsible for this turnaround. The 1990 census shows that there are 581,615 foreign-born Chinese women compared to 560,965 Chinese men. For American-born Chinese, there are still more men than women (260,577 vs. 245,539).

FAMILIES AND CHILDREN

Psychologist George K. Hong has observed that Chinese immigrant families have special problems, such as isolation, adjustment to relocation, cultural and generational gaps, and language difficulties. The impacts of these problems may have been mitigated by strong family bonds. Chinese tradition promotes family solidarity to the extent that individual members will sacrifice for the welfare of the family group. It is not unusual for all members of a family to pool their financial and social resources in times of need. Given the strong family value, it is not surprising that a great majority of the Chinese-American families are intact, consisting of both husband and wife. Eighty-one percent of the Chinese-American families in 1990 were married-couple households, compared with the national figure of 73 percent. Chinese are less likely to have female-headed families with no husband present. There were less than 10 percent of this type of single families among the Chinese, whereas the national figure was 17 percent. Chinese Americans are also less likely to have children outside of marriage. Only 8 percent of all births among Chinese Americans were to unmarried women in 1995, compared with 32 percent in the nation. Teenage parents are also rare among the Chinese in the United States. In 1995, only 1 percent of the Chinese births was to teenage mothers, whereas it was 13 percent in the general population. In general, Chinese Americans have fewer children than the national average. In 1990, the total fertility rate (average number of children a woman will have) for the Chinese was only 1.4, compared with 2.1 in the country as a whole.

Chinese children under age eighteen are more likely to live with both parents in comparison with children nationally, 87 percent versus 70 percent. Chinese households are more likely than the average households to include other relatives in addition to spouses and children. About 10 percent of the individuals in Chinese households were other relatives, compared with only 4.5 percent in the general population. Consequently, the Chinese-American family in 1990 is somewhat larger than the national average (3.6 versus 3.2 persons).

MARRIAGES AND INTERMARRIAGES

The 1990 census showed that 60 percent of Chinese men and women were married. These numbers were lower than those for whites, which were 66 percent for men and 62 percent for women. (All figures were based on individuals who were age fifteen or over.) Chinese were much less likely to be divorced, separated, or widowed than whites. Only 4 percent of the Chinese men and 12 percent of the Chinese women were in these categories, compared with 10 percent of the men and 21 percent of the women in the white population. These data indicate that Chinese tend to marry later and have more stable marriages than the whites.

In a multicultural environment, it is inevitable that there will be romantic attractions between members of different ethnic and racial groups. Although not an issue for many people today, sentiments opposing exogamy (marrying out of one's group) have not completely disappeared in the United States. When it exists, the antiexogamous attitude usually is mutual. For the dominant group, the fear is of losing social status by marrying members of a minority group. For the minority group, the major concern is loss of cultural identity, especially for children of the mixed unions. Historically, many states in the United States had laws prohibiting miscegenation (intermarriages) between whites and racial minorities. It was not until 1967 that the U.S. Supreme Court voided all antimiscegenation laws.

However, even in the old days, when the norm against intermarriage was strong, there were individuals who were able to overcome the societal pressures. Historian John Kuo Wei Tehen has documented numerous marriages between Chinese men and Irish immigrant women in New York City in the nineteenth century. Yung Wing, the first American college graduate of Chinese descent, married a white woman, Mary Louise Kellogg, in 1876. In 1902, Mary Bong married a prospector of Scandinavian descent in Alaska after her first husband, Ah Bong, died. "China Mary," as she was affectionately called by those who knew her, was a trailblazer in many fields, including gold mining, fishing, as well as fox farming, and, at the age of seventy, became the first official matron of a federal prison, in Sitka, Alaska. Lalu Nathoy, a Mongolian Chinese, married Charlie Bemis, a white saloon keeper, in Idaho in the 1870s. Better known by her American name, Polly Bemis, she is remembered as a pioneer woman of exceptional talents.

In spite of the celebrated cases, Chinese-white marriages have been rare throughout the history of Chinese in America. More common, however, were marriages between Chinese men and women from other minority groups. Due to the scarcity of Chinese women and lack of social and legal sanctions against such unions, many Chinese men married Native Americans, Hawaiians, blacks, or Mexicans in the nineteenth century and the early twentieth century. Ruthanne Lum McCunn, a noted scholar on Chinese pioneers, estimated that about 30 percent of the Chinese in Mississippi in 1893 were married to black women.

The 1990 census showed that there were 39,873 Chinese marriages having a non-Chinese spouse (whites and others, including other Asians), representing 12 percent of all the Chinese marriages. The 1990 rate is lower than that of a decade earlier, when it was 15.7 percent. There is an important difference in intermarriage rates between American-born and foreign-born Chinese. About 46 percent of the American-born Chinese married out of their ethnic group, whereas only 9 percent of the foreign-born Chinese did. There is also a gender difference in the intermarriage rates, especially among those foreign-born. While American-born Chinese females have only a slightly higher rate (48.2 percent) than American-born males (44.5 percent), foreign-born Chinese females have a rate signifcantly higher than that of their male counterparts (11.3 percent vs. 6.7 percent). Intermarriage between overseas American military personnel and Chinese women in Asia might have contributed to the significantly higher rate.

Among the Chinese who intermarried, they are

most likely to have married whites (53.7 percent), followed by other Asians (32.7 percent), Hispanics (8.6 percent), Hawaiians (2.5 percent), blacks (1.8 percent), and American Indians (0.5 percent). To some extent, these differences reflect different group sizes, which determine the number of potential partners for marriage. For example, since there are more whites in the population than blacks, there are more potential white partners than black for Chinese to marry. There are also regional variations in Chinese intermarriage rates. In 1980, Hawaii had the highest percent of Chinese men marrying out of their own ethnic group (35.5 percent), while the northeastern part of the country had the lowest (8.1 percent). The Southwest also had a comparatively low rate at about 11 percent. The West, South, and North Central had about the same rates—in the neighborhood of 15 percent. As for Chinese women, the intermarriage rate was also highest in Hawaii (38.5 percent) and lowest in the Northeast (8.9 percent). The West, South, Southwest, and North Central had rates between 14.6 percent and 23.3 percent.

Based on the 1980 census, exogamy may be more prevalent among the more educated Chinese. In an analysis of the data, Betty Lee Sung found that 55 percent of the New York Chinese men who married non-Chinese had some college education, compared to only 29 percent of those who married Chinese. As for the Chinese women who married non-Chinese, 72 percent attended some college as compared to only 20 percent of those who married within their own ethnic group. The non-Chinese spouses of Chinese were also more highly educated than the Chinese spouses in endogamous unions (in-marriages). Sixty-seven percent of the non-Chinese husbands and 35 percent of the non-Chinese wives had some college education, whereas the percentages for Chinese husbands and wives in in-marriages were 29 percent and 20 percent, respectively.

As compared to other Asian groups, children of Chinese mixed marriages are most likely to retain their Chinese identity. Analyzing the 1980 census data, Rogelio Saenz and his colleagues found that 44 percent of the children of Chinese-Anglo marriages identify themselves as Chinese, 38 percent identify themselves as Anglo, and 18 percent other. On the other hand, 47 percent to 64 percent of the children in other Asian-Anglo marriages identify themselves as Anglo. Reflecting the patrilineal tendency in the Asian families, the father appears to be the most influential person in the child's ethnic identification. If the father in the mixed marriage is Asian, the children are more likely to identify themselves as Asian. The community is another important factor in identity formation. If

their Asian parent's ethnic group is large in the area where they live, the children are more likely to retain their parent's Asian identity.

EDUCATION AND BRAIN GAIN

Chinese Americans have been noted for their educational attainment. In 1990, nearly 41 percent of the Chinese in the United States, age twenty-five or older, had a bachelor's degree or higher, compared to 20 percent of the same age group in the general population. Selective immigration has been a factor in the higher educational level of the Chinese. Many immigration laws, including the 1965 Immigration and Nationality Act, favor immigrants with higher education. For example, virtually all the Chinese who adjusted their status to residents under Executive Order 12711 for the year 1991 had earned a college degree before coming to the United States. According to a survey conducted by David Zweig and Changgui Chen, 48.4 percent of these individuals had a baccalaureate education or its equivalent, 44 percent a master's degree, and 3.3 percent a Ph.D. degree. The United States, therefore, has gained the service of a highly educated labor force through immigration.

In addition to selective migration, traditional Chinese culture is another factor in the superior educational attainment of Chinese Americans. Chinese culture places a premium on formal education both as a means for economic advancement and as an end in itself for personal growth. Both American-born and foreign-born Chinese in the United States have a higher percentage of college graduates than the general population. Fifty-four percent of the American-born and 40 percent of the foreign-born Chinese are graduates of college and professional schools, compared to the national average of 20 percent. The story of Toy Len Goon, a widow with eight children, brought national attention to this cultural ideal. In 1952, she was conferred the title Mother of the Year at a White House ceremony for her extraordinary accomplishment in providing a college education to all her children while running a small laundry business.

In California, Chinese enrollments on campuses such as UCLA, UC Irvine, and UC Berkeley have far exceeded their proportion in the population. With less than 3 percent of the state's population, Chinese registered a 21-percent representation in the undergraduate student body at UC Berkeley in 1997, the top-ranked public university in California. Chinese Americans have excelled not only as students but also as teachers and researchers. They are on the faculties of many universities, including the most prestigious ones. Six Chinese-American scientists have won a Nobel Prize between 1957 and 1998. In large measure because of their educational achievement, Chinese have been labeled a model minority. This stereotype, favorable though it may be, diverts attention from the fact that many Chinese Americans have not achieved the level of education that is the minimum requirement for most occupations. The 1990 census shows that 31 percent of the foreign-born Chinese, age twenty-five or older, do not hold a high school certificate, a rate significantly higher than the national average of 25 percent. The drive for educational excellence also has driven a wedge between Chinese and other ethnic minorities on the issue of affirmative action. Many Chinese have felt that affirmative action discriminates against them in admission to the top universities because it favors underrepresented minorities which, statistically, they are not.

WORK, INCOME, AND ECONOMIC ACTIVITY

Chinese Americans have virtually identical labor participation rates as the general population. In 1990, 65.9 percent of the Chinese Americans, age sixteen or over, were working, compared to 65.3 percent of all people in the same age group. Chinese women, however, are slightly more likely to be working than other women. The labor-force participation rate for Chinese women was 59.2 percent, compared to 56.8 percent of the females nationwide. Chinese families tend to have more members active in the labor force than the national average. Nearly 48 percent of the Chinese families have two workers, compared to an average of 45.6 percent nationally. Another 19 percent of the Chinese families have three or more workers, compared to 13.4 percent nationwide.

Having more working members in the family has contributed to higher family income for the Chinese. The median family income for the Chinese was $41,316, compared with $20,056 for all families. Chinese also have higher per capita incomes than the national average, $14,876 versus $14,143. However, the overall favorable statistics have obscured the fact that many Chinese do not share in financial success. As many as 14 percent of the Chinese live in poverty, a rate slightly higher than the 13 percent of all Americans. In terms of families, 11 percent of the Chinese are in poverty, compared to the 10 percent for all families in the nation. (By government definition, the pov-

erty level in 1989 for one person was $6,310, and for a family of four, $12,674.)

Chinese Americans are found in a wide range of occupations and businesses that are very different from those of their predecessors in the nineteenth century. Chinese today are most likely to be employed in the managerial and professional sectors. Nearly 36 percent of the Chinese engage in these lines of work, compared to 26.4 percent of the population at large. The second most common type of work is in the technical, sales, and administrative support areas (31 percent). This is followed by service work (17 percent). Another 17 percent of the Chinese are employed in jobs such as production workers, laborers, operators, and agricultural workers. The high occupational profile is a partial reflection of their work experience prior to immigration. For example, 14 percent of those who immigrated to the United States in 1997 came with a professional or technical background, and 9 percent had an executive or administrator background.

In 1992, Chinese Americans owned 153,096 businesses, with receipts of more than $30 billion. The majority of these firms are located in California, New York, and Texas. Chinese Americans have played a major role in ushering in the Information Age. Chinese run nearly one in five—or more than two thousand—of the high-tech companies in the Silicon Valley. Computer Associates International in New York, the second-largest software company in the world in 1999, behind Microsoft Corporation, was founded by an immigrant from Shanghai. Yahoo, one of the most recognized Internet media companies, was cocreated by a Chinese American. Kingston Technologies, the world's largest hardware company for computer memory-enhancement products in 1999, was founded by two immigrants, one from Taiwan and the other from Shanghai, by way of Germany.

Chinese Americans also have made significant inroads in the nontech sector, such as the fashion industry. Nautica, a name brand in menswear, is sold in retail stores worldwide. Vera Wang's boutique is synonymous with high bridal fashion. Anna Sui and Vivienne Tam are two other top labels for cutting-edge designs. Bugle Boy, a trendy apparel maker, had annual sales exceeding $400 million in 1993. On the less glamorous side of the apparel business, Chinese operate more than two thousand sewing factories in major coastal cities, such as New York, Los Angeles, and San Francisco. While these factories provide needed jobs for a large number of immigrants, wages are usually low and working conditions poor.

In southern California, many Chinese immigrants

have entered the hospitality industry, operating travel agencies, hotels, and motels. According to one estimate, Chinese own about 40 percent of the hotels and motels in the area extending from Los Angeles to San Diego. Chinese have a strong presence in the toy wholesale trade, importing dolls, games, and other playthings from Asia for department stores and other retailers in the American market. In downtown Los Angeles, the growth of this trade has created a Toytown of stores and warehouses.

Among the traditional businesses in the Chinese-American community, two have continued to thrive. One is Chinese grocery stores. Corresponding with the expansion of the Asian population since the 1970s, there has been a marked increase in demands for specialty food items such as rice, fresh fish, and Asian vegetables and condiments. Asian grocery stores have flourished in many neighborhoods, and some of them have grown into supermarket chains. The largest is the 99 Ranch Markets (also known as Tawa Supermarkets), which has sixteen stores in the United States and Canada. In 1997, it had 1,200 employees and annual sales of $150 million. Another rapidly expanding chain is Shun Fat Supermarket, which has five outlets in California. Some of the Tawa and Shun Fat markets are located in large retail plazas that are built as one-stop shopping centers to attract customers outside of their immediate neighborhoods. The demands for foodstuffs special to Asian tastes have spawned local manufacturing plants. One of the largest Chinese frozen and packaged food companies is Wei-Chuan U.S.A. Established by a Chinese immigrant with a single factory in 1972, Wei-Chuan has grown to five branches nationwide, with annual sales of over $50 million. In 2000, Wei-Chuan has entered the mainstream market by introducing the Lotus brand of oriental food, designed for consumers at large.

Another economic activity traditional to the Chinese that has enjoyed remarkable growth is the restaurant business. There were approximately twenty thousand restaurants operated by Chinese Americans in the 1990s. Like the food markets, some of the Chinese restaurant businesses have expanded into chain operations. One of these is Panda Express, which had 320 outlets and annual sales of $153 million in 1998. Panda Express built its success on the concept of a simple menu and efficient service that is employed by many fast-food restaurants. However, unlike other fast-food chains, it concentrates its business in the food malls of shopping centers and on college campuses. (Panda Express was founded in 1983 by a Chinese immigrant couple, Andrew and Peggy Cheung, who, unusually for restaurateurs, had educational backgrounds in the scientific fields. The husband has a master's degree in mathematics and the wife, a Ph.D. in electrical engineering.)

RELIGIOUS LIFE

There were only about one hundred thousand Buddhists in the United States in the 1960s, but the number has grown to 1.5 million in the 1990s. Buddhist facilities, ranging from room-size meditation centers to palatial-sized temples, are now found in nearly every state. There also exist many varieties of Buddhism, each having its own tradition and adaptation to American society. In the past, most American Buddhists were Japanese, whereas today they are of many ethnic backgrounds, including whites and large numbers of Chinese from Taiwan and Southeast Asia. The largest Buddhist temple outside of Asia is Hsi Lai Temple in Hacienda Heights, east of Los Angeles. The $25 million temple, opened for worship in 1988, has become the symbolic center of Buddhism for Chinese Americans. Besides religious services, Hsi Lai Temple offers a variety of classes and workshops in both English and Chinese on subjects such as meditation, chanting, vegetarian cooking, and flower arrangement. The temple also operates a state-licensed university conferring undergraduate and graduate degrees in Buddhist and other studies. Buddhist teachings are available on TV programs that are carried nationwide on Chinese cable channels.

Not all Chinese are adherents of Buddhism. As early as 1852, the Presbyterian Church had established a mission among the Chinese in San Francisco. By the 1950s, there were at least sixty-two Protestant and six Catholic Chinese churches in the United States. In the late 1990s, the Southern Baptists had more than thirty churches for Chinese Christians in California alone. There are also many Chinese Catholics, especially among individuals from Hong Kong. A Web site listed Chinese Catholic organizations in eighteen states: Alabama, California, Delaware, Georgia, Hawaii, Iowa, Illinois, Louisiana, Maryland, Massachusetts, Michigan, New Jersey, New York, Ohio, Pennsylvania, Texas, Washington, and Wisconsin. The same list gave the names of forty-one Chinese-American Catholic priests. Additionally, a large number of Chinese, especially the recent immigrants from mainland China, do not have any formal religious beliefs.

EXTRAORDINARY CHINESE AMERICANS

From the beginning, Chinese immigrants have contributed to the richness of America. No less than their predecessors, contemporary Chinese Americans continue to enrich American society and the world by their endeavors in many different arenas. Gary Lock, the grandson of immigrants, was elected governor of Washington in 1996. Julia Chang Bloch was U.S. ambassador to Nepal (1989). Elaine L. Chao was president of United Way of America (1992–96) and deputy secretary of the Department of Transportation (1989–91); Chang-Lin Tien became the first Asian American to serve as chancellor at the University of California, Berkeley (1990–97). David Ho, a medical researcher at the Aaron Diamond Institute, was named *Time* magazine's 1996 Man of the Year for his contributions to the development of drugs that extend the life of those infected with the HIV virus. Michelle Kwan won the U.S. Figure Skating Championship and the Silver Medal in the Winter Olympics in 1998. For more than a decade, Michael Chang was ranked among the top tennis players in the world.

Henry Lee, a former police officer from Taiwan, has become America's best-known criminologist. As commissioner of the Connecticut Department of Public Safety, Lee has been called upon to provide expert opinions on high-profile murder cases around the world, from war crimes in Bosnia to the O. J. Simpson trial in Los Angeles. In 1993, Connie Chung became one of the two women to coanchor a prime-time news program on a national network (CBS). She left CBS in 1996 and joined ABC in 1999 to become its anchor for the program *20/20*. Doug Chiang is Academy Award winner for best visual effects for *Return of the Jedi* (1983), *Cocoon* (1985), *Who Framed Roger Rabbit?* (1988), and *Death Becomes Her* (1992). David Henry Hwang is a playwright and screenwriter whose Broadway production, *M. Butterfly*, won the 1988 Tony Award. Wayne Wang is the director of many memorable films, such as *The Joy Luck Club* and *Chan Is Missing*. Christopher Lee was president of Motion Picture Production of TriStar/Columbia before heading his own company, Chris Lee Productions, in 1999. Yo-Yo Ma is not only a popular cellist, but an artist who has made the cello popular. His combination of personality and artistry has made him one of music's most endearing performers.

Amy Tan is the author of the best-selling novel, *The Joy Luck Club*. In addition to having been made into a major movie, the book was translated into seventeen languages. Tan's other books include *The Kitchen God's Wife, The Moon Lady, The Chinese Siamese Cat*, and *The Hundred Secret Senses*. Maxine Hong Kingston gained national attention with her semiautobiography, *The Woman Warrior: Memoirs of a Girlhood Ghost*. She further established herself in literary circles with works such as *Tripmaster Monkey: His Fake Book, China Men*, and *Hawai'i One Summer*. The second half of the twentieth century witnessed a prolific production of scholarly works on Chinese Americans by Chinese Americans. Some noted contributors are Sucheng Chan, *This Bittersweet Soil*; Iris Chang, *Thread of the Silkworm* (also the critically acclaimed *The Rape of Nanking*); Marshall Jung, *Chinese American Family Therapy*; Ruthanne Lum McCunn, *Chinese American Portraits*; Him Mark Lai, Genny Lim, and Judy Yung, *Island: Poetry and History of Chinese Immigrants on Angel Island, 1910–1940*; Pei Chi Liu, *The History of Chinese in the United States of America* (in Chinese); Victor G. Nee and Brett de Bary Nee, *Longtime Californ'*; and Betty Lee Sung, *Mountain of Gold: The Story of Chinese in America* and *Chinese American Intermarriage*.

In the field of architecture, Maya Lin and I. M. (Ieoh Ming) Pei are legends. At the age of twenty-one, Lin won an open competition to design the Vietnam Veterans Memorial in Washington, D.C. Partly because of her age, gender, and ethnicity, Lin's design was severely criticized by politicians and veteran groups before it was built. When it was completed in 1982, the memorial instantly won the hearts of the American people, including many of those who had denounced it initially. The Vietnam Veterans Memorial has become one of the most inspiring monuments in the United States. Lin's other noted works include The Women's Table at her alma mater, Yale University, and the Civil Rights Memorial in Montgomery, Alabama. I. M. Pei came to the United States at the age of seventeen, studied at MIT and Harvard, and, over the years, has become one of the world's most honored architects. Among the numerous awards that he has received are the AIA Gold Medal (1979), the highest architectural honor in the United States, the Grande Medaille d'Or from the French Academie d'Architecture (1982), and the Praemium Imperiale from the Japan Art Association (1989). In 1993, Pei was elected an Honorary Academician of the Royal Academy of Arts in London. Pei's designs span the continents. They include the John F. Kennedy Library in Boston; the East Building of the National Gallery of Art in Washington; the Museum of Modern Art in Athens, Greece; the Miho Museum of Shiga, Japan; the Grand Louvre in Paris; Raffles City in Singapore;

Fragrant Hill Hotel in Beijing; and the Bank of China in Hong Kong.

In the realm of science, Chen Ning Yang and Tsung-Dao Lee were the first two of the six Chinese Americans to win the Nobel Prize. Yang and Lee were classmates in China as well as at the University of Chicago and later worked as a team on many research projects. In 1957, they were jointly awarded the Nobel Prize in physics for their investigation of the so-called parity laws, which led to important discoveries regarding elementary particles. Born in the United States and raised in China, Samuel Chao Chung Ting studied mathematics and physics at the University of Michigan, where he received his Ph.D. Ting and Burton Richter were co-winners of the Nobel Prize in physics in 1976 for their pioneering work in the discovery of a heavy elementary particle of a new kind. Yuan Tseh Lee was one of the recipients of the Nobel Prize in chemistry in 1986. He studied in Taiwan before enrolling in the University of California at Berkeley, where he earned a Ph.D. in 1965. He and his colleagues Dudley R. Herschbach and John C. Polanyi were honored by the Nobel Prize committee for their contributions concerning the dynamics of chemical elementary processes. Steven Chu won the Nobel Prize in physics in 1997; he was recognized for his work with Claude Cohen-Tannoudji and William D. Phillips in developing methods to cool and trap atoms with laser light. Born in Garden City, New York, Chu was from an extended family of exceptional educational achievement where almost everyone had an advanced degree. Daniel C. Tsui was born in Henan, China, and came to the United States in 1958. He received his Ph.D. in physics from the University of Chicago in 1967 and was awarded the Nobel Prize in 1998 for his discovery of the fractional quantum Hall effect.

In the corporate world, Andrea Jung broke new ground by becoming the chief executive officer of Avon Products Inc. in 1999. Jung was the first Asian-American woman and only one of four female CEOs of Fortune 500 companies at the beginning of the twenty-first century. A graduate of Princeton University, Jung worked in various management capacities at some of the top retailers, such as Bloomingdale's, I. Magnin, and Neiman Marcus, before accepting an executive vice president position at Avon in 1994. Allen Chao, following in the footsteps of his parents' business in Taiwan, founded Watson Pharmaceuticals, one of the largest generic drug manufacturers in the United States. Reflecting his Confucian filial piety, the name of his company is "Hwa's son" Anglicized, "Hwa" being his mother's maiden name. In the high-tech business, Charles B. Wang and Jerry Yang are leaders in their related industries. Wang left Shanghai and came to the United States with his parents in 1952. He founded Computer Associates International in 1976 and built it into one of the largest software companies in the world. Computer Associates has been named one of the best companies for employees and for working mothers by a number of publications. Jerry Yang and his classmate David Filo created Yahoo in 1994 while they were graduate students at Stanford University. When Yahoo went public in the 1996, it legitimized the Net portal business. By January 2000, Yahoo had a stock capitalization (stock price times number of shares outstanding) of $114.8 billion, the third highest among Internet stocks, behind only America Online and Microsoft. Yang was born in Taiwan and moved to the United States at the age of ten. John Tu and David Sun founded Kingston Technologies in 1987, a top designer and manufacturer of computer memory products, which has been named by *Fortune* magazine as one of the "100 Best Companies" to work for in the United States. Kingston Technologies gained additional fame when Tu and Sun sold the company in 1996 and voluntarily shared a substantial portion of the profit with their employees.

JoMei Chang's career path exemplifies the professional trajectories of the many new techno-entrepreneurs at the turn of the new millennium. After graduating from Purdue University in 1979, Chang first worked for Bell Laboratories and then Sun Microsystems. At Bell, she patented a technology for simultaneously delivering data to multiple users. In the late 1980s, she left Sun and cofounded a software company with her husband where they introduced a trader workstation that has revolutionized Wall Street information systems. They sold the company in 1994 and started a new one, Vitra Technology, Inc., which has become a leading e-business platform provider. The Information Age might not have been the same if it were not for the contributions of An Wang, who died in 1990. Wang held more than thirty-five patents on computer technology and was responsible for developing a magnetic pulse-controlling device, the principle upon which computer data storage is based. Wang was the founder of the Wang Laboratories, an innovative hardware company in the early days of desktop computing.

Lawrence K. Hong

See also: Chinese and Chinese Exclusion Act (Part I, Sec. 2); Los Angeles, New York City, San Francisco (Part II, Sec. 12); Immigration to Australia, Immigration to Canada (Part II, Sec. 13); Page Act, 1875, Angell Treaty, 1881, Chinese Exclusion Act, 1882, Contract

Labor Act (Foran Act), 1885, Scott Act, 1888, Repeal of Chinese Exclusion Acts, 1943 (Part IV, Sec. 1).

BIBLIOGRAPHY

"100 Most Influential Asian Americans of the Decade." *A. Magazine*, (October/November 1999): 79–122.

Bureau of the Census. *We, the American Asians*. Washington, D.C.: Department of Commerce, September 1993.

Claymon, Deborah. "JoMei The Money." *The Red Herring Magazine*, July 1998.

Hong, G. K. "Application of Cultural and Environmental Issues in Family Therapy with Immigrant Chinese Americans." *Journal of Strategic and Systematic Therapies* 8 (1989): 14–21.

Iritani, Evelyn. "In Silicon Valley, China's Brightest Draw Suspicion." *Los Angeles Times*, October 18, 1999.

Lai, H. M. "The United States." In *The Encyclopedia of the Chinese Overseas*, ed. L. Pan. Singapore: Chinese Heritage Centre, 1998.

Lee, R. H. *The Chinese in the United States of America*. Hong Kong: Hong Kong University Press, 1960.

Lee, S. M. "Asian Americans: Diverse and Growing." *Population Bulletin* 53:2 (June 1998).

Lee, S. M., and M. Fernandez. "Trends in Asian American Racial/Ethnic Intermarriage: A Comparison of 1980 and 1990 Census Data." *Sociological Perspectives* 41:2 (Summer 1998): 323–44.

McCunn, R. Lum. *Chinese American Portraits: Personal Histories 1928–1988*. San Francisco: Chronicle Books, 1988.

Saenz, Rogelio, Sean-Shong, Hwang, B. E. Aguirre, and R. N. Anderson. "Persistence and Change in Asian Identity Among Children of Intermarried Couples." *Sociological Perspectives* 38:2, (Summer 1995):175.

Sung, B. L. *Chinese American Intermarriage*. New York: Center for Migration Studies, 1990.

Tung, W. L. *The Chinese in America 1820–1973*. Dobbs Ferry, NY: Oceana, 1974.

Zweig, David, and Chen Changgui. *China's Brain Drain to the United States*. Berkeley, CA: Institute of East Asian Studies, 1995.

𝒯RAN

According to official statistics, in 1990, almost half of the Iranian population in the Western world resided in the United States, which was by far the favored destination of the global Iranian diaspora. The Iranian population in the United States, is however, distinctive from Iranian communities elsewhere in terms of socioeconomic characteristics and ethno-religious diversity.

CAUSES OF MIGRATION

The causes of emigration from Iran before the Iranian revolution of 1978–79 were mainly educational, whereas the causes after the revolution were predominantly political. Iranians who emigrated before the revolution were mostly college students in pursuit of higher education, while those who have left after the revolution are mainly exiles or political refugees. Some Iranians have also emigrated for economic reasons during both waves, especially during the second, when the economic conditions deteriorated at home.

The late shah's industrialization drive began in the 1960s and took off in the 1970s with the rising oil revenues, which increased the demand for skilled workers. Unlike some other oil-producing countries in the Middle East, which imported workers, Iran relied on its own large population to fill these jobs. However, there were not enough universities in Iran to meet the needs of an increasingly large number of high school graduates. For many students, therefore, overseas education was the only alternative to obtain the skills needed in a rapidly industrializing economy. Although Iranian students went to several countries in pursuit of higher education, their favored destination was the United States—half of Iranian students abroad were in the United States in the mid-1970s. They preferred America because of their English fluency (English was the most common foreign language

taught in Iranian high schools), relatively easier admission to numerous American universities, and the state-of-the-art technical education, such as engineering, offered by these universities.

Political factors became the overriding determinants of Iranian immigration during and after the Iranian revolution, which caught most by surprise because it occurred at a time when that country was experiencing an economic boom. The causes of the revolution itself were more political (e.g., populist opposition to the shah's autocratic rule) than economic. Despite Iran's relative religious homogeneity (about 98 percent of its prerevolution population was Muslim), Iranians in the United States include a sizable number of religious minorities who fled Iran because of the revolution and the establishment of the Islamic republic. The Islamic revolution also explains why most Iranian Muslims in the United States are secular; indeed the religious Iranian Muslims had no reason for leaving a strict Muslim society. The first wave of Iranian exiles, immediately after the revolution, consisted of members of the elite and the most modernized segments of Iranian society. The emergence of a theocratic state in Iran—the only one of its kind in the world at present—and its imposition of a strict code of Islamic behavior was particularly intolerable for the modernizing Iranian women, many of whom emigrated.

IMMIGRATION TRENDS

Only 130 Iranians are known to have emigrated to the United States from the mid-nineteenth century to the beginning of the twentieth century. The Immigration and Naturalization Service (INS) did not report data separately for Iranian arrivals in the United States in the first quarter of the twentieth century. In the second quarter (1925–50), less than two thousand Iranians

After the American-supported shah was overthrown in an Islamic revolution in 1979, tens of thousands of Iranians, like this family in Los Angeles, came to the United States. *(Shades of L.A. Archives, Los Angeles Public Library)*

were admitted as immigrants. But in the second half of the twentieth century, immigration increased dramatically, with more than two hundred and fifteen thousand Iranians admitted as immigrants or permanent residents.

Although some had immigrant status upon arrival, most were admitted as students before the revolution or as visitors afterward, and subsequently adjusted their status to permanent residents. For instance, only 35,000 Iranian immigrants were admitted to the United States before the revolution (1950–77), whereas 391,000 nonimmigrants arrived during the same period. Multiple counting notwithstanding, students made up about one-fifth of all nonimmigrants from Iran between 1950 and 1977. Data of the INS further show that the number of nonimmigrants (students and visitors) from Iran dropped precipitously from its peak of 130,000 in 1978 to slightly over 20,000 in 1992. After the revolution, in the decade of 1980, refugee or asylee status became the most common forms of obtaining permanent residency among Iranians. Almost one-quarter of all Iranian immigrants to the United States (59,000) have entered as refugees or were classified as asylees after their arrival. For the first thirty years, from 1950 to 1980, there were only 732 Iranian refugees and asylees, but this number increased dramatically to 58,381 in the next twelve years (1981–93) due to the Iranian revolution.

The trend among Iranians including asylum seekers, is to adjust their status to immigrant after being admitted to the United States on nonimmigrant visas. Of the almost 35,000 Iranian immigrants admitted to the United States before the revolution, less than half (almost 14,000) were new arrivals; the rest had adjusted their status. While a total of about 104,000 Iranian immigrants were admitted in 1978–86, only one-fifth (22,000) were new arrivals—the rest were adjusters, including almost 18,000 refugees and asylees.

Obtaining a U.S. visa in Iran was relatively easy before the seizure of the American embassy in Iran in 1980, but it has become impossible since there is no American embassy in that country. Iranians have to go to a third country to receive a visa to come to the United States. Immigration to the United States has increasingly become less feasible economically, since the Iranian government has imposed restrictions on the sum of money allowed out of the country for travel. Moreover, the Iranian *toman* is weak against the dollar (from 7:1 in the mid-1970s to nearly 1,000:1 in the late 1990s), thus requiring a substantial amount of money to finance the trip.

Despite their initial sojourning intentions, both former students and exiles show signs of settlement in the United States, as reflected in naturalization figures. During the first phase of Iranian immigration to the United States (1950–77), only about 9,000 Iranians had become naturalized U.S. citizens, but this figure increased dramatically during the second phase (e.g., 82,500 from 1978 to 1995). Iranians used to arrive in the United States under student and visitor visas, but as they have increasingly become naturalized citizens, they are able to bring their immediate relatives over through family reunification laws.

Many students have become "self-imposed exiles" by changing their minds about repatriation after the revolution. The exiles, some of whom are members of religious minorities from Iran, have migrated to the United States in family units due to their precarious position in Iran. Moving with family members has further reduced the likelihood of return for these minorities.

The Iranian population in the United States doubled during the 1980s. The 1990 U.S. census counted over 200,000 Iranians in the United States, about 70 percent of whom were foreign-born, indicating that most of this growth was due to recent immigration. Over half of these Iranians resided in California, with the Los Angeles metropolitan area (five-county region) accounting for 100,000 or 35 percent, of the population. About 80,000 or 28 percent, of Iranians were in Los Angeles County alone. The emergence of Los Angeles as perhaps the largest Iranian center outside Iran is mainly due to a combination of two migratory trends: (1) the direct influx of exiles from Iran to be near family and friends, and (2) the regrouping of Iranians from other parts of the United States, San Francisco, New York, Washington, D.C., and Baltimore, Maryland, are also favored destinations of Iranians in the United States.

ECONOMIC INCORPORATION

The combination of former college students and elite exiles makes Iranians one of the most educated immigrant groups in the United States. According to the 1990 census, half of the population twenty-five years and older held a bachelor's degree or higher. Foreign-born Iranians were the third most highly educated major immigrant group (more than 100,000 persons) and also ranked third in percentage in professional specialty occupations in the United States, after Asian Indians and Taiwanese. About half of employed Iranian males and one-third of employed females held top white-collar professional (e.g., physicians, engineers, accountants) and managerial specialty occupations (e.g., supervisors). Sales occupations for males, and sales, clerical, and service occupations for females, were other typical jobs held by Iranians.

The socioeconomic status of Iranian females is lower than that of males. With roughly one-third of females over twenty-five holding a college degree or higher, Iranian women in the United States are very highly educated, even compared to their male counterparts (62 percent). The most puzzling feature of the economic adaptation of Iranian females, however, is their relatively low rate of labor-force participation (LFP) compared to that of many other foreign-born groups. This is partly a carryover of low female LFP in Iran (less than 20 percent in 1990), though Iranian women have adapted to the American norm of working outside of the household. The LFP among Iran-born females increased substantially over time from 29 percent in 1980 to 50 percent in 1990. Although Iranian males registered the same relative gain from 61 percent to 88 percent, this was due to their exile status and ambivalence about working shortly after arrival. Women's employment and economic independence have challenged traditional gender roles and have contributed to family disintegration (e.g., rising divorce).

With a self-employment rate above 11 percent in 1990, Iranians are also one of the most entrepreneurial groups in the United States. But unlike other immigrant groups who turn to self-employment because of disadvantages in the labor market (for example, language barriers among Koreans), premigration self-employment, especially among minorities such as Armenians and Jews, spurs Iranian entrepreneurship. The rate of Iranian self-employment is even higher in Los Angeles than it is in the United States as a whole due to the greater presence of these minorities. Iranians had the second highest self-employment rate (33 percent) after Koreans in Los Angeles in 1990. Availability of capital and the presence of highly skilled self-employed professionals such as doctors and dentists further contribute to the high self-employment rate of Iranians.

The combination of salaried and self-employed professionals, as well as managerial occupations, accounts for the successful economic adaptation of Iranian immigrants. This success, however, is qualified by the downward mobility, at least initially, of exiles and the discrimination Iranians as a whole face in the labor market. As a result, the earnings of Iranians, at least in Los Angeles, are not commensurate with their high level of education and occupational skills.

There are very few social problems associated with Iranian immigrants, yet discrimination and prejudice afflict them more than other similarly high status immigrant groups. This is mostly provoked by the actions of the Iranian regime rather than by the immigrants themselves. Anti-American slogans started during the Iranian revolution and culminated in the hostage crisis in 1979–81 when fifty-two Americans were taken hostage for 444 days in Iran. Ironically, the hostage crisis coincided with the massive influx of Iranian exiles into the United States. According to a presidential order, Iranians who did not have legal status and were in violation of their visas were subjected to deportation. Although fewer than one thousand Iranians were actually deported, this was an unfair targeting and scapegoating of Iranian immigrants, some of whom had been persecuted by the regime that they left behind. Every time conflict has broken out between Iran and the United States since, Iranian immigrants have become scapegoats and have suffered the consequences. Not surprisingly, many Iranians still perceive that there is prejudice against them in the United States.

ASSIMILATION

An immigrant group such as Iranians with high levels of educational and occupational achievement, as well as English proficiency, is expected to assimilate rapidly into American society. Other indicators, such as the lack of a commercial and residential enclave, even in cities with high concentration of Iranians, seem to signal assimilation. However, Iranians, by and large, have not assimilated as much or as fast as other immigrant groups. Some Iranians in the United States are more assimilated, especially students who arrived much earlier, subsequently married Americans, and settled down in college towns where there are few Iranians. But most, especially the postrevolution exiles

that have congregated in major areas of Iranian concentration (Los Angeles, New York, and Washington, D.C.) have resisted the pressures of assimilation. It may appear that the difference between former students and exiles is a function of their length of residence in the United States, that is, the earlier arrivals (students) are more assimilated than the later ones (exiles). But it is not so much time of arrival as the causes and context of immigration that account for the differences in their degree of assimilation. Iranian students were well on their way toward assimilation because they had emigrated on their own and dispersed to college campuses across the nation, until they were joined by parents and other relatives or relocated within the United States to be near other Iranians. Conversely, often having emigrated with family members or reunifying with them soon after immigration, Iranian exiles have maintained close ties with relatives, thus reinforcing their ethnicity. This is particularly the case among religious minorities from Iran, who have frequently migrated with their family members.

Major indicators of ethnicity reflect its high maintenance among Iranians—at least in Los Angeles, where rich data on Iranians are available. Intermarriage is used as the best indicator of assimilation—the higher the rate of intermarriage, the more assimilated the group. With 90 percent of Iranian females in Los Angeles married to Iranian males, Iranians there have not intermarried at a great rate. Besides marriage in Iran, the sizable presence of endogamous minority groups, notably Jews and Armenians, accounts for the low rate of intermarriage among Iranians in Los Angeles.

As another indicator of cultural preservation, the use and maintenance of language is particularly high among foreign-born Iranians. The majority speak their mother tongue at home (frequently Persian), despite their English proficiency. Iranians do not come from a country where English was commonly used, yet their high level of education, which in many cases was obtained in the United States, accounts for their fluency in English. In Los Angeles, among Iranians who speak a language other than English at home, about 80 percent claim that they speak English well or very well.

Iranians in Los Angeles are unassimilated partly because they consist of sizable ethnoreligious minorities (e.g., Armenians and Jews) with a long and well-defined history of minority experience. But even the Muslims resist assimilation because of their exile status, a strong sense of Iranian nationalism, and attachment to the homeland. This is best reflected in the Iranian media, especially its extensive TV programming, which is preoccupied with Iran as opposed to issues confronting the community in the United States.

In light of their ethnoreligious heterogeneity, social integration among Iranians is much more complex than among many other immigrant groups. Particularly interesting is the extent to which Armenians in Los Angeles and Jews in Los Angeles and New York, the two largest minorities from Iran, may become integrated within the general Armenian and Jewish communities, respectively. In Los Angeles, where data on friendship ties and participation in organizations are available, there is no large-scale integration, at least for the immigrant generation. The close friends of most first-generation Iranian Jews and Armenians are Iranian coreligionists. Furthermore, they are more likely than the Muslims to define their ethnicity in terms of both their nationality and religion, thus setting them apart from other Iranians and also from their coreligionists. Although minorities from Iran might find a congenial coreligionist community, their cultural and even class differences are so pronounced as to prevent social integration among the first generation (e.g., between Iranians and American Jews in Long Island, New York).

First-generation differences, however, are slowly disappearing among the second generation; less than half of Armenian and Jewish Iranian children, both second- and one-and-a-half generation (that is, born in Iran and emigrated before the age of twelve) have exclusively Iranian coreligionist close friends. These intergenerational differences suggest that as Iranian Armenian and Jewish children grow up, they may move away from the Iranian community toward the general Armenian- and Jewish-American communities, respectively. Of course, the outcome will also depend on whom they marry. Not surprisingly, the first choice of almost all Armenian and Jewish Iranian parents is that their children marry Iranian coreligionists. Young Iranian Jews in Los Angeles share the same preferences as their parents in terms of mate selection. In general, Iranian Muslims, including the second generation, are more open to intermarriage than are minorities from Iran. Thus, they are more likely to follow the traditional assimilationist path toward the mainstream American society.

Research on second-generation Iranians is sorely lacking, but preliminary evidence suggests that only a small fraction identify themselves as American; a larger percentage consider themselves to be Iranian-American than Iranian only. Not surprisingly, an Iranian ethnic identity is stronger in centers of concentration of Iranians (e.g., California). As this new minority group emerges in the United States, the most interesting thing to watch for will be the effect of the recent political liberalizations in Iran on Iranian national identity in the United States, especially among the second generation. With President Muhammad Khatami's election in 1997 and the landslide victory of moderate politicians in the parliamentary elections in 2000, Iran may finally normalize the relations with the United States, increase travel to and from Iran, and improve the image of Iran in the eyes of Americans. All of these factors are bound to reinforce Iranian ethnicity and identity in the United States.

Mehdi Bozorgmehr

See also: Political, Ethnic, Religious, and Gender Persecution (Part II, Sec. 1); Los Angeles (Part II, Sec. 12).

BIBLIOGRAPHY

Ansari, Abdolmaboud. *Iranian Immigrants in the United States.* New York: Associated Faculty Press, 1988.

Bozorgmehr, Mehdi, Guest Editor. Special Issue on "Iranians in America." *Iranian Studies* 31: 1 (1998): 3–95.

Bozorgmehr, Mehdi, Claudia Der-Martirosian, and Georges Sabagh. "Middle Easterners: A New Kind of Immigrant." In *Ethnic Los Angeles,* ed. Roger Waldinger and Mehdi Bozorgmehr, pp. 345–78. New York: Russell Sage, 1996.

Bozorgmehr, Mehdi, and Georges Sabagh. "High Status Immigrants: A Statistical Profile of Iranians in the United States." *Iranian Studies* 21:3–4 (1988): 4–34.

Dallalfar, Arlene. "Iranian Women as Immigrant Entrepreneurs." *Gender and Society* 8:4 (1994): 541–61.

Fathi, Asghar, ed. *Iranian Refugees and Exiles Since Khomeini.* Costa Mesa, CA: Mazda Publishers, 1991.

Hannasab, Shideh, and Romeria Tidwell. "Intramarriage and Intermarriage: Young Iranians in Los Angeles." *International Journal of Intercultural Relations* 22: 4 (1998): 395–408.

Karim, Persis, and M. M. Khorrami, eds. *A World in Between: Poems, Stories, and Essays by Iranian-Americans.* New York: George Braziller, 1999.

Kelley, R., and Jonathan Friedlander, eds. *Irangeles: Iranians in Los Angeles.* Berkeley and Los Angeles: University of California Press, 1993.

Naficy, Hamid. *The Making of Exile Cultures: Iranian Television in Los Angeles.* Minneapolis: University of Minnesota Press, 1993.

$\mathcal{J}$APAN

The history of Japanese immigration to the present-day United States began in 1868, when 148 illegal contract laborers arrived in Hawaii to work on sugar plantations. By 1925, over 200,000 Japanese had left their homes for Hawaii, and about 180,000 went to the mainland of the United States. This generation of Japanese-born immigrants are known as *Issei*. Their American-born children are known as *Nisei*. After Hawaii was annexed in 1898, massive numbers of Japanese came to the mainland from Hawaii, especially to California. For instance, in 1900 more than twelve thousand Japanese from Hawaii arrived on the West Coast, where many European Americans had clashed with Chinese immigrants since the mid-nineteenth century. By the middle of the twentieth century, most immigration to America from Japan had been effectively halted, first by discriminatory anti-Asian immigration policies from the 1920s, and then by World War II. This anti-Asian feeling on the West Coast was no doubt an impetus for the removal to detention centers of 120,000 people of Japanese ancestry, including their American-born children.

After the war, Japanese immigration restarted, and today, there are some 850,000 people of Japanese descent living in the United States. However, this latter type of immigrant is very different from the earlier ones at the turn of the twentieth century. At that time, most were either laborers looking for better economic conditions, or accomplished farmers who found that their skills worked well in the agricultural areas of the West Coast. Most of them came to the United States with the hope of making money and returning to Japan. Postwar immigration has been quite different, and the majority of immigrants are of two kinds: war brides who married American servicemen during the American occupation of Japan, and long-term professional residents, such as business people, scientists, or students, or permanent immigrants whose spouses are U.S. citizens.

WAR BRIDES

Postwar immigration to the United States began with the War Brides Act of 1945. During World War II and just after, over sixteen million American citizens served overseas. The majority of these people were between the ages of 18 and 30, and most were single. As might be expected—being away from home and family, and residing for long periods of time in foreign countries—these young men often fell in love with local women. About one million American service personnel married foreign nationals during the 1940s and early 1950s. The War Brides Act allowed their spouses to enter the United States; if they were of European stock, these new wives were naturalized upon arrival. However, since the Quota Act of 1924 was still in place, Japanese brides were not eligible even to land in the United States at this time.

About a half-million American soldiers were stationed in Japan during the Occupation. It is not surprising that romances between American soldiers and Japanese women developed. Many of these women were workers employed on, or near, American military installations. However, these women and their mixed-blood children were not really welcome in Japanese society, where notions of cultural purity ran deep, to say nothing of the shame of defeat after the war. At the same time, these women and their children were not allowed to accompany their husbands (or fathers) back to the United States. The American military actively discouraged these intermarriages and put many barriers in their way. As a result, almost 100,000 Japanese women were left in Japan in the 1940s when their American spouses were rotated home.

In July 1947, Congress relaxed some of these restrictions, and finally Japanese brides were allowed to apply for immigration to the United States, even

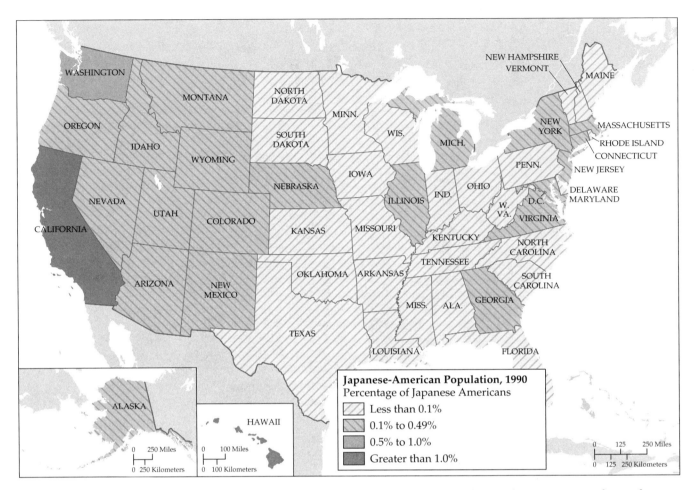

Japanese-American Population, 1990
Percentage of Japanese Americans
- Less than 0.1%
- 0.1% to 0.49%
- 0.5% to 1.0%
- Greater than 1.0%

Although they arrived in relatively small numbers, the Japanese were one of the earlier Asian immigrant groups, and many Japanese Americans trace their ancestry in this country back to the turn of the twentieth century. *(CARTO-GRAPHICS)*

though the time to process their permits often took several years. Even after their arrival, however, Japanese women were not necessarily eligible for automatic naturalization through marriage as other foreign brides were. These women were required to take an examination to become American citizens, but, of course, many of them lacked the English skills required to pass these tests. Having so many difficulties—linguistic, social, economic, and political—to overcome in the new country, great stress was placed on these relationships. One out of three couples of these war-bride marriages separated within a year of their arrival in America.

Normal general immigration from Japan to the United States began again in 1952—seven years after World War II—with the passage of the McCarran–Walter Act (see Table 1). This law removed racial and ethnic barriers for immigration to America. As a result, "alien" Japanese in the United States—or "strangers from a different shore" as President Roosevelt had called them—finally became American citizens. Japanese Americans in Japan could now also reenter the United States. Over the next decade, almost six thousand Japanese a year emigrated to the United States. The majority of these immigrants were the parents, spouses, or siblings of Japanese Americans who had been separated by the war. This law also permitted American women who had lost their U.S. citizenship by marriage to men who were "aliens ineligible for citizenship"—that is, who were married to Japanese nationals—to regain their citizenships (together with their husbands). Furthermore, the McCarran–Walter Act stated explicitly that the right to naturalization would not be contingent upon race or gender. However, the act still contained some racial inequalities, as it established a quota system based on national origins.

Table 1	
Japanese Postwar Immigration to the United States	
Date	Number of Immigrants
1946–1950	1,197
1951–1955	14,660
1956–1960	31,022
1961–1965	21,342
1966–1970	21,911
1971–1975	25,989
1976–1980	21,925
1981–1985	20,020
1986–1990	23,228

Source: H. Barringer, R. W. Gardner, and M. J. Levin, *Asians and Pacific Islanders in the United States* (New York: Russell Sage Foundation, 1995), 24–25.

Despite an early-twentieth-century law that banned land ownership to Japanese immigrants, many—like this California man—became successful farmers. *(Norma Holt/Impact Visuals)*

To show their loyalty and patriotism during World War II, many Japanese Americans placed signs such as these in their store windows. The Asahi Dye Works was located in Los Angeles. *(U.S. Department of the Interior, National Park Service)*

LONG-TERM JAPANESE RESIDENTS AND PERMANENT IMMIGRANTS

The Immigration and Nationality Act of 1965 abolished the national-origin quota system; instead, a hemispheric quota system was introduced. About 170,000 people from the Eastern Hemisphere could enter the United States each year, with a limit of 20,000 from each nation. About 12,000 people could come from the Western Hemisphere, with no limitation by nation. As a result, the Asian-American population—especially the Chinese, Korean, Indian, Filipino, and Vietnamese populations—grew substantially. In 1960 the Asian population in the United States was some 900,000, and by 1980 it had become

Table 2
Permanent and Long-Term Japanese Residents in North America, 1995–1998

Date	Number of Permanent Immigrants	Number of Long-Term Residents	Students, Faculty, Researchers	Total
1995	113,161	175,916	58,032	289,077
1996	115,187	185,144	62,664	300,331
1997	118,541	193,073	65,944	311,614
1998	122,227	195,739	67,762	317,966

Source: Japanese Immigration Department of the Foreign Affairs Office of the Japanese Government, *Kaigai Zairyû hô jinsû chôsa tôkei* (Overseas Japanese Statistical Survey).

Table 3
Japanese Immigration to the United States by Sex

Date	Male	Female	Total	Percent Female
1950	16	29	45	64.4
1951	45	161	206	78.2
1952	153	4,581	4,734	96.8
1953	198	2,291	2,489	92.0
1954	685	3,377	4,062	83.1
1955	708	3,435	4,143	82.9
1956	1,342	4,280	5,622	76.1
1957	765	5,357	6,122	87.5
1958	868	5,559	6,427	86.5
1959	810	5,283	6,093	86.7
1960	824	4,812	5,636	85.4

Source: Roger Daniels, *Asian America: Chinese and Japanese in the United States since 1850* (Seattle: University of Washington Press, 1988), 307.

nearly 3.5 million. By 1990, it had doubled to 7.3 million people.

Unlike some other Asian nations, however, the number of immigrants from Japan is relatively few. Right after World War II, Japanese war-bride immigration held steady at about 6,000 people per year. Since the 1960s the number of Japanese coming to America each year remained at about 4,000. In the early and mid-1990s—the tail end of the Japanese "economic miracle" and the "bubble economy"—the number of immigrants sometimes dropped to less than 3,000 per year. In the late 1990s, however, the numbers rose again: in 1997 and 1998, for example, about 3,500 per year came to the United States (see Table 2).

Since the 1970s, Japanese corporations setting up independent or joint ventures have sent many Japanese nationals to work in North America with long-term visas. These Japanese are extremely sensitive about associating with the local people, and their companies often go to great lengths not to appear to create "Japanese ghettos" or such concentrated areas. These workers have often acquired substantial English skills in Japan, and companies also usually provide English classes for their workers and families while they are in the United States. Thus, upon their arrival these people have sufficient cultural skills and command of the language to reside in the local community. Many become permanent, or quasi-permanent, residents while working for these Japanese corporations. As a kind of reversal of the post-war occupation phenomenon, American women now sometimes marry these highly educated and financially secure men.

However, the proportion of Japanese women marrying American men is still very high. In fact, one of the most outstanding features of postwar permanent

American residency from Japan has always been this high ratio of females to males (see Table 3). It is not surprising that almost all the immigrants in the war-bride era were females; to this day, however, over 80 percent of Japanese permanent residents in America are women. Although there are many Japanese men in the United States with long-term residence permits, these men often come with their spouses or families. Many times, after finishing the several years of their tour of duty for the company, they return to Japan. On the other hand, young women come to America by themselves, with student visas. About one-third of the long-term Japanese resident population are students, faculty members, or scientific researchers. A sizable number of these Japanese women develop relationships with American men, just as they had done during the Occupation. The majority of their children are heavily assimilated into American culture, and often do not speak Japanese. It is said that the popularity of Japanese women marrying American men is somehow related to an image some Japanese women have of American wives being more free and liberated compared to the roles of the typical Japanese housewife married to a Japanese man. While of course such claims are complex, and vary greatly from individual to individual, it is likely that some of these symbols and images influence some Japanese women, especially those already actively seeking experience abroad.

Nobuko Adachi

See also: Immigrants and Westward Expansion (Part I, Sec. 2); Nativist Reaction, Restrictive Legislation, Japanese Internment (Part I, Sec. 4); San Francisco (Part II, Sec. 12); Immigration to Japan (Part II, Sec. 13); Quota Act of 1924, Immigration and Nationality Act, 1965, Gentlemen's Agreement, 1907, President Roosevelt's Executive Order 9066 (Japanese Internment), 1942, *Hirabayashi v. United States,* 1943 (Part IV, Sec. 1); Reparations for Japanese-American Internees, 1988 (Part IV, Sec. 2).

BIBLIOGRAPHY

Barringer, Herbert, Robert W. Gardner, and Michael Levin. *Asians and Pacific Islanders in the United States.* New York: Russell Sage Foundation, 1995.

Daniels, Roger. *Asian America: Chinese and Japanese in the United States since 1850.* Seattle: University of Washington Press, 1988.

———. *Coming to America: A History of Immigration and Ethnicity in American Life.* New York: HarperCollins, 1990.

Kitano, Henry, and Roger Daniels. *Asian Americans: Emerging Minorities.* Englewood Cliffs, NJ: Prentice Hall, 1995.

KOREA

Generally, three factors have been behind most of the immigration of Koreans to the United States: internal conditions within Korea; the political, economic, and cultural links between the United States and Korea; and shifts in the U.S. immigration laws. Historically, Korean migration to the United States can be divided into three main phases. The first wave of immigration occurred between 1902 and 1905, consisting primarily of males, and between 1910 and 1924, when "picture brides" came to unite with some of the Korean bachelors in the United States. War brides, war orphans, and students were the primary immigrants of the second wave, during the post–World War II period between 1945 and 1964. From 1965 to the present is the contemporary—and largest—wave, consisting predominantly of families and professional migrants.

IMMIGRATION TO AMERICA BEFORE 1945

The 8,000 Korean immigrants who came to the United States before World War II was a small number compared to the number of immigrants from other Asian countries. For example, over 440,000 immigrants came from China, while almost 500,000 immigrants came from Japan, and 180,000 immigrants came from the Philippines. Although the number of Korean immigrants was relatively small compared with the number of other Asian immigrants who entered during this time, the 35 million European new arrivals to America within the same period vastly exceeded the total number of all immigrants from all of Asia. It was not until after the passage of the 1965 Immigration Act that immigration from Korea became significant. Within the last thirty-five years, Korea has become a major sending country of immigrants. Currently, there are almost 1 million Korean Americans in the United States.

Cultural and economic ties were created by the United States as early as 1882, twenty years before the first wave of Koreans migrants came to America, when American missionaries established Protestant churches, hospitals, and schools in Korea as part of their undertaking to convert the Korean people to Christianity. At the beginning of the twentieth century, American missionaries, led by Dr. Horace Allen, recruited Koreans to the Hawaiian sugar plantations. For wealthy planters, Koreans were desirable workers, to be used as strikebreakers against the predominantly Japanese workers on the plantations. As a result, approximately seventy-two hundred Korean immigrants entered between 1903 and 1905 to work on the Hawaiian plantations. The role of missionaries as active recruiters in this process is evident, as approximately 40 percent of the first wave were Christian converts. Immigrants in this early wave were mostly students, ex-soldiers, laborers, and farmers, primarily between the ages of twenty and thirty. Moreover, 90 percent of these migrants were single males.

The Korean government made efforts to stop emigration to the United States in 1905 because of the maltreatment of its nationals overseas. However, Japan had occupied Korea by this time (and formally annexed Korea in 1910) and insisted that all Koreans leaving Korea must carry Japanese passports. In compliance with Japan's wishes, the U.S. government ceased to acknowledge Korean passports, and for all political purposes, Koreans were recognized as Japanese nationals. Korean immigration officially ended in 1907, as all laws between the United States and Japan were automatically applied to Koreans as well. Thus, the Gentlemen's Agreement Act of 1907–1908, which officially ended most Japanese immigration to the United States, also effectively terminated Korean immigration.

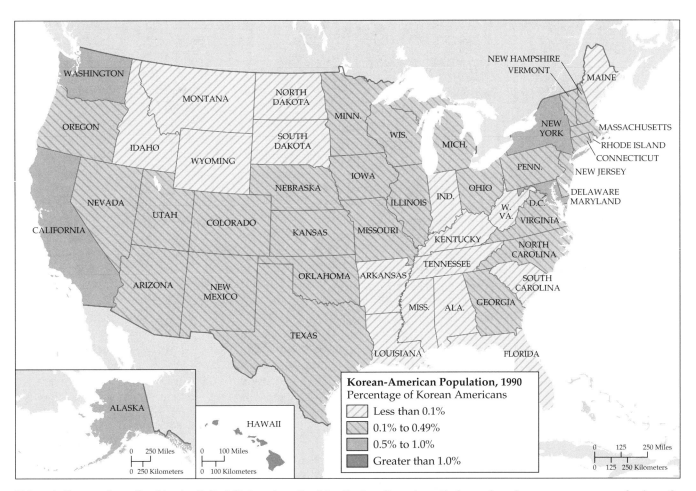

Korean-American Population, 1990
Percentage of Korean Americans

- Less than 0.1%
- 0.1% to 0.49%
- 0.5% to 1.0%
- Greater than 1.0%

Although Koreans have lived in the United States since the late nineteenth century, their numbers have grown enormously since the Immigration and Nationality Act of 1965, with the vast majority settling in Hawaii, California, other West Coast states, and New York. *(CARTO-GRAPHICS)*

For the largely Korean bachelor community, life on the plantations without women and families was dull and lonely. Therefore, gambling and drinking became their primary forms of entertainment. However, a provision within the Gentlemen's Agreement permitted "picture brides" to enter, which allowed single men to wed with women in Korea. Marriage with picture brides took place through the exchange of photographs between bachelors in Hawaii and on the mainland and prospective brides in Korea. Approximately one thousand Korean brides, mostly in their late teens, came to the United States between 1910 and 1920 through the picture bride system. The young brides were devastated to discover that the men they married had sent pictures that had been altered to make them look younger or sent photos that had been taken when they were much younger. The average age difference between picture brides and their husbands was fourteen years. While some women re-turned to Korea upon discovering this deception, most women stayed. As a result, a small group of second-generation Korean Americans emerged, and pockets of Korean communities developed. The presence of families was instrumental in allowing Korean immigrants to save sufficient capital to leave the plantations to start family businesses in urban areas or to move to the mainland to farm or operate small businesses.

POST-WAR IMMIGRANTS (1945–1964)

After World War II ended, Soviet troops occupied northern Korea and American troops occupied southern Korea. Efforts to unify the country failed, and war broke out in 1950. The Korean War lasted until 1953.

During this period, the United States established a strong military presence in South Korea to thwart the spread of communism in Asia. The U.S.–Korean military relationship was the link that paved the road for the second wave of Korean immigration to the United States. Korean wives of U.S. servicemen stationed in South Korea and the children of U.S. servicemen were allowed to come to the United States on a nonquota basis through the War Brides Act of 1945.

Unlike the first wave of immigrants, who were uneducated male farmers, immigrants who entered during the second wave came from two ends of the Korean class system. On one end of the spectrum were war brides and orphans from lower-class backgrounds. On the other end were students, children of the elite from the upper echelons of Korean society, who came to study. Among the almost fourteen thousand immigrants who entered the United States between 1951 and 1964, three-fourths were wives of U.S. servicemen or war orphans who were adopted by American parents. The wives of servicemen and children adopted by established American citizens were scattered throughout the new country and isolated from other Korean immigrants. On the opposite end of the class system were six thousand Korean students who came to the United States seeking higher education and advanced degrees. Most of the students expected to return to South Korea with their prestigious degrees; however, most remained in the United States upon completion of their education and many became important links for the chain migration that was to follow.

IMMIGRATION TO AMERICA AFTER 1965

Although Koreans have been in the United States for almost a century, their numbers remained small until 1965. The passage of the Immigration and Nationality Act of 1965 eliminated the prior discriminatory immigration system based on national-origin quotas to one based on a preferential system. The 1965 law restructured the previous immigration law to give priority to family unification. Preferences were given to spouses, children, parents, and siblings of permanent residents and U.S. citizens, and to individuals with special skills or training. This law had a tremendous influence on immigration from Korea and other parts of Asia, dramatically changing the contours of America's immigrant landscape and radically redefining

the characteristics of Korean immigrants to the United States.

The changes in U.S. immigration policies were vital in allowing Korean immigrants to enter, but other factors propelled the mass immigration of South Koreans to the United States. The need to control population growth and to manage high unemployment within South Korea forced the Korean government to launch a series of actions to encourage emigration. In addition, South Koreans were also motivated to leave by the political instability in their home country. Many Koreans opposed the oppressive military regimes of Park Chung-Hee (1963–79) and Chun Doo-Hwan (1980–88) and feared the possibility of another war in South Korea. Moreover, the relationship between the United States and South Korea led to the diffusion of U.S. cultural, political, and economic influences, which lured immigrants to come. The United States played a key role in reforming South Korea's educational curriculum by instilling into Korean students the ideas of democracy and equality. Other immigrants, particularly college graduates, longed for better economic and educational opportunities, as many encountered high unemployment and barriers to mobility at home. The number of college graduates exceeded demands for a highly educated labor force in a country that relied on low-wage labor for its rapid export-oriented industrialization. The enticement of the U.S. media was one of the strongest hooks for immigrants, who caught the "American fever" as it promised them democracy, prosperity, and gender equality.

The year 1970 was the first time that the U.S. Census Bureau began to classify Koreans as a distinct Asian group. Almost 71,000 persons identified themselves as Korean in 1970; however, by the 1980 census there were over 357,000 Koreans throughout the United States. This 400 percent increase represented the fastest-growing immigrant group at that time. At its peak period between 1985 and 1987, Korea sent over thirty-five thousand immigrants annually; only Mexico and Philippines sent more people to the United States. By 1990, Korean-American population growth in the United States was again very striking. Within a decade, the Korean population in the United States grew over 125 percent. There were about eight hundred thousand Korean Americans in 1990. Currently, Korean Americans are the fifth largest Asian group. It is projected that there were over 1 million Koreans in the United States as of the year 2000.

The socioeconomic composition of the third wave of Korean migrants differed radically from that of the

A Korean immigrant family enjoys a picnic and celebrates their nation's harvest festival in a Queens, New York, park. *(Hazel Hankin, Impact Visuals)*

previous groups. Most post-1965 immigrants came from urban areas, primarily Seoul, and most were educated. They also came from the middle class, and many had held white-collar occupations in technical, managerial, and professional fields before emigrating. The number of professional immigrants increased until the late 1970s, but an amendment of the 1965 Act in 1976 made it difficult for professional immigrants to come to the United States. Hence, the number of professional immigrants has decreased since the late 1970s, while the proportion of the working class has been increasing. The phenomenal growth of the Korean immigrant population in the last two decades of the twentieth century was a direct consequence of chain migration, or immigrants who enter through the invitation of relatives who are permanent residents or citizens in the United States. Another notable difference is that, in contrast to the previous waves of immigrants, most post-1965 immigrants came as families. Indeed, the presence of families for this new wave was highly instrumental in their social and economic adaptation.

KOREANS IN SMALL BUSINESS

The propensity of Korean immigrants toward small business ownership is striking. Nationally, in 1990, over 25 percent of all Korean Americans were self-employed, representing the highest self-employed group among all ethnic and racial groups. Their self-employment rate was double the national average. In a study by Pyung Gap Min, he found that one-half of all Korean immigrants in Los Angeles were self-employed, exceeding the self-employment rates for all other immigrant and native groups.

Self-employment provides benefits to Korean immigrants that they would otherwise not receive from the general labor market. First, self-employment allows Korean immigrants to achieve economic mobility more quickly than working in the secondary labor market. In small businesses, Korean immigrants do not need to be proficient in English, for immigrants can rely on their children to help with language interpretation. Small businesses are family businesses, often named "mom-and-pop" shops, as families provide long hours of unpaid labor. Additionally, self-employment provides Korean immigrants with a sense of autonomy and flexibility that they would not receive in the general labor market. Hence, immigrants set the hours of operation, or leave and return at will, without answering to a higher authority.

Korean immigrants are heavily concentrated in a few principal businesses, such as liquor stores; greengrocers, primarily in New York; dry cleaning; retailers of imported goods from South Korea, such as wigs and low-end fashion items; and the garment manufacturing industry. The characteristics that these businesses share are that they are labor-intensive and require long hours of work.

REASONS WHY KOREAN IMMIGRANTS ENTER ENTREPRENEURSHIP

Various theories help explain the overrepresentation of Korean immigrants in small businesses. The restructuring of the contemporary U.S. labor market into a segmented labor market has made it difficult for Korean immigrants to find work commensurate with their educational attainment. Good wages, promotional opportunities, and job security characterize jobs in the primary sector. However, racial minorities and women have been systematically excluded from this sector. Korean immigrants are unable to participate because of their inability to transfer their occupational skills and credentials and their lack of proficiency in English. The secondary sector of the labor market is not an attractive alternative, as jobs in this sector are labor-intensive, low-paying, and lack job security. Unable to find the kind of white-collar employment for which they had been trained in their native country, Korean immigrants enter small businesses in low-income minority neighborhoods or within their own ethnic communities. Hence, the development of the ethnic economy is tightly integrated with the structural changes in the overall U.S. economy, since Korean immigrants enter into small businesses in reaction to the structural constraints that they encounter.

While the disadvantaged position of Korean immigrants helps explain their predisposition to small businesses, they need access to resources that will aid them in business. The resources theory of entrepreneurship suggests that there are resources on which Korean immigrants rely that facilitate their entrance into and success in small businesses. Family is one of the most valuable resources available to immigrant entrepreneurs. Just as families were vital for the first wave of Korean immigrants to move off the Hawaiian

plantations, family members, and especially spouses, are valuable resources for cheap or unpaid labor. Extended family, such as in-laws, may also contribute indirectly by providing free child-care services. When family labor is unavailable, fellow Korean immigrants and non-Koreans, usually Latino immigrants, are available to work for low wages.

Ethnic resources include material and financial goods and services, such as social networks; ethnic banks; trade guilds; and *kye*, or rotating credit associations. Ethnic social networks such as Korean-American churches, high school or college alumni associations, and Korean-American media channel information to coethnics. Class resources are also instrumental in assisting Korean immigrants into entrepreneurship. Class resources are the material and cultural endowments, such as material resources and middle-class values that immigrants mobilize in small businesses. Researchers attribute working long hours, saving money through delayed gratification, and placing high value on education as class resources that promote entrepreneurial success. Hence, contemporary Korean immigrants who come from middle-class backgrounds, who are educated, and who emigrate with large sums of money are equipped with cultural resources that give them an advantage to succeed in small businesses.

The opportunity structure theory of immigrant entrepreneurship points to business opportunities or niches that Korean immigrant entrepreneurs create. Korean immigrants have created niches in neglected and underserved areas in low-income minority neighborhoods that many middle-class whites and their businesses have left. The high crime rates and shrinking middle-class customer base have dropped the market of the stores, and many buildings are left vacant. It is in such areas that Korean entrepreneurs seize the opportunity to establish businesses. Another area that presents opportunities for Korean entrepreneurs is ethnic enclaves such as Koreatown in Los Angeles and in Flushing, New York, where there is a high concentration of coethnics who seek goods and services that cater specifically to their needs.

THE CASE OF KOREANS IN KOREATOWN, LOS ANGELES

Over 44 percent of all Korean Americans in the United States live in the West, and one-third live in California. Southern California houses the largest concentration of Koreans in the United States. In 1990, there were almost three hundred thousand Koreans in California, with over one hundred forty-five thousand Koreans residing in Los Angeles County. Almost 70 percent of Koreans in California reside in Orange and Los Angeles Counties. The thriving Korean ethnic economies in Los Angeles and Orange Counties have become magnets for newly arriving and established immigrants. While competition is fierce, business opportunities serving the needs of coethnics abound.

The Korean economic enclave in Los Angeles, known as Koreatown, is a commercial and cultural community west of downtown Los Angeles that houses the largest concentration of Korean-owned businesses in the United States. More than a quarter of all Korean-owned firms in Southern California are nestled within its twenty square miles. Korean Americans own 95 percent of the over seven hundred businesses in the heart of Koreatown and 40 percent of the businesses in the immediate surrounding areas. Most of the businesses within this community cater to the cultural, social, and economic needs of coethnic immigrants. While Korean immigrants are the primary business owners within this community, the majority of its residents are recent Mexican immigrants and only 15 percent of the residents in Koreatown are Korean. Due to the poor quality of the schools and high crime rates, most Korean immigrants consider it a temporary place of residence.

CONSEQUENCES OF IMMIGRATION

Significant changes occur in the lives of immigrants as a result of emigration. Women shoulder new roles and expectations, while many educated immigrants face downward mobility, as they are unable to recapture their premigration occupation and social status. For many South Korean women whose identities and roles are traditionally defined as the family caregiver, entry into the labor market is one of the first major changes to occur in their lives upon immigration. One survey of married Korean women, taken before departure, found that while only 30 percent had worked outside of the home before immigration, over 83 percent expected to work after coming to the United States. Studies on Korean communities show that 75 percent of married Korean women worked outside the home (a higher percentage than any other ethnic group), compared with only 20 percent of married women in South Korea who work. Another study reports that over 67 percent of Korean-American women are in the labor force as full- or part-time workers.

Men and women have different motivations and expectations for immigration. Women are enticed by the promise of gender equality and the vision that America is a land that will provide them with material comfort. Immigration also offers women the opportunity to leave their burdensome obligations to their husbands' families and their precarious relationships with their parents-in-law.

Middle-class women in Korea are mostly expected to quit wage work upon marriage. College diplomas are used to secure a good marriage prospect, rather than a lifelong career. Migration has indeed tremendously affected women's lives, as many are expected to enter wage labor in order to supplement their family's income. Women take on a double burden as the sole workers within the domestic sphere and as wage earners doing labor-intensive work. These demanding roles often lead to stress and overwork. Many other women enter small businesses with their spouses, working long hours as unpaid labor, where patriarchal constraints are reproduced at the place of work. It is not surprising, then, that immigration puts strains on the conjugal relationship and increases the divorce rate to five to six times higher than in their homeland.

Downward occupational mobility is another problem that Korean immigrants encounter. Since most Korean immigrants attain economic mobility through self-employment, their educational backgrounds and occupations before migration are not commensurate with their work after migration. This often leads to feelings of regret, but they are unable to return to Korea for fear of loss of face and humiliation. Many are subject to depression and other psychological problems.

The most serious and immediate problem for Korean business owners is interethnic conflict. Korean entrepreneurs who operate businesses in minority neighborhoods are perceived by African Americans as exploiting their community by taking resources as well as their economic autonomy away from them. Although the media have portrayed the hostility between African Americans and Korean Americans solely as an outcome of cultural and linguistical differences, the root of the problem extends beyond these differences. One overlooked factor is that the plight of the African Americans in the inner cities is related to structural changes in the economy. Economic restructuring has led to the loss of heavy manufacturing jobs in Los Angeles and a shift to light manufacturing and service jobs. Most of these jobs are poorly paid, and they are usually taken by Latino immigrants. Korean business owners in the inner cities are treated as scapegoats and bear the frustrations of African Americans' economic woes. Many Korean-owned businesses in Chicago, New York, and Los Angeles have been targets of boycotts and looting. The conflict between the two groups was nowhere more evident than in the Los Angeles riots in April 1992, when approximately thirty-two hundred Korean-American businesses were looted or destroyed by fire. Korean merchants were the targets of hostility from oppressed racial minorities.

The economic, political, and cultural involvement of the United States in Korea paved the path for the 100-year history of Korean immigration to the United States. However, Korean migration to the United States was not very significant until the passage of the Immigration and Nationality Act of 1965. In the years since then, the Korean-American population has reached almost one million. Unlike previous groups, the new wave of immigrants consists of urban, educated professionals, and most come as families.

For many Korean Americans, small business ownership presents one of few options for economic mobility. However, entrepreneurial success is often gained at the price of physical and psychological security. Research is now exploring the outcome of the second-generation Korean Americans. Will they follow in the footsteps of their parents by entering entrepreneurship? Most studies find this not to be true, as most children of immigrants are finding professional jobs.

Yoonies Park

See also: Immigrant-Minority Relations (Part I, Sec. 5); Wars and Civil Unrest (Part II, Sec. 1); Los Angeles, New York City (Part II, Sec. 12); Immigration to Japan (Part II, Sec. 13).

BIBLIOGRAPHY

Abelman, Nancy, and John Lie. *Blue Dreams: Korean Americans and the Los Angeles Riots.* Cambridge, MA: Harvard University Press, 1995.

Asis, Maruja Milagros B. *To the United States and into the Labor Force: Occupational Expectations of Filipino and Korean Immigrant Women.* Papers of the East-West Population Institute, No. 118. Honolulu, HI: East-West Center, 1991.

Barringer, Herbert R., Robert W. Gardner, and Michael J. Levin. *Asians and Pacific Islanders in the United States.* New York: Russell Sage Foundation, 1993.

Bureau of the Census. *1990 Census of Population and Housing.* Washington, DC: U.S. Government Printing Office, 1992.

Bureau of the Census, U.S. Department of Commerce. *We, the Asian and Pacific Islander Americans.* Washington, DC: U.S. Government Printing Office, 1993.

Choy, Bong-Youn. *Koreans in America.* Chicago: Nelson Hall, 1979.

Glenn, Evelyn Nakano. "Split Household, Small Producers, and Dual Wage Earner: An Analysis of Chinese-American Family Strategies." *Journal of Marriage and the Family* 1 (1983): 35–47.

Hondagneu-Sotelo, Pierrette. *Gendered Transitions: Mexican Experiences of Immigration.* Los Angeles: University of California Press, 1994.

Hurh, Won Moo. *The Korean Americans.* Westport, CT: Greenwood Press, 1998.

Kim, K. Chung, and Won Moo Hurh. "The Burden of Double Roles: Korean Immigrant Wives in the USA." *Ethnic and Racial Studies* 11 (1988): 151–67.

Kim, Illsoo. *New Urban Immigrants: The Korean Community in New York.* Princeton, NJ: Princeton University Press, 1981.

Light, Ivan, and Edna Bonacich. *Immigrant Entrepreneurs.* Los Angeles: University of California Press, 1988.

———, and Carolyn Rosenstein. *Race, Ethnicity, and Entrepreneurship in Urban America.* New York: Aldine de Gruyter, 1995.

———, Georges Sabagh, Mehdi Bozorgmehr, and Claudi Der-Martirosian. "Beyond the Ethnic Enclave Economy." *Social Problems* 41:1 (1994): 65–80.

Liu, John. "A Comparative View of Asian Immigration to the USA." In *The Cambridge Survey of World Migration,* ed. Robin Cohen, 253–59. New York: Cambridge University Press, 1995.

———, and Lucie Cheng. "Pacific Rim Development and the Duality of the Post-1965 Asian Immigration to the United States." In *The New Asian Immigration in Los Angeles and Global Restructuring,* ed. Paul Ong, Edna Bonacich, and Lucie Cheng, 74–99. Philadelphia: Temple University Press, 1994.

Mangiafico, Luciano. *Contemporary American Immigrants: Patterns of Filipino, Korean, and Chinese Settlement in the United States.* New York: Praeger, 1988.

Mar, Don. "Another Look at the Enclave Economy Thesis: Chinese Immigrants in the Ethnic Labor Market." *Amerasia* 17: 3 (1991): 5–21.

Min, Pyung Gap. "Problems of Korean Immigrant Entrepreneurs." *International Migration Review* 24:3 (1990): 436–55.

———. "The Entrepreneurial Adaptation of Korean Immigrants." In *Origins and Destinies: Immigration, Race, and Ethnicity in America,* ed. Silvia Pedraza and Ruben Rumbaut, 302–14. San Francisco: Wadsworth, 1996.

———. *Caught in the Middle: Korean Communities in New York and Los Angeles.* Los Angeles: University of California Press, 1996.

Ong, Paul, Edna Bonacich, and Lucie Cheng. "The Political Economy of Capitalist Restructuring and the New Asian Immigration." In *The New Asian Immigration in Los Angeles and Global Restructuring,* ed. Paul Ong, Edna Bonacich, and Lucie Cheng, 3–35. Philadelphia: Temple University Press, 1994.

Park, Kyeyoung. *The Korean American Dream: Immigrants and Small Business in New York City.* Ithaca, NY: Cornell University Press, 1997.

Sanders, Jimy M., and Victor Nee. "Immigrant Self-Employment: The Family as Social Capital and the Value of Human Capital." *American Sociological Review* 61 (April 1996): 231–49.

Waldinger, Roger. "Structural Opportunity or Ethnic Advantage? Immigrant Business Development in New York." *International Migration Review* 23:1 (1989): 48–72.

Yoon, In Jin. "The Changing Significance of Ethnic and Class Resources in Immigrant Businesses: The Case of Korean Immigrant Businesses in Chicago." *International Migration Review* 25:2 (1991): 303–31.

———. *On My Own: Korean: Businesses and Race Relations in America.* Chicago: University of Chicago Press, 1997.

Yu, Eui-Young, and Earl H. Phillips. *Korean Women in Transition.* Los Angeles: Center for Korean American and Korean Studies, California State University, 1987.

MIDDLE EAST

Immigrants from the near Middle East include people from Turkey, Lebanon, Syria, Israel, Jordan, Iraq, the West Bank and Gaza Strip, the Arab Gulf States, Saudi Arabia, and Yemen. The overwhelming majority of the immigrants from these countries and regions are Arab, Christian, and Muslim but also include other ethnic and religious minorities such as Armenians, Jews, Assyrians, and Kurds. An "Arab" is defined in the broadest sense of the term as someone coming from an Arab country, speaking Arabic, and professing to be Arab.

IMMIGRATION FROM THE OTTOMAN EMPIRE (GREATER SYRIA)

The 1990 census placed the number of ethnic Arabs or those who trace their ancestry to immigrants from the Arab countries at about 870,000. Arab sources, however, place the figure at anywhere from 1 to 3 million. Half of the Arabs in the United States are descendants from the first wave of immigrants who came before World War I from what was then known as the Ottoman Empire. For the most part, they trace their roots to Mount Lebanon and Syria. According to some sources, the overwhelming majority of these immigrants, estimated at 90 percent, were Christians who adhered to the eastern rites of Christianity: Maronite, Melchite Catholic, and Eastern Orthodox. Though generally Christian, the early Arab Americans maintained the sectarian divisions from the Middle East. Many fewer Muslims emigrated from the same region during this period. Until 1899, U.S. immigration did not distinguish Arab immigrants from other Ottoman subjects. They were labeled "Turks" and were included with other ethnic groups from the empire, such as Greeks and Armenians. Figures show that between 1899 and 1940, 115,838 Arab Syrians immigrated to the United States. But no estimate exists

of the Arabs who entered the country after living for a time in Canada, South and Central America, and the West Indies.

The early Arab immigrants from the Ottoman Empire called themselves "Syrians" because they came from that part of the Ottoman Empire that was known as Greater Syria. Geographically, Greater Syria consists of present-day Syria, Lebanon, Jordan, and Israel (including the West Bank and Gaza Strip). Yet the early immigrants did not have a clear sense of national identity and instead identified themselves based on their family, religion, and native town or village, as they were accustomed to doing in the Ottoman Empire. This cultural identity was strong and important. Syrians maintained close ties with other immigrants from Greater Syria who belonged to the same religious sect, and most of the cultural and social activities in the United States centered on the church. After World War II, when many of the Middle Eastern countries gained independence and a strong nationalistic Arab feeling swept the region, the term "Arab" became widespread, and immigrants used this term to refer to themselves regardless of religion, sect, or place of origin. Arab immigrants also began to identify themselves as Syrian (coming from the country Syria), Lebanese, and Palestinian based on their or their ancestors' place of origin, according to the new geopolitical map of the Middle East.

The early wave of immigrants left for various economic and political reasons. And not only the poor but also members of the elite left. Many of the poor immigrants were illiterate, unskilled, young, unmarried peasant men who came to the United States to seek their fortune. Many did not speak English. Some returned to their native village after saving enough money to enable them to settle down comfortably. The appearance of wealth on the young men who had left only a few years earlier encouraged others to leave. In 1860, a civil war broke out in Mount Lebanon, and in the aftermath of the conflict, many Christians and

Muslims who were left homeless and without means for a livelihood left for America. They also emigrated to avoid sectarian and religious strife. In 1907, the Turkish government instigated military conscription for the non-Muslim minority, and soon afterward, many young Christian men, Arab or Armenian, left to avoid military duty in the Ottoman army. In addition, a few Syrians who were educated in American missionary schools left for the United States for employment opportunities because jobs were scarce in Syria for learned young men. Although most of the immigrants were peasants, they did not usually seek agricultural work when they arrived in America. Most worked as peddlers, in factories, or in businesses already established by other Arab immigrants.

As more young men brought their families to America, ethnic Syrian communities began to flourish across the United States, most notably in New York City, Boston, and Detroit. As they settled among Americans, they began to assimilate but tried to maintain their distinctive cultural and ethnic values. Syrians in America maintained close ties with the Arab world either due to connections with family still living in the Middle East or to a growing feeling of Arab nationalism, especially after World War II. Early Arab Americans established several organizations and institutions, one of which was the literary society called the Pen League, established in New York City in 1915 by writers led by Khalil Gibran (1883–1931), author of *The Prophet*. This society had greater influence on the arts and literature in the Arab world than on the Syrians in America, evidence of the links maintained with the homeland.

ARAB IMMIGRATION FROM ARAB COUNTRIES

Immigration from the Arab countries in the Middle East continued, albeit in smaller numbers after World War I. The United States curtailed immigration during this period, especially during the depression. At this time, the character of the immigrants changed. Although still predominately Christians from Syria and Lebanon, Arab immigrants from the near Middle East were educated in Western or Western-influenced schools and were more affluent than the first wave of Arab immigrants. Immigrants were not only leaving in search of better economic opportunities but also fleeing war-torn countries, especially the countries waging those wars of independence that followed the end of World War II and the demise of the colonial

era. Syria and Iraq were in the turmoil of successive revolutions that led many of the landed gentry who lost their traditional source of power and livelihood to leave. Palestinians who became refugees after 1948 also immigrated in increasing numbers to the United States.

After the Hart-Celler Act of 1964, which reduced the restrictions on entry to the United States, immigration to the United States increased. Under this new act, preference was given to family unification and individuals with professional skills. The category of "refugee" was expanded to include not only those fleeing political or religious oppression and civil war but also survivors from natural disasters. As a result of these changes, in the 1990 census, over 75 percent of Arab Americans born outside the United States had immigrated after 1964. During this period, the percentage of Arab immigrants who were Muslim increased.

In the 1980s, immigrants from the Arab world were second in number only to immigrants from Asia. According to the 1990 census, 82 percent of Arab Americans were citizens, but only 63 percent were born in the United States. Currently, the majority of Arab Americans are Lebanese or Syrian descendants but include a growing number of Palestinians and Iraqis. It is believed that immigration from these countries will continue, especially if the peace talks between the Arabs and the Israelis falter and the United Nations continues sanctions on Iraq. Immigration from Lebanon, Syria, Iraq, and Jordan remains significant. In the totals of immigrants from these countries, Palestinians figure significantly.

The creation of Israel in 1948 resulted in the displacement of 700,000 Palestinians who became refugees overnight. Another 500,000 were displaced due to the Arab-Israeli War in 1967. The majority of Arab immigrants to the United States between 1948 and 1966 were Palestinians, of whom more than 60 percent were Muslim. These immigrants are highly educated professionals. Because they generally have higher levels of education and achievement, Palestinian Arabs have a higher socioeconomic status than other Arab Americans. Palestinians have settled throughout the United States but can be found mainly in California, Texas, Michigan, New York, Illinois, and Florida.

Iraqi Muslim immigrants have increased in number during the 1980s and 1990s as a result of two wars: the Iran-Iraq War and the Persian Gulf War. According to the 1990 census, there were 14,359 Iraqi immigrants in the United States, many of whom were given refugee status as a result of displacement or persecution by the Iraqi government. They live pre-

Brooklyn, once home to one of the most vibrant Jewish communities in the United States, is now, ironically, a popular destination for Arab immigrants like these two Palestinian women. *(Mel Rosenthal)*

dominantly in Detroit and Dearborn, Michigan; Chicago; and Los Angeles.

Immigration from Jordan has grown steadily over the course of the past two decades. Yet it remains difficult to determine the exact number of ethnic Jordanians because many Palestinians who entered the country did so under the classification of "Jordanian" because they held Jordanian passports.

In addition to Sunni Muslims, there are Shia Muslim immigrants mostly from southern Lebanon and Iraq. The number of immigrant Druze, a Shia Muslim sect, is also increasing. Most of these immigrants come from Lebanon and consider themselves Arab. They have left their homeland as a result of the civil war in Lebanon during the 1970s and 1980s. Large Druze populations can be found in Los Angeles, Houston, and Dearborn. Most are educated, professional, and middle class. As Muslim immigration from Arab countries rises, more mosques and Islamic institutes are being created throughout the United States to cater to their spiritual needs. The increase in recent im-

migration of educated and professional Arabs has led to a loss of valuable professional human resources in many Arab countries.

Although there are Arab Americans living in all fifty states, large communities are found in eleven states: Massachusetts, Rhode Island, New Jersey, New York, Pennsylvania, Virginia, Texas, Michigan, Ohio, Illinois, and California. New immigrants tend to reside in areas where there is an established Arab community. The top destination is California, where there is a high concentration of Arab Americans in the Los Angeles–Long Beach area. The second and third choices for new immigrants are New York City and Detroit, respectively. Recent arrivals are more likely to live in ethnic enclaves with other Arab Americans from the same country of origin.

In addition, Arab immigration has increased from other Middle Eastern countries that traditionally were not sources of immigrants to the United States, such as the Gulf States and Yemen. The most prominent group consists of immigrants from Yemen who began to arrive in the 1960s, mostly single young men in search of work and who settled mainly in Detroit. These workers would remit their earnings to their family members who remained behind in Yemen. As in the case with other immigrant Arabs from the Middle East, especially in the early days, some returned to Yemen while others remained and took advantage of immigration laws to bring their families over to the United States. Though still small in number, the Yemeni community in the United States is increasing at a fast pace. In the ten years between 1982 and 1992, it has increased fourfold to a total of 2,100 Yemenis. Yemeni communities can be found in Michigan, California, and New York. Immigrants from the Gulf States are negligible. In 1992, less than 600 nationals emigrated from Saudi Arabia, and only 200 have left the United Emirates. Only 59 nationals emigrated from Qatar.

As a migrant group, Arab Americans retain certain characteristics that set them apart from the rest of the U.S. population. Arab Americans tend to be younger than other ethnic groups. On the whole, they have a higher level of education, with 82 percent having attained a high school diploma, and 36 percent, a bachelor's degree or higher. Many of the immigrants in the second wave came for the purpose of a higher education and remained to work and live in the United States. As a result of being more educated, they tend to earn higher than the median income for other Americans. The tradition of self-employment remains strong among Arab Americans, especially in retail and professional services. Compared with immigrants from other ethnic groups, they prefer to settle in urban areas, with 91 percent of Arab Americans residing in such locations.

Usually, both spouses in the household are Arab. The extended family residing together is more commonly found among recent immigrants, and then only in small numbers. Many Arab-American families are nuclear, though they may live in neighborhoods with other relatives and members from their native village or town living nearby.

Although early immigrants were relatively unnoticed by the host community, Arab Americans have recently been faced with hostile reactions from the American public and government, especially after the Arab-Israeli War. Antagonism toward the Arab-American community and negative stereotyping in American media and society became widespread, while discrimination against this group was highest during the 1970s and 1980s. In 1970, the Nixon administration launched Operation Boulder, whose aim was to combat terrorism in the United States by targeting Arab Americans through surveillance methods

that were sometimes unconstitutional. After the Arab-Israeli War and the oil crisis of the 1970s, Arabs were vilified and often depicted as bloodthirsty sheikhs. International acts of terrorism and adverse political developments in the Middle East would result in a backlash on Arab Americans. Some became the target of hate mail and assassination. During this period, many Arab Americans were under surveillance by the Federal Bureau of Investigation (FBI) in violation of their civil liberties, and during the Persian Gulf War in 1991, many Iraqi Americans faced hostility.

Arab Americans have established several national organizations to advocate issues of concern to the community at large. The American Arab Anti-Discrimination Committee (ADC) was founded in 1980 to fight the defamation and stereotyping of Arab Americans. The Arab American Institute (AAI) was established in 1985 to mobilize the Arab American community and encourage it to be more involved in the United States's political process. The National Association of Arab Americans (NAAA), in addition to combating negative images of Arab Americans, works on improving the relationship between the United States and Arab nations. The Association of Arab American University Graduates, Inc. (AAUG), founded by a group of academics in 1967 in the aftermath of the Arab-Israeli War, seeks to represent the Arab point of view to Americans.

Arab Americans have contributed in numerous ways to American society and have achieved prominence in all fields in the United States. Among the notable members of this community is Edward Said, a world-renowned scholar and writer. Doug Flutie, quarterback for the Buffalo Bills, has won the Heisman Trophy. Michael De Bakey is a prominent heart surgeon. Entertainer Danny Thomas and his daughter Marlo Thomas have been household names. Paul Anka and Paula Abdul are well known in the music industry, while Casey Kasem achieved prominence in radio. In politics, James Abourezk of South Dakota was the first Arab American to be elected to the Senate, John Sununu served as President George Bush's chief of staff, and Donna Shalala served as secretary of health and human services for President Bill Clinton. Ralph Nader, the influential consumer advocate, maintains a huge influence on national policy.

IMMIGRATION FROM ISRAEL, TURKEY, AND KURDISTAN

Since the founding of Israel in 1948, there has been a steady flow of Jewish immigrants from that country to the United States, in addition to Palestinians, Armenians, and other Middle Eastern groups. From 1948 to 1990, the number of legal immigrants from the Middle East has increased. The largest population of Israeli Americans lives in Los Angeles and New York City. Although itself a country established by Jewish migration from all over the world, many chose to leave Israel for the United States for a variety of reasons, including seeking better economic opportunities, unifying families, and escaping the military service required because of the turbulent political situation in the Middle East. Some of the Jewish minorities left Israel because of discrimination they felt in Israel. In the 1970s and 1980s, Jewish immigrants to the United States were considered to be turning their back on the Zionist dream to establish a Jewish homeland in Israel and were stigmatized by American Jews. But these feelings have subsided, and today, Israeli expatriates are welcomed in Jewish communities across the United States. Israeli Americans also maintain close ties to Israel, which continues to offer benefits and services to them as they reside in the States. Israeli sources indicate that after 1992 and the election of the Labor Party in Israel on a platform to pursue peace with the Arabs, the number of Israelis returning from the United States increased.

Israeli immigrants tend to be young—under forty-five years of age. On the whole, they are well educated, with 58 percent in Los Angeles and 54 percent in New York having some kind of college education. Approximately 50 percent of those between the ages of twenty-four and sixty-five work as administrators, professionals, or technical specialists, and 25 percent work in marketing. Those self-employed work mainly in the real estate, construction, jewelry, garment, engineering, and media industries.

Little information exists on ethnic Turk immigrants in the United States. Turks can be found in New York City, Los Angeles, and Chicago, and they include both the early immigrants who left the Ottoman Empire as well as Turks who came from the state of Turkey after it was founded in 1923. "Turk" was the term designated for immigrants from the Ottoman Empire, who included Arabs, Armenians, Greeks, and individuals from the Balkans. After World War I, "Turk" was used for persons from present-day Turkey who spoke Turkish and were Muslims. Up until 1940, most of these were men who came in search of economic opportunities. They were largely illiterate, worked as unskilled labor and lived with other Turks. Their impact on American life was minimal, and because of their small numbers, they did not become a visible ethnic minority in the United States. After 1940, most of the immigrants from Turkey were well-

educated professionals seeking better jobs and wages in the United States, thus causing a drain on human resources in the home country. As the economic situation in the United States changed, many of these professionals returned to Turkey. The expatriate community maintains strong ties with Turkey. Nationalist sentiments run high, and many continue to hold Turkish passports even as permanent residents of the United States. Turks in the United States closely follow political events in Turkey and have been in contention with Armenian and Greek groups in the United States.

Turkish immigrants have established an estimated one hundred clubs and associations, but membership tends to be small, with less than fifty members. Turkish cultural events are held in areas where there is a sizable community or in universities that offer Turkish studies.

Kurds form a distinct ethnic group and live in an area referred to as Kurdistan that lies in four Middle Eastern countries: Iran, Turkey, Syria, and Iraq. Kurdistan was never an independent country, and Kurds were subjugated by the governments of the countries within whose borders they resided. Since the beginning of this century, Kurds have been involved in efforts to create an independent country for themselves. Kurds in the United States came originally as students but remained to work and eventually settle down. They remain connected to their country of origin and raise funds to support the war efforts there.

OTHER IMMIGRATION FROM THE MIDDLE EAST

Immigration of Armenians commenced in the nineteenth and early twentieth centuries from the region in northeastern Turkey and the former Armenian Soviet Socialist Republic of the Soviet Union. American missionaries who originally went to proselytize among the Turks but found a more willing audience among the Armenians introduced them to the United States. Although not many Armenians did convert (only 50,000 became Protestants by 1914), they were encouraged by the missionaries to go to America to study so they could return and serve their community. In the early years, only a small number of Armenians entered the United States, and they settled in the Northeast, notably in Massachusetts and Rhode Island. For the most part, these early immigrants were educated and skilled laborers and overwhelmingly young men. Some of those immigrants made their fortune and returned to their homeland. For this early period, it is difficult to assess the number of Armenians immigrating to the United States because data are unavailable. After the massacre of Armenians in 1895 in the Ottoman Empire, there was an increase in the number leaving the country. The number of Armenians entering the United States between 1895 and 1899 reached a total of 70,982. The Ottoman Empire prohibited the emigration of Armenians, but the continued oppression and annihilation of Armenians by the Turkish government during the following years greatly influenced migration. In 1915, the Ottomans killed over 1 million Armenians. After World War I and the dismantling of the Ottoman Empire, it remained difficult to determine the number of Armenians entering the United States because they were then emigrating from countries to which they had fled following the massacres. Many had left for France, Egypt, Lebanon, Iran, and Iraq and thereafter entered the United States as citizens of those countries. To this day, Armenian immigration continues from Soviet Armenia and countries in the Middle East. Most of the newcomers are young, educated professionals seeking better economic opportunities and escaping the political tensions in Middle Eastern countries.

By the 1970s, there were 350,000 to 450,000 Armenians living in the United States. Approximately half of the Armenians continue to live in New England, and the rest live in California and the Midwest. Not unlike Arab immigrants, Armenians moved predominantly to the urban areas, with the exception of the community in Fresno, California, which works in the cultivation of vineyards. The earlier immigrants, though skilled and educated, sought employment in factories where both men and women worked. The main aim was to get established and educate their children. It is estimated that 47 percent of Armenian Americans have a college education. The later generations and the newer immigrants worked in the professions and services. Business remains the main lure for the educated and skilled Armenians, and the present community is part of the American middle class.

Like other immigrant groups, Armenians live largely in ethnic neighborhoods and maintain close ties with other Armenians. They pride themselves on their distinct cultural identity, and the early immigrants tried to keep alive the Armenian language, which to many was the cornerstone of their identity. With subsequent generations, however, assimilation into American society was stronger, and the Armenian language lost its appeal. Still, the family remains a solid force in Armenian communities, and there is a strong sense of pride in the solidarity and cohesiveness of the family. Children are reared to be proud of and loyal to the Armenian culture. Incidents of intermarriage with non-Armenians remained low until recently, and many of the older generations decry marrying outside the ethnic group as diluting the distinct Armenian culture.

Armenian cultural and social activities largely revolve around the Armenian Church, a church with a hierarchy separate from Rome, and there are about ninety-two parishes in fifty-two communities throughout the United States. The church currently plays a very important role in preserving the community's culture and traditions. It is estimated that 70 percent of Armenians are baptized in the church, although attendance at Sunday mass has gone down. The liturgy is in both Armenian and English.

Assyrians trace their ancestry to the ancient Assyrian Empire, which flourished in prebiblical times in Mesopotamia, part of present-day Iraq. They are a Christian group speaking in an Aramaic dialect and may refer to themselves as Chaldean or Syrian but are not to be confused with Arabs from Syria. Since the nineteenth century, there has been a steady flow of Assyrians from Iraq in search of employment or to escape oppression. Though they come from an Arab country, they reject the label "Arab." Because U.S. immigration records have not used the designation "Assyrian," no good estimate exists of the number of immigrants in the country. Assyrian leaders, however, place the figure between 60,000 and 75,000, and these populations can be found mainly in California, Illinois, Michigan, New Jersey, and New York.

The early Assyrian immigrants in the late 1880s were young men encouraged to immigrate by American missionaries working in their villages. The lure of streets paved with gold led many to cross the ocean in search of riches. Some returned to their native land or intended to return. The most recent immigrants are refugees from the wars in Iraq over the past two decades. The sanctions imposed on Iraq since the end of the Gulf War in 1991, along with the ensuing economic and social hardships, have further induced Assyrians to leave the country. Many of the emigrants take advantage of U.S. immigration policy favoring family unification. These immigrants tend to be more Arab in character than were the earlier ones, yet for the most part, Assyrians do not associate with other Arab immigrant groups.

Assyrians generally live in ethnic neighborhoods with other Assyrians. They tend to have large families and maintain close ties with extended family members, both in the United States and Iraq. The wishes of the family and community are important in making individual choices, and those family demands have become a source of contention among second- and third-generation Assyrians. Intermarriage is frowned upon, and members of the community are encouraged to sustain their distinct ethnic identity. Cultural activities are promoted by the church, which also strives to keep the ethnic identity alive. The situation during the Gulf War was especially difficult for many Assyrians, some of whom were harassed and had their businesses vandalized. Many worried for the safety of relatives in Iraq, and Assyrian communities in the United States mobilized efforts to help by sending money and medicine through informal channels.

Overall, immigration from the Middle East to the United States presents a varied picture. Some groups—such as Christian Lebanese and Syrians—have been in this country for generations and are as fully assimilated as any white ethnic group from Europe. At the same time, this population is being dramatically augmented by a new Muslim immigration from the region, as well as a continuing trickle of Christians. While the earlier immigrants came at a time when assimilation was the accepted option, newer immigrants insist on maintaining their distinctive culture and religion.

Faedah Totah

See also: Political, Ethnic, Religious, and Gender Persecution (Part II, Sec. 1); Islam, Judaism (Part II, Sec. 11); Houston, Los Angeles, New York City (Part II, Sec. 12).

BIBLIOGRAPHY

Bakalian, Anny. *Armenian-Americans: From Being to Feeling Armenian.* New Brunswick, NJ: Transaction, 1992.

El-badry, Samia. "The Arab Americans." *American Demographics* 16 (January 1994): 22–30.

Bilge, Barbara. "Voluntary Associations in the Old Turkish Community of Metropolitan Detroit." In *Muslim Communities in North America*, ed. Yvonne Yazbeck Haddad and Jane Idelman Smith, pp. 381–406. Albany: State University of New York Press, 1994.

Kass, Drora, and Seymour Martin Lipset. "Jewish Immigration to the United States from 1967 to the Present: Israelis and Others." In *Understanding American Jewry*, ed. Marshall Sklare, pp. 272–94. New Brunswick, NJ: Transaction, 1982.

Mehdi, Beverlee Turner. *The Arabs in America: 1492–1977.* Dobbs Ferry, NY: Oceana, 1978.

Naff, Alixa. *Becoming American: The Early Arab Immigrant Experience.* Carbondale: Southern Illinois University Press, 1985.

Rosenthal, Mirra, and Charles Auerbach. "Cultural and Social Assimilation of Israeli Immigrants in the United States." *International Migration Review* 26:3 (1992): 982–91.

Sengstock, Mary C. "Iraqi Christians in Detroit: An Analysis of an Ethnic Occupation." In *Arabic Speaking Communities in American Cities*, ed. Barbara Aswad, pp. 21–38. Staten Island, NY: Center for Migration Studies of New York, 1974.

Tashjian, James H. *The Armenians of the United States and Canada: A Brief Study.* 1947. Boston: Armenian Youth Federation, 1970.

Zogby, John. *Arab America Today: A Demographic Profile of Arab Americans.* Washington, DC: Arab American Institute, 1990.

GENERAL INDEX

442nd Regimental Combat Team, **1**:163–164
8, Code of Federal Regulations sec. 214.2(o), **2**:707
8, US Code sec. 1101(a)(15)(f), **2**:707
8, US Code sec. 1101(a)(15)(j), **2**:706
8, US Code sec. 1101(a)(15)(m), **2**:708–709
8, US Code sec. 1101(a)(15)(q), **2**:707
8, US Code sec. 1481(a), **4**:1459
8, US Code sec. 1481(b), **4**:1459
8, US Code sec. 1153(b)(1), **2**:705; **3**:837
8, US Code sec. 1153(b)(2), **2**:705–706; **3**:839
8, US Code sec. 1153(b)(3), **2**:706; **3**:840
8, US Code sec. 1153, **3**:837
20, Code of Federal Regulations sec. 656.21, **2**:706

A

Abbott, Grace, **4**:1488
Ability-motivation hypothesis, **2**:601
Academic institutions. *See* Education, higher
Academic Student. *See* F-1 Academic Student
Acadians, **1**:284; **4**:1265
Acculturation, **1**:94–96
  definition of, **4**:1505*g*
  factors aiding, **2**:717–719
  before leaving homeland, **3**:990
  stages in, **2**:721
  types of, **2**:424*t*
ACLU. *See* American Civil Liberties Union

Act Banning Naturalization of Anarchists (1903), **4**:1288
Act Conferring United States Citizenship on American Indians (1924), **4**:1297
Act of Union (Great Britain), **1**:54
Act to Establish a Uniform Rule of Naturalization, An (1790), **4**:1277
Activism. *See* Political activism
Adams, John, **1**:51, 71, 245; **2**:484
Adams, John Quincy, **1**:72
Addams, Jane, **1**:335; **2**:726, 730
Adolescence
  adjustment among, **2**:426–430
  community-based services, **2**:733
  crime, **2**:683–684
  demographics, **2**:422–424
  impact of immigration on, **2**:425
  See also Children
Adoption, **1**:307–310; **2**:506
Adventurer, **3**:858
Advocacy groups. *See* Interest groups
Affidavit of support, **4**:1443, 1449, 1505*g*
Affirmative action, **3**:972
Afghan immigrants, **4**:1210
AFL-CIO. *See* American Federation of Labor-Congress of Industrial Organizations
African Americans
  banned from AFL-affiliated unions, **1**:123
  employment, **2**:573–574, 593
  and Irish immigrant relations, **1**:61, 62
  racial/ethnic conflict, **1**:225
  response to South African immigrants, **3**:1068

African Americans *(continued)*
  San Francisco, **3**:970, 972
  in Union army, **1**:85
  Washington, D.C., **3**:974
African immigrants
  East, **3**:1056–1060
  and evangelicalism, **3**:879
  forced immigration (slave trade), **1**:28, 37–41, 53, 89; **3**:1065, 1072
  North, **3**:1027–1028, 1062–1064
  South, **3**:1065–1068
  Washington, D.C., **3**:981
  West, **1**:37–40; **3**:1070–1077
  women, **3**:1060, 1074
Aggravated felonies, **2**:514
Agribusiness. *See* Agriculture
Agricultural Act of 1949. *See* Bracero Program Act (1949)
Agricultural labor
  contemporary trends, **2**:627
  ethnic and racial shifts, **2**:621–622
  public awareness, **2**:622–623
  social movements, **2**:625–626
  temporary workers, **4**:1318, 1327
  unions. *See* Agricultural organizations
Agricultural laws
  Bracero Program Act. *See* Bracero Program Act (1949)
  California Farm Labor Act (1975), **4**:1305–1312
Agricultural organizations
  Agricultural Workers Organizing Committee (AWCO), **2**:539, 622–623, 626
  Farm Labor Organizing Committee (FLOC), **2**:596, 626

La Unión de Trabajadores del Valle
  Imperial, **1:**171; **2:**626
Labor
  child, **1:**124
  Civil War and, **2:**501
  contract. *See* Contract labor
  discrimination, **2:**487–488
  displacement, **1:**184–185
  ethnicity and, **1:**118, 120, 122–123
  finding jobs, **1:**118–120
  hours, **1:**121–122
  industrial, **1:**118–123
  Irish labor conflict, **1:**61
  legalized aliens, **2:**479–480
  markets. *See* Labor markets
  resistance efforts, **1:**122–123, 124
  shop-floor production, **1:**121
  strikes, **1:**124, 145
  turnover rates, **1:**122
  unions. *See* Labor unions
  unskilled work, **1:**121; **2:**592
  U.S. Labor Department,
    1:184–185
  violations of laws, **2:**596
  work conditions, **1:**120, 121–122,
    124–125; **2:**596
  worker rights, **2:**479, 733
  workforce participation rates,
    2:606–607
  See also Earnings; Economics;
    Employment;
    Entrepreneurship
Labor market outcomes, **2:**629–634
  educational attainment and,
    2:634–636
  English fluency and, **2:**637–638
Labor markets
  competition hypothesis, **2:**565,
    566
  ethnic flux and volatility,
    2:688–689
  formal/informal, **2:**633, 651–652,
    688
  of global cities, **3:**992
  international law and, **3:**997–998
  restructuring of, **2:**688
  segmented, **3:**990–991
Labor unions, **1:**123, 124; **2:**539,
    596, 686–687
  agricultural, **2:**625–626
  garment industry, **2:**665, 675–677
  and legalized aliens, **2:**479

Labor unions *(continued)*
  Mexican, **1:**171
  organizing strategies, **2:**689–692
  service sector, **2:**658–659
  underground economy's effect
    on, **2:**679–680
Laborers International Union of
  North America (LIUNA),
  2:690
Labor-export countries, **1:**270
Labor-import countries, **1:**270
Lambada Legal Defense and
  Education Fund, **2:**449
Lamont Canal Strike Massacre
  (1893), **4:**1241
Land grants, **2:**620
Language
  Americanization of, **1:**126
  assimilation of, **3:**810
  generational shifts, **3:**811–812
  identity and, **3:**817–818
  laws, **1:**230; **2:**486; **3:**815
  linguistic nativism, **1:**230; **3:**804,
    815–817
  rights for minorities, **3:**815
  See also Bilingualism; English
    language
Laos, **1:**186, 188, 191
Laotian immigrants
  refugees, **1:**186–188, 290, 300;
    4:1226–1125
  repatriation, **1:**191
  settlement patterns, **2:**414–415;
    4:1226–1227
    Houston, **3:**906–907
    Washington, D.C., **3:**980
Latin American Club (LAC), **3:**904
Latin American immigrants
  attitude toward immigration,
    2:567
  crime, **2:**682–683
  culture and cultural identity
    film, **3:**788–789
    radio and television, **3:**798
    theater, **2:**762–763
  demographics (post-1965),
    1:357–358
  education/occupation level,
    1:206
  elders, **2:**432–433, 434
  evangelicalism, **3:**878–879
  family relations, **2:**441–442

Latin American immigrants
  (continued)
  gender roles, **2:**441, 458
  health, **2:**712
  immigration challenges,
    1:168–170
  immigration policy, **1:**167–168
  number of, **1:**195–196
  politics
    activism, **2:**540–541
    electoral, **2:**549, 550
  population, **1:**237, 360–361
  and poverty, **1:**208
  racial/ethnic conflict, **1:**225
  refugees, **1:**291
  settlement patterns, **2:**415–416
    Houston, **3:**903–904
    Los Angeles, **3:**914–915
    Washington, D.C., **3:**980
  See also specific ethnic group
Latin Americans, emigration to
  Israel, **3:**1029
Latter Day Saints, **1:**94
  Family History Library, **3:**808
Lattimer Massacre (1897), **4:**1241
Latvian immigrants, **4:**1232, 1243*t*
Lau v. Nichols (1974), **3:**815;
  4:1371–1372, 1511*g*
Laud, William, **1:**18, 20
Laughlin, Harry H., **1:**152
Laundry industry, **1:**79
Laurel Foundation, **1:**230
Lautenberg, Frank, **1:**211, 292
Lautenberg amendment, **1:**211–212
Law, international, **3:**997–999
Law of Return, **3:**1026; **4:**1511*g*
Law of Vacant Lands (1883),
  3:923–924
LDS. *See* Latter Day Saints
League of United Latin American
  Citizens (LULAC), **1:**168;
  2:535–536, 541, 545; **3:**904;
  4:1511*g*
  LULAC et al. v. Wilson et al.
    (1995), **4:**1387
Legal services, **2:**732
Legalized Population Survey
  (LPS), **2:**476–479, 629–630
Legg, Rok v., **2:**516
Lemieux Agreement. *See*
  Gentlemen's Agreement
Lemlich, Clara, **1:**124

Numbers in bold indicate volume; g indicates glossary.

Wobblies. *See* Industrial Workers of the World

Women
community-based services, **2**:733
Convention on the Elimination of All Forms of Discrimination Against Women, **4**:1437
depression in, **2**:720–721
earnings, **2**:633
and education, **2**:457
"feminization of poverty," **1**:361
genital mutilation, **1**:293; **2**:456–457; **4**:1327, 1508*g*
head of household, **2**:441, 444
legalized aliens, **2**:477
marriage. *See* Marriage
in sex industry, **1**:272, 273, 274–275, 329
sweatshop work, **2**:665–666
trafficking of, **1**:365–366; **2**:680
Violence Against Women Act (VAWA), **1**:367
and volunteerism/activism, **2**:455–456
working, **1**:124–125; **2**:453–455, 606
See also Fertility; Gender; Gender roles

Work. *See* Employment; Labor

Workers' rights, **3**:997–998

Working poor, **2**:602

Workingmen's Party of California, **1**:81, 95; **3**:967; **4**:1516*g*

Worksite enforcement, **4**:1433

World Bank, **1**:272

World Refugee Year Law (1960), **1**:167

World War I, **1**:135, 247
antiforeign propaganda, **1**:144
effect on immigration, **1**:105
homeland politics, **2**:554
nativism through, **1**:137–140
restrictive legislation, **1**:150–153, 156; **2**:503–504

World War II, **1**:135
effect on immigration, **1**:105; **2**:537–538
Israel, **3**:1025–1026
Japanese Internment. *See* Japanese internment
nativism, **1**:141–142
political activism, **2**:537–538
post war policies, **1**:159–160, 288
refugee crisis, **1**:158–159
religious/political persecution, **1**:286–288
restrictive legislation, **1**:153–154, 158–159; **2**:505
San Francisco, **3**:969–970

World-system theory, **1**:377

Wyoming, Rock Springs, **1**:81; **2**:623

Y

Yale University, **2**:703

Yamataya v. Fisher, **2**:485

Yasui, Minoru, **1**:165

Yasui v. United States, **1**:165

Yellow Power, **2**:540

Yemenites, **3**:1028

YMCA (Young Men's Christian Association), **2**:725

"Young Irish" rebellion, **1**:58

Young Men's Buddhist Association. *See* Buddhist Mission of North America

Youth. *See* Adolescence

Yugoslavian (former) refugees, **1**:213; **4**:1232, 1243*t*

Z

Zacatecas Federation of Hometown Associations, **2**:598

Zen Buddhism, **3**:861

Zero Immigration Series, **2**:393, 396; **4**:1516*g*

Zero Population Growth (ZPG), **1**:229; **2**:527; **4**:1516*g*

Zionism, **3**:1023–1024; **4**:1516*g*

Zoning measures, **2**:589

Zoot Suit Riots, **1**:168, 171; **2**:495, 496

Zoroastrianism, **3**:861

GEOGRAPHICAL INDEX

Numbers in bold indicate volume; g indicates glossary.

LEGAL AND JUDICIAL INDEX

O

Oakdale Agreement, **4**:1352
Oriental Exclusion Act (1924), **3**:863
Oyama v. California (1948), **2**:515

P

Pacific Railroad Act, **1**:94
Page Act (1875), **3**:1157; **4**:1281
Paris Peace agreement (1991), **1**:190–191
Pax Americana, **1**:267
People v. George W. Hall, **1**:80
Personal Responsibility and Work Opportunity Reconciliation Act (1996), **1**:218–219; **2**:486, 518, 522, 591, 697, 739; **4**:1439
  text, **4**:1328–1329
Petition for Alien Fiancée, **1**:364–365
Petition for Alien Relative, **1**:364, 369–370
Platt Amendment, **1**:173
Plyler v. Doe (1982), **4**:1373–1380
Pole law (1870), **1**:80
Presidential Proclamation No. 4865, **1**:316
Proclamation of 1763, **1**:42, 89
Proposition 63. *See* California Proposition 63
Proposition 187. *See* California Proposition 187
Proposition 227. *See* California Proposition 227
Puerto Rico Citizenship Act (1917), **4**:1292

Q

Quarter Acre Clause. *See* Gregory Clause
Quebec Act of 1774, **1**:42
Querétaro Protocol, **3**:1137
Queue law (1870), **1**:80
Quota Act (1921), **1**:151–152; **2**:724; **4**:1254
  definition of, **4**:1513*g*
  text, **4**:1293–1294
Quota Act (1924), **1**:152; **2**:504, 621, 724; **3**:969; **4**:1263–1264
  definition of, **4**:1513*g*
  text, **4**:1295–1296

R

Racketeering Influenced Corrupt Organization statutes, **1**:372
Rate-in-Aid Act (1849) (Great Britain), **1**:58
Re Examining Board v. Flores de Otero, **2**:520
Refugee Act (1980), **1**:191, 281, 291, 297–298, 358
  definition of, **4**:1514g
  effect on Miami, **3**:934
  history of, **4**:1364–1366
  text, **4**:1313–1314
Refugee-Escapee Act (1957), **1**:160
Refugee Fair Share Law (1960), **1**:160, 281, 293
Refugee Parolees Act (1978), **2**:506
Refugee Relief Act (1953), **1**:281, 288, 297, 346, 358; **2**:505–506
  definition of, **4**:1514*g*
Reno v. American-Arab Anti-Discrimination Committee, **3**:1002
Richardson, Graham v., **2**:516
Ridge v. Verity (1989), **2**:399
Rok v. Legg (1939), **2**:516

S

Scott Act (1888), **1**:81; **4**:1286–1287
Second Quota Act. *See* Quota Act (1924)
Sedition Act (1798), **2**:484
Sedition Act (1918), **1**:140, 144, 151
Sixth Amendment, **2**:515
Skeffington, Colyer et al. v., **1**:148; **4**:1507*g*
Sweatshop Reform Bill, California (1999), **2**:677

T

Temporary Relief Act (1847) (Great Britain), **1**:57
Tenth Amendment, **2**:519
Terrace v. Thompson (1923), **2**:515
Thirteenth Amendment, **1**:87
Thompson, Terrace v., **2**:515
Title IV: Restricting Welfare and Public Benefits from Aliens (1996), **4**:1439–1451
Trade Act, Freedom of Emigration Amendment, **4**:1248

Trading with the Enemy Act (1917), **3**:833
Treaty of Ghent (1814), **4**:1253
Treaty of Guadalupe Hidalgo (1848), **1**:91; **2**:539, 620; **3**:909, 922, 1049, 1136–1140
  definition of, **4**:1509*g*
  text, **4**:1280
Tydings-McDuffie Act (1934), **4**:1201

U

United States, Chae Chan Ping v., **3**:1002
United States, Fong Yue Ting v., **3**:1002
United States, Hirabayashi v., **1**:165; **4**:1369–1370
United States, Korematsu v., **1**:165
United States, Yasui v., **1**:165
United States ex rel. Negron v. New York, **3**:815; **4**:1515*g*
United States v. Bhagat Singh Thind (1923), **4**:1367–1368
United States v. Sakaram Ganesh Pandit, **4**:1208
U.S. Constitution, **1**:44–46, 246; **2**:484, 510; **4**:1276
  government office restrictions, **2**:511
U.S. Declaration of Independence, **1**:42, 43, 245–246

V–W

Verity, Ridge v., **2**:399
Volstead Act, **2**:492
Wagner-Rogers bill, **1**:157–158
White Slave Traffic Act (1910), **2**:503; **4**:1289
Whom We Shall Welcome (1953), **3**:1002; **4**:1336–1344
Wilson et al., LULAC et al. v., **4**:1387
World Refugee Year Law (1960), **1**:167

Y

Yamataya v. Fisher, **2**:485
Yasui v. United States, **1**:165

Numbers in bold indicate volume; g indicates glossary.